# ELEMENTS OF Literature

## FIRST COURSE

## Indiana Edition

These are the stories
that never, never die,
that are carried like seed
into a new country,
are told to you and me
and make in us
new and lasting strengths.

—from *Nancy Hanks of Wilderness Road:*
*A Story of Lincoln's Mother*
by Meridel Le Sueur

# ELEMENTS OF

## Literature

### FIRST COURSE

## Indiana Edition

**HOLT, RINEHART AND WINSTON**

A Harcourt Education Company

**Austin** • Orlando • Chicago • New York • Toronto • London • San Diego

# CREDITS

**EDITORIAL**

**Project Director:** Kathleen Daniel

**Managing Editor:** Richard Sime

**Executive Editor:** Juliana Koenig

**Editorial Staff:** Leora Harris, Jan Watson Collins, Robert Hoyt, Kathryn Rogers, Christopher LeCluyse

**Editorial Support:** Laurie Muir, Dan Hunter

**Editorial Permissions:** Tamara Blanken, Sacha Frey

**Research and Development:** Joan Burditt

**Index:** Robert Zolnerzak

**PRODUCTION, DESIGN, AND PHOTO RESEARCH**

**Director:** Athena Blackorby

**Design Coordinator:** Betty Mintz

**Program Design:** Kirchoff/Wohlberg, Inc.

**Electronic Files:** Preface; H&S Graphics, Inc.

**Design/Production:** Joseph Padial

**Photo Research:** Omni-Photo Communications, Inc.

**Photo Research Coordinator:** Mary Monaco

**Manufacturing:** RR Donnelley & Sons Company, Willard, Ohio

**Cover Artist:** Greg Geisler

**Photo Credits:** Front cover: (frog), K. Griffiths/APL/Corbis and Leo Meier/APL/Corbis; (crown), image copyright © 2001 PhotoDisc, Inc./HRW; (lily pond), Steve Hix/FPG International; (sky), Corbis Images/HRW; (grasses), Russell Dian/HRW; (moon), Chad Ehlers/Tony Stone Images; (grassy knoll), Corbis Images/HRW. Back cover: (detail, pair of frogs), Asian Art Museum of San Francisco/The Avery Brundage Collection/B60 B1082/1083.

**Quotation on Cover:** Meridel Le Sueur (page 591), courtesy of Holy Cow! Press

Requests for permission to make copies of any part of the work should be mailed to the following address: Permissions Department, Holt, Rinehart and Winston, 10801 N. MoPac Expy., Bldg. 3, Austin, Texas 78759.

Acknowledgments appear on pages 797–800, which are an extension of the copyright page.

Printed in the United States of America

ISBN 0-03-067242-2                          2 3 4 5 6 048 03 02

# PROGRAM AUTHORS

**Kylene Beers** wrote the Reading Matters section of the book and developed the accompanying *Reading Skills and Strategies* component. A former middle school teacher, Dr. Beers has turned her commitment to helping readers having difficulty into the major focus of her research, writing, speaking, and teaching. A clinical associate professor at the University of Houston, Dr. Beers is also currently the editor of the National Council of Teachers of English journal *Voices from the Middle*. She is the author of *When Kids Can't Read: The Reading Handbook for Teachers Grades 6–12* and co-editor of *Into Focus: Understanding and Creating Middle School Readers*. She has served on the review boards of the *English Journal* and *The ALAN Review*. Dr. Beers is a recipient of the NCTE Richard W. Halle Award. She currently serves on the board of directors of the International Reading Association's Special Interest Group on Adolescent Literature.

**Robert Anderson** wrote the Elements of Literature essay on drama and contributed to the instructional materials for *Brian's Song*. Mr. Anderson is a playwright, novelist, screenwriter, and teacher. His plays include *Tea and Sympathy; Silent Night, Lonely Night; You Know I Can't Hear You When the Water's Running;* and *I Never Sang for My Father*. His screenplays include *The Nun's Story* and *The Sand Pebbles*. Mr. Anderson has taught at the Writers' Workshop at the University of Iowa, the American Theater Wing Professional Training Program, and the Salzburg Seminar in American Studies. He is a past president of the Dramatists' Guild, past vice president of the Authors' League of America, and a member of the Theater Hall of Fame.

**John Malcolm Brinnin** wrote the Elements of Literature essays on poetry and contributed to the instructional materials on poetry. Mr. Brinnin is the author of six volumes of poetry, which received many prizes and awards. He was a member of the American Academy and Institute of Arts and Letters. He was also a critic of poetry and a biographer of poets and was for a number of years director of New York's famous Poetry Center. His teaching career, begun at Vassar College, included long terms at the University of Connecticut and Boston University, where he succeeded Robert Lowell as Professor of Creative Writing and Contemporary Letters. Mr. Brinnin's books include *Dylan Thomas in America: An Intimate Journal* and *Sextet: T. S. Eliot & Truman Capote & Others*.

**Robert E. Probst** established the pedagogical framework for the 1997, 2000, and current editions of **Elements of Literature**. Dr. Probst is Professor of English Education at Georgia State University. He has taught English in Maryland and been Supervisor of English for the Norfolk, Virginia, Public Schools. He is the author of *Response and Analysis: Teaching Literature in Junior and Senior High School* and has contributed chapters to such books as *Literature Instruction: A Focus on Student Response; Reader Response in the Classroom; Handbook of Research on Teaching the English Language Arts; Transactions with Literature;* and *For Louise M. Rosenblatt*. Dr. Probst has worked on the National Council of Teachers of English Committee on Research, the Commission on Reading, and the Commission on Curriculum. He has also served on the board of directors of the Adolescent Literature Assembly and is a member of the National Conference on Research in Language and Literacy.

**John Leggett** wrote the Elements of Literature essays on the short story and contributed to the instructional materials on short stories. Mr. Leggett is a novelist, biographer, and former teacher. He went to the Writers' Workshop at the University of Iowa in the spring of 1969, expecting to work there for a single semester. In 1970, he assumed temporary charge of the program, and for the next seventeen years he was its director. Mr. Leggett's novels include *Wilder Stone; The Gloucester Branch; Who Took the Gold Away?; Gulliver House;* and *Making Believe*. He also wrote the highly acclaimed biography *Ross and Tom: Two American Tragedies*.

**Judith L. Irvin** established the conceptual basis for the vocabulary and reading strands and developed the Reading Skills and Strategies exercises for grades 6–8. Dr. Irvin teaches courses in curriculum, middle school education, and educational leadership at Florida State University. She is also chair of the Research Committee of the National Middle School Association and was the editor of *Research in Middle Level Education* for five years. She taught middle school for eight years before seeking her doctorate in Reading–Language Arts. Dr. Irvin writes a column, "What Research Says to the Middle Level Practitioner," for the *Middle School Journal*. Her many books include *Transforming Middle Level Education: Perspectives and Possibilities* and *Reading and the Middle School Student: Strategies to Enhance Literacy*.

## SPECIAL CONTRIBUTORS

**Virginia Hamilton** wrote the Elements of Literature essays on fables and folk tales and the commentaries on Aesop's fables. Ms. Hamilton is one of America's most highly acclaimed writers of books for children and young adults. She has received many awards, including the Newbery Award for *M. C. Higgins, the Great;* the Newbery Honor Award for *In the Beginning: Creation Stories from Around the World;* the Coretta Scott King Award for *Sweet Whispers, Brother Rush;* and the Edgar Allan Poe Award for *The House of Dies Drear.* Among her collections of folk tales are *The People Could Fly* and *The Dark Way: Stories from the Spirit World.* The *All Jahdu Storybook* is a collection of Hamilton's own tales about a trickster hero who was born in an oven between two loaves of bread. In 1990, Hamilton received an honorary doctorate from the Bank Street College of Education in New York City. In 1995, she received a MacArthur Fellowship. In 1998, Kent State University established the Virginia Hamilton Literary Award for excellence in multicultural literature for children and young adults.

**David Adams Leeming** wrote the Elements of Literature essay on Greek and Roman myths. Dr. Leeming was a Professor of English and Comparative Literature at the University of Connecticut for many years. He is the author of several books on mythology, including *Mythology: The Voyage of the Hero; The World of Myth;* and *Encyclopedia of Creation Myths.* For several years he taught English at Robert College in Istanbul, Turkey. He also served as secretary and assistant to the writer James Baldwin in New York and Istanbul. He is the author of the biographies *James Baldwin* and *Amazing Grace: A Biography of Beauford Delaney.*

**Naomi Shihab Nye** wrote the Elements of Literature essay "Nonfiction: Encountering Our Lives." Ms. Nye writes poems, essays, and children's books. Her collections of poems include *Words Under the Words: Selected Poems* and *Red Suitcase.* Her picture books include *Benito's Dream Bottle,* a School Library Journal "Best Book," and *Sitti's Secrets,* recipient of the Jane Addams Children's Book Award. She edited the prize-winning *This Same Sky,* a collection of poems from around the world, and *The Tree Is Older Than You Are,* bilingual poems and stories from Mexico, both for young readers. Ms. Nye has been a visiting writer in elementary and high schools, universities, and communities across the country throughout her working life.

## WRITERS

*The writers prepared instructional materials for the text under the supervision of Dr. Probst and the editorial staff.*

**Lynn Hovland**
Former Teacher
Educational Writer and Editor
Berkeley, California

**Erin Hurley**
Former Faculty Member
Brown University
Providence, Rhode Island

**Julith Jedamus**
Educational Writer and Editor
Pacific Palisades, California

**William Kaufman**
Former Teacher
Educational Writer and Editor
Hempstead, New York

**David Pence**
Former Teacher
Educational Writer and Editor
Brooklyn, New York

**Margaret Pickett**
Wellesley Middle School
Wellesley, Massachusetts

**David Snyder**
Wellesley Middle School
Wellesley, Massachusetts

## REVIEWERS AND CONSULTANTS

*Reviewers assisted in choosing selections and evaluated instructional materials. Consultants assisted in securing student active-reading models and provided advice on current pedagogy.*

**Jody Alexander**
Madison School District
Phoenix, Arizona

**Joyce Black-Carson**
Montera Junior High School
Oakland, California

**Alfee Enciso**
Palms Middle School
Los Angeles, California

**Cheryl Greenwood**
Washington Park Middle School
Washington, Pennsylvania

**Carleen Hemric**
Pershing Junior High School
San Diego, California

**Martha Lince**
JMF Ctr. for Eductional Services
Indianapolis, Indiana

**Jan Meeks**
Fairmont Junior High School
Boise, Idaho

**Pamela Moore**
Milford Junior High School
Milford, Ohio

**Phil Simcox**
Carmody Middle School
Lakewood, Colorado

**Nan Worch**
Kennedy-King Middle School
Gary, Indiana

# FIELD-TEST PARTICIPANTS

*The following teachers participated in field-testing of prepublication materials for the series.*

**Janet Blackburn-Lewis**
Western Guilford High School
Greensboro, North Carolina

**Dana E. Bull**
F. J. Turner High School
Beloit, Wisconsin

**Maura Casey**
Skyline High School
Oakland, California

**Deborah N. Dean**
Warner Robins Middle School
Warner Robins, Georgia

**Gloria J. Dolesh**
Friendly High School
Fort Washington, Maryland

**Christina Donnelly**
Parkdale High School
Riverdale, Maryland

**Kay T. Dunlap**
Norview High School
Norfolk, Virginia

**Joseph Fitzgibbon**
West Linn High School
West Linn, Oregon

**Paul Garro**
Taft High School
San Antonio, Texas

**Suzanne Haffamier**
Agoura High School
Agoura, California

**Robert K. Jordan**
Land O' Lakes High School
Land O' Lakes, Florida

**Terry Juhl**
Bella Vista High School
Fair Oaks, California

**Elizabeth Keister**
Blair Middle School
Norfolk, Virginia

**Jane S. Kilgore**
Warner Robins High School
Warner Robins, Georgia

**Janet S. King**
Reading High School
Reading, Pennsylvania

**Cheryl L. Lambert**
Milford Mill Academy
Baltimore, Maryland

**Sarah A. Long**
Robert Goddard Middle School
Seabrook, Maryland

**Margaret E. McKinnon**
Roger L. Putnam Vocational-
  Technical High School
Springfield, Massachusetts

**Donna J. Magrum**
Rogers High School
Toledo, Ohio

**Nancy Maheras**
Western High School
Las Vegas, Nevada

**Mara Malone**
Central High School
Baton Rouge, Louisiana

**Lourdes J. Medina**
Pat Neff Middle School
San Antonio, Texas

**Joan Mohon**
Todd County Central High
  School
Elkton, Kentucky

**Terrence R. Moore**
John Muir High School
Pasadena, California

**Gayle C. Morey**
Countryside High School
Clearwater, Florida

**Beverly Mudd**
Western High School
Las Vegas, Nevada

**Jan Nichols**
Apollo High School
Glendale, Arizona

**Jeffrey S. Norton**
Lewis and Clark High School
Spokane, Washington

**Barbara Powell**
Todd County Central High
  School
Elkton, Kentucky

**Gloria S. Pridmore**
Morrow High School
Morrow, Georgia

**Dee Richardson**
Moore High School
Moore, Oklahoma

**Carole A. Scala**
Southwest Middle School
Orlando, Florida

**Barbara A. Slaughter**
Lewis and Clark High School
Spokane, Washington

**Barbara B. Smith**
Dr. Phillips Ninth-Grade Center
Orlando, Florida

**Sister Eileen Stephens**
Cathedral Preparatory Seminary
Elmhurst, New York

**Sally Thompson**
Andrew Jackson Middle School
Suitland, Maryland

**Blanca M. Valledor**
G. Holmes Braddock Senior
  High School
Miami, Florida

**Charla J. Walton**
John C. Fremont Junior High
  School
Las Vegas, Nevada

**William Ward**
Roger L. Putnam Vocational-
  Technical High School
Springfield, Massachusetts

**Lynn White**
Tascosa High School
Amarillo, Texas

**Noretta M. Willig**
Baldwin High School
Pittsburgh, Pennsylvania

**Deborah K. Woelflein**
Merrimack High School
Merrimack, New Hampshire

# STUDENT CONTRIBUTORS

*The following students wrote annotations for the Dialogue with the Text models.*

**Katharine Gaddis**
Westview Middle School
Longmont, Colorado

**Crystal Hinojos**
Lincoln Middle School
El Paso, Texas

**Rebecca Irizarry**
Maplewood Middle School
Maplewood, New Jersey

**Rana Jaber**
Southwest Middle School
Orlando, Florida

**Hester Reed**
The Dutchess Day School
Millbrook, New York

**Katie Sheldon**
Vista Verde Middle School
Irvine, California

**Cheryl Testa**
William T. Rogers Middle School
Kings Park, New York

INDIANA

# CONTENTS IN BRIEF

# CONTENTS

## Collection One

## Out Here on My Own

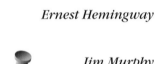

### Language / Grammar Links

## COMMUNICATIONS WORKSHOPS

## Collection Two

# Who Am I?

# Collection Three

# Do the Right Thing

## Language / Grammar Links

- End All End-Mark Errors **201**
- Commas Make Sense of a Series **215**
- Put That Splice on Ice **225**
- End the Apostrophe Glut **243**
- Punctuate Dialogue Correctly—And Punch Up Your Writing **256**

## Collection Four

# We Rookies Have to Stick Together

**Language /
Grammar Link**

• Transitions Make the
Right Connection **324**

## Collection Five

# Living in the Heart

## Collection Six
# This Old Earth

---

## COMMUNICATIONS WORKSHOPS

**Language /
Grammar Links**

## Collection Seven
# Our Classical Heritage

**Language /
Grammar Links**

## COMMUNICATIONS WORKSHOPS

## Collection Eight

# 900 Cinderellas:
# Our World Heritage
# in Folklore

---

## COMMUNICATIONS WORKSHOPS

**Language /
Grammar Links**

# Resource Center

# *Elements of Literature* on the Internet

## TO THE STUDENT

**D**iscover more about the stories, poems, and essays in *Elements of Literature* by logging on to the Internet. At **go.hrw.com** we help you complete your homework assignments, learn more about your favorite writers, and find facts that support your ideas and inspire you with new ones. Here's how to log on:

1. Start your Web browser and enter **go.hrw.com** in the location field.

2. Note the keyword in your textbook.

go.hrw.com
*LEO 7-1*

3. In your Web browser, enter the keyword and click on GO.

Now that you've arrived, you can peek into the palaces and museums of the world, listen to stories of exploration and discovery, or view fires burning on the ocean floor. As you move through *Elements of Literature,* use the best online resources at **go.hrw.com.**

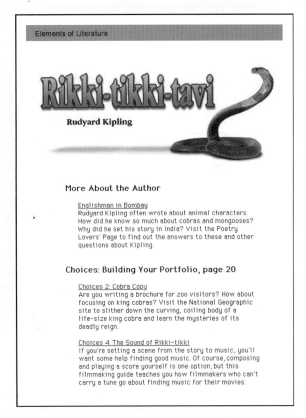

Elements of Literature

## Rikki-tikki-tavi
**Rudyard Kipling**

### More About the Author

**Englishman in Bombay**
Rudyard Kipling often wrote about animal characters. How did he know so much about cobras and mongooses? Why did he set his story in India? Visit the Poetry Lovers' Page to find out the answers to these and other questions about Kipling.

### Choices: Building Your Portfolio, page 20

**Choices 2: Cobra Copy**
Are you writing a brochure for zoo visitors? How about focusing on king cobras? Visit the National Geographic site to slither down the curving, coiling body of a life-size king cobra and learn the mysteries of its deadly reign.

**Choices 4: The Sound of Rikki-tikki**
If you're setting a scene from the story to music, you'll want some help finding good music. Of course, composing and playing a score yourself is one option, but this filmmaking guide teaches you how filmmakers who can't carry a tune go about finding music for their movies.

Enjoy the Internet, but be critical of the information you find there. Always evaluate your sources for credibility, accuracy, timeliness, and possible bias.

Web sites accessed through **go.hrw.com** are reviewed regularly. However, online materials change continually and without notice. Holt, Rinehart and Winston cannot ensure the accuracy or appropriateness of materials other than our own. Students, teachers, and guardians should assume responsibility for checking all online materials. A full description of Terms of Use can be found at **go.hrw.com.**

# Selections by Genre

# Myth, Folk Tale, and Fable

## *Myth*

## *Folk Tale/Urban Legend*

## *Fable*

# Drama

## *Stage Play*

## *Teleplay*

# Song

# FEATURES

## Elements of Literature

## Across the Curriculum

## Student Models

## No Questions Asked

## Writer's Workshops

## Reading for Life

## Learning for Life

## Connections

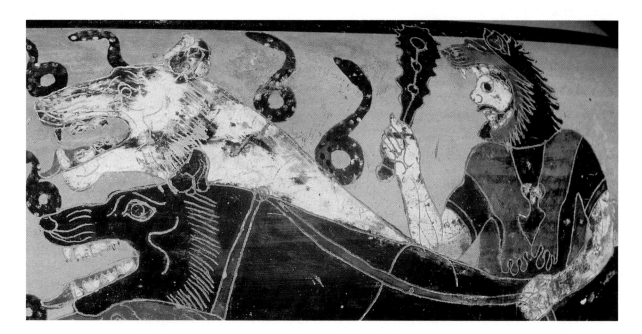

# SKILLS

## Reading Skills and Strategies

## Literature Skills

## Language / Grammar Links

# Vocabulary / Spelling Skills

# Speaking and Listening Workshops

# Sentence Workshops

# Assessment

# Building a Foundation for Success in Literature

# Mastering the Indiana Standards in Reading
## *A Foundation for Reading*

## Reading Matters *By Dr. Kylene Beers*

# Preparing for ISTEP+ and Other Standardized Tests
## *A Foundation for Test Taking*

## Test Smarts

# Reading Matters

## Strategy Lesson 1

# Summarizing the Plot
## Retelling

**"I**s this a plot?" Manuel asked as he pointed to the first paragraph of a story. He didn't understand that plot isn't a single thing he can point to in the story. He didn't know that **plot** is the "what happens" in the story—all the related events that move from the story's beginning to its end.

The first part of a plot is called its **basic situation.** Here you meet the **characters,** learn what they **want,** and discover the **problems** they face getting what they want. The major part of the plot involves a series of events in which **complications** develop as the characters struggle to resolve their conflicts. The plot then moves to a **climax**—the most emotional and suspenseful part of the story, when the character's problem is solved. In the **resolution** all the loose ends of the plot are tied up, and the story is over.

### Retelling Summary Sheet

Keeping up with all the information in a story can be difficult. A strategy called **retelling** can help you identify the elements of a plot and keep all the information about a plot straight in your mind. With this strategy you practice telling the plot of the story using a **retelling summary sheet.** You use the retelling summary sheet as a guide, to be sure you've included all the events in the plot.

### PRACTICE

Retell a short story (or even a movie or TV show), using a retelling summary sheet to help you remember and organize the bare bones of the plot. Score your own retelling. (Zero means you didn't tell

| Retelling Summary Sheet | | | |
| --- | --- | --- | --- |
| Rating of Coverage | | | |
| 0 | 1 | 2 | 3 |
| No coverage | A little | Some | A lot |

1. Introduction
2. Characters
3. Conflict
4. Complications
5. Climax
6. Resolution

about an event at all, and 3 means you did a good job covering the plot.) The sample on the opposite page gives you tips on how to fill out a summary sheet.

# Retelling Summary Sheet

| Rating of Coverage | | | |
|---|---|---|---|
| *0* | *1* | *2* | *3* |
| No coverage | A little | Some | A lot |

**I. Introduction** Begin with the **title** and **author** of the story. Then, tell where and when the story is **set**—if that's important.

Some people use the terms **protagonist** and **antagonist.** The protagonist is the hero, and the antagonist works against the hero. Luke Skywalker is a protagonist, and Darth Vader is his antagonist.

**2. Characters** Tell the **characters'** names, and explain how the characters are related or connected to one another. Tell what the main character **wants.**

**3. Conflict** What is the main character's problem, or **conflict**—that is, who or what is keeping the main character from getting what he or she wants?

**Strategy Tip**
If it's hard to keep events in **chronological,** or time, order, think about how each event caused another event to happen. Use words such as *because of, since, as a result of.*

**4. Complications** Tell the **main events**—what happens as the character tries to solve the conflict.

**Strategy Tip**
This is the moment when you know you are finally about to find out how the protagonist will overcome the conflict (or be defeated).

**5. Climax** Describe the **climax,** the most suspenseful moment in the story, when you discover at last how the conflict ends.

**Strategy Tip**
Avoid linking the events with a string of *and*'s. Here are some good time-order words to use: *first; second; third; next; eventually; later; afterward; finally; in conclusion.*

**6. Resolution** Finally, tell what happens after the **climax.** How does the story end?

# 2

# Understanding
# How Character Affects Plot
## If . . . Then . . .

**W**hat would happen in *Star Wars* if Darth Vader suddenly became afraid of Luke Skywalker? How would the cartoon *Scooby Doo* be different if Scooby became brave? What would happen to *The Flintstones* if Fred suddenly got smart?

In each of those situations, the outcome of the plot would certainly change if the characters changed. In other words, if a character acts one way, then the plot proceeds in a certain way. If a character acts in a different way, the outcome of the plot changes also.

Imagine what would have happened in *How the Grinch Stole Christmas* if the Grinch had not been mean and stingy. Probably he would never have tried to stop Christmas from coming. Think about what would have happened in "Sleeping Beauty" if the princess hadn't been curious. Most likely she wouldn't have wandered into the one room that had the spinning wheel that was to put her and the whole kingdom to sleep for one hundred years.

## We All Have Traits

To understand how character affects plot, you've first got to be able to identify the main character's qualities. A character's qualities, or traits, can be flaws or strengths. We all have character traits. We may be ambitious, shy, generous, fearless, kind, selfish—the possibilities are almost endless.

You discover the traits of a character you meet in a story the same way you discover the traits of real people. You think about how the character acts, how the character looks, and what he or she says. You think about how other people respond to the character. In fact, you think about all the ways writers develop a character.

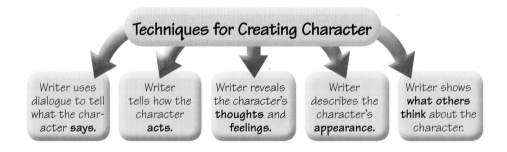

Techniques for Creating Character

| Writer uses dialogue to tell what the character **says.** | Writer tells how the character **acts.** | Writer reveals the character's **thoughts** and **feelings.** | Writer describes the character's **appearance.** | Writer shows **what others think** about the character. |

Here are some adjectives you can use to describe character traits.

> **Character Traits**
>
> | | | |
> |---|---|---|
> | strong/weak | wise/foolish | truthful/sneaky |
> | kind/mean | selfish/unselfish | dependable/unreliable |
> | brave/cowardly | good/bad | generous/stingy |
> | honest/dishonest | clever/silly | |
> | bold/shy | modern/old-fashioned | |

## If . . . Then . . .

When you're trying to figure out how character affects plot, think of what would happen if the character acted differently—or were a different kind of person. Think **If . . . Then . . .** *If* the character is like this, *then* what would happen in the story? On the other hand, *if* the character is like *that, then* what would happen?

## PRACTICE

1. When you read "The Smallest Dragonboy" (page 47), decide which word in each of the following pairs describes Keevan.
   **a.** brave/cowardly
   **b.** truthful/sneaky
   **c.** strong/weak
   Next, decide how the story would change if you were to choose the other word in each pair. If you think Keevan is brave, then how would the story change if he were cowardly? Would he go to the hatching? Would he Impress with the bronze dragon? If you think he is strong, then what would happen if he were weak? Would he stay in bed? Would he find his dragon?

2. When you read "A Day's Wait" (page 81), think about Schatz. Decide which word in each of the following pairs best describes him.
   **a.** stoic/agitated
   **b.** brave/cowardly
   **c.** considerate/selfish
   Now, choose the other word to describe Schatz, and predict how the plot and its resolution would change.

3. In "Rikki-tikki-tavi" (page 3), think about Rikki. Decide which word in each of the following pairs best describes Rikki.
   **a.** brave/shy
   **b.** strong/weak
   **c.** determined/lazy
   Predict how the story would progress and how it would end if Rikki were the opposite of whichever word you chose.

# Uncovering Theme
## Most Important Word

**H**as your teacher ever asked you that dreaded theme question—the one that begins "What is the theme of . . . ?" What do you do when you hear that question? A group of seventh-graders all immediately started turning the pages of their books when their teacher asked them. "Why are you doing that?" she asked. "I'm looking for the theme," one student replied. "Yeah," another said, "I sure hope the writer remembered to include it."

### What Is Theme?

Well, the writer did include it, but not in the way the students were hoping. Writers don't end (or begin) their stories with a nice note to the reader that says, "And the theme of the story is . . ." No, instead writers let their readers meet the characters and share an experience with them. At the end of the experience, the reader, along with the characters, has discovered something about human experience. It might be something the reader already knows but rediscovers under new circumstances. It might be something new. The **theme,** then, is a truth about life or people that we discover as we share the characters' experiences.

When you write or state a theme, remember that a theme isn't a word or a phrase—it's at least one sentence!

## Most Important Word

If you need help writing a theme statement, try a strategy called **Most Important Word.** After you've read a selection, skim through it again looking for the word in the text you think is most important. Here are comments three students made after reading a poem called "The Secret Heart" by Robert P. Tristram Coffin. In this poem a father checks on his son, who is sleeping.

"I say **heart** is the most important word, because it's used a lot and is in the title and because the boy thinks his dad's hands look like they are making a heart, and that's the image the boy always remembers."

"I think the most important word is **father,** because it is the father who is checking on his son when he is sleeping at night."

**What's the most important word and why?**

"I think the most important word is **love,** because if the father didn't love his son, he wouldn't have been checking on him at night, wanting to protect him."

After deciding on the most important word and coming up with reasons for your choice, think about how that word could be related to the theme. Since different readers can pull different themes from the same selection, statements of themes usually differ from reader to reader. Look at the following three themes those three students stated, and match them to the comments above.

1. A parent's love for a child is never-ending—it goes on day and night.

2. Children remember their parents' simple acts of love.

3. A father is his child's protector.

## PRACTICE

Read this short, short poem by Langston Hughes. Select what you think is its most important word (or words—there could be more than one). Write down reasons for your choice. Then, think of how that word could point to the theme of the poem. Try stating, in a sentence, the theme that you have discovered. Be sure to compare your themes in class.

> O God of dust and rainbows help us see
> That without dust the rainbows would not be.
> —Langston Hughes

Strategy Lesson 4

# Analyzing Point of View
## Somebody Wanted But So

**I**s this glass half empty or half full? The very thirsty child would complain that it's half empty. The mom, who doesn't want the child drinking so much soda anyway, would say it's half full. What you're seeing in this situation is the effect of point of view.

It's half empty!

It's half full!

When we talk about **point of view** in stories, we are talking about who is telling the story. Here are the three main points of view:

**First-Person Point of View.** The story is told by "I," a character in the story.

**Omniscient Point of View.** The story is told by an all-knowing narrator who is not a character in the story. This narrator can tell everything about everyone in the story. This narrator can even tell the future.

**Third-Person Limited Point of View.** The story is told by a narrator who is not in the story. This narrator zooms in on only one character and tells the story through that character's eyes and emotions.

Writers are especially aware of point of view, and they experiment with it all the time. Skilled readers also think about how a story would be changed if it were told from a different viewpoint. Try experimenting with point of view by using a strategy called **Somebody Wanted But So (SWBS).**

### Somebody Wanted But So

This simple strategy helps you summarize a story; it can also help you think about the story from various characters' perspectives—or points of view. Here's how the strategy works:

On a sheet of paper, jot down the words *Somebody Wanted But So.* Now, think about a story you've just read. For right now, let's think about "Cinderella," a fairy tale you probably know. First, decide which character in the story you want to think about. Here are some choices: Cinderella, the stepmother, the stepsisters, the prince, maybe even the fairy godmother. Now, write your choice under the heading "Somebody," like this:

| Somebody | Wanted | But | So |
|---|---|---|---|
| The prince | | | |

With a focus on the prince, next think about what the prince wanted. "But" means he faced a problem getting what he wanted. "So" tells what the outcome is. Once you think through all of this, you have an SWBS chart that looks like this:

| Somebody | Wanted | But | So |
|---|---|---|---|
| The prince | to find the young woman he met at the ball, | she left the ball without telling him who she was, | he traveled far and wide until he found her and married her. |

You've just thought about the story from the prince's point of view. Now, try thinking about it from Cinderella's point of view. You might come up with a statement like this:

| Somebody | Wanted | But | So |
|---|---|---|---|
| Cinderella | to escape the kitchen and a cruel family; she also wanted to go to the prince's ball, | her cruel stepmother would not let her get a dress for the ball, | a fairy god-mother visited Cinderella and magically grant-ed her wish. |

Notice that as you change the character under the "Somebody" heading, you are shifting focus. If the prince tells the story or if a storyteller tells the story zooming in on the prince, you will not hear about Cinderella and her sad, ragged state until later. You will hear the prince telling you that he has fallen in love with a mysterious, beautiful young woman wearing the most fantastic gown, who left a tiny glass slipper on the palace steps.

## PRACTICE

Look at "After Twenty Years" (page 193).

1. Create SWBS charts for Jimmy, Bob, and the plainclothes policeman.

2. Be ready to discuss how the story would change if the point of view were narrowed to what only one of these characters knows and sees.

# Identifying Cause and Effect

**H**ere are three situations:

- You punch the right button on your stereo, and music starts to play.
- Someone tells you your clothes are cool, and you feel good about yourself.
- Your brother barges into your room without knocking, and you get angry.

In each of those situations, something has happened (an **effect**) because of something else (a **cause**). Look at this chart, and you can see which part of each sentence is the cause and which is the effect:

| Cause → | Effect |
|---|---|
| punching the stereo's right button | music starting to play |
| hearing your clothes are cool | feeling good about yourself |
| brother barging into your room | getting angry |

## Finding the Cause and Its Effect

If writers showed us cause-and-effect relationships (sometimes called **causal relationships**) by using charts like the one to the left, then finding causes and effects would be easy. Most of the time, information isn't delivered in chart format, so you've got to find causes and effects on your own. Here are some tips for doing that:

1. **Change the words.** Think of *cause* as "source" or "reason" and *effect* as "result" or "outcome."

2. **Check out the question.** If a question in your history book or science book (even in this book!) asks you to identify causes and effects, look carefully at the question. The question itself often lets you know if you are hunting for the cause or the effect.

   - **What are three causes of the Civil War?** In this question you see that you are looking for the causes of (reasons for) the Civil War (outcome or effect).

   - **What are three effects of poor nutrition?** This time you've got the cause (poor nutrition), and you're looking to see what the effects or results of poor nutrition are.

   - **Why is George Washington called the father of our country?** With this question you are given the effect, or outcome: Washington came

to be called the father of our country. Now you've got to find the reason or reasons why, so you are looking for the causes.

3. **Be on the lookout for signal words.** Certain words can signal that a reason for something or a cause of something is about to be mentioned. Other words can signal that a result or an effect is being described.

| Words That Signal Causes | | Words That Signal Effects | |
| --- | --- | --- | --- |
| because | since | therefore | thus |
| due to | were caused by | consequently | so |
| given that | results from | as a result | for that reason |
| as | | then | why |

## Graphic Organizers to Show Causes and Effects

Some causes have more than one effect. For example, unhealthful eating habits can cause many health problems. Some effects, such as the Civil War, have more than one cause. You can show these cause-and-effect relationships by using graphic organizers like the following.

### Three Effects of Unhealthful Eating Habits

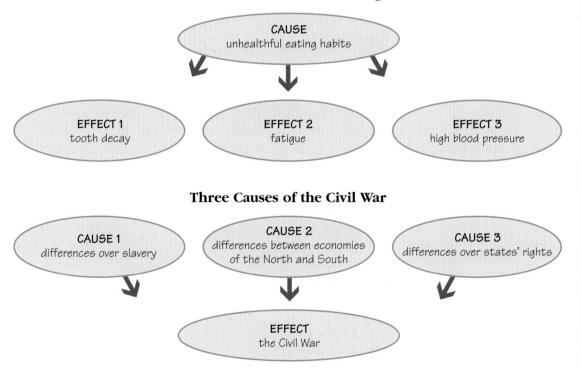

**CAUSE**
unhealthful eating habits

**EFFECT 1**
tooth decay

**EFFECT 2**
fatigue

**EFFECT 3**
high blood pressure

### Three Causes of the Civil War

**CAUSE 1**
differences over slavery

**CAUSE 2**
differences between economies of the North and South

**CAUSE 3**
differences over states' rights

**EFFECT**
the Civil War

### PRACTICE I

Read the sentences that follow, and make a cause-and-effect chart like the one on page xxxviii. Decide which part of each sentence goes under the "Cause" heading and which part goes under the "Effect" heading. Look for signal words that help you spot causes and effects.

1. The California population grew from about 114,000 in 1848 to about 750,000 in 1852 as people moved to California in search of gold.

2. People rushing to California to find gold were called forty-niners because most of them arrived in 1849, the height of the gold rush.

3. Many of the mining towns that sprang up quickly were unsafe because they had no sheriffs.

4. Because so many people came so quickly to California looking for gold, by 1850, much of the easily found surface gold was already gone.

5. Although most people who went to California did not become rich from mining gold, many thousands decided to stay because of the wonderful climate and good farmland.

### PRACTICE 2

Read "A Mason-Dixon Memory" on page 205. Then, read the following sentences and identify the cause-and-effect signal words in each.

- "Why did she look and sound so nervous?"
- "You mean I can't go to the park," I stuttered, "because I'm a Negro?"
- "'They don't allow Negroes in the park,' he said, 'so I'm staying with Clifton.'"

Next, read the following cause-and-effect chain. Then, make a second cause-and-effect chain for the experiences of Dondré Green. Write "Country club has racist admission policy" in the first box. Add as many boxes as you need to show how the policy affected Dondré, what actions his teammates took as a result, and what other effects the incident had.

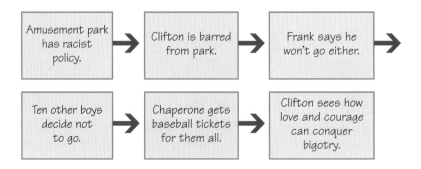

# Test Smarts

## Strategies for Taking Multiple-Choice Tests

If you have ever watched a quiz show on TV, you know how multiple-choice tests work. You get a question and (usually) four choices. Your job is to pick the correct one. Taking multiple-choice tests will get much easier when you apply these Test Smarts:

**T** rack your time.

**E** xpect success.

**S** tudy the directions.

**T** ake it all in.

**S** pot those numbers.

**M** aster the questions.

**A** nticipate the answers.

**R** ely on 50/50.

**T** ry. Try. Try.

**S** earch for skips and smudges.

### Track Your Time

You race through a test for fear you won't finish, or you realize you have only five minutes left to complete eleven zillion questions. Sound familiar? You can avoid both problems if you take a few minutes before you start to estimate how much time you have for each question. Using all the time you are given can help you avoid making errors. Follow these tips to set **checkpoints:**

- How many questions should be completed when one quarter of the time is gone?
- What should the clock read when you are halfway through the questions?
- If you find yourself behind your checkpoints, you can speed up.
- If you are ahead, you can—and should— slow down.

### Expect Success

Top athletes know that attitude affects performance. They learn to deal with their negative thoughts. So can you! Do you compare yourself with others? Most top athletes will tell you that they compete against only one person: themselves. They know they cannot change another person's performance. Instead, they study their own performance and find ways to improve it. That makes sense for you, too. Review your last scores. Figure out just what you need to do to top them. You can!

What if you get anxious? It's OK if you do. A little nervousness will help you focus. Of course, if you're so nervous that you think you might get sick or faint, take time to relax for a few minutes. Calm bodies breathe slowly. You can fool yours into feeling calmer and thinking more clearly by taking a few deep breaths—five slow counts in, five out.

# Test Smarts

## Study the Directions

You're ready to go, go, go, but first it's wait, wait, wait. Pencils. Paper. Answer sheets. Lots of directions. Listen! In order to follow directions, you have to know them. Read all test directions as if they contained the key to lifetime happiness and several years' allowance. Then, read them again. Study the answer sheet. Does it look like this?

1

2

3

4

or like this?

1      2      3      4

What about answer choices? Are they arranged

A      B      C      D

or

A      B          A      C

C      D    or    B      D

**Directions count.** Be very, very sure you know exactly what to do and how to do it before you make your first mark.

## Take It All In

When you finally hear the words "You may begin," briefly **preview the test** to get a mental map of your tasks:

- Know how many questions you have to complete.
- Know where to stop.
- Set your time checkpoints.
- Do the easy sections first; easy questions are worth just as many points as hard ones.

## Spot Those Numbers

"I got off by one and spent all my time trying to fix my answer sheet." *Oops.* Make it a habit to

- match the number of each question to the numbered space on the answer sheet every time
- leave the answer space blank if you skip a question
- keep a list of your blank spaces on scratch paper or somewhere else—but *not* on your answer sheet. The less you have to erase on your answer sheet, the better.

## Master the Questions

Be sure—very sure—that you **know what a question is asking you.** Read the question at least twice before reading the answer choices. Approach it as you would a mystery story or a riddle. Look for clues. Watch especially for words like *not* and *except*—they tell you to look for the choice that is false or different from the other choices or opposite in some way. For a reading-comprehension test, read the selection, master all the questions, and then reread the selection. The answers will be likely to pop out the second time around. Remember: A test isn't trying to trick you; it's trying to test your knowledge and your ability to think clearly.

## Anticipate the Answers

Before you read the answer choices, **answer the question yourself. Then, read the choices.** If the answer you gave is among the choices listed, it is probably correct.

## Rely on 50/50

"I . . . have . . . no . . . clue." You understand the question. You have an answer, but your answer is not listed, or perhaps you drew a complete blank. It happens. Time to **make an educated guess**—not a *wild* guess, but an *educated* guess. Think about quiz shows again, and you'll know the value of the 50/50 play. When two answers are eliminated, the contestant has a 50/50 chance of choosing the correct one. You can use elimination, too.

Always read every choice carefully. **Watch out for distracters**—choices that may be true but are too broad, too narrow, or not relevant to the question. Eliminate the least likely choice. Then, eliminate the next, and so on until you find the best one. If two choices seem equally correct, look to see if "All of the above" is an option. If it is, that might be your choice. If no choice seems correct, look for "None of the above."

## Try. Try. Try.

**Don't give up.** You might be surprised by how many students do give up. Think of tests as a kind of marathon. Just as in any marathon, people get bored, tired, hungry, thirsty, hot, discouraged. They may begin to feel sick or develop aches and pains. They decide the test doesn't matter.

Remember: The last question is worth just as much as the first question, and the questions on a test don't always get harder as you go. If the question you just finished was really hard, an easier one is probably coming up. Take a deep breath, and give it your all, all the way to the finish.

## Search for Skips and Smudges

"Hey! I got that one right, and the machine marked it wrong!" If you have ever—ever—had this experience, pay attention! When this happens in class, your teacher can give you the extra point. On a machine-scored test, however, you would lose the point and never know why. So, listen up: All machine-scored answer sheets have a series of lines marching down the side. The machine stops at the first line and scans across it for your answer, stops at the second line, scans, stops at the third line, scans, and so on, all the way to the end. The machine is looking for a dark, heavy mark. If it finds one where it should be, you get the point. If you leave a question blank or accidentally mark two answers instead of one, you lose a point. If your marks are not very dark, the machine sees blank spaces, and you'll lose more points.

To avoid losing points, take time at the end of the test to make sure you

- did not skip any answers
- gave one answer for each question
- made the marks heavy and dark and within the lines

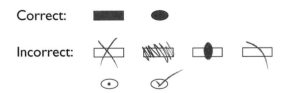

Get rid of smudges. Make sure there are no stray pencil marks on your answer sheet. Cleanly erase those places where you changed your mind. Check for little stray marks from pencil tapping.

## Reading Comprehension

Many tests have a section called **reading comprehension.** The good news is that you do not have to study for this part of the test. Taking a reading-comprehension test is a bit like playing ball. You don't know where the ball will land, so you have to stay alert to all possibilities. However, just as the ball can come at you in only a few ways, there are only a few kinds of questions on reading-comprehension tests. This discussion will help you identify the most common ones. Two kinds of texts are used here. The first one is an informational text. The second is an updated fairy tale.

---

**DIRECTIONS:** Read the following selection. Then, choose the best answer for each question. Mark each answer on your answer sheet in the square provided.

### Night Lights on the High Seas

For centuries, lighthouses have been used to alert sailors that land is near, to point out dangerous rocks and reefs, and to cast a bright light into the night to guide ships on their way. Seafarers have relied on these structures since the days of ancient Egypt. The lighthouse built in 300 B.C. on Pharos, an island near Alexandria, was regarded as one of the Seven Wonders of the World.

Lighthouses help to guide ships at night by giving off an intense beam that flashes every few seconds. Until the eighteenth century, the source of light was an oak-log fire. Coal fire was used for many years after that, until electricity became common in the early twentieth century. Some modern lighthouses also send out radio signals to help ships find their way in foggy weather. Even in their modern form, lighthouses serve their ancient purpose as guiding lights, flashing specks of civilization in the dark, lonely waters of night.

---

**ITEM 1** asks for vocabulary knowledge.

1. In the first paragraph, the word *seafarers* means —

   **A** oceans     **C** fish

   **B** sailors     **D** ships

**Answer:** Look at the surrounding sentences, or **context,** to see which definition fits.

**A is incorrect.** The word *ocean* is another word for "sea," but oceans do not rely on lighthouses.

**B is the best answer.** In the context of the passage, it makes sense that *sailors* have relied on lighthouses for centuries.

**C is incorrect.** Fish live and travel in the sea, but nothing in the passage indicates that they depend on lighthouses.

**D is incorrect.** The safety of ships on the ocean depends on lighthouses. However, it is the *sailors* on the ships who have "relied on these structures for centuries."

**ITEM 2** asks for close reading. Read carefully to see if the answer is stated directly in the text.

2. What was used to produce the light in lighthouses before the eighteenth century?

   **F** Wood     **H** Gas

   **G** Coal     **J** Electricity

**Answer:** Read the passage carefully to find the answer.

**F is the correct answer.** The second sentence of the second paragraph indicates that "until the eighteenth century, the source of light was an oak-log fire." The words *oak* and *log* clearly indicate that "wood" is the right choice.

**ITEM 3** asks for an inference.

3. What is the main idea of this passage?

   **A** Working in a lighthouse is a dangerous job.

   **B** Modern lighthouses are very different from those of long ago.

   **C** The first lighthouse was built in 300 b.c. on the island of Pharos.

   **D** Lighthouses have helped guide ships for thousands of years.

**Answer:** Think about which statement covers the passage as a whole.

**A is incorrect.** The passage does not provide an explanation of working in a lighthouse.

**B is incorrect.** It does not explain the purpose of lighthouses over the years.

**C is incorrect.** It is only one detail in the passage.

**D is the best answer.** It covers most of the details in the passage.

**ITEM 4** asks you to recognize an opinion.

5. Which is an **opinion** expressed in the passage?

   **F** The beam from a lighthouse flashes every few seconds.

   **G** Modern lighthouses send out radio signals.

   **H** Pharos is an island near Alexandria.

   **J** The ocean waters are lonely at night.

**Answer:** A **fact** can be proved true or false. An **opinion,** a personal feeling or belief, cannot be proved true or false. **F, G,** and **H** are facts that can be proved true or false. **J is correct** because it is the only opinion.

**ITEM 5** asks you to decide why the author wrote the passage.

6. What is the author's main **purpose** for writing this passage?

   **A** To entertain readers with an exciting story

   **B** To inform readers about the history of lighthouses

   **C** To persuade readers to visit a lighthouse

   **D** To describe what life in a lighthouse is like

**Answer:** Look at the information given in the passage, and decide what the writer's purpose was in writing.

**A is incorrect.** The writer does not tell a story.

**B is the best answer.** The writer presents information about the function of lighthouses over time.

**C is incorrect.** The writer's purpose is not to persuade readers to visit a lighthouse.

**D is incorrect.** The writer never tells what it's like to live in a lighthouse.

# Test Smarts

### A Technologically Correct Fairy Tale: Jack and the Beanstalk

There once was a poor widow who lived in a small cottage with her son, Jack. Jack was a good-hearted fellow who <u>devoted</u> all his time to a mega-computer game. Since Jack did not have a paying job, he and his widowed mother were very poor.

The day arrived when the widow had sold all her possessions via the Internet, except for an elderly cow. Jack was to sell the cow at the market since his mother was too <u>frail</u> to make the trip.

"Get a good price for her," the widow instructed.

"Yes, Mother," Jack answered.

Off he went with the cow in tow.

Out on the highway, Jack was stopped by a man who offered to trade him a handful of oddly shaped, brightly colored beans for the cow. "These are turbo-beans," the man whispered. While Jack didn't know exactly what that meant, he did know that the word *turbo* made the beans sound special, so he agreed to the trade. When he got home, he proudly handed the beans to his mother. She promptly tossed them out the window, declaring she didn't know what he could have been thinking. . . .

**ITEM 1** is a vocabulary question. To answer it, go back to the fairy tale, and consider the surrounding words, or context, to identify the best definition.

1. In the first paragraph the underlined word *devoted* means —

   **A** donated

   **B** avoided

   **C** captured

   **D** dedicated

**A is incorrect.** *Donated* means "gave someone something of value." It doesn't fit in this context.

**B is incorrect.** It doesn't fit the context, which shows what Jack did with his time, not what he didn't do.

**C is incorrect.** It doesn't fit in the context.

**D is the best answer.** In this context, *devoted* means "dedicated" or "gave one's time to a particular pursuit."

**ITEM 2** is another vocabulary question.

2. In the second paragraph of the fairy tale, *frail* means —

   **F** proud

   **G** weak

   **H** stubborn

   **J** forceful

**The best answer is G,** since it offers the only reason why the widow would not be able to make the trip herself.

**ITEM 3** is a factual question. Reread the fairy tale, and you'll find the answer.

3. How did the widow sell all of her possessions, except for the old cow?

   **A** She sold them via the Internet.

   **B** She set up a shop on the highway.

   **C** She sold them to her neighbors.

   **D** She sold them to the man with the beans.

**A is the answer.** The fairy tale clearly states that she sold her possessions on the Internet.

**B is incorrect.** Jack met the man with the beans on the main highway. The widow did not go there.

**C is incorrect.** Neighbors are not mentioned in the selection.

**D is incorrect.** Jack, not the widow, traded the cow for the beans.

**ITEM 4** asks you to analyze a cause-and-effect relationship. Don't worry, though. The answer is in the text.

4. Because Jack didn't have a paying job, he and his mother were —

    **F** supported by an uncle

    **G** very poor

    **H** reduced to stealing

    **J** very angry

**F is incorrect.** An uncle is not mentioned in the story.

**G is the best answer.** The fairy tale says that they were poor.

**H is incorrect.** Stealing is not mentioned in the story.

**J is incorrect.** Anger is not mentioned in the story.

**ITEM 5** requires that you make an inference based on the text.

5. Jack's mother didn't think beans for a cow was a good trade. How do you know this?

    **A** She explains that a cow is worth more than a handful of beans.

    **B** Jack was supposed to sell the cow.

    **C** The man cheated Jack.

    **D** She tossed the beans out the window.

**A is incorrect.** Jack's mother doesn't say this in the story.

**B is incorrect.** This is true, but it doesn't explain why his mother didn't think it was a good trade.

**C is incorrect.** This may be true, but it doesn't tell us how we know what Jack's mother thought of the trade.

**D is the best answer.** Her actions show what she thought of the trade.

**ITEM 6** asks you to use your **prior knowledge** to predict the outcome.

6. If this story ended like a typical fairy tale, which of the following predictions would you make?

    **F** The beans do, indeed, prove worthless.

    **G** The beans become the key to lifelong happiness for Jack and his mother.

    **H** The beans end up in a stew.

    **J** The cow comes home.

**F is incorrect.** The fairy tale cannot have its "happily ever after" ending if the beans are worthless.

**G is the best answer.** In fairy tales, magical gifts from strangers often bring great rewards in the end.

**H is incorrect.** This is too ordinary an ending for a fairy tale.

**J is incorrect.** This ending is also too ordinary for a fairy tale.

# Strategies for Taking Writing Tests
## Writing a Fictional or Autobiographical Narrative

Some tests may include writing prompts that ask you to write a narrative, or story. The following steps will help you write a **fictional** or **autobiographical narrative.** The responses are based on this prompt.

> **Prompt**
> Write a short fictional narrative. The story should include major and minor characters, a thoroughly developed plot, and a definite setting.

## Thinking It Through: Writing a Fictional or Autobiographical Narrative

■ **STEP 1 Read the prompt carefully.** Does the prompt ask you to write a fictional story (a made-up story) or an **autobiographical story** (a story of something that really happened to you)?

*The word "fictional" tells me that the prompt is asking for a made-up story.*

**STEP 2 Outline the plot of your narrative.** Explain conflict, climax, resolution.

*Conflict—the main character, Sue, wants to win the fencing tournament. Climax—Sue fences against the champion. Resolution—Sue wins but feels bad when she sees her opponent crying.*

**STEP 3 Identify the major and minor characters.** What do they look and act like? How do they sound when they speak?

*Major character—Sue is tall and lanky; she is shy; she is very competitive. Minor character—Sue's competitor, Tory, is tall; she is confident and sometimes rude.*

**STEP 4 Identify the setting of your narrative.** Where and when does your story take place?

*The story takes place in January during the state fencing championships in a gymnasium.*

**STEP 5 Draft your narrative, adding dialogue, suspense, and sensory details.**

*I plan to create suspense by drawing out the moment when Sue must decide what to do when she sees Tory crying. I will use sensory details to describe how she feels. I will also include dialogue of her conversation with Tory.*

**STEP 6 Revise and proofread your narrative.** Make sure that you have organized the events in your story in a logical order. Add transitions that show time, such as *earlier, afterward, at the same time,* and *later.*

# Writing a Summary

Some tests include writing prompts like the one to the right.

To write a **summary** of a passage, you rewrite in your own words the passage's main idea and significant details. The summary should both paraphrase and condense the original. A summary of a short passage should be about one-third as long. For a longer selection, a summary should include no more than one sentence for each paragraph.

> **Prompt**
>
> Read the essay "Fish Cheeks," and then summarize it. In your summary, include the main idea and significant details of the article.

**The following steps will help you write an effective summary in response to a prompt. The student responses are based on the reading selection "Fish Cheeks" on pages 135–137.**

## Thinking It Through: Writing a Summary

■ **STEP 1 Read the passage carefully. Identify the main idea, and restate it in your own words.** What is the most important point the writer is making about the topic? How would *you* say it?

Main idea: The narrator learns that she can fit in with American teens but she should be proud of her Chinese heritage.

**STEP 2 Identify significant details to include in the summary.** Which details directly support the main idea? List at least one key idea or detail from each paragraph.

Significant details: The narrator is Chinese American; she has a crush on the minister's son, who is white; the narrator is embarrassed by the Chinese food her mother prepares and by her relatives' table manners; her mother gives her a miniskirt.

**STEP 3 Write the main idea and most significant details in a paragraph, using your own words.** Give details in the same order they are presented in the passage.

The narrator is a Chinese American teenager struggling to fit in with her friends. When her parents invite the minister and his family to Christmas Eve dinner, the narrator is embarrassed by the food her mother prepares and by the table manners of her relatives. Her mother gives her a miniskirt and tells her that she can look like a typical American girl on the outside but she should always be proud of her Chinese heritage.

## Writing a Response to Literature

On a writing test, you may be asked to write a **literary response.** Often on such tests, you will be given a literary selection to read and a prompt such as the one on the right.

**The following steps and the partial student responses will help you respond to a prompt like the one above. The short story "A Day's Wait" can be found on pages 81–83.**

> ***Prompt***
> What sort of character is Schatz from the short story "A Day's Wait"? Analyze his thoughts, actions, and words.

### Thinking It Through: Writing a Response to Literature

■ **STEP 1** **Read the prompt carefully, noting key words.** Key words might include a verb—such as *analyze, identify,* or *explain*—and a literary element—such as *plot, character, setting,* or *theme.*

The key words are "analyze" and "character."

**STEP 2** **Read the selection at least twice.** Read first for the overall meaning of the work. Then, read the selection a second time, keeping the key words from the prompt in mind.

**STEP 3** **Write a main idea statement.** Your main idea statement should give the title and author of the work and should directly address the prompt.

Schatz, the little boy in "A Day's Wait" by Ernest Hemingway, is similar to my little brother; both hide their feelings.

**STEP 4** **Find specific examples and details from the selection to support your main idea.** If you include quotations from the literary work, remember to enclose them in quotation marks.

When Schatz's father asked Schatz how he was feeling, he replied, "Just the same, so far," although he feared he was dying.

**STEP 5** **Draft, revise, and proofread your response.** To create coherence, use transitions between ideas, such as *for example, however,* and *finally.* When you have written your draft, re-read it to make sure you have presented your ideas clearly. Also, check to see that you have fully addressed all the key words in the prompt. Finally, proofread to correct mistakes in spelling, punctuation, and capitalization.

# Using the T.H.E.M.E.S. Strategy on a Writing Test

Writing tests often ask you to write a **persuasive essay** in response to a prompt. Most of these prompts give you a topic, but you must identify your position and generate support for your position. Thinking of what to say in a limited amount of time is one of the most difficult parts of such a test.

**Use the T.H.E.M.E.S. strategy, explained in the steps below, to generate support for a position quickly. The student responses are based on this prompt.**

> **Prompt**
> The city council is considering building a parking garage or a park on an empty lot. Write an essay that takes a position on the issue and defends the position with relevant support.

## Thinking It Through: Using the T.H.E.M.E.S. Strategy on a Writing Test

■ **Each letter in T.H.E.M.E.S. stands for a category you could use to trigger ideas for supporting your position in a persuasive essay.**

T = Time
H = Health
E = Education
M = Money
E = Environment
S = Safety

**STEP 1 Identify your position on the topic given in the prompt.**

The city council should build a park.

**STEP 2 Use T.H.E.M.E.S. to list benefits for your position.**

T = A park would take less <u>time</u> to build than a garage. H = People could use the park to exercise and remain <u>healthy.</u> E = People might become more aware, or <u>educated,</u> about the wildlife and plants that occupy the area. M = The city would save <u>money</u> because constructing playscapes and jogging trails is less expensive than clearing the land and building a garage. E = The <u>environment</u> would benefit because the trees and homes of animals are not destroyed. S = Without a garage, fewer cars may drive in the area, reducing the <u>safety</u> hazard of automobile accidents.

**STEP 3 Identify the three strongest reasons you developed using T.H.E.M.E.S.** Your strongest reasons will be those for which you have the most evidence and those that address readers' concerns about the topic.

My three strongest reasons for building a park are health benefits, reduced costs, and environmental benefits. These are the issues that I think concern my readers the most.

# Out Here on My Own

*You've got to walk that lonesome valley*
*You've got to walk it by yourself*
*Nobody else can walk it for you…*
                    *—African American spiritual*

# Before You Read

## Make the Connection

### It's a Wild World

People face difficult situations in all kinds of ways. The expressions "Pick yourself up, dust yourself off, and start all over again," "Run for your life," and "Circle the wagons" suggest different strategies for dealing with tough situations.

### What Would You Do?

If you were facing a bully, would you

- run the other way?
- get help from your family and friends?
- face your opponent and fight?
- try to use logic and reasoning to reach an agreement?
- use a strategy other than the ones listed above? (What would it be?)

Talk about your response with a partner or a group.

## Elements of Literature

### Conflict: "Clash" Action

Conflict is what gives any story its energy. When you can't wait to find out what happens next and you care about who wins out in a story, you're reacting to conflict.

> **Conflict** is a struggle or clash between opposing characters or opposing forces.
>
> *For more on Conflict, see pages 22–23 and the Handbook of Literary Terms.*

As the first two paragraphs of "Rikki-tikki-tavi" tell us, this is a story about a "great war" that is fought by a brave little mongoose. Does this bold little creature's conflict with a deadly enemy keep you turning those pages?

## Reading Skills and Strategies

### Dialogue with the Text

When you read a story actively, a great deal goes on in your head:

- You connect what you read with your own experience.
- You ask yourself questions and make predictions about what will happen next.
- You challenge the text.
- You reflect on its meaning.

As you read, you create your own meaning from the text. No two readers will interpret a text in exactly the same way. Your way of reading is unique.

Jotting down notes as you read will help you become aware of yourself as a reader. Try keeping a sheet of paper beside each page so that you can note your thoughts next to the passage you're responding to. One reader's comments appear on the first pages of "Rikki-tikki-tavi" as an example.

**go.hrw.com**
*LEO 7-1*

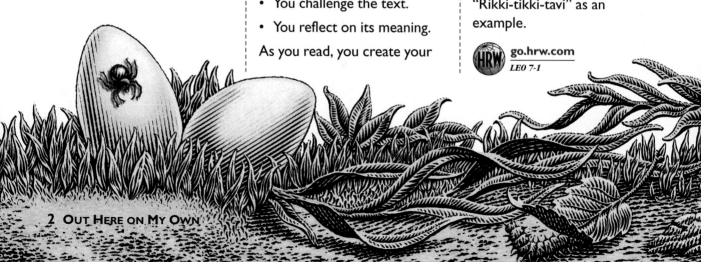

# Rikki-tikki-tavi

## Rudyard Kipling

*Inch by inch rose up the big black cobra . . .*

This is the story of the great war that Rikki-tikki-tavi fought single-handed, through the bathrooms of the big bungalow[1] in Segowlee cantonment.[2] Darzee, the tailorbird, helped him, and Chuchundra, the muskrat, who never comes out into the middle of the floor but always creeps round by the wall, gave him advice; but Rikki-tikki did the real fighting.

He was a mongoose, rather like a little cat in his fur and his tail but quite like a weasel in his head and his habits. His eyes and the end of his

1. **bungalow:** in India, low, one-storied house, named after a type of house found in Bengal, a region of South Asia.
2. **Segowlee** (sē·gouʹlē) **cantonment:** British army post in Segowlee (now Segauli), India.

### Dialogue with the Text

What kind of name is Rikki-tikki-tavi?

I wonder what kind of war is fought in the bathrooms of a bungalow. What are these animals fighting about?

What purpose do Darzee and Chuchundra have in the story? Are they Rikki-tikki-tavi's friends?

These Indian names are very interesting! They are different from the names around here.

restless nose were pink; he could scratch himself anywhere he pleased with any leg, front or back, that he chose to use; he could fluff up his tail till it looked like a bottlebrush, and his war cry as he scuttled through the long grass was *Rikk-tikk-tikki-tikki-tchk!*

One day, a high summer flood washed him out of the burrow where he lived with his father and mother and carried him, kicking and clucking, down a roadside ditch. He found a little wisp of grass floating there and clung to it till he lost his senses. When he revived, he was lying in the hot sun in the middle of a garden path, very draggled[3] indeed, and a small boy was saying: "Here's a dead mongoose. Let's have a funeral."

"No," said his mother; "let's take him in and dry him. Perhaps he isn't really dead."

They took him into the house, and a big man picked him up between his finger and thumb and said he was not dead but half choked; so they wrapped him in cotton wool and warmed him over a little fire, and he opened his eyes and sneezed.

"Now," said the big man (he was an Englishman who had just moved into the bungalow), "don't frighten him, and we'll see what he'll do."

It is the hardest thing in the world to frighten a mongoose, because he is eaten up from nose to tail with curiosity. The motto of all the mongoose family is "Run and find out," and Rikki-tikki was a true mongoose. He looked at the cotton wool, decided that it was not good to eat, ran all round the table, sat up and put his fur in order, scratched himself, and jumped on the small boy's shoulder.

"Don't be frightened, Teddy," said his father. "That's his way of making friends."

"Ouch! He's tickling under my chin," said Teddy.

3. **draggled:** wet and muddy, as if from being dragged around.

## Dialogue with the Text

Rikki-tikki-tavi reminds me of my cat, Charlie. Charlie can scratch himself anywhere he pleases, and when he's scared, his tail also looks like a bottlebrush. That's a good description of how it looks.

I think it is neat that Rikki got his name from the sound he makes.

I wonder where Rikki-tikki-tavi's mother and father ended up after the flood?

The mother must be an animal lover because she wants to save the mongoose.
I wonder what they are going to do with Rikki-tikki-tavi, and I wonder what purpose this family will serve later on in the story?

Rikki-tikki-tavi must be very tiny if the big man picked him up between his thumb and finger.

Is the big man the father? He is also kind to animals.
I think I would also try to save a cute little animal that was dying. I hope I would know what to do.

*Rebecca Irizarry*

—Rebecca Irizarry
Maplewood Middle School
Maplewood, New Jersey

Rikki-tikki looked down between the boy's collar and neck, snuffed at his ear, and climbed down to the floor, where he sat rubbing his nose.

"Good gracious," said Teddy's mother, "and that's a wild creature! I suppose he's so tame because we've been kind to him."

"All mongooses are like that," said her husband. "If Teddy doesn't pick him up by the tail or try to put him in a cage, he'll run in and out of the house all day long. Let's give him something to eat."

They gave him a little piece of raw meat. Rikki-tikki liked it <u>immensely</u>, and when it was finished, he went out into the veranda[4] and sat in the sunshine and fluffed up his fur to make it dry to the roots. Then he felt better.

"There are more things to find out about in this house," he said to himself, "than all my family could find out in all their lives. I shall certainly stay and find out."

He spent all that day roaming over the house. He nearly drowned himself in the bathtubs, put his nose into the ink on a writing table, and burnt it on the end of the big man's cigar, for he climbed up in the big man's lap to see how writing was done. At nightfall he ran into Teddy's nursery to watch how kerosene lamps were lighted, and when Teddy went to bed, Rikki-tikki climbed up too; but he was a restless companion, because he had to get up and attend to every noise all through the night and find out what made it. Teddy's mother and father came in, the last thing, to look at their boy, and Rikki-tikki was awake on the pillow. "I don't like that," said Teddy's mother; "he may bite the child." "He'll do no such thing," said the father. "Teddy's safer with that little beast than if he had a bloodhound to watch him. If a snake came into the nursery now——"

But Teddy's mother wouldn't think of anything so awful.

4. **veranda:** open porch covered by a roof, running along the outside of a building.

Early in the morning, Rikki-tikki came to early breakfast in the veranda riding on Teddy's shoulder, and they gave him banana and some boiled egg; and he sat on all their laps one after the other, because every well-brought-up mongoose always hopes to be a house mongoose someday and have rooms to run about in; and Rikki-tikki's mother (she used to live in the General's house at Segowlee) had carefully told Rikki what to do if ever he came across white men.

Then Rikki-tikki went out into the garden to see what was to be seen. It was a large garden, only half cultivated, with bushes, as big as summerhouses, of Marshal Niel roses; lime and orange trees; clumps of bamboos; and thickets of high grass. Rikki-tikki licked his lips. "This is a splendid hunting ground," he said, and his tail grew bottlebrushy at the thought of it, and he scuttled up and down the garden, snuffing here and there till he heard very sorrowful voices in a thorn bush. It was Darzee, the tailorbird, and his wife. They had made a beautiful nest by pulling two big leaves together and stitching them up the edges with fibers and had filled the hollow with cotton and downy fluff. The nest swayed to and fro as they sat on the rim and cried.

"What is the matter?" asked Rikki-tikki.

"We are very miserable," said Darzee. "One of our babies fell out of the nest yesterday and Nag ate him."

"H'm!" said Rikki-tikki, "that is very sad—but I am a stranger here. Who is Nag?"

Darzee and his wife only <u>cowered</u> down in the nest without answering, for from the thick grass at the foot of the bush there came a low hiss—a horrid, cold sound that made Rikki-tikki jump back two clear feet. Then inch by inch out of the grass rose up the head and

## WORDS TO OWN
**immensely** (im·mens′lē) *adv.*: enormously.
**cowered** (kou′ərd) *v.*: crouched and trembled in fear.

spread hood of Nag, the big black cobra, and he was five feet long from tongue to tail. When he had lifted one third of himself clear of the ground, he stayed balancing to and fro exactly as a dandelion tuft balances in the wind, and he looked at Rikki-tikki with the wicked snake's eyes that never change their expression, whatever the snake may be thinking of.

"Who is Nag," said he. "*I* am Nag. The great God Brahm[5] put his mark upon all our people, when the first cobra spread his hood to keep the sun off Brahm as he slept. Look, and be afraid!"

He spread out his hood more than ever, and Rikki-tikki saw the spectacle mark on the back of it that looks exactly like the eye part of a hook-and-eye fastening. He was afraid for the minute; but it is impossible for a mongoose to stay frightened for any length of time, and though Rikki-tikki had never met a live cobra before, his mother had fed him on dead ones, and he knew that all a grown mongoose's business in life was to fight and eat snakes. Nag knew that too, and at the bottom of his cold heart, he was afraid.

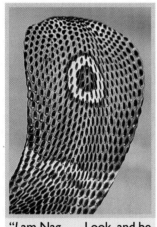

"*I* am Nag. . . . Look, and be afraid!"

"Well," said Rikki-tikki, and his tail began to fluff up again, "marks or no marks, do you think it is right for you to eat fledglings out of a nest?"

Nag was thinking to himself and watching the least little movement in the grass behind Rikki-tikki. He knew that mongooses in the garden meant death sooner or later for him and his family, but he wanted to get Rikki-tikki off his guard. So he dropped his head a little and put it on one side.

"Let us talk," he said. "You eat eggs. Why should not I eat birds?"

"Behind you! Look behind you!" sang Darzee.

Rikki-tikki knew better than to waste time in staring. He jumped up in the air as high as he could go, and just under him whizzed by the head of Nagaina, Nag's wicked wife. She had crept up behind him as he was talking, to make an end of him; and he heard her savage hiss as the stroke missed. He came down almost across her back, and if he had been an old mongoose, he would have known that then was the time to break her back with one bite; but he was afraid of the terrible lashing return stroke of the cobra. He bit, indeed, but did not bite long enough, and he jumped clear of the whisking tail, leaving Nagaina torn and angry.

"Wicked, wicked Darzee!" said Nag, lashing up as high as he could reach toward the nest in the thorn bush; but Darzee had built it out of reach of snakes, and it only swayed to and fro.

Rikki-tikki felt his eyes growing red and hot (when a mongoose's eyes grow red, he is angry), and he sat back on his tail and hind legs like a little kangaroo, and looked all round him, and chattered with rage. But Nag and Nagaina had disappeared into the grass. When a snake misses its stroke, it never says anything or gives any sign of what it means to do next. Rikki-tikki did not care to follow them, for he did not feel sure that he could manage two snakes at once. So he trotted off to the gravel path near the house and sat down to think. It was a serious matter for him. If you read the old books of natural history, you will find they say that when the mongoose fights the snake and happens to get bitten, he runs off and eats some herb that cures him. That is not true. The victory is only a matter of quickness of eye and quickness of foot—snake's blow against the mongoose's jump—and as no eye can follow the motion of

5. **Brahm** (bräm): in the Hindu religion, the creator (also called Brahma).

a snake's head when it strikes, this makes things much more wonderful than any magic herb. Rikki-tikki knew he was a young mongoose, and it made him all the more pleased to think that he had managed to escape a blow from behind. It gave him confidence in himself, and when Teddy came running down the path, Rikki-tikki was ready to be petted. But just as Teddy was stooping, something wriggled a little in the dust and a tiny voice said: "Be careful. I am Death!" It was Karait, the dusty brown snakeling that lies for choice on the dusty earth; and his bite is as dangerous as the cobra's. But he is so small that nobody thinks of him, and so he does the more harm to people.

Rikki-tikki's eyes grew red again, and he danced up to Karait with the peculiar rocking, swaying motion that he had inherited from his family. It looks very funny, but it is so perfectly balanced a <u>gait</u> that you can fly off from it at any angle you please; and in dealing with snakes this is an advantage. If Rikki-tikki had only known, he was doing a much more dangerous thing

"Be careful. I am Death!" It was Karait. . . .

than fighting Nag, for Karait is so small and can turn so quickly that unless Rikki bit him close to the back of the head, he would get the return stroke in his eye or his lip. But Rikki did not know; his eyes were all red, and he rocked back and forth, looking for a good place to hold. Karait struck out, Rikki jumped sideways and tried to run in, but the wicked little dusty gray head lashed within a fraction of his shoulder, and he had to jump over the body, and the head followed his heels close.

Teddy shouted to the house: "Oh, look here! Our mongoose is killing a snake," and Rikki-

tikki heard a scream from Teddy's mother. His father ran out with a stick, but by the time he came up, Karait had lunged out once too far, and Rikki-tikki had sprung, jumped on the snake's back, dropped his head far between his forelegs, bitten as high up the back as he could get hold, and rolled away. That bite paralyzed Karait, and Rikki-tikki was just going to eat him up from the tail, after the custom of his family at dinner, when he remembered that a full meal makes a slow mongoose, and if he wanted all his strength and quickness ready, he must keep himself thin. He went away for a dust bath under the castor-oil bushes, while Teddy's father beat the dead Karait. "What is the use of that?" thought Rikki-tikki; "I have settled it all"; and then Teddy's mother picked him up from the dust and hugged him, crying that he had saved Teddy from death, and Teddy's father said that he was a providence,[6] and Teddy looked on with big, scared eyes. Rikki-tikki was rather amused at all the fuss, which, of course, he did not understand. Teddy's mother might just as well have petted Teddy for playing in the dust. Rikki was thoroughly enjoying himself.

That night at dinner, walking to and fro among the wineglasses on the table, he might have stuffed himself three times over with nice things; but he remembered Nag and Nagaina, and though it was very pleasant to be patted and petted by Teddy's mother and to sit on Teddy's shoulder, his eyes would get red from time to time, and he would go off into his long war cry of *Rikk-tikk-tikki-tikki-tchk!*

Teddy carried him off to bed and insisted on Rikki-tikki's sleeping under his chin. Rikki-tikki was too well bred to bite or scratch, but as soon as Teddy was asleep, he went off for his

6. **providence:** favor or gift from God or nature.

**WORDS TO OWN**
**gait** *n.:* way of walking or running.

nightly walk round the house, and in the dark he ran up against Chuchundra, the muskrat, creeping round by the wall. Chuchundra is a brokenhearted little beast. He whimpers and cheeps all night, trying to make up his mind to run into the middle of the room; but he never gets there.

Chuchundra, a brokenhearted little beast.

"Don't kill me," said Chuchundra, almost weeping. "Rikki-tikki, don't kill me!"

"Do you think a snake killer kills muskrats?" said Rikki-tikki scornfully.

"Those who kill snakes get killed by snakes," said Chuchundra, more sorrowfully than ever. "And how am I to be sure that Nag won't mistake me for you some dark night?"

"There's not the least danger," said Rikki-tikki, "but Nag is in the garden, and I know you don't go there."

"My cousin Chua, the rat, told me——" said Chuchundra, and then he stopped.

"Told you what?"

"H'sh! Nag is everywhere, Rikki-tikki. You should have talked to Chua in the garden."

"I didn't—so you must tell me. Quick, Chuchundra, or I'll bite you!"

Chuchundra sat down and cried till the tears rolled off his whiskers. "I am a very poor man," he sobbed. "I never had spirit enough to run out into the middle of the room. H'sh! I mustn't tell you anything. Can't you *hear,* Rikki-tikki?"

Rikki-tikki listened. The house was as still as still, but he thought he could just catch the faintest *scratch-scratch* in the world—a noise as faint as that of a wasp walking on a windowpane—the dry scratch of a snake's scales on brickwork.

"That's Nag or Nagaina," he said to himself, "and he is crawling into the bathroom sluice.[7] You're right, Chuchundra; I should have talked to Chua."

He stole off to Teddy's bathroom, but there was nothing there, and then to Teddy's mother's bathroom. At the bottom of the smooth plaster wall there was a brick pulled out to make a sluice for the bathwater, and as Rikki-tikki stole in by the masonry[8] curb where the bath is put, he heard Nag and Nagaina whispering together outside in the moonlight.

"When the house is emptied of people," said Nagaina to her husband, "*he* will have to go away, and then the garden will be our own again. Go in quietly, and remember that the big man who killed Karait is the first one to bite. Then come out and tell me, and we will hunt for Rikki-tikki together."

"But are you sure that there is anything to be gained by killing the people?" said Nag.

"Everything. When there were no people in the bungalow, did we have any mongoose in the garden? So long as the bungalow is empty, we are king and queen of the garden; and remember that as soon as our eggs in the melon bed hatch (as they may tomorrow), our children will need room and quiet."

"I had not thought of that," said Nag. "I will go, but there is no need that we should hunt for Rikki-tikki afterward. I will kill the big man and his wife, and the child if I can, and come away quietly. Then the bungalow will be empty, and Rikki-tikki will go."

Rikki-tikki tingled all over with rage and hatred at this, and then Nag's head came through the sluice, and his five feet of cold body followed it. Angry as he was, Rikki-tikki was very frightened as he saw the size of the big cobra. Nag coiled himself up, raised his head, and looked into the bathroom in the dark, and Rikki could see his eyes glitter.

7. **sluice** (slo͞os): drain.
8. **masonry:** built of stone or brick.

"Now, if I kill him here, Nagaina will know; and if I fight him on the open floor, the odds are in his favor. What am I to do?" said Rikki-tikki-tavi.

Nag waved to and fro, and then Rikki-tikki heard him drinking from the biggest water jar that was used to fill the bath. "That is good," said the snake. "Now, when Karait was killed, the big man had a stick. He may have that stick still, but when he comes in to bathe in the morning, he will not have a stick. I shall wait here till he comes. Nagaina—do you hear me?—I shall wait here in the cool till daytime."

There was no answer from outside, so Rikki-tikki knew Nagaina had gone away. Nag coiled himself down, coil by coil, round the bulge at the bottom of the water jar, and Rikki-tikki stayed still as death. After an hour he began to move, muscle by muscle, toward the jar. Nag was asleep, and Rikki-tikki looked at his big back, wondering which would be the best place for a good hold. "If I don't break his back at the first jump," said Rikki, "he can still fight; and if he fights—O Rikki!" He looked at the thickness of the neck below the hood, but that was too much for him; and a bite near the tail would only make Nag savage.

"It must be the head," he said at last, "the head above the hood; and when I am once there, I must not let go."

Then he jumped. The head was lying a little clear of the water jar, under the curve of it; and as his teeth met, Rikki braced his back against the bulge of the red earthenware to hold down the head. This gave him just one second's purchase,[9] and he made the most of it. Then he was battered to and fro as a rat is shaken by a dog—to and fro on the floor, up and down, and round in great circles, but his eyes were red and he held on as the body cartwhipped over the floor, upsetting the tin dipper and the soap dish and the flesh brush, and banged against the tin side of the bath. As he held, he closed his jaws tighter and tighter, for he made sure[10] he would be banged to death, and for the honor of his family, he preferred to be found with his teeth locked. He was dizzy, aching, and felt shaken to pieces, when something went off like a thunderclap just behind him; a hot wind knocked him senseless and red fire singed his fur. The big man had been wakened by the noise and had fired both barrels of a shotgun into Nag just behind the hood.

Rikki-tikki held on with his eyes shut, for now he was quite sure he was dead; but the head did not move, and the big man picked him up and said: "It's the mongoose again, Alice; the little chap has saved *our* lives now." Then Teddy's mother came in with a very white face and saw what was left of Nag, and Rikki-tikki dragged himself to Teddy's bedroom and spent half the rest of the night shaking himself tenderly to find out whether he really was broken into forty pieces, as he fancied.

When morning came, he was very stiff but well pleased with his doings. "Now I have Nagaina to settle with, and she will be worse than five Nags, and there's no knowing when the eggs she spoke of will hatch. Goodness! I must go and see Darzee," he said.

Without waiting for breakfast, Rikki-tikki ran to the thorn bush, where Darzee was singing a song of triumph at the top of his voice. The news of Nag's death was all over the garden, for the sweeper had thrown the body on the rubbish heap.

"Oh, you stupid tuft of feathers!" said Rikki-tikki angrily. "Is this the time to sing?"

"Nag is dead—is dead—is dead!" sang Darzee. "The valiant Rikki-tikki caught him by the head and held fast. The big man brought

9. **purchase:** firm hold.

10. **made sure:** here, felt sure.

- - - - - - - - - - - - - - - - - - - - - - - - - - - -

**WORDS TO OWN**

**valiant** (val′yənt) *adj.*: brave and determined.

- - - - - - - - - - - - - - - - - - - - - - - - - - - -

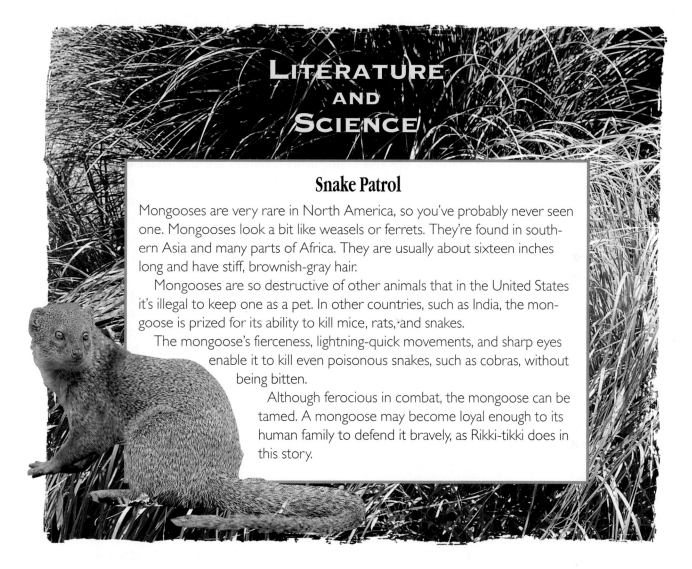

## Snake Patrol

Mongooses are very rare in North America, so you've probably never seen one. Mongooses look a bit like weasels or ferrets. They're found in southern Asia and many parts of Africa. They are usually about sixteen inches long and have stiff, brownish-gray hair.

Mongooses are so destructive of other animals that in the United States it's illegal to keep one as a pet. In other countries, such as India, the mongoose is prized for its ability to kill mice, rats, and snakes.

The mongoose's fierceness, lightning-quick movements, and sharp eyes enable it to kill even poisonous snakes, such as cobras, without being bitten.

Although ferocious in combat, the mongoose can be tamed. A mongoose may become loyal enough to its human family to defend it bravely, as Rikki-tikki does in this story.

the bang-stick, and Nag fell in two pieces! He will never eat my babies again."

"All that's true enough, but where's Nagaina?" said Rikki-tikki, looking carefully round him.

"Nagaina came to the bathroom sluice and called for Nag," Darzee went on; "and Nag came out on the end of a stick—the sweeper picked him up on the end of a stick and threw him upon the rubbish heap. Let us sing about the great, the red-eyed Rikki-tikki!" and Darzee filled his throat and sang.

"If I could get up to your nest, I'd roll your babies out!" said Rikki-tikki. "You don't know when to do the right thing at the right time.

You're safe enough in your nest there, but it's war for me down here. Stop singing a minute, Darzee."

"For the great, beautiful Rikki-tikki's sake I will stop," said Darzee. "What is it, O Killer of the terrible Nag?"

"Where is Nagaina, for the third time?"

"On the rubbish heap by the stables, mourning for Nag. Great is Rikki-tikki with the white teeth."

"Bother[11] my white teeth! Have you ever heard where she keeps her eggs?"

"In the melon bed, on the end nearest the

11. **bother:** here, never mind.

wall, where the sun strikes nearly all day. She hid them there weeks ago."

"And you never thought it worthwhile to tell me? The end nearest the wall, you said?"

"Rikki-tikki, you are not going to eat her eggs?"

"Not eat exactly; no. Darzee, if you have a grain of sense, you will fly off to the stables and pretend that your wing is broken and let Nagaina chase you away to this bush. I must get to the melon bed, and if I went there now, she'd see me."

Darzee was a featherbrained little fellow who could never hold more than one idea at a time in his head, and just because he knew that Nagaina's children were born in eggs like his own, he didn't think at first that it was fair to kill them. But his wife was a sensible bird, and she knew that cobra's eggs meant

Darzee, a featherbrained little fellow.

young cobras later on; so she flew off from the nest and left Darzee to keep the babies warm and continue his song about the death of Nag. Darzee was very like a man in some ways.

She fluttered in front of Nagaina by the rubbish heap and cried out, "Oh, my wing is broken! The boy in the house threw a stone at me and broke it." Then she fluttered more desperately than ever.

Nagaina lifted up her head and hissed, "You warned Rikki-tikki when I would have killed him. Indeed and truly, you've chosen a bad place to be lame in." And she moved toward Darzee's wife, slipping along over the dust.

"The boy broke it with a stone!" shrieked Darzee's wife.

"Well! It may be some <u>consolation</u> to you when you're dead to know that I shall settle accounts with the boy. My husband lies on the rubbish heap this morning, but before night the boy in the house will lie very still. What is the use of running away? I am sure to catch you. Little fool, look at me!"

Darzee's wife knew better than to do *that,* for a bird who looks at a snake's eyes gets so frightened that she cannot move. Darzee's wife fluttered on, piping sorrowfully and never leaving the ground, and Nagaina quickened her pace.

Rikki-tikki heard them going up the path from the stables, and he raced for the end of the melon patch near the wall. There, in the warm litter above the melons, very cunningly hidden, he found twenty-five eggs about the size of a bantam's[12] eggs but with whitish skins instead of shells.

"I was not a day too soon," he said, for he could see the baby cobras curled up inside the skin, and he knew that the minute they were hatched, they could each kill a man or a mongoose. He bit off the tops of the eggs as fast as he could, taking care to crush the young cobras, and turned over the litter from time to time to see whether he had missed any. At last there were only three eggs left, and Rikki-tikki began to chuckle to himself, when he heard Darzee's wife screaming:

"Rikki-tikki, I led Nagaina toward the house, and she has gone into the veranda, and—oh, come quickly—she means killing!"

Rikki-tikki smashed two eggs, and tumbled backward down the melon bed with the third egg in his mouth, and scuttled to the veranda as hard as he could put foot to the ground. Teddy and his mother and father were there at early

12. **bantam's:** small chicken's.

**WORDS TO OWN**
**consolation** (kän′sə·lā′shən) n.: comfort.

breakfast, but Rikki-tikki saw that they were not eating anything. They sat stone still, and their faces were white. Nagaina was coiled up on the matting by Teddy's chair, within easy striking distance of Teddy's bare leg, and she was swaying to and fro, singing a song of triumph.

"Son of the big man that killed Nag," she hissed, "stay still. I am not ready yet. Wait a little. Keep very still, all you three! If you move, I strike, and if you do not move, I strike. Oh, foolish people, who killed my Nag!"

Teddy's eyes were fixed on his father, and all his father could do was to whisper, "Sit still, Teddy. You mustn't move. Teddy, keep still."

Then Rikki-tikki came up and cried: "Turn round, Nagaina; turn and fight!"

"All in good time," said she, without moving her eyes. "I will settle my account with *you* presently. Look at your friends, Rikki-tikki. They are still and white. They are afraid. They dare not move, and if you come a step nearer, I strike."

"Look at your eggs," said Rikki-tikki, "in the melon bed near the wall. Go and look, Nagaina!"

The big snake turned half round and saw the egg on the veranda. "Ah-h! Give it to me," she said.

Rikki-tikki put his paws one on each side of the egg, and his eyes were blood-red. "What price for a snake's egg? For a young cobra? For a young king cobra? For the last—the very last of the brood? The ants are eating all the others down by the melon bed."

Nagaina spun clear round, forgetting everything for the sake of the one egg; and Rikki-tikki saw Teddy's father shoot out a big hand, catch Teddy by the shoulder, and drag him across the little table with the teacups, safe and out of reach of Nagaina.

"Tricked! Tricked! Tricked! *Rikk-tck-tck!*" chuckled Rikki-tikki. "The boy is safe, and it was I—I—I—that caught Nag by the hood last night in the bathroom." Then he began to jump up and down, all four feet together, his head close to the floor. "He threw me to and fro, but he could not shake me off. He was dead before the big man blew him in two. I did it! *Rikki-tikki-tck-tck!* Come then, Nagaina. Come and fight with me. You shall not be a widow long."

Nagaina saw that she had lost her chance of killing Teddy, and the egg lay between Rikki-tikki's paws. "Give me the egg, Rikki-tikki. Give me the last of my eggs, and I will go away and never come back," she said, lowering her hood.

"Yes, you will go away, and you will never come back; for you will go to the rubbish heap with Nag. Fight, widow! The big man has gone for his gun! Fight!"

Rikki-tikki was bounding all round Nagaina, keeping just out of reach of her stroke, his little eyes like hot coals. Nagaina gathered herself together and flung out at him. Rikki-tikki jumped up and backwards. Again and again and again she struck, and each time her head came with a whack on the matting of the veranda and she gathered herself together like a watch spring. Then Rikki-tikki danced in a circle to get behind her, and Nagaina spun round to keep her head to his head, so that the rustle of her tail on the matting sounded like dry leaves blown along by the wind.

He had forgotten the egg. It still lay on the veranda, and Nagaina came nearer and nearer to it, till at last, while Rikki-tikki was drawing breath, she caught it in her mouth, turned to the veranda steps, and flew like an arrow down the path, with Rikki-tikki behind her. When the cobra runs for her life, she goes like a whiplash flicked across a horse's neck. Rikki-tikki knew that he must catch her or all the trouble would begin again. She headed straight for the long grass by the thorn bush, and as he was running, Rikki-tikki heard Darzee still singing his foolish little song of triumph. But Darzee's wife was wiser. She flew off her nest as Nagaina came along and flapped her wings about Nagaina's head. If Darzee had helped, they might have turned her, but Nagaina only lowered her hood and went on. Still, the instant's delay brought Rikki-tikki up to her, and as she plunged into the rat hole where she and Nag used to live, his little white teeth were clenched on her tail and he went down with her—and very few mongooses, however wise and old they may be, care to follow a cobra into its hole. It was dark in the hole, and Rikki-tikki never knew when it might open out and give Nagaina room to turn and strike at him. He held on savagely and stuck out his feet to act as brakes on the dark slope of the hot, moist earth. Then the grass by the mouth of the hole stopped waving, and Darzee said: "It is all over with Rikki-tikki! We must sing his death song. Valiant Rikki-tikki is dead! For Nagaina* will surely kill him underground."

So he sang a very mournful song that he made up on the spur of the minute, and just as he got to the most touching part, the grass quivered again, and Rikki-tikki, covered with dirt, dragged himself out of the hole leg by leg, licking his whiskers. Darzee stopped with a little shout. Rikki-tikki shook some of the dust out of his fur and sneezed. "It is all over," he said. "The widow will never come out again." And the red ants that live between the grass stems heard him and began to troop down one after another to see if he had spoken the truth.

Rikki-tikki curled himself up in the grass and slept where he was—slept and slept till it was late in the afternoon, for he had done a hard day's work.

"Now," he said, when he awoke, "I will go back to the house. Tell the Coppersmith, Darzee, and he will tell the garden that Nagaina is dead."

The Coppersmith is a bird who makes a noise exactly like the beating of a little hammer on a copper pot; and the reason he is always making it is because he is the town crier to every Indian garden and tells all the news to everybody who cares to listen. As Rikki-tikki went up the path, he heard his "attention" notes like a tiny dinner gong and then the steady *"Ding-dong-tock!* Nag is dead—*dong!* Nagaina

The Coppersmith, the town crier.

is dead! *Ding-dong-tock!"* That set all the birds in the garden singing and the frogs croaking, for Nag and Nagaina used to eat frogs as well as little birds.

When Rikki got to the house, Teddy and Teddy's mother (she looked very white still, for she had been fainting) and Teddy's father came out and almost cried over him; and that night he ate all that was given him till he could eat no more and went to bed on Teddy's shoulder, where Teddy's mother saw him when she came to look late at night.

"He saved our lives and Teddy's life," she said to her husband. "Just think, he saved all our lives."

Rikki-tikki woke up with a jump, for the mongooses are light sleepers.

"Oh, it's you," said he. "What are you bothering for? All the cobras are dead; and if they weren't, I'm here."

Rikki-tikki had a right to be proud of himself, but he did not grow too proud, and he kept that garden as a mongoose should keep it, with tooth and jump and spring and bite, till never a cobra dared show its head inside the walls.

### Darzee's Chant
#### Sung in honor of Rikki-tikki-tavi

Singer and tailor am I—
    Doubled the joys that I know—
Proud of my lilt[13] to the sky,
    Proud of the house that I sew.
Over and under, so weave I my music—
    so weave I the house that I sew.

Sing to your fledglings again,
    Mother, O lift up your head!
Evil that plagued us is slain,
    Death in the garden lies dead.
Terror that hid in the roses is impotent[14]—
    flung on the dunghill and dead!

Who has delivered us, who?
    Tell me his nest and his name.
*Rikki,* the valiant, the true,
    *Tikki,* with eyeballs of flame—
*Rikk-tikki-tikki,* the ivory-fanged,
    the hunter with eyeballs of flame!

Give him the Thanks of the Birds,
    Bowing with tail feathers spread,
Praise him with nightingale words—
    Nay, I will praise him instead.
Hear! I will sing you the praise of the bottle-tailed Rikki with eyeballs of red!

*(Here Rikki-tikki interrupted, so the rest of the song is lost.)*

---

13. **lilt:** light, graceful way of singing or speaking.
14. **impotent** (im′pə·tənt): powerless.

# MEET THE WRITER

## On His Own

India, the setting of "Rikki-tikki-tavi," is a place **Joseph Rudyard Kipling** (1865–1936) knew well. His father was a professor of art in Bombay, and Kipling was born in that city when India was still under British rule. India was a fascinating place, and young Kipling loved it.

When he was six, his parents shipped Kipling and his sister off to a boardinghouse in England. Throughout his life he called this place "the House of Desolation." Feeling very much on his own in England, he made a discovery:

> 66 [Books] were among the most important affairs in the world . . . I could read as much as I chose and ask the meaning of things from anyone I met. I had found out, too, that one could take pen and set down what one thought, and that nobody accused one of 'showing off' by doing so. 99

*The Cat That Walked by Himself:* Illustration by Rudyard Kipling for the first edition of his *Just So Stories,* published in 1902.

The Granger Collection, New York.

When he was seventeen, Kipling returned to India and took a job as an editor with an English-language newspaper. He was fascinated by the lives of British colonials in India and the vivid contrast they made with the Indian people they ruled. Soon the paper was printing Kipling's poems and tales about the life he saw around him. Other newspapers reprinted them, and readers clamored for more. Kipling's fame grew; over the next half century he wrote dozens of books, and in 1907, he won the Nobel Prize in literature. Although he later lived in many places around the world, including Brattleboro, Vermont, India always remained close to his heart.

### More Stories by Kipling

You can read more of Kipling's animal stories in *Just So Stories* (Bantam) and *The Jungle Book* (Bantam). *The Jungle Book* is about a boy named Mowgli who is raised by wolves. *Kim* (Penguin), Kipling's best-known novel, traces the adventures of an Irish orphan who is raised as an Indian and eventually becomes a British spy.

# The Dinner Party

*retold by* **Mona Gardner**

*I first heard this story in India, where it is told as if true—though any naturalist[1] would know it couldn't be. Later I learned that a magazine version of it appeared shortly before World War I. This account, and its author, I have never been able to track down.*

The country is India. A colonial official and his wife are giving a large dinner party. They are seated with their guests—army officers and government attachés[2] and their wives, and a visiting American naturalist—in their spacious dining room, which has a bare marble floor, open rafters, and wide glass doors opening onto a veranda.

A spirited discussion springs up between a young girl who insists that women have outgrown the jumping-on-a-chair-at-the-sight-of-a-mouse era and a colonel who says that they haven't.

"A woman's unfailing reaction in any crisis," the colonel says, "is to scream. And while a man may feel like it, he has that ounce more of nerve control than a woman has. And that last ounce is what counts."

The American does not join in the argument but watches the other guests. As he looks, he sees a strange expression come over the face of the hostess. She is staring straight ahead, her muscles contracting slightly. With a slight gesture she summons the native boy standing behind her chair and whispers to him. The boy's eyes widen; he quickly leaves the room.

Of the guests, none except the American notices this or sees the boy place a bowl of milk on the veranda just outside the open doors.

---

1. **naturalist:** person who studies nature by observing animals and plants.
2. **attachés** (at′ə·shāz′): diplomatic officials.

*(continued on next page)*

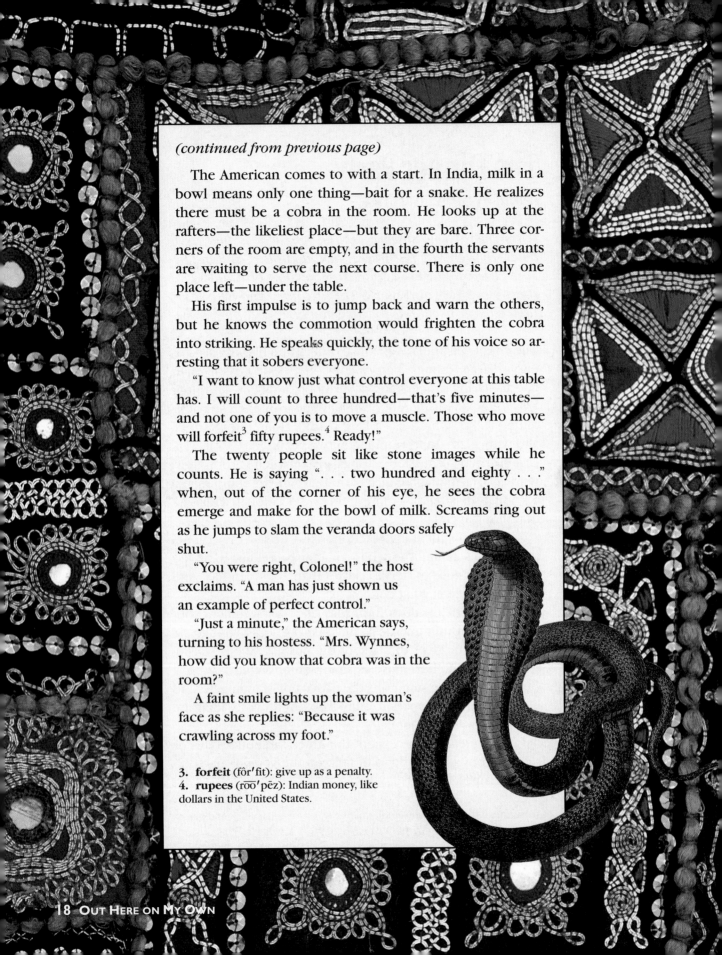

*(continued from previous page)*

The American comes to with a start. In India, milk in a bowl means only one thing—bait for a snake. He realizes there must be a cobra in the room. He looks up at the rafters—the likeliest place—but they are bare. Three corners of the room are empty, and in the fourth the servants are waiting to serve the next course. There is only one place left—under the table.

His first impulse is to jump back and warn the others, but he knows the commotion would frighten the cobra into striking. He speaks quickly, the tone of his voice so arresting that it sobers everyone.

"I want to know just what control everyone at this table has. I will count to three hundred—that's five minutes—and not one of you is to move a muscle. Those who move will forfeit[3] fifty rupees.[4] Ready!"

The twenty people sit like stone images while he counts. He is saying ". . . two hundred and eighty . . ." when, out of the corner of his eye, he sees the cobra emerge and make for the bowl of milk. Screams ring out as he jumps to slam the veranda doors safely shut.

"You were right, Colonel!" the host exclaims. "A man has just shown us an example of perfect control."

"Just a minute," the American says, turning to his hostess. "Mrs. Wynnes, how did you know that cobra was in the room?"

A faint smile lights up the woman's face as she replies: "Because it was crawling across my foot."

3. **forfeit** (fôr′fit): give up as a penalty.
4. **rupees** (roo′pēz): Indian money, like dollars in the United States.

# MAKING MEANINGS

## First Thoughts

1. Respond to "Rikki-tikki-tavi" by completing these sentences. Look back at your Dialogue with the Text notes for ideas.

   - I thought this story was . . .
   - I was frightened for Rikki-tikki when . . .
   - The scene I liked best was . . .

## Shaping Interpretations

2. Describe three **conflicts** that Rikki-tikki faces. Which conflict do you think is his greatest challenge, and why?

3. Like all great heroes, Rikki is celebrated by the society he saves. How does Darzee's chant make Rikki into a super-hero? What kind of music would you set the song to?

4. "The Dinner Party" (see *Connections* on page 17) is another story about an encounter with a snake. How does the hostess deal with *her* snake problem?

### Reading Check

a. Explain how Rikki-tikki comes to Teddy's home.

b. Why is it "the hardest thing in the world to frighten a mongoose"?

c. Whom does Rikki-tikki fight in the "great war"? Why does he fight?

d. Rikki-tikki fights alone, but he gets a little help from his friends. Who are they? How do they help him?

e. What does Rikki-tikki do with Nagaina's eggs?

## Connecting with the Text

5. Did Rikki-tikki's conflicts with the deadly garden bullies remind you of your own experiences? For ideas, think back to what you said about bullies before you read the story. You might also check your reading notes.

## Extending the Text

6. The animal world of "Rikki-tikki-tavi" is filled with conflict and danger. What causes the war in this animal story? What causes most wars among people?

## Challenging the Text

7. Is Kipling fair to the snakes in this story? What could you say in defense of Nag and Nagaina?

8. The animals in this story talk and think as if they were human. How do you feel about stories like this? Do you like them, or do you prefer to read about real animals without human characteristics? Use examples from the story to help explain your feelings about animal stories.

# CHOICES: Building Your Portfolio

## Writer's Notebook

### 1. Collecting Ideas for a Story

Writers get ideas for stories from all kinds of places. Some writers find stories in photographs or paintings. Look at the picture on page 14, or pick another in this book that grabs your attention. Jot down ideas about the following:

- what you see in the picture
- what you think will happen next
- what you think the character should do
- conflicts the character might face that aren't shown in the picture

> **Story Idea from Photograph:**
> —Young girl stranded at dusk on lonely road
> —Her bike has a flat.
> —She's nervous, looking over her shoulder.

## Expository Writing/Science

### 2. Cobra Copy

Create a brochure that will inform zoo visitors about cobras. Before you do research, decide on the questions you'd like to answer. Here are some possibilities:

- How many kinds of cobras exist?
- Where do they live, and what do they eat?
- How dangerous are they?
- Can cobras hypnotize their prey?

Make a brochure by folding a sheet of notebook paper into thirds and presenting your information on it. You may want to include photographs or artwork.

## Speaking and Listening

### 3. Rikki-tikki-2

Suppose that Nagaina's last egg was left on the veranda during the battle and lay there until it hatched. With a group of classmates, create a sequel to the story. Tell the story of the baby cobra in a "talk-around." Form a circle with three or four classmates; then, have someone start with this sentence: "The baby cobra wriggled into the sunlight." Go around the circle, with each person adding a sentence or two to develop the story. Consider how Rikki-tikki might respond by referring to the choices listed under What Would You Do? on page 2.

## Storytelling/Music

### 4. The Sound of Rikki-tikki

Get together with three or four music-loving classmates. With the group, choose one key scene from the story for each person; then, find music to use as background for your scene. Record the different pieces of music on one tape to create a "soundtrack." Perform a dramatic reading of the scenes with your group, weaving the soundtrack into the performance.

# LANGUAGE LINK

## Style: Choosing Specific Verbs

**Language Handbook HELP**

*See Action Verbs, page 714.*

**Technology HELP**

*See* Language Workshop CD-ROM. *Key word entry: verbs.*

SOME OF KIPLING'S VERBS

creep
cower
roam
trot
scuttle
dance

This story moves at a fast pace, in part because Kipling uses strong, vivid verbs to help us see all the action in the cobra wars. Chuchundra doesn't just walk; he *creeps.* Darzee and his wife don't just sit; they *cower.* Rikki-tikki himself *roams, trots, scuttles,* and *dances.* Consider this sentence about a scene from the story:

> Darzee moved along the branch, his eye on Nag.

How did Darzee move? Replace *moved* with *hopped, strolled,* and *stormed.* How does each verb change what you see? What does each verb tell you about Darzee's feelings and plans?

Go back to Kipling's story and find verbs you can add to the list on the left. Keep a verb bank like this one in your notebook for reference when you revise your own writing.

Cover for *The Jungle Book* by Rudyard Kipling.
Rare Books and Manuscripts Division. The New York Public Library. Astor, Lenox and Tilden Foundations.

### Try It Out

➤ Rewrite the sentences below, replacing each tame verb with a more specific (and more interesting) verb.

1. That night, Nag went into the bungalow.
2. Rikki-tikki gave a warning.
3. Teddy's parents stood and looked at the cobra.

➤ Be a verb spotter. Choose a piece of your own writing.

- Underline all the verbs.
- Replace at least three verbs with ones that are sharper, more vivid, and more specific.
- Get together with a partner, and explain why you chose the verbs you did—what do you want the reader to see?

## VOCABULARY — HOW TO OWN A WORD

**WORD BANK**

*immensely*
*cowered*
*gait*
*valiant*
*consolation*

### You've Been There

1. Describe a time when you or someone you know was immensely proud.
2. Describe how a large dog would look if it cowered before a kitten.
3. Draw pictures suggested by the words *gait* and *gate* to help you remember their meanings. Use the letters of the words in your pictures.
4. Name three people in the world who are valiant.
5. What consolation could you offer a friend who didn't make the team?

# Elements of Literature

## THE SHORT STORY: A Story's Building Blocks

### Plot: "What Happens?"

**Plot** is what happens in a story. Plot consists of a series of related episodes, one growing out of another. These episodes create **suspense,** a feeling of anxious curiosity. Suspense is what keeps us reading: It keeps us glued to the story because we are curious to find out what happens next. In fact, the real power of a story lies in its ability to create suspense. A good storyteller makes us worry about those campers cooking their trout over the campfire by letting us see the bear watching from the trees nearby.

A plot has four parts, which are like building blocks.

1. The first part of a plot tells us about the story's **basic situation:** Who are the characters, and what do they want? This is usually where we find out about the conflict in a story. A **conflict** is a struggle between opposing characters or opposing forces. In an **external conflict** a character struggles with another person, with a group of people, or with a force of nature (a tornado, a bear, an icy mountain path). An **internal conflict** takes place in a character's mind (he suffers from shyness; she struggles to accept a loss). Here is the introduction to a new version of a tale you know well. A hungry wolf provides the external conflict.

"Hi there, Red," said a wolf to a little girl in a red velvet hood. "How'd ya like a ride on my motorcycle?"

"Thank you, sir, but I can't," replied Little Red Riding Hood. "As you can see, I'm carrying this basket of ginger cookies to my grandmother, and I mustn't be late."

"Tell you what, Red. You just hop on the back, and I'll run you over to Granny's in five seconds flat."

"My grandmother lives way out at the end of Lonely Road," Red protested. "It's miles and miles."

"This here motorcycle eats miles. We'll be there before you can say 'ginger cookies.' "

"No, thank you," said Little Red Riding Hood. "I've made up my mind." She began to walk faster.

2. In the second part of a plot, one or more of the characters act to resolve the conflict. Now **complications** develop.

"Suit yourself," chuckled the wolf, who had conceived a wicked plan. He would go alone to the end of Lonely Road, eat Red's grandma, and then, when the delicious little girl turned up, he would eat her and her delicious ginger cookies, too.

3. Now comes the **climax,** the story's most emotional or suspenseful moment. This is the point where the conflict is decided one way or another.

It was nearly dark when Red arrived, but as she approached her grandma's bed, she sensed something was wrong.

"Are you all right, Granny?" Red asked. "Your eyes look bloodshot."

*by* **John Leggett**

"All the better to see you with," replied the wolf.

"And your teeth. Suddenly they look like fangs."

"All the better to eat—" the wolf began, but he stopped at the sound of his motorcycle engine thundering in the front yard. "Wait right there, Red," said the wolf, bounding from the bed.

The wolf was startled to find Grandma Riding Hood astride the motorcycle.

"Hey!" he shouted. "Stop fooling with my bike." As he lunged for her, Grandma found the gearshift and the cycle leaped forward, catching the wolf up on its handlebars and hurling him into a giant thornbush—which is where the police found him when they arrived.

4. The last part of a story is its **resolution.** This is where the loose ends of the story are tied up and the story is closed.

Little Red and her grandma let the police make a cap of the wolf's fur. And they all lived happily ever after.

## Theme: The Story's Main Idea

All good stories have **themes.** This is the main idea of the story, the discovery about life that we take away from it. Here are some steps to take to identify a story's theme.

1. Think about how the main character has changed in the course of the story and what the character has learned. Sometimes what the character has learned can be stated as the theme. ("If you are self-centered, you can hurt yourself as well as others.")

2. Think about the title of the story and its meaning.

3. Identify some important passages in the story and think about what they suggest to you about our lives.

## Sharing Feelings

There is no better mark of a well-told story than the sense of special understanding it creates between the writer and the reader. Whether the story is about a teenage romance, revenge among criminals, or a dog who rescues a rancher's child, each reader will approach it differently and respond to it in a unique way. If the story moved us deeply, we can hardly wait to talk about our feelings with someone else. That sense of unique communication between writer and reader—and between reader and reader—is the true joy of reading.

---

### *A Writer on the Short Story*

"Of all the writing forms, I've always been partial to the short story. It suits my temperament. It makes a modest appeal for attention, allowing me to slip up alongside the reader on her/his blind side and grab'm."

—Toni Cade Bambara

# Before You Read

## THE RUNAWAY

## Make the Connection

### Not Just Horsing Around

In "The Runaway," Robert Frost introduces us to a colt who's never seen snow before. Even if the only horses you've met are in the movies, you can probably identify with the colt in this poem. Find a partner and talk about some of the things that children have to learn in life as they grow to adulthood.

## Quickwrite

Freewrite about a time when you learned something important about life. Who helped you?

## Elements of Literature

### Symbol: What Does It Stand For?

A **symbol** is a person, place, or thing that has meaning in itself and stands for something else as well.

Many symbols are traditional. We easily understand them because people have agreed on their meaning. A dove, for example, often symbolizes peace. The image of Uncle Sam is a symbol of the United States.

Writers sometimes create their own symbols. On one level, Frost's "The Runaway" is a simple story about some people who take a walk in a snowstorm and come across a colt who is seeing snow for the first time. On another level the poem may be seen as symbolic. What do you sense the frightened little colt stands for?

> **A** **symbol** is a person, place, or thing that has meaning in itself and stands for something beyond itself as well.
>
> *For more on Symbol, see the Handbook of Literary Terms.*

## Background

### Literature and Science

The subject of "The Runaway" is a Morgan colt. Morgans are a breed of swift, strong horses named for Justin Morgan (1747–1798), a Vermont schoolteacher who owned the stallion that founded the line. Morgans are small, sturdy horses that excel at weight-pulling contests. Today they are used mostly for riding and in herding cattle.

**go.hrw.com**
*LEO 7-1*

# The Runaway

**Robert Frost**

Once when the snow of the year was beginning to fall,
We stopped by a mountain pasture to say, "Whose colt?"
A little Morgan had one forefoot on the wall,
The other curled at his breast. He dipped his head
5   And snorted at us. And then he had to bolt.
We heard the miniature thunder where he fled,
And we saw him, or thought we saw him, dim and gray,
Like a shadow against the curtain of falling flakes.
"I think the little fellow's afraid of the snow.
10   He isn't winter-broken. It isn't play
With the little fellow at all. He's running away.
I doubt if even his mother could tell him, 'Sakes,
It's only weather.' He'd think she didn't know!
Where is his mother? He can't be out alone."
15   And now he comes again with clatter of stone,
And mounts the wall again with whited eyes
And all his tail that isn't hair up straight.
He shudders his coat as if to throw off flies.
"Whoever it is that leaves him out so late,
20   When other creatures have gone to stall and bin,
Ought to be told to come and take him in."

## A Poem "Begins as a Lump in the Throat"

While in high school in Lawrence, Massachusetts, **Robert Frost** (1874–1963) decided to become a poet. Not only did he succeed, but he became for a time America's most celebrated living poet.

"Rob" Frost lived most of his life on farms in Vermont and New Hampshire. There, he grew corn, edited a local newspaper, taught, and raised a family. Frost filled his poems with images of the people of New England and their _hay_ barns, farmhouses, pastures, apple orchards, and woods. His work speaks to people everywhere because it springs from intense feelings.

Frost says this about poetry: A poem "begins as a lump in the throat, a sense of wrong, a home-sickness, a loneliness." The feeling then "finds the thought and the thought finds the words." Frost felt that "it is most important of all to reach the heart of the reader."

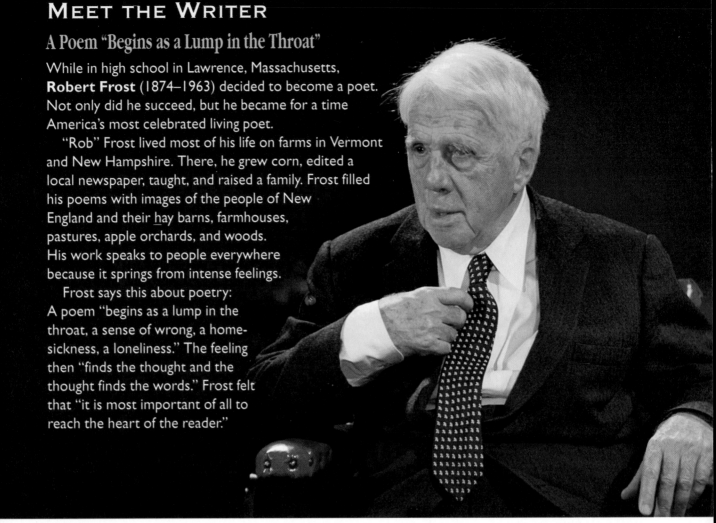

# MAKING MEANINGS

### First Thoughts

1. How would you complete each of these sentences?

   • As he faced his first snowfall alone, the colt felt . . .

   • As I read about him, I felt . . .

### Shaping Interpretations

2. To break a colt is to get him used to being ridden. What do you think the expression _winter-broken_ (line 10) means?

3. How do you think the speaker feels about the person who has left the colt alone in the pasture?

4. Why do you think Frost called the poem "The Runaway"? (What is the colt running away from?)

5. Some people think that the colt **symbolizes** a lost child or someone who is too young or too innocent to understand what he or she is experiencing. Do you agree with this interpretation, or do you have another one? Support your interpretation with details from the poem.

6. When you read, you form **mental images** of people, settings, and events. Describe what you see as you read (and reread) this poem. Compare your mental images with those of your classmates.

### Extending the Text

7. Reread the last three lines of "The Runaway." What other situations in life do you think these lines could be applied to? Explain.

8. *Runaway* can refer to people, too. What other "runaways" are found in our world? What lines from the poem could apply to them?

## CHOICES: Building Your Portfolio

### Writer's Notebook

#### 1. Collecting Ideas for a Story

WORK IN PROGRESS

Robert Frost said that a poem begins with a feeling. That's true of stories, too. To find a feeling that you want to write about, go through some of your souvenirs—photographs, ticket stubs, score cards. When you find an item that stirs a strong memory, start jotting down notes. Record as many details of the memory as you can. Describe what you felt. You might find some ideas in your notes for the Quickwrite on page 24.

### Creative Writing

#### 2. Straight from the Horse's Mouth

Throughout "The Runaway" the observers guess what the colt is thinking and feeling. Do you think they're right? In poetry or prose, rewrite "The Runaway" from the colt's point of view. Have him share his feelings about the weather, about his mother—and about the people watching him. If you write a poem, you could present it in the following form, with the first letters of the lines spelling out the word *runaway*.

R _____
U _____
N _____
A _____
W _____
A _____
Y _____

### Performance

#### 3. Choral Reading

With several classmates, prepare a group reading of "The Runaway." Decide which lines you will assign to a chorus and which lines you'll assign to a single voice. Practice reading aloud so that the poet's use of normal speech rhythms comes through.

# *Before You Read*

## SONG OF THE TREES

## Make the Connection

### Agree? Disagree?

disagree 0 1 2 3 4 agree

1. People gain self-respect by standing up for their beliefs.

2. Given the chance, most people will never take advantage of another person.

3. Some people are treated unfairly because of the color of their skin.

4. Nobody owns the earth.

Rate each of the statements above with a number from 0 to 4. (Zero means that you completely disagree; 4 means you completely agree.)

## Quickwrite

Which statement do you agree or disagree with most strongly? Explain very briefly what you think about that statement and why. You might want to jot down notes on an experience that shaped your opinion. Share your Quickwrite with a partner; then, discuss these issues with the rest of the class.

## Elements of Literature

### Theme: A Revelation About Life

Have you ever asked after reading a story: "What does it *mean?*" What you are asking about is the story's theme. **Theme** is what a story reveals about people and life. It is the meaning that we take away from the story. Stories like "Song of the Trees" often have several themes, but one usually stands out from the others.

> **T**heme is the idea about life revealed in a piece of literature.
>
> *For more on Theme, see pages 22–23 and the Handbook of Literary Terms.*

## Reading Skills and Strategies

### Making Generalizations: Putting It All Together

A **generalization** is a broad statement that tells about something "in general." A statement about a story's theme is a kind of generalization. From specific evidence in the story you make a broad, universal statement about life. To make a statement about the theme of "Song of the Trees," you have to

- think about the main events and conflicts in the story

- decide what the characters have learned by the end of the story

- think about how the story relates to your experiences

## Background

### Literature and Social Studies

The depression referred to in this story is the Great Depression, the severe economic decline that lasted from 1929 to 1942 in the United States. During the Depression many banks and businesses closed. People lost their jobs, their savings, and their homes, and many had barely enough to eat. This was also a time when the segregation of African Americans was still a sad reality in parts of the United States.

go.hrw.com
*LEO 7-1*

*I stared at the trees,
aware of an eerie silence
descending.*

# Song of the Trees

Mildred D. Taylor

"Cassie. Cassie, child, wake up now," Big Ma called gently as the new sun peeked over the horizon.

I looked sleepily at my grandmother and closed my eyes again.

"Cassie! Get up, girl!" This time the voice was not so gentle.

I jumped out of the deep, feathery bed as Big Ma climbed from the other side. The room was still dark, and I stubbed my toe while stumbling sleepily about looking for my clothes.

"Shoot! Darn ole chair," I fussed, rubbing my injured foot.

"Hush, Cassie, and open them curtains if you can't see," Big Ma said. "Prop that window open, too, and let some of that fresh morning air in here."

I opened the window and looked outside. The earth was draped in a cloak of gray mist as the sun chased the night away. The cotton stalks, which in another hour would glisten greenly toward the sun, were gray. The ripening corn, wrapped in jackets of emerald and gold, was gray. Even the rich brown Mississippi earth was gray.

Only the trees of the forest were not gray. They stood dark, almost black, across the dusty road, still holding the night. A soft breeze stirred, and their voices whispered down to me in a song of morning greeting.

"Cassie, girl, I said open that window, not stand there gazing out all morning. Now, get moving before I take something to you," Big Ma threatened.

I dashed to my clothes. Before Big Ma had unwoven her long braid of gray hair, my pants and shirt were on and I was hurrying into the kitchen.

A small kerosene lamp was burning in a corner as I entered. Its light reflected on seven-year-old Christopher-John, short, pudgy, and a year younger than me, sitting sleepily upon a side bench drinking a large glass of clabber milk.[1] Mama's back was to me. She was dipping flour from a near-empty canister, while my older brother, Stacey, built a fire in the huge iron-bellied stove.

"I don't know what I'm going to do with you, Christopher-John," Mama scolded. "Getting up in the middle of the night and eating all that cornbread. Didn't you have enough to eat before you went to bed?"

"Yes'm," Christopher-John murmured.

"Lord knows I don't want any of my babies going hungry, but times are hard, honey. Don't you know folks all around here in Mississippi are struggling? Children crying cause they got no food to eat, and their daddies crying cause they can't get jobs so they can feed their babies? And you getting up in the middle of the night, stuffing yourself with cornbread!"

Her voice softened as she looked at the sleepy little boy. "Baby, we're in a depression. Why do you think Papa's way down in Louisiana laying tracks on the railroad? So his children can eat—but only when they're hungry. You understand?"

"Yes'm," Christopher-John murmured again, as his eyes slid blissfully shut.

"Morning, Mama," I chimed.

"Morning, baby," Mama said. "You wash up yet?"

"No'm."

"Then go wash up and call Little Man again. Tell him he's not dressing to meet President Roosevelt[2] this morning. Hurry up, now, cause I want you to set the table."

---

1. **clabber milk:** thickly curdled sour milk.
2. **President Roosevelt:** Franklin Delano Roosevelt (1882–1945) was president of the United States from 1933 to 1945.

Little Man, a very small six-year-old and a most finicky dresser, was brushing his hair when I entered the room he shared with Stacey and Christopher-John. His blue pants were faded, but except for a small grass stain on one knee, they were clean. Outside of his Sunday pants, these were the only pants he had, and he was always careful to keep them in the best condition possible. But one look at him and I knew that he was far from pleased with their condition this morning. He frowned down at the spot for a moment, then continued brushing.

"Man, hurry up and get dressed," I called. "Mama said you ain't dressing to meet the president."

"See there," he said, pointing at the stain. "You did that."

"I did no such thing. You fell all by yourself."

"You tripped me!"

"Didn't!"

"Did, too!"

"Hey, cut it out, you two!" ordered Stacey, entering the room. "You fought over that stupid stain yesterday. Now get moving, both of you. We gotta go pick blackberries before the sun gets too high. Little Man, you go gather the eggs while Christopher-John and me milk the cows."

Little Man and I decided to settle our dispute later when Stacey wasn't around. With Papa away, eleven-year-old Stacey thought of himself as the man of the house, and Mama had instructed Little Man, Christopher-John, and me to mind him. So, like it or not, we humored him. Besides, he was bigger than we were.

I ran to the back porch to wash. When I returned to the kitchen, Mama was talking to Big Ma.

"We got about enough flour for two more meals," Mama said, cutting the biscuit dough. "Our salt and sugar are practically down to nothing and——" She stopped when she saw me. "Cassie, baby, go gather the eggs for Mama."

"Little Man's gathering the eggs."

"Then go help him."

"But I ain't set the table yet."

"Set it when you come back."

I knew that I was not wanted in the kitchen. I looked suspiciously at my mother and grandmother, then went to the back porch to get a basket.

Big Ma's voice drifted through the open window. "Mary, you oughta write David and tell him somebody done opened his letter and stole that ten dollars he sent," she said.

"No, Mama. David's got enough on his mind. Besides, there's enough garden foods so we won't go hungry."

"But what 'bout your medicine? You're all out of it and the doctor told you good to——"

"Shhhh!" Mama stared at the window. "Cassie, I thought I told you to go gather those eggs!"

"I had to get a basket, Mama!" I hurried off the porch and ran to the barn.

After breakfast, when the sun was streaking red across the sky, my brothers and I ambled into the coolness of the forest, leading our three cows and their calves down the narrow cow path to the pond. The morning was already muggy, but the trees closed out the heat as their leaves waved restlessly, high above our heads.

"Good morning, Mr. Trees," I shouted. They answered me with a soft, swooshing sound. "Hear 'em, Stacey? Hear 'em singing?"

"Ah, cut that out, Cassie. Them trees ain't singing. How many times I gotta tell you that's just the wind?" He stopped at a sweet alligator gum, pulled out his knife, and scraped off a glob of gum that had seeped through its cracked bark. He handed me half.

------------------------------------------------

## WORDS TO OWN

**finicky** (fin′ik·ē) *adj.:* fussy and extremely careful.
**dispute** (di·spyo͞ot′) *n.:* argument.
**ambled** (am′bəld) *v.:* walked easily, without hurrying.

------------------------------------------------

As I stuffed the gooey wad into my mouth, I patted the tree and whispered, "Thank you, Mr. Gum Tree."

Stacey frowned at me, then looked back at Christopher-John and Little Man walking far behind us, munching on their breakfast biscuits.

"Man! Christopher-John! Come on, now," he yelled. "If we finish the berry picking early, we can go wading before we go back."

Christopher-John and Little Man ran to catch up with us. Then, resuming their leisurely pace, they soon fell behind again.

A large gray squirrel scurried across our path and up a walnut tree. I watched until it was settled amidst the tree's featherlike leaves; then, poking one of the calves, I said, "Stacey, is Mama sick?"

"Sick? Why you say that?"

"Cause I heard Big Ma asking her 'bout some medicine she's supposed to have."

Stacey stopped, a worried look on his face. "If she's sick, she ain't bad sick," he decided. "If she was bad sick, she'd been in bed."

We left the cows at the pond and, taking our berry baskets, <u>delved</u> deeper into the forest looking for the wild blackberry bushes.

"I see one!" I shouted.

"Where?" cried Christopher-John, eager for the sweet berries.

"Over there! Last one to it's a rotten egg!" I yelled, and off I ran.

Stacey and Little Man followed at my heels. But Christopher-John puffed far behind. "Hey, wait for me," he cried.

"Let's hide from Christopher-John," Stacey suggested.

The three of us ran in different directions. I plunged behind a giant old pine and hugged its warm trunk as I waited for Christopher-John.

Christopher-John puffed to a stop, then, looking all around, called, "Hey, Stacey! Cassie! Hey, Man! Y'all cut that out!"

I giggled and Christopher-John heard me.

"I see you, Cassie!" he shouted, starting toward me as fast as his chubby legs would carry him. "You're it!"

"Not 'til you tag me," I laughed. As I waited for him to get closer, I glanced up into the boughs of my wintry-smelling hiding tree, expecting a song of laughter. But the old pine only tapped me gently with one of its long, low branches. I turned from the tree and dashed away.

"You can't, you can't, you can't catch me," I taunted, dodging from one beloved tree to the next. Around shaggy-bark hickories and sharp-needled pines, past blue-gray beeches and sturdy black walnuts I sailed, while my laughter resounded through the ancient forest, filling every chink. Overhead, the boughs of the giant trees hovered protectively, but they did not join in my laughter.

Deeper into the forest I plunged.

Christopher-John, unable to keep up, plopped on the ground in a pant. Little Man and Stacey, emerging from their hiding places, ran up to him.

"Ain't you caught her yet?" Little Man demanded, more than a little annoyed.

"He can't catch the champ," I boasted, stopping to rest against a hickory tree. I slid my back down the tree's shaggy trunk and looked up at its long branches, heavy with sweet nuts and slender green leaves, perfectly still. I looked around at the leaves of the other trees. They were still also. I stared at the trees, aware of an eerie silence descending over the forest.

Stacey walked toward me. "What's the matter with you, Cassie?" he asked.

"The trees, Stacey," I said softly, "they ain't singing no more."

"Is that all?" He looked up at the sky. "Come on, y'all. It's get-

## WORDS TO OWN
delved (delvd') v.: searched.

ting late. We'd better go pick them berries." He turned and walked on.

"But, Stacey, listen. Little Man, Christopher-John, listen."

The forest echoed an uneasy silence.

"The wind just stopped blowing, that's all," said Stacey. "Now stop fooling around and come on."

I jumped up to follow Stacey, then cried, "Stacey, look!" On a black oak a few yards away was a huge white X. "How did that get there?" I exclaimed, running to the tree.

"There's another one!" Little Man screamed.

"I see one too!" shouted Christopher-John.

Stacey said nothing as Christopher-John, Little Man, and I ran wildly through the forest counting the ghostlike marks.

"Stacey, they're on practically all of them," I said when he called us back. "Why?"

Stacey studied the trees, then suddenly pushed us down.

"My clothes!" Little Man wailed indignantly.

"Hush, Man, and stay down," Stacey warned. "Somebody's coming."

Two white men emerged. We looked at each other. We knew to be silent.

"You mark them all down here?" one of the men asked.

"Not the younger ones, Mr. Andersen."

"We might need them, too," said Mr. Andersen, counting the X's. "But don't worry 'bout marking them now, Tom. We'll get them later. Also them trees up past the pond toward the house."

"The old woman agree to you cutting these trees?"

"I ain't been down there yet," Mr. Andersen said.

"Mr. Andersen . . ." Tom hesitated a moment, looked up at the silent trees, then back at Mr. Andersen. "Maybe you should go easy with them," he cautioned. "You know that David can be as mean as an ole jackass when he wanna be."

"He's talking about Papa," I whispered.

"Shhhh!" Stacey hissed.

Mr. Andersen looked uneasy. "What's that gotta do with anything?"

"Well, he just don't take much to any dealings with white folks." Again, Tom looked up at the trees. "He ain't afraid like some."

Mr. Andersen laughed weakly. "Don't worry 'bout that, Tom. The land belongs to his mama. He don't have no say in it. Besides, I guess I oughta know how to handle David Logan. After all, there are ways. . . .

"Now, you get on back to my place and get some boys and start chopping down these trees," Mr. Andersen said. "I'll go talk to the old woman." He looked up at the sky. "We can almost get a full day's work in if we hurry."

Mr. Andersen turned to walk away, but Tom stopped him. "Mr. Andersen, you really gonna chop all the trees?"

"If I need to. These folks ain't got no call for them. I do. I got me a good contract for these trees and I aim to fulfill it."

Tom watched Mr. Andersen walk away; then, looking sorrowfully up at the trees, he shook his head and disappeared into the depths of the forest.

"What we gonna do, Stacey?" I asked anxiously. "They can't just cut down our trees, can they?"

"I don't know. Papa's gone. . . ." Stacey muttered to himself, trying to decide what we should do next.

"Boy, if Papa was here, them ole white men wouldn't be messing with our trees," Little Man declared.

"Yeah!" Christopher-John agreed. "Just let Papa get hold of 'em and he gonna turn 'em every which way but loose."

"Christopher-John, Man," Stacey said finally, "go get the cows and take them home."

"But we just brought them down here," Little Man protested.

"And we gotta pick the berries for dinner," said Christopher-John mournfully.

"No time for that now. Hurry up. And stay clear of them white men. Cassie, you come with me."

We ran, brown legs and feet flying high through the still forest.

By the time Stacey and I arrived at the house, Mr. Andersen's car was already parked in the dusty drive. Mr. Andersen himself was seated comfortably in Papa's rocker on the front porch. Big Ma was seated too, but Mama was standing.

Stacey and I eased quietly to the side of the porch, unnoticed.

"Sixty-five dollars. That's an awful lot of money in these hard times, Aunt Caroline," Mr. Andersen was saying to Big Ma.

I could see Mama's thin face harden.

"You know," Mr. Andersen said, rocking familiarly in Papa's chair, "that's more than David can send home in two months."

"We do quite well on what David sends home," Mama said coldly.

Mr. Andersen stopped rocking. "I suggest you encourage Aunt Caroline to sell them trees, Mary. You know, David might not always be able to work so good. He could possibly have . . . an accident."

Big Ma's soft brown eyes clouded over with fear as she looked first at Mr. Andersen, then at Mama. But Mama clenched her fists and said, "In Mississippi, black men do not have accidents."

"Hush, child, hush," Big Ma said hurriedly. "How many trees for the sixty-five dollars, Mr. Andersen?"

"Enough 'til I figure I got my sixty-five dollars' worth."

"And how many would that be?" Mama persisted.

Mr. Andersen looked haughtily at Mama. "I said I'd be the judge of that, Mary."

"I think not," Mama said.

Mr. Andersen stared at Mama. And Mama stared back at him. I knew Mr. Andersen didn't like that, but Mama did it anyway. Mr. Andersen soon grew uneasy under that piercing gaze, and when his eyes swiftly shifted from Mama to Big Ma, his face was beet red.

"Caroline," he said, his voice low and menacing, "you're the head of this family and you've got a decision to make. Now, I need them trees and I mean to have them. I've offered you a good price for them and I ain't gonna haggle over it. I know y'all can use the money. Doc Thomas tells me that Mary's not well." He hesitated a moment, then hissed venomously, "And if something should happen to David . . ."

"All right," Big Ma said, her voice trembling. "All right, Mr. Andersen."

"No, Big Ma!" I cried, leaping onto the porch. "You can't let him cut our trees!"

Mr. Andersen grasped the arms of the rocker, his knuckles chalk white. "You certainly ain't taught none of your younguns how to behave, Caroline," he said curtly.

"You children go on to the back," Mama said, shooing us away.

"No, Mama," Stacey said. "He's gonna cut them all down. Me and Cassie heard him say so in the woods."

"I won't let him cut them," I threatened. "I won't let him! The trees are my friends and ain't no mean ole white man gonna touch my trees——"

Mama's hands went roughly around my body as she carried me off to my room.

"Now, hush," she said, her dark eyes flashing wildly. "I've told you how dangerous it is . . ."

She broke off in midsentence. She stared at me a moment, then hugged me tightly and went back to the porch.

Stacey joined me a few seconds later, and we sat there in the heat of the quiet room, listening miserably as the first whack of an ax echoed against the trees.

That night I was awakened by soft sounds outside my window. I reached for Big Ma, but she wasn't there. Hurrying to the window, I saw Mama and Big Ma standing in the yard in their nightclothes and Stacey, fully dressed, sitting atop Lady, our golden mare. By the time I got outside, Stacey was gone.

"Mama, where's Stacey?" I cried.

"Be quiet, Cassie. You'll wake Christopher-John and Little Man."

"But where's he going?"

"He's going to get Papa," Mama said. "Now be quiet."

"Go on, Stacey, boy," I whispered. "Ride for me, too."

As the dust billowed after him, Mama said, "I should've gone myself. He's so young."

Big Ma put her arm around Mama. "Now, Mary, you know you couldn't've gone. Mr. Andersen would miss you if he come by and see you ain't here. You done right, now. Don't worry, that boy'll be just fine."

Three days passed, hot and windless.

Mama forbade any of us to go into the forest, so Christopher-John, Little Man, and I spent the slow, restless days hovering as close to the dusty road as we dared, listening to the foreign sounds of steel against the trees and the thunderous roar of those ancient loved ones as they crashed upon the earth. Sometimes Mama would scold us and tell us to come back to the house, but even she could not ignore the continuous pounding of the axes against the trees.

----

**WORDS TO OWN**

**curtly** (kurt'lē) *adv.*: rudely and with few words.

----

Or the sight of the loaded lumber wagons rolling out of the forest. In the middle of washing or ironing or hoeing, she would look up sorrowfully and listen, then turn toward the road, searching for some sign of Papa and Stacey.

On the fourth day, before the sun had risen, bringing its cloak of miserable heat, I saw her walking alone toward the woods. I ran after her.

She did not send me back.

"Mama," I said. "How sick are you?"

Mama took my hand. "Remember when you had the flu and felt so sick?"

"Yes'm."

"And when I gave you some medicine, you got well soon afterward?"

"Yes'm."

"Well, that's how sick I am. As soon as I get my medicine, I'll be all well again. And that'll be soon, now that Papa's coming home," she said, giving my hand a gentle little squeeze.

The quiet surrounded us as we entered the forest. Mama clicked on the flashlight, and we walked silently along the cow path to the pond. There, just beyond the pond, pockets of open space loomed before us.

"Mama!"

"I know, baby, I know."

On the ground lay countless trees. Trees that had once been such strong, tall things. So strong that I could fling my arms partially around one of them and feel safe and secure. So tall and leafy green that their boughs had formed a forest temple.

And old.

So old that Indians had once built fires at their feet and had sung happy songs of happy days. So old they had hidden fleeing black men in the night and listened to their sad tales of a foreign land.

In the cold of winter, when the ground lay frozen, they had sung their frosty ballads of years gone by. Or on a muggy, sweat-drenched day, their leaves had rippled softly, lazily, like restless green fingers strumming at a guitar, echoing their epic tales.

But now they would sing no more. They lay forever silent upon the ground.

Those trees that remained standing were like defeated warriors mourning their fallen dead. But soon they, too, would fall, for the white X's had been placed on nearly every one.

"Oh, dear, dear trees," I cried as the gray light of the rising sun fell in ghostly shadows over the land. The tears rolled hot down my cheeks. Mama held me close, and when I felt her body tremble, I knew she was crying too.

When our tears eased, we turned sadly toward the house. As we emerged from the forest, we could see two small figures waiting impatiently on the other side of the road. As soon as they spied us, they hurried across to meet us.

"Mama! You and Cassie was in the forest," Little Man accused. "Big Ma told us!"

"How was it?" asked Christopher-John, rubbing the sleep from his eyes. "Was it spooky?"

"Spooky and empty," I said listlessly.

"Mama, me and Christopher-John wanna see too," Little Man declared.

"No, baby," Mama said softly as we crossed the road. "The men'll be done there soon, and I don't want y'all underfoot."

"But, Mama——" Little Man started to protest.

"When Papa comes home and the men are gone, then you can go. But until then, you stay out of there. You hear me, Little Man Logan?"

"Yes'm," Little Man reluctantly replied.

But the sun had been up only an hour when Little Man decided that he could not wait for Papa to return.

"Mama said we wasn't to go down there," Christopher-John warned.

"Cassie did," Little Man cried.

"But she was with Mama. Wasn't you, Cassie?"

"Well, I'm going too," said Little Man. "Every-

body's always going someplace 'cepting me." And off he went.

Christopher-John and I ran after him. Down the narrow cow path and around the pond we chased. But neither of us was fast enough to overtake Little Man before he reached the lumbermen.

"Hey, you kids, get away from here," Mr. Andersen shouted when he saw us. "Now, y'all go on back home," he said, stopping in front of Little Man.

"We are home," I said. "You're the one who's on our land."

"Claude," Mr. Andersen said to one of the black lumbermen, "take these kids home." Then he pushed Little Man out of his way. Little Man pushed back. Mr. Andersen looked down, startled that a little black boy would do such a thing. He shoved Little Man a second time, and Little Man fell into the dirt.

Little Man looked down at his clothing covered with sawdust and dirt and wailed, "You got my clothes dirty!"

I rushed toward Mr. Andersen, my fist in a mighty hammer, shouting, "You ain't got no right to push on Little Man. Why don't you push on somebody your own size—like me, you ole——"

The man called Claude put his hand over my mouth and carried me away. Christopher-John trailed behind us, tugging on the man's shirt.

"Put her down. Hey, mister, put Cassie down."

The man carried me all the way to the pond. "Now," he said, "you and your brothers get on home before y'all get hurt. Go on, get!"

As the man walked away, I looked around. "Where's Little Man?"

Christopher-John looked around too.

"I don't know," he said. "I thought he was behind me."

Back we ran toward the lumbermen.

We found Little Man's clothing first, folded neatly by a tree. Then we saw Little Man, dragging a huge stick and headed straight for Mr. Andersen.

"Little Man, come back here," I called.

But Little Man did not stop.

Mr. Andersen stood alone, barking orders, unaware of the oncoming Little Man.

"Little Man! Oh, Little Man, don't!"

It was too late.

Little Man swung the stick as hard as he could against Mr. Andersen's leg.

Mr. Andersen let out a howl and reached to where he thought Little Man's collar was. But, of course, Little Man had no collar.

"Run, Man!" Christopher-John and I shouted. "Run!"

"Why, you little . . ." Mr. Andersen cried, grabbing at Little Man. But Little Man was too quick for him. He slid right through Mr. Andersen's legs. Tom stood nearby, his face crinkling into an amused grin.

"Hey, y'all!" Mr. Andersen yelled to the lumbermen. "Claude! Get that kid!"

But sure-footed Little Man dodged the groping hands of the lumbermen as easily as if he were <u>skirting</u> mud puddles. Over tree stumps, around legs, and through legs he dashed. But in the end, there were too many lumbermen for him, and he was handed over to Mr. Andersen.

For the second time, Christopher-John and I went to Little Man's rescue.

"Put him down!" we ordered, charging the lumbermen.

I was captured much too quickly, though not before I had landed several stinging blows. But Christopher-John, furious at seeing Little Man handled so roughly by Mr. Andersen, managed to <u>elude</u> the clutches of the lumbermen until he was fully upon Mr. Andersen. Then, with his mightiest thrust, he kicked Mr. Andersen

---

**WORDS TO OWN**
**skirting** v.: narrowly avoiding.
**elude** (ē·lōōd') v.: escape by quickness or cleverness.

---

solidly in the shins, not once, but twice, before the lumbermen pulled him away.

Mr. Andersen was fuming. He slowly took off his wide leather belt. Christopher-John, Little Man, and I looked woefully at the belt, then at each other. Little Man and Christopher-John fought to escape, but I closed my eyes and awaited the whining of the heavy belt and its painful bite against my skin.

What was he waiting for? I started to open my eyes, but then the zinging whirl of the belt began and I tensed, awaiting its fearful sting. But just as the leather tip lashed into my leg, a deep, familiar voice said, "Put the belt down, Andersen."

I opened my eyes.

"Papa!"

"Let the children go," Papa said. He was standing on a nearby ridge with a strange black box in his hands. Stacey was behind him, holding the reins to Lady.

The chopping stopped as all eyes turned to Papa.

"They been right meddlesome," Mr. Andersen said. "They need teaching how to act."

"Any teaching, I'll do it. Now, let them go."

Mr. Andersen looked down at Little Man struggling to get away. Smiling broadly, he motioned our release. "Okay, David," he said.

As we ran up the ridge to Papa, Mr. Andersen said, "It's good to have you home, boy."

Papa said nothing until we were safely behind him. "Take them home, Stacey."

"But, Papa——"

"Do like I say, son."

Stacey herded us away from the men. When we were far enough away so Papa couldn't see us, Stacey stopped and handed me Lady's reins.

"Y'all go on home now," he said. "I gotta go help Papa."

"Papa don't need no help," I said. "He told you to come with us."

"But you don't know what he's gonna do."

"What?" I asked.

"He's gonna blow up the forest if they don't get out of here. So go on home where y'all be safe."

"How's he gonna do that?" asked Little Man.

"We been setting sticks of dynamite since the middle of the night. We ain't even been up to the house cause Papa wanted the sticks planted and covered over before the men came. Now, Cassie, take them on back to the house. Do like I tell you for once, will ya?" Then, without waiting for another word, he was gone.

"I wanna see," Little Man announced.

"I don't," protested Christopher-John.

"Come on," I said.

We tied the mare to a tree, then belly-crawled back to where we could see Papa and joined Stacey in the brush.

"Cassie, I told you . . ."

"What's Papa doing?"

The black box was now set upon a sawed-off tree stump, and Papa's hands were tightly grasping a T-shaped instrument which went into it.

"What's that thing?" asked Little Man.

"It's a plunger," Stacey whispered. "If Papa presses down on it, the whole forest will go *pfffff*!"

Our mouths went dry and our eyes went wide. Mr. Andersen's eyes were wide, too.

"You're bluffing, David," he said. "You ain't gonna push that plunger."

"One thing you can't seem to understand, Andersen," Papa said, "is that a black man's always gotta be ready to die. And it don't make me any difference if I die today or tomorrow. Just as long as I die right."

Mr. Andersen laughed uneasily. The lumbermen moved nervously away.

"I mean what I say," Papa said. "Ask anyone. I always mean what I say."

"He sure do, Mr. Andersen," Claude said, eyeing the black box. "He always do."

"Shut up!" Mr. Andersen snapped. "And the rest of y'all stay put." Then turning back to Papa, he smiled cunningly. "I'm sure you and me can work something out, David."

"Ain't nothing to be worked out," said Papa.

"Now, look here, David, your mama and me, we got us a contract. . . ."

"There ain't no more contract," Papa replied coldly. "Now, either you get out or I blow it up. That's it."

"He means it, Mr. Andersen," another frightened lumberman ventured. "He's crazy and he sure 'nough means it."

"You know what could happen to you, boy?" Mr. Andersen exploded, his face beet red again. "Threatening a white man like this?"

Papa said nothing. He just stood there, his hands firmly on the plunger, staring down at Mr. Andersen.

Mr. Andersen could not bear the stare. He turned away, cursing Papa. "You're a fool, David. A crazy fool." Then he looked around at the lumbermen. They shifted their eyes and would not look at him.

"Maybe we better leave, Mr. Andersen," Tom said quietly.

Mr. Andersen glanced at Tom, then turned back to Papa and said as lightly as he could, "All right, David, all right. It's your land. We'll just take the logs we got cut and get out." He motioned to the men. "Hey, let's get moving and get these logs out of here before this crazy fool gets us all killed."

"No," Papa said.

Mr. Andersen stopped, knowing that he could not have heard correctly. "What you say?"

"You ain't taking one more stick out of this forest."

"Now, look here——"

"You heard me."

"But you can't sell all these logs, David," Mr. Andersen exclaimed incredulously.

Papa said nothing. Just cast that piercing look on Mr. Andersen.

"Look, I'm a fair man. I tell you what I'll do. I'll give you another thirty-five dollars. An even hundred dollars. Now, that's fair, ain't it?"

"I'll see them rot first."

"But——"

"That's my last word," Papa said, tightening his grip on the plunger.

Mr. Andersen swallowed hard. "You won't always have that black box, David," he warned. "You know that, don't you?"

"That may be. But it won't matter none. Cause I'll always have my self-respect."

Mr. Andersen opened his mouth to speak, but no sound came. Tom and the lumbermen were quietly moving away, putting their gear in the empty lumber wagons. Mr. Andersen looked again at the black box. Finally, his face ashen, he too walked away.

Papa stood unmoving until the wagons and the men were gone. Then, when the sound of the last wagon rolling over the dry leaves could no longer be heard and a hollow silence filled the air, he slowly removed his hands from the plunger and looked up at the remaining trees standing like lonely sentries in the morning.

"Dear, dear old trees," I heard him call softly, "will you ever sing again?"

I waited. But the trees gave no answer.

- - - - - - - - - - - - - - - - - - - - - - - - - - - - - -
**WORDS TO OWN**
**incredulously** (in·krej′ oo·ləs·lē) *adv.:* unbelievingly.
**ashen** (ash′ən) *adj.:* pale.
**sentries** (sen′trēz) *n.:* guards.
- - - - - - - - - - - - - - - - - - - - - - - - - - - - - -

## MEET THE WRITER

### "We Were Somebody . . ."

**Mildred D. Taylor** (1943–    ) grew up in Toledo, Ohio. In high school she was an honor student, a newspaper editor, and a class officer—but, she says, she wasn't able to do what she really wanted: be a cheerleader.

Every summer she and her family visited Mississippi relatives, and she listened to their stories. By the time she was nine or ten, she knew that she wanted to write.

**66** I wanted to show a Black family united in love and pride, of which the reader would like to be a part. **99**

Her first effort, *Song of the Trees*, introduced the Logan family and won first prize in the African American category of a competition for children's books. In 1977, when she accepted the Newbery Award for her second work about the Logan family, *Roll of Thunder, Hear My Cry,* Taylor talked about her father:

**66** Throughout my childhood he impressed upon my sister and me that we were somebody, that we were important and could do anything we set our minds to do or be. He was not the kind of father who demanded A's on our report cards. He was more concerned about how we carried ourselves, how we respected ourselves and others, and how we pursued the principles upon which he hoped we would build our lives. He was constantly reminding us that how we saw ourselves was far more important than how others saw us. . . .

If the Logans seem real, it is because I had my own family upon which to base characterizations. Through David Logan have come the words of my father, and through the Logan family the love of my own family. If people are touched by the warmth of the Logans, it is because I had the warmth of my own youthful years from which to draw. And if people believe the book to be biographical, it is because I have tried to distill the essence of Black life, so familiar to most Black families, to make the Logans an embodiment of that spiritual heritage. **99**

### More of Mildred Taylor's Heritage

You can rejoin Cassie Logan and her family in the novels *Let the Circle Be Unbroken* (Bantam) and *The Road to Memphis* (Puffin).

# MAKING MEANINGS

## First Thoughts

1. What scene from the story do you remember most vividly?

## Shaping Interpretations

2. Cassie gives the trees human characteristics, describing them as if they could talk and sing. Find two passages in the story where the trees seem human. Why do you think Cassie loves her trees so much?

3. Which character in this story is "out there on his or her own"? How does this person deal with the problem confronting him or her?

4. When you read on page 35 that Mr. Andersen "hissed venomously," what are you reminded of? How do you feel about Mr. Andersen's behavior?

5. "Song of the Trees" is told by Cassie. How would the story be different if it were told by her father?

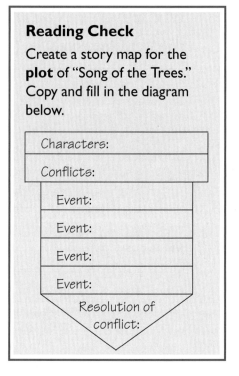

**Reading Check**

Create a story map for the **plot** of "Song of the Trees." Copy and fill in the diagram below.

Characters:

Conflicts:

Event:

Event:

Event:

Event:

Resolution of conflict:

## Connecting with the Text

6. Look at the story map that you made for the Reading Check on this page. **Analyze** the **plot** by thinking about its major parts. At what point does the main conflict begin, and who is involved in the struggle? What problems make it difficult for Cassie and her family to resolve the conflict? How do they finally solve their problems?

7. Have you ever felt as strongly about a place as Cassie feels about her forest? Describe that special place.

8. Go back to the statements you rated on page 28. Individually and with the class, rate the four statements again, using the same scale. Have any of your opinions changed now that you've read the story?

9. Suppose you needed money but the only valuable thing you owned was a beautiful piece of land that had been home to your family for generations. Would you sell this land to be more comfortable for a time? Why or why not?

# CHOICES: Building Your Portfolio

## Writer's Notebook

### 1. Collecting Ideas for a Story

Taylor says that in writing "Song of the Trees," she "drew upon people and places I had known all my life." In creating the character of Cassie, for example, she drew on the personalities of her sister and an aunt. Do you know anyone about whom you could write a story? Create a character based partly on a real person (or on a combination of people). Then, think of a problem, real or imaginary, for your character to solve.

**Name:** Martita
**Age:** 13
**Personality:** reliable, shy, softhearted
**Problem:** Her dad died. She wants to convince her mom to let her adopt a skinny stray cat.

## Stating a Theme

### 2. What Did the Main Characters Learn?

**Theme,** as you learned earlier (pages 23 and 28), is the *meaning* of a story. Theme points to what the main characters learned in the story, and to what *you* learned as you shared their experiences.

In a paragraph, state what you think the theme of this story is. Remember that no two statements of theme will be alike. Share your ideas on theme with the class.

## Music

### 3. Sound Decisions

A movie's soundtrack does more than just fill the time between conversations. It establishes a mood and, with repeated hearings, may even remind moviegoers of a movie's theme. If you were creating the soundtrack for a film version of Taylor's work, what music would you use for the song of the trees that Cassie hears: an African American folk song or spiritual? a popular song of the 1930s? classical music that suggests the beauty of nature? Play a recording of the music you select, and explain to the class why you think it sings the song of the trees.

## Science/Art

### 4. Trees' Company

Cassie Logan plays among "shaggy-bark hickories and sharp-needled pines, . . . blue-gray beeches and sturdy black walnuts." Imagine taking a class hike through Cassie's forest. With three or four classmates, research some of the trees you might expect to see. (Leaves from several kinds of trees mentioned in the story are used as illustrations.) Using heavy paper, make a fact sheet for each kind of tree. Show a picture of the tree, its leaves, and its seeds, and give hikers some information about it. Post your fact sheets around the room and lead an in-class "nature hike."

# GRAMMAR LINK

## Subject-Verb Agreement Is Unanimous!

Probably the most common error people make in writing (and in speaking) is in subject-verb agreement. The rule is simple: Subjects and their verbs must always agree—that is, a singular subject takes a singular verb, and a plural subject takes a plural verb. The problem comes with identifying the subject and deciding whether it's singular or plural.

EXAMPLES

1. Either Cassie or her brother has/~~have~~ entered the woods. [Singular subjects joined by *or* or *nor* take a singular verb.]

2. Neither Mr. Andersen nor his workers know/~~knows~~ what to do with Little Man. [When a singular and a plural subject are joined by *or* or *nor*, the verb agrees with the subject closer to the verb.]

3. The pounding of axes ~~echo~~/echoes sadly through their woods. [The number of the subject is not changed by a phrase following the subject.]

**Language Handbook HELP**

*See Problems in Agreement, page 721.*

**Technology HELP**

*See* Language Workshop CD-ROM. *Key word entry: subject-verb agreement.*

### Try It Out

As the editor of the paragraph below, rewrite the text to correct errors in subject-verb agreement.

The most important moments in this story comes when Papa and Mr. Andersen meet along the ridge. Mr. Andersen tries to scare and bribe Cassie's father, but neither threats nor the promise of money move Papa. Mr. Andersen, in front of his workers, back down and leave.

---

# VOCABULARY

**WORD BANK**

*finicky*
*dispute*
*ambled*
*delved*
*curtly*
*skirting*
*elude*
*incredulously*
*ashen*
*sentries*

## Connotations: What's the Difference Between . . .

Would you rather be described as *curious* or *nosy*? The two words have the same basic meaning, or **denotation,** but different connotations. **Connotations** are the feelings and associations that have come to be attached to certain words. Most people wouldn't mind being called curious, but *nosy* suggests putting your nose into other people's business.

Test your skills at recognizing shades of meaning. What's the difference between . . .

1. *finicky* and *careful*?
2. a *dispute* and a *brawl*?
3. *ambled* and *walked*?
4. *delved* and *looked for*?
5. *matter-of-factly* and *curtly*?
6. *passing* and *skirting*?
7. *escape* and *elude*?
8. *incredulously* and *doubtfully*?
9. *creamy* and *ashen*?
10. *watchers* and *sentries*?

# Reading Skills and Strategies

## METACOGNITION: THINKING ABOUT THINKING

What do readers do when they read a story? Here are some responses:

- "I always count the pages to see how long it is."

- "I sort of look through the story to see whether the words are hard or easy to read. If they're hard, I know I'll have to spend a little more time reading it."

- "Sometimes if I don't understand something, I just keep reading to see if the rest of the story explains it. Other times I just ask someone."

The readers are engaged in a process called **metacognition.** This word comes from Greek and Latin roots: *Meta-* is a prefix that comes from Greek and means "along with" or "beyond," and *cognition* comes from the Latin word for "knowing." So *metacognition* just means "thinking about thinking." Here are a few study strategies to help you practice metacognition.

### Before Reading: Preview

Flip through the pages of the story, and look at the illustrations. Then, ask yourself these questions:

- What does the story seem to be about?

- Do I see any difficult words as I look through the story?

### During Reading: Question, Reread, and Record

Be aware of your reactions to the story as you are reading. Strike up a dialogue with the text by asking questions and making observations along the way.

- Ask yourself if you understand everything that has happened so far. If your answer is no, reread the sections you found difficult or talk about what's happening with a friend who's also reading the story.

- Are you bothered by anything in the story? Does a particular event or statement seem especially meaningful to you? Record

ideas and details that seem important.

### After Reading: Reflect

Take a few minutes to think about your reactions to the story.

- Decide how you feel about the story. Did you like it as much as you thought you would? Did you like it better?

- Were you asked to complete an assignment after reading the story? Which of your responses and reflections can help with the assignment?

There. You are now using metacognition.

**Apply the strategy on the next page.**

# Before You Read

## THE SMALLEST DRAGONBOY

## Make the Connection

### Underdogs

If anyone can say "I'm out here on my own," it's an underdog. An underdog is supposed to be a loser—so when an underdog unexpectedly wins, say, in football, sportscasters and fans make a big fuss. In fact, most of us love to see underdogs win—maybe because in some ways we identify with them.

## Quickwrite

Anne McCaffrey's brother Kevin was the inspiration for "The Smallest Dragonboy." As a twelve-year-old, Kevin suffered from a painful bone disease. He seemed to be marked as an underdog, but his courage made him the model for Keevan in the story. Quickwrite about someone you know who was an underdog but unexpectedly triumphed.

## Reading Skills and Strategies

### Metacognition: Thinking About Your Thinking

When you read "The Smallest Dragonboy," you'll enter the imaginary world of Pern. As you explore this new world, ask yourself questions and make observations. Jot down your thoughts as they occur to you.

When you finish the story, reconsider your questions and observations. What new questions come to mind that did not occur to you earlier, as you were reading? Take a moment to reflect on what you've read and what you're thinking.

For other hints on making reading a thought-provoking process, see page 45.

## Background

### Literature and Science

"The Smallest Dragonboy" takes place on the planet Pern, an imaginary world somewhere in outer space. Pern is threatened by the dangerous Red Star, which rains deadly threadlike plant spores on the planet every two hundred years or so. If the hungry Thread falls on Pern soil and grows there, it will devour every living thing.

To protect their planet, colonists on Pern have bioengineered a race of great winged dragons. When fed a special rock called firestone, the dragons breathe flames that char Thread to ashes. During Threadfall the dragons and their dragonriders charge into battle in midair while the other colonists hide safely in their cave towns. During periods of Threadfall, the protectors of Pern live inside the cones of old volcanoes in cave colonies called Weyrs.

As the story opens, young candidates for dragonrider in Benden Weyr, a colony in the Benden Mountains, await the hatching of a clutch of dragon eggs. According to custom, each newborn dragon will choose its own rider—and lifelong partner— through a kind of telepathic communication called Impression.

go.hrw.com

LEO 7-1

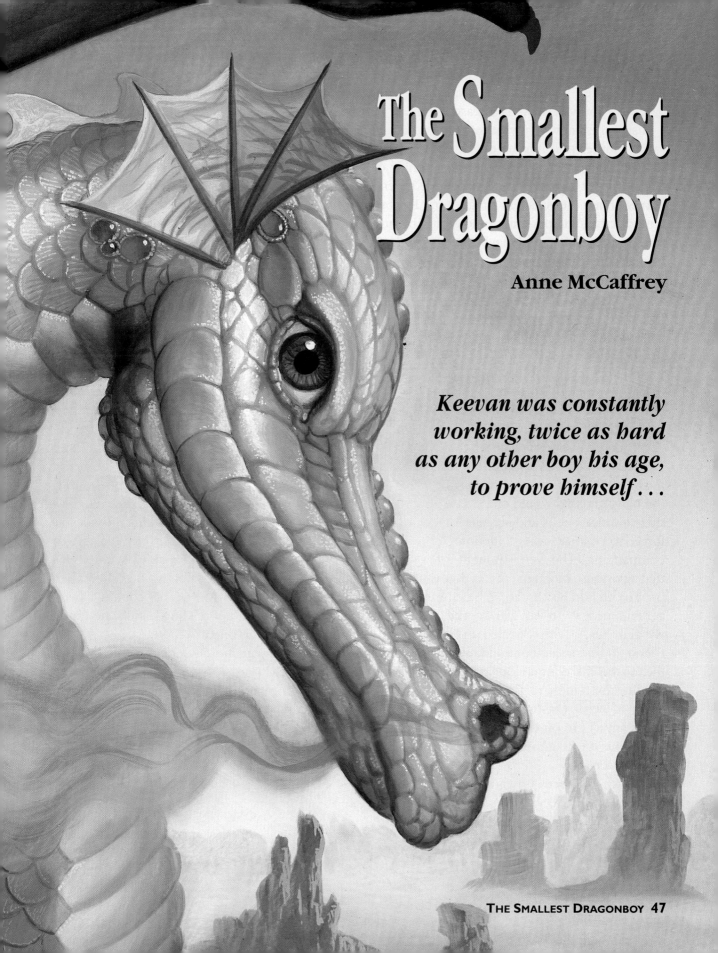

# The Smallest Dragonboy

**Anne McCaffrey**

*Keevan was constantly working, twice as hard as any other boy his age, to prove himself...*

Although Keevan lengthened his walking stride as far as his legs would stretch, he couldn't quite keep up with the other candidates. He knew he would be teased again.

Just as he knew many other things that his foster mother told him he ought not to know, Keevan knew that Beterli, the most senior of the boys, set that spanking pace just to embarrass him, the smallest dragonboy. Keevan would arrive, tail fork-end of the group, breathless, chest heaving, and maybe get a stern look from the instructing wingsecond.

Dragonriders, even if they were still only hopeful candidates for the glowing eggs which were hardening on the hot sands of the Hatching Ground cavern, were expected to be punctual and prepared. Sloth was not tolerated by the Weyrleader of Benden Weyr. A good record was especially important now. It was very near hatching time, when the baby dragons would crack their mottled shells and stagger forth to choose their lifetime companions. The very thought of that glorious moment made Keevan's breath catch in his throat. To be chosen—to be a dragonrider! To sit astride the neck of a winged beast with jeweled eyes; to be his friend, in telepathic communion[1] with him for life; to be his companion in good times and fighting extremes; to fly effortlessly over the lands of Pern! Or, thrillingly, *between* to any point anywhere on the world! Flying *between* was done on dragonback or not at all, and it was dangerous.

Keevan glanced upward, past the black mouths of the Weyr caves, in which grown dragons and their chosen riders lived, toward the Star Stones that crowned the ridge of the old volcano that was Benden Weyr. On the height, the blue watch dragon, his rider mounted on his neck, stretched the great transparent pinions[2] that carried him on the winds of Pern to fight the evil Thread that fell at certain times from the skies. The many-faceted rainbow jewels of his eyes glistened fleetingly in the greeny sun. He folded his great wings to his back, and the watch pair resumed their statuelike pose of alertness.

Then the enticing view was obscured as Keevan passed into the Hatching Ground cavern. The sands underfoot were hot, even through heavy wher-hide boots. How the boot maker had protested having to sew so small! Keevan was forced to wonder why being small was reprehensible. People were always calling him "babe" and shooing him away as being "too small" or "too young" for this or that. Keevan was constantly working, twice as hard as any other boy his age, to prove himself capable. What if his muscles weren't as big as Beterli's? They were just as hard. And if he couldn't overpower anyone in a wrestling match, he could outdistance everyone in a footrace.

"Maybe if you run fast enough," Beterli had jeered on the occasion when Keevan had been goaded to boast of his swiftness, "you could catch a dragon. That's the only way you'll make a dragonrider!"

> "Maybe if you run fast enough, you could catch a dragon . . ."

1. **telepathic communion:** communication of thoughts without speaking.

2. **pinions** (pin′yənz): wings.

----

### WORDS TO OWN

**goaded** (gōd′id) v.: pushed or driven. A goad is a stick with a sharp point used to herd oxen.

----

"You just wait and see, Beterli, you just wait," Keevan had replied. He would have liked to wipe the contemptuous smile from Beterli's face, but the guy didn't fight fair even when a wingsecond was watching. "No one knows what Impresses a dragon!"

"They've got to be able to *find* you first, babe!"

Yes, being the smallest candidate was not an enviable position. It was therefore imperative that Keevan Impress a dragon in his first hatching. That would wipe the smile off every face in the cavern and accord him the respect due any dragonrider, even the smallest one.

Besides, no one knew exactly what Impressed the baby dragons as they struggled from their shells in search of their lifetime partners.

"I like to believe that dragons see into a man's heart," Keevan's foster mother, Mende, told him. "If they find goodness, honesty, a flexible mind, patience, courage—and you've got that in quantity, dear Keevan—that's what dragons look for. I've seen many a well-grown lad left standing on the sands, Hatching Day, in favor of someone not so strong or tall or handsome. And if my memory serves me"—which it usually did: Mende knew every word of every Harper's tale worth telling, although Keevan did not interrupt her to say so—"I don't believe that F'lar, our Weyrleader, was all that tall when bronze Mnementh chose him. And Mnementh was the only bronze dragon of that hatching."

Dreams of Impressing a bronze were beyond Keevan's boldest reflections, although that goal dominated the thoughts of every other hopeful candidate. Green dragons were small and fast and more numerous. There was more prestige to Impressing a blue or brown than a green. Being practical, Keevan seldom dreamed as high as a big fighting brown, like Canth, F'nor's fine fellow, the biggest brown on all Pern. But to fly a bronze? Bronzes were almost as big as the queen, and only they took the air when a queen flew at mating time. A bronze rider could aspire to become Weyrleader! Well, Keevan would console himself, brown riders could aspire to become wingseconds, and that wasn't bad. He'd even settle for a green dragon; they were small, but so was he. No matter! He simply had to Impress a dragon his first time in the Hatching Ground. Then no one in the Weyr would taunt him anymore for being so small.

Shells, Keevan thought now, but the sands are hot!

"Impression time is imminent, candidates," the wingsecond was saying as everyone crowded respectfully close to him. "See the extent of the striations on this promising egg." The stretch marks *were* larger than yesterday.

Everyone leaned forward and nodded thoughtfully. That particular egg was the one Beterli had marked as his own, and no other candidate dared, on pain of being beaten by Beterli at his first opportunity, to approach it. The egg was marked by a large yellowish splotch in the shape of a dragon backwinging to land, talons outstretched to grasp rock. Everyone knew that bronze eggs bore distinctive markings. And naturally, Beterli, who'd been presented at eight Impressions already and was the biggest of the candidates, had chosen it.

"I'd say that the great opening day is almost upon us," the wingsecond went on, and then his face assumed a grave expression. "As we well know, there are only forty eggs and seventy-two candidates. Some of you may be disappointed on the great day. That doesn't necessarily mean you aren't dragonrider material, just that *the* dragon for you hasn't been shelled. You'll have other hatchings, and it's no

**WORDS TO OWN**
imminent (im′ə·nənt) *adj.*: about to happen.

disgrace to be left behind an Impression or two. Or more."

Keevan was positive that the wingsecond's eyes rested on Beterli, who'd been stood off at so many Impressions already. Keevan tried to squinch down so the wingsecond wouldn't notice him. Keevan had been reminded too often that he was eligible to be a candidate by one day only. He, of all the hopefuls, was most likely to be left standing on the great day. One more reason why he simply had to Impress at his first hatching.

"Now move about among the eggs," the wingsecond said. "Touch them. We don't know that it does any good, but it certainly doesn't do any harm."

Some of the boys laughed nervously, but everyone immediately began to circulate among the eggs. Beterli stepped up officiously to "his" egg, daring anyone to come near it. Keevan smiled, because he had already touched it—every inspection day, when the others were leaving the Hatching Ground and no one could see him crouch to stroke it.

Keevan had an egg he concentrated on, too, one drawn slightly to the far side of the others. The shell had a soft greenish blue tinge with a faint creamy swirl design. The consensus was that this egg contained a mere green, so Keevan was rarely bothered by rivals. He was somewhat perturbed, then, to see Beterli wandering over to him.

"I don't know why you're allowed in this Impression, Keevan. There are enough of us without a babe," Beterli said, shaking his head.

"I'm of age." Keevan kept his voice level, telling himself not to be bothered by mere words.

"Yah!" Beterli made a show of standing on his toe tips. "You can't even see over an egg; Hatching Day, you better get in front or the dragons won't see you at all. 'Course, you could get run down that way in the mad scramble. Oh, I forget, you can run fast, can't you?"

"You'd better make sure a dragon sees *you* this time, Beterli," Keevan replied. "You're almost overage, aren't you?"

Beterli flushed and took a step forward, hand half raised. Keevan stood his ground, but if Beterli advanced one more step, he would call the wingsecond. No one fought on the Hatching Ground. Surely Beterli knew that much.

Fortunately, at that moment, the wingsecond called the boys together and led them from the Hatching Ground to start on evening chores. There were "glows" to be replenished in the main kitchen caverns and sleeping cubicles, the major hallways, and the queen's apartment. Firestone sacks had to be filled against Thread attack, and black rock brought to the kitchen hearths. The boys fell to their chores, tantalized by the odors of roasting meat. The population of the Weyr began to assemble for the evening meal, and the dragonriders came in from the Feeding Ground on their sweep checks.

It was the time of day Keevan liked best: Once the chores were done but before dinner was served, a fellow could often get close enough to the dragonriders to hear their talk. Tonight, Keevan's father, K'last, was at the main dragonrider table. It puzzled Keevan how his father, a brown rider and a tall man, could *be* his father—because he, Keevan, was so small. It obviously puzzled K'last, too, when he deigned to notice his small son: "In a few more Turns, you'll be as tall as I am—or taller!"

K'last was pouring Benden wine all around the table. The dragonriders were relaxing. There'd be no Thread attack for three more days, and they'd be in the mood to tell tall tales, better than Harper yarns, about impossible

----

**WORDS TO OWN**

perturbed (pər·tʉrbd′) v. used as *adj.*: disturbed; troubled.

----

maneuvers they'd done a-dragonback. When Thread attack was closer, their talk would change to a discussion of tactics of evasion, of going *between,* how long to suspend there until the burning but fragile Thread would freeze and crack and fall harmlessly off dragon and man. They would dispute the exact moment to feed firestone to the dragon so he'd have the best flame ready to sear Thread midair and render it harmless to ground—and man—below. There was such a lot to know and understand about being a dragonrider that sometimes Keevan was overwhelmed. How would he ever be able to remember everything he ought to know at the right moment? He couldn't dare ask such a question; this would only have given additional weight to the notion that he was too young yet to be a dragonrider.

"Having older candidates makes good sense," L'vel was saying as Keevan settled down near the table. "Why waste four to five years of a dragon's fighting prime until his rider grows up enough to stand the rigors?" L'vel had Impressed a blue of Ramoth's first clutch. Most of the candidates thought L'vel was marvelous because he spoke up in front of the older riders, who awed them. "That was well enough in the Interval when you didn't need to mount the full Weyr complement to fight Thread. But not now. Not with more eligible candidates than ever. Let the babes wait."

"Any boy who is over twelve Turns has the right to stand in the Hatching Ground," K'last replied, a slight smile on his face. He never argued or got angry. Keevan wished he were more like his father. And oh, how he wished he were a brown rider! "Only a dragon—each particular dragon—knows what he wants in a rider. We certainly can't tell. Time and again, the theorists," K'last's smile deepened as his eyes swept those at the table, "are surprised by dragon choice. *They* never seem to make mistakes, however."

"Now, K'last, just look at the roster this Impression. Seventy-two boys and only forty eggs. Drop off the twelve youngest, and there's still a good field for the hatchlings to choose from. Shells! There are a couple of Weyrlings unable to see over a wher egg, much less a dragon! And years before they can ride Thread."

"True enough, but the Weyr is scarcely under fighting strength, and if the youngest Impress, they'll be old enough to fight when the oldest of our current dragons go *between* from senility."

"Half the Weyr-bred lads have already been through several Impressions," one of the bronze riders said then. "I'd say drop some of *them* off this time. Give the untried a chance."

"There's nothing wrong in presenting a clutch with as wide a choice as possible," said the Weyrleader, who had joined the table with Lessa, the Weyrwoman.

"Has there ever been a case," she said, smiling in her odd way at the riders, "where a hatchling didn't choose?"

Her suggestion was almost heretical and drew astonished gasps from everyone, including the boys.

F'lar laughed. "You say the most outrageous things, Lessa."

"Well, *has* there ever been a case where a dragon didn't choose?"

"Can't say as I recall one," K'last replied.

"Then we continue in this tradition," Lessa said firmly, as if that ended the matter.

"Any boy who is over twelve Turns has the right to stand in the Hatching Ground . . ."

But it didn't. The argument ranged from one table to the other all through dinner, with some favoring a weeding out of the candidates to the most likely, lopping off those who were very young or who had had multiple opportunities to Impress. All the candidates were in a swivet,[3] though such a departure from tradition would be to the advantage of many. As the evening progressed, more riders were favoring eliminating the youngest and those who'd passed four or more Impressions unchosen. Keevan felt he could bear such a dictum[4] only if Beterli were also eliminated. But this seemed less likely than that Keevan would be turfed out,[5] since the Weyr's need was for fighting dragons and riders.

By the time the evening meal was over, no decision had been reached, although the Weyrleader had promised to give the matter due consideration.

He might have slept on the problem, but few of the candidates did. Tempers were uncertain in the sleeping caverns next morning as the boys were routed out of their beds to carry water and black rock and cover the "glows." Twice Mende had to call Keevan to order for clumsiness.

"Whatever is the matter with you, boy?" she demanded in exasperation when he tipped black rock short of the bin and sooted up the hearth.

"They're going to keep me from this Impression."

"What?" Mende stared at him. "Who?"

"You heard them talking at dinner last night. They're going to turf the babes from the hatching."

Mende regarded him a moment longer before touching his arm gently. "There's lots of talk around a supper table, Keevan. And it cools as soon as the supper. I've heard the same nonsense before every hatching, but nothing is ever changed."

"There's always a first time," Keevan answered, copying one of her own phrases.

"That'll be enough of that, Keevan. Finish your job. If the clutch does hatch today, we'll need full rock bins for the feast, and you won't be around to do the filling. All my fosterlings make dragonriders."

"The first time?" Keevan was bold enough to ask as he scooted off with the rockbarrow.

Perhaps, Keevan thought later, if he hadn't been on that chore just when Beterli was also fetching black rock, things might have turned out differently. But he had dutifully trundled the barrow to the outdoor bunker for another load just as Beterli arrived on a similar errand.

"Heard the news, babe?" Beterli asked. He was grinning from ear to ear, and he put an unnecessary emphasis on the final insulting word.

"The eggs are cracking?" Keevan all but dropped the loaded shovel. Several anxieties flicked through his mind then: He was black with rock dust—would he have time to wash before donning the white tunic of candidacy? And if the eggs were hatching, why hadn't the candidates been recalled by the wingsecond?

"Naw! Guess again!" Beterli was much too pleased with himself.

With a sinking heart, Keevan knew what the news must be, and he could only stare with intense desolation at the older boy.

"C'mon! Guess, babe!"

"I've no time for guessing games," Keevan managed to say with indifference. He began to shovel black rock into the barrow as fast as he could.

"I said, guess." Beterli grabbed the shovel.

"And I said I have no time for guessing games."

Beterli wrenched the shovel from Keevan's hands. "Guess!"

"I'll have that shovel back, Beterli." Keevan

3. **in a swivet:** frustrated and annoyed.
4. **dictum:** pronouncement or judgment.
5. **turfed out:** British expression meaning "removed; expelled."

straightened up, but he didn't come to Beterli's bulky shoulder. From somewhere, other boys appeared, some with barrows, some mysteriously alerted to the prospect of a <u>confrontation</u> among their numbers.

"Babes don't give orders to candidates around here, babe!"

Someone sniggered, and Keevan, incredulous, knew that he must've been dropped from the candidacy.

He yanked the shovel from Beterli's loosened grasp. Snarling, the older boy tried to regain possession, but Keevan clung with all his strength to the handle, dragged back and forth as the stronger boy jerked the shovel about.

With a sudden, unexpected movement, Beterli rammed the handle into Keevan's chest, knocking him over the barrow handles. Keevan felt a sharp, painful jab behind his left ear, an unbearable pain in his left shin, and then a painless nothingness.

Mende's angry voice roused him, and, startled, he tried to throw back the covers, thinking he'd overslept. But he couldn't move, so firmly was he tucked into his bed. And then the constriction of a bandage on his head and the dull sickishness in his leg brought back recent occurrences.

"Hatching?" he cried.

"No, lovey," Mende said in a kind voice. Her hand was cool and gentle on his forehead. "Though there's some as won't be at any hatching again." Her voice took on a stern edge.

Keevan looked beyond her to see the Weyrwoman, who was frowning with irritation.

"Keevan, will you tell me what occurred at the black-rock bunker?" asked Lessa in an even voice.

He remembered Beterli now and the quarrel over the shovel and . . . what had Mende said about some not being at any hatching? Much as he hated Beterli, he couldn't bring himself to tattle on Beterli and force him out of candidacy.

"Come, lad," and a note of impatience crept into the Weyrwoman's voice. "I merely want to know what happened from you, too. Mende said she sent you for black rock. Beterli—and every Weyrling in the cavern—seems to have been on the same errand. What happened?"

"Beterli took my shovel. I hadn't finished with it."

"There's more than one shovel. What did he *say* to you?"

"He'd heard the news."

"What news?" The Weyrwoman was suddenly amused.

"That . . . that . . . there'd been changes."

"Is that what he said?"

"Not exactly."

"What did he say? C'mon, lad, I've heard from everyone else, you know."

"He said for me to guess the news."

"And you fell for that old gag?" The Weyrwoman's irritation returned.

"Consider all the talk last night at supper, Lessa," Mende said. "Of course the boy would think he'd been eliminated."

"In effect, he is, with a broken skull and leg." Lessa touched his arm in a rare gesture of sympathy. "Be that as it may, Keevan, you'll have other Impressions. Beterli will not. There are certain rules that must be observed by all candidates, and his conduct proves him unacceptable to the Weyr."

She smiled at Mende and then left.

"I'm still a candidate?" Keevan asked urgently.

"Well, you are and you aren't, lovey," his foster mother said. "Is the numbweed working?" she asked, and when he nodded, she said, "You just rest. I'll bring you some nice broth."

At any other time in his life, Keevan would

---

## WORDS TO OWN

**confrontation** (kän′frən·tā′shən) *n.:* face-to-face meeting between opposing sides.

---

have relished such cosseting, but now he just lay there worrying. Beterli had been dismissed. Would the others think it was his fault? But everyone was there! Beterli provoked that fight. His worry increased, because although he heard excited comings and goings in the passageway, no one tweaked back the curtain across the sleeping alcove he shared with five other boys. Surely one of them would have to come in sometime. No, they were all avoiding him. And something else was wrong. Only he didn't know what.

Mende returned with broth and beachberry bread.

"Why doesn't anyone come see me, Mende? I haven't done anything wrong, have I? I didn't ask to have Beterli turfed out."

Mende soothed him, saying everyone was busy with noontime chores and no one was angry with him. They were giving him a chance to rest in quiet. The numbweed made him drowsy, and her words were fair enough. He permitted his fears to dissipate. Until he heard a hum. Actually he felt it first, in the broken shinbone and his sore head. The hum began to grow. Two things registered suddenly in Keevan's groggy mind: The only white candidate's robe still on the pegs in the chamber was his, and the dragons hummed when a clutch was being laid or being hatched. Impression! And he was flat abed.

Bitter, bitter disappointment turned the warm broth sour in his belly. Even the small voice telling him that he'd have other opportunities failed to alleviate his crushing depression. *This* was the Impression that mattered! This was his chance to show *everyone,* from Mende to K'last to L'vel and even the Weyrleader, that he, Keevan, was worthy of being a dragonrider.

He twisted in bed, fighting against the tears that threatened to choke him. Dragonmen don't cry! Dragonmen learn to live with pain.

Pain? The leg didn't actually pain him as he rolled about on his bedding. His head felt sort of stiff from the tightness of the bandage. He sat up, an effort in itself since the numbweed made exertion difficult. He touched the splinted leg; the knee was unhampered. He had no feeling in his bone, really. He swung himself carefully to the side of his bed and stood slowly. The room wanted to swim about him. He closed his eyes, which made the dizziness worse, and he had to clutch the wall.

Gingerly, he took a step. The broken leg dragged. It hurt in spite of the numbweed, but what was pain to a dragonman?

No one had said he couldn't go to the Impression. "You are and you aren't" were Mende's exact words.

Clinging to the wall, he jerked off his bed shirt. Stretching his arm to the utmost, he jerked his white candidate's tunic from the peg. Jamming first one arm and then the other into the holes, he pulled it over his head. Too bad about the belt. He couldn't wait. He hobbled to the door and hung on to the curtain to steady himself. The weight on his leg was unwieldy. He wouldn't get very far without something to lean on. Down by the bathing pool was one of the long crook-necked poles used to retrieve clothes from the hot washing troughs. But it was down there, and he was on the level above. And there was no one nearby to come to his aid; everyone would be in the Hatching Ground right now, eagerly waiting for the first egg to crack.

The humming increased in volume and tempo, an urgency to which Keevan responded, knowing that his time was all too limited if he was to join the ranks of the hopeful boys standing around the cracking eggs. But if he hurried down the ramp, he'd fall flat on his face.

He could, of course, go flat on his rear end,

---

**WORDS TO OWN**
alleviate (ə·lē′vē·āt′) v.: relieve; reduce.

---

the way crawling children did. He sat down, sending a jarring stab of pain through his leg and up to the wound on the back of his head. Gritting his teeth and blinking away tears, Keevan scrabbled down the ramp. He had to wait a moment at the bottom to catch his breath. He got to one knee, the injured leg straight out in front of him. Somehow, he managed to push himself erect, though the room seemed about to tip over his ears. It wasn't far to the crooked stick, but it seemed an age before he had it in his hand.

Then the humming stopped!

Keevan cried out and began to hobble frantically across the cavern, out to the bowl of the Weyr. Never had the distance between living caverns and the Hatching Ground seemed so great. Never had the Weyr been so breathlessly silent. It was as if the multitude of people and dragons watching the hatching held every breath in suspense. Not even the wind muttered down the steep sides of the bowl. The only sounds to break the stillness were Keevan's ragged gasps and the thump-thud of his stick on the hard-packed ground. Sometimes he had to hop twice on his good leg to maintain his balance. Twice he fell into the sand and had to pull himself up on the stick, his white tunic no longer spotless. Once he jarred himself so badly he couldn't get up immediately.

Then he heard the first exhalation of the crowd, the oohs, the muted cheer, the susurrus[6] of excited whispers. An egg had cracked, and the dragon had chosen his rider. Desperation increased Keevan's hobble. Would

6. **susurrus** (sə·sûr′əs): rustling sound.

he never reach the arching mouth of the Hatching Ground?

Another cheer and an excited spate of applause spurred Keevan to greater effort. If he didn't get there in moments, there'd be no unpaired hatchling left. Then he was actually staggering into the Hatching Ground, the sands hot on his bare feet.

No one noticed his entrance or his halting progress. And Keevan could see nothing but the backs of the white-robed candidates, seventy of them ringing the area around the eggs. Then one side would surge forward or back and there'd be a cheer. Another dragon had been Impressed. Suddenly a large gap appeared in the white human wall, and Keevan had his first sight of the eggs. There didn't seem to be *any* left uncracked, and he could see the lucky boys standing beside wobble-legged dragons. He could hear the unmistakable plaintive crooning of hatchlings and their squawks of protest as they'd fall awkwardly in the sand.

*If he didn't get there in moments, there'd be no unpaired hatchling left.*

Suddenly he wished that he hadn't left his bed, that he'd stayed away from the Hatching Ground. Now everyone would see his ignominious failure. So he scrambled as desperately to reach the shadowy walls of the Hatching Ground as he had struggled to cross the bowl. He mustn't be seen.

He didn't notice, therefore, that the shifting group of boys remaining had begun to drift in his direction. The hard pace he had set himself and his cruel disappointment took their double toll of Keevan. He tripped and collapsed, sobbing, to the warm sands. He didn't see the consternation in the watching Weyrfolk above the Hatching Ground, nor did he hear the excited whispers of speculation. He didn't know that

the Weyrleader and Weyrwoman had dropped to the arena and were making their way toward the knot of boys slowly moving in the direction of the entrance.

"Never seen anything like it," the Weyrleader was saying. "Only thirty-nine riders chosen. And the bronze trying to leave the Hatching Ground without making Impression."

"A case in point of what I said last night," the Weyrwoman replied, "where a hatchling makes no choice because the right boy isn't there."

"There's only Beterli and K'last's young one missing. And there's a full wing of likely boys to choose from. . . ."

"None acceptable, apparently. Where is the creature going? He's not heading for the entrance after all. Oh, what have we there, in the shadows?"

Keevan heard with dismay the sound of voices nearing him. He tried to burrow into the sand. The mere thought of how he would be teased and taunted now was unbearable.

*Don't worry! Please don't worry!* The thought was urgent, but not his own.

Someone kicked sand over Keevan and butted roughly against him.

"Go away. Leave me alone!" he cried.

*Why?* was the injured-sounding question inserted into his mind. There was no voice, no tone, but the question was there, perfectly clear, in his head.

Incredulous, Keevan lifted his head and stared into the glowing jeweled eyes of a small bronze dragon. His wings were wet, the tips drooping in the sand. And he sagged in the middle on his unsteady legs, although he was making a great effort to keep erect.

Keevan dragged himself to his knees, oblivious of the pain in his leg. He wasn't even aware that he was ringed by the boys passed over, while thirty-one pairs of resentful eyes watched him Impress the dragon. The Weyrmen looked on, amused and surprised at the draconic[7] choice, which could not be forced. Could not be questioned. Could not be changed.

*Why?* asked the dragon again. *Don't you like me?* His eyes whirled with anxiety, and his tone was so piteous that Keevan staggered forward and threw his arms around the dragon's neck, stroking his eye ridges, patting the damp, soft hide, opening the fragile-looking wings to dry them, and wordlessly assuring the hatchling over and over again that he was the most perfect, most beautiful, most beloved dragon in the Weyr, in all the Weyrs of Pern.

"What's his name, K'van?" asked Lessa, smiling warmly at the new dragonrider. K'van stared up at her for a long moment. Lessa would know as soon as he did. Lessa was the only person who could "receive" from all dragons, not only her own Ramoth. Then he gave her a radiant smile, recognizing the traditional shortening of his name that raised him forever to the rank of dragonrider.

*My name is Heth,* the dragon thought mildly, then hiccuped in sudden urgency. *I'm hungry.*

"Dragons are born hungry," said Lessa, laughing. "F'lar, give the boy a hand. He can barely manage his own legs, much less a dragon's."

K'van remembered his stick and drew himself up. "We'll be just fine, thank you."

"You may be the smallest dragonrider ever, young K'van," F'lar said, "but you're one of the bravest!"

And Heth agreed! Pride and joy so leaped in both chests that K'van wondered if his heart would burst right out of his body. He looped an arm around Heth's neck, and the pair, the smallest dragonboy and the hatchling who wouldn't choose anybody else, walked out of the Hatching Ground together forever.

---

7. **draconic** (drə·kän′ik): of a dragon. *Drakōn* is the Greek word for "dragon."

## MEET THE WRITER

### "I Can't NOT Write"

**Anne McCaffrey** (1926– ) is known to her many readers as "the Dragon lady." When asked why she defends dragons, McCaffrey said, "Dragons have always had bad press. And I liked the thought of them being so big, and controlled by a bond of love."

Anne McCaffrey grew up in Essex County, New Jersey. As a "lonely tomboy," she decided on two things she most wanted. "When I was a very young girl, I promised myself fervently (usually after I'd lost another battle with one of my brothers) that I would become a famous author and I'd own my own horse." McCaffrey's books are now known all over the world and have been translated into many languages. Since she moved to County Wicklow in Ireland, she has owned her own horse—a large dapple-gray Irish hunter she calls Horseface. McCaffrey lives and works in Ireland at her home, called Dragonhold. Fans of her books rejoice in McCaffrey's promise: "I shall continue to write—I can't NOT write—until I am too frail to touch the keys of my word processor." When asked how she writes stories, McCaffrey responds:

**66** First I find interesting people to write about (I have written an anthology series, *Crystal Singer*, because I wanted to name a feminine character Killeshandra), and then I find something for them to argue about or fight for or against. Or I think about an interesting concept—the dragons of Pern—telepathic, huge, flame-throwing dragons who fly because they 'think' they can. Aerodynamically, they can't. I like to write better than anything else, including riding Horseface. And I write because I can't always get the kind of story I like to read on library shelves. **99**

### The Worlds of Anne McCaffrey

If you want to continue riding with the dragon-riders, read *Dragonsong* (Bantam), *Dragonsinger* (Bantam), and *Dragondrums* (Bantam), a series of science fantasy novels about the dragons of Pern.

Student TO Student

# Sir Kensley the Brave

My name is Sir Kensley the Brave,
A mighty, prestigious knight.
I have no fears nor weaknesses;
Foes tremble at my sight.

5   I do not care for dragons,
And they don't care for me.
For every time I duel with them,
It ends in victory.

The maidens all adore me
10  And attend my every need.
Their love for me increases
With my every knightly deed.

Oh no, my master approaches me
And bellows with much rage,
15  "Get up, daydreaming imbecile,
You lowly servant page!"

—Megan Washam
Pinehurst Elementary School
Alexandria, Virginia

Armor of George Clifford, third earl of Cumberland, made in the royal workshops in Greenwich, England (c. 1580–1585) (69$^1$/$_2$" high).

The Metropolitan Museum of Art, Munsey Fund, 1932. (32.130.6) Photograph ©1991 The Metropolitan Museum of Art.

# MAKING MEANINGS

## First Thoughts

1. Describe or draw three vivid **images** that you remember from this story. Compare your pictures with your classmates'. Are any of your images the same as theirs?

## Shaping Interpretations

2. Make a chart showing all the **conflicts** Keevan faced. Which conflict do you think was the hardest one for Keevan?

| External Conflicts | Internal Conflicts |
|---|---|
|  |  |

3. What is the **climax** of this story—its most emotional moment? How did you feel at this point in the story?

4. When the Impression is over, Lessa calls Keevan K'van. What do you think this change of name will mean for Keevan's future?

5. Why do you think Beterli never Impressed a dragon?

## Connecting with the Text

6. Describe what you imagine is going on in Keevan's mind as Heth makes his choice. When has something wonderful like this happened to you?

## Extending the Text

7. How does it feel to be an underdog—to be teased about your looks or height or age? How should people like Keevan handle such teasing?

## Challenging the Text

8. List all the women in this story. Do you think they have powerful positions in Pern society, or do only men hold power? If you were writing about Pern, what roles and responsibilities would you give to men and women?

9. Think back to how you responded to this story as you read it. Did you find some passages confusing? Were all your questions eventually answered? Discuss your reading experiences in class.

### Reading Check

a. What does Keevan want as the story opens? Why does he fear he won't get it?

b. How are dragonriders chosen? Why does Keevan fear he'll be kept from this Impression?

c. How does the bully Beterli try to ruin Keevan's chances on Hatching Day?

d. Describe Keevan's struggle to reach the Hatching Ground.

e. What happens to Keevan at the Impression, just when he is most unhappy and discouraged?

# CHOICES: Building Your Portfolio

## Writer's Notebook

### 1. Collecting Ideas for a Story

Anne McCaffrey says she hatches a plot by creating fascinating characters and then finding something for them to fight for or against. Go back to your notes for the Quickwrite on page 46, and use McCaffrey's technique to expand your notes into the beginning of a story. Ask yourself,

- Who is my main character?
- Why is my main character an underdog?
- What is he or she fighting to get or to get away from?

*Name: Lydia*
*—a girl struggling to be a dancer*
*—has hearing loss*
*—concentrates on sensing vibrations of music through floor as she dances*

---

## Science/ Speaking and Listening

### 2. Weyr Science

Although dragons are traditionally creatures of fantasy, Pern's dragons are products of bioengineering. What other references to science do you find in the story?

With one classmate or more, choose and research a scientific topic suggested by the text. You might explore one of these:

- animals that use warm sand to incubate their eggs
- weeds and herbs used as medicine
- the formation of volcanic cones

Present your findings to the class. Use charts, drawings, and other visual aids to illustrate your report.

## Language and Vocabulary/Writing

### 3. What's the Word?

To describe life on Pern, Anne McCaffrey has invented new words, like *Weyr* and *Weyrling,* and new compound words, like *dragonboy* and *wingsecond.* You won't find any of these words in a dictionary, so you must guess their meanings from context clues or from what you already know about parts of the words. Help other readers by creating a "Pern glossary" of invented words

from the story. Besides giving definitions and pronunciations, you may want to illustrate some of the words.

## Creative Writing/ Music

### 4. Dragonballads (Working on Your Scales)

On Pern, Harpers compose songs about brave dragons and their riders. Alone or with a partner, write a song about an adventure shared by K'van and Heth. Use the melody of a familiar song, or create your own tune. Work with other students to perform your song in a Pernian concert.

# GRAMMAR LINK   MINI-LESSON

## Keeping Verb Tenses Consistent

**Language Handbook HELP**

*See Consistency of Tense, page 731.*

**Technology HELP**

*See* Language Workshop CD-ROM. *Key word entry: verb tenses.*

In "The Smallest Dragonboy," Anne McCaffrey relies on verbs to tell readers *what* happened and on verb tenses to tell *when* it happened. Verb tenses help show the sequence of events in a plot; if the writer jumps from one tense to another, the order of events becomes unclear.

When writing about events that take place in the present, use verbs that are in the present tense.

EXAMPLE

"'I don't know why you're allowed in this Impression, Keevan. There are enough of us without a babe.'"

When writing about events that occurred in the past, use verbs that are in the past tense.

EXAMPLE

"Someone kicked sand over Keevan and butted roughly against him."

Be careful not to shift tenses unnecessarily. Unless you want to show a shift in time, be consistent—use one tense.

INCONSISTENT   An egg cracks, and the dragon had chosen his rider.

CONSISTENT   "An egg had cracked, and the dragon had chosen his rider."

### Try It Out

➤ Make the verb tenses in each sentence consistent.

1. Keevan watches as the blue dragon stretched its wings.

2. Keevan drops his cane and fell to his knees.

3. Do all the dragons choose, or was one waiting for him?

➤ Keeping your tenses consistent can be difficult. Double-check your "tense sense" by asking a peer reviewer to go over a piece of writing with you. Circle all your verbs; their tenses should all be the same—unless, of course, you are writing about events that take place at different times.

## VOCABULARY   HOW TO OWN A WORD

**WORD BANK**

goaded
imminent
perturbed
confrontation
alleviate

### Write About It and Own It

1. Write a line of dialogue for Mende, using the word *goaded*.
2. Use the word *imminent* to describe a danger to Pern.
3. Write a line of dialogue for K'van, using the word *perturbed*.
4. Use the word *confrontation* in a description of Beterli.
5. Use the word *alleviate* to describe what Heth wants.

# *Before You Read*

## Make the Connection

### A Living Nightmare

Movies, TV, and books are full of horror tales. You might think that horror stories are something new, but since ancient times, storytellers have scared people with tales that make them want to check under their beds or behind the rocks in the back of their caves.

## Quickwrite

If you were writing a horror story or directing a horror movie, what details would you use to create a scary setting? Freewrite your ideas.

## Elements of Literature

### Suspense and Foreshadowing: It Was a Dark and Stormy Night

Like many storytellers, the writer of this story hooks our interest with his very first words: "My most terrifying experience?" Once a question like this is asked in a story, we want to know the answer. We want to know what happens next. This feeling of anxious curiosity is called **suspense.**

Writers often intensify suspense by dropping hints that suggest what will happen later in the story. This use of clues is called **foreshadowing.**

> **S**uspense is the uncertainty or anxiety that we feel about what will happen next in a story. **Foreshadowing** is the use of clues to suggest events that will happen later in the story. Foreshadowing often heightens suspense.
>
> *For more on Foreshadowing and Suspense, see pages 22–23 and the Handbook of Literary Terms.*

## Reading Skills and Strategies

### Making Predictions: What Will Happen Next?

Part of the fun of reading is trying to guess what will happen next. This process is called **making predictions.** Here is how you make predictions:

- Look for clues that foreshadow what will happen.

- As the suspense builds, predict possible outcomes. See if you can guess where the writer is leading you.

- Ask yourself questions while you read. Revise your predictions as you go.

- Draw on your own experiences and knowledge in making your predictions.

Remember: A good writer always surprises you.

## Background

### Literature and Geography

The title of this story is the name of a key, or low-lying island, off the coast of French Guiana (gē·an′ə), in South America. At the time the story was written, French Guiana was a colony of France. Cayenne (kī·en′), the capital, was the site of one of several prison camps maintained by France in French Guiana until 1945.

For more information, see the map on page 76.

**go.hrw.com**
*LEO 7-1*

# Three Skeleton Key

### George G. Toudouze

I did not give the
warnings of the
old-timers a
second thought.

**M**y most terrifying experience? Well, one does have a few
in thirty-five years of service in the Lights, although it's
mostly monotonous, routine work—keeping the light in order,
making out the reports.

When I was a young man, not very long in the service, there
was an opening in a lighthouse newly built off the coast of
Guiana, on a small rock twenty miles or so from the mainland.
The pay was high, so in order to reach the sum I had set out to
save before I married, I volunteered for service in the new light.

Three Skeleton Key, the small rock on which the light stood,
bore a bad reputation. It earned its name from the story of the
three convicts who, escaping from Cayenne in a stolen dugout

canoe, were wrecked on the rock during the night, managed to escape the sea, but eventually died of hunger and thirst. When they were discovered, nothing remained but three heaps of bones, picked clean by the birds. The story was that the three skeletons, gleaming with phosphorescent[1] light, danced over the small rock, screaming. . . .

But there are many such stories and I did not give the warnings of the old-timers at the *Île-de-Seine*[2] a second thought. I signed up, boarded ship, and in a month I was installed at the light.

## The story was that the three skeletons, gleaming with phosphorescent light, danced over the small rock, screaming . . .

Picture a gray, tapering cylinder,[3] welded to the solid black rock by iron rods and concrete, rising from a small island twenty-odd miles from land. It lay in the midst of the sea, this island, a small, bare piece of stone, about one hundred fifty feet long, perhaps forty wide. Small, barely large enough for a man to walk about and stretch his legs at low tide.

This is an advantage one doesn't find in all lights, however, for some of them rise sheer from the waves, with no room for one to move save within the light itself. Still, on our island, one must be careful, for the rocks were treacherously smooth. One misstep and down you would fall into the sea—not that the risk of

drowning was so great, but the waters about our island swarmed with huge sharks, who kept an eternal patrol around the base of the light.

Still, it was a nice life there. We had enough provisions to last for months, in the event that the sea should become too rough for the supply ship to reach us on schedule. During the day we would work about the light, cleaning the rooms, polishing the metalwork and the lens and reflector of the light itself, and at night we would sit on the gallery and watch our light, a twenty-thousand-candlepower lantern, swinging its strong white bar of light over the sea from the top of its hundred-twenty-foot tower. Some days, when the air would be very clear, we could see the land, a threadlike line to the west. To the east, north, and south stretched the ocean. Landsmen, perhaps, would soon have tired of that kind of life, perched on a small island off the coast of South America for eighteen weeks until one's turn for leave ashore came around. But we liked it there, my two fellow tenders and myself—so much so that for twenty-two months on end, with the exception of shore leaves, I was greatly satisfied with the life on Three Skeleton Key.

I had just returned from my leave at the end of June, that is to say, midwinter in that latitude, and had settled down to the routine with my two fellow keepers, a Breton[4] by the name of Le Gleo and the head keeper, Itchoua, a Basque[5] some dozen years or so older than either of us.

Eight days went by as usual; then on the ninth night after my return, Itchoua, who was on night duty, called Le Gleo and me, sleeping in our rooms in the middle of the tower, at two in the morning. We rose immediately and,

---

1. **phosphorescent** (fäs′fə·res′ənt): glowing.
2. **Île-de-Seine** (ēl′ də sen′).
3. **tapering cylinder:** tube shape that gradually narrows toward one end, in this case toward the top.

4. **Breton** (bret′′n): person from Brittany, a region of northern France.
5. **Basque** (bask): Basques are people living in the Pyrenees, a mountain range in France and Spain.

*Le Séducteur* by René Magritte. Oil on canvas (19" × 23").

climbing the thirty or so steps that led to the gallery, stood beside our chief.

Itchoua pointed, and following his finger, we saw a big three-master, with all sail set, heading straight for the light. A queer course, for the vessel must have seen us; our light lit her with the glare of day each time it passed over her.

Now, ships were a rare sight in our waters, for our light was a warning of treacherous reefs, barely hidden under the surface and running far out to sea. Consequently we were always given a wide berth, especially by sailing vessels, which cannot maneuver as readily as steamers.

No wonder that we were surprised at seeing this three-master heading dead for us in the gloom of early morning. I had immediately recognized her lines, for she stood out plainly, even at the distance of a mile, when our light shone on her.

She was a beautiful ship of some four thousand tons, a fast sailer that had carried cargoes to every part of the world, plowing the seas unceasingly. By her lines she was identified as Dutch built, which was understandable, as

Paramaribo and Dutch Guiana are very close to Cayenne.

Watching her sailing dead for us, a white wave boiling under her bows, Le Gleo cried out:

"What's wrong with her crew? Are they all drunk or insane? Can't they see us?"

Itchoua nodded soberly and looked at us sharply as he remarked: "See us? No doubt—if there *is* a crew aboard!"

## "Are you saying that she's the *Flying Dutchman?*" His sudden fright had been so evident that the older man laughed.

"What do you mean, chief?" Le Gleo had started, turned to the Basque. "Are you saying that she's the *Flying Dutchman?*"[6]

His sudden fright had been so evident that the older man laughed:

"No, old man, that's not what I meant. If I say that no one's aboard, I mean she's a derelict."[7]

Then we understood her queer behavior. Itchoua was right. For some reason, believing her doomed, her crew had abandoned her. Then she had righted herself and sailed on, wandering with the wind.

The three of us grew tense as the ship seemed about to crash on one of our numerous reefs, but she suddenly lurched with some change of the wind, the yards[8] swung around, and the derelict came clumsily about and sailed dead away from us.

In the light of our lantern she seemed so sound, so strong, that Itchoua exclaimed impatiently:

"But why the devil was she abandoned? Nothing is smashed, no sign of fire—and she doesn't sail as if she were taking water."

Le Gleo waved to the departing ship:

"Bon voyage!" he smiled at Itchoua and went on. "She's leaving us, chief, and now we'll never know what——"

"No, she's not!" cried the Basque. "Look! She's turning!"

As if obeying his words, the derelict three-master stopped, came about, and headed for us once more. And for the next four hours the vessel played around us—zigzagging, coming about, stopping, then suddenly lurching forward. No doubt some freak of current and wind, of which our island was the center, kept her near us.

Then suddenly the tropic dawn broke, the sun rose, and it was day, and the ship was plainly visible as she sailed past us. Our light extinguished, we returned to the gallery with our glasses[9] and inspected her.

The three of us focused our glasses on her poop[10] and saw, standing out sharply, black letters on the white background of a life ring, the stenciled name "*Cornelius de Witt,* Rotterdam."

We had read her lines correctly: She was Dutch. Just then the wind rose and the *Cornelius de Witt* changed course, leaned to port, and headed straight for us once more. But this time she was so close that we knew she would not turn in time.

"Thunder!" cried Le Gleo, his Breton soul aching at seeing a fine ship doomed to smash upon a reef, "she's going to pile up! She's gone!"

6. *Flying Dutchman:* fabled Dutch ghost ship whose captain is said to be condemned to sail the seas until Judgment Day. Seeing the *Flying Dutchman* is supposed to bring bad luck.
7. **derelict** (der′ə·likt′): here, abandoned ship.
8. **yards:** in nautical terms, rods fastened across the masts to support the sails.

9. **glasses:** here, binoculars.
10. **poop:** in nautical terms, the stern (back) deck of a ship.

I shook my head:

"Yes, and a shame to see that beautiful ship wreck herself. And we're helpless."

There was nothing we could do but watch. A ship sailing with all sail spread, creaming the sea with her forefoot as she runs before the wind, is one of the most beautiful sights in the world—but this time I could feel the tears stinging in my eyes as I saw this fine ship headed for her doom.

All this time our glasses were riveted on her and we suddenly cried out together:

"The rats!"

Now we knew why this ship, in perfect condition, was sailing without her crew aboard. They had been driven out by the rats. Not those poor specimens of rats you see ashore, barely reaching the length of one foot from their trembling noses to the tip of their skinny tails, wretched creatures that dodge and hide at the mere sound of a footfall.

No, these were ships' rats, huge, wise creatures, born on the sea, sailing all over the world on ships, transferring to other, larger ships as they multiply. There is as much difference between the rats of the land and these maritime rats as between a fishing smack[11] and an armored cruiser.

The rats of the sea are fierce, bold animals. Large, strong, and intelligent, clannish and sea-wise, able to put the best of mariners to shame with their knowledge of the sea, their uncanny ability to foretell the weather.

And they are brave, these rats, and vengeful. If you so much as harm one, his sharp cry will bring <u>hordes</u> of his fellows to swarm over you, tear you, and not cease until your flesh has been stripped from the bones.

The ones on this ship, the rats of Holland, are the worst, superior to other rats of the sea as their brethren are to the land rats. There is a well-known tale about these animals.

11. **smack:** here, small sailboat.

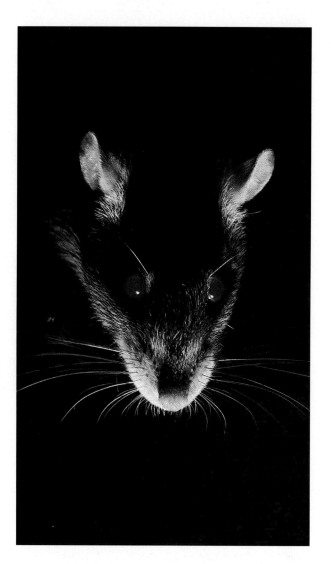

## The rats of the sea are fierce, bold animals.

A Dutch captain, thinking to protect his cargo, brought aboard his ship not cats but two terriers, dogs trained in the hunting, fighting, and killing of vicious rats. By the time the ship, sailing from Rotterdam, had passed the Ostend

**WORDS TO OWN**
**hordes** (hôrdz) *n.:* large, moving crowds.

## Thousands of heads rose, felt the wind, and we were scented, seen!

light, the dogs were gone and never seen again. In twenty-four hours they had been overwhelmed, killed, and eaten by the rats.

At times, when the cargo does not <u>suffice</u>, the rats attack the crew, either driving them from the ship or eating them alive. And studying the *Cornelius de Witt*, I turned sick, for her small boats were all in place. She had not been abandoned.

Over her bridge, on her deck, in the rigging, on every visible spot, the ship was a writhing mass—a starving army coming toward us aboard a vessel gone mad!

Our island was a small spot in that immense stretch of sea. The ship could have grazed us or passed to port or starboard with its ravening[12] cargo—but no, she came for us at full speed, as if she were leading the regatta at a race, and impaled herself on a sharp point of rock.

There was a dull shock as her bottom stove in,[13] then a horrible crackling as the three masts went overboard at once, as if cut down with one blow of some gigantic sickle. A sighing groan came as the water rushed into the ship; then she split in two and sank like a stone.

But the rats did not drown. Not these fellows! As much at home in the sea as any fish, they formed ranks in the water, heads lifted, tails stretched out, paws paddling. And half of them, those from the forepart of the ship,

12. **ravening** (rav′ən·iŋ): greedily searching for animals to kill for food. A more common related word is *ravenous* (rav′ə·nəs), meaning "wildly, greedily hungry."
13. **stove in:** caved in.

### WORDS TO OWN
**suffice** (sə·fis′) *v.:* be enough.

sprang along the masts and onto the rocks in the instant before she sank. Before we had time even to move, nothing remained of the three-master save some pieces of wreckage floating on the surface and an army of rats covering the rocks left bare by the <u>receding</u> tide.

Thousands of heads rose, felt the wind, and we were scented, seen! To them we were fresh meat, after possible weeks of starving. There came a scream, composed of innumerable screams, sharper than the howl of a saw attacking a bar of iron, and in the one motion, every rat leaped to attack the tower!

We barely had time to leap back, close the door leading onto the gallery, descend the stairs, and shut every window tightly. Luckily the door at the base of the light, which we never could have reached in time, was of bronze set in granite and was tightly closed.

The horrible band, in no measurable time, had swarmed up and over the tower as if it had been a tree, piled on the embrasures[14] of the windows, scraped at the glass with thousands of claws, covered the lighthouse with a furry mantle, and reached the top of the tower, filling the gallery and piling atop the lantern.

Their teeth grated as they pressed against the glass of the lantern room, where they could plainly see us, though they could not reach us. A few millimeters of glass, luckily very strong, separated our faces from their gleaming, beady eyes, their sharp claws and teeth. Their odor filled the tower, poisoned our lungs, and rasped our nostrils with a pestilential, nauseating smell. And there we were, sealed alive in our own light, prisoners of a horde of starving rats.

That first night, the tension was so great that we could not sleep. Every moment, we felt that some opening had been made, some window given way, and that our horrible besiegers were pouring through the breach. The rising tide, chasing those of the rats which had stayed on the bare rocks, increased the numbers clinging to the walls, piled on the balcony—so much so that clusters of rats clinging to one another hung from the lantern and the gallery.

With the coming of darkness we lit the light and the turning beam completely maddened the beasts. As the light turned, it successively blinded thousands of rats crowded against the glass, while the dark side of the lantern room gleamed with thousands of points of light, burning like the eyes of jungle beasts in the night.

## And there we were, sealed alive in our own light, prisoners of a horde of starving rats.

All the while we could hear the enraged scraping of claws against the stone and glass, while the chorus of cries was so loud that we had to shout to hear one another. From time to time, some of the rats fought among themselves and a dark cluster would detach itself, falling into the sea like a ripe fruit from a tree. Then we would see phosphorescent streaks as triangular fins slashed the water—sharks, permanent guardians of our rock, feasting on our jailers.

The next day we were calmer and amused ourselves teasing the rats, placing our faces against the glass which separated us. They could not fathom the invisible barrier which separated them from us, and we laughed as we watched them leaping against the heavy glass.

But the day after that, we realized how serious our position was. The air was foul; even the heavy smell of oil within our stronghold could

---

14. **embrasures** (em·brā′zhərz): slanted openings.

**WORDS TO OWN**
**receding** (ri·sēd′iŋ) v. used as adj.: moving back.

# LITERATURE AND HISTORY

---

## Night Lights on the High Seas

For centuries, lighthouses have been used to alert sailors that land is near, to point out dangerous rocks and reefs, and to cast a bright light into the night to guide ships on their way. Seafarers have relied on these structures since the days of ancient Egypt. The lighthouse built in 300 B.C. on Pharos, an island near Alexandria, was regarded as one of the Seven Wonders of the World.

Lighthouses help to guide ships at night by giving off an intense beam of light that flashes every few seconds. Until the eighteenth century the source of light was an oak-log fire. Coal fire was used for many years after that, until electricity became common in the early twentieth century. Some modern lighthouses also send out radio signals to help ships find their way in foggy weather. Even in their modern form, lighthouses still serve their ancient purpose as a guiding light, a flashing speck of civilization in the dark, lonely waters of the night.

---

not dominate the fetid odor of the beasts massed around us. And there was no way of admitting fresh air without also admitting the rats.

The morning of the fourth day, at early dawn, I saw the wooden framework of my window, eaten away from the outside, sagging inwards. I called my comrades and the three of us fastened a sheet of tin in the opening, sealing it tightly. When we had completed that task, Itchoua turned to us and said dully:

"Well—the supply boat came thirteen days ago, and she won't be back for twenty-nine." He pointed at the white metal plate sealing the opening through the granite. "If that gives way"—he shrugged—"they can change the name of this place to Six Skeleton Key."

The next six days and seven nights, our only distraction was watching the rats whose holds were insecure fall a hundred and twenty feet into the maws of the sharks—but they were so many that we could not see any diminution in their numbers.

Thinking to calm ourselves and pass the time, we attempted to count them, but we soon gave up. They moved incessantly, never still. Then we tried identifying them, naming them.

One of them, larger than the others, who

seemed to lead them in their rushes against the glass separating us, we named "Nero";[15] and there were several others whom we had learned to distinguish through various peculiarities.

But the thought of our bones joining those of the convicts was always in the back of our minds. And the gloom of our prison fed these thoughts, for the interior of the light was almost completely dark, as we had had to seal every window in the same fashion as mine, and the only space that still admitted daylight was the glassed-in lantern room at the very top of the tower.

Then Le Gleo became morose and had nightmares in which he would see the three skeletons dancing around him, gleaming coldly, seeking to grasp him. His maniacal, raving descriptions were so vivid that Itchoua and I began seeing them also.

It was a living nightmare, the raging cries of the rats as they swarmed over the light, mad with hunger; the sickening, strangling odor of their bodies——

True, there is a way of signaling from lighthouses. But to reach the mast on which to hang the signal, we would have to go out on the gallery where the rats were.

There was only one thing left to do. After debating all of the ninth day, we decided not to light the lantern that night. This is the greatest breach of our service, never committed as long as the tenders of the light are alive; for the light is something sacred, warning ships of danger in the night. Either the light gleams a quarter-hour after sundown, or no one is left alive to light it.

Well, that night, Three Skeleton Light was dark, and all the men were alive. At the risk of causing ships to crash on our reefs, we left it unlit, for we were worn out—going mad!

At two in the morning, while Itchoua was

**15. Nero** (nir′ō): emperor of Rome (A.D. 54–68), known for his cruelty.

dozing in his room, the sheet of metal sealing his window gave way. The chief had just time enough to leap to his feet and cry for help, the rats swarming over him.

But Le Gleo and I, who had been watching from the lantern room, got to him immediately, and the three of us battled with the horde of maddened rats which flowed through the gaping window. They bit, we struck them down with our knives—and retreated.

We locked the door of the room on them,

**The chief had just time enough to leap to his feet and cry for help, the rats swarming over him.**

but before we had time to bind our wounds, the door was eaten through and gave way, and we retreated up the stairs, fighting off the rats that leaped on us from the knee-deep swarm.

I do not remember, to this day, how we ever managed to escape. All I can remember is wading through them up the stairs, striking them off as they swarmed over us; and then we found ourselves, bleeding from innumerable bites, our clothes shredded, sprawled across the trapdoor in the floor of the lantern room— without food or drink. Luckily, the trapdoor was metal, set into the granite with iron bolts.

The rats occupied the entire light beneath us, and on the floor of our retreat lay some twenty of their fellows, who had gotten in with us before the trapdoor closed and whom we had killed with our knives. Below us, in the tower, we could hear the screams of the rats as they devoured everything edible that they found. Those on the outside squealed in reply and writhed in a horrible curtain as they stared at us through the glass of the lantern room.

## "The Three Skeletons!
## Hee! Hee!
## The Three Skeletons
## are now *six* skeletons!
## *Six* skeletons!"

Itchoua sat up and stared silently at his blood trickling from the wounds on his limbs and body and running in thin streams on the floor around him. Le Gleo, who was in as bad a state (and so was I, for that matter), stared at the chief and me vacantly, started as his gaze swung to the multitude of rats against the glass, then suddenly began laughing horribly:

"Hee! Hee! The Three Skeletons! Hee! Hee! The Three Skeletons are now *six* skeletons! *Six* skeletons!"

He threw his head back and howled, his eyes glazed, a trickle of saliva running from the corners of his mouth and thinning the blood flowing over his chest. I shouted to him to shut up, but he did not hear me, so I did the only thing I could to quiet him—I swung the back of my hand across his face.

The howling stopped suddenly, and his eyes swung around the room; then he bowed his head and began weeping softly, like a child.

Our darkened light had been noticed from the mainland, and as dawn was breaking, the patrol was there to investigate the failure of our light. Looking through my binoculars, I could see the horrified expression on the faces of the officers and crew when, the daylight strengthening, they saw the light completely covered by a seething mass of rats. They thought, as I

afterwards found out, that we had been eaten alive.

But the rats had also seen the ship or had scented the crew. As the ship drew nearer, a solid phalanx[16] left the light, plunged into the water, and swimming out, attempted to board her. They would have succeeded, as the ship was hove to;[17] but the engineer connected his steam to a hose on the deck and scalded the head of the attacking column, which slowed them up long enough for the ship to get under way and leave the rats behind.

Then the sharks took part. Belly up, mouths gaping, they arrived in swarms and scooped up the rats, sweeping through them like a sickle through wheat. That was one day that sharks really served a useful purpose.

The remaining rats turned tail, swam to the shore, and emerged dripping. As they neared the light, their comrades greeted them with shrill cries, with what sounded like a derisive note predominating. They answered angrily and mingled with their fellows. From the several tussles that broke out, it seemed as if they resented being ridiculed for their failure to capture the ship.

But all this did nothing to get us out of our jail. The small ship could not approach but steamed around the light at a safe distance, and the tower must have seemed fantastic, some weird, many-mouthed beast hurling defiance at them.

Finally, seeing the rats running in and out of the tower through the door and the windows, those on the ship decided that we had perished and were about to leave when Itchoua,

16. **phalanx** (fā′laŋks′): closely packed group. A phalanx is an ancient military formation, and the word still has war-like connotations.
17. **hove to:** stopped by being turned into the wind.

---

## WORDS TO OWN
**edible** (ed′ə·bəl) *adj.*: fit to be eaten.
**derisive** (di·rī′siv) *adj.*: scornful and ridiculing.

---

regaining his senses, thought of using the light as a signal. He lit it and, using a plank placed and withdrawn before the beam to form the dots and dashes, quickly sent out our story to those on the vessel.

Our reply came quickly. When they understood our position—how we could not get rid of the rats, Le Gleo's mind going fast, Itchoua and myself covered with bites, cornered in the lantern room without food or water—they had a signalman send us their reply.

His arms swinging like those of a windmill, he quickly spelled out:

"Don't give up, hang on a little longer! We'll get you out of this!"

Then she turned and steamed at top speed for the coast, leaving us little reassured.

She was back at noon, accompanied by the supply ship, two small coast guard boats, and the fireboat—a small squadron. At twelve-thirty the battle was on.

After a short reconnaissance,[18] the fireboat picked her way slowly through the reefs until she was close to us, then turned her powerful jet of water on the rats. The heavy stream tore the rats from their places and hurled them screaming into the water, where the sharks gulped them down. But for every ten that were dislodged, seven swam ashore, and the stream could do nothing to the rats within the tower. Furthermore, some of them, instead of returning to the rocks, boarded the fireboat, and the men were forced to battle them hand to hand. They were true rats of Holland, fearing no man, fighting for the right to live!

Nightfall came, and it was as if nothing had been done; the rats were still in possession. One of the patrol boats stayed by the island; the rest of the flotilla[19] departed for the coast. We had to

18. **reconnaissance** (ri·kän′ə·səns): exploratory survey or examination.
19. **flotilla** (flō·til′ə): small fleet of boats.

spend another night in our prison. Le Gleo was sitting on the floor, babbling about skeletons, and as I turned to Itchoua, he fell unconscious from his wounds. I was in no better shape and could feel my blood flaming with fever.

Somehow the night dragged by, and the next afternoon I saw a tug, accompanied by the fireboat, come from the mainland with a huge barge in tow. Through my glasses, I saw that the barge was filled with meat.

Risking the treacherous reefs, the tug dragged the barge as close to the island as possible. To the last rat, our besiegers deserted the rock, swam out, and boarded the barge reeking with the scent of freshly cut meat. The tug dragged the barge about a mile from shore, where the fireboat drenched the barge with gasoline. A well-placed incendiary shell from the patrol boat set her on fire.

The barge was covered with flames immediately, and the rats took to the water in swarms, but the patrol boat bombarded them with shrapnel from a safe distance, and the sharks finished off the survivors.

A whaleboat from the patrol boat took us off the island and left three men to replace us. By nightfall we were in the hospital in Cayenne. What became of my friends?

Well, Le Gleo's mind had cracked and he was raving mad. They sent him back to France and locked him up in an asylum, the poor devil! Itchoua died within a week; a rat's bite is dangerous in that hot, humid climate, and infection sets in rapidly.

As for me—when they fumigated the light and repaired the damage done by the rats, I resumed my service there. Why not? No reason why such an incident should keep me from finishing out my service there, is there?

Besides—I told you I liked the place—to be truthful, I've never had a post as pleasant as that one, and when my time came to leave it forever, I tell you that I almost wept as Three Skeleton Key disappeared below the horizon.

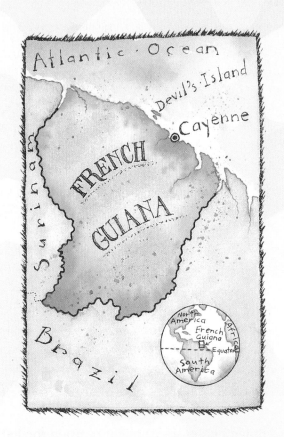

## MEET THE WRITER

### Sea Fever

**George G. Toudouze** (1847–1904) was born in France and had many literary interests—he was a playwright, an essayist, and an illustrator. He also had a great interest in the sea and worked on a history of the French Navy. One critic says of his storytelling style, "It has the impact of a powerful man at a fair who, for the fun of it, takes the hammer and at one blow sends the machine to the top, rings the bell, and walks off." "Three Skeleton Key" first appeared in *Esquire* magazine.

# MAKING MEANINGS

## First Thoughts

1. Describe your reaction to "Three Skeleton Key" by completing these sentences:

   • When I first read about the rats, I felt . . .

   • For me, the scariest part of the story was . . .

## Shaping Interpretations

2. Early in the story the narrator explains how Three Skeleton Key got its name. How does this **foreshadow**—or hint at—the danger the three lighthouse keepers face later on?

3. On the fourth day of the invasion, a wooden window frame in the lighthouse sags inward. How does this incident increase **suspense**? What other details create suspense?

4. The three characters in the lighthouse respond differently to the invasion. Describe each man's reactions to the rats. Which character (if any) did you identify with?

## Connecting with the Text

5. If you were the narrator, would you have returned to Three Skeleton Key? Why or why not?

6. The writer Isaac Asimov once said, "When I was a lad . . . I found myself fearfully attracted to stories that scared me. Don't ask why—I hate being scared, but I didn't mind, as long as I knew in my heart that I was safe." Do you enjoy tales of terror like "Three Skeleton Key"? Explain why or why not.

7. At what point in the story did you **predict** that the crew would survive the rat attack? On what evidence did you base your prediction?

## Extending the Text

8. This is a story of nature gone berserk. What other stories or movies can you name that have used this same frightening idea? (A well-known old movie is Alfred Hitchcock's *The Birds,* in which birds attack human beings.)

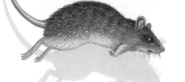

### Reading Check

To review the story line, imagine you are the narrator filling out a report on your adventure at Three Skeleton Key.

| Lighthouse Log |
| --- |
| Day 1: |
| Day 2: |
| Day 3: |
| Day 4: |

| |
| --- |
| Day 9: |
| Day 10: |
| Day 11: |

# CHOICES: Building Your Portfolio

## Writer's Notebook

### 1. Collecting Ideas for a Story

Much of the suspense in "Three Skeleton Key" comes from the fact that the characters are out there on their own. A lonely, forsaken setting like a tiny island can often inspire an idea for a frightening story. Jot down some ideas for the setting of a horror story. Look back at your notes for the Quickwrite on page 64 for more ideas.

> **Scene:**
> Cabin in the woods far from the main road. Starless night. Electricity sputters off. A knock on the door. Faint scraping sound heard outside.

## Creative Writing/ Reader's Theater

### 2. On-Air Scare

In 1949, a drama called "Three Skeleton Key" was broadcast on a radio series called *Escape,* a half-hour program of horror-adventure stories. Work with three or four class-mates to write a radio script for the whole story or for the part of the story you find most exciting. You might want to start with lines from the narrator to set the scene. Then, let the **dialogue,** or conversation, among the keepers carry the action of the story. Sound effects are important in a radio drama, so de-scribe briefly any sound ef-fects you'd use. Put these notes in parentheses right where you want the sounds heard. You may also de-scribe background music. Schedule some class time to present a tape recording of your radio drama.

## Science/Speaking

### 3. Oh, Rats!

What are the real facts about rats? As part of a team, research one of these questions:

- What role did rats play in European history during the 1300s?

- Are sea rats really as fierce, knowledgeable, and vengeful as they are in the story?

- In what ways are rats still a problem today?

Don't limit your research to encyclopedias. Try other resources, such as history books, computer databases, and knowledgeable mem-bers of your community.

What conclusions about rats can you draw from your research? Regroup and share what you have learned. Then, work to-gether to create a presen-tation for the class.

## Design/ Creative Writing

### 4. Career: Keeper

Design a job listing for the position of lighthouse keeper at Three Skeleton Key. Describe the personal characteristics and skills necessary for the job. Be sure to describe the work environment, duties, and pay. If possible, use com-puter graphics and special typefaces to attract the at-tention of the best possible candidates.

# GRAMMAR LINK    MINI-LESSON

## Those Troublesome Verbs

**Language Handbook HELP**

*See Irregular Verbs, pages 727-729.*

**Technology HELP**

*See Language Workshop CD-ROM. Key word entry: irregular verbs.*

Use this chart to help you navigate the choppy seas of troublesome verbs:

| Base Form | Past | Past Participle |
|-----------|------|-----------------|
| lie (recline) | lay | (have) lain |
| lay (put) | laid | (have) laid |
| sit (rest) | sat | (have) sat |
| set (place) | set | (have) set |
| rise (go up) | rose | (have) risen |
| raise (lift) | raised | (have) raised |

EXAMPLES

1. The keepers <u>lay</u> ill while men <u>laid</u> meat on the barge.

2. The men <u>sat</u> behind a metal door that was <u>set</u> in granite.

3. The sailors <u>rose</u> from the bench and <u>raised</u> the ship's sails.

### Try It Out

➤ Complete the sentences below by choosing the correct word from each underlined pair.

1. The keepers <u>sit/set</u> a light in the window and <u>rise/raise</u> a distress flag.

2. They <u>lie/lay</u> awake and <u>sit/set</u> their minds on rescue. (Use the present tense.)

3. No ship had <u>raised/risen</u> their hopes or had <u>laid/lain</u> their fears to rest.

➤ Keep an eye out for these troublesome verbs in your writing, and check the chart when you proofread.

# VOCABULARY    HOW TO OWN A WORD

**WORD BANK**

*hordes*
*suffice*
*receding*
*edible*
*derisive*

## And the Answer Is . . .

1. Hordes of rats would be a terrifying sight. Describe two other <u>hordes</u> that you would not like to see coming at you.

2. How much food will <u>suffice</u> for you for a day?

3. If you were a flood victim, how would you feel when you saw the flood waters <u>receding</u>?

4. What's your favorite <u>edible</u> plant? Why do you like it?

5. Write a <u>derisive</u> remark that a skeptic would make on hearing this rat story.

## Make the Connection

### Things That Go Bump in the Night

**Think-pair-share.** Read the cartoon on this page; then, take five minutes to talk with a partner about the reasons children have so many fears.

## Quickwrite

Make a list of suggestions you could give a young child about what to do when he or she is feeling afraid. You might want to begin each suggestion with "Whenever I feel afraid . . .".

## Elements of Literature

### What's in a Character?

"A Day's Wait" introduces two characters: a father, called Papa, and Schatz, his young son. The writer doesn't tell you directly what Papa and Schatz are like. You have to figure out their personalities for yourself, by watching what they say and do and think.

> **A** **character** is a person or animal who takes part in the action of a story.
>
> *For more on Character, see the Handbook of Literary Terms.*

## Reading Skills and Strategies

### Making Inferences: Finding Clues

An **inference** is an educated guess based on evidence. When you make inferences about characters, you try to guess what they are like. Here is how you do it:

• Take note of any information that the writer gives you directly. For instance, what does the character look like?

• Pay attention to what the character thinks, says, and does.

• Watch how other people react to the character.

• Think about people you know in real life—or from other stories—who resemble this character.

## Background

### Literature and Science

To understand this story, you have to know that there are two kinds of thermometers, each using a different temperature scale. On the Celsius thermometer, used in Europe, the boiling point of water is 100 degrees. On the Fahrenheit thermometer, the boiling point is much higher, 212 degrees.

go.hrw.com

*LE0 7-1*

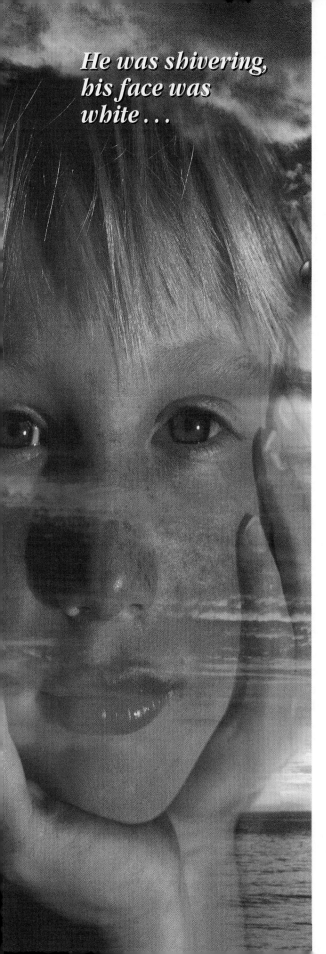

*He was shivering, his face was white . . .*

*The events in this story really happened to Hemingway and his nine-year-old son Bumby. (In this story Bumby is called Schatz, a German word meaning "treasure.") Hemingway and his family lived in France for many years; in this story they are back in the United States.*

# A Day's Wait

### Ernest Hemingway

He came into the room to shut the windows while we were still in bed and I saw he looked ill. He was shivering, his face was white, and he walked slowly as though it ached to move.

"What's the matter, Schatz?"

"I've got a headache."

"You better go back to bed."

"No. I'm all right."

"You go to bed. I'll see you when I'm dressed."

But when I came downstairs he was dressed, sitting by the fire, looking a very sick and miserable boy of nine years. When I put my hand on his forehead I knew he had a fever.

"You go up to bed," I said, "you're sick."

"I'm all right," he said.

When the doctor came he took the boy's temperature.

"What is it?" I asked him.

"One hundred and two."

Downstairs, the doctor left three different medicines in different-colored capsules with instructions for giving them. One was to bring down the fever, another a purgative,[1] the third to overcome an acid

---

1. **purgative** (pʉr′gə·tiv): laxative.

condition. The germs of influenza can only exist in an acid condition, he explained. He seemed to know all about influenza and said there was nothing to worry about if the fever did not go above one hundred and four degrees. This was a light epidemic of flu and there was no danger if you avoided pneumonia.

Back in the room I wrote the boy's temperature down and made a note of the time to give the various capsules.

"Do you want me to read to you?"

"All right. If you want to," said the boy. His face was very white and there were dark areas under his eyes. He lay still in the bed and seemed very detached from what was going on.

I read aloud from Howard Pyle's *Book of Pirates;* but I could see he was not following what I was reading.

"How do you feel, Schatz?" I asked him.

"Just the same, so far," he said.

I sat at the foot of the bed and read to myself while I waited for it to be time to give another capsule. It would have been natural for him to go to sleep, but when I looked up he was looking at the foot of the bed, looking very strangely.

"Why don't you try to go to sleep? I'll wake you up for the medicine."

"I'd rather stay awake."

After a while he said to me, "You don't have to stay in here with me, Papa, if it bothers you."

"It doesn't bother me."

"No, I mean you don't have to stay if it's going to bother you."

I thought perhaps he was a little lightheaded and after giving him the prescribed capsules at eleven o'clock I went out for a while.

It was a bright, cold day, the ground covered with a sleet that had frozen so that it seemed as if all the bare trees, the bushes, the cut brush, and all the grass and the bare ground had been varnished with ice. I took the young Irish setter for a little walk up the road and along a frozen creek, but it was difficult to stand or walk on the glassy surface and the red dog slipped and slithered and I fell twice, hard, once dropping my gun and having it slide away over the ice.

We flushed a covey of quail[2] under a high clay bank with overhanging brush and I killed two as they went out of sight over the top of the bank. Some of the covey lit in trees, but most of them scattered into brush piles and it was necessary to jump on the ice-coated mounds of brush several times before they would flush. Coming out while you were poised unsteadily on the icy, springy brush, they made difficult shooting and I killed two, missed five, and started back

---

2. **flushed a covey** (kuv′ē) **of quail:** frightened a small group of wild birds called quail from their hiding place.

---

---

pleased to have found a covey close to the house and happy there were so many left to find on another day.

At the house they said the boy had refused to let anyone come into the room.

"You can't come in," he said. "You mustn't get what I have."

I went up to him and found him in exactly the position I had left him, white-faced, but with the tops of his cheeks flushed by the fever, staring still, as he had stared, at the foot of the bed.

I took his temperature.

"What is it?"

"Something like a hundred," I said. It was one hundred and two and four tenths.

"It was a hundred and two," he said.

"Who said so?"

"The doctor."

"Your temperature is all right," I said. "It's nothing to worry about."

"I don't worry," he said, "but I can't keep from thinking."

"Don't think," I said. "Just take it easy."

"I'm taking it easy," he said and looked straight ahead. He was evidently holding tight onto himself about something.

"Take this with water."

"Do you think it will do any good?"

"Of course it will."

I sat down and opened the *Pirate* book and commenced to read, but I could see he was not following, so I stopped.

"About what time do you think I'm going to die?" he asked.

"What?"

"About how long will it be before I die?"

"You aren't going to die. What's the matter with you?"

"Oh, yes, I am. I heard him say a hundred and two."

"People don't die with a fever of one hundred and two. That's a silly way to talk."

"I know they do. At school in France the boys told me you can't live with forty-four degrees. I've got a hundred and two."

He had been waiting to die all day, ever since nine o'clock in the morning.

"You poor Schatz," I said. "Poor old Schatz. It's like miles and kilometers. You aren't going to die. That's a different thermometer. On that thermometer thirty-seven is normal. On this kind it's ninety-eight."

"Are you sure?"

"Absolutely," I said. "It's like miles and kilometers. You know, like how many kilometers we make when we do seventy miles in the car?"

"Oh," he said.

But his gaze at the foot of the bed relaxed slowly. The hold over himself relaxed too, finally, and the next day it was very slack and he cried very easily at little things that were of no importance.

---

## WORDS TO OWN

**commenced** (kə·menst′) *v.:* began.
**slack** *adj.:* loose.

---

# MEET THE WRITER

## Grace Under Pressure

**Ernest Hemingway** (1899–1961) was born in Oak Park, Illinois. The son of a doctor, he spent his first seventeen summers in northern Michigan, where his father introduced him to hunting and fishing. In high school, Hemingway boxed and played football, but he also wrote poetry, stories, and the gossip column for his school newspaper.

When the United States entered World War I, Hemingway volunteered and became an American Red Cross ambulance driver in Italy. He was nineteen when a bomb that landed three feet away filled his right leg with 227 pieces of shrapnel.

After returning from the war, Hemingway wrote many stories and novels that are now considered classics. In them he portrays men who show "grace under pressure"—that is, calm courage in the face of great danger or death. In his own life, Hemingway relentlessly pursued excitement and danger. He hunted and fished all over the world, surviving several plane crashes and the fierce charges of the large animals he loved to hunt. His exploits made him as famous as any movie star.

In "A Day's Wait," Hemingway again explores the theme of grace under pressure. This time he focuses on a young boy's first awareness of his own mortality. The silences and sparse dialogue in the story reflect the belief of Hemingway's heroes that they should keep a tight rein on their fears and other emotions. The story also illustrates Hemingway's approach to writing: "I always try to write on the principle of the iceberg. There is seven eighths of it underwater for every part that shows."

Hemingway worked hard to keep up his image of toughness, but his son Gregory ("Gig") remembers a more human side:

66 He told me about the times he'd been scared as a boy, how he used to dream about a furry monster who would grow *taller and taller* every night and then, just as it was about to eat him, would jump over the fence. He said fear was perfectly natural and nothing to be ashamed of. The trick to mastering it was controlling your imagination; but he said he knew how hard that was for a boy.

He said he loved to read the Bible when he was seven or eight because it was so full of battles. 'But I wasn't much good at reading at first, Gig, just like you. It was years before I realized that *Gladly the cross I'd bear* didn't refer to a kindly animal. I could easily imagine a cross-eyed bear and Gladly seemed like such a lovely name for one.'

Mainly he just told me stories—about how he had fished and hunted in the Michigan north woods and about how he wished he could have stayed my age and lived there forever—until I fell asleep. 99

Hemingway won the Nobel Prize in literature in 1954. Today he is regarded as one of the great writers of the twentieth century.

# MAKING MEANINGS

## First Thoughts

1. Finish these sentences:

   - If I were Schatz and thought that I was about to die, I would . . .

   - If I were Papa and saw the way Schatz looked and acted, I would . . .

## Shaping Interpretations

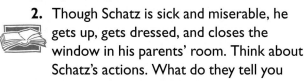

2. Though Schatz is sick and miserable, he gets up, gets dressed, and closes the window in his parents' room. Think about Schatz's actions. What do they tell you about his **character**?

3. What makes us believe that the boy's mother is present? Why do you suppose she does not appear in the story?

4. What do you think of Papa's choice of reading material for his son? (Would it teach a child to be tough and macho?)

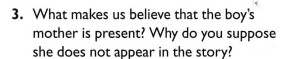

5. During the day the father goes hunting and kills two birds. Think about this activity and other details in the story. What do they tell you about the father's **character**? Do you think the father shows his son that he loves him?

6. Why would so young a boy behave so heroically in the face of death? What do you think of this kind of behavior?

## Connecting with the Text

7. Look back at your notes for the Quickwrite on page 80. What items on your list might help Schatz deal with his fears? If you could talk with Schatz, what else would you share with him?

## Extending the Text

8. Why do you think people like Schatz often hesitate to share their feelings? How could this lack of communication cause misunderstandings?

## Challenging the Text

9. How much did you care about Schatz and Papa as you read? Do you think Hemingway's way of telling a story gets readers involved with the characters? Why or why not?

10. Explain what the **title** means. Do you think it is a good title? If you were to give this story a different title, what would it be?

**Reading Check**

Go back through "A Day's Wait," and then fill in a story map like the one below.

| | |
|---|---|
| Title: | |
| Author: | |
| Characters: | |
| Conflict: | |
| Resolution: | |
| Setting: | |

## Writer's Notebook

### 1. Collecting Ideas for a Story

Papa in "A Day's Wait" represents Hemingway's idea of a hero because he values courage and self-reliance. What qualities do *you* think make someone a hero? Using a word web, describe someone who displays the qualities you admire. Your character could be someone you know or imagine, someone famous, or even someone from a book or a movie.

funny — patient — Mrs. Lopez — helps others — cares for foster children — volunteers at Senior Center

## Creative Writing

### 2. Journal Jottings

Pretend that you are Schatz waiting for his father to return from hunting. Write a journal entry giving your version of the story's events.

Caricature of Ernest Hemingway.

Drawing by David Levine. Reprinted with permission from The New York Review of Books. Copyright ©1964 Nyrev, Inc.

## Analyzing Character

### 3. Sketching Schatz

Write a brief **character sketch** of Schatz. Before you begin, review the story for information on

- Schatz's **actions** (what he does)
- his **words** (what he says)
- **how other people respond** to him

As you gather details, think of words you can use to describe Schatz.

## Math

### 4. By the Numbers

Schatz confuses the numbers on Celsius and Fahrenheit thermometers. Help Schatz out by teaching him about the metric system. (You can find out about the metric system in an encyclopedia or a science textbook.) Imagine that Schatz and Papa take a camping trip. Convert these numbers (and others you invent yourself) into metric measurements:

- Papa carries provisions weighing 34 pounds.
- Schatz's knapsack weighs 7 pounds.
- They travel 13.5 miles.
- The temperature ranges from 55°F to 75°F.

# GRAMMAR LINK

## Irregular Verbs Dare to Be Different

**Language Handbook HELP**

*See Irregular Verbs, pages 727-729.*

**Technology HELP**

*See* Language Workshop CD-ROM. *Key word entry: irregular verbs.*

Many people have trouble with irregular verbs. You don't form the past tense of irregular verbs by adding *-d* or *-ed,* as you do with regular verbs. The only way to be sure you know the various forms of irregular verbs is to memorize them. Don't suffer in silence, as Schatz did—reading this list aloud several times will help you remember these odd verb forms.

| Base Form | Past | Past Participle |
| --- | --- | --- |
| am/is/are | was/were | (has/have) been |
| begin | began | (has/have) begun |
| break | broke | (has/have) broken |
| bring | brought | (has/have) brought |
| do | did | (has/have) done |
| find | found | (has/have) found |
| freeze | froze | (has/have) frozen |
| go | went | (has/have) gone |
| see | saw | (has/have) seen |
| swim | swam | (has/have) swum |
| throw | threw | (has/have) thrown |

**Try It Out**

➤ Act as an editor: Provide the correct irregular verb forms in the paragraph below.

I had went with my Irish setter to the froze creek. There he had broke the ice, and then we begun a game. I throwed a stick, and he swum out after it. I seen him circling, looking for that stick. When he had founded it, he done what he's always did. He bringed it right back and begun to chew it up.

➤ Find out if irregular verbs are a trouble spot for you. As you edit your own work, circle all the verbs in the past or past participle form. If you suspect you've used the wrong form, check a dictionary.

# VOCABULARY   HOW TO OWN A WORD

**WORD BANK**
*detached*
*poised*
*commenced*
*slack*

## Vocabulary for the Workplace: The Job Interview

1. Imagine that you have just conducted two job interviews. Which candidate would you hire: the one who was excitedly <u>poised</u> on the edge of the seat or the one who seemed <u>detached</u>? Why?

2. Describe how you feel about this scenario: You're at an interview that just <u>commenced</u>, and the interviewer's interest seems very <u>slack</u>.

**The giant flesh eater stepped from the forest, snapping his mouth to reveal seven-inch-long slashing teeth.**

# The Last Dinosaur

## Jim Murphy

The sun came up slowly, fingers of light poking into and brightening the tangled forest of pine and poplar and hemlock trees. The drone of insects quieted, and the tiny mammals scampered to hide.

In a clearing a small triceratops herd began their day. The female triceratops blinked several times before moving to get the light out of her eyes. Then she went back to the frond she'd ripped from a cycadeoid.[1]

The frond was tough and spiky, but her sharp-edged beak and rows of teeth chopped the plant into easily swallowed pieces. She was about to tug at another frond when a male triceratops began stamping his feet in alarm.

He had been feeding at the base of a tree when his horns became entangled in a mass of grapevines. He shook his head violently to get free. When that didn't work, he backed away, yanking his head from side to side. Still covered with vines, he halted. His breathing came in short, grunting pants.

Suddenly he lowered his head and charged the tree. He hit it solidly, backed up, and hit it again, and then again. The fourth butt splintered the tree's base, and it leaned over. A few wiggles of his head and the vine slipped off.

He snorted at the vine, challenging it. When it didn't move, he walked around it and left the clearing. He was the largest triceratops and leader of the herd, so the smaller male and the female followed him.

The three wandered through the forest, always staying near the stream that was their source of water. They did not hurry, and often stopped to nibble at figs or tender tree saplings. On the second day they came to a hillside covered with tasty ferns. The spot was cool and quiet, so they stayed the afternoon, browsing.

A sudden noise made the female jerk up her head to look and listen. They had not seen another dinosaur in a very long time, but she was still wary. A hungry tyrannosaur might have picked up their scent and followed, hoping one of them would stray from the herd.

The two males sensed her unease and also looked around. A giant dragonfly circled the

---

1. **cycadeoid** (sī·kad′ē·oid′): extinct plant that existed at the time of the dinosaurs.

triceratopses, then flew away. A bird chattered briefly. Then the forest grew still. Was a tyrannosaur out there, watching, waiting? Nothing moved and the noise did not return, but the herd was nervous. They left the hillside and continued their journey.

The next day, the land sloped downward and the stream widened to become a series of falls, pools, and swirling rapids. The path twisted to follow the water and dipped sharply in places. Despite their great size, the tricer-atopses walked the narrow ledges and leaped boulders with an easy grace.

The female triceratops smelled something. Her sense of sight was very poor, so she turned to face what was causing the strange odor. Wisps of smoke trailed through the trees.

The smoke was from a fire started the night before by heat lightning.[2] The female couldn't

2. **heat lightning:** lightning flashes that appear near the horizon on hot nights.

see the fire or know that it was advancing toward them. But the smoke was growing thicker and more unpleasant, so the three animals trotted away.

All night they moved quickly to stay clear of the smoke. At dawn, the ground leveled, and the smell seemed to disappear. The two males stopped, exhausted, and bent to drink the cool water. The female continued along the path.

Weeks before, the female triceratops had mated with the leader of the herd. She was hunting now for a spot to build her nest.

The leader stamped his feet and snorted for her to stop, but it did no good. The female would not obey until the nest was completed and her eggs laid. This time, the males followed.

A mile downstream, the forest thinned and the stream emptied into a broad marsh. In the past, dome-headed pachycephalosaurs or armored ankylosaurs would be browsing in the cattails and rushes. Now only the bones of a long-dead anatosaur, half buried in mud, were there to greet the herd.

The female walked the edge of the marsh carefully. The ground was either too wet or too rocky for the nest. On the opposite side of the marsh she found a warm, sandy area with low-growing shrubs.

Immediately she began digging, using the toes of her front and rear feet to shovel out the sand. The hole she dug was six feet across and a foot deep.

## A Dino Dictionary

Did you know that the names of the dinosaurs come from Greek and Latin words? Read about these terrifying beasts and look at their pictures. Do they resemble the Greek and Latin words that form their names?

**anatosaur** (ə·nat′ō·sôr′): two-legged, plant-eating dinosaur with a wide jaw resembling the bill of a duck, webbed feet, and a long tail. The name comes from *anas,* the Latin word for "duck."

**ankylosaur** (aŋ′kə·lō·sôr′): four-legged, plant-eating dinosaur with thick, leathery skin covered by bony plates. *Ankylos* is Greek for "crooked."

**pachycephalosaur** (pak′ə·sef′ə·lō·sôr′): two-legged, plant-eating dinosaur with a dome-shaped plate nine inches thick covering its brain. The

name comes from Greek: *pachys* (thick) + *kephalē* (head) + *sauros* (lizard).

**tyrannosaur** (tə·ran′ə·sôr′): fierce two-legged meat eater, about forty feet in length. Its name comes from Greek: *tyrannos* (tyrant, or cruel ruler) + *sauros* (lizard).

**Tyrannosaurus rex** (reks): best-known species of tyrannosaur. In Latin, *rex* means "king."

**triceratops** (trī·ser′ə·täps′): four-legged, plant-eating dinosaur of North America. The triceratops had three horns on its head, grew to about twenty-five feet in length, and weighed up to four or five tons. Its name comes from Greek: *tri-* (three) + *kerat-* (horn) + *ōps* (eye, face).

When the hole was finished, she laid fifteen eggs in it to form a circle. Gently she covered the eggs with sand. The sun would warm the sand and eggs, and eventually baby triceratopses would emerge.

The two males were feeding a little distance from the nest. The smaller male approached the nest.

When the female saw him, she placed herself between him and her eggs and lowered her head as a warning. The curious male kept coming, so the female charged him. Only when he backed away did the female stop her charge.

When the herd had been larger, many females would make nests in the same area. They would then take turns guarding the nests or feeding and sleeping. But the female triceratops was alone now. It would be her job to keep clumsy males and egg-eating creatures away from her eggs. The quick shrewlike[3] mammals were especially annoying at night.

Two days later the smell of smoke returned. It was faint, distant, and yet the three triceratopses grew nervous. The female paced near her nest.

Late in the day, a heavy line of smoke appeared on the other side of the marsh. Flames erupted, reaching into the air.

A flock of birds flew overhead, screeching an alarm. Mammals, made bold by their fear, left their hiding places and ran from the fire. The two males edged away, but the female stayed to guard her eggs.

In the smoke and dark forest shadows, something moved. The shape was big, as big as many of the trees, and had a massive head. Tyrannosaurus rex. The giant flesh eater stepped from the forest, snapping his mouth to reveal seven-inch-long slashing teeth.

Instinctively the two triceratops males rejoined the female and formed a semicircle barrier in front of the nest. The leader lowered his head and stared at his enemy. Neither moved.

**3. shrewlike:** resembling a shrew, a small mammal that looks like a mouse.

Ordinarily, the tyrannosaur would not attack a triceratops, especially near its nest. But a wall of flames and heat had cut off his retreat. Besides, the tyrannosaur had not had a large meal in weeks.

The tyrannosaur darted at the herd, skidded to a sudden halt, then began circling warily, watching for a chance to strike. He hissed and snapped his teeth. At that instant, the largest triceratops charged, his powerful legs driving him directly at the soft belly of his attacker.

With the aid of his long tail and thickly muscled legs, the tyrannosaur leaped aside to avoid the sharp horns. He spun and dove, mouth wide open, and sank his teeth into the back of the triceratops.

Then the smaller triceratops lunged at the giant, but he was an inexperienced fighter. The tyrannosaur's teeth closed on his neck, and with a quick, deadly yank, he tore a chunk of flesh from the triceratops. The smaller triceratops fell, dying.

The other triceratops tried to charge again, but his right leg was dragging and his movements were slow. Again the tyrannosaur moved aside easily. Using his tail as a spring, the tyrannosaur launched himself for the kill. His teeth sank into the triceratops, while his clawed feet struck him in the stomach. The two rolled, kicking and biting each other.

At this moment, the female triceratops abandoned her eggs and rammed the tyrannosaur full in the side. He bellowed painfully, releasing his hold on the male. The female pushed forward with all her strength, pinning the tyrannosaur against a tree and driving her horns in deeper.

She stepped away and watched her enemy, ready to charge if he got up. His legs and tail flailed weakly, his breathing became labored. Then, with a violent shudder, the great killer died.

During the battle, the fire had spread, leaping and dancing from tree to tree until it reached the edge of the sandy area. Flames rolled through the reeds.

The male triceratops struggled to get up, but his legs buckled under him. He crawled a few feet but had to stop. His wounds were too severe. A choking wave of smoke surrounded him.

The female triceratops went back to protect her eggs. To one side a tree crashed to the ground, sending up an explosion of sparks. A bush nearby caught fire. The female charged it, slashing at it blindly with her horns.

The roar of the fire became deafening, and the heat and smoke grew painful. Reluctantly the female moved away from her eggs to find air.

She went only a short distance and turned to go back. The smoke stung her lungs and burned her eyes. She shook her head, but the choking pain would not go away. She backed away some more and lost sight of her nest.

Immediately the tiny mammals pounced on the unguarded nest. Low to the ground the smoke was not so thick. Digging hastily, they uncovered the eggs and devoured them. Then they scurried from the approaching fire.

The female triceratops hurried through the forest. Several times she stopped to look back toward her eggs. A wall of smoke and flames was all she could see. Finally she gave up.

A tongue of flames reached out at her, and she broke into a gallop. She crashed through branches and vines, leaped over fallen logs heedlessly, with the fire just behind her. At last she came to a rock ledge overlooking a wide river.

The water was dark and deep. Branches and tree roots floated near the banks. The female wanted to find another retreat, but she was surrounded by flames. She hesitated a second, then jumped into the water.

Legs churning frantically, she swam across the river and away from the fire. The river's current caught her, pulling her swiftly along.

She struggled to keep her head above water, to breathe, all the while moving her legs. At last her feet touched the river bottom.

Exhausted, her breathing fast, she hauled herself onto solid ground. Across from her, the fire had stopped at the river's edge. She was safe. It was then she noticed the streams of mammals that had also crossed the river to escape the fire.

The light grew dim and the air became chilly. The female's breath gave off thin vapor streams.

The triceratops shook her head and snorted. She hadn't eaten much in days and wanted to find some tender plants. And maybe, somewhere deep in the forest, there was another triceratops herd she could join.

Slowly, as the sun went down, the female pushed through the bushes to begin her search.

## MEET THE WRITER

### Digging Dinosaurs

**Jim Murphy** (1947–    ) says that dinosaurs have always fascinated him.

66 Our knowledge of them suggests that they were amazing survivors, occupying every corner of the world and adapting to changing climates and food sources for millions of years. 99

Murphy feels that studying dinosaurs and finding out how they survived for so long may help humans adapt and survive.

**Good Reads About the Past**

Other books by Murphy that present information in an entertaining way are *The Great Fire* (Scholastic) and *Across America on an Emigrant Train* (Clarion).

# READ ON

## Survival of the Fittest

Young Brian finds himself stranded alone in the Canadian wilderness after a plane crash. With only his wits and a hatchet to rely on for survival, Brian learns some memorable lessons about nature, growing up, and himself in Gary Paulsen's *Hatchet* (Puffin). (This title is available in the HRW Library.)

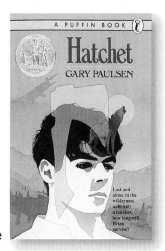

## Working Girl

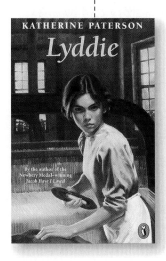

In Katherine Paterson's *Lyddie* (Puffin), set in the 1840s, Lyddie Worthen has to grow up fast when her mother is forced to abandon the family farm. After she finds a job in a textile mill, Lyddie faces a grim new world of poverty and eighteen-hour workdays. A true heroine, Lyddie fights against injustice as she struggles to earn enough to buy back the family farm.

## Hot on the Trail

It is 1882 in the Old West, and fifteen-year-old Artemis is the last surviving male of the Bonner family after his rich uncle is killed by the wicked Catfish Grimes. Artemis sets out on a wild cross-country chase to avenge the murder and recover his uncle's treasure in Walter Dean Myers's *The Righteous Revenge of Artemis Bonner* (HarperCollins).

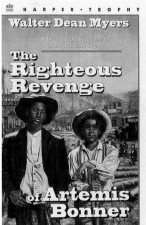

## Other Picks

- Patricia Beatty, *Lupita Mañana* (Beech Tree Books). In order to find work, Lupita Torres enters California illegally. Her search for a better life becomes a struggle in a place where laws are not always fair and growing up is not always easy. (This title is available in the HRW Library.)
- Jack London, *The Call of the Wild* (Macmillan). When Buck is taken from his comfortable home and forced into service as a sled dog, he must draw on his instincts in order to survive. As he adapts to his harsh surroundings, Buck finds himself responding to "the call of the wild." (This title is available in the HRW Library.)

# Writer's Workshop

*See* Writer's Workshop 1
CD-ROM. *Assignment:*
*Story.*

**ASSIGNMENT**

**Write a story on a topic of your choice.**

**AIM**

**To be creative.**

**AUDIENCE**

**Children, teenagers, or adults. (You decide.)**

## NARRATIVE WRITING

## STORY

We all want to know what happened and what's going to happen next. Drivers slow down when they pass an accident, trying to figure out how it happened. When we overhear a story told by one stranger to another, we want to know who did what and why.

### Professional Model

In movies, geniuses have frizzy white hair, right? They wear thick glasses and have names like Dr. Zweistein.

Peter Lu didn't have frizzy white hair. He had straight hair, as black as licorice. He didn't wear thick glasses, either, since his vision was normal.

Peter's family, like ours, had immigrated from China, but they had settled here first. When we moved into a house just two doors down from the Lus, they gave us some good advice on how to get along in America.

I went to the same school as Peter, and we walked to the school bus together every morning. Like many Chinese parents, mine made sure that I worked very hard in school.

In spite of all I could do, my grades were nothing compared to Peter's. He was at the top in all his classes. We walked to the school bus without talking, because I was a little scared of him. Besides, he was always deep in thought.

*The first sentence grabs our attention.*

*A character is introduced and described.*

*The narrator tells us about herself.*

*The narrator describes her feelings.*

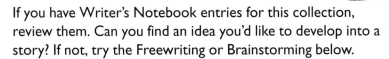

*(continued)*

> Peter didn't have any friends. Most of the kids thought he was a nerd because they saw his head always buried in books. I didn't think he even tried to join the rest of us or cared what the others thought of him.
>
> Then on Halloween he surprised us all.
>
> —from "Lafff" by Lensey Namioka

*The events of the plot begin. The writer hints at a conflict.*

*We start to feel suspense.*

## Prewriting

### 1. Writer's Notebook

**WORK IN PROGRESS**

If you have Writer's Notebook entries for this collection, review them. Can you find an idea you'd like to develop into a story? If not, try the Freewriting or Brainstorming below.

### 2. Freewriting

Stories are likely to come from personal experience. Try to find the kernel of a story in your memory. Prod your memory with a few of these prompts:

- Of all the people you've known, who was the most unusual? the most often in trouble? the most serious?

- What place do you know best? What happens there?

- What interesting experiences have your friends told you about?

- Do you have a dream of an adventure you'd like to have?

### 3. Brainstorming

Try writing down at least ten characters, ten settings, and ten problems on separate slips of paper. For each story element, use a different-colored paper. To start, see the ideas at the right. Then, mix and match the characters, settings, and problems until you come up with an interesting combination for a story.

| Characters |
| --- |
| park ranger |
| veterinarian |
| seventh-grader |
| shy teenager |

| Settings |
| --- |
| Yosemite |
| suburb in summer |
| big city |
| shopping mall |

| Problems |
| --- |
| battles a fire |
| is hit by a car |
| hates dirty streets |
| needs a friend |

**Story Plan**
My main character is

_____, who
   (name)

_____.
  (basic situation)

This character wants

_____, but
    (goal)

_____.
  (main conflict)

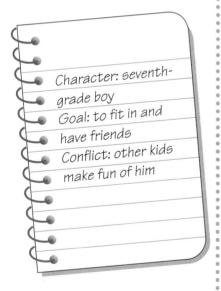

Character: seventh-
grade boy
Goal: to fit in and
have friends
Conflict: other kids
make fun of him

**Language/Grammar Link**
**H E L P**

*Problems with verbs:*
*pages 44, 63, 79, and 87.*

## 4. Creating Interesting Characters

One of the best ways to hold your readers' interest is to create vivid, true-to-life characters. To develop your characters, concentrate on specific physical descriptions, actions, realistic speech, and others' opinions of the characters.

## 5. Plotting Your Story

To come up with the events, or **plot**, of your story, think about the character's problem. What is the **conflict** that arises? What goal does your character have? What events lead to solving the problem? The story-plan framework at the left might serve as a guide, or you may prefer to start writing once you have the initial situation and a few of the characters.

## 6. Where in the World?

Look for opportunities to give your reader a clear picture of the **setting**—where and when the events of the story take place. Don't just describe the setting and then forget about it when you move on to the action. Try to blend the two.

## Drafting
### 1. Getting Started

If you can come up with a good opening now, that's great, but if you can't, don't worry. Just start writing. Pick an event or a character or a place, and begin.

## 2. What Did They Say?

Readers can learn a lot about characters through **dialogue**, or what the characters say. As you write, ask yourself if there's a way to use dialogue to *show* rather than *tell* about a character. For example, if you want to show that a character is kind, try having her speak gently to someone. Let readers hear your character talk so that they can make their own judgments.

## 3. Whose Story Is It?

From whose point of view do you want to tell your story? Do you want to tell it from the **point of view** of one of the characters, who refers to himself or herself as "I"? Do you want to tell it from the point of view of someone outside the story who knows everything about all the characters? Perhaps you want to use a narrator who is outside the story but knows the thoughts

*This is the beginning of a student's short story.*

## from BEING DIFFERENT

The top edge of the sun was visible over the roof of the barn. There was a slight chill in the air like every dusk. I spotted the slumped figure in the wooden swing across the field and walked to it.

"Momma is worried. You didn't go tell her you were home from school," I said, noticing the pile of books at his feet. "She thought something happened to you."

He didn't answer, just shrugged.

"Why didn't you kiss Momma hello?"

"Didn't want to." He looked in the other direction. "I just needed time to think about things alone." He faced me, a tear in his left eye glistened.

"What things?" I asked. I had never seen my brother so upset.

He looked up at the dusk sky and then down at his feet. "About important things."

I didn't mean to pry, I knew he disliked me to do so, but I felt so close to him now, closer than ever before, and I knew I had to pry.

"I don't fit in with the other boys at school."

"Who told you that?"

"It's so obvious, Angie. Don't you notice who always gets the good grades but never the good friends? I'm so different."

—Amy Yustein
Suffern Junior High School
Suffern, New York

*The first paragraph introduces us to the setting and the main characters.*

*The realistic dialogue creates believable characters.*

*The main character's actions clearly show he is sad and upset.*

*We get inside the narrator's mind and know how she feels.*

*This is the main character's problem. His goal is to fit in.*

---

### Strategies for Elaboration

To create believable, interesting characters, start carefully observing the people around you—at a mall or fast-food restaurant, for example. Look at people's appearance—their clothing, hairstyles, and so on. Listen carefully. How do people talk? What does realistic speech sound like? Take notes on what you see and hear. Your notes may help you write your story. Remember that the more you observe in the world around you, the better you'll write.

---

### ■ *Evaluation Criteria*

*A good story*

1. *centers on a major conflict that the characters must resolve*

2. *uses dialogue and actions to develop the characters*

3. *provides a description of the setting*

4. *ends with a resolution of the conflict*

5. *reveals a theme*

**Sentence Workshop**
**H E L P**

*Sentence fragments: page 99.*

---

### Proofreading Tips

- Check your writing for errors in spelling, grammar, and punctuation.
- Make sure you have punctuated dialogue correctly.
- Correct any sentence fragments.

---

**Communications Handbook**
**H E L P**

*See Proofreaders' Marks.*

---

### Publishing Tip

Collect your class stories in a booklet. Provide a table of contents, and assign someone to write a preface explaining your story-writing project. Leave your story anthology in your classroom as an inspiration and resource for other students.

---

and feelings of just one character. (Learn more about point of view on pages 202–203.)

## Evaluating and Revising

### 1. Peer Editing

After writing the first draft, share your work with a partner. Exchange papers, and answer the following questions:

- Did the story hold my interest? If not, why didn't it?
- What did I like best about the characters? What would I change about them?
- What is the best part of the story?

### 2. Self-Evaluation

**Plot**

1. Are the character's problem and its resolution believable? If not, can I add more true-to-life details?

2. Which events need to be elaborated on or eliminated?

**Character**

1. Have I conveyed the main character's personality?

2. What details can I add to make the character more vivid?

**Setting**

Are there other details about time and place I can add to develop the setting?

**Point of View**

1. What point of view did I choose? Why?

2. Are there any places where the point of view seems weak?

**Theme**

1. What is the main idea about life that I wanted to communicate?

2. What details can I add (to the characterization or to the story events, for example) to make my theme clearer?

# Sentence Workshop

## SENTENCE FRAGMENTS

To be a complete sentence, a group of words must (1) have a subject, (2) have a verb, and (3) express a complete thought. A **sentence fragment** is punctuated like a sentence—it begins with a capital letter and ends with a period—but it lacks one or more of the key elements that make up a complete sentence.

FRAGMENT    Wished that he hadn't left his bed. [Who wished? The sentence's subject is missing.]

SENTENCE    Keevan wished that he hadn't left his bed. [Adding the subject *Keevan* makes it a complete sentence.]

FRAGMENT    Then suddenly the tropic dawn. [The sentence's verb is missing.]

SENTENCE    Then suddenly the tropic dawn broke. [Adding the verb *broke* makes this a complete sentence.]

FRAGMENT    When the cobra runs for her life. [Even with a subject and verb, this group of words does not express a complete thought.]

SENTENCE    When the cobra runs for her life, she goes like a whiplash.

## Writer's Workshop Follow-up: Revision

Take out a story you've written, and exchange papers with a classmate. Note any sentence fragments you find and suggest a correction for each. Exchange papers again and revise any fragments that you feel are genuine errors. (You can check with your teacher.) You will want to use some fragments in the dialogue you write, because real people often talk in fragments. In "The Dinner Party," for example, a character remarks, "Because it was crawling across my foot" (page 18). This is a fragment, but it's correct because it's in dialogue.

**Language Handbook
HELP**

*See Sentence or Sentence Fragment?, pages 750–751.*

**Technology
HELP**

*See* Language Workshop CD-ROM. *Key word entry: sentence fragments.*

### Try It Out

Copy the following paragraph onto a separate sheet of paper, and revise it, correcting any sentence fragments. Compare your rewritten versions in class. How many variations are possible?

Robert Frost earned a poor living. As a schoolteacher and editor. Before deciding to try farming. The stony New Hampshire soil on thirty acres. Which his grandfather had bought for him. The great physical effort of working the land too hard to write poetry. After a few years of discouragement. Frost returned to teaching.

# Reading for Life
## Using Text Organizers

### Situation

It's the beginning of another school year. You're in English class, and you've just been handed this literature textbook. Use the following strategies to get to know your new book and to **locate specific information.**

### Strategies

**Use the table of contents.**

- The **table of contents** (TOC) is always near the front of the book. Turn to the TOC to get an idea of what's in the book. You'll find a list of writers and selections (with authors' names at left) and special features in the order in which they appear in the book.

**Look at the headings.**

- A **heading** is a kind of title. Textbook headings are usually printed in a color or size that grabs your attention.

- Glance through the book and look for headings (like *Before You Read* and *Making Meanings*) that jump out at you. A repeated heading always signals the same kind of material.

**CONTENTS**

**Collection One**
**Out Here on My Own**

**Use graphic features.**

- **Graphic features** like charts, tables, and maps organize or present information visually. Graphic features like color, boldface words, and logos (tiny pictures—like computer icons) help you find what you're looking for. For example, you'll find an open-book logo like the one on page 2 near every reading lesson, question, and activity.

### Using the Strategies

Turn to page viii, and use the strategies you've just learned to answer these questions about the TOC.

1. What is the title of Collection One?

2. On what page does the lesson on the short story begin?

3. Make a list of all the special features that are included in Collection One.

4. What headings in this TOC are you curious about?

5. If you needed help in writing, could you find it in this book? If so, where?

### Extending the Strategies

Give a classmate a guided tour of this textbook. Explain how the book is organized.

# Learning for Life
## Making a Presentation

## Problem

As in real life, characters in literature face challenges they sometimes have to deal with alone. Who in our world can be called courageous? What can we learn from courageous people?

## Project

**Analyze the personal qualities that make people courageous. Create a presentation that teaches others about courage.**

## Preparation

1. Either alone or with a group, identify someone you know, or someone currently in the news, who shows courage. Remember that courage is shown not only in a daring rescue attempt but also in more ordinary actions, such as standing up for something you believe in even if your opinion is unpopular.

2. Write down the person's specific actions that show courage.

## Procedure

1. For each of the person's actions, make a list of qualities the person showed—

for example, determination, a desire to help others, and emotional strength.

2. If the person is someone you know, interview him or her. Ask questions like these:

   • What actions do you think require courage?

   • What personal qualities help you act courageously?

   • How can a person develop those qualities?

## Presentation

Present what you have learned in one of the following ways:

## 1. Role-Play

Role-play and deliver a speech to your class. Try to be as much like the courageous person you've researched as possible. Talk about the personal qualities that make someone courageous.

## 2. Public-Service Announcement

Write and audiotape or videotape a public-service announcement about acting courageously. The person you researched will be the spokesperson of the announcement. Make the point that courage can be shown in many ways, some of them bold and some of them quiet.

## 3. Design

Design a symbol for each personal quality that contributes to courage. Label each symbol. Display your symbols in any form you wish. Consider writing a short article and sending your designs to a magazine for possible publication.

## Processing

Complete this sentence: The most important thing I learned about courage is. . . .

# Who Am I?

I am myself,
of all my atom parts I am the sum.
And out of my blood and my brain
I make my own interior weather,
my own sun and rain.

—Eve Merriam

# Before You Read

## HOMESICK

## Make the Connection

### Do You Speak My Language?

If you lived in France or Spain or Korea, people might ask you if you could speak their language:

**Parlez-vous français?** (pàr′lā vōō frän·sā′)

**¿Habla español?** (ä′blä es·pä·nyôl′)

한국말을 할수 있습니까? (hän gōōk mär·əl häl sōō its·ōōm′ nē kä)

Suppose you had to live for a time in another country, far away from the place you call home. What would you miss? How could living far away help you find out who you are and what you like about your own country?

**Round table.** Divide into small groups and brainstorm the pros and cons ("fors and againsts") of living in a different land, in a different culture. (Perhaps you or someone you know is doing exactly that.) List your pros and cons, and then share your findings with the class.

As you read "Homesick," keep a sheet of paper next to the book so that you can record your responses to Jean Fritz's account of living in two cultures. One student's responses appear on the first page.

## Elements of Literature

### Autobiography and Biography: Who's Telling?

An **autobiography** is the story of a person's life, written by that very person. A **biography** is the story of a person's life, told by *another* person. In her autobiography, "Homesick," Jean Fritz tells what it was like to grow up in China.

The first chapter of her account begins on the next page. The year is 1925, and Jean is ten years old. To learn what happened to Jean when she grew up, read her biography and "meet the writer" on page 117.

**I**n an **autobiography** the writer tells the story of his or her own life. In a **biography** the writer tells the story of someone else's life.

*For more on Autobiography and Biography, see pages 121–122 and the Handbook of Literary Terms.*

## Reading Skills and Strategies

### Distinguishing Fact from Opinion: Checking It Out

When you read an autobiography, it's important to be able to tell facts from opinions. A **fact** can be proved true or false. "The Yangtze River is in China" is a fact. An **opinion,** a personal feeling or belief, can't be proved true or false. In autobiographies, like "Homesick," writers share their feelings and opinions, but they also present facts.

Don't be fooled: People may state an opinion as if it were a fact. If you're in doubt, ask yourself: Can this statement be proved, or is it someone's personal feeling or belief?

go.hrw.com
*LEO 7-2*

# *from* Homesick

## Jean Fritz

### *I belonged on the other side of the world. In America . . .*

In my father's study there was a large globe with all the countries of the world running around it. I could put my finger on the exact spot where I was and had been ever since I'd been born. And I was on the wrong side of the globe. I was in China in a city named Hankow, a dot on a crooked line that seemed to break the country right in two. The line was really the Yangtze River, but who would know by looking at a map what the Yangtze River really was?

Orange-brown, muddy mustard colored. And wide, wide, wide. With a river smell that was old and came all the way up from the bottom. Sometimes old women knelt on the riverbank, begging the River God to return a son or grandson who may have drowned. They would wail and beat the earth to make the River God pay attention, but I knew how busy the River God must be. All those people on the Yangtze River! Coolies[1] hauling water. Women washing clothes. Houseboats swarming with old people and young, chickens and pigs. Big crooked-sailed junks[2] with eyes painted on their prows so they could see where they were going. I loved the Yangtze River, but of course, I belonged on the other side of the world. In America, with my grandmother.

1. **coolies:** workers who do heavy work for little pay. English-speakers visiting the East took this name from the Hindi word *qulī*, meaning "hired servant."
2. **junks:** Chinese ships with flat bottoms and square sails.

### Dialogue with the Text

Where does she live? Who's telling the story?

That person must have lived near the river.

That reminds me of a story in our literature book, "The Old Demon."

I think that the people made up the River God as an explanation for people's deaths.

Why did the person telling the story move?

*Katie Sheldon*

— Katie Sheldon
Vista Verde Middle School
Irvine, California

*Twenty-five fluffy little yellow chicks hatched from our eggs today, my grandmother wrote.*

*I wrote my grandmother that I had watched a Chinese magician swallow three yards of fire.*

The trouble with living on the wrong side of the world was that I didn't feel like a *real* American.

For instance. I could never be president of the United States. I didn't want to be president; I wanted to be a writer. Still, why should there be a *law* saying that only a person born in the United States could be president?[3] It was as if I wouldn't be American enough.

Actually, I was American every minute of the day, especially during school hours. I went to a British school and every morning we sang "God Save the King." Of course the British children loved singing about their gracious king. Ian Forbes stuck out his chest and sang as if he were saving the king all by himself. Everyone sang. Even Gina Boss, who was Italian. And Vera Sebastian, who was so Russian she dressed the way Russian girls did long ago before the Revolution,[4] when her family had to run away to keep from being killed.

But I wasn't Vera Sebastian. I asked my mother to write an excuse so I wouldn't have to sing, but she wouldn't do it. "When in Rome," she said, "do as the Romans do." What she meant was, "Don't make trouble. Just sing."

So for a long time I did. I sang with my fingers crossed but still I felt like a traitor.

Then one day I thought: If my mother and father were really and truly in Rome, they wouldn't do what the Romans did at all. They'd probably try to get the Romans to do what *they* did, just as they were trying to teach the Chinese to do what Americans did. (My mother even gave classes in American manners.)

So that day I quit singing. I kept my mouth locked tight against the king of England. Our teacher, Miss Williams, didn't notice at first. She stood in front of the room, using a ruler for a baton, striking each syllable so hard it was as if she were making up for the times she had nothing to strike.

(Miss Williams was pinch-faced and bossy. Sometimes I wondered what had ever made her come to China. "Maybe to try and catch a husband," my mother said.

A husband! Miss Williams!)

"Make him vic-tor-i-ous," the class sang. It was on the strike of "vic" that Miss Williams noticed. Her eyes lighted on my mouth and when we sat down, she pointed her ruler at me.

"Is there something wrong with your voice today, Jean?" she asked.

"No, Miss Williams."

"You weren't singing."

"No, Miss Williams. It is not my national anthem."

"It is the national anthem we sing here," she snapped. "You have always sung. Even Vera sings it."

I looked at Vera with the big blue bow tied on the top of her head. Usually I felt sorry for her but not today. At recess I might even untie that bow, I thought. Just give it a yank. But if I'd

---

**3.** This is not a fact. The U.S. Constitution states only that a presidential candidate must be a "natural-born" U.S. citizen. This term applies to citizens born in the United States and its territories. But no law or court case has yet decided whether "natural-born" also describes children born to U.S. citizens in other countries.
**4. Revolution:** In 1917, a revolution drove the czars (emperors) and other nobility from power, and Russia became the first nation to set up a Communist government.

been smart, I wouldn't have been looking at Vera. I would have been looking at Ian Forbes and I would have known that no matter what Miss Williams said, I wasn't through with the king of England.

Recess at the British School was nothing I looked forward to. Every day we played a game called prisoner's base, which was all running and shouting and shoving and catching. I hated the game, yet everyone played except Vera Sebastian. She sat on the sidelines under her blue bow like someone who had been dropped out of a history book. By recess I had forgotten my plans for that bow. While everyone was getting ready for the game, I was as usual trying to look as if I didn't care if I was the last one picked for a team or not. I was leaning against the high stone wall that ran around the schoolyard. I was looking up at a little white cloud skittering across the sky when all at once someone tramped down hard on my right foot. Ian Forbes. Snarling bulldog face. Heel grinding down on my toes. Head thrust forward the way an animal might before it strikes.

"You wouldn't sing it. So say it," he ordered. "Let me hear you say it."

I tried to pull my foot away but he only ground down harder.

"Say what?" I was telling my face please not to show what my foot felt.

"*God save the king.* Say it. Those four words. I want to hear you say it."

Although Ian Forbes was short, he was solid and tough and built for fighting. What was more, he always won. You had only to look at his bare knees between the top of his socks and his short pants to know that he would win. His knees were square. Bony and unbeatable. So of course it was crazy for me to argue with him.

"Why should I?" I asked. "Americans haven't said that since George the Third."[5]

He grabbed my right arm and twisted it behind my back.

"Say it," he hissed.

I felt the tears come to my eyes and I hated myself for the tears. I hated myself for not staying in Rome the way my mother had told me.

"I'll never say it," I whispered.

They were choosing sides now in the schoolyard and Ian's name was being called—among the first, as always.

He gave my arm another twist. "You'll sing tomorrow," he snarled, "or you'll be bloody sorry."

As he ran off, I slid to the ground, my head between my knees.

*Oh, Grandma, I thought, why can't I be there with you? I'd feed the chickens for you. I'd pump water from the well, the way my father used to do.*

It would be almost two years before we'd go to America. I was ten years old now; I'd be twelve then. But how could I think about *years*? I didn't even dare to think about the next day. After school I ran all the way home, fast so I couldn't think at all.

Our house stood behind a high stone wall, which had chips of broken glass sticking up from the top to keep thieves away. I flung open the iron gate and threw myself through the front door.

"I'm home!" I yelled.

Then I remembered that it was Tuesday, the day my mother taught an English class at the YMCA[6] where my father was the director.

I stood in the hall, trying to catch my breath, and as always I began to feel small. It was a huge hall with ceilings so high it was as if they would have nothing to do with people. Certainly not with a mere child, not with me—the only child in the house. Once I asked my best friend, Andrea, if the hall made her feel little too. She said no. She was going to be a dancer

**5. George the Third** (1738–1820): king of Great Britain at the time of the Revolutionary War (1775–1783), fought by the American colonies to gain independence from Great Britain.

**6. YMCA:** short for "Young Men's Christian Association."

and she loved space. She did a high kick to show how grand it was to have room.

Andrea Hull was a year older than I was and knew about everything sooner. She told me about commas, for instance, long before I took punctuation seriously. How could I write letters without commas? she asked. She made me so ashamed that for months I hung little wagging comma-tails all over the letters to my grandmother. She told me things that sounded so crazy I had to ask my mother if they were true. Like where babies came from. And that someday the whole world would end. My mother would frown when I asked her, but she always agreed that Andrea was right. It made me furious. How could she know such things and not tell me? What was the matter with grown-ups anyway?

I wished that Andrea were with me now, but she lived out in the country and I didn't see her often. Lin Nai-Nai, my amah,[7] was the only one around, and of course I knew she'd be there. It was her job to stay with me when my parents were out. As soon as she heard me come in, she'd called, "Tsai loushang," which meant that she was upstairs. She might be mending or ironing but most likely she'd be sitting by the window embroidering. And she was. She even had my embroidery laid out, for we had made a bargain. She would teach me to embroider if I would teach her English. I liked embroidering: the cloth stretched tight within my embroidery hoop while I filled in the stamped pattern with cross-stitches and lazy daisy flowers. The trouble was that lazy daisies needed French knots for their centers and I hated making French knots. Mine always fell apart, so I left them to the end. Today I had twenty lazy daisies waiting for their knots.

Lin Nai-Nai had already threaded my needle with embroidery floss.

"Black centers," she said, "for the yellow flowers."

7. **amah:** in Asia, a woman who looks after children.

I felt myself glowering. "American flowers don't have centers," I said, and gave her back the needle.

Lin Nai-Nai looked at me, puzzled, but she did not argue. She was different from other amahs. She did not even come from the servant class, although this was a secret we had to keep from the other servants, who would have made her life miserable had they known. She had run away from her husband when he had taken a second wife. She would always have been Wife Number One and the Boss no matter how many wives he had, but she would rather be no wife than head of a string of wives. She was modern. She might look old-fashioned, for her feet had been bound up tight when she was a little girl so that they would stay small, and now, like many Chinese women, she walked around on little stumps stuffed into tiny cloth shoes. Lin Nai-Nai's were embroidered with butterflies. Still, she believed in true love and one wife for one husband. We were good friends, Lin Nai-Nai and I, so I didn't know why I felt so mean.

She shrugged. "English lesson?" she asked, smiling.

I tested my arm to see if it still hurt from the twisting. It did. My foot too. "What do you want to know?" I asked.

We had been through the polite phrases— Please, Thank you, I beg your pardon, Excuse me, You're welcome, Merry Christmas (which she had practiced but hadn't had a chance to use since this was only October).

"If I meet an American on the street," she asked, "how do I greet him?"

I looked her straight in the eye and nodded my head in a greeting. "Sewing machine," I said. "You say, 'Sew-ing ma-chine.'"

---

**WORDS TO OWN**
**glowering** (glou′ər·iŋ) v. used as adj.: staring angrily; scowling.

---

She repeated after me, making the four syllables into four separate words. She got up and walked across the room, bowing and smiling. "Sew Ing Ma Shing."

Part of me wanted to laugh at the thought of Lin Nai-Nai maybe meeting Dr. Carhart, our minister, whose face would surely puff up, the way it always did when he was <u>flustered</u>. But part of me didn't want to laugh at all. I didn't like it when my feelings got tangled, so I ran downstairs and played "Chopsticks" on the piano. Loud and fast. When my sore arm hurt, I just beat on the keys harder.

Then I went out to the kitchen to see if Yang Sze-Fu, the cook, would give me something to eat. I found him reading a Chinese newspaper, his eyes going up and down with the characters. (Chinese words don't march across flat surfaces, the way ours do; they drop down cliffs, one cliff after another from right to left across a page.)

"Can I have a piece of cinnamon toast?" I asked. "And a cup of cocoa?"

Yang Sze-Fu grunted. He was smoking a cigarette, which he wasn't supposed to do in the kitchen, but Yang Sze-Fu mostly did what he wanted. He considered himself superior to common workers. You could tell because of the fingernails on his pinkies. They were at least two inches long, which was his way of showing that he didn't have to use his hands for rough or dirty work. He didn't seem to care that his fingernails were dirty, but maybe he couldn't keep such long nails clean.

He made my toast while his cigarette dangled out of the corner of his mouth, collecting a long ash that finally fell on the floor. He wouldn't have kept smoking if my mother had been there, although he didn't always pay attention to my mother. Never about butter pagodas,[8] for instance. No matter how many times my mother told him before a dinner party, "No butter pagoda," it made no difference. As soon as everyone was seated, the serving boy, Wong Sze-Fu, would bring in a pagoda and set it on

8. **pagodas:** Asian temples with several levels.

## WORDS TO OWN

**flustered** (flus′tərd) *v.* used as *adj.:* confused; upset.

the table. The guests would "oh" and "ah," for it was a masterpiece: a pagoda molded out of butter, curved roofs rising tier upon tier, but my mother could only think how unsanitary it was. For, of course, Yang Sze-Fu had molded the butter with his hands and carved the decorations with one of his long fingernails. Still, we always used the butter, for if my mother sent it back to the kitchen, Yang Sze-Fu would lose face[9] and quit.

When my toast and cocoa were ready, I took them upstairs to my room (the blue room) and while I ate, I began *Sara Crewe*[10] again. Now there was a girl, I thought, who was worth crying over. I wasn't going to think about myself. Or Ian Forbes. Or the next day. I wasn't. I wasn't.

9. **lose face:** lose dignity or self-respect.
10. *Sara Crewe:* famous children's book by Frances Hodgson Burnett about a rich girl who becomes a poor orphan. Burnett also wrote *A Little Princess, Little Lord Fauntleroy,* and *The Secret Garden.*

And I didn't. Not all afternoon. Not all evening. Still, I must have decided what I was going to do because the next morning when I started for school and came to the corner where the man sold hot chestnuts, the corner where I always turned to go to school, I didn't turn. I walked straight ahead. I wasn't going to school that day.

I walked toward the Yangtze River. Past the store that sold paper pellets that opened up into flowers when you dropped them in a glass of water. Then up the block where the beggars sat. I never saw anyone give money to a beggar. You couldn't, my father explained, or you'd be mobbed by beggars. They'd follow you everyplace; they'd never leave you alone. I had learned not to look at them when I passed and yet I saw. The running sores, the twisted legs, the mangled faces. What I couldn't get over was that, like me, each one of those beggars had only one life to live. It just happened that they had drawn rotten ones.

*Oh, Grandma, I thought, we may be far apart but we're lucky, you and I. Do you even know how lucky? In America do you know?*

This part of the city didn't actually belong to the Chinese, even though the beggars sat there, even though upper-class Chinese lived there. A long time ago other countries had just walked into China and divided up part of Hankow (and other cities) into sections, or concessions, which they called their own and used their own rules for governing. We lived in the French concession on Rue de Paris. Then there was the British concession and the Japanese. The Russian and German concessions had been officially returned to China, but the people still called them concessions. The Americans didn't have one, although, like some of the other countries, they had gunboats on the river. In case, my father said. In case what? Just in case. That's all he'd say.

The concessions didn't look like the rest of China. The buildings were solemn and orderly, with little plots of grass around them. Not like those in the Chinese part of the city: a jumble of rickety shops with people, vegetables, crates of quacking ducks, yard goods, bamboo baskets, and mangy[11] dogs spilling onto a street so narrow it was hardly there.

The grandest street in Hankow was the Bund, which ran along beside the Yangtze River. When I came to it after passing the beggars, I looked to my left and saw the American flag flying over the American consulate building. I was proud of the flag and I thought maybe today it was proud of me. It flapped in the breeze as if it were saying ha-ha to the king of England.

Then I looked to the right at the Customs House, which stood at the other end of the Bund. The clock on top of the tower said nine-thirty. How would I spend the day?

I crossed the street to the promenade part of the Bund. When people walked here, they weren't usually going anyplace; they were just out for the air. My mother would wear her broad-brimmed beaver hat when we came, and my father would swing his cane in that jaunty way that showed how glad he was to be a man. I thought I would just sit on a bench for the morning. I would watch the Customs House clock, and when it was time, I would eat the lunch I had brought along in my schoolbag.

I was the only one sitting on a bench. People did not generally "take the air" on a Wednesday morning, and besides, not everyone was allowed here. The British had put a sign on the Bund, NO DOGS, NO CHINESE. This meant that I could never bring Lin Nai-Nai with me. My father couldn't even bring his best friend, Mr. T. K. Hu. Maybe the British wanted a place where they could pretend they weren't in China, I thought. Still, there were always Chinese coolies around. In order to load and unload boats in the river, coolies had to cross the Bund. All day they went back and forth, bent double under their loads, sweating and chanting in a tired, singsong way that seemed to get them from one step to the next.

To pass the time, I decided to recite poetry. The one good thing about Miss Williams was that she made us learn poems by heart and I liked that. There was one particular poem I didn't want to forget. I looked at the Yangtze River and pretended that all the busy people in the boats were my audience.

"'Breathes there the man, with soul so dead,'" I cried, "'Who never to himself hath said, This is my own, my native land!'"

I was so carried away by my performance that I didn't notice the policeman until he was right in front of me. Like all policemen in the British

---

11. **mangy** (mān′jē): diseased. Animals with mange lose their hair and become covered with sores and scabs.

**WORDS TO OWN**
**rickety** (rik′it·ē) *adj.*: weak and shaky.

concession, he was a bushy-bearded Indian with a red turban wrapped around his head.

He pointed to my schoolbag. "Little miss," he said, "why aren't you in school?"

He was tall and mysterious-looking, more like a character in my *Arabian Nights* book than a man you expected to talk to. I fumbled for an answer. "I'm going on an errand," I said finally. "I just sat down for a rest." I picked up my schoolbag and walked quickly away. When I looked around, he was back on his corner, directing traffic.

So now they were chasing children away too, I thought angrily. Well, I'd like to show them. Someday I'd like to walk a dog down the whole length of the Bund. A Great Dane. I'd have him on a leash—like this—(I put out my hand as if I were holding a leash right then) and he'd be so big and strong I'd have to strain to hold him back (I strained). Then of course sometimes he'd have to do his business and I'd stop (like this) right in the middle of the sidewalk and let him go to it. I was so busy with my Great Dane I was at the end of the Bund before I knew it. I let go of the leash, clapped my hands, and told my dog to go home. Then I left the Bund and the concessions and walked into the Chinese world.

My mother and father and I had walked here but not for many months. This part near the river was called the Mud Flats. Sometimes it was muddier than others, and when the river flooded, the flats disappeared underwater. Sometimes even the fishermen's huts were washed away, knocked right off their long-legged stilts and swept down the river. But today the river was fairly low and the mud had dried so that it was cracked and cakey. Most of the men who lived here were out fishing, some not far from the shore, poling their sampans through the shallow water. Only a few people were on the flats: a man cleaning fish on a flat rock at the water's edge, a woman spreading clothes on the dirt to dry, a few small children.

But behind the huts was something I had never seen before. Even before I came close, I guessed what it was. Even then, I was excited by the strangeness of it.

It was the beginnings of a boat. The skeleton of a large junk, its ribs lying bare, its backbone running straight and true down the bottom. The outline of the prow was already in place, turning up wide and snub-nosed, the way all junks did. I had never thought of boats starting from nothing, of taking on bones under their bodies. The eyes, I supposed, would be the last thing added. Then the junk would have life.

The builders were not there, and I was behind the huts where no one could see me as I walked around and around, marveling. Then I climbed inside, and as I did, I knew that something wonderful was happening to me. I was a-tingle, the way a magician must feel when he swallows fire, because suddenly I knew that the boat was mine. No matter who really owned it, it was mine. Even if I never saw it again, it would be my junk sailing up and down the Yangtze River. My junk seeing the river sights with its two eyes, seeing them for me whether I was there or not. Often I had tried to put the Yangtze River into a poem so I could keep it. Sometimes I had tried to draw it, but nothing I did ever came close. But now, *now* I had my junk and somehow that gave me the river too.

I thought I should put my mark on the boat. Perhaps on the side of the spine. Very small. A secret between the boat and me. I opened my schoolbag and took out my folding penknife that I used for sharpening pencils. Very carefully I carved the Chinese character that was our name. Gau. (In China my father was Mr. Gau, my mother was Mrs. Gau, and I was Little Miss Gau.) The builders would paint right over the character, I thought, and never notice. But I would know. Always and forever I would know.

For a long time I dreamed about the boat,

imagining it finished, its sails up, its eyes wide. Someday it might sail all the way down the Yangtze to Shanghai, so I told the boat what it would see along the way because I had been there and the boat hadn't. After a while I got hungry and I ate my egg sandwich. I was in the midst of peeling an orange when all at once I had company.

A small boy, not more than four years old, wandered around to the back of the huts, saw me, and stopped still. He was wearing a ragged blue cotton jacket with a red cloth pincushion-like charm around his neck which was supposed to keep him from getting smallpox. Sticking up straight from the middle of his head was a small pigtail, which I knew was to fool the gods and make them think he was a girl. (Gods didn't bother much with girls; it was boys that were important in China.) The weather was still warm so he wore no pants, nothing below the waist. Most small boys went around like this so that when they had to go, they could just let loose and go. He walked slowly up to the boat, stared at me, and then nodded as if he'd already guessed what I was. "Foreign devil," he announced gravely.

I shook my head. "No," I said in Chinese. "American friend." Through the ribs of the boat, I handed him a segment of orange. He ate it slowly, his eyes on the rest of the orange. Segment by segment, I gave it all to him. Then he wiped his hands down the front of his jacket.

"Foreign devil," he repeated.

"American friend," I corrected. Then I asked him about the boat. Who was building it? Where were the builders?

He pointed with his chin upriver. "Not here today. Back tomorrow."

I knew it would only be a question of time before the boy would run off to alert the people in the huts. "Foreign devil, foreign devil," he would cry. So I put my hand on the prow of the boat, wished it luck, and climbing out, I started back toward the Bund. To my surprise the boy walked beside me. When we came to the edge of the Bund, I squatted down so we would be on the same eye level.

"Goodbye," I said. "May the River God protect you."

For a moment the boy stared. When he spoke, it was as if he were trying out a new sound. "American friend," he said slowly.

When I looked back, he was still there, looking soberly toward the foreign world to which I had gone.

The time, according to the Customs House clock, was five after two, which meant that I couldn't go home for two hours. School was dismissed at three-thirty and I was home by three-forty-five unless I had to stay in for talking in class. It took me about fifteen minutes to write "I will not talk in class" fifty times, and so I often came home at four o'clock. (I wrote up and down like the Chinese: fifty "I's," fifty "wills," and right through the sentence so I never had to think what I was writing. It wasn't as if I were making a promise.) Today I planned to arrive home at four, my "staying-in" time, in the hope that I wouldn't meet classmates on the way.

Meanwhile I wandered up and down the streets, in and out of stores. I weighed myself on the big scale in the Hankow Dispensary[12] and found that I was as skinny as ever. I went to the Terminus Hotel and tried out the chairs in the lounge. At first I didn't mind wandering about like this. Half of my mind was still on the river with my

12. **dispensary:** place where medicine and first aid are provided.

junk, but as time went on, my junk began slipping away until I was alone with nothing but questions. Would my mother find out about today? How could I skip school tomorrow? And the next day and the next? Could I get sick? Was there a kind of long lie-abed sickness that didn't hurt?

I arrived home at four, just as I had planned, opened the door, and called out, "I'm home!" Cheery-like and normal. But I was scarcely in the house before Lin Nai-Nai ran to me from one side of the hall and my mother from the other.

"Are you all right? Are you all right?" Lin Nai-Nai felt my arms as if she expected them to be broken. My mother's face was white. "What happened?" she asked.

Then I looked through the open door into the living room and saw Miss Williams sitting there. She had beaten me home and asked about my absence, which of course had scared everyone. But now my mother could see that I was in one piece and for some reason this seemed to make her mad. She took me by the hand and led me into the living room. "Miss Williams said you weren't in school," she said. "Why was that?"

I hung my head, just the way cowards do in books.

My mother dropped my hand. "Jean will be in school tomorrow," she said firmly. She walked Miss Williams to the door. "Thank you for stopping by."

Miss Williams looked satisfied in her mean, pinched way. "Well," she said, "ta-ta." (She always said "ta-ta" instead of "goodbye." Chicken language, it sounded like.)

As soon as Miss Williams was gone and my mother was sitting down again, I burst into tears. Kneeling on the floor, I buried my head in her lap and poured out the whole miserable story. My mother could see that I really wasn't in one piece after all, so she listened quietly, stroking my hair as I talked, but gradually I

could feel her stiffen. I knew she was remembering that she was a Mother.

"You better go up to your room," she said, "and think things over. We'll talk about it after supper."

I flung myself on my bed. What was there to think? Either I went to school and got beaten up. Or I quit.

After supper I explained to my mother and father how simple it was. I could stay at home and my mother could teach me, the way Andrea's mother taught her. Maybe I could even go to Andrea's house and study with her.

My mother shook her head. Yes, it was simple, she agreed. I could go back to the British School, be sensible, and start singing about the king again.

I clutched the edge of the table. Couldn't she understand? I couldn't turn back now. It was too late.

So far my father had not said a word. He was leaning back, teetering on the two hind legs of his chair, the way he always did after a meal, the way that drove my mother crazy. But he was not the kind of person to keep all four legs of a chair on the floor just because someone wanted him to. He wasn't a turning-back person so I hoped maybe he would understand. As I watched him, I saw a twinkle start in his eyes and suddenly he brought his chair down slambang flat on the floor. He got up and motioned for us to follow him into the living room. He sat down at the piano and began to pick out the tune for "God Save the King."

A big help, I thought. Was he going to make me practice?

Then he began to sing:

"My country 'tis of thee,
Sweet land of liberty . . ."

Of course! It was the same tune. Why hadn't I thought of that? Who would know what I was singing as long as I moved my lips? I joined in now, loud and strong.

"Of thee I sing."

My mother laughed in spite of herself. "If you sing that loud," she said, "you'll start a revolution."

"Tomorrow I'll sing softly," I promised. "No one will know." But for now I really let freedom ring.

Then all at once I wanted to see Lin Nai-Nai. I ran out back, through the courtyard that separated the house from the servants' quarters, and upstairs to her room.

"It's me," I called through the door and when she opened up, I threw my arms around her. "Oh, Lin Nai-Nai, I love you," I said. "You haven't said it yet, have you?"

"Said what?"

"Sewing machine. You haven't said it?"

"No," she said, "not yet. I'm still practicing."

"Don't say it, Lin Nai-Nai. Say 'Good day.' It's shorter and easier. Besides, it's more polite."

"Good day?" she repeated.

"Yes, that's right. Good day." I hugged her and ran back to the house.

The next day at school when we rose to sing the British national anthem, everyone stared at me, but as soon as I opened my mouth, the class lost interest. All but Ian Forbes. His eyes never left my face, but I sang softly, carefully, proudly. At recess he <u>sauntered</u> over to where I stood against the wall.

He spat on the ground. "You can be bloody glad you sang today," he said. Then he strutted off as if he and those square knees of his had won again.

And, of course, I was bloody glad.

---

**WORDS TO OWN**
saundered (sôn′tərd) v.: strolled.

---

# MEET THE WRITER

## "I Wander About in History . . ."

**Jean Fritz** (1915–    ) spent the first thirteen years of her life in Hankow, China, a memorable childhood she recalls in *Homesick: My Own Story*, a 1983 Newbery Honor Book and an American Book Award winner.

© Jill Krementz.

66 Until I was eleven years old I attended an English school. I felt very American and often thought I had to speak up for my country. At recess, for instance. The English children would sometimes tease me by making fun of America. I never let that pass even if it meant a fight. 99

After moving to the United States and graduating from college, Jean Fritz became a librarian. "When I ran the children's department of our local library," she recalls, "I found that I not only wanted to read children's stories, I wanted to write them too."

One of Fritz's first books was *The Cabin Faced West* (1958). This account of a lonely girl in frontier Pennsylvania is based on the experiences of her own grandmother's grandmother. While working on this historical novel, Fritz discovered the joy of research— reading old newspapers, letters, church records, and county histories filled with colorful bits and pieces of the past.

66 Digging into American history also seemed to satisfy a need that I had . . . of finding my roots, of trying to come to terms with just what it has meant historically to be an American. 99

Today Jean Fritz is best known for her fascinating and funny biographies of great historical figures:

66 I have never felt that one lifetime is long enough to meet all the people you would like to meet and to have all the experiences you would like to have. So I wander about in history, getting to know the people I find there. 99

### Biographies by Jean Fritz

Jean Fritz's "wanderings" have led her to write more than a dozen biographies for young adults, including *Why Don't You Get a Horse, Sam Adams?; Can't You Make Them Behave, King George?;* and *Where Do You Think You're Going, Christopher Columbus?* (all published by Putnam).

# MAKING MEANINGS

## First Thoughts

1. What would you do if you were in Jean's shoes at the British school?

## Shaping Interpretations

2. How do Jean's parents react to her decision to stop singing the British national anthem?

3. Why does Jean feel it is so important to carve her name on the framework of the junk?

4. Suppose Jean Fritz had described her experiences in an encyclopedia article on Americans living in China, rather than in an **autobiography.** How would the story be different? Which kind of writing do you like better?

5. In "Homesick," Jean Fritz reveals some opinions about her life in China. Like other writers of autobiography, however, she also presents facts. Give one example of a **fact** and one example of an **opinion** in "Homesick."

6. Why do you think Jean goes back to Lin Nai-Nai to tell her the right words to use in greeting an American?

7. What is Jean "bloody glad" about in the end?

### Reading Check

a. Why doesn't Jean wish to sing the British national anthem?

b. What **conflicts** arise from her decision? (You should be able to name three people who try to make her sing.)

c. What trick does Jean play on Lin Nai-Nai?

d. What does Jean see and do while playing hooky in the Chinese section of town?

e. How does her father help her solve her problem?

## Connecting with the Text

8. You've probably gotten angry at least once at someone who didn't deserve it, as Jean does with Lin Nai-Nai. What other feelings expressed by Jean remind you of feelings you've had?

9. Think back to your round-table discussion about the pros and cons of living in a different land. How do your feelings about living in another culture compare with Jean's? Did her story change any of your opinions?

## Extending the Text

10. Today the culture of the United States and its ideas about democracy travel throughout the world. Do you think the Americanization of countries like China through movies, music, malls, and fast-food restaurants is a good thing or a bad thing? Defend your position in a class or group discussion.

# Choices: Building Your Portfolio

## Writer's Notebook

### 1. Collecting Ideas for an Autobiographical Incident

In "Homesick," Jean Fritz looks back more than fifty years to the incident in which the little Chinese boy calls her a "foreign devil" and then an "American friend." Look back at something surprising or unusual that happened to you. Maybe it's something that made you happy or very sad. Try to remember exactly what happened—recall details about the people, time, and place. What events led up to the experience? How did you feel at the time, and how do you feel about the experience now? You might focus on answering the questions shown in the notebook at the right.

**What** happened? Traveled alone on a bus to N. Carolina, got lost

**Who** was involved?

**Where** did it happen?

**When?**

**Why?**

**How** did I feel at the time?

**How** do I feel about it now?

## Research/Expository Writing

### 2. China Back Then

When you got to page 111 in "Homesick," you might have asked, "What's this about American gunboats on the Yangtze?" In your library, find out about China—especially Hankow—in the 1920s. Why did countries have "concessions" there? Write a short report and present it to the class.

## Art

### 3. Made in America

How would you convey to someone living in another country what the United States means to you? What image would you choose to show how living in this country affects who you are? Draw a picture or make a collage of the image you select. Give your work a title. (You also might consider sending your personal image to a pen pal in another country.)

## Dramatic Reading

### 4. From Page to Stage

Working in a small group, select a passage from "Homesick" to present in a dramatic reading. Find a passage that includes dialogue and takes about five minutes to read aloud. (Ask your teacher to approve your selection.) In your group, assign one person to read the narrator's (Jean Fritz's) commentary. Assign others to read the dialogue. (The narrator will have to read all the dialogue "tags"—phrases like "she asked," "he hissed," and so on.) Read with all the emotions you think the people in the narrative are feeling. When you present your reading, stand in a line in front of your class, with the narrator at the center.

# LANGUAGE LINK  | MINI-LESSON |

**Handbook of Literary Terms**
**HELP**

*See Connotation and Denotation.*

## Style: Shades of Meaning—Denotations and Connotations

The literal "dictionary definition" of a word is called its **denotation.** All the feelings and associations we attach to certain words are called their **connotations.**

Jean Fritz carefully chose words with particular connotations to describe her tormentor, Ian Forbes. She wanted to make sure you, the reader, knew exactly what she thought of him.

| She could have written: | She wrote instead: |
| --- | --- |
| He walked. | He sauntered. |
| He was strong. | He was tough. |
| He whispered. | He hissed. |

It's easy to see the difference. You don't really mind if someone *whispers* to you. On the other hand, you wouldn't want to spend much time with someone who *hisses* at you like a snake.

### Try It Out

In the following sentences, identify words that have negative or positive connotations. Then, change the meaning of each sentence by choosing words that suggest different feelings. Follow the directions in parentheses.

1. "Twenty-five fluffy little yellow chicks hatched from our eggs today, my grandmother wrote." (Rewrite the sentence to make the chicks seem ugly.)

2. "Miss Williams was pinch-faced and bossy." (Make Miss Williams seem attractive.)

3. "Then he strutted off as if he and those square knees of his had won again." (Make the bully seem like a hero.)

4. "The buildings were solemn and orderly, with little plots of grass around them." (Paint a negative picture of the buildings.)

# VOCABULARY  | HOW TO OWN A WORD |

**WORD BANK**
*glowering*
*flustered*
*rickety*
*sauntered*

## Body Language

A good way to own a word is to interpret it with your body and face. Try these exercises for the words in the Word Bank.

1. How are you at glowering? Give a partner a glowering look.
2. How do you look and what do you do when you are flustered?
3. Now get your body into the act. Pretend you are on a rickety ladder. Be careful!
4. Saunter to the door. Your walk should suggest you've got time and are in a good mood. Ask your partner to tell you what you looked like as you sauntered.

# Elements of Literature

## NONFICTION: Encountering Our Lives *by* Naomi Shihab Nye

### Experiment with Nonfiction

Try an experiment with non-fiction. Think of an event that happened in your family. Invite someone in your family—sister, grandmother, father—to tell the story as he or she remembers it, including as many details as possible.

Then, ask another family member, one who wasn't present at this telling, to share his or her own version of the very same events. Compare both versions with your own. Is the story the same or has it changed? Almost always, people remember the same event differently. One person may describe how delicious the split-open watermelons looked at a family picnic. Another might not remember those watermelons at all but might remember the joke someone told or how blisteringly hot the sun felt. Very quickly you will see how much "fictionalizing" enters the telling and writing of nonfiction.

Conduct another experiment: Take your journals and go on a silent "observation walk" with some of your classmates around the edge of your schoolyard. Each of you should write down at least ten sensory details you experience on your walk. Afterward compare your details. Someone may have described the pattern of links in the chain fence. Someone else may have noted the scent of honeysuckle in the air or the woman waiting at a bus stop down the block. What can you tell about yourselves simply from what you notice?

### Nonfiction Happens to Everybody

Readers sometimes think that since fiction is basically "invented," its opposite, nonfiction, must be basically "true." It would be more accurate to say that fiction writers *claim* to make things up, while nonfiction writers *claim* to base their work on real happenings. In fact, many of the same elements—plots, characters, conflicts, settings, points of view, and themes—may be used in both fiction and nonfiction. Both fiction and nonfiction often contain elements we associate with poetry as well—rhythm, sensory images, and figures of speech. Some people try to separate literature into distinctly different compartments, but it's really a big family whose members all secretly get along.

Nonfiction happens all the time to everybody. It can include what we ate for breakfast, whom we saw in the street and what they said—as well as everything we may be dreaming or remembering.

The world of nonfiction is wide-ranging. It includes **personal histories** (also called **autobiographies** and **memoirs**), **biographies** (accounts of other people's lives), **personal essays,** and **reports** or **feature stories,** such as we read in newspapers.

*(continued on next page)*

*(continued from previous page)*

## Subjective and Objective Writing: The Snapshot and the Big Picture

Some nonfiction is richly, frankly **subjective,** which means that its purpose is to express the writer's opinions, feelings, and point of view. That is, it is personal. For example, Elroy Bode, a writer in Texas, has written eloquent short essays on such ordinary topics as selecting a pair of pants at a discount store or returning to his old neighborhood to stare at his childhood home. By speaking directly and intimately, personal essays like Bode's pull us in. They earn our trust and remind us of ourselves.

Other nonfiction pieces maintain a more **objective** tone. This means the writers try to be unbiased, to present the "big picture" rather than a private snapshot. The purpose of such writers is often to inform. A news-paper story that reports on an earthquake, for example, will usually not tell us how the reporter feels about earthquakes. A personal essay on earthquakes, on the other hand, might well focus entirely on the writer's feelings and sensations and not even mention the Richter scale.

## The Appeal of Nonfiction: Telling It Your Way

Many novelists, poets, and short-story writers find themselves writing nonfiction today. Perhaps writing nonfiction satisfies a deep, important urge—when we write personal nonfiction, we can sit back, take our shoes off, and tell the story. We can tell it straight, we can tell it twisted and mysterious, we can tell it any way we like. People write essays about everything from eating to traveling to growing older. When you write nonfiction, no subject is too large—or too small.

Jean Fritz, whose vivid story about growing up in China is included in this collection, has talked about the reasons she writes **biographies,** or stories about other people's lives. "We all seek insight into the human condition," she says, "and it is helpful to find familiar threads running through the lives of others. . . . We need to know more people in all circumstances and times so we can pursue our private, never-to-be-fulfilled quest to find out what life is all about."

CALVIN AND HOBBES © Watterson. Dist. by UNIVERSAL PRESS SYNDICATE.

## COMPARING AND CONTRASTING

### Finding Similarities and Differences

There you are at your favorite mall, but something weird is going on. In the store that sells jeans, all the jeans look exactly alike. All the shoes in the shoe store look like clones. Even the music store is selling just one CD, and you can't stand that group. Is this a nightmare, or are you about to be bored out of your mind?

### Variety's the Spice

Shopping's no fun when there are no decisions to make, nothing to compare and contrast. When you **compare,** you look at two or more things to see how they are similar. When you **contrast,** you look for differences. You may not realize it, but you do a lot of comparing and contrasting every day. When you decide what you'll eat for lunch, you may compare and contrast different foods. Even when you think about whether to do your homework right after school or later, you're comparing and contrasting the advantages of one choice with those of the other.

Comparing and contrasting are important skills at school, too. In English class, for instance, your teacher may ask you to look for similarities and differences between two characters or two poems.

To find similarities and differences between poems, look at elements like these:

- figures of speech
- sound effects
- subjects
- themes

To compare and contrast stories, you might look at these elements:

- characters
- plots
- settings
- themes
- conflicts

Here are some words that writers use in comparing and contrasting:

| Comparing | Contrasting |
|---|---|
| both, similar, like, as, too, also | in contrast, different, although, but, yet |

### The Venn Diagram

A Venn diagram like the one below can help you sort out and analyze the similarities and differences between two texts. In each circle, you note differences. In the center, where the circles overlap, you note similarities. This diagram shows how you might begin comparing and contrasting "Homesick" and "Barrio Boy."

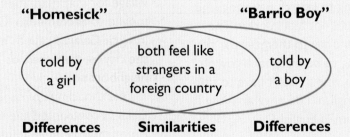

**"Homesick"**                    **"Barrio Boy"**

told by a girl | both feel like strangers in a foreign country | told by a boy

**Differences**          **Similarities**          **Differences**

**Apply the strategy on the next page.**

# *Before You Read*

## BARRIO BOY

## Make the Connection

### "I Wasn't Able to Be Myself"

Here is a brief true story that connects to the autobiography you're about to read: Guadalupe Solis immigrated to the United States from Monterrey, Mexico. When she arrived, one of her first big jobs was to learn English. She remembers that "when I moved here . . . I wasn't able to be myself because I couldn't speak. People couldn't know me because I couldn't communicate."

Guadalupe learned English by writing down the words she heard and then looking them up in the dictionary. She also found patient people who helped her with her new language: "Sometimes I would go to the store to practice my English—the store clerks had to be patient with me because they were trying to sell me something. . . . People who are trying to learn a new language should not feel inferior. They should say to themselves, 'I'm going to be bilingual.' Now, even when I don't have to talk in English, I do anyway. Now I dream in English."

go.hrw.com
*LEO 7-2*

## Quickwrite

Describe what you would do if you lived in a place where you did not speak the language. If you are in this situation now, describe what you are doing to learn the language.

## Reading Skills and Strategies

### Comparing and Contrasting: Alike or Unlike?

When you **compare,** you look for ways that things are alike. When you **contrast,** you look for ways that things are different. Jean Fritz and Ernesto Galarza grew up in different countries, half a world apart. Yet, in some ways, their stories are similar. As you read "Barrio Boy," think about the similarities and the differences between the two autobiographies. To find similarities and differences between texts, focus on these elements:

- subject
- theme, or main idea
- setting
- plot

## Background

### Literature and Social Studies

Ernesto Galarza was born in 1905 in Jalcocotán, a village in western Mexico with a main street that he says "was just wide enough to park six automobiles hub to hub."

In 1910, when the Mexican Revolution threatened their peaceful mountain home, Ernesto, his mother, and two uncles left their village for Mazatlán, Mexico. Eventually they moved to Sacramento, California, and lived in what Galarza called "a rented corner of the city"—the *barrio,* or Spanish-speaking neighborhood.

Like thousands of other immigrants, Galarza confronted the values and customs of American city life—adjusting gradually, and often with difficulty, to his adopted country.

# from
# Barrio Boy

**Ernesto Galarza**

*At Lincoln, making us into Americans did not mean scrubbing away what made us originally foreign.*

The two of us [the narrator, Ernesto, and his mother] walked south on Fifth Street one morning to the corner of Q Street and turned right. Half of the block was occupied by the Lincoln School. It was a three-story wooden building, with two wings that gave it the shape of a double T connected by a central hall. It was a new building, painted yellow, with a shingled roof that was not like the red tile of the school in Mazatlán. I noticed other differences, none of them very reassuring.

We walked up the wide staircase hand in hand and through the door, which closed by itself. A mechanical contraption screwed to the top shut it behind us quietly.

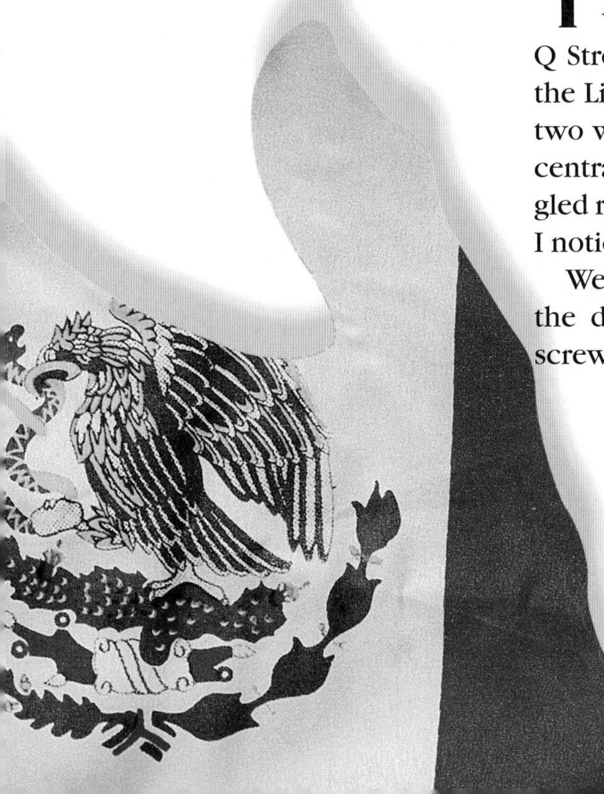

---

### WORDS TO OWN

**reassuring** (rē′ə·shoor′iŋ) v. used as *adj.*: comforting; giving hope or confidence; from the Latin word *securus,* meaning "secure." Look for the related word *assured* on page 126.
**contraption** (kən·trap′shən) *n.*: strange machine or gadget.

---

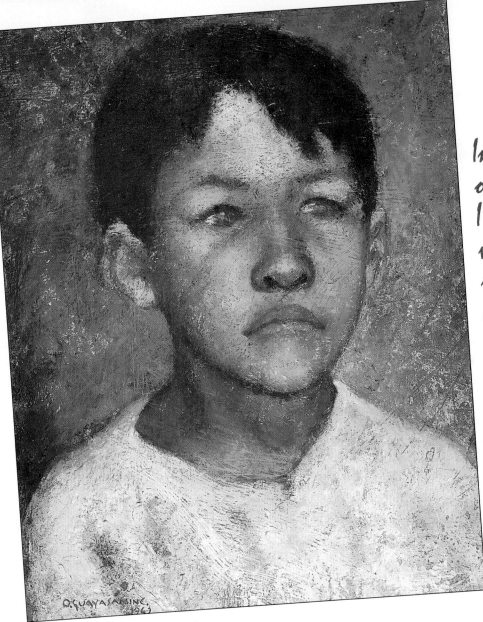

*In a matter of seconds I had to decide whether she was a possible friend or a menace.*

*My Brother* (1942) by Oswaldo Guayasamín (Oswaldo Guayasamín Calero). Oil on wood (15⅞" × 12¾"; 40.3 cm × 32.4 cm)

The Museum of Modern Art, New York. Inter-American Fund. Photograph ©2000 The Museum of Modern Art, New York.

Up to this point the adventure of enrolling me in the school had been carefully rehearsed. Mrs. Dodson had told us how to find it and we had circled it several times on our walks. Friends in the barrio explained that the director was called a principal, and that it was a lady and not a man. They <u>assured</u> us that there was always a person at the school who could speak Spanish.

Exactly as we had been told, there was a sign on the door in both Spanish and English: "Principal." We crossed the hall and entered the office of Miss Nettie Hopley.

Miss Hopley was at a roll-top desk to one side, sitting in a swivel chair that moved on wheels. There was a sofa against the opposite

### WORDS TO OWN
**assured** (ə·shoord′) *v.:* guaranteed; promised confidently.

wall, flanked by two windows and a door that opened on a small balcony. Chairs were set around a table, and framed pictures hung on the walls of a man with long white hair and another with a sad face and a black beard.

The principal half turned in the swivel chair to look at us over the pinch glasses crossed on the ridge of her nose. To do this, she had to duck her head slightly, as if she were about to step through a low doorway.

What Miss Hopley said to us we did not know, but we saw in her eyes a warm welcome, and when she took off her glasses and straightened up, she smiled wholeheartedly, like Mrs. Dodson. We were, of course, saying nothing, only catching the friendliness of her voice and the sparkle in her eyes while she said words we did not understand. She signaled us to the table. Almost tiptoeing across the office, I maneuvered myself to keep my mother between me and the gringo[1] lady. In a matter of seconds I had to decide whether she was a possible friend or a menace. We sat down.

Then Miss Hopley did a <u>formidable</u> thing. She stood up. Had she been standing when we entered, she would have seemed tall. But rising from her chair, she soared. And what she carried up and up with her was a buxom superstructure, firm shoulders, a straight sharp nose, full cheeks slightly molded by a curved line along the nostrils, thin lips that moved like steel springs, and a high forehead topped by hair gathered in a bun. Miss Hopley was not a giant in body, but when she mobilized it to a standing position she seemed a match for giants. I decided I liked her.

She strode to a door in the far corner of the office, opened it, and called a name. A boy of about ten years appeared in the doorway. He sat down at one end of the table. He was brown like us, a plump kid with shiny black hair combed straight back, neat, cool, and faintly obnoxious.

Miss Hopley joined us with a large book and some papers in her hand. She, too, sat down and the questions and answers began by way of our interpreter. My name was Ernesto. My mother's name was Henriqueta. My birth certificate was in San Blas. Here was my last report card from the Escuela Municipal Numero 3 para Varones[2] of Mazatlán, and so forth. Miss Hopley put things down in the book and my mother signed a card.

As long as the questions continued, Doña Henriqueta could stay and I was secure. Now that they were over, Miss Hopley saw her to the door, dismissed our interpreter, and without further ado took me by the hand and strode down the hall to Miss Ryan's first grade.

Miss Ryan took me to a seat at the front of the room, into which I shrank—the better to survey her. She was, to skinny, somewhat runty me, of a withering height when she patrolled the class. And when I least expected it, there she was, crouching by my desk, her blond, radiant face level with mine, her voice patiently maneuvering me over the awful idiocies of the English language.

During the next few weeks Miss Ryan overcame my fears of tall, energetic teachers as she bent over my desk to help me with a word in the pre-primer. Step by step, she loosened me and my classmates from the safe anchorage of the desks for recitations at the blackboard and consultations at her desk. Frequently she burst into happy announcements to the whole class. "Ito can read a sentence," and small Japanese Ito, squint-eyed and shy, slowly read aloud while the class listened in wonder: "Come,

2. **Escuela Municipal Numero 3 para Varones:** Spanish for "Municipal School Number 3 for Boys."

---

**WORDS TO OWN**

**formidable** (fôr′mə·də·bəl) *adj.*: awe-inspiring; impressive.

---

1. **gringo** (griŋ′gō): in Latin America, insulting term for "foreigner"; from the Spanish *griego,* meaning "Greek."

Skipper, come. Come and run." The Korean, Portuguese, Italian, and Polish first-graders had similar moments of glory, no less shining than mine the day I conquered "butterfly," which I had been persistently pronouncing in standard Spanish as boo-ter-flee. "Children," Miss Ryan called for attention. "Ernesto has learned how to pronounce *butterfly*!" And I proved it with a perfect imitation of Miss Ryan. From that celebrated success, I was soon able to match Ito's progress as a sentence reader with "Come, butterfly, come fly with me."

Like Ito and several other first-graders who did not know English, I received private lessons from Miss Ryan in the closet, a narrow hall off the classroom with a door at each end. Next to one of these doors Miss Ryan placed a large

*It was as if in that closet we were both discovering together the secrets of the English language . . .*

chair for herself and a small one for me. Keeping an eye on the class through the open door, she read with me about sheep in the meadow and a frightened chicken going to see the king, coaching me out of my phonetic ruts in words like *pasture, bow-wow-wow, hay,* and *pretty,* which to my Mexican ear and eye had so many unnecessary sounds and letters. She made me watch her lips and then close my eyes as she repeated words I found hard to read. When we came to know each other better, I tried interrupting to tell Miss Ryan how we said it in Spanish. It didn't work. She only said "oh" and went on with *pasture, bow-wow-wow,* and *pretty.* It was as if in that closet we were both discovering together the secrets of the English language and grieving together over the tragedies of Bo-Peep. The main reason I was graduated with honors from the first grade was that I had fallen

## MEET THE WRITER

### "Anecdotes I Told My Family . . ."

For young **Ernesto Galarza** (1905–1984), coming to the United States meant abandoning everything he had ever known and confronting an alien landscape. He couldn't understand the language; the customs and values were strange. Like millions of other immigrants, he felt lost. He soon discovered that education was the key to making sense of his new life. Eventually he earned his Ph.D. from Columbia University in New York and then returned to California to teach. Although he was a beloved teacher, Galarza is best remembered for *Barrio Boy,* his best-selling 1971 account of his journey from Mexico to the United States. Galarza explains how he came to write *Barrio Boy*:

66 *Barrio Boy* began as anecdotes I told my family about Jalcocotán, the mountain village in western Mexico where I was born. Among this limited public (my wife, Mae, and daughters, Karla and Eli Lu) my thumbnail sketches became best-sellers. Hearing myself tell them over and over, I began to agree with my captive audience that they were not only interesting but possibly good.

in love with Miss Ryan. Her radiant, no-nonsense character made us either afraid not to love her or love her so we would not be afraid, I am not sure which. It was not only that we sensed she was with it, but also that she was with us.

Like the first grade, the rest of the Lincoln School was a sampling of the lower part of

Quite by accident I told one of these vignettes at a meeting of scholars and other boring people. It was recorded on tape, printed in a magazine, and circulated among schools and libraries here and there. I received letters asking for reprints, and occasionally a tempting suggestion that I write more of the same, perhaps enough to make a book.

Adding up the three listeners in my family and the three correspondents made a public of six. I didn't need more persuasion than this to link the anecdotes into a story. **"**

### Be One of Ernesto Galarza's Public

The selection you've read is from one chapter of Galarza's *Barrio Boy* (University of Notre Dame Press). If you liked it, you'll enjoy reading the entire book.

town, where many races made their home. My pals in the second grade were Kazushi, whose parents spoke only Japanese; Matti, a skinny Italian boy; and Manuel, a fat Portuguese who would never get into a fight but wrestled you to the ground and just sat on you. Our assortment of nationalities included Koreans, Yugoslavs, Poles, Irish, and home-grown Americans.

Miss Hopley and her teachers never let us forget why we were at Lincoln: for those who were alien, to become good Americans; for those who were so born, to accept the rest of us. Off the school grounds we traded the same insults we heard from our elders. On the playground we were sure to be marched up to the principal's office for calling someone a wop, a chink, a dago, or a greaser. The school was not so much a melting pot as a griddle where Miss Hopley and her helpers warmed knowledge into us and roasted racial hatreds out of us.

At Lincoln, making us into Americans did not mean scrubbing away what made us originally foreign. The teachers called us as our parents did, or as close as they could pronounce our names in Spanish or Japanese. No one was

*The teachers called us as our parents did, or as close as they could pronounce our names . . .*

ever scolded or punished for speaking in his native tongue on the playground. Matti told the class about his mother's down quilt, which she had made in Italy with the fine feathers of a thousand geese. Encarnación acted out how boys learned to fish in the Philippines. I astounded the third grade with the story of my travels on a stagecoach, which nobody else in the class had seen except in the museum at Sutter's Fort. After a visit to the Crocker Art Gallery and its collection of heroic paintings of the golden age of California, someone showed a silk scroll with a Chinese painting. Miss Hopley herself had a way of expressing wonder over these matters before a class, her eyes wide open until they popped slightly. It was easy for me to feel that becoming a proud American, as she said we should, did not mean feeling ashamed of being a Mexican.

# An Immigrant in the United States

I am a Cambodian immigrant refugee living in the United States. My family and I left Cambodia because of the war in my country where I was born. I can't believe that we are free in this country. I was eight years old when I first saw different-colored people. How strange, scary, and frightening to see white- and black-colored people, red and brown and yellow hair, blue, green, and brown eyes. I thought they had costumes on. My eyes had only seen brown-skinned people with black hair. The only pictures in books I had ever seen in my country were of Cambodian people who are of the brown race. Everything was different. The climate was so cold, and when I saw something white on the ground I thought somebody went up in an airplane and dropped lots and lots of tiny pieces of paper down on the ground. It was the first time I saw snow.

When I went to school I couldn't speak English and the teacher didn't speak Khmer. I couldn't understand what to do. It was very difficult. Eating in the cafeteria at the beginning was so different. I had never seen or tasted milk and never eaten cheese or butter. I had never used a fork or knife. There were about five other Cambodian kids in my room who had been in America longer, so they showed me how to use a fork and a knife. At first I didn't like the foods—cheese, salad, pizza, and milk—so I threw them away. The foods I hated are some of my favorite foods now, like pizza, cheese, and milk.

American kids showed me how to play American sports and we became friends. Today I feel very happy to be in a free country in America.

The color of people doesn't scare me anymore. I think how silly it was to be afraid. Everyone is the same inside with the same feelings.

—Ponn Pet
Lowell, Massachusetts

# MAKING MEANINGS

• ## First Thoughts

1. Finish these sentences:
   - If I went to a school where I did not speak the language, I would . . .
   - I have been in the same situation as Ernesto, and I . . .

## Shaping Interpretations

2. What did you **predict** would happen to Ernesto, and why? (Were you correct?) How else could his story have ended?

3. In many ways this story is a tribute to Ernesto's teachers. What do you think Galarza means when he says that Miss Ryan was not only "with it" but "with us"?

4. The **metaphor** of the melting pot comes from a 1908 play by Israel Zangwill: "America is . . . a great melting pot, where all the races of Europe are melting and reforming!" Ernesto thinks of Lincoln School not as a melting pot—which makes everyone the same—but as a warm griddle. What do you think this means? Which metaphor would you use to describe the United States, and why?

5. Reread the ending of Ponn Pet's essay (page 130). Do you think the teachers at Lincoln School would agree with him? Why or why not?

6. How is Ernesto's experience at an American school different from Jean Fritz's experience at the Hankow British school in "Homesick" (page 105)? Are the experiences of the two outsiders similar at all? Explain.

## Connecting with the Text

7. At school Ernesto learns tolerance for other cultures and races. Where does he learn intolerance? Where have you seen tolerance and intolerance in your community and in the wider world?

8. Refer to your notes for the Quickwrite on page 124. How has this story helped you understand the difficulties of learning a second language?

## Extending the Text

9. Ernesto Galarza and many of his classmates are immigrants. What special problems do you think immigrants face today? What are some ways that schools and local governments try to solve these problems?

---

### Reading Check

a. How does Ernesto feel about Miss Hopley and Miss Ryan?

b. How is the makeup of Ernesto's class a lot like that of his neighborhood?

c. How does Miss Ryan encourage her students to learn English?

d. According to Miss Hopley and the teachers at Lincoln School, what are the children to remember about *why* they are at school?

e. How does Lincoln School honor its students' original languages and customs?

# CHOICES: Building Your Portfolio

## Writer's Notebook

### 1. Collecting Ideas for an Autobiographical Incident

Ernesto's autobiography might have given you ideas for an autobiography of your own. Develop your ideas by freewriting on one of the following topics in your Writer's Notebook. Use words that express the feelings you associate with a time when

- you felt anxious about going somewhere or doing something new
- a teacher helped you learn or do something
- you realized what it means to live in the United States

> First day of school:
> — Everything was **so big**.
> — J.J. spilled milk on me. I was soaked and smelly.
> — When I visited as a seventh-grader, everything seemed so small.

## Comparing and Contrasting

### 2. Looking Back

Both Ernesto Galarza and Jean Fritz wrote autobiographies in which they look back at their childhood. At first their stories may seem quite different. Yet, when you look closely, you'll find some important similarities, especially in the problems and feelings they experienced. Write a paragraph or two comparing and contrasting "Homesick" and "Barrio Boy." Before you write, use a Venn diagram like the one on page 123 to organize your ideas.

## Research/Math

### 3. American Pie

Students from all over the world attended Ernesto's school. Is the same true in your class? Take a poll to find out. List the various ethnic groups you find among your classmates (ask them to consider the backgrounds of their parents and grandparents). Then, figure out the percentage of the whole that each group represents. Show your results on a pie graph.

## Speaking and Listening

### 4. Connecting Across Cultures

Recall how Ernesto's classmates share simple stories that help reveal to one another their diverse ethnic and racial backgrounds. With a group of classmates, arrange a "Telling Our Stories" session. Talk about something from your heritage that will help your classmates learn who you are. Then, as a class, discuss the ways details in your stories "cross cultures."

# GRAMMAR LINK    MINI-LESSON

## Making the Most of Comparing Adjectives

**Language Handbook**
**H E L P**

*See Comparison of Modifiers, pages 737-739.*

**Technology**
**H E L P**

*See* Language Workshop CD-ROM. *Key word entry: degrees of comparison.*
.

The **comparative degree** of an adjective compares two people or things. The **superlative degree** compares more than two people or things.

| Comparative Degree | |
|---|---|
| Add the ending -*er* or the the word *more* when you compare two items. | The Lincoln School was a sampling of the <u>lower</u> part of town. . . . |

| Superlative Degree | |
|---|---|
| When you compare more than two, add the ending -*est* or the word *most.* | To the children, their beloved Miss Ryan was the <u>most wonderful</u> teacher in the world. |

1. When comparing, don't use both *more* and -*er,* and don't use both *most* and -*est.*

   Ernesto felt mo~~re~~ <u>safer</u> when his mother was present.

   Matti was the mo~~st~~ <u>thinnest</u> boy in the second grade.

2. Don't use the superlative form when you compare only two people or things.

   *prouder*
   Do you think Ernesto was prou~~dest~~ of being an American or a Mexican?

   *more*
   Of the two boys, Ito learned mo~~st~~ quickly.

### Try It Out

Act as an editor and show how you'd correct these sentences:

1. Ernesto thought American schools were more stranger than Mexican schools.

2. Ernesto spoke Spanish and English, but his Spanish was best.

3. Was Ernesto proudest of pronouncing *butterfly* or of reading "Little Bo-Peep"?

---

# VOCABULARY    HOW TO OWN A WORD

**WORD BANK**

*reassuring*
*contraption*
*assured*
*formidable*

## Rest Assured—The Words Are in the Bank

Write some sentences of your own.

1. What are the most <u>reassuring</u> words you've ever heard? Tell about when you heard them.
2. Describe some <u>contraption</u> that makes your life easier.
3. Have you ever <u>assured</u> a friend that something would happen? Recall what you said.
4. Who is the most <u>formidable</u> person in your school? What makes him or her so?

# Before You Read

## Make the Connection

### Oops!

A girl is walking down the hall at school. She spots a boy she's been dying to meet coming toward her. They are almost right next to each other when she slips, loses her balance, and falls to the floor in a clumsy heap. How could a moment like this possibly have a positive outcome?

## Quickwrite

Jot down your responses to the question above. Then, in a group, share your possible outcomes.

## Elements of Literature

### Description: Putting You There

People who write autobiographies, or personal histories, try to let the reader share their experiences. They do this by using descriptive language. In "Fish Cheeks," Amy Tan describes holiday guests arriving "in a clamor of doorbells and rumpled Christmas packages." These vivid images help us to hear and see the scene—to be right in the thick of it.

**D**escription is the kind of writing that creates a clear image of something, usually by using details that appeal to one or more of our senses: sight, hearing, smell, taste, and touch.

*For more on Description, see the Handbook of Literary Terms.*

## Reading Skills and Strategies

### Describing Mental Images: Appealing to the Senses

When writers describe things, they create **mental images,** pictures drawn with words. To help you imagine places, events, and characters, they use language that appeals to the senses, as Amy Tan does in this true story. When you read description, notice that

- most images are visual, but images often appeal to several senses at once

- writers often choose details that show how they feel about what they describe

 go.hrw.com
LEO 7-2

# FISH CHEEKS

Amy Tan

ON CHRISTMAS EVE
I SAW THAT MY MOTHER
HAD OUTDONE HERSELF IN
CREATING A STRANGE MENU.

I fell in love with the minister's son the winter I turned fourteen. He was not Chinese, but as white as Mary in the manger. For Christmas I prayed for this blond-haired boy, Robert, and a slim new American nose.

When I found out that my parents had invited the minister's family over for Christmas Eve dinner, I cried. What would Robert think of our shabby *Chinese* Christmas? What would he think of our noisy *Chinese* relatives who lacked proper American manners? What terrible disappointment would he feel upon seeing not a roasted turkey and sweet potatoes but *Chinese* food?

On Christmas Eve I saw that my mother had outdone herself in creating a strange menu. She was pulling black veins out of the backs of fleshy prawns. The kitchen was littered with appalling mounds of raw food: A slimy rock cod with bulging fish eyes that pleaded not to be thrown into a pan of hot oil. Tofu, which looked like stacked wedges of rubbery white sponges. A bowl soaking dried fungus back to life. A plate of squid, their backs crisscrossed with knife markings so they resembled bicycle tires.

And then they arrived—the minister's family and all my relatives in a clamor of doorbells and rumpled Christmas packages. Robert grunted hello, and I pretended he was not worthy of existence.

> **THE KITCHEN WAS LITTERED WITH APPALLING MOUNDS OF RAW FOOD...**

------------------------------------------------------------

### WORDS TO OWN

**appalling** (ə·pôl′iŋ) *adj.*: shocking, horrifying.
**wedges** (wej′iz) *n.*: pieces of material thick at one end and narrowing to a thin edge.
**clamor** (klam′ər) *n.*: loud, confused noise.
**rumpled** (rum′pəld) *v.* used as *adj.*: wrinkled and untidy.

------------------------------------------------------------

Dinner threw me deeper into despair. My relatives licked the ends of their chopsticks and reached across the table, dipping them into the dozen or so plates of food. Robert and his family waited patiently for platters to be passed to them. My relatives murmured with pleasure when my mother brought out the whole steamed fish. Robert grimaced. Then my father poked his chopsticks just below the fish eye and plucked out the soft meat. "Amy, your favorite," he said, offering me the tender fish cheek. I wanted to disappear.

At the end of the meal my father leaned back and belched loudly, thanking my mother for her fine cooking. "It's a polite Chinese custom to show you are satisfied," explained my father to our astonished guests. Robert was looking down at his plate with a reddened face. The minister managed to <u>muster</u> up a quiet burp. I was stunned into silence for the rest of the night.

> "YOU WANT TO BE THE SAME AS AMERICAN GIRLS ON THE OUTSIDE."

After everyone had gone, my mother said to me, "You want to be the same as American girls on the outside." She handed me an early gift. It was a miniskirt in beige tweed. "But inside you must always be Chinese. You must be proud you are different. Your only shame is to have shame."

And even though I didn't agree with her then, I knew that she understood how much I had suffered during the evening's dinner. It wasn't until many years later—long after I had gotten over my crush on Robert—that I was able to fully appreciate her lesson and the true purpose behind our particular menu. For Christmas Eve that year, she had chosen all my favorite foods.

**WORDS TO OWN**
**muster** (mus′tər) v.: call forth.

## LITERATURE AND SCIENCE

### Queen Bean

Whenever you have Chinese food, it's there: In a restaurant it's in the small, tapered beaker nestled between the salt and pepper shakers; in your take-out bag it's in bulgy tiny plastic packets. Yes, it's the soy sauce, as reliable and reassuring a companion to Chinese food as ketchup is to some American foods. Yet, this tasty sauce is only one of dozens of uses for the amazing soybean, a staple of Chinese cuisine for centuries.

The soybean is a member of the legume family, a high-protein vegetable group that includes such familiar items as peanuts, chickpeas, lentils, lima beans, navy beans, and split peas. Soybeans are used in a wide variety of products: tofu (a high-protein bean curd popular among vegetarians), soy milk, soy flour, and tempeh (a fermented soy product high in protein and vitamin $B_{12}$). In fact, soybeans so far surpass all other legumes in protein, B vitamins, and versatility that in comparison, the other members of the family seem like mere has-beans.

# MEET THE WRITER
## Finding Answers in Stories

66 I was the only Chinese girl in class from third grade on. I remember trying to belong and feeling isolated. I felt ashamed of being different and ashamed of feeling that way. When I was a teenager, I rejected everything Chinese. . . . The only people I could think I wanted to be like were fictional characters. In part, that is one of the reasons I began to write. You're looking for answers in your life, and you can't find them in anyone else. You end up finding them in stories. 99

**Amy Tan** (1952–    ) found her friends in books—fairy tales, the *Little House* novels of Laura Ingalls Wilder, and later, the British novels of the Brontë sisters. Later still, she began to write books of her own, about a life half a world away from America's prairies and Britain's moors.

Tan spent her childhood in Oakland, California, where her parents had settled after leaving China. When she was fourteen, both her father and her brother died from brain tumors. After these losses, her mother revealed a long-kept secret: Amy had three half-sisters still living in China. These upheavals in her family changed Amy Tan's sense of who she was. Suddenly her Chinese heritage became important to her. She began to read whatever she could about China, later taking college courses in Chinese literature and history. Most of all, Tan became fascinated by her mother's stories about her experiences in China during the war-torn 1930s and 1940s.

Eventually these experiences inspired Tan to write *The Joy Luck Club* (1989) and *The Kitchen God's Wife* (1991). Tan explains:

66 I took images from my mother's stories and painted a larger picture. The voice in my mother and in my novels is one and the same. 99

In recent years, Amy Tan has made several trips to China, where she has come to know the sisters who once seemed lost to her forever. She now loves the Chinese culture she once tried so hard to reject.

In rediscovering her heritage, Tan has not abandoned American ways. She is the lead vocalist in a rock band called the Rock Bottom Remainders. The humorist Dave Barry plays lead guitar, and the writer Stephen King plays rhythm guitar. All three band members claim to have no musical talent whatsoever.

Scene from the 1993 movie version of *The Joy Luck Club.*
© Buena Vista Pictures Distribution, Inc.

# Immigrants  Pat Mora

wrap their babies in the American flag,
feed them mashed hot dogs and apple pie,
name them Bill and Daisy,
buy them blonde dolls that blink blue
5    eyes or a football and tiny cleats
before the baby can even walk,
speak to them in thick English,
            hallo, babee, hallo,
whisper in Spanish or Polish
10    when the babies sleep, whisper
in a dark parent bed, that dark
parent fear, "Will they like
our boy, our girl, our fine american
boy, our fine american girl?"

# MAKING MEANINGS

## First Thoughts

1. Have you ever felt the way Amy does? What would you have done that Christmas Eve if you had been Amy?

## Shaping Interpretations

2. Why do you think Amy is ashamed of her family's Chinese traditions? What does Amy's mother mean when she says, "Your only shame is to have shame"?

3. Reread Tan's **description** of the food her mother is preparing for dinner. How does Amy feel about the dinner? How can you tell?

4. Find one visual **image** in the story that creates a vivid picture in your mind. Then, find three more images that appeal to more than one sense.

5. What do you think Robert and his family think of the Christmas Eve dinner? Use details from the essay to support your response. (How did *you* predict this evening would turn out?)

6. Why do you suppose it isn't until many years later that Amy realizes her mother chose all of Amy's favorite foods for Christmas Eve dinner? What do you think are her mother's "lesson" and "true purpose" in preparing these foods?

7. How are the new Americans in "Immigrants" (see *Connections* on page 140) similar to Amy Tan's family? How are they different?

## Connecting with the Text

8. Amy's mother tells her that she can be an American girl on the outside but must always be Chinese on the inside. Do you think this is possible? Is it a good idea? Explain your answer.

## Extending the Text

9. Think about Jean in "Homesick" (page 105), Ernesto in "Barrio Boy" (page 125), and Amy in "Fish Cheeks." How do you think each would answer the question "Who am I?"

## Challenging the Text

10. Where does the **title** "Fish Cheeks" come from? Do you think it's a good title? Tell why or why not.

> ### Reading Check
>
> Imagine that it is Christmas Eve twenty years later. With a partner, retell the **main events** of "Fish Cheeks." Let one person play the role of Amy and the other person play her mother. Let Amy retell the story. Let her mother add details.

# CHOICES: Building Your Portfolio

## Writer's Notebook

### 1. Collecting Ideas for an Autobiographical Incident

Have you ever been in an embarrassing situation that somehow ended with a positive outcome (like the one you wrote about for the Quickwrite on page 134)? Write about this experience, or write about a time when you were anxious to make a good impression.

*Wanted to look grown-up. Wore high heels to interview for camp counselor. Couldn't play with kids. Felt embarrassed and awkward. Interviewer helped. Said "Just take off the heels!"*

## Descriptive Writing

### 2. Different Tastes

*Slimy, bulging, rubbery*—Amy Tan uses specific **adjectives** to make us feel disgust for the foods that her mother has lovingly prepared for Christmas Eve. Actually these foods are young Amy's favorites, but she uses these adjectives to show her feelings about the meal at the time.

Describe a meal from two different points of view: the point of view of someone who loves everything on the plate, and the point of view of someone who thinks the food is strange and can't eat a thing. You might gather your details in a chart like the one in the next column. The Language Links on pages 120 and 143 might help you with your adjectives.

| Meal |
| --- |
| **Delicious** |
| Buttery, fluffy potatoes with a lake of rich gravy |
| **Horrible** |
| Some mashed-up white stuff flooded with a gluey liquid |

## Home Economics

### 3. World-Class Dining

Bring in the recipe for a dish that is one of your favorites. If possible, choose a dish that you associate with your ethnic or racial heritage. Collect the recipes in a class cookbook. Before each recipe, write a few sentences describing the dish in words that make it sound delicious.

## Style: Using Precise Adjectives

Amy Tan's **descriptive writing** is vivid because she uses specific adjectives that paint an exact picture of the nouns they modify. Overall, these small details work together to give us a clear impression of Amy's feelings. How would your sense of her experience change if she had left out the adjectives?

| Tan's Sentences Without Adjectives | Tan's Sentences With Adjectives |
|---|---|
| What would Robert think of our Christmas? | "What would Robert think of our shabby _Chinese_ Christmas?" |
| The kitchen was littered with mounds of food. | "The kitchen was littered with appalling mounds of raw food." |

Notice how the precise adjectives—_shabby, appalling, raw_—help you see how Amy feels about this Chinese Christmas.

### Try It Out

► Do adjectives sometimes fail you? Take out a description you've written that you want to revise. Place a check mark above each adjective. Decide if it is a general adjective or a precise adjective that paints an exact picture. For example:

| General Adjective | Precise Adjective |
|---|---|
| big | colossal, gigantic |
| nice | generous, kind |
| strong | forceful, muscular |

Change any adjective that does not give readers a precise and vivid impression. You may want to use a **thesaurus** to find the exact word.

## VOCABULARY | HOW TO OWN A WORD

### Analogies: Pairs of Pairs

An analogy begins with a pair of items that are related in some way. You figure out that relationship and then complete another pair that has a similar relationship. For example:

**1.** _Sad_ is to _happy_ as _____ is to _delightful._

The relationship of _sad_ to _happy_ is one of opposites. Complete the analogy with a vocabulary word from the Word Bank that is the opposite of _delightful._ Then, complete each analogy below.

**2.** _Pressed_ is to _neat_ as _____ is to _sloppy._
**3.** _Whisper_ is to _soft_ as _____ is to _loud._
**4.** _Receive_ is to _get_ as _____ is to _summon._
**5.** _Slices_ is to _pizza_ as _____ is to _cheese._

# *Before You Read*

## Make the Connection

### The Name Game

How would you feel if someone mispronounced or misspelled your name? or introduced you as Judy, though your name was really Julie? or made fun of your name?

**Round robin.** Share your thoughts about the following questions with a group of three or four other students:

- How does your name affect how you see yourself and how others see you?

- Would you like to have a different name? What would you like it to be?

## Quickwrite

Write about your family name, given name, nickname, or pet name. Explain when and how you got the name and how you feel about it. Is it an accurate representation of who you are?

## Elements of Literature

### Main Idea

Have you ever heard someone say "Just get to the point"? Often, in real life as well as in literature, that point, or **main idea,** is not directly stated; it is **implied.** When a main idea is implied, you must draw your own conclusions to decide what the point is.

## Reading Skills and Strategies

### Discovering the Main Idea: It's in the Details

The **main idea** of a story is the idea that all the important details add up to. It's the central idea in the story, the one that the writer wants you to remember. In some stories, like "Names/Nombres," the writer **implies,** or suggests, the main idea. You have to **infer,** or guess, the point that the writer is getting at. To infer a main idea, follow these steps:

- Identify the important details in the selection.

- Think about the point that the important details make.

- From this information, figure out what the main idea is, and state it in your own words.

**go.hrw.com**
**LEO 7-2**

> The **main idea** is the most important thing a writer has to say in a paragraph or selection. The main idea may be directly stated or implied.
>
> *For more on Main Idea, see page 443 and the Handbook of Literary Terms.*

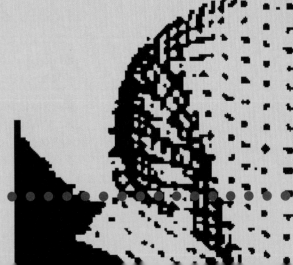

A name as chaotic with sounds as a Middle Eastern bazaar . . .

# Names/Nombres

### Julia Alvarez

When we arrived in New York City, our names changed almost immediately. At Immigration, the officer asked my father, *Mister Elbures,* if he had anything to declare. My father shook his head no, and we were waved through. I was too afraid we wouldn't be let in if I corrected the man's pronunciation, but I said our name to myself, opening my mouth wide for the organ blast of the *a,* trilling my tongue for the drumroll of the *r, All-vah-rrr-es!* How could anyone get *Elbures* out of that orchestra of sound?

At the hotel my mother was Missus Alburest, and I was *little girl,* as in, "Hey, little girl, stop riding the elevator up and down. It's *not* a toy."

When we moved into our new apartment building, the super called my father *Mister Alberase,* and the neighbors who became mother's friends pronounced her name *Jew-lee-ah* instead of *Hoo-lee-ah.* I, her namesake, was known as *Hoo-lee-tah* at home. But at school I was *Judy* or *Judith,* and once an English teacher mistook me for *Juliet.*

It took a while to get used to my new names. I wondered if I shouldn't correct my teachers and new friends. But my mother argued that it didn't matter. "You know what your friend Shakespeare said, *'A rose by any other name would smell as sweet.'"*[1] My family had gotten into the habit of calling any famous author "my friend" because I had begun to write poems and stories in English class.

By the time I was in high school, I was a popular kid, and it showed in my name. Friends called me *Jules* or *Hey Jude,* and once a group of troublemaking friends my mother forbade me to hang out with called me *Alcatraz.* I was *Hoo-lee-tah* only to Mami and Papi and uncles and aunts who came over to eat sancocho[2] on Sunday afternoons—old world folk whom I would just as soon go back to where they came from and leave me to pursue whatever mischief I wanted to in America. *JUDY ALCATRAZ,* the name on the "Wanted" poster would read. Who would ever trace her to me?

My older sister had the hardest time getting an American name for herself because *Mauricia* did not translate into English. Ironically, although she had the most foreign-sounding name, she and I were the Americans in the family. We had been born in New York City when our parents had first tried immigration and then gone back "home," too homesick to stay. My mother often told the story of how she had almost changed my sister's name in the hospital.

After the delivery, Mami and some other new mothers were cooing over their new baby sons and daughters and exchanging names and weights and delivery stories. My mother was embarrassed among the Sallys and Janes and Georges and Johns to reveal the rich, noisy name of *Mauricia,* so when her turn came to brag, she gave her baby's name as *Maureen.*

"Why'd ya give her an Irish name with so many pretty Spanish names to choose from?" one of the women asked.

My mother blushed and admitted her baby's real name to the group. Her mother-in-law had recently died, she apologized, and her husband had insisted that the first daughter be named after his mother, *Mauran.* My mother thought it the ugliest name she had ever heard, and she talked my father into what she believed was an improvement, a combination of *Mauran* and her own mother's name, *Felicia.*

"Her name is *Mao-ree-shee-ah,*" my mother said to the group of women.

"Why, that's a beautiful name," the new mothers cried. *"Moor-ee-sha, Moor-ee-sha,"* they cooed into the pink blanket. *Moor-ee-sha* it was when we returned to the States eleven years later. Sometimes, American tongues found even that mispronunciation tough to say and called her *Maria* or *Marsha* or *Maudy* from her nickname *Maury.* I pitied her. What an awful name to have to transport across borders!

My little sister, Ana, had the easiest time of all. She was plain *Anne*—that is, only her name was plain, for she turned out to be the pale, blond "American beauty" in the family. The only Hispanic thing about her was the affectionate nicknames her boyfriends sometimes gave her. *Anita,* or, as one goofy guy used to sing to her to the tune of the banana advertisement, *Anita Banana.*

Later, during her college years in the late sixties, there was a push to pronounce Third

---

1. *"A rose . . . as sweet":* Julia's mother is quoting from the play *Romeo and Juliet.*
2. **sancocho** (sän·kō′chō): stew of meats and fruit.

World[3] names correctly. I remember calling her long distance at her group house and a roommate answering.

"Can I speak to Ana?" I asked, pronouncing her name the American way.

"Ana?" The man's voice hesitated. "Oh! You must mean *Ah-nah*!"

Our first few years in the States, though, ethnicity was not yet "in." Those were the blond, blue-eyed, bobby-sock years of junior high and high school before the sixties ushered in peasant blouses, hoop earrings, serapes.[4] My initial desire to be known by my correct Dominican name faded. I just wanted to be Judy and merge with the Sallys and Janes in my class. But, inevitably, my accent and coloring gave me away. "So where are you from, Judy?"

"New York," I told my classmates. After all, I had been born blocks away at Columbia-Presbyterian Hospital.

"I mean, *originally.*"

"From the Caribbean," I answered vaguely, for if I specified, no one was quite sure on what continent our island was located.

"Really? I've been to Bermuda. We went last April for spring vacation. I got the worst sunburn! So, are you from Portoriko?"

"No," I sighed. "From the Dominican Republic."

"Where's that?"

"South of Bermuda."

They were just being curious, I knew, but I burned with shame whenever they singled me out as a "foreigner," a rare, exotic friend.

"Say your name in Spanish, oh, please say it!" I had made mouths drop one day by rattling off my full name, which, according to Dominican custom, included my middle names, Mother's and Father's surnames for four generations back.

"Julia Altagracia María Teresa Álvarez Tavares Perello Espaillat Julia Pérez Rochet González." I pronounced it slowly, a name as chaotic with sounds as a Middle Eastern bazaar or market day in a South American village.

My Dominican heritage was never more apparent than when my extended family attended school occasions. For my graduation, they all came, the whole lot of aunts and uncles and the many little cousins who snuck in without tickets. They sat in the first row in order to better understand the Americans' fast-spoken English. But how could they listen when they were constantly speaking among themselves in florid-sounding[5] phrases, rococo[6] consonants, rich, rhyming vowels?

Introducing them to my friends was a further trial to me. These relatives had such complicated names and there were so many of them, and their relationships to myself were so convoluted. There was my Tía[7] Josefina, who was not really an aunt but a much older cousin. And her daughter, Aida Margarita, who was adopted, una hija de crianza.[8] My uncle of affection, Tío José, brought my madrina[9] Tía Amelia and her comadre[10] Tía Pilar. My friends rarely had more than a "Mom and Dad" to introduce.

After the commencement ceremony, my family waited outside in the parking lot while my friends and I signed yearbooks with nicknames which recalled our high school good times: "Beans" and "Pepperoni" and "Alcatraz." We hugged and cried and promised to keep in touch.

5. **florid-sounding:** flowery; using fancy words.
6. **rococo** (rə·kō′kō): fancy. Rococo is a style of art and architecture of the early eighteenth century known for its fancy ornamentation.
7. **Tía** (tē′ä): Spanish for "Aunt." *Tío* is "Uncle."
8. **una hija de crianza** (ōō′nä ē′hä de krē·än′sä): Spanish for "an adopted daughter." *Crianza* means "upbringing."
9. **madrina** (mä·drē′nä): Spanish for "godmother."
10. **comadre** (kô·mä′drā): Spanish for "close friend" (informal). *Comadre* is the name used by the mother and the godmother of a child for each other.

3. **Third World:** the developing countries of Latin America, Africa, and Asia.
4. **serapes** (sə·rä′pēs): woolen shawls worn in Latin American countries.

Our goodbyes went on too long. I heard my father's voice calling out across the parking lot, "*Hoo-lee-tah!* Vámonos!"[11]

Back home, my tíos and tías and primas,[12] Mami and Papi, and mis hermanas[13] had a party for me with sancocho and a store-bought pudín,[14] inscribed with *Happy Graduation, Julie.* There were many gifts—that was a plus to a large family! I got several wallets and a suitcase with my initials and a graduation charm from my godmother and money from my uncles. The biggest gift was a portable typewriter from my parents for writing my stories and poems.

Someday, the family predicted, my name would be well-known throughout the United States. I laughed to myself, wondering which one I would go by.

11. **Vámonos!** (vä′mô·nôs): Spanish for "Let's go!"
12. **primas** (prē′mäs): Spanish for "female cousins."
13. **mis hermanas** (mēs är·mä′näs): Spanish for "my sisters."
14. **pudín** (poo·dēn′): Spanish cake.

## MEET THE WRITER

### "Just Do Your Work and Put in Your Heart . . ."

Born in New York City, **Julia Alvarez** (1950–    ) spent her childhood in the Dominican Republic, returning with her family to New York when she was ten years old. Adjusting to her new surroundings in the early 1960s wasn't easy for young Julia:

66 I can tap into that struggling English speaker, that skinny, dark-haired, olive-skinned girl in a sixth grade of mostly blond and blue-eyed giants. Those tall, freckled boys would push me around in the playground. 'Go back to where you came from!' 'No comprendo!' I'd reply, though of course there was no misunderstanding the fierce looks on their faces. 99

Despite the difficulties, being an immigrant gave Julia a special point of view. "We [immigrants] travel on that border between two worlds," she explains, "and we can see both points of view." Later, as a writer, she used these sometimes conflicting perspectives—American and Latino—to describe brilliantly the cultures of the United States and the Dominican Republic.

After college and graduate school, Alvarez taught poetry for twelve years in Kentucky, California, Vermont, Washington, D.C., and Illinois. Now she lives in Vermont, where she writes novels and teaches at Middlebury College.

66 Day to day, I guess I follow my papi's advice. When we first came [to the United States], he would talk to his children about how to make it in our new country. 'Just do your work and put in your heart, and they will accept you!' 99

If you judge by Julia Alvarez's experience, that's good advice.

**More by Julia Alvarez**

In her funny, touching first novel, *How the García Girls Lost Their Accents* (Algonquin Books of Chapel Hill), Alvarez tells about an immigrant Dominican family—something like her own—adjusting to American life. One remarkable thing about this novel is that it moves backward, rather than forward, in time.

# MAKING MEANINGS

## First Thoughts

1. Think back to what you said about names in your notes for the Quickwrite on page 144. How has "Names/Nombres" either changed or strengthened your ideas?

## Shaping Interpretations

2. What picture does Alvarez create of the people who mispronounce her name?

3. As a teenager, why does Alvarez "just [want] to be Judy"? How do you think her attitudes have changed since then?

4. Why do you think the writer chooses Julia Alvarez as the name she'll be known by?

5. Why do you think Julia Alvarez gave this piece the **title** "Names/Nombres" instead of just "Names" (or just "Nombres")? What connection can you see between this title and Alvarez's comment about being "on that border between two worlds"?

6. State in your own words the **main idea** of "Names/Nombres." List three significant **details** or **quotes** from the story that you think back up the main idea.

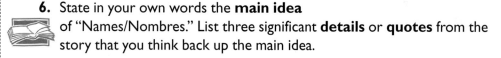

> **Reading Check**
>
> Julia Alvarez has been known by the different names listed below. Explain who uses each name or group of names and what the names mean to Alvarez.
>
> - "little girl"
> - Julita (pronounced *hoo-LEE-tah*)
> - Judith, Juliet
> - Jules, Jude
> - Alcatraz
> - Judy
> - Julia Altagracia María Teresa Álvarez Tavares Perello Espaillat Julia Pérez Rochet González
> - Julia Alvarez

## Connecting with the Text

7. Have you ever wanted to change your name or nickname? Explain.

## Extending the Text

8. What advantages do you see in being part of two cultures? What problems do you see?

## Challenging the Text

9. "Names/Nombres" includes many Spanish words and phrases. In your opinion, do they make it harder for non–Spanish speakers to read the essay, or do they add something valuable to it?

# CHOICES: Building Your Portfolio

---

## Writer's Notebook

### 1. Collecting Ideas for an Autobiographical Incident

Jot down some notes about your own experiences with names. Here are some ways to get started:

- comments people have made about your name in the past
- the perfect name for you and why (it could be the one you have now or one you make up)
- feelings you've had about other people's names
- names you've given (nicknames, names of pets)

> Little sister couldn't say "Elizabeth"—She shouted "Belizet! Belizet!" Big hug— smell of baby powder—Her love stopped me from being jealous.

---

### Creative Writing

## 2. I Am a Poem

Imagine that you are writing from the point of view of Julia Alvarez, and complete the following "I Am" poem. Use what you have learned about Alvarez in "Names/ Nombres" to help you capture her personality.

"I Am"
I am …
I wonder …
I hear …
I see …
I want …
I am …

### Research/ Speaking and Listening

## 3. What's in Your Name?

Research your own names to find out as much as you can about them—first, middle, and last names, as well as any additional names you've been given as part of your ethnic or religious heritage. You could begin by interviewing your family members to record what they know. Then, check the name books at your library. See if you can find out the **origins** of all your names. Prepare a short talk in which you tell your classmates about the meanings of your names.

### Writing/Art

## 4. Pen Names

What do Mark Twain, Dr. Seuss, Lewis Carroll, M. E. Kerr, and O. Henry have in common? Answer: They all wrote their books using pen names. Invent a pen name that you might use someday. Then, think of a title for a book you might write. Create a book cover with that title and pen name. On the back cover, place a photo of yourself, accompanied by notes about your life.

# GRAMMAR LINK  **MINI-LESSON**

## • Don't Leave Your Modifiers Dangling

**Language Handbook H E L P**

*See Participial Phrases, page 740.*

**Technology H E L P**

*See* Language Workshop CD-ROM. *Key word entry: dangling modifiers.*

It's easy to make the mistake of "hanging" a modifying phrase on a sentence (usually at the beginning) and forgetting to include the word it modifies:

DANGLING
> Arriving in New York City, our names changed almost immediately.

Who arrived in New York City? It sounds as if the names came on their own!

Phrases that hang, or dangle, on a sentence without clearly modifying a word are called **dangling modifiers.** You can correct a dangling modifier by adding, subtracting, or rearranging words:

CLEAR
> Arriving in New York City, <u>we noticed that</u> our names changed almost immediately.

The first sentence of "Names/Nombres" shows this even better solution:

CLEAR
> "<u>When we arrived</u> in New York City, our names changed almost immediately."

### Try It Out

➤ Find and fix the dangling modifiers in these sentences.

1. Tracing the fugitive, the name on the wanted poster was JUDY ALCATRAZ.

2. Moving into our new apartment, our name became *Alberase*.

3. Equipped with a typewriter, the stories were easier to write.

➤ Exchange a sample of your writing with a partner. Then, be a dangler detector: Read through each other's work carefully to see that every sentence makes sense and that every modifier or phrase has something to modify. Your first step should be to identify the modifying phrases (with the permission of the writer, use a colored pen). Dangling modifiers usually appear, or "dangle," at the opening of a sentence.

# SPELLING  **HOW TO OWN A WORD**

**VERB LIST**

*combine*
*generate*
*graduate*
*pronounce*
*immigrate*

## • Suffixes: The Verb-Noun Connection

How do you turn a verb into a noun? Often you can do it simply by adding the **suffix** *-ion* (or its variation *-sion, -tion, -ation,* or *-iation*) to the verb. A **suffix** is a word part that is added to the end of a word. (A **prefix** is added to the beginning.) You may have to make a spelling change when you add one of these suffixes to a verb. For example, when you add *-ion, -ation,* or *-iation* to a word that ends with an e, you must drop the e:

> *complicate + -ion = complication*

Change the verbs in the list into nouns. Then, check the story to see if you have formed each noun correctly.

## THE NAMING OF NAMES

## Make the Connection

### What's in a Name?

From Walla Walla to Winnemucca, from Mooseheart to King of Prussia, from Devil's Hopyard to Saint Cloud— every part of our country has wonderful names that give us clues to the identity and background of the people who have lived there. With a group of classmates, look over a map of your community, region, or state. Pick out and list some unusual names. Consider names of roads, neighborhoods, buildings, rivers, and mountains, as well as towns. Discuss these names with your group. How does each name reflect the culture of the people who have lived in the region?

## Quickwrite

Imagine you were among the first people to settle your town. Decide on a new name that you think captures the spirit or the setting of your new home. Write your new name and the reason you think it's a good one.

## Elements of Literature

### Setting: Out of the Imagination

You won't recognize Mars in this science fiction story. The story's imaginary and fantastic setting springs from the imagination of Ray Bradbury. On his Mars, twenty-first-century colonists from Earth settle in a place where the wind roars through "the violet grass, shaking out green rose petals." As you'll see, in this strange Martian setting everything is subject to a kind of magic.

> **S**etting is the time and place in which a story takes place.
>
> *For more on Setting, see the Handbook of Literary Terms.*

## Reading Skills and Strategies

### Monitoring Comprehension: Modify Your Reading

Luckily, **monitoring comprehension** is easier to do than to say. It just means checking your understanding of a story as you go along. To prevent breakdown, you monitor and modify, or adjust, your reading style—just as astronauts monitor and adjust computerized controls on a spaceflight. If your understanding of "The Naming of Names" breaks down, here are some ways to get back into orbit:

- Stop and take reading notes whenever the setting changes.

- Reread paragraphs aloud.

- Use reference aids, such as footnotes and dictionaries.

- Ask questions. Look for clues with your classmates and teacher.

go.hrw.com
LE0 7-2

# The Naming of Names

**Ray Bradbury**

*"I wonder if those Martians mind us living here."*

The rocket metal cooled in the meadow winds. Its lid gave a bulging *pop.* From its clock interior stepped a man, a woman, and three children. The other passengers whispered away across the Martian meadow, leaving the man alone among his family.

The man felt his hair flutter and the tissues of his body draw tight as if he were standing at the center of a vacuum.[1] His wife, before him, seemed almost to whirl away in smoke. The children, small seeds, might at any instant be sown to all the Martian climes.[2]

The children looked up at him, as people look to the sun to tell what time of their life it is. His face was cold.

"What's wrong?" asked his wife.

"Let's get back on the rocket."

"Go back to Earth?"

"Yes! Listen!"

The wind blew as if to flake away their identities. At any moment the Martian air might draw his soul from him, as marrow comes from a white bone. He felt submerged in a chemical that could dissolve his intellect and burn away his past.

They looked at Martian hills that time had worn with a crushing pressure of years. They saw the old cities, lost in their meadows, lying like children's delicate bones among the blowing lakes of grass.

"Chin up, Harry," said his wife. "It's too late. We've come over sixty million miles."

The children with their yellow hair hollered at the deep dome of Martian sky. There was no answer but the racing hiss of wind through the stiff grass.

He picked up the luggage in his cold hands. "Here we go," he said—a man standing on the edge of a sea, ready to wade in and be drowned.

They walked into town.

1. **vacuum:** closed space with the air sucked out.
2. **climes:** regions.

Their name was Bittering. Harry and his wife, Cora; Dan, Laura, and David. They built a small white cottage and ate good breakfasts there, but the fear was never gone. It lay with Mr. Bittering and Mrs. Bittering, a third, unbidden partner at every midnight talk, at every dawn awakening.

"I feel like a salt crystal," he said, "in a mountain stream, being washed away. We don't belong here. We're Earth people. This is Mars. It was meant for Martians. For heaven's sake, Cora, let's buy tickets for home!"

But she only shook her head. "One day the atom bomb will fix Earth. Then we'll be safe here."

"Safe and insane!"

*Tick-tock, seven o'clock,* sang the voice-clock; *time to get up.* And they did.

Something made him check everything each morning—warm hearth, potted blood-geraniums—precisely as if he expected something to be amiss. The morning paper was toast-warm from the 6:00 A.M. Earth rocket. He broke its seal and tilted it at his breakfast place. He forced himself to be convivial.

"Colonial days all over again," he declared. "Why, in ten years there'll be a million Earthmen on Mars. Big cities, everything! They said we'd fail. Said the Martians would resent our invasion. But did we find any Martians? Not a living soul! Oh, we found their empty cities, but no one in them. Right?"

A river of wind submerged the house. When the windows ceased rattling, Mr. Bittering swallowed and looked at the children.

"I don't know," said David. "Maybe there're

---

**WORDS TO OWN**

**interior** (in·tir′ē·ər) *n.:* inside.
**submerged** (sub·mʉrjd′) *v.* used as *adj.:* sunk; covered with liquid.
**amiss** (ə·mis′) *adj.:* wrong; improper.
**convivial** (kən·viv′ē·əl) *adj.:* sociable or friendly.
**ceased** (sēst) *v.:* stopped.

---

Martians around we don't see. Sometimes nights I think I hear 'em. I hear the wind. The sand hits my window. I get scared. And I see those towns way up in the mountains where the Martians lived a long time ago. And I think I see things moving around those towns, Papa. And I wonder if those Martians *mind* us living here. I wonder if they won't do something to us for coming here."

"Nonsense!" Mr. Bittering looked out the windows. "We're clean, decent people." He looked at his children. "All dead cities have some kind of ghosts in them. Memories, I mean." He stared at the hills. "You see a staircase and you wonder what Martians looked like climbing it. You see Martian paintings and you wonder what the painter was like. You make a little ghost in your mind, a memory. It's quite natural. Imagination." He stopped. "You haven't been prowling up in those ruins, have you?"

"No, Papa." David looked at his shoes.

"See that you stay away from them. Pass the jam."

"Just the same," said little David, "I bet something happens."

Something happened that afternoon. Laura stumbled through the settlement, crying. She dashed blindly onto the porch.

"Mother, Father—the war, Earth!" she sobbed. "A radio flash just came. Atom bombs hit New York! All the space rockets blown up. No more rockets to Mars, ever!"

"Oh, Harry!" The mother held on to her husband and daughter.

"Are you sure, Laura?" asked the father quietly.

Laura wept. "We're stranded on Mars, forever and ever!"

For a long time there was only the sound of the wind in the late afternoon.

*Alone,* thought Bittering. *Only a thousand of us here. No way back. No way. No way.* Sweat poured from his face and his hands and his body; he was drenched in the hotness of his fear. He wanted to strike Laura, cry, "No, you're lying! The rockets will come back!" Instead, he stroked Laura's head against him and said, "The rockets will get through someday."

"Father, what will we do?"

"Go about our business, of course. Raise crops and children. Wait. Keep things going until the war ends and the rockets come again."

The two boys stepped out onto the porch.

"Children," he said, sitting there, looking beyond them, "I've something to tell you."

"We know," they said.

In the following days, Bittering wandered often through the garden to stand alone in his fear. As long as the rockets had spun a silver web across space, he had been able to accept Mars. For he had always told himself: *Tomorrow, if I want, I can buy a ticket and go back to Earth.*

But now: the web gone, the rockets lying in jigsaw heaps of molten girder[3] and unsnaked wire. Earth people left to the strangeness of Mars, the cinnamon dusts and wine airs, to be baked like gingerbread shapes in Martian summers, put into harvested storage by Martian winters. What would happen to him, the others? This was the moment Mars had waited for. Now it would eat them.

He got down on his knees in the flower bed, a spade in his nervous hands. *Work,* he thought, *work and forget.*

He glanced up from the garden to the Martian mountains. He thought of the proud old Martian names that had once been on those peaks. Earthmen, dropping from the sky, had gazed upon hills, rivers, Martian seas left nameless in spite of names. Once Martians had built cities, named cities; climbed mountains, named mountains; sailed seas, named seas.

---

3. **molten girder:** A girder is a metal beam that helps to support a framework; *molten* means "melted."

Mountains melted, seas drained, cities tumbled. In spite of this, the Earthmen had felt a silent guilt at putting new names to these ancient hills and valleys.

Nevertheless, man lives by symbol and label. The names were given.

Mr. Bittering felt very alone in his garden under the Martian sun, an anachronism bent here, planting Earth flowers in a wild soil.

*Think. Keep thinking. Different things. Keep your mind free of Earth, the atom war, the lost rockets.*

He perspired. He glanced about. No one watching. He removed his tie. *Pretty bold,* he thought. *First your coat off, now your tie.* He hung it neatly on a peach tree he had imported as a sapling from Massachusetts.

He returned to his philosophy of names and mountains. The Earthmen had changed names. Now there were Hormel Valleys, Roosevelt Seas, Ford Hills, Vanderbilt Plateaus, Rockefeller Rivers, on Mars. It wasn't right. The American settlers had shown wisdom, using old Indian prairie names: Wisconsin, Minnesota, Idaho, Ohio, Utah, Milwaukee, Waukegan, Osseo. The old names, the old meanings.

Staring at the mountains wildly, he thought: *Are you up there? All the dead ones, you Martians? Well, here we are, alone, cut off! Come down, move us out! We're helpless!*

The wind blew a shower of peach blossoms.

He put out his sun-browned hand, gave a small cry. He touched the blossoms, picked them up. He turned them, he touched them again and again. Then he shouted for his wife.

"Cora!"

She appeared at a window. He ran to her.

"Cora, these blossoms!"

She handled them.

"Do you see? They're different. They've changed! They're not peach blossoms any more!"

"Look all right to me," she said.

"They're not. They're *wrong*! I can't tell how. An extra petal, a leaf, something, the color, the smell!"

The children ran out in time to see their father hurrying about the garden, pulling up radishes, onions, and carrots from their beds.

"Cora, come look!"

They handled the onions, the radishes, the carrots among them.

"Do they look like carrots?"

"Yes . . . no." She hesitated. "I don't know."

"They're changed."

"Perhaps."

"You know they have! Onions but not onions, carrots but not carrots. Taste: the same but different. Smell: not like it used to be." He felt his heart pounding, and he was afraid. He dug his fingers into the earth. "Cora, what's happening? What is it? We've got to get away from this." He ran across the garden. Each tree felt his touch. "The roses. The roses. They're turning green!"

And they stood looking at the green roses.

And two days later Dan came running. "Come see the cow. I was milking her and I saw it. Come on!"

They stood in the shed and looked at their one cow.

It was growing a third horn.

And the lawn in front of their house very quietly and slowly was coloring itself like spring violets. Seed from Earth but growing up a soft purple.

"We must get away," said Bittering. "We'll eat this stuff and then we'll change—who knows to what? I can't let it happen. There's only one thing to do. Burn this food!"

"It's not poisoned."

"But it is. Subtly, very subtly. A little bit. A very little bit. We mustn't touch it."

---

**WORDS TO OWN**

anachronism (ə·nak'rə·niz'əm) *n.*: something out of its proper time in history, like a television in the Middle Ages or penicillin in ancient Rome.

---

# LITERATURE AND SCIENCE

## Live from Mars

Mars is called the red planet because its surface is covered with red dust. The strong Martian winds create huge dust storms. Depending on how much dust is in the air, the Martian sky ranges from pink on a clear day to purple on a stormy one. People associate the color red with fury. This may be why Mars was named after the Roman god of war.

About "The Naming of Names" Bradbury says, "I charted my own Mars and went through a naming of names, building cities and towns, and creating a wild and special new world." In fact, the real Mars is so cold and has so little oxygen and water that humans could not survive there without special equipment. Its atmosphere consists mainly of carbon dioxide, and the average temperature near the planet's surface is an icy −80°F.

In the nineteenth century, astronomers noticed what looked like canals on the surface of Mars. They wondered if intelligent beings had dug these trenches. Scientists now know that the "canals" are actually the outlines of large craters. Still, evidence from a recently discovered 4.5-billion-year-old meteorite suggests that life (in the form of tiny, single-celled organisms) may have existed on Mars billions of years ago.

Mars continues to fascinate scientists. In 1996, NASA sent two spacecraft to Mars. The first, the Mars Pathfinder, landed on Mars on July 4, 1997. The second, the Mars Global Surveyor, reached Mars's orbit about two months later. Future missions will study the climate, terrain, and water conditions. Scientists are planning for the next step in the exploration of the planet: As early as 2020, humans may be landing on Mars!

---

He looked with dismay at their house. "Even the house. The wind's done something to it. The air's burned it. The fog at night. The boards, all warped out of shape. It's not an Earthman's house anymore."

"Oh, your imagination!"

He put on his coat and tie. "I'm going into town. We've got to do something now. I'll be back."

"Wait, Harry!" his wife cried.

But he was gone.

In town, on the shadowy step of the grocery store, the men sat with their hands on their knees, conversing with great leisure and ease.

Mr. Bittering wanted to fire a pistol in the air.

*What are you doing, you fools!* he thought. *Sitting here! You've heard the news—we're stranded on this planet. Well, move! Aren't you frightened? Aren't you afraid? What are you going to do?*

"Hello, Harry," said everyone.

"Look," he said to them. "You did hear the news, the other day, didn't you?"

They nodded and laughed. "Sure. Sure, Harry."

"What are you going to do about it?"

"Do, Harry, do? What *can* we do?"

"Build a rocket, that's what!"

"A rocket, Harry? To go back to all that trouble? Oh, Harry!"

"But you *must* want to go back. Have you noticed the peach blossoms, the onions, the grass?"

"Why, yes, Harry, seems we did," said one of the men.

"Doesn't it scare you?"

"Can't recall that it did much, Harry."

"Idiots!"

"Now, Harry."

Bittering wanted to cry. "You've got to work with me. If we stay here, we'll all change. The air. Don't you smell it? Something in the air. A Martian virus, maybe; some seed, or a pollen. Listen to me!"

They stared at him.

"Sam," he said to one of them.

"Yes, Harry?"

"Will you help me build a rocket?"

"Harry, I got a whole load of metal and some blueprints. You want to work in my metal shop on a rocket, you're welcome. I'll sell you that metal for five hundred dollars. You should be able to construct a right pretty rocket, if you work alone, in about thirty years."

Everyone laughed.

"Don't laugh."

Sam looked at him with quiet good humor.

"Sam," Bittering said. "Your eyes——"

"What about them, Harry?"

"Didn't they used to be gray?"

"Well, now, I don't remember."

"They were, weren't they?"

"Why do you ask, Harry?"

"Because now they're kind of yellow-colored."

"Is that so, Harry?" Sam said, casually.

"And you're taller and thinner——"

"You might be right, Harry."

"Sam, you shouldn't have yellow eyes."

"Harry, what color eyes have *you* got?" Sam said.

"My eyes? They're blue, of course."

"Here you are, Harry." Sam handed him a pocket mirror. "Take a look at yourself."

Mr. Bittering hesitated and then raised the mirror to his face.

There were little, very dim flecks of new gold captured in the blue of his eyes.

"Now look what you've done," said Sam a moment later. "You've broken my mirror."

Harry Bittering moved into the metal shop and began to build the rocket. Men stood in the open door and talked and joked without raising their voices. Once in a while they gave him a hand on lifting something. But mostly they just idled and watched him with their yellowing eyes.

"It's supper time, Harry," they said.

His wife appeared with his supper in a wicker basket.

"I won't touch it," he said. "I'll eat only food from our deep freezer. Food that came from Earth. Nothing from our garden."

His wife stood watching him. "You can't build a rocket."

"I worked in a shop once, when I was twenty. I know metal. Once I get it started, the others will help," he said, not looking at her, laying out the blueprints.

"Harry, Harry," she said, helplessly.

"We've got to get away, Cora. We've *got* to!"

The nights were full of wind that blew down the empty moonlit sea meadows past the little white chess cities lying for their twelve-thousandth year in the shallows. In the Earthmen's settlement, the Bittering house shook with a feeling of change.

Lying abed, Mr. Bittering felt his bones shifted, shaped, melted like gold. His wife, lying beside him, was dark from many sunny afternoons. Dark she was, and golden-eyed, burnt almost black by the sun, sleeping, and the children metallic in their beds, and the wind roaring forlorn and changing through the old peach trees, the violet grass, shaking out green rose petals.

The fear would not be stopped. It had his throat and heart. It dripped in a wetness of the arm and the temple and the trembling palm.

A green star rose in the east.

A strange word emerged from Mr. Bittering's lips.

*Iorrt. Iorrt.* He repeated it.

It was a Martian word. He knew no Martian.

In the middle of the night he arose and dialed a call through to Simpson, the archaeologist.

"Simpson, what does the word *Iorrt* mean?"

"Why, that's the old Martian word for our planet Earth. Why?"

"No special reason."

The telephone slipped from his hand.

"Hello, hello, hello, hello," it kept saying while he sat gazing out at the green star. "Bittering? Harry, are you there?"

The days were full of metal sound. He laid the frame of the rocket with the reluctant help of three indifferent men. He grew very tired in an hour or so and had to sit down.

"The altitude," laughed a man.

"Are you *eating,* Harry?" asked another.

"I'm eating," he said, angrily.

"From your deep freezer?"

"Yes!"

"You're getting thinner, Harry."

"I'm not!"

"And taller."

"Liar!"

His wife took him aside a few days later. "Harry, I've used up all the food in the deep freezer. There's nothing left. I'll have to make sandwiches using food grown on Mars."

He sat down heavily.

"You must eat," she said. "You're weak."

"Yes," he said.

He took a sandwich, opened it, looked at it, and began to nibble at it.

"And take the rest of the day off," she said. "It's hot. The children want to swim in the canals and hike. Please come along."

"I can't waste time. This is a crisis!"

"Just for an hour," she urged. "A swim'll do you good."

He rose, sweating. "All right, all right. Leave me alone. I'll come."

"Good for you, Harry."

The sun was hot, the day quiet. There was only an immense staring burn upon the land. They moved along the canal, the father, the mother, the racing children in their swimsuits. They stopped and ate meat sandwiches. He saw their skin baking brown. And he saw the yellow eyes of his wife and his children, their eyes that were never yellow before. A few tremblings shook him but were carried off in waves of pleasant heat as he lay in the sun. He was too tired to be afraid.

"Cora, how long have your eyes been yellow?"

She was bewildered. "Always, I guess."

"They didn't change from brown in the last three months?"

She bit her lips. "No. Why do you ask?"

"Never mind."

They sat there.

"The children's eyes," he said. "They're yellow, too."

"Sometimes growing children's eyes change color."

"Maybe *we're* children, too. At least to Mars. That's a thought." He laughed. "Think I'll swim."

They leaped into the canal water, and he let himself sink down and down to the bottom like a golden statue and lie there in green silence. All was water-quiet and deep, all was

---

**WORDS TO OWN**

**forlorn** (fôr·lôrn′) *adj.:* hopeless. *Forlorn* may also mean "deserted" or "abandoned."

---

peace. He felt the steady, slow current drift him easily.

*If I lie here long enough,* he thought, *the water will work and eat away my flesh until the bones show like coral. Just my skeleton left. And then the water can build on that skeleton—green things, deep-water things, red things, yellow things. Change. Change. Slow, deep, silent change. And isn't that what it is up* there?

He saw the sky submerged above him, the sun made Martian by atmosphere and time and space.

*Up there, a big river,* he thought, *a Martian river, all of us lying deep in it, in our pebble houses, in our sunken boulder houses, like crayfish hidden, and the water washing away our old bodies and lengthening the bones and——*

He let himself drift up through the soft light.

Dan sat on the edge of the canal, regarding his father seriously.

"*Utha,*" he said.

"What?" asked his father.

The boy smiled. "You know. *Utha*'s the Martian word for 'father.'"

"Where did you learn it?"

"I don't know. Around. *Utha!*"

"What do you want?"

The boy hesitated. "I—I want to change my name."

"Change it?"

"Yes."

His mother swam over. "What's wrong with Dan for a name?"

Dan fidgeted. "The other day you called Dan, Dan, Dan. I didn't even hear. I said to myself, that's not my name. I've a new name I want to use."

Mr. Bittering held to the side of the canal, his body cold and his heart pounding slowly. "What is this new name?"

"Linnl. Isn't that a good name? Can I use it? Can't I, please?"

Mr. Bittering put his hand to his head. He thought of the silly rocket, himself working alone, himself alone even among his family, so alone.

He heard his wife say, "Why not?"

He heard himself say, "Yes, you can use it."

"Yaaa!" screamed the boy. "I'm Linnl, Linnl!"

Racing down the meadowlands, he danced and shouted.

Mr. Bittering looked at his wife. "Why did we do that?"

"I don't know," she said. "It just seemed like a good idea."

They walked into the hills. They strolled on old mosaic⁴ paths, beside still-pumping fountains. The paths were covered with a thin film of cool water all summer long. You kept your bare feet cool all the day, splashing as in a creek, wading.

They came to a small deserted Martian villa with a good view of the valley. It was on top of a hill. Blue marble halls, large murals, a swimming pool. It was refreshing in this hot summertime. The Martians hadn't believed in large cities.

"How nice," said Mrs. Bittering, "if we could move up here to this villa for the summer."

"Come on," he said. "We're going back to town. There's work to be done on the rocket."

But as he worked that night, the thought of the cool blue marble villa entered his mind. As the hours passed, the rocket seemed less important.

In the flow of days and weeks, the rocket receded and dwindled. The old fever was gone. It frightened him to think he had let it slip this way. But somehow the heat, the air, the working conditions——

He heard the men murmuring on the porch of his metal shop.

"Everyone's going. You heard?"

"All going. That's right."

Bittering came out. "Going where?" He saw a couple of trucks, loaded with children and furniture, drive down the dusty street.

"Up to the villas," said the man.

"Yeah, Harry. I'm going. So is Sam. Aren't you, Sam?"

"That's right, Harry. What about you?"

"I've got work to do here."

"Work! You can finish that rocket in the autumn, when it's cooler."

He took a breath. "I got the frame all set up."

"In the autumn is better." Their voices were lazy in the heat.

"Got to work," he said.

"Autumn," they reasoned. And they sounded so sensible, so right.

*Autumn would be best,* he thought. *Plenty of time, then.*

*No!* cried part of himself, deep down, put away, locked tight, suffocating. *No! No!*

"In the autumn," he said.

"Come on, Harry," they all said.

"Yes," he said, feeling his flesh melt in the

---

4. **mosaic** (mō·zā′ik): made of small pieces of colored glass, stone, and so on.

---

**WORDS TO OWN**

**receded** (ri·sēd′id) v.: withdrew; became more distant.
**dwindled** (dwin′dəld) v.: shrank.

---

hot liquid air. "Yes, in the autumn. I'll begin work again then."

"I got a villa near the Tirra Canal," said someone.

"You mean the Roosevelt Canal, don't you?"

"Tirra. The old Martian name."

"But on the map——"

"Forget the map. It's Tirra now. Now I found a place in the Pillan mountains——"

"You mean the Rockefeller range," said Bittering.

"I mean the Pillan mountains," said Sam.

"Yes," said Bittering, buried in the hot, swarming air. "The Pillan mountains."

Everyone worked at loading the truck in the hot, still afternoon of the next day.

Laura, Dan, and David carried packages. Or, as they preferred to be known, Ttil, Linnl, and Werr carried packages.

The furniture was abandoned in the little white cottage.

"It looked just fine in Boston," said the mother. "And here in the cottage. But up at the villa? No. We'll get it when we come back in the autumn."

Bittering himself was quiet.

"I've some ideas on furniture for the villa," he said after a time. "Big, lazy furniture."

"What about your encyclopedia? You're taking it along, surely?"

Mr. Bittering glanced away. "I'll come and get it next week."

They turned to their daughter. "What about your New York dresses?"

The bewildered girl stared. "Why, I don't want them anymore."

They shut off the gas, the water; they locked the doors and walked away. Father peered into the truck.

"Gosh, we're not taking much," he said. "Considering all we brought to Mars, this is only a handful!"

He started the truck.

Looking at the small white cottage for a long moment, he was filled with a desire to rush to it, touch it, say goodbye to it, for he felt as if he were going away on a long journey, leaving something to which he could never quite return, never understand again.

Just then Sam and his family drove by in another truck.

"Hi, Bittering! Here we go!"

The truck swung down the ancient highway out of town. There were sixty others traveling the same direction. The town filled with a silent, heavy dust from their passage. The canal waters lay blue in the sun, and a quiet wind moved in the strange trees.

"Goodbye, town!" said Mr. Bittering.

"Goodbye, goodbye," said the family, waving to it.

They did not look back again.

Summer burned the canals dry. Summer moved like flame upon the meadows. In the empty Earth settlement, the painted houses flaked and peeled. Rubber tires upon which children had swung in backyards hung suspended like stopped clock pendulums[5] in the blazing air.

At the metal shop, the rocket frame began to rust.

In the quiet autumn Mr. Bittering stood, very dark now, very golden-eyed, upon the slope above his villa, looking at the valley.

"It's time to go back," said Cora.

"Yes, but we're not going," he said quietly. "There's nothing there anymore."

"Your books," she said. "Your fine clothes."

"Your *Illes* and your fine *ior uele rre,*" she said.

"The town's empty. No one's going back," he said. "There's no reason to, none at all."

The daughter wove tapestries and the sons

5. **pendulums** (pen′dyoo·ləmz): hanging weights that swing back and forth; used to regulate the movement of old-fashioned clocks.

played songs on ancient flutes and pipes, their laughter echoing in the marble villa.

Mr. Bittering gazed at the Earth settlement far away in the low valley. "Such odd, such ridiculous houses the Earth people built."

"They didn't know any better," his wife mused. "Such ugly people. I'm glad they've gone."

They both looked at each other, startled by all they had just finished saying. They laughed.

"Where did they go?" he wondered. He glanced at his wife. She was golden and slender as his daughter. She looked at him, and he seemed almost as young as their eldest son.

"I don't know," she said.

"We'll go back to town maybe next year, or the year after, or the year after that," he said, calmly. "Now—I'm warm. How about taking a swim?"

They turned their backs to the valley. Arm in arm they walked silently down a path of clear-running spring water.

Five years later a rocket fell out of the sky. It lay steaming in the valley. Men leaped out of it, shouting.

"We won the war on Earth! We're here to rescue you! Hey!"

But the American-built town of cottages, peach trees, and theaters was silent. They found a <u>flimsy</u> rocket frame rusting in an empty shop.

The rocket men searched the hills. The captain established headquarters in an abandoned bar. His lieutenant came back to report.

"The town's empty, but we found native life in the hills, sir. Dark people. Yellow eyes. Martians. Very friendly. We talked a bit, not much. They learn English fast. I'm sure our relations will be most friendly with them, sir."

"Dark, eh?" mused the captain. "How many?"

"Six, eight hundred, I'd say, living in those marble ruins in the hills, sir. Tall, healthy. Beautiful women."

"Did they tell you what became of the men and women who built this Earth settlement, Lieutenant?"

"They hadn't the foggiest notion of what happened to this town or its people."

"Strange. You think those Martians killed them?"

"They look surprisingly peaceful. Chances are a plague[6] did this town in, sir."

"Perhaps. I suppose this is one of those mysteries we'll never solve. One of those mysteries you read about."

The captain looked at the room, the dusty windows, the blue mountains rising beyond, the canals moving in the light, and he heard the soft wind in the air. He shivered. Then, recovering, he tapped a large fresh map he had thumbtacked to the top of an empty table.

"Lots to be done, Lieutenant." His voice droned on and quietly on as the sun sank behind the blue hills. "New settlements. Mining sites, minerals to be looked for. Bacteriological specimens taken. The work, all the work. And the old records were lost. We'll have a job of remapping to do, renaming the mountains and rivers and such. Calls for a little imagination.

"What do you think of naming those mountains the Lincoln Mountains, this canal the Washington Canal, those hills—we can name those hills for you, Lieutenant. Diplomacy. And you, for a favor, might name a town for me. Polishing the apple. And why not make this the Einstein Valley, and further over . . . are you *listening*, Lieutenant?"

The lieutenant snapped his gaze from the blue color and the quiet mist of the hills far beyond the town.

"What? Oh, *yes*, sir!"

6. **plague:** deadly disease that spreads quickly.

------

**WORDS TO OWN**

**flimsy** (flim′zē) *adj.:* poorly made; easily broken or damaged.

------

# MEET THE WRITER

## Extra! Extra! Shouting Stories Bite Writer on Leg!

**Ray Bradbury** (1920–    ) decided at the age of twelve to become a writer. He credits this decision to a circus performer called Mr. Electrico. Bradbury recalls one performance:

66 Mr. Electrico twitched his blazing sword. He touched me on the right shoulder, the left shoulder, and then gently on my brow and the tip of my nose. I felt the storms jiggling in my eardrums, the blue fire swarming into my brain and down my arms and out my fingertips. . . . 99

Bradbury went home and shortly afterward began to write.

Eventually Bradbury enjoyed great success with works such as *Fahrenheit 451* (1951) (the title refers to the temperature at which book paper burns), *Dandelion Wine* (1957), *Something Wicked This Way Comes* (1983) (its main character is based on Mr. Electrico), and *The Martian Chronicles* (1958).

In writing about Mars, Bradbury says:

66 I have always looked on myself as some sort of Martian. . . . Some twenty-three years ago, I wrote a strange tale entitled 'Dark They Were, and Golden-Eyed' [another title for 'The Naming of Names']. In that Martian story, I told of a man and his family who helped colonize Mars, who eat of its foods and live in its strange seasons, and stay on when everyone else goes back to Earth, until the day finally comes when they find that the odd weathers and peculiar temperatures of the Red Planet have melted their flesh into new shapes, tinted their skin, and put flecks of gold into their now most fantastic eyes, and they move up into the hills to live in old ruins and become—Martians. Which is the history I predict for us on that far world. The ruins may not be there. But if necessary we will *build* the ruins, and live in them and name them ourselves as my

transplanted Earthmen did. And will not be of Earth anymore but will truly be Martians. 99

Bradbury has been called the "world's greatest science fiction writer," but he thinks of himself as an "idea writer." Of the products of his ideas Bradbury says:

66 My stories have led me through my life. They shout, I follow. They run up and bite me on the leg—I respond by writing down everything that goes on during the bite. When I finish, the idea lets go, and runs off. 99

### Bite into a Bradbury

Catch up on more of Ray Bradbury's stories by sampling some of his short-story collections. In collections such as *The Illustrated Man* (Bantam), *R Is for Rocket* (Bantam), and *The Stories of Ray Bradbury* (Knopf), you'll find popular stories like "Mars Is Heaven," "The Sound of Summer Running," and "The Flying Machine."

# Making Meanings

- ## First Thoughts

    1. Does the life on Mars appeal to you or scare you? Would you want to stay on Mars—or get back to Earth?

## Shaping Interpretations

2. Why do you think Harry Bittering resists change so fiercely? Do you think Bradbury wants us to admire Harry's resistance or to think it's foolish?

3. How does the **setting,** especially the Martian wind, affect the Earth people? Think of how it changes their attitudes and their identities.

4. What **inferences,** or guesses, can you make about the fate of the original Martians who lived in the villas? (Look for clues in the first few paragraphs of the story.)

5. Which group—the Martians or the Earth people—do you think Bradbury likes better, and what are his reasons?

> **Reading Check**
>
> Suppose that Harry Bittering kept a journal on Mars. Write the entries he might have made about these **main events:**
>
> a. how he feels when he first looks around the Martian landscape
>
> b. what changes he notices in things and people
>
> c. why he begins to build a rocket
>
> d. what he does and thinks during the picnic by the canal
>
> e. what he thinks when he leaves for the Martian villa
>
> f. why he decides not to go back to the town

## Connecting with the Text

6. Do you think it's good for newcomers to a society or culture to change their ways? Should they try to hold on to their old ways of doing things instead? Explain.

## Extending the Text

7. What do you predict will happen to the lieutenant who arrives on Mars at the end of the story?

## Challenging the Text

8. At one point the **title** of this story was "Dark They Were, and Golden-Eyed." Why do you think Bradbury changed it to "The Naming of Names"? Which title do you think is more interesting?

9. Did your understanding break down at any point as you read this story? If so, what did you do to get back on track? If you could write to Ray Bradbury about the way his story is written, what would you say?

# CHOICES: Building Your Portfolio

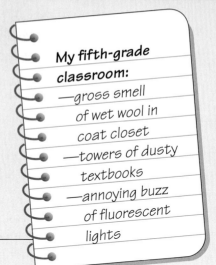

## Writer's Notebook

### 1. Collecting Ideas for an Autobiographical Incident

Details of his new home—the weird Martian wind, green roses, the strange-tasting vegetables—give Mr. Bittering the creeps. Like him, we've all spent time in places that unsettle us. Describe a real **setting** that you disliked or that made you feel strange. Begin with **sensory details** that tell what you saw, smelled, heard, felt, or tasted in that place.

*My fifth-grade classroom:*
*—gross smell of wet wool in coat closet*
*—towers of dusty textbooks*
*—annoying buzz of fluorescent lights*

## Research/Science

### 2. Get Real

Suppose you read this story aloud to a third-grader. She decides to report on Mars to her science class, and now she thinks Mars is exactly like Bradbury's fantasy. Help her out. Look back at the information about Mars on page 157. **Compare and contrast** each fact with events from the story. Make a chart listing all the contradictions you find.

## Creative Writing/Science

### 3. Once upon a Planet . . .

Take another planet in our solar system, and describe it as the **setting** for a fantasy. Before you write, create a science data sheet for your planet. Focus on details like climate, atmosphere, colors, and physical features.

## Mapping/Speaking

### 4. Name That Dune

Pretend you have just conquered your region. You have decided to put your mark on this territory by choosing new names. First, review your notes for the Quickwrite on page 152. Then, choose names for other places in the area— geographical features, towns, roads, universities, malls. Show your classmates a map with your new names in place, and explain the reasoning behind your choices.

## Art

### 5. Martian Makeover

Imagine you're the art director of a team making a film of "The Naming of Names." First, you must decide how to present the Bitterings as typical Americans newly arrived from Earth. Then, you will choose makeup, costumes, and special effects to show their transformation, or **metamorphosis,** into Martians. Draw "before" and "after" pictures of the family to show the changes you imagine. Label each set of drawings to call attention to particularly important details of each character's costumes, makeup, and special effects.

# GRAMMAR LINK  MINI-LESSON

**Language Handbook HELP**

See Placement of Modifiers, pages 739-741.

## All Modifiers! Places, Please!

To work well, modifiers have to be in the right place. Here's an example of a **misplaced modifier:**

> Today I read a story about a Martian settlement that disappeared in my literature book.

Did the settlement disappear into the book? No, the phrase *in my literature book* is misplaced. To fix the sentence, place the modifier as close as possible to the word it modifies—*story*.

> Today I read a story in my literature book about a Martian settlement that disappeared.

### Try It Out

➤Move the misplaced modifier in each sentence to the right place.

1. The picnic is a key scene in this story beside the canal.

2. The lieutenant saw people in the villas named Linnl and Ttil.

3. I almost understood every word of the story.

# VOCABULARY  HOW TO OWN A WORD

**WORD BANK**

interior
submerged
amiss
convivial
ceased
anachronism
forlorn
receded
dwindled
flimsy

## Using Glossaries and Dictionaries

A **glossary** is an alphabetical list of difficult words used in a book, along with their definitions. A glossary usually gives only meanings that apply to the way the words are used in the book. Look at the glossary for this book (pages 789–796). Besides the definition, what information about each word can you find? For more information on a word, you need to look in a **dictionary.** Many dictionaries give the **derivation** (or **etymology**) of words, the origins of the words and their parts. At the back or front of the dictionary, you'll find a list of definitions for symbols and abbreviations used in the derivations. One important symbol is <, which means "comes from." To indicate that the derivation of a word or word part is unknown, the symbols < ? are used.

Here is a word map for the word *interior*. Make similar word maps, using the same labels, for three other words from the Word Bank.

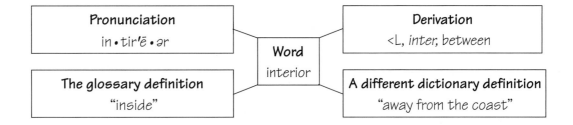

| Pronunciation | | Derivation |
|---|---|---|
| in•tir′ē•ər | Word | <L, *inter,* between |
| The glossary definition | interior | A different dictionary definition |
| "inside" | | "away from the coast" |

# Before You Read

## I'm Nobody!

### Make the Connection

**Fame for Fifteen**

"In the future everyone will be world-famous for fifteen minutes."
                    —Andy Warhol

**Pair and share.** Discuss Warhol's statement with a partner. Do you agree with Warhol? Why or why not? What do you feel are the privileges and pitfalls of fame?

### Quickwrite

Pretend that you became a celebrity overnight. Fill in a chart like the one below showing how sudden fame might change you and your private life.

FAME

| Pluses | Minuses |
|--------|---------|
| + _____ | - _____ |
| + _____ | - _____ |
| + _____ | - _____ |
| + _____ | - _____ |

### Elements of Literature

**Figures of Speech: Painting with Words**

In "I'm Nobody!" Emily Dickinson throws a spotlight on her ideas by using **figures of speech.** Figures of speech compare things that at first glance seem very different.

Thinking about these comparisons of unlike things lets you see familiar people and objects in a new light. The comparisons in figures of speech are imaginative and are not meant to be understood as literally true.

The most common types of figures of speech are similes and metaphors. A **simile** compares two unlike things, using the word *like* or *as:* The sleeping calico cat is *like* a cushion. A **metaphor** equates two things: The sleeping calico cat *is* a cushion.

> A **figure of speech** is a word or phrase that describes one thing in terms of something else, something very different from it. A **simile** is a comparison between two unlike things, using a word such as *like* or *as*. A **metaphor** is a comparison in which one thing is said to be another thing. A metaphor does not use *like* or *as*.
>
> *For more on Figure of Speech, Simile, and Metaphor, see page 397 and the Handbook of Literary Terms.*

**HRW** go.hrw.com
*LE0 7-2*

*Senecio* (1922) by Paul Klee. Oil on gauze on cardboard (40.5 cm x 38 cm) (accession number 1569).

# I'm Nobody!

## Emily Dickinson

I'm Nobody! Who are you?
Are you Nobody too?
Then there's a pair of us!
Don't tell! they'd banish us, you know!

How dreary to be Somebody!
How public—like a Frog—
To tell your name the livelong June
To an admiring Bog!

## MEET THE WRITER

### Who Is That Mysterious Woman in White?

Today **Emily Dickinson** (1830–1886) ranks as one of America's—and the world's—greatest poets. During her lifetime, however, she was anything but famous. Of the seventeen hundred poems she wrote, only seven were published while she was alive—and she refused to have her name put on any of them.

After a normal, sociable childhood and adolescence, Dickinson became a recluse at the age of twenty-six. By the time she was forty, she dressed only in white and rarely left her family's house in Amherst, Massachusetts. She never married, and except for family and a few old friends, she saw no one. Why? No one knows for sure. Her poems often deal with the relationship between her inner self and the outer world. Perhaps she had to draw back from the world and study it from a distance in order to write about it.

Many successful poets in the nineteenth century used regular rhymes and dum-de-dum rhythms. Emily Dickinson did not. Her rhythms were irregular and her rhymes slightly "off." More important, she chose strong images to express her bold ideas. All in all, she was a true American original.

The Granger Collection, New York.

After Emily Dickinson died, her sister discovered more than a thousand poems written on envelopes, paper bags, and scraps of paper, all neatly sewn into little packets. It looked as if the poet was hoping someone would find the poems and publish them. Yet in her lifetime, no one had really understood what poetry meant to Emily Dickinson. Here is how she once defined it:

66 If I read a book and it makes my whole body so cold no fire can ever warm me, I know that is poetry. If I feel physically as if the top of my head were taken off, I know that is poetry. These are the only ways I know it. Is there any other way? 99

# MAKING MEANINGS

- ## First Thoughts

    1. How do you think the speaker feels about fame? Do you agree?

- ## Shaping Interpretations

    2. What does "Nobody" mean in this poem? What does "Somebody" mean?

    3. Who are "they" in line 4? Why would "they" banish the speaker?

    4. The **simile** in the second stanza compares a celebrity to a frog. How could a frog and a public person be similar? Is this a flattering comparison?

    5. In the **metaphor** in the last line, admirers of famous people are compared to creatures in a bog (a marshy place) that admire a croaking frog. How do you think the poet feels about people who idolize celebrities?

    6. Whom do you think the speaker is talking to?

- ## Connecting with the Text

    7. Look back at the pluses and minuses of fame you listed for the Quickwrite on page 168. Do you think your pluses would convince the poet? Explain.

# CHOICES: Building Your Portfolio

### Writer's Notebook

## 1. Collecting Ideas for an Autobiographical Incident

A person can be a "No-body" to the world but a "Somebody" to you. List a few of your personal "Somebodies." Choose one you'd like to write about. Make notes to show what that person has meant to you. Include something the person has said to you, and try to describe the way you feel about this person.

### Letter Writing

## 2. Dear Ms. Dickinson

If you could talk to Emily Dickinson, what would you want to tell her? What would you want to ask her? Write her a letter letting her know what you think of her poem and what you wonder about her life. You could make a class collection of Letters to a Poet.

### Art/Design

## 3. Judging by the Cover

Sometimes you *can* judge a book by its cover. Design a cover for a collection of Emily Dickinson's poetry, entitled *I'm Nobody and Other Selected Poems*. Using "I'm Nobody" as your inspiration, decide what art you want to put on the front cover to give readers an idea of what's inside. On the back cover, create more art or draw a picture of the author.

Let's examine a little creature who is feeling mighty bad, mighty sad, mighty mad . . .

# The Frog Who Wanted to Be a Singer

Linda Goss

Well, friends, I got a question for you. Have you ever been frustrated? That's right, I said *frustrated*. Tell the truth now. Everybody in this room should be screaming, "Yeah, I've been frustrated," because you know you have, at least once in your lives. And some of us here are frustrated every single day.

How do you tell when you are frustrated? Do you feel angry? Do you feel depressed? Are you full of anxiety? Are you tense? Are you nervous? Confused? Sometimes you can't stop eating. Sometimes you don't want to eat at all. Sometimes you can't sleep. And sometimes you don't want to wake up. *You are frustrated!*

Well, friends, let's go back. Back to the forest. Back to the motherland. Back to the days when the animals talked and walked upon the earth, as folks do now.

Let's examine a little creature who is feeling mighty bad, mighty sad, mighty mad, and mighty frustrated. We call him the frog. There's nothing wrong in being a frog. But this particular frog feels that he has talent. You see, he wants to be a singer. And there's nothing wrong in wanting to be a singer except that in this particular forest where this particular frog lives, frogs don't sing. Only the birds are allowed to sing. The birds are considered the most beautiful singers in the forest.

So, for a while, the frog is cool. He's quiet. He stays to himself and practices on his lily pad, jumping up and down, singing to himself. But one day all of this frustration begins to swell inside him. He becomes so swollen that frustration bubbles start popping from his mouth, his ears, his nose, even from his eyes, and he says to himself (in a froglike voice): "You know, I'm tired of feeling this way. I'm tired of holding all this inside me. I've got talent. I want to be a singer."

The little frog decides to share his ambitions with his parents. His parents are somewhat worried about his desires, but since he is their son, they encourage him and say: "Son, we're behind you one hundred percent. If that's what you want to be, then go right ahead. You'll make us very proud."

This makes the frog feel better. It gives him some confidence, so much so that he decides to share the good news with his friends. He jumps over to the other side of the pond and says, "Fellows, I want to share something with you."

"Good!" they reply. "You got some flies we can eat."

"No, not flies. I got talent. I want to be a singer."

"Fool, are you crazy?" says one friend. "Frogs don't sing in this place. You'd better keep your big mouth shut."

They laugh at the frog, so he jumps back over to his lily pad.

He rocks back and forth, meditating and contemplating his situation, and begins to realize that perhaps he should go and talk with the birds. They seem reasonable enough; maybe they will allow him to join their singing group.

He gathers up his confidence, jumps over to their tree house, and knocks on their trunk. The head bird flies to the window, looks down on the frog's head, and says: "Oh, it's the frog. How may we help you?"

"Can I come up? I got something to ask you," says the frog.

"Very well, Frog. Do jump up."

Frog enters the tree house, and hundreds of birds begin fluttering around him.

"Come on in, Frog. Why don't you sit over there in the corner," says the head bird. Frog sits down but he feels a little shy. He begins to chew on his tongue.

"Frog, how may we help you?"

"Uh, well, uh, you see," says Frog, "I would like to become a part of your group."

"That's wonderful," says the head bird.

"Yes, wonderful," echo the other birds.

"Frog, you may help us carry our worms," said the head bird.

"That's not what I had in mind," says Frog.

"Well, what do you have in mind?"

Frog begins to stutter: "I-I-I-I want to-to-to sing wi-wi-with your group."

"What! You must be joking, of course. An ugly green frog who is full of warts sing with us delicate creatures. You would cause us great embarrassment."

"B-b-but . . ." Frog tries to plead his case, but the head bird becomes angry.

"Out! Out! Out of our house you go." He kicks the frog from the house. Frog rolls like a ball down the jungle path.

When he returns home, he feels very sad. The frog wants to cry but doesn't, even though he aches deep inside his gut. He wants to give up, but he doesn't. Instead he practices and practices and practices and practices.

Then he begins to think again and realizes that even though the birds sing every Friday night at the Big Time Weekly Concert, they don't control it. The fox is in charge. The frog jumps over to the fox's place and knocks on his cave.

"Brother Fox, Brother Fox, it's me, Frog. I want to talk to you."

The fox is a fast talker and a busy worker, and really doesn't want to be bothered with the frog.

"Quick, quick, quick, what do you want?" says the fox.

"I want to be in the concert this Friday night."

"Quick, quick, what do you want to do?"

"I want to sing," says the frog.

"Sing? Get out of here, quick, quick, quick!"

"Please, Brother Fox. Please give me a chance."

"Hmmm," says the fox, shifting his eyes. "Uh, you know something, Froggie? Maybe I could use you. Why don't you show up Friday, at eight o'clock sharp, OK?"

"You mean I can do it?"

"That's what I said. Now, get out of here. Quick, quick, quick!"

Oh, the frog is happy. He is going to "do his thing." He is going to present himself to the world.

Meanwhile, the fox goes around to the animals in the forest and tells them about the frog's plans. Each animal promises to be there and give the frog a "little present" for his singing debut.

And so Monday rolls around, Tuesday rolls around, Wednesday rolls around, Thursday rolls around, and it is Friday. The frog is so excited, he bathes all day. He combs his little green hair, parts it in the middle, and slicks down the sides. He scrubs his little green fingers and his little green toes. He looks at his little reflection in the pond, smiles, and says, "Um, um, um, I am *beauuuutiful*! And I am going to 'do my thing' tonight." And soon it is seven o'clock, and then it is seven thirty, and then it is seven forty-five, and there is the frog trembling, holding on to the edge of the curtain.

He looks out at the audience and sees all the animals gathering in their seats. The frog is scared, so scared that his legs won't stop trembling and his eyes won't stop twitching. Brother Fox strolls out onstage and the show begins.

"Thank you, thank you, thank you. Ladies and gentlemen, we have a wonderful show for you tonight. Presenting, for your entertainment, the frog who thinks he's a singer. Come on, let's clap. Come on out here, Frog, come on, come on. Let's give him a big hand." The animals clap and roar with laughter. The frog jumps out and slowly goes up to the microphone.

"For-for-for-for my first number, I-I-I-I——"

Now, before that frog can put the period at the end of that sentence, the elephant stands up, pulls down a pineapple, and throws it right at the frog's head.

"Ow!" cries the frog. And the lion pulls down a banana, throws it, and hits that frog

Oh, the frog is happy. He is going to "do his thing." He is going to present himself to the world.

right in the mouth. "Oh," gulps the frog. Other animals join in the act of throwing things at the frog. Some of them shout and yell at him, "Boo! Boo! Get off the stage. You stink! You're ugly. We don't want to hear a frog sing. Boo, you jive turkey!"

The poor little frog has to leap off the stage and run for his life. He hides underneath the stage. Brother Fox rushes back on the stage.

"OK, OK, OK, calm down—just trying out our comic routine. We have some real talent for your enjoyment. Presenting the birds, who really can sing. Let's hear it for the birds." The audience claps loudly. The birds fly onto the stage, their heads held up high. Their wings slowly strike a stiff, hypnotic pose as if they are statues. Their stage presence demands great respect from the audience. They chirp, tweet, and whistle, causing the audience to fall into a soft, peaceful nod.

Everyone is resting quietly except the frog, who is tired of being pushed around. The frog is tired of feeling frustrated. He leaps over the fox. He grabs him, shakes him, puts his hands

"I don't care if you are asleep. I'm gonna wake you up. I came here to sing a song tonight . . ."

around the fox's throat, and says, "You tricked me. You tried to make a fool out of me."

"Leave me alone," says the fox. "If you want to go back out there and make a fool of yourself, go right ahead."

"Hmph," says the frog. "That's just what I'm going to do."

Now that little green frog hippity-hops back onto the stage. He is shaking but determined to sing his song.

"I don't care if you are asleep. I'm gonna wake you up. I came here to sing a song tonight, and that's what I'm going to do."

In the style of what we call boogie-woogie, the frog begins to "do his thing":

> *DOOBA DOOBA DOOBA DOOBA DOOBA DOOBA DOOBA DOOBA*
> *DOOBA DOOBA DOOBA DOOBA DOOBA DOOBA DOOBA DOOBA*

The frog bops his head about as though it were a jazzy saxophone. His fingers move as though they were playing a funky bass fiddle.

> *DOOBA DOOBA DOOBA DOOBA DOOBADEE DOOBADEE DOOBADEE DOOBADEE*
> *DOOBA DOOBA DOOBA DOOBA DOOBADEE DOOBADEE DOOBADEE DOOBADEE*
> *DOOBA DOOBA DOOBA DOOBA DOOBA DOOBA DOOBA DOOBA*
> *DOOBA! DOOBA! DOOP-DEE-DOOP! . . . BLUR-RRRRRP!*

The elephant opens one eye. He roars "Uuumphf!" He jumps from his seat. He flings his hips from side to side, doing a dance we now call the "bump." The lion is the next animal to jump up from his seat. He shouts: "I love it! I love it!" He shakes his body thisaway and thataway and every whichaway, doing a dance we now call the "twist." Soon the snakes are boogalooing and the giraffes are doing the jerk. The hyenas do the "slop" and the fox does the "mashed potato." The birds also want to join in: "We want to do Dooba Dooba, too." They chirp and sway through the trees.

*Tweet Tweet Tweet Dooba*
*Tweet Tweet Tweet Dooba*

The whole forest is rocking. The joint is jumping. The animals are snapping their fingers. They are *dancing,* doing something that they have never done before.

The fox runs back on the stage, grabs the mike, and shouts: "Wow, Frog, you are a genius. You have given us something new."

From then on, the frog is allowed to sing every Friday night at the Big Time Weekly Concert.

And, as my granddaddy used to say, that is how Rhythm and Blues was born.

*DOOBA DOOBA DOOBA DOOBA DOOBA DOOBA DOOBA DOOBA*
*DOOBA! DOOBA! DOOP-DEE-DOOP! . . . BLURRRRRRP!*

## MEET THE WRITER
### "It's Storeee-Tellin' Time!"

Storyteller **Linda Goss** is hardly ever sitting at a desk when she begins to create a story.

66 When I'm in the kitchen, I become very creative. I have created stories when washing dishes or sweeping my kitchen floor. I have created when I've been on planes, trains, buses, sometimes in the car. I don't necessarily put it down on paper. The kind of storytelling I do is oral, so I think of telling it instead of writing it. That's the whole thing about a storyteller. It's memory. 99

Linda Goss was born and raised in Alcoa, Tennessee. "Everybody in the town was a storyteller," she recalls. In college she studied drama and immersed herself in folklore. After teaching school she decided to become a full-time storyteller, and she is now Philadelphia's official storyteller.

When Goss tells stories, she dresses in African clothes and beaded jewelry, wrapping her hair in colorful cloth hung with charms and decorations. She sometimes walks in front of an audience, clanging cowbells and calling, "It's storeee-tellin' time!" Then she brings her tales to life with singing, talking, and dramatic expressions and gestures.

Goss aims to inspire people with her stories. In "The Frog Who Wanted to Be a Singer," she wants to show that if people believe in themselves, they can realize their dreams.

### More "Storeee-Tellin' "

Linda Goss has collected more magical tales in *Talk That Talk* (Simon and Schuster), an anthology of African American storytelling.

# A Place in the Choir

**Bill Staines**

All God's critters got a place in the choir,
Some sing low, some sing higher,
Some sing out loud on the telephone wire,
And some just clap their hands,
    Or paws,
    Or anything they got now.

Listen to the bass, it's the one on the bottom
Where the bullfrog croaks and the hippopotamus
Moans and groans with a big t'do,
And the old cow just goes "moo."

The dogs and the cats they take up the middle,
While the honeybee hums and the cricket fiddles,
The donkey brays and the pony neighs
And the old coyote howls.

CHORUS: *All God's critters . . .*

Listen to the top where the little birds sing
On the melodies with the high notes ringing,
The hoot owl hollers over everything
And the jaybird disagrees.

Singing in the nighttime, singing in the day,
The little duck quacks, then he's on his way,
The 'possum ain't got much to say,
And the porcupine talks to himself.

CHORUS: *All God's critters . . .*

It's a simple song of living sung everywhere
By the ox and the fox and the grizzly bear,
The grumpy alligator and the hawk above,
The sly raccoon and the turtledove.

CHORUS: *All God's critters . . .*

A Curiosity Bedspread
(1935) by Mrs. Avery
Burton.

Collection of Shelly Zegart,
Louisville, Kentucky.

# READ ON

## Great Pumpkins

In *Squashed* (Delacorte) by Joan Bauer, sixteen-year-old Ellie Morgan wants to lose twenty pounds and grow a two-hundred-pound pumpkin. If she can become a famous pumpkin grower with a trim figure, her life will be perfect. When uncontrollable pressures threaten her plans, Ellie discovers her strengths and learns to believe in herself.

## Sentimental Journey

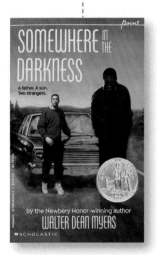

Suffering from kidney disease and confined to a prison hospital, Cephus "Crab" Little decides to make up for lost time with his fifteen-year-old son, Jimmy, in *Somewhere in the Darkness* (Scholastic) by Walter Dean Myers. Together they journey to Crab's hometown in Arkansas, where Jimmy's growing understanding of his father's past helps him come to terms with his father and himself.

## Growing Up Absurd

Gracie, a sophomore in high school, finds her road to self-discovery fraught with the hurdles of family turmoil: an unhappy mother, a newly adopted brother, and an impending family move. A. E. Cannon's *Amazing Gracie* (Delacorte) is a moving account of a girl's discovery of herself through the power of love.

## Other Picks

- Minfong Ho, *Rice Without Rain* (Lothrop, Lee & Sheperd). The ancient traditions of Jinda's Thai village are challenged, and Jinda faces questions of loyalty when young strangers from the city arrive.

- Louise Fitzhugh, *Harriet the Spy* (Dell). Harriet Welsch longs to be a writer, and when her secret spy notebook is discovered, she suddenly finds out what being a writer really means.

# Speaking and Listening Workshop

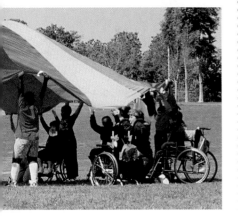

## GROUP DISCUSSION

### TWO (OR THREE OR FOUR) HEADS ARE BETTER THAN ONE

When was the last time you worked with other people to discuss an issue, solve a problem, or find an answer to a question? Maybe you and a group of classmates talked about a story in this collection. Maybe you and some of your friends planned a walkathon or a weekend soccer match.

People work in groups because it's a good way to get things done. In fact, more and more businesses are finding that when people work in groups, they are more efficient and more creative. Here are some guidelines that will help any group work together smoothly.

### 1. Choose Your Roles

In small groups, people seem to take on certain roles naturally. Some are leaders; others prefer to work behind the scenes. Some may create conflict; others may help settle arguments.

Each person in the group has a role to play, and each role has special responsibilities. For example, your group may choose a chairperson or moderator to help keep the discussion moving and make sure everyone speaks up, stays on the subject, and listens to others. Someone else may be named secretary or recorder. This person has the responsibility of taking notes during the discussion. You can rotate these roles if the people in your group work together often.

### 2. State Your Goals

Everyone in the group should agree on a specific task or goal. Your goal may be to

- discuss and share ideas
- cooperate in group learning
- solve problems
- arrive at a decision or make a specific recommendation

**Try It Out**

Get together with a group of three or four classmates to discuss one of the stories in this collection that you all have read. First, explain what you liked or disliked about the story. Then, tell if you think the story fits the theme of this collection, "Who Am I?"

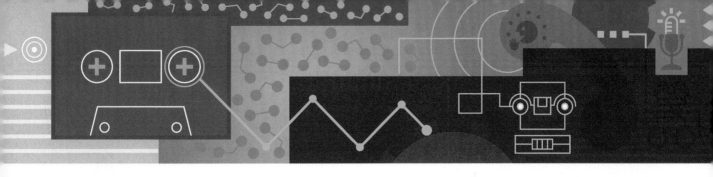

## 3. Brainstorm to Gather Ideas

Brainstorming lets you find out each person's ideas about reaching the group's goal. Here are some tips on brainstorming:

- Be silent for several minutes so that everyone has a chance to collect his or her thoughts.

- Take turns expressing your ideas. Don't worry if you think your ideas are boring or impractical. Keep going around the group until you have plenty of good ideas.

- Take only your fair share of time to talk. Be friendly and polite and listen when it's someone else's turn to speak.

## 4. Reach a Consensus

After brainstorming, begin to work cooperatively to meet your goal. Discuss your ideas and decide as a group which to pursue. Coming to a general agreement as a group is called reaching a consensus. Here are some hints about what to do during this part of the discussion:

- Listen carefully and be willing to learn from what others have to say. Don't interrupt, and speak only when it is your turn.

- Stay on the discussion topic. If you have to remind others to stick to the subject, be polite about it.

- Ask questions if you don't understand something.

Shoe, ©Tribune Media Services, Inc. All Rights Reserved. Reprinted with permission.

## 5. Present Your Information

You may need to present your ideas to other people. Think about the information you need to communicate. Be sure to include enough details so that your listeners can understand and relate to your ideas.

**Try It Out**

Form a group with three or four class-mates. Your goal is to answer this question: What would make your school a better place to learn in? After brain-storming, reach a con-sensus on your three best ideas. Then, choose a group representative to present your ideas to the rest of the class.

# Writer's Workshop

**Technology
HELP**

*See* Writer's Workshop 1
CD-ROM. *Assignment:
Autobiographical
Incident.*

### ASSIGNMENT

**Write a narrative
about an experience
you've had.**

### AIM

**To record an incident
in your life; to express
your feelings.**

### AUDIENCE

**Your teacher,
classmates, friends, or
family or people who
were involved in the
incident.**

## NARRATIVE WRITING

# AUTOBIOGRAPHICAL INCIDENT

When something important happens to you, you probably want
to tell a friend about it right away. When you write an **autobiographical incident** (or personal narrative), you tell about
an event in your life that has special significance for you.

### Professional Model

That night I asked Mother, "What are
the long words for what's wrong
with my eyes?" . . .
　She rhymed off a whole list.
"Say it again. Slowly."
"Strabismus, nystagmus corneal
opacities, and eccentric pupils."
　I practiced.
　The next day I was late coming
out of school. The same grade-seven
boy was waiting for me. He had his
first snowball ready.
"Cross-eyed, cross-eyed," he
chanted and waited for me to start
running so that he could chase me,
pelting me with hard-packed snow-
balls.
　I turned on him instead.
"I am not cross-eyed," I said in a
strong, clear voice. "I have corneal
opacities and eccentric pupils."
　I glared at him as I spoke, and my
eyes were as crossed as ever. But he
was so surprised that he stood there,
his mouth gaping open like a fish's.
　Then I turned my back and

*Dialogue and a
question grab our
attention.*

*The writer uses
dialogue to give
background.*

*Dialogue and
details make the
experience real
and vivid.*

*Action and
dialogue reveal
character.*

*The writer's
feelings are clear.*

*Description
of the boy's
surprise.*

(continued)

walked away. Perhaps his aim was off because he was so used to firing his missiles at a running target. But the first snowball flew past harmlessly. The second exploded with a smack against a nearby tree.

    I kept walking, chin in the air. . . .

    I had found out what mere words could do. I would not forget.

*The writer tells why the incident was important to her.*

        —from *Little by Little* by Jean Little

## Prewriting

### 1. Check Your Writer's Notebook

Look at your Writer's Notebook entries for this collection. Is there one you'd like to develop further? If not, freewrite about one of the subjects listed below or another topic of your choice until you've found an incident you want to write about.

### 2. Freewrite

**a.** Freewrite for two minutes about one or two of the following subjects:

    surprises • conflicts • vacation • helping others • secrets • athletic events • losing a friend • thinking about the future • special memories • luck • honesty

**b.** Complete one of these starters in as many ways as possible:

- The happiest time in my life was . . .

- The most unforgettable time in my life was . . .

- I still feel sad thinking about . . .

- I felt caught in the middle when . . .

---

**Framework for an Autobiographical Incident**

What the incident means to me:

_____

_____

**Introduction** (dialogue, question, statement, or description that grabs readers' attention):

_____

_____

**Order of events:**

1._____
2._____
3._____
4._____

**Conclusion** (summary of the importance of the incident):

_____

_____

c. **Favorites.** Make a list of your favorite things: people, places, hobbies, sports, clothes, animals, vacations, and so on. Is there an incident involving one of your favorite things that you want to write about? Explore your ideas by freewriting.

d. **Souvenirs.** Do you have souvenirs (ticket stubs, photos, letters) that remind you of special times in your life? Try developing your thoughts about one of these times by freewriting.

## 3. Choose Your Topic

To choose an incident to expand on, ask yourself:

- Do any of these incidents mean something special to me?
- Which of the incidents do I remember especially well?
- Am I willing to share any of these incidents with others?

## 4. Explain Why It's Important

After choosing an incident to write about, explain in a sentence or two why the experience was important. For example: "I felt so happy—as if I were my team's hero. Great feeling."

As you draft and redraft, keep looking back at this statement. As you write, you may develop a different sense of what your experience means. If so, change your statement. Some writers say they never know what an experience really means to them until they write about it.

## Drafting
### 1. Get It on Paper: First Draft

The best way to start your draft is to get the basics of your story down on paper as quickly as you can. Try answering the 5W questions as you write: *Who* was involved in the incident? *What* happened? *When* did it happen? *Where* did it happen? *Why* did it happen? Filling in a framework like the one on page 183 can help you organize your draft. Have you left out anything important? Have you emphasized what needs to be emphasized?

**Student Model**

### THE CLUTCH MOMENT

Nine, eight, seven, six, five, four.
I was fouled with four seconds left

*Suspenseful opener.*

in the game. The fans roared out of their seats, cheering and howling. I couldn't believe it. My dream had come true. These two free throws would decide if we won, lost, or tied.

*Background information.*

I stepped up to the free throw line with sweat dripping off my head into my eyes. Chills ran through my body, making my arms feel numb and loose. The only thing I could think of was making these two free throws. I blocked all the cheers out of my head and took a deep breath to relax. I turned the ball in my hands and took four dribbles. I looked at the goal and released the ball. Swish! The game was tied 49–49. The Jefferson Junior fans grew quiet and the Cubs were cheering loudly.

*Detailed description of the writer's actions, thoughts, and feelings.*

I stepped up to the free throw line for the last time that night. After dribbling again four times I raised my arms to shoot the ball.

*Descriptive details make us feel as if we were there.*

It felt like a piece of flab as I released the ball, letting it fly through the air. I knew the ball was not going to miss. I had made the shot of my life to win the game 50–49. It was our ball out of bounds and I threw it in and the time ran out. The game was over! As soon as I raised my hands, I was tackled by Ben Meldrum and the rest of the team. Even the B-team joined in the fun and piled on me.

I knew right then while I was on the floor that I could never have that feeling again.

*The writer tells why the incident was important.*

—Vinnie Merrill
Simonsen Junior High School
Jefferson City, Missouri

---

## Strategies for Elaboration

You can help your readers see, hear, feel, smell, and even taste what you've experienced by including **sensory details** in your autobiographical incident.

Try capturing your memories by completing these statements:

- I see . . .
- I hear . . .
- I smell . . .
- I taste . . .
- I feel . . .

If you have photographs that help you remember the incident, look them over.

- Who's in the picture?
- How would you describe the people's expressions?
- What are they wearing?
- What year or season is it?
- Are any objects visible in the photo that bring back special memories?

*A good autobiographical incident*

1. *focuses on a single incident*

2. *opens in a way that grabs readers' attention*

3. *includes enough background information to allow readers to understand the story*

4. *narrates events in time order or in another order that readers can follow*

5. *includes descriptive details that bring the story to life*

6. *shows what the incident means to the writer*

**Sentence Workshop
H E L P**

*Combining sentences using subordinate clauses: page 187.*

**Communications Handbook
H E L P**

*See Proofreaders' Marks.*

---

**Publishing Tip**

Collect your class's stories in a book, and present it to your school library.

---

## 2. Elaborate

Once you've written down the basics of your incident, add details to make your story come alive.

**a. Run your mental videotape.** Replay the experience in your mind as if you were watching it on videotape. What did the people involved *say* to one another? How did they *look*? What exactly did they *do*? Jot down the details.

**b. Return to the scene.** To jog your memory about what happened and what you were thinking and feeling at the time, try returning to the place where the incident happened.

**c. Interview others.** Talk to other people involved in the experience. What details do they remember?

## Evaluating and Revising

### 1. Peer Review

When you finish your second draft, trade papers with a partner. Read your partner's paper, and answer the following questions:

- Does the beginning grab my attention?

- Are there any missing or unnecessary details?

- Are there parts where I would like more details?

- Do I understand why the incident is important to the writer?

### 2. Self-Evaluation

If you can, put your paper aside briefly. When you look at it again, ask yourself if it has the characteristics of a good autobiographical incident. (See the Evaluation Criteria at the left.)

*"'What I Did This Summer.' This summer, I went to camp. I hated it. I hated every minute of it. I hated my counsellor. I hated the food. I hated the woods. I hated the nature walks and the nature talks. I hated the outings. I hated the campfires. I hated the overnights. I hated . . ."*

# Sentence Workshop

## COMBINING SENTENCES USING SUBORDINATE CLAUSES

When you have a string of short choppy sentences, you can often combine them by changing some of them into subordinate clauses.

A **subordinate clause** is a clause that does not stand alone as a complete sentence. A subordinate clause is attached to a main clause and tells things like *who, what, where, why, when, how,* or *to what extent.*

You can change a sentence into a subordinate clause by adding a word that tells the time or place, such as *after, before, until, where, wherever, when, whenever,* or *while.*

| | |
|---|---|
| CHOPPY SENTENCES | I found out that my parents had invited the minister's family over for Christmas Eve dinner. I cried. |
| COMBINED | "When I found out that my parents had invited the minister's family over for Christmas Eve dinner, I cried." |

—Amy Tan, "Fish Cheeks" (page 136)

In this case the subordinate clause precedes the independent clause. You could easily have reversed the order.

I cried <u>when I found out that my parents had invited the minister's family over for Christmas Eve dinner.</u>

Note: If you put your time or place clause at the beginning of the sentence, you must put a comma after the clause.

## Writer's Workshop Follow-up: Revision

Exchange your autobiographical incident for a partner's. Circle groups of sentences you could combine by making one or more a time or place clause. Then, suggest a revision for each group. Exchange papers again, and review your partner's suggestions.

**Language Handbook**
**H E L P**

*See Combining Sentences, pages 760-761.*

**Technology**
**H E L P**

*See* Language Workshop CD-ROM. *Key word entry: subordinate clauses.*

---

### Try It Out

Make each of the following items a single sentence by changing one or more sentences into subordinate clauses. Then, find the original passage and see how the writer combined these ideas.

**1.** We sat down. She pointed her ruler at me.

—"Homesick" (page 106)

**2.** The commencement ceremony ended. My family waited outside in the parking lot. I signed yearbooks with nicknames.

—"Names/Nombres" (page 147)

**3.** They looked at Martian hills. Time had worn those hills with a crushing pressure of years.

—"The Naming of Names" (page 154)

# Reading for Life

## Situation

Your teacher wants everyone in your class to read a novel. You look at the Read On suggestions on page 179. How about *Rice Without Rain*? You liked "Homesick"; it might be fun to read a whole novel set in another country. Here are some things to think about as you select and read a book for independent reading.

## Strategies

### Find a book to read.

- When you read independently, outside school, you are reading for a purpose. Maybe you are reading for enjoyment. Maybe you have to write a book report. Keep your purpose in mind as you select your book.

- Whenever you're looking for something to read on your own, check the Read On and Meet the Writer features in this book.

- Be picky! If reading a particular book feels like taking medicine, try the opening chapter of a few others until you find one you like.

### Read regularly and often.

- Reading regularly helps you

---

### Reading List: Science Fiction and Fantasy

- Lois Lowry, *The Giver* **A**
  Twelve-year-old Jonas looks forward to training for his first job. At first his community of the future seems ideal: Injustice, poverty, and inequality no longer exist. Gradually it becomes apparent that things are terribly wrong.

- Monica Furlong, *Wise Child* **E/A**
  A wise woman shares her knowledge and "magic" with a young girl in this tale of long ago.

- Robert Louis Stevenson, *Dr. Jekyll and Mr. Hyde* **C**
  A classic horror fantasy that examines the forces of good and evil as embodied in one tortured man.

> **Key to reading levels**
> E = easy
> A = average
> C = challenging

---

get into the reading habit. Try setting a reading goal for yourself—a certain number of pages or a certain amount of time each day.

### Speed up; slow down.

- When you read a novel, set your own pace, adjusting your reading rate to your purpose.

- When you bump into a difficult word, try to infer its meaning from its context, the words around it.

### Use your reading skills.

Even when you're reading for enjoyment, keep using the skills you've learned at school.

- Notice how the writer creates character and keeps you asking questions.

---

- Make inferences and predictions.

- Connect what you read with your own life.

### Using the Strategies

1. Which book do you think is the most difficult on the list above? How can you tell?

2. Which book seems to be fantasy? science fiction? a combination of the two?

3. If you were looking for something to read on your own, which book on the list would you choose? Why?

### Extending the Strategies

Write a letter or send e-mail to the author of your novel. Tell how you felt about the book.

# Learning for Life

## Evaluating Advertising

### Problem

Like the characters in this collection, you may have asked yourself, "Who am I?" Companies that try to sell you their products also want to know who you are. A good advertising company tries to understand you, the buyer, so that it can create an effective advertisement to persuade you to buy something. How can you learn to view advertisements critically and make well-informed decisions?

### Project

**Evaluate advertising aimed at your age group.**

### Preparation

1. Look through magazines, and find advertisements targeted to your age group. Select six advertisements to bring to class.

2. People read ads very quickly, so the ads have to work on our emotions instantly. Take a few minutes to think about how you feel when you look at these advertisements. Jot down some notes. How do you think the advertisers want you to feel?

### Procedure

1. Write answers to these questions about the advertisements you have chosen:

   - What group is each ad directed to? (What age, gender, interests, and so on are targeted?)

   - What desires does each ad appeal to? (To be cool, to look great, to be popular, to be like everyone else, to be successful, to have fun?)

   - What in the ad creates the appeal (pictures, slogans, and so on)?

   - Are the ads' claims realistic?

   - Would you buy the products on the basis of the ads? Explain.

2. Form a group with four or five classmates, and compare your responses to your advertisements.

### Presentation

Use your evaluation of the advertisements to do one of the following:

### 1. Advertisement

With a small group, create your own ad for a product. Be sure you make realistic claims, and appeal to your own age group. Include illustrations that you create or find in magazines. Select the wording you feel would be most effective.

### 2. Opinion Poll

Do a survey of students in your grade to find out how effective some of the advertisements are. Select five to eight advertisements, and display them around the classroom. Prepare a brief list of questions to ask. When you've finished, write up the results of the poll. Try to draw conclusions from the information you gathered in the poll.

### 3. Consumer-Response Letter

Write a letter to one of the advertisers, commenting on the company's ad. Tell what you liked and what you didn't like about the ad. With your teacher's permission, send the letter to the company's public relations manager.

### Processing

Have your reactions to advertisements changed as a result of doing this project? Write a reflection on what you learned.

# Do the Right Thing

*It is the ability to choose which makes us human.*

*—Madeleine L'Engle*

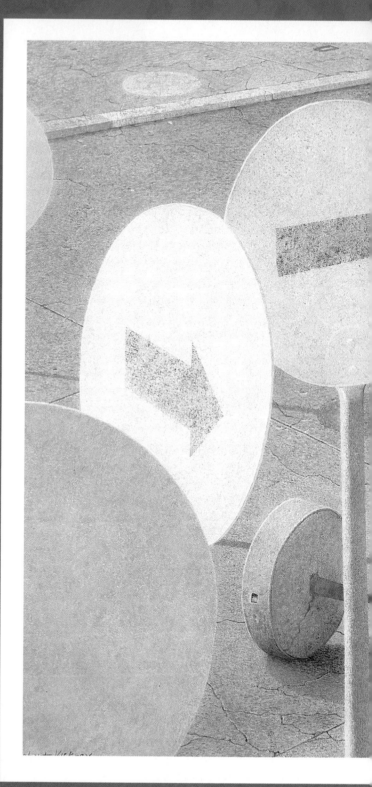

*Signs* (1961) by Robert Remsen Vickrey.
Tempera on board (27¾" × 41¾").

## AFTER TWENTY YEARS

## Make the Connection

### Do What's Right

Imagine that you write an advice column for your school newspaper. One day you receive this letter from someone in your school.

*Last Friday I saw my friend Lucy (not her real name) take a wallet that was left on the cafeteria table. I know she needs the money because her dad is between jobs. I don't know what to do! I mean, I want to do what's right—but I don't know how to handle this. She's just never done anything like this before.*

*Sincerely,*
*Confused and Can't Sleep*

## Quickwrite

In a letter, advise "Confused and Can't Sleep." How would you suggest she resolve her problem?

## Elements of Literature

### Foreshadowing

O. Henry is famous for writing stories with surprise endings. When most readers finish one of his stories, they like to go back to see if he dropped any clues that should have helped them **predict** how the story was going to end. These clues planted in a story are called **foreshadowing**.

## Reading Skills and Strategies

### Attacking Strange Words

O. Henry loved long words and fancy words. (He read dictionaries for pleasure!) For example, in the second paragraph of this story, he says "pacific thoroughfare." Most people would just say "peaceful street." You can figure out some of O. Henry's difficult words by examining their structure, by looking at **context clues,** or by thinking of words that the unfamiliar word resembles. *Pacific,* for example, resembles *pacifist,* "a person who loves peace." It also resembles *pacifier,* the device you give babies to keep them peaceful.

As you read "After Twenty Years," keep a sheet of paper next to each page so that you can record your thoughts.

> **F**oreshadowing is the use of clues to hint at events that will happen later in a story.
>
> *For more on Foreshadowing, see the Handbook of Literary Terms.*

Pause after the sixth paragraph, after the face of the man in the doorway is revealed. From the description of this man, what do you guess he is like? What do you **predict** is going to happen next? One student's comments appear on the first page, showing her "dialogue with the text."

**HRW** go.hrw.com
*LEO 7-3*

Inset, *The City from Greenwich Village* (1922) by John Sloan. Oil on canvas.

Inset, Gift of Helen Farr Sloan, © 1998 Board of Trustees, National Gallery of Art, Washington, D.C.

Background image, Courtesy of The Valentine Museum, Richmond, Virginia.

# After Twenty Years

**O. Henry**

*"We agreed that we would meet here again exactly twenty years from that date and time . . ."*

The policeman on the beat moved up the avenue impressively. The impressiveness was <u>habitual</u> and not for show, for spectators were few. The time was barely ten o'clock at night, but chilly gusts of wind with a taste of rain in them had well nigh depeopled the streets.

Trying doors as he went, twirling his club with many <u>intricate</u> and artful movements, turning now and then to cast his watchful eye down the pacific[1] thoroughfare, the officer, with his stalwart form and slight swagger, made a fine picture of a guardian of the peace. The vicinity was one that kept early hours. Now and then you might see the lights of a cigar store or of an all-night lunch counter, but the majority of the doors belonged to business places that had long since been closed.

When about midway of a certain block, the policeman suddenly slowed his walk. In the doorway of a darkened hardware store a man leaned with an unlighted cigar in his mouth. As the policeman walked up to him, the man spoke up quickly.

"It's all right, officer," he said reassuringly. "I'm just waiting for a friend. It's an appointment made twenty years ago. Sounds a little funny to you, doesn't it? Well, I'll explain if you'd like to make certain it's all straight. About that long ago there used to be a restaurant where this store stands— 'Big Joe' Brady's restaurant."

"Until five years ago," said the policeman. "It was torn down then."

The man in the doorway struck a match and lit his cigar. The light showed a pale, square-jawed face with keen eyes and a little white scar near his right eyebrow. His scarf pin was a large diamond, oddly set.

"Twenty years ago tonight," said the man, "I dined here at 'Big Joe' Brady's with Jimmy Wells, my best chum and the finest chap in the world. He and I were raised here in New York, just like two brothers, together. I was eighteen and Jimmy was twenty. The next morning I was to start for the West to make my fortune. You couldn't have dragged Jimmy out of New York; he thought it was the only place on earth.

1. **pacific:** here, peaceful.

---

## WORDS TO OWN
**habitual** (hə·bich′oō·əl) *adj.*: done or fixed by habit; customary.
**intricate** (in′tri·kit) *adj.*: complicated; full of detail.

---

**Dialogue with the Text**

What was impressive about the policeman?

Does this take place in a city?

Were these movements what made him impressive?

He was obviously an experienced "guardian of the peace."

Did he slow his walk because of apprehension or curiosity?

Why did the man assume that the policeman was going to question him and that he needed to supply an answer before a question was even asked?

The man is obviously familiar with the town.

Has the policeman let down his guard?

Extremely descriptive—gives a nice picture of the man in a few sentences.

—Hester Reed
The Dutchess Day School
Millbrook, New York

Well, we agreed that night that we would meet here again exactly twenty years from that date and time, no matter what our conditions might be or from what distance we might have to come. We figured that in twenty years each of us ought to have our destiny worked out and our fortunes made, whatever they were going to be."

"It sounds pretty interesting," said the policeman. "Rather a long time between meets, though, it seems to me. Haven't you heard from your friend since you left?"

"Well, yes, for a time we corresponded," said the other. "But after a year or two we lost track of each other. You see, the West is a pretty big proposition, and I kept hustling around over it pretty lively. But I know Jimmy will meet me here if he's alive, for he always was the truest, staunchest old chap in the world. He'll never forget. I came a thousand miles to stand in this door tonight, and it's worth it if my old partner turns up."

The waiting man pulled out a handsome watch, the lids of it set with small diamonds.

"Three minutes to ten," he announced. "It was exactly ten o'clock when we parted here at the restaurant door."

"Did pretty well out West, didn't you?" asked the policeman.

"You bet! I hope Jimmy has done half as well. He was a kind of plodder, though, good fellow as he was. I've had to compete with some of the sharpest wits going to get my pile. A man gets in a groove in New York. It takes the West to put a razor edge on him."

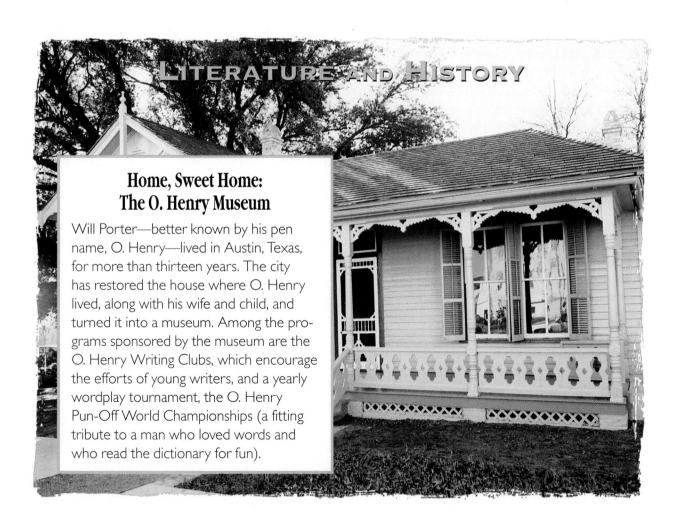

LITERATURE AND HISTORY

### Home, Sweet Home: The O. Henry Museum

Will Porter—better known by his pen name, O. Henry—lived in Austin, Texas, for more than thirteen years. The city has restored the house where O. Henry lived, along with his wife and child, and turned it into a museum. Among the programs sponsored by the museum are the O. Henry Writing Clubs, which encourage the efforts of young writers, and a yearly wordplay tournament, the O. Henry Pun-Off World Championships (a fitting tribute to a man who loved words and who read the dictionary for fun).

The policeman twirled his club and took a step or two.

"I'll be on my way. Hope your friend comes around all right. Going to call time on him sharp?"

"I should say not!" said the other. "I'll give him half an hour at least. If Jimmy is alive on earth, he'll be here by that time. So long, officer."

"Good night, sir," said the policeman, passing on along his beat, trying doors as he went.

There was now a fine, cold drizzle falling, and the wind had risen from its uncertain puffs into a steady blow. The few foot passengers astir in that quarter hurried <u>dismally</u> and silently along with coat collars turned high and pocketed hands. And in the door of the hardware store the man who had come a thousand miles to fill an appointment, uncertain almost to absurdity, with the friend of his youth, smoked his cigar and waited.

About twenty minutes he waited, and then a tall man in a long overcoat, with collar turned up to his ears, hurried across from the opposite side of the street. He went directly to the waiting man.

"Is that you, Bob?" he asked, doubtfully.

"Is that you, Jimmy Wells?" cried the man in the door.

"Bless my heart!" exclaimed the new arrival, grasping both the other's hands with his own. "It's Bob, sure as fate. I was certain I'd find you here if you were still in existence. Well, well, well!—twenty years is a long time. The old restaurant's gone, Bob; I wish it had lasted, so we could have had another dinner there. How has the West treated you, old man?"

"Bully;[2] it has given me everything I asked it for. You've changed lots, Jimmy. I never thought you were so tall by two or three inches."

"Oh, I grew a bit after I was twenty."

"Doing well in New York, Jimmy?"

2. **bully:** informal term meaning "very well."

"Moderately. I have a position in one of the city departments. Come on, Bob; we'll go around to a place I know of and have a good long talk about old times."

The two men started up the street, arm in arm. The man from the West, his <u>egotism</u> enlarged by success, was beginning to outline the history of his career. The other, submerged in his overcoat, listened with interest.

At the corner stood a drugstore, brilliant with electric lights. When they came into this

glare, each of them turned <u>simultaneously</u> to gaze upon the other's face.

The man from the West stopped suddenly and released his arm.

"You're not Jimmy Wells," he snapped. "Twenty years is a long time, but not long enough to change a man's nose from a Roman to a pug."

"It sometimes changes a good man into a bad one," said the tall man. "You've been under arrest for ten minutes, 'Silky' Bob. Chicago thinks you may have dropped over our way and wires us she wants to have a chat with you. Going quietly, are you? That's sensible. Now, before we go to the station, here's a note I was asked to hand to you. You may read it here at the window. It's from Patrolman Wells."

The man from the West unfolded the little piece of paper handed him. His hand was steady when he began to read, but it trembled a little by the time he had finished. The note was rather short.

> Bob: I was at the appointed place on time. When you struck the match to light your cigar, I saw it was the face of the man wanted in Chicago. Somehow I couldn't do it myself, so I went around and got a plainclothes man to do the job.
>
> Jimmy

---

## WORDS TO OWN

**simultaneously** (sī′məl·tā′nē·əs·lē) *adv.*: at the same time.

---

## MEET THE WRITER

### "Stories in Everything"

**O. Henry** (1862–1910) is the pen name of William Sydney Porter, who was born in Greensboro, North Carolina. He left school at fifteen and eventually moved to Texas. There he edited a humor magazine called *The Rolling Stone* and worked for a few years in a bank in Austin. Unfortunately, Porter was a careless record keeper. Two years after he left the bank, he was accused of embezzling its money. Although he was probably innocent, Porter panicked and ran off to Honduras. A year or so later, he returned to Austin to be with his dying wife. There, he was convicted and spent three years in a federal prison in Ohio.

Porter found the plots of many of his stories (including "After Twenty Years") in jail. He may also have found his famous pen name there: The name of a prison guard was Orrin Henry.

After he was released from prison in 1901, Porter moved to New York. Soon, as O. Henry, he became one of the country's most popular short-story writers. His stories are known for their snappy surprise endings. Many of his best-known stories are set in New York's streets and tenements and cheap hotels.

One day, while O. Henry was dining with friends at a New York restaurant, a young writer asked him where he got his plots. "Oh, everywhere," replied O. Henry. "There are stories in everything." He picked up the menu on which the dishes of the day were typewritten. "There's a story in this," he said. And then he outlined the story called "Springtime à la Carte." (On menus, *à la carte* means that each item is priced separately.)

### More from the Pen of O. Henry

"After Twenty Years" is from a collection called *The Four Million and Other Stories* (Airmont). This title refers to the population of New York City in O. Henry's day. Other O. Henry stories set in New York include "The Gift of the Magi" and "The Last Leaf."

# The Pitch That Didn't Work

"Steeeeriiike two!" called the umpire.

"Way to go, Joe!" Sam yelled out of his thick catcher's mask. Sam was always on the bright side of things. Even when he went zero for four, made two errors behind the plate, and his team was losing by five runs, he would still have a positive attitude and continue to try, despite the obviousness of his not being a good athlete.

Joe stared down as Sam gave the sign for the curve. Joe shook it off because he always wanted to put on the heat with two strikes.

"Time!" yelled Joe. "Listen," he said as Sam came out to meet him on the mound, "I'll throw what I want to throw! If I want to throw heat, I'll do it!" Joe had always been very stubborn and very critical. He didn't have one friend in the world besides Sam, who looked up to him as the star pitcher of the league for three years in a row but who also relied on him to be his friend. There was an odd relationship between the two, but somehow they had always worked it out one way or another.

Sam returned to home plate, a little frustrated that Joe wouldn't listen to him but knowing it wasn't anything new, as Joe did this all the time.

"Let's fire it in here, buddy!" yelled Sam.

Joe kicked up, released, and as the fastball came out, there was a loud crack of the bat. As Sammy had foreseen, Brad Newsome, a fifteen-year-old and the biggest player in the league, crushed it deep to left-center field. Everyone knew it was gone.

This was the first game Joe had lost this whole year, and Joe blamed it on Sam for stirring everything up.

At the end of the inning, Joe and Sam's coach, Harvey Mulock, gave a lecture to the team, who were sulking around the dugout. He chewed them out about how they had to get their attitudes straightened out, and after that he took Joe and Sam outside the dugout to have a private talk.

"Which one of you is responsible for the home run by Brad Newsome? If it just got away and it was a mistake, then tell me, Joe, why did you give him that pitch? You know better."

"It was my fault, Coach Mulock," answered Sam. "I gave the wrong sign when I knew that Brad grooves on fastballs, and I just wasn't thinking. I'm really sorry."

"That's OK; just try to get things worked out on what you're going to throw before you do it."

*Phew,* was what was going through both Joe's and Sam's heads. Joe knew he had done the wrong thing and not spoken up, but then again, he thought to himself, if Sam's going to stick up for me and apologize even though it was really my fault, then let him be that stupid. I'm not going to stop him.

After the game, Joe and Sam walked off together as always, Sam carrying the bats, balls, and gloves, and Joe carrying nothing.

—Michael Levitin
Forestville School
Forestville, California

# MAKING MEANINGS

## First Thoughts

1. What would you have done if you'd been in Jimmy's situation? Talk about whether or not you think he did the right thing.

## Shaping Interpretations

2. Two old friends keep an appointment made twenty years earlier. What does the fact that they both turn up say about their friendship?

3. Why did the police officer need to know if the man would wait for his friend or "call time on him sharp"? What do you think the officer would have done if the man had said he would leave at ten o'clock?

4. Did you guess who the police officer was? Go back to the text and find clues that hint at, or **foreshadow,** something sinister about the man in the doorway.

5. Jimmy Wells had an **internal conflict:** He had to decide what to do about his friend. How did he resolve his problem? Why do you think he didn't do the job himself?

## Connecting with the Text

6. Take a look at the advice you gave to "Confused and Can't Sleep" in your Quickwrite notes. What do you think Jimmy Wells would say about your advice?

7. "After Twenty Years" and "The Pitch That Didn't Work" (page 198) raise interesting questions about friendship. What do you think of Joe and Sam's friendship? How should friends treat one another?

### Reading Check

a. Why had the stranger come back to the old neighborhood after twenty years?

b. What did the police officer realize when the man in the doorway lit his cigar?

c. What had the man from the West done to make his fortune?

d. What did the police officer do after saying good night to the man in the doorway?

Courtesy of the Valentine Museum, Richmond, Virginia.

# CHOICES: Building Your Portfolio

## Writer's Notebook

### 1. Collecting Ideas for Supporting a Position

Jimmy Wells took a stand. He did what he thought was the right thing, even though he had to betray someone who had been like a brother to him. If you knew that your best friend had done something wrong, what would you do? Think about a situation like this that you might face. Take a few minutes to describe the situation. Then, take a position, and list some reasons supporting it.

> My best friend told me a secret about another friend. I think my other friend should know. If I tell, my best friend will be mad.

## News Article

### 2. Cop Busts Best Buddy

New York, 1906—You are a reporter for the *New York World,* the newspaper O. Henry once worked for. You cover the police beat, and you hear the story of Jimmy Wells and his chum "Silky" Bob from the plain-clothes man who brought Bob in. Write an article about it for the morning edition. A news story should answer these questions at the beginning of the article:

- *What* happened?
- *Who* was involved?
- *Why* did it happen?
- *When* and *where* did it happen?
- *How* did it happen?

## Speaking/Using Another Point of View

### 3. "I'd Traveled a Thousand Miles ..."

Retell "After Twenty Years" from Bob's point of view. Imagine you are "Silky" Bob talking to a fellow prisoner, telling the story of how you got caught by your old friend Jimmy Wells. Tape-record your account the first time you tell it. Then, play back the tape, and polish your wording and your delivery until you're ready to tell the class "Silky" Bob's story.

## Performance/Radio Play

### 4. Play It by Ear

With a group of four class-mates, read "After Twenty Years" aloud as if you were performing a radio play. One of you can be the nar-rator. Three can read the parts of Bob, Jimmy Wells, and the plainclothes man. The fifth person can do sound effects—wind, foot-steps, and the striking of a match—at the points where they're heard in the story. Practice varying the loudness and softness of your voice. When you've got it just right, tape-record your performance. Take turns giving the tape to schoolmates, family, and friends to listen to.

# GRAMMAR LINK    MINI-LESSON

**Language Handbook HELP**

*See Sentences Classified by Purpose, pages 759–760; End Marks, page 768.*

**Technology HELP**

*See* Language Workshop CD-ROM. *Key word entry: end marks.*

## End All End-Mark Errors

If you mean yes, nod and you'll be understood—unless you're in Turkey, where a nod means no. Every language has its own conventions, or accepted rules. In written English the accepted rule states that every sentence must begin with a capital letter and end with one of these **end marks:** a period, a question mark, or an exclamation point. Follow these simple rules:

1. Use a period at the end of a statement.

   EXAMPLE    "It's an appointment made twenty years ago."

2. Use a question mark at the end of a question.

   EXAMPLE    "Is that you, Bob?"

3. Use an exclamation point at the end of an exclamation or a command.

   EXAMPLES    "You bet!"
   "Bless my heart!"

### Try It Out

Rewrite the following paragraph, adding capitalization and end punctuation marks. (The paragraph contains a total of seven sentences.)

Charlie tried out for the baseball team what did he have to lose it's not as if you have to be Ken Griffey, Jr., to play a position who imagined what would happen it was such a surprise unbelievably, he's hitting lead-off I guess you never know

# VOCABULARY    HOW TO OWN A WORD

**WORD BANK**

*habitual*
*intricate*
*dismally*
*egotism*
*simultaneously*

## Attacking Strange Words

When you come across a word you don't know, ask yourself these questions: First, are there any clues in the **context,** the surrounding words and sentences, that might help me guess the word's meaning? Second, does the strange word sound like a familiar word?

Try to guess the meaning of *habitual* from this sentence on page 194: "The policeman on the beat moved up the avenue impressively. The impressiveness was *habitual* and not for show, for spectators were few."

The first clue is that *habitual* looks and sounds like *habit,* which means "usual way of doing something." The second clue is in the sentence itself. We learn that the police officer doesn't move impressively just to show off. It is a habit with him.

How are you at building in clues? Write five sentences about the story using the Word Bank words. Fill the sentences with context clues.

# Elements of Literature

## POINT OF VIEW: Through Whose Eyes? *by* John Leggett

When you were little, you probably imagined at one time or another that there was something terrifying under your bed. Did it ever occur to you that that something might find *you* just as terrifying? As the saying goes, "It all depends on your point of view." When you're telling a story, you look at things one way—your way. When someone else tells the story, he or she will put a slightly different spin on the same events.

Novels and short stories are also told from a particular **point of view,** or vantage point. When you're reading, you should ask, "Who is the narrator?" and "What is the narrator's relationship to the story?"

### The Big Three

The three most common points of view are the omniscient, the first person, and the third-person limited.

The **omniscient** (äm·nish′ənt) **point of view** is the all-knowing point of view. (In Latin, *omnis* means "all" and *sciens* means "knowing.")

**THE FAR SIDE**     By GARY LARSON

*"I've got it again, Larry . . . an eerie feeling there's something on top of the bed."*

You can think of an omniscient narrator as being above the action, looking down on it like a god. This narrator can tell you everything about all the characters, even their most private thoughts.

Once upon a time there lived a princess who would have been perfectly happy except for one thing: In a moment of weakness, she had promised to marry a frog.

Her father felt sorry for her, but he insisted that she keep her word. (In fact, he was a little nervous—he'd never met a talking frog before.) "After all, a promise is a promise," agreed her mother, who thought the frog was better looking than the princess's last boyfriend. Little did any of the royal family know who the frog really was.

A story can also be told by one of the characters. In this viewpoint the character speaks as "I." We call this the **first-person point of view.** ("I" is the first-person pronoun.) In this point of view, we know only what this one character can tell us. Sometimes that isn't very reliable.

I couldn't believe that my parents were actually going to make me marry a slimy, ugly, bulgy-eyed frog! They didn't feel sorry for me at all! All they cared about was a stupid promise I never thought I'd have to keep.

Often a story is seen through the eyes of one character, but the character is *not* telling the story as "I." This is called the **third-person limited point of view.** In this point of view, a narrator zooms in on the thoughts and feelings of just one character in the story. This point of view helps us share that character's reactions to the story's events.

The princess tried desperately to get out of her promise. It was all her parents' fault, she thought. They were so unfair. But she had a nagging feeling that she had only herself to blame—and the frog. "I wonder if the royal chef knows how to cook frogs' legs?" she said to herself.

Point of view is very important in storytelling, and writers love to experiment with it. Someone who wanted to tell the frog-and-princess story from a really unusual point of view might choose to let the frog tell it.

*"Personally, I can't imagine what he sees in her."*

# Reading Skills and Strategies

Booking space on the Net: Used-booksellers take a page from other on-line vendors

## MAKING PREDICTIONS: FORECASTING MORE THAN JUST THE WEATHER

One reason we get pulled into good stories is that as we get more and more caught up in the plot, we crank up our antennas and begin to make predictions. The process of making predictions is simply forecasting what will happen next. Think about your own process of making predictions as you read these two story beginnings.

ZIGGY

STORY A    The young campers have just settled down to cook the trout they caught in the lake. (What do you predict will happen next?)

STORY B    "I'm famished," said the bear to himself as he watched the young campers building a fire to cook their hard-won trout. (What do you predict happens next?)

### I Told You So

Weather forecasters base their predictions on prior knowledge of things like cloud formations and barometric pressure. Good readers constantly add their **prior knowledge** to what they are reading to make good educated guesses. An interesting story will constantly trigger **predictions.** The reader adjusts those predictions as he or she continues reading the text. A chart of this process of predicting and adjusting might look like this:

| Prior Knowledge | + | Prediction | + | Information from Text | = | Adjusted Prediction |

You've been making and confirming and adjusting predictions ever since you began to listen to bedtime stories as a child. As you read "A Mason-Dixon Memory," practice your predicting strategies. Ask yourself if the events are turning out the way you thought they would. Can you make new predictions as you read more of the selection? Making and confirming and adjusting predictions is a process you can engage in right up to the end of the story.

**Apply the strategy on the next page.**

# *Before You Read*

## Make the Connection

### What If . . . ?

How far would you go to "do the right thing"? Think of something you really care about. It could be a possession. It could be an event you're looking forward to—a party, a tournament, or a field trip—anything you'd hate to give up. Talk with a partner about the thing you really value, and then have your partner tell you about what he or she values.

## Quickwrite

Think about your partner's choice, and imagine situations in which making the right choice could mean that your partner would have to give up the thing he or she prizes so much. Write a brief *what if* question for your partner—for example, "What if going to the party means you have to break a date with a friend who wasn't invited?"

go.hrw.com
*LEO 7-3*

## Elements of Literature

### Flashback: We Interrupt This Story . . .

Most stories are written in **chronological order**—the writer tells about events in the order they happen. Just as Clifton Davis starts his story, though, he remembers a childhood experience. He interrupts his story with a **flashback** that takes you back to earlier times and events in his life. The flashback and the main story are connected: They both tell about people who "did the right thing."

> A **flashback** is a scene that breaks the normal time order of a plot to show a past event.
>
> *For more on Flashback, see the Handbook of Literary Terms.*

## Reading Skills and Strategies

### Making and Confirming Predictions

As you read this story, do some guesswork about what will happen. Remember, the best thing about guessing or predicting is that you can always change your prediction (and often should) once you've read more of the story. Put a slip of paper on this page to hold your place. Briefly respond to the questions that follow as you reach the points in the story marked by the star, square, triangle, diamond, and circle.

★ Look at the title and the illustrations. What do you think this story will be about? What do you know about the Mason-Dixon line?

■ What do you think will happen? What will the seniors' response be?

▲ Does your prior knowledge from guessing about the title of the story match what you now know? Will Clifton get to go to the amusement park?

◆ What do you predict these characters will do? (Think about what you already know about their friendship.)

● Confirm your predictions about what the seniors' response will be. How does what really happened compare with your prediction?

# A Mason-Dixon Memory*

**Clifton Davis**

Sponsor: Fred Matte

Dondré Green

Damon Marsala

Jef McN

"If we leave, we forfeit this tournament.

If we stay, Dondré can't play."

Golf team photograph from the 1991 *Warrior* yearbook.

Dondré Green glanced uneasily at the civic leaders and sports figures filling the hotel ballroom in Cleveland. They had come from across the nation to attend a fund-raiser for the National Minority College Golf Scholarship Foundation. I was the banquet's featured entertainer. Dondré, an eighteen-year-old high school senior from Monroe, Louisiana, was the evening's honored guest.

"Nervous?" I asked the handsome young man in his starched white shirt and rented tuxedo.

"A little," he whispered, grinning.

One month earlier, Dondré had been just one more black student attending a predominantly white Southern school. Although most of his friends and classmates were white, Dondré's race had never been an issue. Then, on April 17, 1991, Dondré's black skin provoked an incident that made nationwide news.

"Ladies and gentlemen," the emcee[1] said, "our special guest, Dondré Green."

As the audience stood applauding, Dondré walked to the microphone and began his story. "I love golf," he said quietly. "For the past two years, I've been a member of the St. Frederick High School golf team. And though I was the only black member, I've always felt at home playing at the mostly white country clubs across Louisiana."

The audience leaned forward; even the waiters and busboys stopped to listen. As I listened, a memory buried in my heart since childhood began fighting its way to life.

"Our team had driven from Monroe," Dondré continued. "When we arrived at the Caldwell Parish Country Club in Columbia, we walked to the putting green."

Dondré and his teammates were too absorbed to notice the conversation between a man and St. Frederick athletic director James Murphy. After disappearing into the clubhouse, Murphy returned to his players.

"I want to see the seniors," he said. "On the double!" His face seemed strained as he gathered the four students, including Dondré.

"I don't know how to tell you this," he said, "but the Caldwell Parish Country Club is reserved for whites only." Murphy paused and looked at Dondré. His teammates glanced at each other in disbelief. "I want you seniors to decide what our response should be," Murphy continued. "If we leave, we forfeit this tournament. If we stay, Dondré can't play." ■

As I listened, my own childhood memory from thirty-two years ago broke free.

In 1959 I was thirteen years old, a poor black kid living with my mother and stepfather in a small black ghetto on Long Island, New York. My mother worked nights in a hospital, and my stepfather drove a coal truck. Needless to say, our standard of living was somewhat short of the American dream.

Nevertheless, when my eighth-grade teacher announced a graduation trip to Washington, D.C., it never crossed my mind that I would be left behind. Besides a complete tour of the nation's capital, we would visit Glen Echo Amusement Park in Maryland. In my imagination, Glen Echo was Disneyland, Knott's Berry Farm, and Magic Mountain rolled into one.

My heart beating wildly, I raced home to deliver the mimeographed letter describing the journey. But when my mother saw how much the trip would cost, she just shook her head. We couldn't afford it.

After feeling sad for ten seconds, I decided to try to fund the trip myself. For the next eight weeks, I sold candy bars door-to-door, delivered newspapers, and mowed lawns. Three

1. **emcee** (em′sē′): master of ceremonies.

---

**WORDS TO OWN**

**civic** (siv′ik) *adj.*: of a city or citizenship.
**predominantly** (prē·däm′ə·nənt·lē) *adv.*: mainly.

---

days before the deadline, I'd made just barely enough. I was going!

The day of the trip, trembling with excitement, I climbed onto the train. I was the only nonwhite in our section.

Our hotel was not far from the White House. My roommate was Frank Miller, the son of a businessman. Leaning together out of our window and dropping water balloons on passing tourists quickly cemented our new friendship.

Every morning, almost a hundred of us loaded noisily onto our bus for another adventure. We sang our school fight song dozens of times—en route[2] to Arlington National Cemetery and even on an afternoon cruise down the Potomac River.

We visited the Lincoln Memorial twice, once in daylight, the second time at dusk. My classmates and I fell silent as we walked in the shadows of those thirty-six marble columns, one for every state in the Union that Lincoln labored to preserve. I stood next to Frank at the base of the nineteen-foot seated statue. Spotlights made the white Georgian marble seem to glow. Together, we read those famous words from Lincoln's speech at Gettysburg, remembering the most bloody battle in the War Between the States: ". . . we here highly <u>resolve</u> that these dead shall not have died in vain—that this nation, under God, shall have a new birth of freedom. . . ."

As Frank motioned me into place to take my picture, I took one last look at Lincoln's face. He seemed alive and so terribly sad.

The next morning I understood a little better why he wasn't smiling. "Clifton," a chaperone said, "could I see you for a moment?"

The other guys at my table, especially Frank, turned pale. We had been joking about the previous night's direct water-balloon hit on a fat lady and her poodle. It was a stupid, dangerous act, but luckily nobody got hurt. We were celebrating our escape from punishment when the chaperone asked to see me.

2. **en route** (en ro͞ot′): on the way.

"Clifton," she began, "do you know about the Mason-Dixon line?"

"No," I said, wondering what this had to do with drenching fat ladies.

"Before the Civil War," she explained, "the Mason-Dixon line was originally the boundary between Maryland and Pennsylvania—the dividing line between the slave and free states." Having escaped one disaster, I could feel another brewing. I noticed that her eyes were damp and her hands shaking.

"Today," she continued, "the Mason-Dixon line is a kind of invisible border between the North and the South. When you cross that invisible line out of Washington, D.C., into Maryland, things change."

There was an <u>ominous</u> drift to this conversation, but I wasn't following it. Why did she look and sound so nervous? ▲

"Glen Echo Amusement Park is in Maryland," she said at last, "and the management doesn't allow Negroes inside." She stared at me in silence.

I was still grinning and nodding when the meaning finally sank in. "You mean I can't go to the park," I stuttered, "because I'm a Negro?"

She nodded slowly. "I'm sorry, Clifton," she said, taking my hand. "You'll have to stay in the hotel tonight. Why don't you and I watch a movie on television?"

I walked to the elevators feeling confusion, disbelief, anger, and a deep sadness. "What happened, Clifton?" Frank said when I got back to the room. "Did the fat lady tell on us?"

Without saying a word, I walked over to my bed, lay down, and began to cry. Frank was stunned into silence. Junior-high boys didn't cry, at least not in front of each other.

It wasn't just missing the class adventure that made me feel so sad. For the first time in

**WORDS TO OWN**

**resolve** (ri·zälv′) v.: decide; make a formal statement.
**ominous** (äm′ə·nəs) adj.: threatening, like a bad sign; warning of something bad.

my life, I was learning what it felt like to be a "nigger." Of course there was discrimination in the North, but the color of my skin had never officially kept me out of a coffee shop, a church—or an amusement park.

"Clifton," Frank whispered, "what is the matter?"

"They won't let me go to Glen Echo Park tonight," I sobbed.

"Because of the water balloon?" he asked.

"No," I answered, "because I'm a Negro."

"Well, that's a relief!" Frank said, and then he laughed, obviously relieved to have escaped punishment for our caper with the balloons. "I thought it was serious!"

Wiping away the tears with my sleeve, I stared at him. "It *is* serious. They don't let Negroes into the park. I can't go with you!" I shouted. "That's pretty serious to me." ◆

I was about to wipe the silly grin off Frank's face with a blow to his jaw when I heard him say, "Then I won't go either."

For an instant we just froze. Then Frank grinned. I will never forget that moment. Frank was just a kid. He wanted to go to that amusement park as much as I did, but there was something even more important than the class night out. Still, he didn't explain or expand.

The next thing I knew, the room was filled with kids listening to Frank. "They don't allow Negroes in the park," he said, "so I'm staying with Clifton."

"Me too," a second boy said.

"Those jerks," a third muttered. "I'm with you, Clifton." My heart began to race. Suddenly, I was not alone. A pint-sized revolution had been born. The "water-balloon brigade," eleven white boys from Long Island, had made its decision: "We won't go." And as I sat on my bed in the center of it all, I felt grateful. But above all, I was filled with pride.

Dondré Green's story brought that childhood memory back to life. His golfing teammates, like my childhood friends, had an important decision to make. Standing by their friend would cost them dearly. But when it came time to decide, no one hesitated. "Let's get out of here," one of them whispered.

"They just turned and walked toward the van," Dondré told us. "They didn't debate it. And the younger players joined us without looking back." ●

Dondré was astounded by the response of his friends—and the people of Louisiana. The whole state was outraged and tried to make it right. The Louisiana House of Representatives proclaimed a Dondré Green Day and passed legislation permitting lawsuits for damages, attorneys' fees, and court costs against any private facility that invites a team, then bars any member because of race.

As Dondré concluded, his eyes glistened with tears. "I love my coach and my teammates for sticking by me," he said. "It goes to show that there are always good people who will not give in to bigotry. The kind of love they showed me that day will conquer hatred every time."

Suddenly, the banquet crowd was standing, applauding Dondré Green.

My friends, too, had shown that kind of love. As we sat in the hotel, a chaperone came in waving an envelope. "Boys!" he shouted. "I've just bought thirteen tickets to the Senators-Tigers game. Anybody want to go?"

The room erupted in cheers. Not one of us had ever been to a professional baseball game in a real baseball park.

On the way to the stadium, we grew silent as our driver paused before the Lincoln Memorial. For one long moment, I stared through the marble pillars at Mr. Lincoln, bathed in that

---

**WORDS TO OWN**
erupted (ē·rup′tid) v.: exploded or burst forth.

---

warm yellow light. There was still no smile and no sign of hope in his sad and tired eyes.

". . . we here highly resolve . . . that this nation, under God, shall have a new birth of freedom. . . ."

In his words and in his life, Lincoln had made it clear that freedom is not free. Every time the color of a person's skin keeps him out of an amusement park or off a country-club fairway, the war for freedom begins again. Sometimes the battle is fought with fists and guns, but more often the most effective weapon is a simple act of love and courage.

Whenever I hear those words from Lincoln's speech at Gettysburg, I remember my eleven white friends, and I feel hope once again. I like to imagine that when we paused that night at the foot of his great monument, Mr. Lincoln smiled at last. As Dondré said, "The kind of love they showed me that day will conquer hatred every time."

## MEET THE WRITER

### A Man of Many Talents

**Clifton Davis** (1946–      ) may be better known for writing tunes than for writing prose. He wrote the song "Never Can Say Goodbye," which sold two million records. He's still involved with music today, as a composer, recording artist, and host of a gospel-music radio program.

Besides being a singer and a songwriter, Clifton Davis is an actor. He has acted in several plays on Broadway and received a Tony nomination for his performance in *Two Gentlemen of Verona*. Davis has also appeared in movies and TV shows. The role he is best known for is Reverend Reuben Gregory on the television series *Amen*. The curious thing about casting Davis in the role of the minister is that he really *is* a minister, in the Seventh-Day Adventist Church.

Davis believes it's important to do what's right, even if you're making a living amid the glitz and glamour of Hollywood.

# Buddies Bare Their Affection for Ill Classmate

OCEANSIDE, California, March 19 (Associated Press)—In Mr. Alter's fifth-grade class, it's difficult to tell which boy is undergoing chemotherapy. Nearly all the boys are bald. Thirteen of them shaved their heads so a sick buddy wouldn't feel out of place.

"If everybody has their head shaved, sometimes people don't know who's who. They don't know who has cancer and who just shaved their head," said eleven-year-old Scott Sebelius, one of the baldies at Lake Elementary School.

For the record, Ian O'Gorman is the sick one. Doctors recently removed a malignant tumor from his small intestine, and a week ago he started chemotherapy to treat the disease, called lymphoma.

"Besides surgery, I had tubes up my nose. I had butterflies in my stomach," said Ian, who'll have eight more weeks of chemotherapy in an effort to keep the cancer from returning.

Ian decided to get his head shaved before all his hair fell out in clumps. To his surprise, his friends wanted to join him.

"The last thing he would want is to not fit in, to be made fun of, so we just wanted to make him feel better and not left out," said ten-year-old Kyle Hanslik.

Kyle started talking to other boys about the idea, and then one of their parents started a list. Last week, they all went to the barber shop together.

"It's hard to put words to," said Ian's father, Shawn, choking back tears as he talked about the boys. "It's very emotional to think about kids like that who would come together, to have them do such a thing to support Ian."

The boy's teacher, Jim Alter, was so inspired that he, too, shaved his head.

Ian left the hospital March 2. Although he has lost twenty pounds and is pale, he is eager to get back to the business of being an eleven-year-old playing baseball and basketball. "I think I can start on Monday," he said.

—from the *Austin American-Statesman*

*Ian O'Gorman (center), who is undergoing chemotherapy for cancer, is surrounded by his classmates, who shaved their heads as a show of support.*

# MAKING MEANINGS

## First Thoughts

1. Finish these sentences:
   - If I were a teammate of Dondré Green's (or a classmate of Clifton Davis's), I would . . .
   - Being a friend means . . .

**Reading Check**

How were the experiences of Dondré Green and Clifton Davis alike? Fill in a chart like the one below to compare their experiences.

|       | Experience | Friends' Response |
|-------|------------|-------------------|
| Green |            |                   |
| Davis |            |                   |

## Shaping Interpretations

2. How did Dondré Green's teammates and the people of Louisiana react to the fact that he had been barred from the tournament? Why do you think Dondré was astounded by this response?

3. The narrator says there was "something even more important" than going to the amusement park. Frank never explained what that "something" was. How would you explain it?

4. Compare the actions of Dondré's coach and teammates with those of Ian O'Gorman's teacher and classmates (see *Connections* on page 212). In your opinion, which group sacrifices more than the other in order to "do the right thing"? Explain.

5. Where does the **flashback** begin and end? What does it have to do with the main story?

## Connecting with the Text

6. Have you or a friend ever felt unwelcome someplace? How did your experience compare with Clifton Davis's or Dondré Green's?

7. When has a friend ever done the right thing and stood by you? How did you feel?

8. Look back at the *what if* question you wrote for the Quickwrite on page 205. Did reading this story change the way you look at choices that might force you to give up something you value? If so, explain how and why.

9. Reflect on the **predicting** you did as you read the story. Compare your predictions with a partner's. Discuss the evidence from the story that led you to make those predictions. How much of your predicting was based on your own experiences with people?

## Challenging the Text

10. Green and Davis both believe that a simple act of love and courage is the most effective weapon against prejudice. Do you agree? Explain.

# CHOICES: Building Your Portfolio

## Writer's Notebook

### 1. Collecting Ideas for Supporting a Position

Many people devote their lives to fighting for important causes, such as civil rights. Think of some issues that *you* really care about. Try to come up with issues that matter to other people too. Write a sentence that identifies each issue and states your opinion of it. Then, list one or two supporting reasons.

> • All nuclear weapons should be destroyed.
> • Girls should be allowed to play football on school teams.

## Creative Writing

### 2. Love's the Thing

In a brief essay, write about a time when people showed that they cared about and supported someone who was different from them or who needed a helping hand. You can write about your own experience or the experience of someone you know or an incident in the news. (See *Connections* on page 212.) You might use one of these statements from "A Mason-Dixon Memory" as your opener:

- "... there are always good people...."
- "... love will conquer hatred...."

## Research

### 3. Questioning a Witness

Find the name of a person who participated in any way in the 1960s civil rights movement. (You might want to look in your social studies book.) Research what the person did and how working for civil rights might have affected what your subject achieved later in life. Once you've gathered your information, write down three questions that you'd like to ask the person. Make one question about the past, one about the present, and one about the future.

## Panel Discussion

### 4. A Color-Blind Society

Martin Luther King, Jr., the famous civil rights leader, once said, "Racial understanding is not something that we find but something that we must create." Do you think the United States can create a "color-blind" society? Can we make sure that Americans of different racial and ethnic backgrounds are all treated fairly? With a small group of classmates, form a team to research the subject. Use the Internet and news magazines as sources. Then, hold a panel discussion to present your findings and views.

# GRAMMAR LINK

## Commas Make Sense of a Series

**Language Handbook HELP**

*See Items in a Series, page 769.*

**Technology HELP**

*See Language Workshop CD-ROM. Key word entry: commas.*

1. Use commas to separate words, phrases, or clauses in a series.

   INCORRECT    Davis felt confusion disbelief anger and a deep sadness.

   CORRECT    Davis felt "confusion, disbelief, anger, and a deep sadness."

2. In most cases, use commas to separate two or more adjectives that come before a noun.

   INCORRECT    It was a stupid dangerous act.

   CORRECT    It was a stupid, dangerous act.

3. Do not place a comma between an adjective and a noun immediately following it.

   INCORRECT    Green's teammates made a fast, important, costly, decision.

   CORRECT    Green's teammates made a fast, important, costly decision.

4. If the last adjective in a series is closely connected in meaning to the noun, do not use a comma before that adjective.

   INCORRECT    Spotlights made the white, Georgian marble seem to glow.

   CORRECT    "Spotlights made the white Georgian marble seem to glow."

To decide whether a comma is needed, add the word *and* between the adjectives. If the *and* sounds strange, don't use a comma. ("White and Georgian marble" sounds strange, so don't use a comma.)

### Try It Out

Copy the sentences below. Add commas where necessary to separate the items in a series. Compare your answers with those of a partner.

1. Davis sold candy bars delivered newspapers and mowed lawns.

2. Lincoln's sad wise tired face impressed them.

3. Sincere courageous acts of love can conquer hatred.

4. They saw many famous national landmarks in Washington, D.C.

---

# VOCABULARY    HOW TO OWN A WORD

**WORD BANK**

*civic*
*predominantly*
*resolve*
*ominous*
*erupted*

## Synonyms: Shades of Meaning

Words with the same or almost the same meaning are called **synonyms.** Synonyms give different shades of meaning. A dictionary or a **thesaurus,** a book of synonyms, can help you pick exactly the word you need. Make a word map like the one below for the rest of the Word Bank words. Find two synonyms for each word, and put them all in a word map.

# *Before You Read*

## Make the Connection

### How Much Is It Worth to You?

Suppose there's something you think you just *have* to have. The trouble is you don't have the money to pay for it.

Look at some of the options listed below. Which would you do to get what you want?

1. Work and save until you can afford it.

2. Persuade a relative to give it to you.

3. Ask your parents for it.

4. Find a friend to share the item and help you pay for it.

5. Borrow the money, though you don't know how you'll pay it back.

## Quickwrite

Which of the options listed above are the most popular with your class? In a secret ballot, have classmates write down the numbers of the options they would choose. Work with several classmates to collect and tally the ballots. Ask the class whether they have additional ideas to suggest. Then, write a **summary** of the results.

## Elements of Literature

### Point of View

Every story you read, every story you tell, comes from a particular **point of view,** or vantage point. "The No-Guitar Blues" is told from the **third-person limited point of view.** This means that the narrator zooms in on the thoughts and feelings of just one character—in this case, Fausto. You'll get inside Fausto's head and share his thoughts and feelings. By the story's end you might feel that you know Fausto better than you know some of your friends.

> **P**oint of view is the vantage point from which a story is told.
>
> *For more on Point of View, see pages 202–203 and the Handbook of Literary Terms.*

## Reading Skills and Strategies

### Regional and Cultural Sayings: You Say "Potato," and I Say . . .

People from different backgrounds and cultures have different words for things. Sometimes they make mistakes and misunderstand one another. In this story, Fausto is confused by the word *turnover* (a pastry). He thinks it means he should turn something over. When he sees a turnover, he realizes that it looks exactly like a Mexican pastry called an *empanada.*

As you read the story, keep an eye out for more regional and cultural sayings.

Los Lobos (The Wolves), the popular rock group mentioned in the story.

go.hrw.com
LEO 7-3

# THE NO-GUITAR BLUES

**GARY SOTO**

Fausto had come this far, so he figured he might as well go through with it.

The moment Fausto saw the group Los Lobos on *American Bandstand,* he knew exactly what he wanted to do with his life—play guitar. His eyes grew large with excitement as Los Lobos ground out a song while teenagers bounced off each other on the crowded dance floor.

He had watched *American Bandstand* for years and had heard Ray Camacho and the Teardrops at Romain Playground, but it had never occurred to him that he too might become a musician. That afternoon Fausto knew his mission in life: to play guitar in his own band; to sweat out his songs and prance around the stage; to make money and dress weird.

Fausto turned off the television set and walked outside, wondering how he could get enough money to buy a guitar. He couldn't ask his parents because they would just say, "Money doesn't grow on trees" or "What do you think we are, bankers?" And besides, they hated rock music. They were into the *conjunto*[1] music of Lydia Mendoza, Flaco Jimenez, and Little Joe and La Familia. And, as Fausto recalled, the last album they bought was *The Chipmunks Sing Christmas Favorites.*

But what the heck, he'd give it a try. He returned inside and watched his mother make tortillas. He leaned against the kitchen counter, trying to work up the nerve to ask her for a guitar. Finally, he couldn't hold back any longer.

"Mom," he said, "I want a guitar for Christmas."

She looked up from rolling tortillas. "Honey, a guitar costs a lot of money."

"How 'bout for my birthday next year," he tried again.

"I can't promise," she said, turning back to her tortillas, "but we'll see."

Fausto walked back outside with a buttered tortilla. He knew his mother was right. His fa-

ther was a warehouseman at Berven Rugs, where he made good money but not enough to buy everything his children wanted. Fausto decided to mow lawns to earn money and was pushing the mower down the street before he realized it was winter and no one would hire him. He returned the mower and picked up a rake. He hopped onto his sister's bike (his had two flat tires) and rode north to the nicer section of Fresno in search of work. He went door-to-door, but after three hours he managed to get only one job, and not to rake leaves. He was asked to hurry down to the store to buy a loaf of bread, for which he received a grimy, dirt-caked quarter.

He also got an orange, which he ate sitting at the curb. While he was eating, a dog walked up and sniffed his leg. Fausto pushed him away and threw an orange peel skyward. The dog caught it and ate it in one gulp. The dog looked at Fausto and wagged his tail for more. Fausto tossed him a slice of orange, and the dog snapped it up and licked his lips.

"How come you like oranges, dog?"

The dog blinked a pair of sad eyes and whined.

"What's the matter? Cat got your tongue?" Fausto laughed at his joke and offered the dog another slice.

At that moment a dim light came on inside Fausto's head. He saw that it was sort of a fancy dog, a terrier or something, with dog tags and a shiny collar. And it looked well-fed and healthy. In his neighborhood, the dogs were never licensed, and if they got sick they were placed near the water heater until they got well.

This dog looked as if he belonged to rich people. Fausto cleaned his juice-sticky hands on his pants and got to his feet. The light in his head grew brighter. It just might work. He called the dog, patted its muscular back, and bent down to check the license.

"Great," he said. "There's an address."

The dog's name was Roger, which struck

---

**1. conjunto** (kôn·hōōn′tô): Northern Mexican polka music played with accordion, bass guitar, and drums.

Fausto as weird, because he'd never heard of a dog with a human name. Dogs should have names like Bomber, Freckles, Queenie, Killer, and Zero.

Fausto planned to take the dog home and collect a reward. He would say he had found Roger near the freeway. That would scare the daylights out of the owners, who would be so happy that they would probably give him a reward. He felt bad about lying, but the dog *was* loose. And it might even really be lost, because the address was six blocks away.

Fausto stashed the rake and his sister's bike behind a bush and, tossing an orange peel every time Roger became distracted, walked the dog to his house. He hesitated on the porch until Roger began to scratch the door with a muddy paw. Fausto had come this far, so he figured he might as well go through with it. He knocked softly. When no one answered, he rang the doorbell. A man in a silky bathrobe and slippers opened the door and seemed confused by the sight of his dog and the boy.

"Sir," Fausto said, gripping Roger by the collar. "I found your dog by the freeway. His dog license says he lives here." Fausto looked down at the dog, then up to the man. "He does, doesn't he?"

The man stared at Fausto a long time before saying in a pleasant voice, "That's right." He pulled his robe tighter around him because of the cold and asked Fausto to come in. "So he was by the freeway?"

"Uh-huh."

"You bad, snoopy dog," said the man, wagging his finger. "You probably knocked over some trash cans, too, didn't you?"

Fausto didn't say anything. He looked around, amazed by this house with its shiny furniture and a television as large as the front window at home. Warm bread smells filled the air and music full of soft tinkling floated in from another room.

"Helen," the man called to the kitchen. "We

have a visitor." His wife came into the living room, wiping her hands on a dish towel and smiling. "And who have we here?" she asked in one of the softest voices Fausto had ever heard.

"This young man said he found Roger near the freeway."

Fausto repeated his story to her while staring at a perpetual clock with a bell-shaped glass, the kind his aunt got when she celebrated her twenty-fifth anniversary. The lady frowned and said, wagging a finger at Roger, "Oh, you're a bad boy."

"It was very nice of you to bring Roger home," the man said. "Where do you live?"

"By that vacant lot on Olive," he said. "You know, by Brownie's Flower Place."

The wife looked at her husband, then Fausto. Her eyes twinkled triangles of light as she said, "Well, young man, you're probably hungry. How about a turnover?"

"What do I have to turn over?" Fausto asked, thinking she was talking about yardwork or something like turning trays of dried raisins.

"No, no, dear, it's a pastry." She took him by the elbow and guided him to a kitchen that sparkled with copper pans and bright yellow wallpaper. She guided him to the kitchen table and gave him a tall glass of milk and something that looked like an empanada.[2] Steamy waves of heat escaped when he tore it in two. He ate with both eyes on the man and woman, who stood arm in arm smiling at him. They were strange, he thought. But nice.

"That was good," he said after he finished the turnover. "Did you make it, ma'am?"

"Yes, I did. Would you like another?"

"No, thank you. I have to go home now."

As Fausto walked to the door, the man opened his wallet and took out a bill. "This is for you," he said. "Roger is special to us, almost like a son."

Fausto looked at the bill and knew he was in

---

**2. empanada** (em′pä·nä′dä): pastry filled with meat or fruit.

trouble. Not with these nice folks or with his parents, but with himself. How could he have been so deceitful? The dog wasn't lost. It was just having a fun Saturday walking around.

"I can't take that."

"You have to. You deserve it, believe me," the man said.

"No, I don't."

"Now don't be silly," said the lady. She took the bill from her husband and stuffed it into Fausto's shirt pocket. "You're a lovely child. Your parents are lucky to have you. Be good. And come see us again, please."

Fausto went out, and the lady closed the door. Fausto clutched the bill through his shirt pocket. He felt like ringing the doorbell and begging them to please take the money back, but he knew they would refuse. He hurried away and, at the end of the block, pulled the bill from his shirt pocket: It was a crisp twenty-dollar bill.

"Oh, man, I shouldn't have lied," he said under his breath as he started up the street like a zombie. He wanted to run to church for Saturday confession,[3] but it was past four-thirty, when confession stopped.

He returned to the bush where he had hidden the rake and his sister's bike and rode home slowly, not daring to touch the money in his pocket. At home, in the privacy of his room, he examined the twenty-dollar bill. He had never had so much money. It was probably enough to buy a secondhand guitar. But he felt bad, like the time he stole a dollar from the secret fold inside his older brother's wallet.

Fausto went outside and sat on the fence. "Yeah," he said. "I can probably get a guitar for twenty. Maybe at a yard sale—things are cheaper."

His mother called him to dinner.

The next day he dressed for church without anyone telling him. He was going to go to eight o'clock mass.

"I'm going to church, Mom," he said. His mother was in the kitchen cooking papas and chorizo con huevos.[4] A pile of tortillas lay warm under a dish towel.

"Oh, I'm so proud of you, Son." She beamed, turning over the crackling papas.

His older brother, Lawrence, who was at the table reading the funnies, mimicked, "Oh, I'm so proud of you, my son," under his breath.

At Saint Theresa's he sat near the front. When Father Jerry began by saying that we are all sinners, Fausto thought he looked right at him. Could he know? Fausto fidgeted with guilt. No, he thought. I only did it yesterday.

Fausto knelt, prayed, and sang. But he couldn't forget the man and the lady, whose names he didn't even know, and the empanada they had given him. It had a strange name but tasted really good. He wondered how they got rich. And how that dome clock worked. He had asked his mother once how his aunt's clock worked. She said it just worked, the way the refrigerator works. It just did.

Fausto caught his mind wandering and tried to concentrate on his sins. He said a Hail Mary and sang, and when the wicker basket came his way, he stuck a hand reluctantly in his pocket and pulled out the twenty-dollar bill. He ironed it between his palms and dropped it into the basket. The grown-ups stared. Here was a kid dropping twenty dollars in the basket while they gave just three or four dollars.

There would be a second collection for Saint Vincent de Paul,[5] the lector[6] announced. The wicker baskets again floated in the pews, and

---

**3. confession:** in the Roman Catholic Church, a ritual in which a person seeks God's forgiveness by telling a priest his or her sins.

**4. papas** (pä′päs) **and chorizo con huevos** (chô·rē′sô kôn wā′vôs): Spanish for "potatoes" and "sausage with eggs," respectively.

**5. Saint Vincent de Paul** (1580–1660): founder of religious orders that care for the sick and poor. Saint Vincent de Paul societies today minister to the needy.

**6. lector** (lek′tər): person who reads the Scripture lessons in a church service.

*Empanadas* (Turnovers) (1991) by Carmen Lomas Garza.
Courtesy of the Artist.

this time the adults around him, given a second chance to show their charity, dug deep into their wallets and purses and dropped in fives and tens. This time Fausto tossed in the grimy quarter.

Fausto felt better after church. He went home and played football in the front yard with his brother and some neighbor kids. He felt cleared of wrongdoing and was so happy that he played one of his best games of football ever. On one play, he tore his good pants, which he knew he shouldn't have been wearing. For a second, while he examined the hole, he wished he hadn't given the twenty dollars away.

Man, I coulda bought me some Levi's, he thought. He pictured his twenty dollars being spent to buy church candles. He pictured a priest buying an armful of flowers with *his* money.

Fausto had to forget about getting a guitar. He spent the next day playing soccer in his good pants, which were now his old pants. But that night, during dinner, his mother said she remembered seeing an old bass guitarron[7] the last time she cleaned out her father's garage.

"It's a little dusty," his mom said, serving his favorite enchiladas. "But I think it works. Grandpa says it works."

Fausto's ears perked up. That was the same kind the guy in Los Lobos played. Instead of

7. **guitarron** (gē'tä·rôn'): type of large guitar.

asking for the guitar, he waited for his mother to offer it to him. And she did, while gathering the dishes from the table.

"No, Mom, I'll do it," he said, hugging her. "I'll do the dishes forever if you want."

It was the happiest day of his life. No, it was the second-happiest day of his life. The happiest was when his grandfather Lupe placed the guitarron, which was nearly as huge as a washtub, in his arms. Fausto ran a thumb down the strings, which vibrated in his throat and chest. It sounded beautiful, deep and eerie. A pumpkin smile widened on his face.

"OK, hijo,[8] now you put your fingers like this," said his grandfather, smelling of tobacco and after-shave. He took Fausto's fingers and placed them on the strings. Fausto strummed a chord on the guitarron, and the bass resounded[9] in their chests.

The guitarron was more complicated than Fausto imagined. But he was confident that after a few more lessons he could start a band that would someday play on *American Bandstand* for the dancing crowds.

8. **hijo** (ē′hô): Spanish for "son."
9. **resounded:** vibrated.

## MEET THE WRITER

### "Stories Sometimes Begin with Memory"

Like Fausto in this story, **Gary Soto** (1952– ) grew up in a Mexican American family in Fresno, California. Much of Soto's award-winning fiction and poetry draws on his Mexican American heritage and his childhood memories. Here's how he recalls the incident that years later inspired "The No-Guitar Blues":

❝ I was sucking on a popsicle, playing checkers with my sister, doing nothing on a hot summer day, when a lawn-sniffing beagle wandered onto our block. Immediately, I got it into my head to rescue that dog because I thought it was lost. I hopped off the porch, with my sister in tow, and called, 'Here, boy,' snapping my fingers, patting my thigh. Foolishly, the dog stopped. I pulled on his collar, the jingle of dog tags rattling under his chin. Sure enough, he was lost: The dog tag was etched with the name of a faraway street. I hauled the poor pooch into our backyard and telephoned the owner to inform her that her dog was found. The owner arrived at our house after a few hours. She was glad to see the dog, and I was glad when she opened her purse and gave me and my sister each a two-dollar bill. So stories sometimes begin with memory, and a memory is what initiated 'No-Guitar Blues,' way back in the mid-sixties when there were no leash laws and plenty of roaming dogs. ❞

### Prose and Poetry by Gary Soto

You might want to read one of Soto's novels, like *Taking Sides,* or its sequel, *Pacific Crossing* (both, Harcourt Brace). If you like poetry, look at Soto's *A Fire in My Hands* (Scholastic). The book includes a "question and answer" section in which he talks about writing poetry.

# MAKING MEANINGS

• ## First Thoughts

1. If you had been Fausto, what would you have done with the twenty dollars?

## Shaping Interpretations

2. When Fausto saw his reward money, he "knew he was in trouble . . . with himself." What does Fausto's reaction tell you about the kind of person he is?

3. Fausto thought Roger's owners were "strange . . . but nice." Why do you think he had that impression of them?

4. Before you read this story, you and your class discussed ways to get something you really want. Refer now to the summary that you wrote for the Quickwrite. How does Fausto's experience compare with the solutions you discussed?

5. What lesson about life do you think Fausto's experience teaches? At what point in the story does he "do the right thing"?

6. Compare and contrast the experiences of Jimmy Wells in "After Twenty Years" (page 193) with those of Fausto. How are they similar? How are they different?

## Challenging the Text

7. The happy ending of this story rewards Fausto's good behavior. Do you think the story would have been more realistic with a different ending? Would it have been better? Explain.

## Extending the Text

8. What does the title of the story mean? What are the blues? Check a dictionary for different meanings of the word. What region and culture in the United States are often connected with the blues?

9. Have you heard any regional or cultural sayings recently? Do you use any when you speak? If so, what are they?

Dick Clark, host of *American Bandstand,* a popular TV show in the 1950s and 1960s.

# CHOICES: Building Your Portfolio

## Writer's Notebook

### 1. Collecting Ideas for Supporting a Position

Sometimes you can get ideas for a writing assignment from something you are reading. All of the following topics are part of Soto's story about Fausto: television, music, money, family, foods, animals, morals. With two or three classmates, brainstorm your opinions on these subjects. Jot down some opinions you think you could support.

> **Music:** Students who want to learn to play a musical instrument should be able to take lessons at school.
> **Money:** Kids should get an allowance if they work for it.

## Creative Writing

### 2. The Eyes Have It

In "The No-Guitar Blues" you see everything that happens from Fausto's **point of view.** Try seeing an event through another character's eyes. Choose a character from one scene in the story—for example, Fausto's mother, one of the churchgoers, or one of Roger's owners. Get inside the head of this character, and write the scene from his or her point of view. Reveal your character's thoughts and feelings about Fausto. Write as "I," the person telling the story.

## Multimedia Presentation

### 3. Fausto's Music

The story talks about two kinds of music—the rock music Fausto likes and the *conjunto* music his parents like—and it names some real musicians and groups, such as Los Lobos. Look for information in the library about these groups and find recordings of their music in audio stores. Share what you learn in a multimedia presentation, perhaps showing photographs and playing recordings.

## Language/ Home Economics

### 4. De la cocina de . . . (From the Kitchen of . . .)

This story mentions a number of Mexican foods (for example, empanadas, enchiladas, chorizo con huevos). Choose one of these foods, and make a recipe card for it, complete with a drawing or photograph of the food. On a separate sheet of paper, rewrite this recipe, translating as many words as you can into Spanish. Ask a friend to help, or use a bilingual dictionary.

## Art/Creative Writing

### 5. Kitchen Chronicle

Look at the picture "Empanadas" on page 221. Imagine that you're one of the people (or the cat) in the picture. Tell a story about the painting, using the **first-person point of view** (that is, speak as "I"). Describe yourself, and tell what you were doing before the moment captured by the picture. Then, tell what you're doing in the picture and what will happen next.

# GRAMMAR LINK

## Put That Splice on Ice

**Language Handbook HELP**

*See Revising Run-on Sentences, page 761.*

**Technology HELP**

*See Language Workshop CD-ROM. Key word entry: run-on sentences.*

Can you see what's wrong with this sentence?

> Fausto had come this far, he figured he might as well go through with it.

It's a case of the wrong connection: It's what is called a **comma splice**—two sentences joined together by just a comma. When you are tying two sentences together, a comma alone can't do the job. Here are two ways you can correct the sentence:

1. Break it into two simple sentences.

   > Fausto had come this far. **H**e figured he might as well go through with it.

2. Create a compound sentence by using a conjunction like *and, or, but,* or *so.* (This is the solution Soto used.)

   > "Fausto had come this far, **so** he figured he might as well go through with it."

---

**Try It Out**

Edit these sentences so that they are correct:

1. The dog looked well-fed, Fausto figured he belonged to rich people.

2. He knocked, no one answered.

3. He'd beg them to take the money, they'd refuse.

**A tip for writers:** To spot comma splices, try reading your writing aloud. A natural, distinct pause in your voice usually marks the end of one thought and the beginning of another. If you stop at a place where you have a comma, you may have found a comma splice.

---

# SPELLING

**Language Handbook HELP**

*See Spelling Rules, page 781.*

## Words with *ie* and *ei*

> *I* before *e*,
> Except after *c*,
> Or when sounded as *a*,
> As in *neighbor* and *weigh*.

Every rule has its exceptions.
Which of these words from the story breaks the rule: *deceitful, terrier,* or *weird*?

Choose the correct spelling of the word in each underlined pair in the paragraph below. Check your choices in a dictionary. Do all the words follow the "*i* before *e*" rule?

After Fausto received/recieved the guitarron, he formed a band. In their leisure/liesure time they seized/siezed every chance to play. Finally, Fausto achieved/acheived his goal: The priest/preist asked his band to play for a youth dance. In an eerei/eerie dream before the dance, Fausto played, and everyone booed. In real life everyone clapped.

## MADAM AND THE RENT MAN

## Make the Connection

### Face to Face

- "Grin and bear it."
- "Stand up for yourself."

What does "grin and bear it" mean? Have you ever been in a situation where you had to "grin and bear it"? What does "stand up for yourself" mean? When do people have to stand up for themselves?

## Quickwrite

Write down your thoughts in response to the following questions:

1. Which is harder—to grin and bear it or to stand up for yourself?

2. Can you stand up for yourself and still be polite? still be popular?

3. Will people respect you if you always deal with situations you don't like by grinning and bearing it?

go.hrw.com
**LEO 7-3**

*The Apartment* (1943) by Jacob Lawrence. Gouache on paper (21¼" × 29¼") (HMA 1982.10).

## Elements of Literature

### Tone

Has anyone ever said to you, "Don't use that tone of voice with me"? Your tone can change the meaning of what you say. Tone can turn a statement like "You're a big help" into a genuine compliment or a cruel, sarcastic remark.

Poems and stories have tones, too. As you read "Madam and the Rent Man," think about the **tone,** or the writer's attitude, and how that tone is conveyed to the reader.

> **T**one is the attitude a writer takes toward the audience, the subject, or a character. Tone is conveyed through the writer's choice of words and details.
>
> *For more on Tone, see the Handbook of Literary Terms.*

Hunter Museum of American Art, Chattanooga, Tennessee. Museum purchase with funds provided by the Benwood Foundation and the 1982 Collectors' Group. Courtesy of the artist and the Francine Seders Gallery, Seattle, Washington.

# Madam and the Rent Man

## Langston Hughes

The rent man knocked.
He said, Howdy-do?
I said, What
Can I do for you?
5   He said, You know
Your rent is due.

I said, Listen,
Before I'd pay
I'd go to Hades°
10   And rot away!

The sink is broke,
The water don't run,
And you ain't done a thing
You promised to've done.

15   Back window's cracked,
Kitchen floor squeaks,
There's rats in the cellar,
And the attic leaks.

He said, Madam,
20   It's not up to me.
I'm just the agent,
Don't you see?

I said, Naturally,
You pass the buck.
25   If it's money you want
You're out of luck.

He said, Madam,
I ain't pleased!
I said, Neither am I.

30   So we agrees!

**9. Hades** (hā′dēz′): in Greek mythology, the underworld, or world of the dead.

## Background

### Literature and Place

This poem is set in Harlem, a section of New York City where most people live in rented apartments. The speaker of the poem is a woman who has reason to be angry with her landlord.

## MEET THE WRITER

### "I Knew Only the People I Had Grown Up With"

**Langston Hughes** (1902–1967) was one of the first African American writers to win worldwide favor. Still, he never lost his popularity with the people he wrote about. Hughes once said:

66 I knew only the people I had grown up with, and they weren't people whose shoes were always shined, who had been to Harvard, or who had heard of Bach. 99

Langston Hughes was born in Joplin, Missouri, and worked at many different jobs in various cities while writing poetry in his spare time. For two years he worked as a busboy at a hotel in Washington, D.C. During this time he wrote many poems, among them blues poems, which he would make up in his head and sing on his way to work. His talent as a poet far exceeded his talent as a singer, as is evident from this story:

66 One evening, I was crossing Rock Creek Bridge, singing a blues I was trying to get right before I put it down on paper. A man passing on the opposite side of the bridge stopped and looked at me, then turned around and cut across the roadway.

He said 'Son, what's the matter? Are you ill?'

'No,' I said. 'Just singing.'

'I thought you were groaning,' he commented. 'Sorry!' And he went on his way.

So after that I never sang my verses aloud in the street any more. 99

Hughes became a major literary figure in what is now known as the Harlem Renaissance of the 1920s. His poems often echo the rhythms of blues and jazz. "Madam and the Rent Man" is from a collection called *One-Way Ticket*.

### Popular Poet

Hughes wrote his first poem *after* he was elected class poet when he was in elementary school. The position inspired him to write poetry, and he went on to become a celebrated poet. You can find some of his best poems in a collection called *The Dream Keeper* (Knopf).

# MAKING MEANINGS

## First Thoughts

1. Which of the following would you say to Madam, and why?

   - "Wait a minute, Madam—you might be evicted."

   - "Why are you picking on the agent? It's not his fault."

   - "You tell him, Madam!"

## Shaping Interpretations

2. What does "pass the buck" mean? How has the rent man "passed the buck"?

3. The woman in the poem speaks plainly and bluntly. Do you think she is right to speak this way? Explain. Refer to your Quickwrite notes for ideas.

4. What **tones** do you hear expressed in this poem?

5. Do you think this poem has a **message**? Explain.

# CHOICES: Building Your Portfolio

**Writer's Notebook**

## 1. Collecting Ideas for Supporting a Position

In "Madam and the Rent Man" the characters are deadlocked. Madam won't pay the rent until her apartment is fixed up. The rent man won't do repairs—it's not his building. This sometimes happens in real life—tenants withhold rent; landlords let buildings fall apart. Suppose that you are an advocate for the rights of tenants who live in rundown buildings. What positions would you take in support of the tenants? How would you make your positions known?

**Creative Writing/ Dialogue**

## 2. She Said, He Said

Write a dialogue between two people who disagree about something: perhaps money, noise, or food. The dialogue could be funny or serious. Use the vocabulary and speech patterns of everyday conversation to make your characters sound real.

**Reading Aloud**

## 3. The Rent Man Knocked

Prepare a read-aloud of "Madam and the Rent Man" in which you and a partner (as Madam and the rent man) read the dialogue. Practice changing the **tone** of your voice as the argument intensifies. Perform your read-aloud for the class. Afterward, ask your listeners to analyze your interpretation of the poem. Did they notice anything new about the poem as they heard it read aloud?

## BARGAIN

## Make the Connection

### Justice or Revenge?

What is the difference between justice and revenge? What do these two concepts have in common?

## Quickwrite

Get together with a group of classmates to talk about your opinions. A chart can help you explore some ideas. Copy the chart on this page, add questions of your own, and fill in the answers.

## Reading Skills and Strategies

### Drawing Conclusions: Looking for Evidence

Writers don't come right out and tell you everything you want to know about their characters. You are supposed to take part in the story. You draw your own **conclusions** about the characters you meet in a story, using information you find in the text and your own life experiences. To draw conclusions about the characters in a story, use these strategies:

- Watch what the characters say and do.

|  | Justice | Revenge |
|---|---|---|
| How is it defined in the dictionary? |  |  |
| Is it right or wrong for a person to seek it? Why? |  |  |
| Is it fair to all parties? Why or why not? |  |  |
| Does it help anyone? Does it hurt anyone? |  |  |
| Give some examples. |  |  |

- Watch the way other characters respond to them.
- Think about how they are like people you know in real life.

## Elements of Literature

### Point of View

"Bargain" is told by a character in the story. We call this the **first-person point of view:** The narrator tells the story using the pronoun *I* to talk about his or her own part in the action. In this story the narrator is a boy about your age.

> **I**n the **first-person point of view**, a character tells the story, using the pronoun *I*.
>
> *For more on Point of View, see pages 202–203 and the Handbook of Literary Terms.*

## Background

### Historical Fiction

This story takes place in Moon Dance, a town where we have all been in our imaginations. You will recognize Moon Dance from TV and movie westerns—its muddy street, its saloon, and its general store. This story is a kind of **historical fiction.** Setting is important in historical fiction. This writer wants you to feel what it was like to live in a rough frontier town. If you took away Moon Dance and all the historical details, you'd have a different story.

go.hrw.com
*LE0 7-3*

# BARGAIN

## A. B. Guthrie

**M**r. Baumer and I had closed the Moon Dance Mercantile Company and were walking to the post office, and he had a bunch of bills in his hand ready to mail. There wasn't anyone or anything much on the street because it was suppertime. A buckboard[1] and a saddle horse were tied at Hirsches' rack, and a rancher in a wagon rattled for home ahead of us, the sound of his going fading out as he prodded his team. Freighter[2] Slade stood alone in front of the Moon Dance Saloon, maybe wondering whether to have one more before going to supper. People said he could hold a lot without showing it except in being ornerier[3] even than usual.

Mr. Baumer didn't see him until he was almost on him, and then he stopped and fingered through the bills until he found the right one. He stepped up to Slade and held it out.

1. **buckboard:** open carriage.
2. **freighter:** here, person who transports goods.
3. **ornerier** (ôr′nər·ē·ər): dialect for "meaner and more stubborn."

Slade said, "What's this, Dutchie?"

Mr. Baumer had to tilt his head up to talk to him. "You know vat it is."

Slade just said, "Yeah?" You never could tell from his face what went on inside his skull. He had dark skin and shallow cheeks and a thick-growing moustache that fell over the corners of his mouth.

"It is a bill," Mr. Baumer said. "I tell you before, it is a bill. For twenty-vun dollars and fifty cents."

He was a man you wouldn't remember from meeting once.

"You know what I do with bills, don't you, Dutchie?" Slade asked.

Mr. Baumer didn't answer the question. He said, "For merchandise."

Slade took the envelope from Mr. Baumer's hand and squeezed it up in his fist and let it drop on the plank sidewalk. Not saying anything, he reached down and took Mr. Baumer's nose between the knuckles of his fingers and twisted it up into his eyes. That was all. That was all at the time. Slade half turned and slouched to the door of the bar and let himself in. Some men were laughing in there.

Mr. Baumer stooped and picked up the bill and put it on top of the rest and smoothed it out for mailing. When he straightened up, I could see tears in his eyes from having his nose screwed around.

He didn't say anything to me, and I didn't say anything to him, being so much younger and feeling embarrassed for him. He went into the post office and slipped the bills in the slot, and we walked on home together. At the last, at the crossing where I had to leave him, he remembered to say, "Better study, Al. Is good to know to read and write and figure." I guess he felt he had to push me a little, my father being dead.

I said, "Sure. See you after school tomorrow"—which he knew I would anyway. I had been working in the store for him during the summer and after classes ever since pneumonia took my dad off.

Three of us worked there regularly: Mr. Baumer, of course, and me and Colly Coleman, who knew enough to drive the delivery wagon but wasn't much help around the store except for carrying orders out to the rigs[4] at the hitchpost and handling heavy things like the whiskey barrel at the back of the store which Mr. Baumer sold quarts and gallons out of.

The store carried quite a bit of stuff—sugar and flour and dried fruits and canned goods and such on one side and yard goods and coats and caps and aprons and the like of that on the other, besides kerosene and bran and buckets and linoleum and pitchforks in the storehouse at the rear—but it wasn't a big store like Hirsch Brothers up the street. Never would be, people guessed, going on to say, with a sort of slow respect, that it would have gone under long ago if Mr. Baumer hadn't been half mule and half beaver. He had started the store just two years before and, the way things were, worked himself close to death.

He was at the high desk at the end of the grocery counter when I came in the next afternoon. He had an eyeshade on and black sateen protectors on his forearms, and his pencil was in his hand instead of behind his ear and his glasses were roosted on the nose that Slade had twisted. He didn't hear me open and close the door or hear my feet as I walked back to him, and I saw he wasn't doing anything with the pencil but holding it over paper. I stood and studied him for a minute, seeing a small, stooped man with a little paunch bulging through his unbuttoned vest. He was a man you wouldn't remember from meeting once. There was nothing in his looks to set itself in your mind unless maybe it was his chin, which was a small pink hill in the gentle plain of his face.

While I watched him, he lifted his hand and felt carefully of his nose. Then he saw me. His eyes had that kind of mistiness that seems to go with age or illness, though he wasn't really old or sick, either. He brought his hand down quickly and picked up the pencil, but he saw I still was looking at the nose, and finally he sighed and said, "That Slade."

Just the sound of the name brought Slade to my eye. I saw him slouched in front of the bar, and I saw him and his string[5] coming down the grade from the buttes,[6] the wheel horses held

4. **rigs:** carriages with their horses.

5. **string:** here, a group of horses.
6. **buttes** (by$\overline{oo}$ts): steep, flat-topped hills that stand alone on a plain.

snug and the rest lined out pretty, and then the string leveling off and Slade's whip lifting hair from a horse that wasn't up in the collar.[7] I had heard it said that Slade could make a horse scream with that whip. Slade's name wasn't Freighter, of course. Our town had nicknamed him that because that was what he was.

"I don't think it's any good to send him a bill, Mr. Baumer," I said. "He can't even read."

"He could pay yet."

"He don't pay anybody," I said.

"I think he hate me," Mr. Baumer went on. "That is the thing. He hate me for coming not from this country. I come here, sixteen years old, and learn to read and write, and I make a business, and so I think he hate me."

"He hates everybody."

Mr. Baumer shook his head. "But not to pinch the nose. Not to call Dutchie."

The side door squeaked open, but it was only Colly Coleman coming in from a trip, so I said, "Excuse me, Mr. Baumer, but you shouldn't have trusted him in the first place."

"I know," he answered, looking at me with his misty eyes. "A man make mistakes. I think some do not trust him, so he will pay me because I do. And I do not know him well then. He only came back to town three, four months ago, from being away since before I go into business."

"People who knew him before could have told you," I said.

"A man make mistakes," he explained again.

"It's not my business, Mr. Baumer, but I would forget the bill."

His eyes rested on my face for a long minute, as if they didn't see me but the problem itself. He said, "It is not twenty-vun dollars and fifty cents now, Al. It is not that anymore."

"What is it?"

He took a little time to answer. Then he brought his two hands up as if to help him shape the words. "It is the thing. You see, it is the thing."

I wasn't quite sure what he meant.

He took his pencil from behind the ear where he had put it and studied the point of it. "That Slade. He steal whiskey and call it evaporation. He sneak things from his load. A thief, he is. And too big for me."

I said, "I got no time for him, Mr. Baumer, but I guess there never was a freighter didn't steal whiskey. That's what I hear."

It was true, too. From the railroad to Moon Dance was fifty miles and a little better—a two-day haul in good weather, heck knew how long in bad. Any freight string bound home with a load had to lie out at least one night. When a freighter had his stock tended to and maybe a little fire going against the dark, he'd tackle a barrel of whiskey or of grain alcohol if he had one aboard consigned to Hirsch Brothers or Mr. Baumer's or the Moon Dance Saloon or the Gold Leaf Bar. He'd drive a hoop out of place, bore a little hole with a nail or bit and draw off what he wanted. Then he'd plug the hole with a whittled peg and pound the hoop back. That was

7. **up in the collar:** pulling as hard as the other horses.

evaporation. Nobody complained much. With freighters you generally took what they gave you, within reason.

"Moore steals it, too," I told Mr. Baumer. Moore was Mr. Baumer's freighter.

"Yah," he said, and that was all, but I stood there for a minute, thinking there might be something more. I could see thought swimming in his eyes, above that little hill of chin. Then a customer came in, and I had to go wait on him.

Nothing happened for a month, nothing between Mr. Baumer and Slade, that is, but fall drew on toward winter and the first flight of ducks headed south and Mr. Baumer hired Miss Lizzie Webb to help with the just-beginning Christmas trade and here it was, the first week in October, and he and I walked up the street again with the monthly bills. He always sent them out. I guess he had to. A bigger store, like Hirsches', would wait on the ranchers until their beef or wool went to market.

Up to a point things looked and happened almost the same as they had before, so much the same that I had the crazy feeling I was going through that time again. There was a wagon and a rig tied up at Hirsches' rack and a saddle horse standing hipshot[8] in front of the harness shop. A few more people were on the street now, not many, and lamps had been lit against the shortened day.

It was dark enough that I didn't make out Slade right away. He was just a figure that came out of the yellow wash of light from the Moon Dance Saloon and stood on the boardwalk and with his head made the little motion of spitting. Then I recognized the lean, raw shape of him and the muscles flowing down into the sloped shoulders, and in the settling darkness I filled the picture in—the dark skin and the flat cheeks and the peevish eyes and the moustache growing rank.

8. **hipshot:** with one hip lower than the other.

There was Slade and here was Mr. Baumer with his bills and here I was, just as before, just like in the second go-round of a bad dream. I felt like turning back, being embarrassed and half scared by trouble even when it wasn't mine. Please, I said to myself, don't stop, Mr. Baumer! Don't bite off anything! Please, short-sighted the way you are, don't catch sight of him at all! I held up and stepped around behind Mr. Baumer and came up on the outside so as to be between him and Slade, where maybe I'd cut off his view.

But it wasn't any use. All along I think I knew it was no use, not the praying or the walking between or anything. The act had to play itself out.

Mr. Baumer looked across the front of me and saw Slade and hesitated in his step and came to a stop. Then in his slow, business way, his chin held firm against his mouth, he began fingering through the bills, squinting to make out the names. Slade had turned and was watching him, munching on a cud of tobacco like a bull waiting.

"You look, Al," Mr. Baumer said without lifting his face from the bills. "I cannot see so good."

So I looked, and while I was looking, Slade must have moved. The next I knew, Mr. Baumer was staggering ahead, the envelopes spilling out of his hands. There had been a thump, the clap of a heavy hand swung hard on his back.

Slade said, "Haryu, Dutchie?"

Mr. Baumer caught his balance and turned around, the bills he had trampled shining white between them and at Slade's feet the hat that Mr. Baumer had stumbled out from under.

Slade picked up the hat and scuffed through the bills and held it out. "Cold to be goin' without a skypiece," he said.

Mr. Baumer hadn't spoken a word. The lampshine from inside the bar caught his eyes, and in them, it seemed to me, a light came and

*The Apprentice* by Robert Duncan.

went as anger and the uselessness of it took turns in his head.

Two men had come up on us and stood watching. One of them was Angus McDonald, who owned the Ranchers' Bank, and the other was Dr. King. He had his bag in his hand.

Two others were drifting up, but I didn't have time to tell who. The light came in Mr. Baumer's eyes, and he took a step ahead and swung. I could have hit harder myself. The fist landed on Slade's cheek without hardly so much as jogging his head, but it let the devil loose in the man. I didn't know he could move so fast. He slid in like a practiced fighter and let Mr. Baumer have it full in the face.

Mr. Baumer slammed over on his back, but he wasn't out. He started lifting himself. Slade leaped ahead and brought a boot heel down on the hand he was lifting himself by. I heard meat

and bone under that heel and saw Mr. Baumer fall back and try to roll away.

Things had happened so fast that not until then did anyone have a chance to get between them. Now Mr. McDonald pushed at Slade's chest, saying, "That's enough, Freighter. That's enough, now," and Dr. King lined up, too, and another man I didn't know, and I took a place, and we formed a kind of screen between them. Dr. King turned and bent to look at Mr. Baumer.

"Fool hit me first," Slade said.

"That's enough," Mr. McDonald told him again while Slade looked at all of us as if he'd spit on us for a nickel. Mr. McDonald went on, using a half-friendly tone, and I knew it was because he didn't want to take Slade on any more than the rest of us did. "You go on home and sleep it off, Freighter. That's the ticket."

Slade just snorted.

From behind us, Dr. King said, "I think you've broken this man's hand."

"Lucky for him I didn't kill him," Slade answered. "Dutch penny pincher!" He fingered the chew out of his mouth. "Maybe he'll know enough to leave me alone now."

Dr. King had Mr. Baumer on his feet. "I'll take him to the office," he said.

Blood was draining from Mr. Baumer's nose and rounding the curve of his lip and dripping from the sides of his chin. He held his hurt right hand in the other. But the thing was that he didn't look beaten even then, not the way a man who has given up looks beaten. Maybe that was why Slade said, with a show of that fierce anger, "You stay away from me! Hear? Stay clear away, or you'll get more of the same!"

Dr. King led Mr. Baumer away, Slade went back into the bar, and the other men walked off, talking about the fight. I got down and picked up the bills, because I knew Mr. Baumer would want me to, and mailed them at the post office, dirty as they were. It made me sorer, someway, that Slade's bill was one of the few that wasn't marked up. The cleanness of it seemed to say that there was no getting the best of him.

Mr. Baumer had his hand in a sling the next day and wasn't much good at waiting on the trade. I had to hustle all afternoon and so didn't have a chance to talk to him even if he had wanted to talk. Mostly he stood at his desk, and once, passing it, I saw he was practicing writing with his left hand. His nose and the edges

of the cheeks around it were swollen some.

At closing time I said, "Look, Mr. Baumer, I can lay out of school a few days until you kind of get straightened out here."

"No," he answered as if to wave the subject away. "I get somebody else. You go to school. Is good to learn."

I had a half notion to say that learning hadn't helped him with Slade. Instead, I blurted out that I would have the law on Slade.

"The law?" he asked.

"The sheriff or somebody."

"No, Al," he said. "You would not."

I asked why.

"The law, it is not for plain fights," he said. "Shooting? Robbing? Yes, the law come quick. The plain fights, they are too many. They not count enough."

He was right. I said, "Well, I'd do something anyhow."

"Yes," he answered with a slow nod of his head. "Something you vould do, Al." He didn't tell me what.

Within a couple of days he got another man to clerk for him—it was Ed Hempel, who was always finding and losing jobs—and we made out. Mr. Baumer took his hand from the sling in a couple or three weeks, but with the tape on it, it still wasn't any use to him. From what you could see of the fingers below the tape, it looked as if it never would be.

He spent most of his time at the high desk, sending me or Ed out on the errands he used to run, like posting and getting the mail. Sometimes I wondered if that was because he was afraid of meeting Slade. He could just as well have gone himself. He wasted a lot of hours just looking at nothing, though I will have to say he worked hard at learning to write left-handed.

Then, a month and a half before Christmas, he hired Slade to haul his freight for him.

Ed Hempel told me about the deal when I showed up for work. "Yessir," he said, resting his foot on a crate in the storeroom where we were supposed to be working. "I tell you he's throwed in with Slade. Told me this morning to go out and locate him if I could and bring him in. Slade was at the saloon, o' course, and says to the devil with Dutchie, but I told him this was honest-to-God business, like Baumer had told me to, and there was a quart of whiskey right there in the store for him if he'd come and get it. He was out of money, I reckon, because the quart fetched him."

"What'd they say?" I asked him.

"Search me. There was two or three people in the store and Baumer told me to wait on 'em, and he and Slade palavered[9] back by the desk."

"How do you know they made a deal?"

Ed spread his hands out. "'Bout noon, Moore came in with his string, and I heard Baumer say he was makin' a change. Moore didn't like it too good, either."

It was a hard thing to believe, but there one day was Slade with a pile of stuff for the Moon Dance Mercantile Company, and that was proof enough with something left for boot.

Mr. Baumer never opened the subject up with me, though I gave him plenty of chances. And I didn't feel like asking. He didn't talk much these days but went around absent-minded, feeling now and then of the fingers that curled yellow and stiff out of the bandage like the toes on the leg of a dead chicken. Even on our walks home he kept his thoughts to himself.

I felt different about him now and was sore inside. Not that I blamed him exactly. A hundred and thirty-five pounds wasn't much to throw against two hundred. And who could tell what Slade would do on a bellyful of whiskey? He had promised Mr. Baumer more of the same, hadn't he? But I didn't feel good. I couldn't look up to Mr. Baumer like I used to and still wanted to. I didn't have the beginning of an answer when men cracked jokes or shook their heads in sympathy with Mr. Baumer, saying Slade had made him come to time.

Slade hauled in a load for the store, and another, and Christmastime was drawing on and trade heavy, and the winter that had started early and then pulled back came on again. There was a blizzard and then a still cold and another blizzard and afterwards a sunshine that was iceshine on the drifted snow. I was glad to be busy, selling overshoes and sheep-lined coats and mitts and socks as thick as saddle blankets and Christmas candy out of buckets and hickory nuts and the fresh oranges that the people in our town never saw except when Santa Claus was coming.

One afternoon, when I lit out from class, the thermometer on the school porch read forty-two degrees below. But you didn't have to look at it to know how cold the weather was. Your nose and fingers and toes and ears and the bones inside you told you. The snow cried when you stepped on it.

I got to the store and took my things off and scuffed my hands at the stove for a minute so's to get life enough in them to tie a parcel. Mr. Baumer—he was always polite to me—said, "Hello, Al. Not so much to do today. Too cold for customers." He shuddered a little, as if he hadn't got the chill off even yet, and rubbed his broken hand with the good one. "Ve need

9. **palavered** (pə·lav′ərd): talked; met to discuss something.

*The Fall of the Cowboy* (1895) by Frederic S. Remington. Oil on canvas (1961. 230).     © Amon Carter Museum, Fort Worth, Texas.

Christmas goods," he said, looking out the window to the furrows that wheels had made in the snow-banked street, and I knew he was thinking of Slade's string, inbound from the railroad, and the time it might take even Slade to travel those hard miles.

Slade never made it at all.

Less than an hour later our old freighter, Moore, came in, his beard white and stiff with frost. He didn't speak at first but looked around and clumped to the stove and took off his heavy mitts, holding his news inside him.

Then he said, not pleasantly, "Your new man's dead, Baumer."

"My new man?" Mr. Baumer said.

"Who do you think? Slade. He's dead."

All Mr. Baumer could say was "Dead!"

"Froze to death, I figger," Moore told him, while Colly Coleman and Ed Hempel and Miss Lizzie and I and a couple of customers stepped closer.

"Not Slade," Mr. Baumer said. "He know too much to freeze."

"Maybe so, but he sure's froze now. I got him in the wagon."

We stood looking at one another and at Moore. Moore was enjoying his news, enjoying feeding it out bit by bit so's to hold the stage.

"Heart might've give out, for all I know."

The side door swung open, letting in a cloud of cold and three men who stood, like us, waiting on Moore. I moved a little and looked through the window and saw Slade's freight outfit tied outside with more men around it. Two of them were on a wheel of one of the wagons, looking inside.

"Had a extra man, so I brought your stuff in," Moore went on. "Figgered you'd be glad to pay for it."

"Not Slade," Mr. Baumer said again.

"You can take a look at him."

Mr. Baumer answered no.

"Someone's takin' word to Connor to bring his hearse. Anyhow, I told 'em to. I carted old Slade this far. Connor can have him now."

Moore pulled on his mitts. "Found him there by the Deep Creek crossin', doubled up in the snow an' his fire out." He moved toward the door. "I'll see to the horses, but your stuff'll have to set there. I got more'n enough work to do at Hirsches'."

Mr. Baumer just nodded.

I put on my coat and went out and waited my turn and climbed on a wagon wheel and looked inside, and there was Slade piled on some bags of bran. Maybe because of being frozen, his face was whiter than I ever saw it, whiter and deader, too, though it never had been lively. Only the moustache seemed still alive, sprouting thick like greasewood from alkali.[10] Slade was doubled up all right, as if he

10. **greasewood from alkali:** Greasewood is a thorny desert plant. Alkali is dry, salty soil that might look white and chalky, like Slade's face.

had died and stiffened leaning forward in a chair.

I got down from the wheel, and Colly and then Ed climbed up. Moore was unhitching, tossing off his pieces of information while he did so. Pretty soon Mr. Connor came up with his old hearse, and he and Moore tumbled Slade into it, and the team, which was as old as the hearse, made off, the tires squeaking in the snow. The people trailed on away with it, their breaths leaving little ribbons of mist in the air. It was beginning to get dark.

Mr. Baumer came out of the side door of the store, bundled up, and called to Colly and Ed and me. "We unload," he said. "Already is late. Al, better you get a couple lanterns now."

We did a fast job, setting the stuff out of the wagons onto the platform and then carrying it or rolling it on the one truck that the store owned and stowing it inside according to where Mr. Baumer's good hand pointed.

A barrel was one of the last things to go in. I edged it up and Colly nosed the truck under it, and then I let it fall back. "Mr. Baumer," I said, "we'll never sell all this, will we?"

"Yah," he answered. "Sure we sell it. I get it cheap. A bargain, Al, so I buy it."

I looked at the barrel head again. There in big letters I saw "Wood Alcohol—Deadly Poison."

"Hurry now," Mr. Baumer said. "Is late." For a flash and no longer I saw through the mist in his eyes, saw, you might say, that hilly chin repeated there. "Then ve go home, Al. Is good to know to read."

# MEET THE WRITER

## "Real People in Real Times"

**A. B. Guthrie** (1901–1991) wanted to portray the West as it was, not create myths about it. He said:

66 I want to talk about real people in real times. For every Wyatt Earp or Billy the Kid, there were thousands of people just trying to get along. 99

Most readers agree that Guthrie succeeded. His most famous work, a trilogy about the opening of the West, is noted for its historical accuracy. Guthrie also wrote the screenplay for *Shane,* a famous movie about a Western gunslinger who takes justice into his own hands to save a family and pays a bitter price.

Albert Bertram Guthrie, Jr., grew up in the little town of Choteau, Montana. After graduating from college, he traveled extensively and worked at various jobs—ranching in Sonora, Mexico; selling groceries in California; working as a census taker in Montana; laboring at his uncle's feed mill in Attica, New York. After the mill burned down, he finally settled in Lexington, Kentucky, where he worked at a newspaper for more than twenty years.

Guthrie became a fiction writer when he took time out from his newspaper job to visit his sick mother. During his visit, he had time to write his first novel, *Murders at Moon Dance* (1943). In this book he introduces the setting of "Bargain" and many of his other short stories.

Thinking back to his childhood in Montana early in the century, Guthrie said that the best Christmas gift he ever got was a dictionary and that his warmest memories were the arguments he used to have with his family about the meanings of words. In talking about choosing words in his own writing, Guthrie said:

66 For me, writing is a slow and painful business. It demands concentration and search and presents the obstacles of dissatisfaction with what could be said better. And there's no immediate reward in putting words on paper. The reward, great but fugitive, is in having written, in having found the word, the line, the paragraph, the chapter that is as good as ever you can make it. I spent a full day on one line of dialogue and knocked off satisfied. 99

### More Words, Lines, and Paragraphs by A. B. Guthrie

Guthrie's novels about the opening of the West are *The Big Sky* (Houghton Mifflin); *The Way West* (Bantam), which won the Pulitzer Prize; and *These Thousand Hills* (Buccaneer).

# MAKING MEANINGS

- ### First Thoughts

  1. What do you think of what Mr. Baumer does to Slade? Does he do the right thing? Why or why not?

  ### Shaping Interpretations

  2. Look again at the Quickwrite on page 230 and the chart the class filled in. Would you say that this story is about justice or revenge? Why?

  3. When Al suggests that Mr. Baumer forget Slade's bill, Mr. Baumer says that it isn't the money anymore; it is "the thing." What do you think Mr. Baumer means by "the thing"?

  4. A writer helps you to predict future events by dropping clues **foreshadowing** what will happen later. Early in "Bargain," Mr. Baumer says, "Better study, Al. Is good to know to read and write and figure." How do these words foreshadow the story's ending?

  5. Writers do not always tell you in so many words what a character in a story is thinking or feeling. You are given various clues and must draw your own **conclusions.** At the end of "Bargain," Guthrie doesn't tell you exactly what Mr. Baumer thinks about Slade's fate. What conclusions can you draw about what Mr. Baumer is thinking? What details in the story support your conclusions?

  6. Who do you think is responsible for Slade's death—Mr. Baumer or Slade himself? Give two or three reasons to support your view.

## Connecting with the Text

  7. If you were in Al's situation, would you keep silent about the likely cause of Slade's death? Why or why not?

## Challenging the Text

  8. "Bargain" is written in the **first-person point of view,** from Al's vantage point. What would you have known if Mr. Baumer had told the story himself?

> ### Reading Check
>
> Suppose that Al decides he has to confide to someone what he knows about Baumer's feud with Slade and the likely cause of Slade's death. He chooses to tell the whole story to Dr. King. With a partner, role-play Al and Dr. King. As Al tells what happened, Dr. King should comment and ask questions. Be sure to cover all the **main events** in the story.

# CHOICES: Building Your Portfolio

---

### Writer's Notebook

## 1. Collecting Ideas for Supporting a Position

How would you solve a problem like Mr. Baumer's? Suppose someone owes you ten dollars. This person refuses to pay you and even insults you in public. What would you do? Take a position and list reasons supporting it.

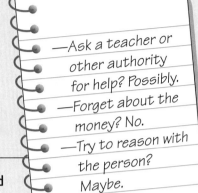

—Ask a teacher or other authority for help? Possibly.
—Forget about the money? No.
—Try to reason with the person? Maybe.

---

### Writing a Summary

## 2. Accident or Plan?

Imagine that Mr. Baumer is put on trial for causing Slade's death. In one paragraph, **summarize** the case *against* Mr. Baumer. Give reasons and evidence to inform and persuade the jury that Mr. Baumer is guilty. In another paragraph, summarize the case *for* Mr. Baumer. Present evidence to show that Slade is responsible for his own death.

### Research/ Speaking and Listening

## 3. Frontier Teacher

What was it like to be a teacher when the frontier was a land of strong men and women and brutal violence? Guthrie says that his father taught school in Montana when "male teachers were few in cattle country and often were belittled because of their occupation." Find information about the people who taught in classrooms in the midst of this rugged country. Present your findings in an oral report to the class.

### Research/Art

## 4. The Moon Dance Movie

You are a properties manager on a film set, the person who finds or creates objects to use in movie scenes. You've been hired to help create the town of Moon Dance. Because you know about A. B. Guthrie's concern for historical accuracy, you want your props to be as realistic as possible. Choose a setting from the story to bring to life—perhaps the inside of the Moon Dance Mercantile Company. What props will you use?

Reread the scenes that take place in that setting, and analyze them. Then, outline your plans on the basis of the story's descriptions and your research. Sketch particular items if you wish, and display your plans in the classroom.

### Analyzing Setting

## 5. Rewriting History

Can you imagine this piece of historical fiction taking place anywhere else—say, in the town or neighborhood you live in? Write a brief essay about how Mr. Baumer's problem might be translated to another time and place. What details in the story would have to change?

## End the Apostrophe Glut

**Language Handbook HELP**

*See Personal Pronouns, page 734; Apostrophes, page 777.*

**Technology HELP**

*See Language Workshop CD-ROM. Key word entry: apostrophes.*

Basically, apostrophes have two jobs: They are used to indicate possession (*Al's problem*) or to indicate where letters are missing in a contraction (*it's serious*).

1. Use apostrophes with nouns to show possession.

> Mr. <u>Baumer</u>**'s** nose [With singular nouns, use an apostrophe and s.]
>
> the <u>horses</u>**'** saddles [With plural nouns ending in s, use just an apostrophe.]
>
> <u>Mercedes</u>**'** sister [Use an apostrophe alone with a singular noun when an apostrophe and s would sound awkward.]

Do *not* add apostrophes to possessive personal pronouns. They already show possession.

> ours [not our**'s**]
>
> hers [not her**'s**]
>
> its [not it**'s**; *it's* means "it is"]

2. The apostrophe's other big job is to take the place of missing letters. You need to use apostrophes in contractions.

> "I <u>don't</u> [do not] think <u>it's</u> [it is] any good to send him a bill. . . . He <u>can't</u> [cannot] even read."

### Try It Out

Proofread the following sentences, adding apostrophes where necessary and removing them where they don't belong.

1. Everyone in town knew Slades way's, and all of them tried to steer clear of him.

2. Its no use sending Slade a bill, because he wouldnt even recognize its purpose.

3. Moore just stood for a while soaking up the fires heat before he said to Mr. Baumer, "You'r new mans dead."

4. Its easy to understand about the wood alcohol and it's role in Slades death when Mr. Baumer reminds Al that its good to know how to read.

**Language Handbook HELP**

*See Spelling Rules, page 781.*

### Silent Letters

Some words are difficult to spell because they contain silent letters—that is, vowels or consonants that are not pronounced. Say aloud these words from the story: *climbed, edged.* What silent letters do you notice?

Which of these words is hard for you to spell? Write both words correctly in your spelling log. Then, underline the silent letters. Add other words with silent letters to your spelling log as you encounter them. You might want to start by finding five words with silent letters in the story.

# Before You Read

## Make the Connection

### Some Friendly Advice

Have you ever had to compete against a good friend in a contest or sport? Did your friendship stay the same after the competition? What advice would you give two friends competing against each other?

## Quickwrite

In a group, create a list titled "Rules for Competing Against a Friend."

## Elements of Literature

### Internal Conflict

In this story two best friends competing for the same prize must fight each other in a boxing ring. This fight is a perfect example of an **external conflict.** The boys are supposed to literally knock each other out. Each boy also struggles with an **internal conflict:** How can he do his best without hurting and even losing his closest friend?

**A**n **internal conflict** takes place within a character's own mind. In an internal conflict, a character struggles with opposing needs or desires or emotions.

*For more on Conflict, see pages 22–23 and the Handbook of Literary Terms.*

## Reading Skills and Strategies

### Comparison and Contrast: Finding Similarities and Differences

Piri Thomas begins his story by contrasting the two best friends: "Antonio was fair, lean, and lanky, while Felix was dark, short, and husky." A **comparison** points out similarities between things; a **contrast** points out differences. After you read the story, go back over it and use a Venn diagram to help you identify the ways in which Felix and Antonio are alike and different. Write their likenesses in the parts of the circles that overlap.

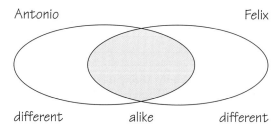

Antonio        Felix

different     alike     different

go.hrw.com
*LEO 7-3*

## Background

### Literature and Social Studies

This story is about two friends (*amigos* in Spanish) living on the Lower East Side of New York City. Many boys from the Lower East Side have dreamed of building a better life by winning the New York Golden Gloves, a tournament started in 1927 by Paul Gallico, a newspaper writer. This tournament marks an amateur's entry into the world of big-time boxing.

Antonio Cruz and Felix Vargas were both seventeen years old. They were so together in friendship that they felt themselves to be brothers. They had known each other since childhood, growing up on the Lower East Side of Manhattan in the same tenement building on Fifth Street between Avenue A and Avenue B.

Antonio was fair, lean, and lanky, while Felix was dark, short, and husky. Antonio's hair was always falling over his eyes, while Felix wore his black hair in a natural Afro style.

Each youngster had a dream of someday becoming lightweight champion of the world. Every chance they had, the boys worked out, sometimes at the Boys' Club on 10th Street and Avenue A and sometimes at the pro's gym on 14th Street. Early morning sunrises would find them running along the East River Drive, wrapped in sweat shirts, short towels around their necks, and handkerchiefs Apache style around their foreheads.

While some youngsters were into street negatives, Antonio and Felix slept, ate, rapped, and dreamt positive. Between them, they had a collection of *Fight* magazines second to none, plus a scrapbook filled with torn tickets to every boxing match they had ever attended, and some clippings of their own. If asked a question about any given fighter, they would immediately zip out from their memory banks divisions, weights, records of fights, knockouts, technical knockouts, and draws or losses.

Each had fought many bouts representing their community and had won two gold-plated medals plus a silver and bronze medallion. The difference was in their style. Antonio's lean form and long reach made him the better boxer, while Felix's short and muscular frame made him the better slugger. Whenever they had met in the ring for sparring sessions,[1] it had always been hot and heavy.

Now, after a series of elimination bouts, they had been informed that they were to meet each other in the division finals that were scheduled for the seventh of August, two weeks away—the winner to represent the Boys' Club in the Golden Gloves Championship Tournament.

The two boys continued to run together along the East River Drive. But even when joking with each other, they both sensed a wall rising between them.

One morning less than a week before their bout, they met as usual for their daily workout. They fooled around with a few jabs at the air, slapped skin, and then took off, running lightly along the dirty East River's edge.

Antonio glanced at Felix, who kept his eyes purposely straight ahead, pausing from time to time to do some fancy leg work while throwing one-twos followed by uppercuts to an imaginary jaw. Antonio then beat the air with a barrage of body blows and short devastating lefts with an overhead jaw-breaking right.

After a mile or so, Felix puffed and said, "Let's stop a while, bro. I think we both got something to say to each other."

Antonio nodded. It was not natural to be acting as though nothing unusual was happening when two ace-boon buddies were going to be blasting each other within a few short days.

They rested their elbows on the railing separating them from the river. Antonio wiped his face with his short towel. The sunrise was now creating day.

Felix leaned heavily on the river's railing and

---

1. **sparring sessions:** practice matches in which boxers use light punches.

## WORDS TO OWN

**tenement** (ten′ə·mənt) *n.* used as *adj.*: apartment. Tenement buildings are often cheaply built and poorly maintained.

**bouts** *n.*: matches; contests.

**elimination** (ē·lim′ə·nā′shən) *n.* used as *adj.*: removal from competition.

**barrage** (bə·räzh′) *n.*: heavy, prolonged attack.

stared across to the shores of Brooklyn. Finally, he broke the silence.

"Man. I don't know how to come out with it."

Antonio helped. "It's about our fight, right?"

"Yeah, right." Felix's eyes squinted at the rising orange sun.

"I've been thinking about it too, panin.[2] In fact, since we found out it was going to be me and you, I've been awake at night, pulling punches on you, trying not to hurt you."

"Same here. It ain't natural not to think about the fight. I mean, we both are cheverote[3] fighters and we both want to win. But only one of us can win. There ain't no draws in the eliminations."

Felix tapped Antonio gently on the shoulder. "I don't mean to sound like I'm bragging, bro. But I wanna win, fair and square."

Antonio nodded quietly. "Yeah. We both know that in the ring the better man wins. Friend or no friend, brother or no . . ."

Felix finished it for him. "Brother. Tony, let's promise something right here. OK?"

"If it's fair, hermano,[4] I'm for it." Antonio ad-mired the courage of a tugboat pulling a barge five times its welterweight size.

"It's fair, Tony. When we get into the ring, it's gotta be like we never met. We gotta be like two heavy strangers that want the same thing and only one can have it. You understand, don't cha?"

"Sí, I know." Tony smiled. "No pulling punches. We go all the way."

"Yeah, that's right. Listen, Tony. Don't you think it's a good idea if we don't see each other until the day of the fight? I'm going to stay with my Aunt Lucy in the Bronx. I can use Gleason's Gym for working out. My manager says he got some sparring partners with more or less your style."

Tony scratched his nose pensively. "Yeah, it would be better for our heads." He held out his hand, palm upward. "Deal?"

---

**WORDS TO OWN**
pensively (pen′siv·lē) adv.: thoughtfully.

---

2. **panin** (pä·nēn′) n.: Puerto Rican Spanish slang for "pal" or "buddy."
3. **cheverote** (chev′er·ôt′te) adj.: Puerto Rican Spanish slang for "good" or "fine."
4. **hermano** (er·mä′nô) n.: Spanish for "brother."

They were so together in friendship that they felt themselves to be brothers. They had known each other since childhood . . .

"Deal." Felix lightly slapped open skin.

"Ready for some more running?" Tony asked lamely.

"Naw, bro. Let's cut it here. You go on. I kinda like to get things together in my head."

"You ain't worried, are you?" Tony asked.

"No way, man." Felix laughed out loud. "I got too much smarts for that. I just think it's cooler if we split right here. After the fight, we can get it together again like nothing ever happened."

The amigo brothers were not ashamed to hug each other tightly.

"Guess you're right. Watch yourself, Felix. I hear there's some pretty heavy dudes up in the Bronx. Suavecito,[5] OK?"

"OK. You watch yourself too, sabe?"[6]

Tony jogged away. Felix watched his friend disappear from view, throwing rights and lefts. Both fighters had a lot of psyching up to do before the big fight.

The days in training passed much too slowly. Although they kept out of each other's way, they were aware of each other's progress via the ghetto grapevine.

The evening before the big fight, Tony made his way to the roof of his tenement. In the quiet early dark, he peered over the ledge. Six stories below, the lights of the city blinked and the sounds of cars mingled with the curses and the laughter of children in the street. He tried not to think of Felix, feeling he had succeeded in psyching his mind. But only in the ring would he really know. To spare Felix hurt, he would have to knock him out, early and quick.

Up in the South Bronx, Felix decided to take in a movie in an effort to keep Antonio's face away from his fists. The flick was *The Champion* with Kirk Douglas, the third time Felix was seeing it.

The champion was getting beaten, his face being pounded into raw, wet hamburger. His eyes were cut, jagged, bleeding, one eye swollen, the other almost shut. He was saved only by the sound of the bell.

Felix became the champ and Tony the challenger.

The movie audience was going out of its head, roaring in blood lust at the butchery going on. The champ hunched his shoulders, grunting and sniffing red blood back into his broken nose. The challenger, confident that he had the championship in the bag, threw a left. The champ countered with a dynamite right that exploded into the challenger's brains.

Felix's right arm felt the shock. Antonio's face, superimposed on the screen, was shattered and split apart by the awesome force of the killer blow. Felix saw himself in the ring, blasting Antonio against the ropes. The champ had to be forcibly restrained. The challenger was allowed to crumble slowly to the canvas, a broken bloody mess.

When Felix finally left the theater, he had figured out how to psych himself for tomorrow's fight. It was Felix the Champion vs. Antonio the Challenger.

He walked up some dark streets, deserted except for small pockets of wary-looking kids wearing gang colors. Despite the fact that he was Puerto Rican like them, they eyed him as a stranger to their turf. Felix did a fast shuffle, bobbing and weaving, while letting loose a torrent of blows that would demolish whatever got in its way. It seemed to impress the brothers, who went about their own business.

Finding no takers, Felix decided to split to his aunt's. Walking the streets had not relaxed him; neither had the fight flick. All it had done was to stir him up. He let himself quietly into his Aunt Lucy's apartment and went straight to

---

5. **suavecito** (swä′vä·sē′tô) *adj.:* Puerto Rican Spanish slang for "be cool."
6. **sabe** (sä′bā) *v.:* Spanish for "you know."

**WORDS TO OWN**
**torrent** (tôr′ənt) *n.:* flood or rush.

bed, falling into a fitful sleep with sounds of the gong for Round One.

Antonio was passing some heavy time on his rooftop. How would the fight tomorrow affect his relationship with Felix? After all, fighting was like any other profession. Friendship had nothing to do with it. A gnawing doubt crept in. He cut negative thinking real quick by doing some speedy fancy dance steps, bobbing and weaving like mercury. The night air was blurred with perpetual motions of left hooks and right crosses. Felix, his amigo brother, was not going to be Felix at all in the ring. Just an opponent with another face. Antonio went to sleep, hear-

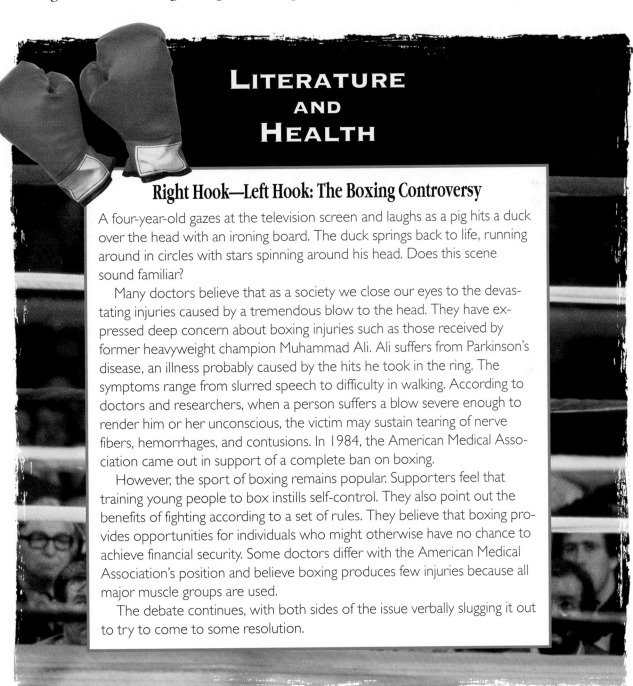

## LITERATURE AND HEALTH

### Right Hook—Left Hook: The Boxing Controversy

A four-year-old gazes at the television screen and laughs as a pig hits a duck over the head with an ironing board. The duck springs back to life, running around in circles with stars spinning around his head. Does this scene sound familiar?

Many doctors believe that as a society we close our eyes to the devastating injuries caused by a tremendous blow to the head. They have expressed deep concern about boxing injuries such as those received by former heavyweight champion Muhammad Ali. Ali suffers from Parkinson's disease, an illness probably caused by the hits he took in the ring. The symptoms range from slurred speech to difficulty in walking. According to doctors and researchers, when a person suffers a blow severe enough to render him or her unconscious, the victim may sustain tearing of nerve fibers, hemorrhages, and contusions. In 1984, the American Medical Association came out in support of a complete ban on boxing.

However, the sport of boxing remains popular. Supporters feel that training young people to box instills self-control. They also point out the benefits of fighting according to a set of rules. They believe that boxing provides opportunities for individuals who might otherwise have no chance to achieve financial security. Some doctors differ with the American Medical Association's position and believe boxing produces few injuries because all major muscle groups are used.

The debate continues, with both sides of the issue verbally slugging it out to try to come to some resolution.

ing the opening bell for the first round. Like his friend in the South Bronx, he prayed for victory via a quick clean knockout in the first round.

Large posters plastered all over the walls of local shops announced the fight between Antonio Cruz and Felix Vargas as the main bout.

The fight had created great interest in the neighborhood. Antonio and Felix were well liked and respected. Each had his own loyal following. Betting fever was high and ranged from a bottle of Coke to cold hard cash on the line.

Antonio's fans bet with unbridled faith in his boxing skills. On the other side, Felix's admirers bet on his dynamite-packed fists.

Felix had returned to his apartment early in the morning of August 7th and stayed there, hoping to avoid seeing Antonio. He turned the radio on to salsa[7] music sounds and then tried to read while waiting for word from his manager.

The fight was scheduled to take place in Tompkins Square Park. It had been decided that the gymnasium of the Boys' Club was not large enough to hold all the people who were sure to attend. In Tompkins Square Park, everyone who wanted could view the fight, whether from ringside or window fire escapes or tenement rooftops.

The morning of the fight Tompkins Square was a beehive of activity with numerous workers setting up the ring, the seats, and the guest speakers' stand. The scheduled bouts began shortly after noon and the park had begun filling up even earlier.

The local junior high school across from Tompkins Square Park served as the dressing room for all the fighters. Each was given a separate classroom with desk tops, covered with mats, serving as resting tables. Antonio thought he caught a glimpse of Felix waving to him from a room at the far end of the corridor. He waved back just in case it had been him.

The fighters changed from their street clothes into fighting gear. Antonio wore white trunks, black socks, and black shoes. Felix wore sky-blue trunks, red socks, and white boxing shoes. They had dressing gowns to match their fighting trunks with their names neatly stitched on the back.

The loudspeakers blared into the open windows of the school. There were speeches by dignitaries, community leaders, and great boxers of yesteryear. Some were well prepared; some improvised on the spot. They all carried the same message of great pleasure and honor at being part of such a historic event. This great day was in the tradition of champions emerging from the streets of the Lower East Side.

Interwoven with the speeches were the sounds of the other boxing events. After the sixth bout, Felix was much relieved when his trainer, Charlie, said, "Time change. Quick knockout. This is it. We're on."

Waiting time was over. Felix was escorted from the classroom by a dozen fans in white T-shirts with the word FELIX across their fronts.

Antonio was escorted down a different stairwell and guided through a roped-off path.

As the two climbed into the ring, the crowd exploded with a roar. Antonio and Felix both bowed gracefully and then raised their arms in acknowledgment.

Antonio tried to be cool, but even as the roar was in its first birth, he turned slowly to meet Felix's eyes looking directly into his. Felix nodded his head and Antonio responded. And both as one, just as quickly, turned away to face his own corner.

Bong—bong—bong. The roar turned to stillness.

---

**WORDS TO OWN**

**interwoven** (in′tər·wō′vən) v. used as adj.: connected closely; blended.

---

7. **salsa** (säl′sə) n.: Latin American dance music, usually played at fast tempos.

"Ladies and Gentlemen, Señores y Señoras."

The announcer spoke slowly, pleased at his bilingual efforts.

"Now the moment we have all been waiting for—the main event between two fine young Puerto Rican fighters, products of our Lower East Side."

"Loisaida,"[8] called out a member of the audience.

"In this corner, weighing 134 pounds, Felix Vargas. And in this corner, weighing 133 pounds, Antonio Cruz. The winner will represent the Boys' Club in the tournament of champions, the Golden Gloves. There will be no draw. May the best man win."

The cheering of the crowd shook the window panes of the old buildings surrounding Tompkins Square Park. At the center of the ring, the referee was giving instructions to the youngsters.

"Keep your punches up. No low blows. No punching on the back of the head. Keep your heads up. Understand? Let's have a clean fight. Now shake hands and come out fighting."

Both youngsters touched gloves and nodded. They turned and danced quickly to their corners. Their head towels and dressing gowns were lifted neatly from their shoulders by their trainers' nimble fingers. Antonio crossed himself. Felix did the same.

BONG! BONG! ROUND ONE. Felix and Antonio turned and faced each other squarely in a fighting pose. Felix wasted no time. He came in fast, head low, half-hunched toward his right shoulder, and lashed out with a straight left. He missed a right cross as Antonio slipped the punch and countered with one-two-three lefts that snapped Felix's head back, sending a mild shock coursing through him. If Felix had any small doubt about their friendship affecting their fight, it was being neatly dispelled.

Antonio danced, a joy to behold. His left hand was like a piston pumping jabs one right after another with seeming ease. Felix bobbed and weaved and never stopped boring in. He knew that at long range he was at a disadvantage. Antonio had too much reach on him. Only by coming in close could Felix hope to achieve the dreamed-of knockout.

Antonio knew the dynamite that was stored in his amigo brother's fist. He ducked a short right and missed a left hook. Felix trapped him against the ropes just long enough to pour some punishing rights and lefts to Antonio's hard midsection. Antonio slipped away from Felix, crashing two lefts to his head, which set Felix's right ear to ringing.

*Bong!* Both amigos froze a punch well on its way, sending up a roar of approval for good sportsmanship.

Felix walked briskly back to his corner. His right ear had not stopped ringing. Antonio gracefully danced his way toward his stool none the worse, except for glowing glove burns showing angry red against the whiteness of his midribs.

"Watch that right, Tony." His trainer talked into his ear. "Remember Felix always goes to the body. He'll want you to drop your hands for his overhand left or right. Got it?"

Antonio nodded, spraying water out between his teeth. He felt better as his sore midsection was being firmly rubbed.

Felix's corner was also busy.

"You gotta get in there, fella." Felix's trainer

8. **Loisaida** (loi·sī′dä): Puerto Rican English dialect for "Lower East Side."

---

**WORDS TO OWN**

**dispelled** (di·speld′) *v.*: driven away.

---

poured water over his curly Afro locks. "Get in there or he's gonna chop you up from way back."

*Bong! Bong!* Round two. Felix was off his stool and rushed Antonio like a bull, sending a hard right to his head. Beads of water exploded from Antonio's long hair.

Antonio, hurt, sent back a blurring barrage of lefts and rights that only meant pain to Felix, who returned with a short left to the head followed by a looping right to the body. Antonio countered with his own flurry, forcing Felix to give ground. But not for long.

Felix bobbed and weaved, bobbed and weaved, occasionally punching his two gloves together.

Antonio waited for the rush that was sure to come. Felix closed in and feinted with his left shoulder and threw a right instead. Lights suddenly exploded inside Felix's head as Antonio slipped the blow and hit him with a pistonlike left, catching him flush on the point of his chin.

Bedlam broke loose as Felix's legs momentarily buckled. He fought off a series of rights and lefts and came back with a strong right that taught Antonio respect.

Antonio danced in carefully. He knew Felix had the habit of playing possum when hurt, to sucker an opponent within reach of the powerful bombs he carried in each fist.

A right to the head slowed Antonio's pretty dancing. He answered with his own left at Felix's right eye that began puffing up within three seconds.

Antonio, a bit too eager, moved in too close, and Felix had him entangled into a rip-roaring, punching toe-to-toe slugfest that brought the whole Tompkins Square Park screaming to its feet.

Rights to the body. Lefts to the head. Neither fighter was giving an inch. Suddenly a short right caught Antonio squarely on the chin. His long legs turned to jelly and his arms flailed out desperately. Felix, grunting like a bull, threw wild punches from every direction. Antonio, groggy, bobbed and weaved, evading most of the blows. Suddenly his head cleared. His left flashed out hard and straight, catching Felix on the bridge of his nose.

Felix lashed back with a haymaker, right off the ghetto streets. At the same instant, his eye caught another left hook from Antonio. Felix swung out, trying to clear the pain. Only the frenzied screaming of those along ringside let him know that he had dropped Antonio. Fighting off the growing haze, Antonio struggled to his feet, got up, ducked, and threw a smashing right that dropped Felix flat on his back.

Felix got up as fast as he could in his own corner, groggy but still game. He didn't even hear the count. In a fog, he heard the roaring of the crowd, who seemed to have gone insane. His head cleared to hear the bell sound at the end of the round. He was glad. His trainer sat him down on the stool.

In his corner, Antonio was doing what all fighters do when they are hurt. They sit and smile at everyone.

The referee signaled the ring doctor to check the fighters out. He did so and then gave his OK. The cold-water sponges brought clarity to both amigo brothers. They were rubbed until their circulation ran free.

*Bong!* Round three—the final round. Up to now it had been tic-tac-toe, pretty much even. But everyone knew there could be no draw and that this round would decide the winner.

This time, to Felix's surprise, it was Antonio who came out fast, charging across the ring. Felix braced himself but couldn't ward off the barrage of punches. Antonio drove Felix hard against the ropes.

---

## WORDS TO OWN

**evading** (ē·vād′iŋ) *v.* used as *adj:* avoiding.
**frenzied** (fren′zēd) *adj.:* wild.

---

The crowd ate it up. Thus far the two had fought with mucho corazón.[9] Felix tapped his gloves and commenced his attack anew. Antonio, throwing boxer's caution to the winds, jumped in to meet him.

Both pounded away. Neither gave an inch and neither fell to the canvas. Felix's left eye was tightly closed. Claret-red blood poured from Antonio's nose. They fought toe-to-toe.

The sounds of their blows were loud in contrast to the silence of a crowd gone completely mute. The referee was stunned by their savagery.

*Bong! Bong! Bong!* The bell sounded over and over again. Felix and Antonio were past hearing. Their blows continued to pound on each other like hailstones.

9. **mucho corazón** (mo͞o′chô côr·ä·sôn′): Spanish for "a lot of heart."

Finally the referee and the two trainers pried Felix and Antonio apart. Cold water was poured over them to bring them back to their senses.

They looked around and then rushed toward each other. A cry of alarm surged through Tompkins Square Park. Was this a fight to the death instead of a boxing match?

The fear soon gave way to wave upon wave of cheering as the two amigos embraced.

No matter what the decision, they knew they would always be champions to each other.

*BONG! BONG! BONG!* "Ladies and Gentlemen. Señores and Señoras. The winner and representative to the Golden Gloves Tournament of Champions is . . ."

The announcer turned to point to the winner and found himself alone. Arm in arm the champions had already left the ring.

## MEET THE WRITER

### A Survivor from the Mean Streets

Like Antonio and Felix in "Amigo Brothers," **Piri Thomas** (1928–    ) grew up in a rough neighborhood in New York City. Unfortunately, he wasn't as lucky as Antonio and Felix— he didn't have a sport like boxing to help him escape the lures of drugs and crime. As a result, Thomas spent time in prison. While in prison, Thomas discovered he could write, and after his release he published an autobiography called *Down These Mean Streets* (1967). Thomas has worked for many years to help drug addicts give up their addictions and start new lives.

# MAKING MEANINGS

## First Thoughts

1. How did you react to the end of the story? Were you surprised by what Felix and Antonio did? Were you disappointed not to find out who won the fight?

## Shaping Interpretations

2. Do you think that Felix and Antonio were right to stop seeing each other before the fight? Were they right to fight so hard? What did you predict they would do, based on what you knew about their friendship?

3. Why do both boys wish for an early knockout? What does this wish show about them and their feelings for each other?

4. Describe what you think is the moment of truth for the boys in the story. What do you think they learn at this moment?

5. The last sentence refers to both boys as "champions." In what sense are they both champions?

6. Which do you think is more important to the story: the **external conflict**—the fight itself—or the **internal conflict**—the feelings the boys struggled with before and during the fight? Why?

## Connecting with the Text

7. Would *you* be able to walk away from a contest like this fight without finding out if you had won? Why or why not?

8. Look back at your "Rules for Competing Against a Friend" from the Quickwrite on page 244. How many of them did Antonio and Felix follow? If you had been in their situation, would you have acted differently?

## Challenging the Text

9. Did you find this story, particularly its ending, true to life? Do you think two good friends can fight each other and stay friends? Give reasons for your opinion.

## Writer's Notebook

### 1. Collecting Ideas for Supporting a Position

If Felix and Antonio were asked to write a paper supporting a position, they might start with the general subject of sports. They might narrow their subject down to a more specific topic, such as prizefighting. They might then think of issues relating to that topic that matter to them.

Making a cluster map like the one in the notebook is one way to gather ideas for an essay supporting a position. Think of a broad subject that interests you. Then, create a cluster map to collect and organize ideas for an essay supporting a position.

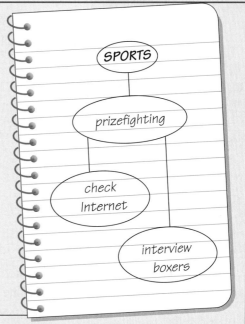

## Creative Writing/ Speaking

### 2. This Just In . . .

Pretend you are a sportscaster for a cable sports channel. Write a news story about the fight between Felix and Antonio. A good news story includes details that tell *who* was involved, *what* happened, *when* and *where* it happened, *why* it happened, and *how* it happened. To grab your listeners' attention, try to give your news story a catchy first sentence. Practice reading your account of the fight aloud; then, read it to your class.

## Comparing Characters

### 3. Side by Side

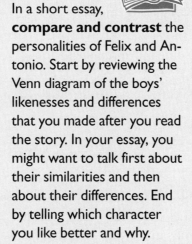

In a short essay, **compare and contrast** the personalities of Felix and Antonio. Start by reviewing the Venn diagram of the boys' likenesses and differences that you made after you read the story. In your essay, you might want to talk first about their similarities and then about their differences. End by telling which character you like better and why.

## Language/Writing

### 4. Slangfest

People in almost every age group, occupation, and area use **slang**—informal language that includes invented words and familiar words that have been given new meanings. Slang words are often colorful. Here are a few of the slang expressions used in "Amigo Brothers": *worked out, slapped skin, ace-boon buddies, fair and square, smarts, get it together, dude, split, flick,* and *cooler.* Create a dictionary of slang from the story. First, list all the slang you can locate. Then, try to figure out the meaning of each word or expression from its **context.** (Check a dictionary to see if you're right, or ask an adult.) Write your definitions, put the entries in alphabetical order, and share your dictionary with the class.

# GRAMMAR LINK  **MINI-LESSON**

## Punctuate Dialogue Correctly—And Punch Up Your Writing

**Language Handbook HELP**

*See Quotation Marks, pages 774-776.*

**Technology HELP**

*See Language Workshop CD-ROM. Key word entry: quotation marks.*

Dialogue, or conversation, puts a lot of punch in a story. When you include what characters say, your story comes to life. It's important to get the punctuation right when you write dialogue. Just follow these rules:

1. Put quotation marks around direct quotations of words spoken aloud:

> Antonio helped. "It's about our fight, right?"

> Antonio helped by asking if it was about the fight.

2. Begin a quotation with a capital letter:

> After a mile or so, Felix puffed and said, "Let's stop a while, bro. I think we both got something to say to each other."

3. Use a comma, a question mark, or an exclamation point (never a period) to set off a quotation from the rest of the sentence:

> "Loisaida," called out a member of the audience.

> "Ready for some more running?" Tony asked lamely.

### Try It Out

Add commas and quotation marks to set off the dialogue in these passages.

1. Felix and Antonio decided they'd each fight to win. Tony said No pulling punches. We go all the way.

2. Did the announcer say There will be no draw. May the best man win?

3. A woman in the crowd said to her friend with alarm What's going on? It looks as if they're trying to kill each other!

4. Let's have a clean fight said the referee. No low blows. No punching on the back of the head. Got it?

## VOCABULARY   **HOW TO OWN A WORD**

**WORD BANK**

tenement
bouts
elimination
barrage
pensively
torrent
interwoven
dispelled
evading
frenzied

### Vocabulary for the Workplace: Sports Reporting

1. You're a reporter interviewing a Little League coach. Write questions that include the words *tenement*, *interwoven*, and *evading*.

2. You're writing a news article about tryouts for the Olympic Games. Write sentences using the words *bouts*, *elimination*, and *barrage*.

3. You're a retired tennis player. Write sentences for your autobiography using the words *pensively* and *dispelled*.

4. You're a sportscaster describing the crowd at a hockey game. Write a description using the words *torrent* and *frenzied*.

# Sarah Cynthia Sylvia Stout Would Not Take the Garbage Out

## Shel Silverstein

Sarah Cynthia Sylvia Stout
Would not take the garbage out!
She'd scour the pots and scrape the pans,
Candy the yams and spice the hams,
5   And though her daddy would scream and shout,
She simply would not take the garbage out.
And so it piled up to the ceilings:
Coffee grounds, potato peelings,
Brown bananas, rotten peas,
10   Chunks of sour cottage cheese.
It filled the can, it covered the floor,
It cracked the window and blocked the door
With bacon rinds and chicken bones,
Drippy ends of ice cream cones,
15   Prune pits, peach pits, orange peel,
Gloppy glumps of cold oatmeal,
Pizza crusts and withered greens,
Soggy beans and tangerines,
Crusts of black burned buttered toast,
20   Gristly bits of beefy roasts . . .
The garbage rolled on down the hall,
It raised the roof, it broke the wall . . .
Greasy napkins, cookie crumbs,
Globs of gooey bubble gum,
25   Cellophane from green baloney,
Rubbery blubbery macaroni,
Peanut butter, caked and dry,
Curdled milk and crusts of pie,
Moldy melons, dried-up mustard,

30 Eggshells mixed with lemon custard,
Cold french fries and rancid meat,
Yellow lumps of Cream of Wheat.
At last the garbage reached so high
That finally it touched the sky.

35 And all the neighbors moved away,
And none of her friends would come to play.
And finally Sarah Cynthia Stout said,
"OK, I'll take the garbage out!"
But then, of course, it was too late . . .

40 The garbage reached across the state,
From New York to the Golden Gate.
And there, in the garbage she did hate,
Poor Sarah met an awful fate,
That I cannot right now relate

45 Because the hour is much too late.
But children, remember Sarah Stout
And always take the garbage out!

## MEET THE WRITER

### "I Couldn't Dance. . . . So I Started to Draw and Write."

**Shel Silverstein** (1932–1999) began drawing and writing when he was a young boy growing up in Chicago. He wrote:

66 When I was a kid—12, 14 around there—I would much rather have been a good baseball player or a hit with the girls. But I couldn't play ball. I couldn't dance. Luckily, the girls didn't want me; not much I could do about that. So I started to draw and write. I was also lucky I didn't have anyone to copy, be impressed by. I . . . developed my own style. 99

When Silverstein grew up, he became a writer of children's books, a poet, a cartoonist, and a songwriter. He created and

illustrated two of the world's most popular collections of poems for children: *Where the Sidewalk Ends* (1974), which includes "Sarah Cynthia Sylvia Stout," and *A Light in the Attic* (1981). Silverstein said:

66 I would hope that people, no matter what age, would find something to identify with in my books, pick one up and experience a personal sense of discovery. 99

# READ ON

## Wonderful Wool

Twelve-year-old Miguel Chavez longs for his family to treat him like an adult. For a year he tries to show that he is ready to make the difficult journey driving sheep into the mountains. It is not until some sheep are missing and a serious letter arrives that Miguel is truly able to prove himself in Joseph Krumgold's Newbery Winner . . . and now Miguel (HarperCollins).

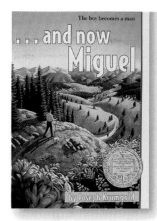

## Struggle at Sea

Lincoln Noah Stonewright is going to Alaska to explore his Eskimo roots and search for his missing uncle. In *Water Sky* (HarperCollins) by Jean Craighead George, Lincoln's search leads him to join the crew of a whaling ship and forces him to face a serious conflict.

## Pride and Prejudice

Virginia Hamilton's *Many Thousand Gone: African Americans from Slavery to Freedom* (Knopf) tells of the brave choices made by people desperate to be free. You'll read about Prince Ukawsaw, who was tricked into slavery; Henry Box Brown, who mailed himself to freedom in a homemade crate; and Jackson, who dressed as a maid to escape his owner. This incredible collection of true stories shows the pain and power of some courageous people.

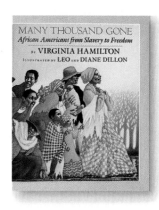

## Other Picks

- Lensey Namioka, *The Coming of the Bear* (HarperCollins). Friends Zenta and Matsuzo, two shipwrecked samurai, may be forced to fight on opposite sides of a war in sixteenth-century Japan.

- Scott Johnson, *One of the Boys* (Macmillan). Eric Atwater enjoys popularity in the "cool" gang led by magnetic Marty Benbow, until the gang's pranks turn cruel.

# Writer's Workshop

## ASSIGNMENT

**Write an essay in which you state your position on an issue that is important to you and provide reasons supporting your position.**

## AIM

**To persuade.**

## AUDIENCE

**Your classmates, newspaper readers, or anyone affected by the issue. (You choose.)**

## PERSUASIVE WRITING

# SUPPORTING A POSITION

In this collection you've been reading about people who take a stand to do the right thing. In this Writer's Workshop you'll have a chance to take and defend a stand on an issue you care about. You'll write a paper in which you

- discuss an issue about which people disagree
- talk about the **pros** and **cons**—the reasons for and against different positions on the issue
- tell where *you* stand on the issue
- give at least three reasons for supporting your position

---

### Professional Model

*Itzhak Perlman, a world-famous violinist, was disabled as a child by polio.*

I've been in public buildings throughout the world, and it's clear that the people who design them have no idea what it feels like to use crutches or sit in a wheelchair. One of the great architectural catastrophes of all time, from the point of view of any concertgoer, much less one who is disabled, is the Sydney Opera House in Sydney, Australia. A design contest was held and the winner was an architect who had conceived a truly fantastic-looking place with about a hundred steps leading to the entrance. There is no elevator— not for the general public, not for the poor musicians who have to lug

*The writer introduces the issue.*

*The writer gives a detailed example as support.*

*The writer states a fact as support.*

---

The history
of the written
word is rich and
Page 1

Once upon a time

(continued)

instruments up all those stairs, and certainly not for the disabled. Why couldn't the prize have been given to the best design that was also barrier-free? Why, when it's possible to make *everyone* comfortable, is so little attention paid to accessibility? . . .

*The writer restates the issue as a question.*

If you want to be sensitive to the indignities and frustrations suffered by the disabled, spend a day or two in a wheelchair. Tell yourself that you cannot get up—then try to get into a car. Try to go shopping or use the toilet in a restaurant. See what it feels like to be all dressed up and have to ride to your appointment in a freight elevator with the garbage. I can tell you how that makes *me* feel—furious.

*The writer tries to convince readers by asking them to put themselves in his place.*

*The writer cites a personal experience as support.*

We don't need more equal-rights laws. What we need is an attitude that we're all human beings, and as such, we all care about each other.

*The essay ends with a call to action.*

—from "To Help the Handicapped, Talk to Them" by Itzhak Perlman

## Looking at the Good and Bad on School Issues

| | |
|---|---|
| Uniforms | Good: They'd save money. Bad: They're boring! |
| Length of school day | Longer: Kids could do their home-work at school. Shorter: Kids need fresh air! |
| Metal detectors | Good: safety Bad: They'd make students feel like criminals! |

## Prewriting

### 1. Writer's Notebook

Look at your Writer's Notebook entries for this collection. Could you use any of your ideas as the basis for a paper supporting a position? For more ideas, try the brainstorming suggestion on the next page.

Chris Britt/Copley News Service

**WRITER'S WORKSHOP 261**

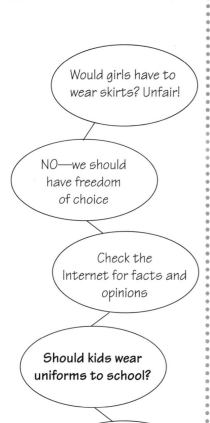

Would girls have to wear skirts? Unfair!

NO—we should have freedom of choice

Check the Internet for facts and opinions

Should kids wear uniforms to school?

YES—everyone would be equal

Tell about Nina's experience

**Language/Grammar Link**
H E L P

*End marks: page 201. Commas in a series: page 215. Comma splice: page 225. Apostrophes: page 243. Punctuating dialogue: page 256.*

## 2. Brainstorming

Remember that you will have to come up with good reasons to support a particular course of action. To find a topic people disagree on, get together with a group of classmates and brainstorm issues in several areas—for instance, school, community, national, and world. Each group member should pick a category and write down the issues, along with opinions on them.

## 3. Choosing an Issue and Finding Reasons

You've got a lot of issues on the table. How do you choose one to work with? First, look for an issue that matters to you. Second, make sure you see reasons to support different sides.

**Clustering** is one way to walk around an issue and look at it from different sides. Here is how it works. State the issue in the form of a question. Write the question in the middle of a sheet of paper, and draw a circle around it. Around the circle, write down another position people might take on the issue, along with reasons to support that position. Then, write down evidence—facts, examples, personal experiences—supporting the reasons. The model on the left is an example of clustering.

**Student Model**

### KIDS SHOULD BE PAID FOR CHORES

I strongly believe that kids should be paid for doing chores around the house. Kids all across the country constantly nag their parents for money to go to the movies, buy CDs, go to McDonalds, and do many other things. Many parents complain about kids' always asking for money.

Parents constantly complain that kids don't help out around the house enough. Lots of times parents nag kids until they clean up their rooms, put out the trash, cut the lawn, do the dishes, shovel the snow, and do many other chores.

Why can't kids and parents reach a compromise about money and chores? Parents would pay kids who remember to do their chores without

*A strong statement of position on a problem is used to grab readers' attention.*

*The writer gives examples to illustrate the problem.*

*The writer restates the issue as a question and*

being reminded a small fee for the work done. Kids would no longer ask for money.

This compromise teaches kids responsibility. They would learn that you don't get anything for doing nothing. When their chores are completed, with no nagging, they'd be paid whatever the parents had agreed to pay them. Kids could spend the money on things they like. They'd learn to save money for the expensive items.

No more nagging kids begging for money. No more nagging parents begging kids to clean up. Both kids and parents would be getting something that they want.

—T. J. Wilson
Atlantic Middle School
North Quincy, Massachusetts

*gives two reasons to support his position.*

*The writer elaborates by giving several more reasons to support his position.*

*The writer ends with a strong statement citing the benefits of the recommended course of action.*

## 4. Targeting Your Audience

In persuasive writing, your goal is to convince your readers to agree with your position and, if possible, to take the actions you recommend. "Whom am I trying to persuade?" is an important question to answer. Here are other questions to think about:

- What does my audience know about the issue? What do I need to explain?

- What is my audience likely to agree with me about?

- What **counterarguments,** or arguments against my position, could my audience make? How could I answer these counterarguments?

## Drafting
### 1. Drafting a Strong Beginning

Grab your readers' attention right from the start. One way to do this is to make your first sentence short. Another way is to begin with a question like "Who has the right to tell us what to

---

### Framework for an Essay Supporting a Position

**Introduction** (statement of the issue, the pros and cons of different positions on the issue, and your position): _____

_____

**Reason 1** and two items of support (support for your position, including facts, examples, and personal experiences): _____

_____

**Reason 2** and two items of support: _____

_____

**Reason 3** and two items of support: _____

_____

**Conclusion** (restatement of your opinion and a call to action): _____

_____

**Sentence Workshop**
**H E L P**

*Run-on sentences: page 265.*

**Communications Handbook**
**H E L P**

*See Proofreaders' Marks.*

---

■ *Evaluation Criteria*

*A good position paper*

1. *clearly states the issue*

2. *presents two or more positions on the issue or courses of action*

3. *clearly states the writer's position on the issue*

4. *gives sound, persuasive reasons to support this position*

5. *stays on track from beginning to end*

6. *is organized logically, with transitions connecting ideas*

---

wear to school?" Let the first paragraph set the stage. Tell what the issue is, and explain why it's important and why it interests you. Then, briefly explain the pros and cons of the issue. Finally, tell which side of the issue you're on.

## 2. Laying Out the Evidence

In the next three paragraphs, you'll try to persuade your audience to agree with you. In each paragraph, give one convincing reason to support your position. Then, elaborate with two items of support—a fact, an example, a personal experience. Try to use several kinds of support. If your evidence is limited to personal experiences, for example, your audience may suspect that you can't find other kinds of support.

## 3. Organizing the Evidence

It's important to arrange your reasons and support in a logical way. Many writers use **order of importance** for this kind of paper, saving their strongest reason for last. You may want to put your best reason in your fourth paragraph.

## 4. Ending with a Bang

In your conclusion, present a strong statement of your position. Leave no doubt in your readers' minds. Drive your point home by telling what's wrong with the other side. End by urging readers to agree with you or to take the course of action you support. Use the Framework for an Essay Supporting a Position (page 263) to organize your ideas.

## Evaluating and Revising

Trade drafts with a classmate, and read your partner's draft. Then, respond to the following questions:

- How does the writer interest me in the issue?

- Does the writer present the issue clearly?

- Does the writer present enough support to convince me?

- What support is strongest? weakest?

- What's the best thing I can say about the introduction and conclusion? What still needs work in those parts of the essay?

Make all the changes that you think will improve your paper.

# Sentence Workshop

## RUN-ON SENTENCES

A **run-on sentence** is two complete sentences punctuated as if they were one sentence. In a run-on the thoughts just run into each other. You can't tell where one idea ends and another one begins.

RUN-ON    I was eighteen the next morning I was to start for the West to make my fortune.

CORRECT   I was eighteen. **T**he next morning I was to start for the West to make my fortune.

A comma does not mark the end of a sentence.

RUN-ON    Fausto went to church, he put twenty dollars in the basket.

CORRECT   Fausto went to church, **and** he put twenty dollars in the basket.

There are several ways to revise run-on sentences:

- You can make two sentences. In the first run-on above, adding the period after *eighteen* clears up the confusion.

- You can add a comma and the coordinating conjunction *and, but,* or *or.*

RUN-ON    Fausto got an orange while he was eating, a dog walked up and sniffed his leg.

CORRECT   Fausto got an orange, **and** while he was eating, a dog walked up and sniffed his leg.

## Writer's Workshop Follow-up: Revision

Take out your essay supporting a position, and exchange papers with a classmate. To spot run-ons, try reading your partner's essay aloud. As you read, you will probably pause where one thought ends and another begins. If you pause at a place where there is no end punctuation, you may have found a run-on sentence. Underline any run-ons you find, and suggest a revision for each. Exchange essays again, and revise any run-ons your partner found in your writing.

**Language Handbook**
**H E L P**

*See Revising Run-on Sentences, page 761.*

**Technology**
**H E L P**

*See* Language Workshop CD-ROM. *Key word entry: run-on sentences.*

---

### Try It Out

Copy the following paragraph onto a separate sheet of paper, and revise it, correcting any run-on sentences.

Gary Soto's love of reading made him want to be a writer, he didn't start trying to be a writer, until he went to college. As a student in Catholic school, he wanted to be a priest when he went to public school he wanted to be a barber. He discovered poetry in college he says he was "hooked for good" on writing.

# Reading for Life

## Situation

In the paragraph on the right, students at Juniper Academy tell why they think wearing school uniforms is the right thing to do. Do you find their message convincing? Use the following strategies to evaluate this and any other persuasive writing.

## Strategies

### Identify the writer and the main idea.

- Who is the writer (or writers), and what special expertise or interest does he or she have in the topic?

- Does the writer clearly state a position on the issue? How much does the writer know about the subject? Can you believe what he or she says?

### Analyze the writer's perspective, or point of view.

- Does the writer present more than one point of view, or is the writing slanted toward one side of the argument?

- Does the writer give convincing reasons to support his or her position?

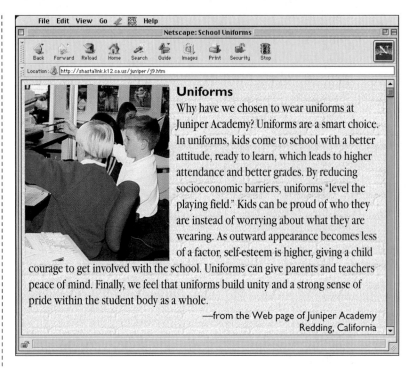

File  Edit  View  Go    Help

Netscape: School Uniforms

Back  Forward  Reload  Home  Search  Guide  Images  Print  Security  Stop

Location: http://shastalink.k12.ca.us/juniper/j9.htm

### Uniforms

Why have we chosen to wear uniforms at Juniper Academy? Uniforms are a smart choice. In uniforms, kids come to school with a better attitude, ready to learn, which leads to higher attendance and better grades. By reducing socioeconomic barriers, uniforms "level the playing field." Kids can be proud of who they are instead of worrying about what they are wearing. As outward appearance becomes less of a factor, self-esteem is higher, giving a child courage to get involved with the school. Uniforms can give parents and teachers peace of mind. Finally, we feel that uniforms build unity and a strong sense of pride within the student body as a whole.

—from the Web page of Juniper Academy
Redding, California

## Evaluate the writer's choice of words.

- Does the vocabulary fit the purpose and the audience?

- Does the writer use loaded words (words that call up strong feelings, like *greatest* or *rotten*) to make a point?

## Using the Strategies

1. What is the subject of the paragraph by the students at Juniper Academy? Describe how the writers' **perspective,** or point of view, affects what they have to say.

2. Give three reasons to support wearing uniforms.

3. Find two or three words or phrases in the last two sentences that could be considered loaded words.

4. Did the paragraph convince you? Why or why not?

## Extending the Strategies

- Read an editorial in your school paper or local newspaper. Evaluate the message, using the strategies you've just learned.

# Learning for Life

## Using Multiple Sources to Conduct Research on Volunteering

### Problem

You've read about people who made decisions to "do the right thing." For many people, volunteering to help others is "doing the right thing." What are the benefits of volunteering?

### Project

**Find out about volunteer opportunities for middle-school students in your community, and make the information available to other students.**

### Preparation

1. Make a list of your interests and skills. Include your favorite activities in and out of school and the causes you feel strongly about.

2. In groups of four or five, brainstorm to come up with a list of places where you might volunteer, for example:

   • an animal shelter

   • a park

   • a hospital

   • a library

   • a senior citizens' center

3. Make a list of volunteer positions to investigate.

### Procedure

1. Design a volunteers-needed card to record information about volunteer jobs. Include such items as the volunteer position, the agency it is with, the location, the name and phone number of the person to contact, how to apply, qualifications looked for in an applicant, the time commitment required, and any special comments.

2. Elect one classmate to call Volunteers of America and the office of the mayor. Find out if there is a government agency nearby that assigns volunteers. Then, call at least one place where you would like to volunteer. Fill in a volunteers-needed card for each place.

### Presentation

Present your findings in one of the following ways:

#### 1. Public-Service Announcement

Create an audio or a video public-service announcement encouraging young people to volunteer in the community. Talk about the benefits of volunteering and the kinds of work available. Play your announcement for your school. You might ask if a local radio or TV station will broadcast your announcement.

#### 2. "Volunteer Fair"

Organize a "volunteer fair" for your class or school. Set up tables with information about volunteer work. Use separate tables for different kinds of work—for example, work with animals or work in hospitals. "Volunteers" at each table can answer questions.

#### 3. On-line Index

If you have access to a computer program that can make an index, enter your volunteers-needed information. Then, students can get information by searching under any of several categories—for example, they should be able to look under the specific position (animal-shelter helper) or the general category (outdoor work) or the part of town in which a job is located.

### Processing

Finish this sentence: "I want to help my community by. . .".

# We Rookies Have to Stick Together

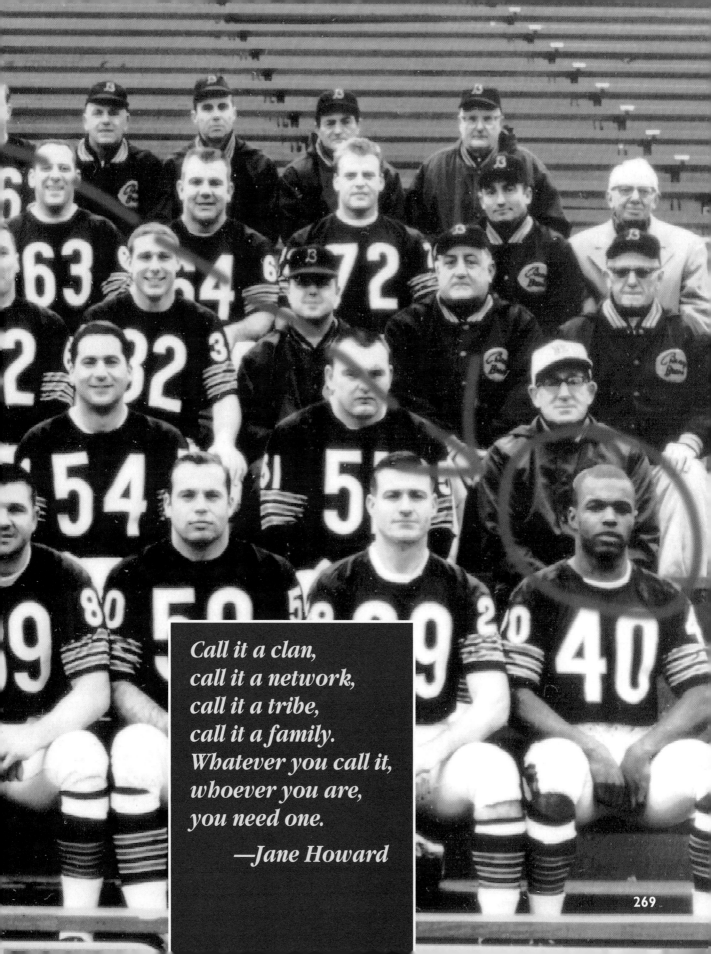

Call it a clan,
call it a network,
call it a tribe,
call it a family.
Whatever you call it,
whoever you are,
you need one.

—Jane Howard

269

# Elements of Literature

## DRAMA: An Introduction *by* Robert Anderson

A play is not written to be read. It is written to be performed on a stage by actors using speech and movements. You shouldn't have to read a program before you see a play. A good playwright reveals everything you need to know right on the stage.

In a short story a writer might write this:

Mary said, "Yes, I agree with you." But she really didn't.

In a play this might be written:

**Mary.** Yes, I agree with you. (*She really doesn't.*)

The actor must find a way of delivering this line that shows that Mary doesn't mean what she says. A play has no all-knowing storyteller who can take us inside Mary's mind and tell us what she is thinking.

In a movie or television show the director might zoom in for a close-up of Mary's face as she says the line, so that we can see the contradiction in her eyes. In the theater the director might have the actor pause a moment before saying the line or make a movement indicating that she doesn't mean what she says.

### "Show, Don't Tell!"

"Show, don't tell," a prime rule in the theater, points up one of the differences between novels and plays. A novelist tells a story largely through narration and, usually, some description and dialogue. In contrast, a playwright must convey the *whole story* through **dialogue** (the characters' words) and stage action alone. Unlike dialogue in a novel, which might simply give you a feel for a character's personality, dialogue in a play must carry the whole story forward.

### The Bare Bones of Drama

In drama, as in fiction, "story" consists of certain elements, which seem to have been part of storytelling from the beginning of time.

In the play's **exposition** the playwright introduces us to the characters and their environment (that is, to their **setting**). In some old-fashioned plays the exposition is delivered by a maid speaking on the phone. "Mr. and Mrs. Jones are not at home," she might say. "Mrs. Jones has gone away with her daughter, Daphne, and Mr. Jones has gone to live in a hotel." Thus we would learn that things are not going well in the Jones family.

Once we know something about the characters, we wait for a conflict to develop. **Conflict** is a struggle between opposing forces.

A clash between a character and an outside force is an **external conflict.** In the movie *Return of the Jedi,* for example, Luke Skywalker struggles with his father, Darth Vader. If the struggle occurs inside a character's mind, it is an **internal conflict.** Scrooge, the heartless miser in Charles Dickens's *A Christmas Carol,* for example, struggles with his own greed and selfishness before he emerges a changed man at the end of the story.

As the characters struggle with their conflicts, more problems, or **complications,** arise. This is what people mean when they say "The plot thickens." It has been said that a playwright first

gets a character up a tree, then throws stones at him, and then gets him down. In this scenario the stones are the complications.

Then we reach the most exciting part of the play, the **climax.** This is the moment, near the end of the play, when the conflict must be resolved. Now the tension is at its peak. In an action-adventure movie the climax would be the scene where the hero single-handedly lands a burning plane full of terrified passengers.

Finally, in the **resolution** of the play, the major problems are more or less resolved. At last the dramatic question posed at the beginning of the play is answered. Mrs. and Mrs. Jones get back together. Luke Skywalker defeats Darth Vader. The story ends.

## Staging a Play: People Working Together

A playwright has to call on a large group of collaborators to help a play become a reality: a producer, a director, actors, set designers, lighting designers. All these people have their own talents and temperaments—and tempers! When I taught playwriting, I used to say, "Half the job is learning how to write a play. The other half is learning how to get along with people."

## Television: A Special Type of Drama

Television may be the most intimate form of drama. It can make you feel close to characters, because it brings them right into your home.

Television plays share many characteristics with stage plays and movies, but they also have some special features. A television play often has a **narrator**—a voice that comments on the action. This narrator may create **suspense,** a feeling of anxious curiosity. For example, a narrator might begin the play by saying, "If I had known then what I know now, I never would have entered the dark house."

A television play can also switch scenes more quickly than a stage play. Many kinds of action that might be hard to represent realistically onstage—a car chase, an underwater scene—can more easily be filmed for television.

The written form of any drama is called a **script.** A script for a movie is called a **screenplay.** A script for a television drama is called a **teleplay.** Like all scripts, a teleplay includes directions for props, setting, and the actors' movements and speech. A teleplay also contains instructions for the camera and for sound effects. These instructions allow you to imagine the drama as you read it. (For an explanation of terms used in a teleplay, see Reading a Teleplay, page 276.)

## The Important Ingredient: Feeling

These elements of conflict, character, and story are only the bare bones of drama. They are like the wire frame on which a sculptor places layer upon layer of clay. What makes a play great is the talents of the writer. These include the ability to tell a good story and to tell it truly.

## MAKING DECISIONS: PREVIEWING THE TEXT

Movie producers know how important previews are. Previews show us a movie's most exciting scenes or funniest lines and leave us curious about what we *didn't* see. Producers know we will decide whether to see a movie largely on the basis of a preview we've seen.

Readers also make decisions on the basis of previews. Walk into any bookstore and you'll see a lot of previewing going on. People are examining book jackets and illustrations, skimming the texts, looking at the tables of contents or indexes.

Previewing can also be useful when you're assigned a text to read in school. Previewing helps you predict what you'll find in the text. It can also help you decide what strategies to use as you read. As you preview a text, ask yourself these questions:

- **Format.** What kind of text is this? (A play, a novel, a history book?)

- **Titles and subtitles.** What is the general topic? Do I already know something about this topic that will help me as I read? Does the topic interest me? What could the title mean? Is it a good title?

- **Difficulty.** Does the text contain a lot of factual information? Should I take notes as I read?

- **Vocabulary.** Does it contain technical terms or other challenging words? Will I need to read this slowly?

- **Visuals.** Are there special features such as maps, graphs, or stage directions?

### Time for the Feature Presentation

As you look through *Brian's Song,* you'll notice that it's set up in the format of a teleplay. There are camera directions, descriptions of sets, sound instructions, directions for the actors. If you flip to page 276, you'll find a list of terms used in a typical screenplay. You should be familiar with these terms; they'll help you visualize the action of the play—as if you were viewing it on a TV screen.

Preview the play for a few minutes. What else do you notice about the text? What is your first response to the text—does it look interesting to you?

**Apply the strategy on the next page.**

# Before You Read

## BRIAN'S SONG

## Make the Connection

### Friendly Foes

Some people say that we need friends more than anything else in life. We are also competitive, though—we want to win—and sometimes competition can cause conflicts between even the closest of friends. Suppose that you and a friend are competing for the same thing—a part in a play, a spot on the team, a special honor or award. Would you

- go all out to win, no matter what?
- talk over the problem and hope you can remain friends?
- put your friendship ahead of your desire to win?

## Quickwrite

Write briefly about your responses to these questions about competition and friendship. What matters more to you—winning or friendship? Save your notes.

## Reading Skills and Strategies

### Previewing the Text

A play usually opens with an introductory scene that gives you some information about its **setting,** or the place and time in which the events occur. Preview the beginning of *Brian's Song.* What details in the **stage and camera directions** (instructions for actors and camera operators) tell you *where* the characters are?

## Background

### A Tale of Two Rookies

*Brian's Song* is a television drama based on the true story of Gale Sayers and Brian Piccolo, two new recruits for the Chicago Bears football team. It is what Hollywood would call a buddy movie, the story of two men who compete with each other, joke with each other, get angry with each other, and finally learn to love each other.

The two rookies couldn't be more different. Gale, an African American, is quiet and shy. Brian, an Italian American, is outgoing and talkative. What the two players have in common is a strong desire to make the team. Many struggles, small and large, take place in this play, with everything from a place on the team to a human life at stake. Sometimes what happens will make you laugh, but just as often this story will make you want to cry.

go.hrw.com
*LEO 7-4*

# Brian's Song

William Blinn

They came to know each other,

fight each other,

and help each other . . .

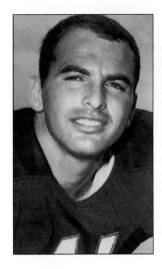

## Reading a Teleplay

In a **screenplay** (a script for a movie) or a **teleplay** (a script for TV) the camera directions are very important. Camera directions help you imagine what you would see on the screen. Like many teleplays, *Brian's Song* uses a **narrator,** or unseen speaker, to comment on the action.

Study this list of terms so that you can recognize and understand them as you read *Brian's Song*.

**Voice-over:** the voice of a character who is off camera or who is on camera but not shown to be speaking.

**Fade In:** The picture slowly appears on the screen.

**Fade Out:** The picture slowly disappears from the screen.

**Exterior:** outdoors.

**Interior:** indoors.

**Beat:** pause.

**Long shot:** a view from a distance.

**Tight on; close shot:** a close-up camera shot.

**Full shot:** a camera shot showing a complete view of the character(s) or scene.

**Pan:** short for *panorama;* the camera swings slowly from one side of the set to the other.

**Hard cut to:** shift abruptly to (a different scene).

**Angle on or to:** position the camera on (a character or scene).

**Zoom:** move in quickly for a close view or away for a distant view.

**Freeze frame; hold:** remain focused on one image for a few seconds.

*For a Glossary of Football Terms used in* Brian's Song, *see Literature and Sports, pages 280–281.*

# Characters

**NARRATOR,** *voice that comments on the action*

**BRIAN PICCOLO** }
**GALE SAYERS** } *running backs for the Chicago Bears*

**GEORGE HALAS,** *coach of the Bears*

**J. C. CAROLINE** }
**ABE GIBRON** } *assistant coaches of the Bears*
**ED MCCASKEY** }

**ATKINS** }
**EVEY** } *players for the Bears*
**O'BRADOVICH** }

**REPORTERS**

**LINDA SAYERS,** *Gale's wife*

**JOY PICCOLO,** *Brian's wife*

**SPEAKER,** *at an awards ceremony*

**JACK CONCANNON,** *quarterback of the Bears*

**ANNOUNCER,** *radio sportscaster*

**DR. FOX,** *who treats Gale*

**NURSES**

**HOTEL OFFICIAL**

**PLAYER,** *Gale's new roommate*

**MR. EBERLE,** *hospital official*

**DOCTOR,** *who gives Brian anesthesia*

**M.C.,** *master of ceremonies*

# Part One

**Exterior—Rolling countryside—Day
(helicopter shot)**

*The terrain is farmland, flat, tranquil, soothing in its simplicity. As our view gets closer to the ground, we start to hear the Narrator's voice.*

> NARRATOR (*voice-over*). This is a story about two men, one named Gale Sayers, the other Brian Piccolo. They came from different parts of the country. They competed for the same job. One was white; the other black. One liked to talk; the other was as shy as a three-year-old. Our story's about how they came to know each other, fight each other, and help each other. . . .
> (*beat*)
> Ernest Hemingway said that every true story ends in death. Well, this *is* a true story.

*As the helicopter continues its descent, we now find ourselves following a cab down a two-lane asphalt road. We follow the cab as we roll opening credits.*

**Direct cut to:**

**Exterior—Campus-type area—Day—
On sign**

*Reading "Training Camp of the Chicago Bears," an NFL insignia beneath the lettering. We pan off the sign, moving by a number of red-brick buildings, the kind of ivied architecture seen at any number of small universities in the Middle West. Coming up the curving blacktopped drive is the cab.*

**Exterior—Practice field—Series of cuts**

*The Bears are going through the various routines and exercises. Defensive linemen scuttling crablike back and forth as a coach switches a ball from hand to hand. Men working on the blocking sled, throwing their bulk against the padded metal arm. Players negotiating the rope framework, some alternating, crossing over, others hopping from square to square. Throughout these cuts, the sounds of men under strain, struggling for breath, grunting with effort as they bear down.*

*As we zoom toward the far end of the field, we see Gale Sayers standing by the driver's side of the cab, his suitcase next to him.*

*Sayers is in his early twenties, his handsome face normally <u>enigmatic</u>, guarded. He's dressed in slacks and sport coat, but even in this kind of "civilian" garb, it doesn't take a practiced eye to note the lean, hard compactness of a born athlete.*

> BRIAN (*voice-over*). Heads up! Look out!

*Gale looks toward the sound of the voice just in time to react to the football hurtling down toward him. He gets a hand up and slaps it away, over the cab. Gale walks across to the other side of the road to get the football and throws it to the young man now approaching him. He's wearing a Bears sweat shirt, workout shorts, football cleats. This is Brian Piccolo—early twenties, with a smile that comes easily and nicely. He takes life and people as he finds them, and he generally finds them worthwhile, enjoyable, and a little funny. The face is strong and handsome. Gale throws the ball back across the road to him.*

> GALE. Here you go.
> BRIAN. Thanks.

*Brian heaves the ball back to the practice area offstage, though he makes no move to*

---

**WORDS TO OWN**

**enigmatic** (en′ig·mat′ik) *adj.*: mysterious; like a riddle.

---

return there himself. *Gale is a little ill at ease as Brian just stands there looking at him with a half smile.*

BRIAN. You're Gale Sayers.
GALE. Yeah.
BRIAN. I'm Brian Piccolo. We met at the All-America game last June in Buffalo.

*Brian has extended his hand, but Gale is holding his suitcase. A short beat as Gale switches hands, but by the time it's done, Brian has taken back his hand, and there's a moment of stuttering reactions. Finally, they shake hands. Gale's head is down, face guarded.*

GALE. Sorry I didn't remember, but I'm not very good at that kind of stuff.

*Piccolo's smile is a nice one.*

BRIAN (*a quiet put-on*). Golly, that's okay. I can see why you might forget, but I sure couldn't. No way. That was a heckuva talk we had, man. I mean, I walked up and said: "I'm Brian Piccolo. I hear we'll both be playing for the Bears." And you said—I'll never forget it—you said: "Uh-huh." Just like that. "Uh-huh." And whenever I'm feeling depressed or low, why, I think about that advice. Lot of guys wouldn't have taken the time to talk to me like that, but not you. "Uh-huh," you said. Just like that. Right out.

*Brian grins. Gale does not. His expression is neutral. A short beat.*

GALE. Where do I go to check in?

*Piccolo's smile goes. The total lack of reaction from Gale is puzzling. He nods toward one of the buildings offstage.*

BRIAN. That building over there. That's where Halas is.
GALE. Thanks.

*The word comes in a characteristic flat tone. Gale moves off for the building. Brian stands there a moment, looking after him thoughtfully.*

BRIAN. Hey . . .

*Gale stops, looking back.*

GALE. What?
BRIAN. You ever met Halas before?
GALE. Talked to him on the phone a couple times. That's all.

*Brian's manner is calm, pleasant, helpful.*

BRIAN. Well, look, let me give you a little hint. He's a good guy and all, but he's deaf in his left ear and he's too vain to admit it. So stay on his right-hand side, or he won't hear a word you say.
   (*beat*)
GALE. Uh—okay. Thanks.
BRIAN. Rookies have to stick together, man.

*With a wave of his hand, Brian starts off, moving at an easy lope back onto the practice field. Sayers stands there, watching Brian, not knowing precisely what to make of him. After a moment, he turns and starts for the building pointed out by Piccolo.*

> **Direct cut to:**
> **Interior—Bears' main office corridor—Full shot**

*Gale comes in looking about uneasily, then heads for the end of the corridor. He stops in front of a door with a nameplate reading "Coach George Halas," wipes his sweating palms on his trouser legs, then knocks on the door.*

HALAS (*impatiently, offstage*). Yeah. Come in.

*Gale stands motionless for a second, gathering his forces, then opens the door and steps inside.*

**Interior—Halas's office—Full shot**

*As Gale comes into the office, he starts to speak, but his voice is only a dry croak. The office is in a state of organized chaos. Cardboard filing boxes, cartons of books, and papers. Reels of film and, standing behind an ancient desk, a large man of some years, some strength, and much power: Halas. He holds a framed picture, hammer, and nails. He looks at the young man standing in the doorway.*

> **HALAS.** I'm George Halas.
> **GALE.** I know. (*Quickly*) I mean, everyone knows who you are. I'm Gale Sayers.
> **HALAS.** Come on in, Gale. You can give me a hand hanging this thing. My good luck picture. First professional team I ever played on. The Decatur Staleys in 1920.

*Gale steps in, closing the door, still awed and afraid. Halas moves to an empty place on the wall, his back to Gale.*

> **HALAS.** How's your leg? I read where it was hurt.
> **GALE.** It's fine. Hundred percent.
> **HALAS.** How about your head?
> **GALE.** My head? Nothin' wrong with my head.
> **HALAS.** Good. Because being in the All-Star game puts you three weeks behind everybody else. New terminology, new plays to learn. Won't be easy.
> > (*beat*)
> **GALE.** NFL[1] ain't supposed to be easy.

*A smile and look from Halas. He nods.*

> **HALAS.** Right. Give me a hand.

*Gale moves behind the desk, where Halas is holding the picture up against the wall. Halas starts hammering a nail.*

> **HALAS.** About all I can promise you is a fair

---

1. **NFL:** National Football League.

shot at running back. But you're going to have a lot of company. Jon Arnett, Ralph Kurek, Brian Piccolo . . . going to be very crowded out there.

*Gale looks at Halas for a second, realizing he's on the man's left side, recalling the advice given him by Brian earlier. He rumbas around behind and then to the other side of the Coach.*

> **GALE.** Well, a fair shot is all I want. Can't ask for more than that.

*Halas notes Gale's shift with a puzzled look, then drives the nail home. He turns back to the desk, once more placing Gale on his left side.*

> **HALAS.** We plan to use our backs a good deal as receivers this year. You do much pass catching when you were in college?

*He looks back to where Gale was, only to find that Gale has crossed behind him.*

> **GALE.** Well, yes sir, I did, but it was usually safety-valve stuff. Once in a while we'd screen.

*Halas moves to one of the filing cabinets nearby.*

> **HALAS.** Well, I generally prefer to get a back into the pattern, unless the other team has a tendency to blitz. That's another thing you'll have to get used to, checking out the linebackers, make sure they aren't coming.

*Halas looks back to Gale, but once again, he's the man who isn't there. Gale has managed to cross behind him again, squeezing in between Halas and the wall, struggling to make the move seem casual.*

> **GALE.** Yes sir, I know . . .

*Halas starts back to the desk, once again forcing Gale to do an end around.*

> **GALE.** . . . and, especially on teams like the Cardinals, I guess . . .

## A Glossary of Football Terms

All sports and jobs have their special vocabularies. What's an end run? a punt return? What's the difference between a flanker and a kicker? If you're a rookie when it comes to football vocabulary, this glossary will help.

**defensive linemen:** players who hold the line (the team's position) against the advancing offense, which has the ball.

**blocking sled:** device with a padded metal arm against which players hurl themselves during practice to increase their capacity to block the opposition.

**rope framework:** rope grid through which players run during practice to increase their agility.

**rookie:** first-year player.

**running back:** offensive player who handles the ball.

**screen:** protect the receiver of a pass with a wall of players known as blockers.

**blitz:** have more than the usual number of defensive players charge the opposing team's quarterback while he is trying to pass.

**offensive back:** running back.

---

**HALAS** (*exasperated*). Sayers—what's the matter with you?

**GALE.** I—I don't know what you mean . . .

**HALAS.** I know you've got moves, but you don't have to show them to me now! You're hopping around here like a pauper[2] in a pay toilet!

**GALE** (*sputtering*). Well, I—I was just trying to stay on the side with your good ear . . .

**HALAS.** Good ear? What are you talking about, good ear?

**GALE.** Well, Brian Piccolo told me that—he said—uh—he—uh . . .

*Halas waits for the sentence to end, but it's not going to. For the realization is slowly dawning on Gale that he has been had. Gale struggles to manufacture a smile as Halas stares at him.*

2. **pauper** (pô′pər): person without any money.

**Direct cut to:**

**Interior—Dining hall—Night—Angle on steam table**

*The table is piled with food being assaulted by a number of large men, who ladle on portions that would choke a garbage disposal. At a centrally placed table, we can see Halas, his coaches, and key players.*

**Closer angle—Coaches' table**

*Seated on one side of Halas is Ed McCaskey, a handsome man in his early fifties. On the other side is Abe Gibron, a man who is all football. One man at the table is standing. This is J. C. Caroline, a man in his late twenties, tall and lean, built for speed. He has a packet of three-by-five index cards he consults as he speaks.*

**CAROLINE.** Some of you guys who pulled in today haven't had a chance to hear what's

**three-point stance:** crouched down with one hand touching the ground in a "ready" position.

**halfback option:** choice of the halfback to run with the ball or throw it when he gets it from the quarterback.

**flanker:** wide receiver who catches passes and is a fast runner.

**scrimmage:** here, a practice game.

**second string:** alternate players.

**fullback:** bigger, stronger running back who often leads interference and blocks the opposition's attempts to reach the carrier of the ball.

**pitch-out:** play in which the quarterback tosses the ball behind him to the running back instead of handing it off to him.

**carries:** acts of holding the ball and running with it.

**game ball:** ball that's used in game and may be awarded to the most valuable player in that game.

**number two halfback:** substitute or alternate halfback.

**punt return:** attempt by a player (the punt returner) to gain yards toward his team's goal by catching the ball after it has been punted (kicked) to the other team.

**kicker:** player who kicks to start the play or kicks field goals. Kickers don't have to be strong or quick since they usually don't have to block or run.

**end run:** a strategy whereby the quarterback hands the ball back to the running back, who runs around the line to score a touchdown.

---

going to be expected of you, so pipe down for a little bit, let me talk.

### Angle on Gale

*He is seated at one of the rear tables, exchanging "pass-the-salt" conversations with the other men nearby, all of whom are black. The man next to Gale finishes his plate and vacates the chair as Caroline continues to speak offstage. Brian Piccolo approaches and starts to unload his tray in the place next to Gale. Gale tries to hide his displeasure.*

**CAROLINE** (*droning offstage*). You new guys are going to be given a playbook tomorrow. It's like the Bible, except the Gideons[3] don't replace it for free. Neither do the Bears. Lose the playbook and the fine is five hundred dollars. No exceptions, no appeal. Five-double-o. Second thing is

3. **Gideons** (gid′ē·ənz): Gideons International, a Protestant organization that places Bibles in hotels and hospitals.

curfew. You don't like it; I don't like it. Well, that's just tough sleddin', because that fine is ten bucks for every fifteen minutes and there's no appeal from that either. Now—for talking in team meeting . . .

*Caroline becomes aware of Gale and Brian speaking offstage.*

**BRIAN.** Sayers, we can't go on meeting like this—my wife's getting suspicious.

**GALE.** Buzz off. I'm trying to listen to the Man.

**BRIAN.** No need, no need. I've been through this lecture twice already. If you lose the playbook, a fine of five big ones. Lose the playbook a second time, and they cut off your foot and feed it to the defensive platoon.

**GALE.** Just cool it, would you, please?

**BRIAN.** Just trying to be helpful.

**GALE.** Yes—like you "helped" me with Halas. Well, I don't need your kind of . . .

**CAROLINE** (*loudly offstage*). *Mister* Sayers!

## Wider angle

*J. C. Caroline fixes Gale with the look that's chilled any number of feckless[4] flankers. Every eye in the room is on Gale, and most are relishing his pained reaction.*

> **CAROLINE** (*continuing*). I was mentioning the fine for talking in a team meeting. Did you happen to hear me?
>
> **GALE.** No, I did not.
>
> **CAROLINE.** The fine is twenty-five dollars, Mr. Sayers. And it's just been levied on you, *dig*?
>
> **GALE** (*seething*). Yeah.

*Piccolo stares straight ahead, lips trembling as he tries to mask the laughter building up within him.*

> **BRIAN** (*sotto*). Sorry, man . . .

*Gale glares at him, homicide[5] in mind. Slow homicide.*

*Caroline gets to his feet, tapping the water glass for attention.*

> **CAROLINE.** It's been brought to my attention that unless Sayers was saying his beads[6] it might be fair if Mr. Piccolo was to give us a little song. Say—a fight song. Wake Forest, wasn't it, Mr. Piccolo?

## Angle to Brian and Gale

*Gale's look acknowledges that there may be some justice in this old world after all. To his surprise, however, the singing troubles Brian not at all. He smiles, rising, and when he sees the surprise on Gale's face, leans over to whisper.*

> **BRIAN.** Can't let it get to you, man—it's all a question of *style*. Style, I say . . .

*He is up on the chair, launching into the Wake Forest fight song, giving it a rousing tempo and booming volume. Brian thrives on this kind of thing. Gale's eye falls on something offstage in the direction of Brian's plate.*

## Gale's point of view—The plate

*Shot is centered on two mammoth dollops of mashed potatoes swimming in rich brown gravy.*

## Angle on Gale

*He takes a spoon and fork, glancing up to make sure Brian is still concentrating on the song, then moves to transfer the potatoes to the seat of Brian's chair.*

*As he finishes the song, Brian waves a cordial hand to those clapping, then hops down lightly and sits—without looking. Gale just sits there, looking at Brian, enjoying the rush of expressions that go rolling across his face. Disbelief. Dread. Realization. A look to the absent mashed potatoes on his plate. Acceptance. By the time he slowly swings his look over to Gale, Gale is just getting to his feet, face composed. Before he goes, however, he reminds Brian.*

> **GALE.** It's all a question of style— style, I say . . .

*He moves off, camera closing on Piccolo. He turns squishily, watching Gale* saunter *off. He can't quite work up a smile, but neither can he get to a point of being very angry about it. He can take it as well as hand it out, it seems.*

**Direct cut to:**

## Exterior—Practice field—Day—Tight on Gibron

*Abe Gibron is an assistant coach possessed of*

---

4. **feckless:** careless.
5. **homicide** (häm′ə·sīd): murder.
6. **beads:** rosary beads, a string of beads used by Roman Catholics to keep count while saying certain prayers.

---

**WORDS TO OWN**

**saunter** (sôn′tər) *v.:* stroll; walk in an unhurried way.

---

*a voice that could shatter glass. When we pull back, we will see that Gibron is presently riding herd on a number of offensive backs, Sayers and Piccolo in the forefront, as they lower their heads and dig against the resistance of the harness looped about their shoulders and fastened to a stone wall. Gibron will not be happy until one of the men pulls down the wall.*

> GIBRON. Dig! Dig! Dig! Come on! What's wrong with you? You're not trying! You're not trying! You make me sick! Dig—dig—dig!

**Hard cut to:**
## Exterior—Practice field—Day—Full shot

*Fifty men hit the dirt, then are up on their feet, running in place.*

> GIBRON. Mark! Set! Go!

*Sayers and Piccolo come out of a sprinter's crouch, taking each other on in wind sprints, their faces locked with drive and desire.*

## Angle to the forty-yard line

*Halas and a number of other coaches are standing. Gale tears across the line a full stride ahead of the others. Stopwatches are held out for Halas's perusal.[7] He notes the results and is pleased.*

## Angle on Gale and Brian

*They draw up, both sagging, leaning forward, hands on knees as they try to pull more air in. This may be the tenth wind sprint they've run today. Between gasps of breath:*

> BRIAN. Well—I think it's working.
> GALE. What's working?
> BRIAN. I'm getting you overconfident.

**Hard cut to:**
## Interior—Team meeting room—Day—On blackboard

---

7. **perusal** (pə·rōō′zəl): studying; careful reading.

*A play is diagrammed on the blackboard, the area covered with circles and X's, dotted lines, and arrows. Halas is the man with the chalk. No need to hear what he's saying—his look and the manner in which he raps the chalk against the slate get the message across.*

## Angle on Sayers and Piccolo

*They are seated near the front with the rest of the players, all of whom are studying the board as if their lives depended on it. Which, in one sense, it does. The look of exhaustion is shared by all as they listen and frantically scribble notes.*

**Direct cut to:**
## Exterior—Practice field—Day—Full shot

*The offense and defense take measure of one another. They line up, the ball is snapped. There is a brief flurry of motion, then the quarterback is downed by a large man from the defensive unit. As they all untangle themselves to the accompaniment of the whistles, Brian gets up and finds himself being glared at by Abe Gibron.*

> GIBRON. Pic! You bonehead! That was a fake draw, screen right! What's your assignment on a fake draw, screen right?
> BRIAN. My assignment on a fake draw, screen right, is to pick up the linebacker, if he's coming, unless the linebacker is Dick Butkus. Then I simply notify the quarterback and send for a priest.

*Laughter from the others on this, which only further enrages Gibron.*

## Angle on Gale

*He is smiling broadly at Piccolo's reply—smiling, perhaps, in spite of himself.*

> GIBRON (*offstage*). Come on, you guys, don't! You just encourage him, that's all! Knock it off!

**Direct cut to:**
**Exterior—Practice field—Night—Full shot**

*Gale moves along the walk bordering the practice area, dressed in casual sports clothes, an after-dinner stroll. He nears us, then stops, looking offstage, expression puzzled.*

### His point of view—On Brian

*In the middle of the empty practice field, he falls into a three-point stance, counts off a whispered series of signals, then breaks to his right. Just as he's about to turn upfield, he brakes sharply and cocks his arm, letting an imaginary pass go. Apparently, the imaginary receiver caught the ball, because Piccolo's expression is pleased as he turns back—and sees Gale watching his pantomime.[8] He shrugs.*

> BRIAN. I'm dynamite until there's someone playing against me.

### Another angle

*Gale moves to him, still a little puzzled.*

> BRIAN. Practicing the halfback option. I'm not too good at it, and it looks as if they want to use it a lot.
> GALE (*politely*). Oh, you'll get the hang of it.

*Brian smiles.*

> BRIAN. Wish I was as sure of that as you are. Tell you the truth, Sayers—I envy you.
> GALE. How come?
> BRIAN. Because they've got a lot of money tied up in you. They can't cut you.

*Gale just looks at him for a second, then turns abruptly and starts off.*

> BRIAN (*simply*). And you're too good to get cut, bonus or no bonus.

8. **pantomime** (pan′tə·mīm′): dramatic presentation using only silent actions and gestures.

*Gale stops, turns back slowly.*
> (*beat*)

> BRIAN. And I'm too good, too, but I'm not sure I've proved that to the Old Man yet.

*Gale is thrown off stride mentally. Piccolo's easy directness takes some getting used to. Brian views him with a small smile.*

> BRIAN. Sayers—I am bending over backwards to get through that turtle shell of yours. Can't you at least say thank you or something?
> GALE. Well—I don't do things like you do—telling jokes and all that kind of—you know—I—I'm more of a . . . (*Considers*) Thanks.

*A quick nod, then Gale turns and heads back in the direction of the dormitory. Piccolo smiles, taking even this small breakthrough as some kind of progress. He gets to his feet and is about to go through the halfback option once more.*

> GALE. Hey, Piccolo?
> BRIAN. Yeah?
> GALE. Try it going to your left. They don't look for a right-handed guy to throw going to his left.

*Brian nods, smiling as their eyes meet; Gale's look still a guarded one.*
> (*beat*)

> BRIAN. Thanks.

*Gale shrugs, glances down.*

> GALE. Well, like you said—us rookies got to stick together.

**Hard cut to:**
**Interior—Hallway outside Halas's office—Day—On door**

*Gale raps on the door several times.*

> HALAS (*offstage*). Come on in, Gale.

*Gale opens the door and steps in, camera following to reveal Halas behind the desk, Ed McCaskey seated nearby, and J. C. Caroline doodling on the blackboard. Gale views the three with a mixture of fear and curiosity.*

HALAS. You know Ed McCaskey, don't you, Gale? And J.C.?

*Affirmative ad-libs[9] come from Gale and the other two men. Gale takes the chair that has obviously been left vacant for him. Halas nods toward a pitcher of iced tea.*

HALAS. Want some iced tea?
GALE. Uh, yeah. Please.

*Halas pours him a glass, the cubes tinkling. Gale fidgets. Halas hands him the glass.*

HALAS. Tell you what we wanted to talk to you about, Gale . . . See, I'm an old-timer in a lot of ways . . . (*A look to Caroline and McCaskey*) At least that's what people keep telling me—but I don't think it's all that uncommon for a man my age to get used to the way things are—to be comfortable with things. You understand what I'm saying?
GALE (*baffled*). I guess so. . . .
HALAS. Well, what it comes down to is that J.C. here had a notion and he talked to Ed about it, and Ed thinks it's a good idea—and I guess maybe it's time for some changes around here. You follow me?
GALE. You want me to play flanker, not running back.

*The other three exchange a smile at this.*

MCCASKEY. Not that simple, Gale. J.C.'s point—and one I agree with—is that it's 1965 and it's time the Bears roomed together by position—without any regard to race.
CAROLINE. We'd like you and Brian Piccolo to room together.

9. **affirmative ad-libs:** remarks improvised by the actors, meaning "yes."

*Gale smiles with relief.*

GALE. Is that all? Is that what this is about?
CAROLINE. Is that *all*?
GALE. Yeah. You had me worried. I thought it was something really . . .

**Tight on Caroline**

*His index finger shoots out, pinning Gale to the chair.*

CAROLINE. Sayers—this *is* something, really. This is a white man and a black man rooming together on a team where that's never been done before. You're going to be called a Tom by some blacks and uppity by some whites. And when we go on the road, we'll be going to Atlanta and Dallas and Houston and Miami—and don't think it's going to get any better in Los Angeles and Detroit and Chicago, and every other town we play in, 'cause it *won't*.
   (*beat*)
You're going to rock the boat, Sayers—and there's plenty of people around who are already seasick.

*A beat, as Caroline holds Gale's gaze, then straightens up. Halas has a small smile on his face.*

HALAS. Have a glass of iced tea, J.C.

*Halas leans forward.*

HALAS. What J.C. is saying is that there may be pressures, Gale. Severe ones. (*Simply*) Now! What do *you* say?

*Gale takes a breath, looking beyond the three men, giving the question the introspection it deserves.*

**Direct cut to:**
**Interior—Dormitory hallway—Night—On Brian**

*Brian comes down the hallway, wearing a windbreaker and casual slacks. Offstage we* can hear the sound of muted rock music. Brian's face is set, _dour_ and depressed. He stops in front of one of the doors, pulls a key out of his pocket, then registers: That music is coming from his room. He looks down at the space between the door and the floor. There's light peeping out from within the room. Puzzled, he puts the key in the lock and opens the door cautiously.

### Interior—The room

_A picture is thumbtacked to the bulletin board, of Joy Piccolo and a baby girl. We pan over to reveal another picture tacked up on the bulletin board next to Joy's. The second picture is of Linda Sayers. We pan down from this picture to find Gale sprawled out on the bed, the radio blaring by his side. He reaches out and turns off the radio._

**GALE.** Hi. We're rooming together.

**BRIAN.** Says who?

**GALE.** Who else?

**BRIAN** (_sourly_). Terrific. Sort of a shame he couldn't ask me how I felt about it, isn't it?

**GALE** (_warily_). Look, if you want me out . . .

**BRIAN.** No, stay, I don't want you out. I'm just steamed at the Old Man for not putting me in the scrimmage this afternoon.

 (_beat_)

Is that your wife?

**GALE.** Yeah.

**BRIAN.** She's pretty.

**GALE.** So's yours. And the little girl.

**BRIAN** (_still down_). Thanks. I'm supposed to call her tonight—tell her how I'm doing. Be the shortest phone call in history.

**GALE.** Maybe not.

_When Piccolo looks over at him, Gale smiles._

**GALE.** Pic—they wouldn't assign us to room together unless we _both_ made the team.

_Brian looks over at Gale and it hits him. He moves to Gale, pulling him off the bed and shoving him toward the door._

**BRIAN.** Come on! We've got to call our wives!

**GALE.** I already called Linda, right after . . .

**BRIAN.** That was just practice! This is for real! Come on!

_And the two of them go tumbling out into the corridor._

### Full shot—The corridor

_Atkins, O'Bradovich, and Evey are standing a few feet away—huge men, arms like hams, necks like tree stumps. Their expressions are insolent, challenging, but not cruel. Each of them has a coffee can in hand. Each container holds a sticky-looking, evil-smelling conglomeration[10] of honey, cereal, sand, catsup, and whatever they could lay their hands on. They move in unison toward Brian and Gale._

**ATKINS.** Congratulations on making the team, gentlemen. Well done.

**EVEY.** As you know, Coach Halas frowns on the hazing[11] of new men.

**O'BRADOVICH.** But now that you've made the team—it's really like—you're one of us.

_All three have wooden spoons in the ooze, lifting the dripping, brown gunk for all to see. In a second, they're all tearing down the hall. Gale and Brian are bent low, the three pursuers bellowing with the thrill of the hunt. The last words echo in the corridor as all the_

---

10. **conglomeration** (kən·gläm′ər·ā′shən): mixture of different sorts of things.
11. **hazing:** initiating of new members by bullying them or making them do ridiculous things.

---

### WORDS TO OWN

**dour** (door) _adj._: gloomy; sullen.
**insolent** (in′sə·lənt) _adj._: boldly disrespectful.

---

*doors are opened and men stick their heads out to see which rookies are getting it now.*

**ATKINS** (*yelling*). Welcome to the Chicago Bears!

## Interior—Bears' locker room—Day—Full shot

*Gale is in front of his locker, just pulling off his jersey, which is muddy and torn. Two reporters are on each side of him. Piccolo, whose uniform looks as if he stepped out of a catalog, is seated in front of his locker, taking it all in with a certain objective humor. Gale, typically, is ill at ease in this kind of situation.*

**REPORTER #1.** Is playing in the NFL easier than you thought it would be?

**GALE.** Only played one game. Not exactly an expert.

**REPORTER #2.** But you didn't look as if you were having too much trouble out there.

**GALE.** The blocks were there.

**BRIAN.** Sure is different from the way you were talking last night, Gale. (*To reporters*) He calls the offensive line the "seven blocks of Silly Putty."

**GALE.** Pic——

**REPORTER #1.** You're Brian Piccolo?

**BRIAN.** P—I—C—C—O—L—O, yes.

**Direct cut to:**

## NFL footage

*A long run from scrimmage by Sayers.*

**BRIAN** (*voice-over*). Gale, when you run, do you think about what you're doing, or do you just do it?

**GALE** (*voice-over*). I just do it.

**BRIAN** (*voice-over*). Well, start thinking about it, will you? I want to play, too.

**Direct cut to:**

## Interior—Pizza parlor—Night—Full shot

*Grouped about one of the tables are Gale, Brian, and their wives, Joy Piccolo and Linda*

*Sayers. They're at ease with one another, just now finishing off a casual, enjoyable evening on the town. They are listening to one of Brian's stories. He's telling it well, laughing as he does so, and it's a catching kind of thing for the women. Gale, being Gale, allows himself a small smile, but little beyond that.*

**BRIAN.** Now—picture this—Concannon calls a trap, see. . . . (*To Linda and Joy*) You know what a trap is?

**LINDA** (*unsure*). I think so, but—maybe . . .

**BRIAN.** Well—uh—all the linemen go one way and hopefully the defense guys go that way, too. If they do, there's a big hole, see? If they don't—bad news. Anyway—Concannon calls a trap up the middle, Gale carrying the ball. It works like they draw it on the blackboard. Forty-three yards. Beautiful. So, Halas sees Gale's winded; he tells me to go in. So, I go in; Gale comes out. We get in the huddle—Concannon decides he's going to get foxy. He calls the *same* play. The very same play. Last thing they'll be looking for, he says. Now—the trap play is also called the "sucker play" because the defense really looks bad when it works— and defenses don't like to look bad— makes 'em <u>surly</u>.

*Joy, who's heard this story a hundred times already, has started to laugh, anticipating Brian's big finish.*

**BRIAN.** So—we come out of the huddle— ball's snapped—all our linemen go one way—and it's like I'm looking at a team portrait of the Los Angeles Rams—Hello, Deacon . . . Merlin, how's the family . . . Rosey . . .

*Laughter from them all, ad-libs between the*

**WORDS TO OWN**

**surly** (sʉr′lē) *adj*.: bad-tempered, rude, and hostile.

girls. *Gale's smile has broadened now and Brian's just having a fine old time.*

> BRIAN. I mean—I was afraid to get up. I figured not everything was going to come with me. . . .
>
> JOY (*nicely*). You never saw anyone so black and blue.
>
> GALE. Yeah—it was like rooming with a black player again.

*Gale grins—and the other three gape, looking at him with expressions of shock. His smile turns uneasy, bewildered. He checks to make sure there's no anchovy hanging off his chin.*

> LINDA. Gale—you told a *joke.*
>
> BRIAN. Joy—did you hear it? The great Stone Face from Kansas told a joke!

*Brian turns to the other patrons, cupping his hands about his mouth.*

> BRIAN (*yelling*). Chicago! There's hope for us all! Sayers *speaks!*
>
> GALE. Aw, come *on,* Pic. . . .

*But Gale's smiling, pleased with himself if the truth were known, as is Linda Sayers. The camera holds on them.*

**Direct cut to:**
**NFL footage of a Sayers run—Slow motion**

*This footage should be the most impressive of all, selling the power and grace of Sayers's ability.*

> BRIAN (*voice-over*). Magic—I think I'm going to write you a speech.
>
> GALE (*voice-over*). What kind of speech?
>
> BRIAN (*voice-over*). Acceptance speech for "Rookie of the Year." You can't miss.
>
> GALE (*voice-over*). And I got to give a *speech?* You're putting me on!

**Direct cut to:**
**Interior—Banquet dais—Night—Tight spot**

*Offstage the sound of a speaker drones on.*

*Gale, Linda, Brian, and Joy are on the dais—the men in tuxedos, the women in formal gowns. Brian has a crumpled piece of paper in his hand. He leans into Gale, speaking in an urgent whisper.*

**BRIAN.** From the top. One more time.

**GALE** (*harried, by rote*). I'd like to thank you all for this honor, though it's really not right to give it to one man. Football is a—team sport, and I . . .

**SPEAKER** (*offstage*). Gale Sayers!

*A spotlight floods the area and we hear off-stage applause. Gale is urged to his feet by Brian and Linda. He moves toward the speaker's platform, petrified. All we can see is Gale; the harsh pinpoint of the carbon arc is centered on him with no residual spillage.*[12] *He looks at the trophy for a second.*

**GALE** (*trembling*). I'd—I'd like to thank you all for this honor, though it's really not right . . .

*He stops. He stops because he can't think of the next word. It's gone. Nothing there. Joy and Linda agonize in the silence, trying to pray more words out of Gale. Brian can't believe it. He starts to slowly tear the speech up, shaking his head, grinning. Gale's mouth is like Death Valley.*

**GALE.** Thank you.

*Brian tosses the pieces of paper in the air, like confetti, smiling.*

**BRIAN.** Who'd believe it—who'd ever believe it. . . .

**Direct cut to:**

**Exterior—Sayers's house—Night**

**BRIAN.** Hey, Gale?

*Gale holds on the porch. Linda waves a hand toward the car, her words intended for Gale.*

**LINDA.** Too cold out here. I'll warm your side of the bed.

*She moves into the house as Brian gets out of the car and trots to Gale, both men with shoulders hunched against the cold. Brian moves to him.*

**GALE.** What do you want, man? It's freezing out here!

**BRIAN.** Something I've got to tell you.

**GALE.** What is it?

*Gale notes an edge to Brian's voice, an under-current*[13] *of* reluctance, *shyness. Brian looks him directly in the eye.*

**BRIAN.** Joy and I had a long talk last night—about whether or not I should ask to be traded. We decided that I wouldn't ask. I like the guys on the team; I like the town.
   (*beat*)
What I *don't* like is playing second string.

**GALE** (*quietly*). I don't blame you.

**BRIAN.** Now—*maybe* I've got a shot at full-back. But I don't think Halas thinks I'm big enough. He'll probably go with Ralph Kurek. The other spot is yours—and that's the job I'm gunning for, Gale.

*Gale starts to reply, but Brian silences him with a gesture.*

**BRIAN.** Let me get it said.
   (*beat*)
I'm a better blocker than you are and I'm as good a receiver. And if I can't break

13. **undercurrent:** unspoken feeling. Literally, *undercurrent* refers to a stream of water flowing beneath the surface.

12. **carbon arc . . . spillage:** The carbon arc, or spotlight, is turned directly on Gale, with no light spilling off onto anyone else (no "residual spillage").

**WORDS TO OWN**

**reluctance** (ri•luk′tən s) *n.*: unwillingness.

away for sixty, I can still get ten sixes, and it adds up the same way. I'm going to come into camp next year in the best shape ever, and I think I've got a realistic chance to blow you out of the lineup. . . . And that's just what I'm going to try to do.

**GALE.** I understand, man—that's your job.

**BRIAN.** Yeah—but I don't like to do "a job" on a friend.

**GALE** (*small smile*). Don't worry; you won't.

*There's no anger between them, just resolve. After a beat, there is a light tap on the car horn. Brian looks at the trophy: He touches it lightly.*

**BRIAN** (*as Bogart*).[14] It's a Maltese Falcon, kid—get this inside—and the free world is safe.

*With that, Brian moves back to the car, camera holding on Gale as he looks after his nutty friend, then down to the trophy. He heads for the door.*

**Direct cut to:**

**Interior—Halas's office—Day—On picture**

*Another team picture is being tacked on the wall, the printing identifying it as last year's Bears.*

**Direct cut to:**

**Exterior—Practice field area—Day— Full shot**

*Gale and Brian take positions in a line for wind sprints. Their look to each other is friendly, but neither has precisely a fix on what attitude is the working one. They speak as the line moves forward. There are sounds of the other men yelling offstage.*

**BRIAN.** Hi. You just pull in?

14. **Humphrey Bogart** (1899-1957): American actor who starred in *The Maltese Falcon,* a film in which the main characters pursue a treasured sculpture of a falcon.

**GALE.** Yeah. Would have been here this morning, but the flight got fogged in in Detroit. You look in good shape.

**BRIAN.** I am. Worked hard this winter.

**GIBRON** (*yelling offstage*). *Go!*

**Full shot**

*Brian takes off, arms pumping, but Gale is laughing at a joke Brian has just told. Brian is past the forty at least three seconds before Gale, grinning from ear to ear.*

*Gale draws up from his leisurely sprint. They haven't even kept the clock on his effort.*

**GALE.** Mind if I try it again?

**HALAS.** Might be a good idea.

*Gale starts to retrace his steps to the goal line, then draws up, looking back to Gibron and Halas.*

**GALE.** What was Pic's time like?

*Gibron consults the clipboard.*

**GIBRON.** Must be out to get you. . . . He's about half a second faster this year than last.

*Gale is not frightened, but properly impressed. He nods, taking it in. His expression denies his statement.*

**GALE.** That's really terrific. . . .

**Direct cut to:**

**Exterior—Practice field—Day—Full shot**

*A number of men dot the area, going through calisthenics. We find Gale and Brian doing sit-ups, each being helped by another player who anchors their feet. They're facing in opposite directions so that, as they come up, they're looking at each other. The looks are not hostile, but there's very little "give" in each man's expression.*

## Exterior—Practice field—Day—Full shot

*The offense and defense are performing the one-on-one drill. This time, it's Brian who's the offensive back and the move he puts on the defensive man is a beauty. As Brian tears out of frame, we zoom in on Gale,* impassive *outwardly, but fully aware of what's going on.*

**Direct cut to:**

## Interior—Dormitory hallway—Night—Full shot

*Gale and Brian come in from the outside, both wearing light jackets, Brian carrying a pizza box.*

**BRIAN.** That's why you'll never cut it, Sayers—pizza has magical properties that give Italian guys strength and speed.
**GALE.** Yeah—a lot of great Italian running backs, all right.
**BRIAN.** Yeah. Jim Brownanelli. Lennie Moorelli. All those guys.

## Angle to stairway

*At the bottom is a bulletin board, where J. C. Caroline stands putting up a large sheet of paper. Brian moves by him, taking the stairs two at a time, and ad-libs a greeting, which is returned by J.C. Gale comes by.*

**GALE.** What's that, J.C.?
**CAROLINE.** Starting lineups for the first exhibition.

*Gale's eye moves toward the landing of the second floor. The shadow of Brian Piccolo can be seen. His head turns slowly, listening.*

**GALE.** What's the backfield?
**CAROLINE** (*as he goes*). Concannon, Ralph Kurek, and you.

*If ever there were mixed emotions in a man, now is that time. Gale looks up.*

## His point of view—Brian's shadow

*Sagging, head lowered. A long beat, then Brian takes a breath, straightens his shoulders and moves off, the shadow disappearing.*

**BRIAN** (*offstage*). Come on, Magic. . . . Pizza's getting cold.

## Tight on Gale

*He leans against the wall, disappointed and yet relieved at the same time. He looks toward the second-story landing once more, as we start to hear the growing roar of a large crowd, the unwavering roar of the hero seekers.*

**Direct cut to:**

## Exterior—Wrigley Field—Day—NFL footage

*The stands are crowded with spectators. The day is damp and gray.*

## Angle to field—NFL footage

*The Bears are playing the San Francisco 49ers.*

## Angle to Bears' bench

*Gale's uniform, muddy and begrimed; Piccolo's with only a smudge or two. Halas and Gibron pace restlessly up and down the sidelines, yelling to the defensive unit, as are all the other players. Concannon is on the phones, listening intently.*

## Angle to field

*The ball is snapped to 49er quarterback John Brodie and he backpedals, looking for a receiver going deep. Brodie gets the pass off, but it falls into the hands of a defensive back from the Chicago Bears.*

---

**WORDS TO OWN**

**impassive** (im·pas′iv) *adj.*: not showing emotion.

## Angle to bench

*Every man is on his feet yelling. There is a flurry of activity—Gale is pulling on his helmet, receiving a pat from Brian. Concannon takes off the earphones and moves with the rest of the offensive team onto the field.*

## Angle to stands

> LINDA. Go get 'em, Gale!! You can do it, honey!

## Tight on Joy Piccolo

*Happy at this turn of events but also painfully aware of something else, her eyes move from the field to the bench.*

## Her point of view—On Brian

*With his back to the stands, helmet off, Number 41 paces restlessly back and forth along the sidelines. His attention is on the game, but the gaze drops a few times as inward moments take over.*

## Angle to Bears' huddle

> CONCANNON. Yours, Gale. Twenty-eight toss. South. Line. On three. *Break!*

## Full shot

*The team comes out of the huddle, moving with precision into formation. Concannon looks over the defense and calls out the signals in a rhythmic cadence.[15] The ball is snapped and Concannon* pivots, *the move coordinated with the pulling of the guards and Gale's instantaneous break to his left. The ball is tossed back to Gale. He takes the pitch-out and has the ball well in hand as he starts to look for an opening in the upfield area.*

## On Brian

*He is at the water bucket, dipper poised as he stops to watch the play develop.*

15. **cadence** (kād''ns): beat.

## Back on Gale

*Seemingly from nowhere, a San Francisco 49er uniform comes hurtling into frame and we freeze frame just before the shoulder of the player tears into Gale's knee. All crowd noises are killed. Only silence. The frame moves again now and we can see the awful impact. Freeze frame on this instant. The picture comes to life in short bursts as Gale crumples, knee landing at an angle to set one's teeth on edge, in jerky, grainy images.*

## On Brian

*A freeze frame slowly moves forward half a step; he realizes what he's witnessing.*

## On Linda and Joy

*They are very much afraid of what they're seeing. Linda's hand flies to her mouth.*

## Back on Gale

*He hits the ground, one hand already going to the knee, the ball forgotten about. He tries to get to his feet, and the instant he puts any pressure on the knee, his head snaps back in reaction to the agony that assaults him. We freeze frame on Gale, every muscle contorted, and we hear the sound of a siren wailing, wailing, wailing.*

**Hard cut to:**

## Exterior—Sayers's home—Day—Full shot

*The car, driven by Linda, pulls to a halt in the driveway. Gale opens the door and starts to get out. He's using two metal canes, the right leg swung out before him, stiff and unbending. His face is chiseled with tension and anger—cold, acid anger.*

> LINDA. Can I help?
> GALE. No.

---

**WORDS TO OWN**

**pivots** (piv'əts) *v.:* rotates; turns around as if on an axis.

---

He makes his way slowly toward the front door, still not used to the canes, not yet using his body weight to help himself. Instead, it's a halting, unnatural motion—painful to execute, more painful for Linda to watch. She hurries past him to open the front door.

## Interior—The living room—Day—Full shot

Gale comes in, no reaction to being home in his eyes. He moves to the first chair and sits.

> LINDA. It's good to have you home, Gale.
> GALE. Yeah. Good to be home.

But his eyes admit it was a reply made because it was the reply expected.

> LINDA. Can I get you anything?
> GALE. No. I'm fine.
> LINDA. It's about lunch time. You want a sandwich or anything?
> GALE. Not hungry; you go ahead, though.
> LINDA. Are you sure?
> GALE (with an edge). Yes, I'm sure.

The emotional moat he's built up is too wide to be crossed at this point. Linda kisses him lightly on the cheek, then rises and moves to the kitchen. She pauses at the door, looking back at him, a tentative smile on her face, but Gale's expression doesn't match or encourage the smile. Disheartened, Linda leaves the room.

## Tight on Gale

His hand moves to the injured knee, the cast large beneath the trouser leg. Alone, the mask falters slightly and the fear is unmistakable. Then, after a moment or two, we, and Gale, start to hear the sound of a man singing. We've heard the song before. It's Brian singing the Wake Forest fight song. Gale looks with disbelief toward another door off of the living room. Using the canes, Gale pulls himself to an upright position and makes his way slowly across the room to the door. He pulls it open.

## Angle down basement stairway

The singing is louder now. A beat, then Brian's smiling face appears at the bottom. He's wearing old clothes, carries a crescent wrench in one hand.

> BRIAN. Hey, Magic . . . thought you'd never get here.

He moves back out of sight and we hear the sound of something metal being tapped upon. Gale enters frame and starts down the steps carefully.

> GALE. Pic—what are you doing down there?

## Interior—Basement—Full shot—Day

This is not a recreation room. The walls are cement block, gun-metal gray; a washer and dryer are in a corner. Opposite them, Brian Piccolo is tightening bolts on a metal framework that will eventually be used as a leg-lift machine. Gale negotiates the last few steps.

> BRIAN. It's not a bad act, Gale, but Peg Leg Bates[16] does it better.
> GALE (indicating machine). What's that supposed to be?
> BRIAN. It's not "supposed" to be anything but what it is—a leg-lift machine.
> GALE. What for?
> BRIAN. What for? Gale—getting that knee back into shape is not going to be a take-it-easy number. If you're afraid, that's understandable, but . . .

16. **Peg Leg Bates:** Clayton Bates (1908–1998), a famous jazz dancer who continued to dance even after his leg was amputated.

- - - - - - - - - - - - - - - - - - - - - - - - - - - - - -

### WORDS TO OWN
**disheartened** (dis·härt′nd) v. used as adj.: discouraged.

- - - - - - - - - - - - - - - - - - - - - - - - - - - - - -

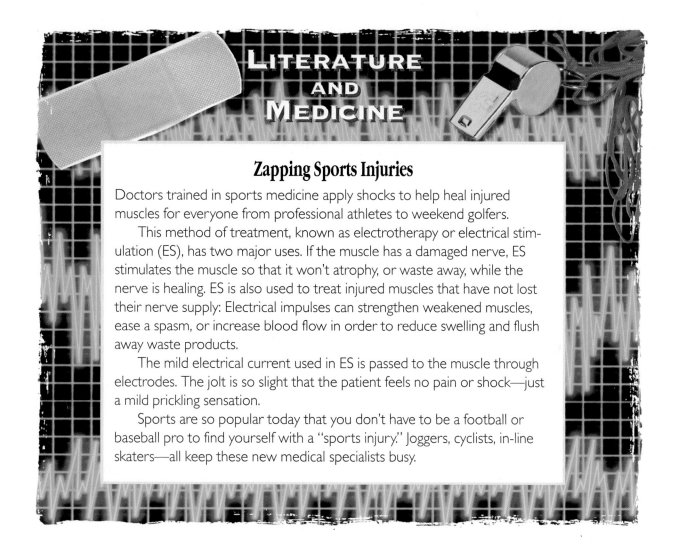

## Zapping Sports Injuries

Doctors trained in sports medicine apply shocks to help heal injured muscles for everyone from professional athletes to weekend golfers.

This method of treatment, known as electrotherapy or electrical stimulation (ES), has two major uses. If the muscle has a damaged nerve, ES stimulates the muscle so that it won't atrophy, or waste away, while the nerve is healing. ES is also used to treat injured muscles that have not lost their nerve supply: Electrical impulses can strengthen weakened muscles, ease a spasm, or increase blood flow in order to reduce swelling and flush away waste products.

The mild electrical current used in ES is passed to the muscle through electrodes. The jolt is so slight that the patient feels no pain or shock—just a mild prickling sensation.

Sports are so popular today that you don't have to be a football or baseball pro to find yourself with a "sports injury." Joggers, cyclists, in-line skaters—all keep these new medical specialists busy.

**GALE** (*hard*). I am *not* afraid!

*Piccolo is out of patience. He picks up the tools and starts for the stairway.*

**BRIAN** (*quietly*). You ought to be, Gale.
**GALE.** Pic, maybe you think this is a real friendly thing you're doing, but . . .
**BRIAN.** And you can put that in your ditty bag, too, you stupid jackass—friendship hasn't got one thing to do with this. . . .

*Piccolo is halfway up the steps now. He stops, looking back at Gale, weighing whether or not to go on. Sayers's expression is stubborn and angry, but no more so than Brian's. A beat, then Brian sits on one of the steps.*

**BRIAN.** Gale—when I was in high school—I was one of the best backs in the state. Unfortunately for me, *the* best back in the state, Tucker Fredrickson, went to the same school. And the colleges would come down to watch us and Tuck ended up at Auburn—and I ended up at Wake Forest. Good school, nice place, but not exactly center ring, you follow?

(*beat*)

So—I work my butt off at Forest. And my senior year—I led the nation in rushing and scoring. . . . (*Softly*) I mean—I led the *entire* nation.

(*beat*)

So, I look around for a pro team, and I pick the Bears. Then, who else comes to the Bears—Sayers. Big gun from a big school, and I'm number two all over again.

(beat)

Well, Gale—I'm number one guy now, but for all the wrong reasons. And if you don't come back one hundred percent, people are always going to say that I got in on a pass, a lucky break, and I won't take it that way. (Rises) I am going to beat you, Magic, but it won't mean a thing unless you're at your best, not one second slower, one degree weaker. I'm going to work your tail off getting you into shape again—for *my* sake.

**Full shot**

*Brian turns and goes to the top of the stairs. Gale stands there, rage stilled, cooled, then turns, looking steadily at the leg-lift machine. He moves to it, running his fingertips over it lightly, seeking reassurance from the chilled metal.*

**Direct cut to:**
**Exterior—City park—Day—On Gale**

*It's a blustery, cold day. The wind drives ribbons of dry snow along the walk. Gale moves toward us, using a wooden cane, the limp noticeable but not as bad as previously seen. He wears an overcoat, the collar turned up, and a grim expression. In his free hand he carries a small radio. A sportscaster is heard over the sound of the wind.*

ANNOUNCER (*voice-over*). And in Los Angeles, the Chicago Bears trimmed the Rams by a score of seventeen to sixteen. Quarterback Jack Concannon was eight for fourteen passing, and the running game was ably manned by Brian Piccolo, who gained 105 yards in fourteen carries. Piccolo was awarded the game ball.

*Gale is adjacent to a litter basket. He stops for a beat, his back to us, then deposits the cane into the basket. His step seems to have more drive to it when he moves on.*

**Direct cut to:**
**Exterior—Park area—Day—On Gale**

*It's early morning as Gale, dressed in a sweatsuit, comes jogging toward us. His expression is stoic, the pace quite slow, the sort of speed one recommends to those just discharged from the hospital after hernial surgery. But the pace is steady and dogged.*

DR. FOX (*voice-over*). (*Filter*) Hello?
BRIAN (*voice-over*). (*Filter*) Dr. Fox? This is Brian Piccolo. How's he doing?
DR. FOX (*voice-over*). (*Filter*) Very well, I think. Though it's boring going through those exercises all by yourself. It's drudgery and it's painful, and a lot of people just give up when they're alone in that situation.

**Direct cut to:**
**Interior—Sayers's basement—Night—Tight on Gale**

*Gale is lying on his back, feet in the air, as he strains to lift the platform bearing a sizable portion of weights. He's drenched with sweat, puffing. We pan up from his face to the knee, seeing the wicked-looking scar that creases the flesh. As he starts to lift the platform, we pull back to reveal Piccolo seated nearby. He has a small kitchen egg timer in his hand.*

BRIAN. And—ten. (*Setting timer*) Minute rest, then one more set.
GALE. *Another* one?
BRIAN. Last one tonight. Hang in there.

---

**WORDS TO OWN**

**stoic** (stō′ik) *adj.*: not showing or complaining about pain. Stoics were philosophers of ancient Greece who tried not to let pleasure or pain affect them.

---

*Gale remains on the floor under the weight machine. He sighs, getting his breath back.*

**BRIAN.** How's the knee feel?

**GALE** (*dispirited*). Oh, one day it feels as strong as ever; the next day it's like I got spaghetti for ligaments.[17]

> (*beat*)

**BRIAN.** You know—if it doesn't come all the way back—it won't be the end of the world, Gale.

**GALE.** That so?

**BRIAN.** Football's terrific, man, but it's still just a job.

**GALE.** It's the only job I know how to do.

> (*beat*)

I'm not like you—I can't talk and all that stuff.

**BRIAN.** Talking now . . .

**GALE.** It's different.

> (*beat*)

**BRIAN.** You'll learn how to talk, once you find something that's got to be said.

*The egg timer chirps once and Gale lifts his legs to the underside of the platform bearing the weights.*

**BRIAN.** Third set. Ten reps. *Go.*

*Gale starts to lift. The first three or four times go smoothly enough, but about halfway through the fifth one . . .*

**GALE** (*straining*). I'll never make ten, man—no juice left . . .

**BRIAN.** Don't bone me! Come on, Magic! Hang tough! Five. Way to go—six—lookin' good, Magic. Come on. . . .

**GALE.** No—way . . .

**BRIAN.** You aren't getting out that easy! Come on! You can do it! Seven! Fantastic! Three more, man! Work on it! Are these the legs of a murderer? Come on, Gale! Eight! Got it! Two more!

17. **ligaments:** bands of tough tissue connecting bones.

**GALE.** No—way . . .

## Tight on Brian

*He is leaning over Gale, mind seeking a ploy.*

**BRIAN.** Can't make it, huh, weakling? Giving up, is that it? Is that what you're doing?

## Tight on Gale

*Looking up at Brian expressionlessly—then a stifled laugh breaks from his lips. He smiles.*

**GALE.** Come on, man—don't make me laugh.

*Gale starts to laugh and lets the weights come to rest on the stops. Brian just stands there without any comprehension of how his maneuver could have backfired so badly.*

**Direct cut to:**

## Exterior wooded area—Day—Long shot

*Brian and Gale move along a narrow dirt road that winds through the trees. Their pace is no longer that of a jog, but one more suited to a brisk 880.[18]*

## Closer—Trucking

*We move back in front of the two of them as they run, both in control, arms pumping smoothly, the motion fluid and easy. After a few seconds, Brian looks over briefly at Gale, then he picks up the pace a little, opening a few yards between them. Gale takes this with some surprise but matches Brian and closes the gap. But it's only temporary, for Brian ups the ante once more, the pace now at 440[19] clip. Gale's eyes flash as Brian moves away, but he picks it up again. He's shoulder to shoulder with Pic.*

**BRIAN.** A beer for the first man to the bridge!

18. **880:** referring to a race of 880 yards, or half a mile. The pace is slower than a dash but faster than a long-distance run.

19. **440:** referring to a race of 440 yards, or a quarter-mile. The pace is much faster than that of an 880-yard race.

**GALE.** You're on!

## Different angle

*Brian peels off from the road and crashes into the trees flanking the road. Gale is a little surprised at this cross-country route, but he's right after Brian, though he's got about five or six yards to make up due to the momentary hesitation.*

## On Brian

*There are no paths here, no easy routes. The trees and shrubs make it necessary to dart this way and that, hurdle logs, scramble up steep slopes and gullies. Brian is in the lead, but Gale's responding to the challenge, charging after him at full bore.*

## Various cuts—The chase

*The two of them are bound together by an invisible rope, though the rope has developed a tendency to shrink slightly. It's almost imperceptible, but Gale is making up ground on Brian. They come to a creek bed five or six inches deep, and as they go splashing through it, we go to slow motion—droplets exploding into the sunlight, the two men calling on reserves from deep within. The small stream dwindles to loose shale.*

## The fall

*A scant step behind Piccolo, Gale loses his footing on the stones and takes a head-over-heels tumble, a really bad one, pinwheeling over and over violently. Piccolo halts immediately, looking back at Gale with concern.*

## On Brian

*He is gasping for breath, looking to Gale.*

## On Gale

*He meets Brian's look. Every breath hurts, sears. He glances down at the knee, then stands slowly, brushing the stones from the palms of his hands. He meets Brian's look. He nods.*

## Full shot

*Like catapults,[20] they both turn and take off. They burst out of the trees, Gale a step behind. This is the final all-out sprint for the tape. Nothing held in reserve at this point, they pull great gulps of air in, straining, eyes frozen on the finish up ahead. And with each step, Gale moves up. An inch, no more, but that inch is repeated with each step, every stride bringing him closer to Brian's shoulder.*

## Long shot

*As they near a small wooden footbridge, they move, it seems, as one, mirror images of black and white. They both literally hurl themselves at the imaginary tape and go tumbling across the bridge with their momentum, sprawling in the soft grass on the other side.*

*They are both lying there, having given it all they had to give. They're shiny as seals with perspiration, their eyes bright with fatigue, focusing on the blue sky overhead. After a long moment, they both sit up, shaky smiles on their faces, though they're still puffing like a Saint Bernard in Palm Springs.*

> **BRIAN.** I—think—I—owe—you—a—beer.
> **GALE** (*shakes head*). I—think—I—owe—you—a—lot—more—than—that.
> **BRIAN.** Yeah—you're—healthy.
> **GALE.** Yeah.

*And they look at each other, the expressions of both growing a little serious, aware that, as friends, they are still competitors; there's only one brass ring on this merry-go-round.*

---

20. **catapults** (kat′ə·pultz′): devices like giant slingshots, used for throwing objects.

# The Day the Butterfly Came

He never really had a name, the Butterfly. Jenny and her grandfather had just found him there, on the windowsill.

It was a quiet day in spring, and not much was going on. Jenny was pushing her grandfather around in his wheelchair. Just as she was about to suggest they go inside, there he was, the Butterfly.

Jenny quickly wheeled her grandfather over to it. Afraid to scare it, she just stood there. "It's not going anywhere," her grandfather told her. Sometimes Jenny thought he knew everything about animals, even what they were thinking.

"How come he's not with the rest of the butterflies in the old maple?" Jenny questioned the old man.

"Not all animals belong together, Jenny," he answered her.

And every day after that, the Butterfly came to the windowsill. Sometimes only for a while, but he always came. It puzzled Jenny because he never joined the others.

One morning she asked her grandfather, "Should we take him to the others in the old maple?"

*Victor and Ernest*, sculpture by John Ahearn.

"No," replied the old man. "Just because he doesn't have any butterfly friends doesn't mean he doesn't have friends. The Butterfly has us. Even if we are different from him, we can still be his friends."

Jenny remembered this all her life. Many years after her grandfather died, she realized what he was trying to tell her. It doesn't matter if your friends are different from you; they can still be the most important people in your life.

— Kristin Sparks
The Abbotsford High School
Abbotsford, Wisconsin

# MAKING MEANINGS (PART ONE)

## First Thoughts

1. Using your notes from the Quick-write on page 273, discuss with a partner your responses to the play. Here are some starters to help you if you're stuck:

   • What most surprises me about the two players' friendship is . . .

   • I admire Gale because . . .

   • I admire Brian because . . .

## Shaping Interpretations

2. **Change** is important in most dramas. How do Brian's feelings about Gale change in the first part of the play? How do Gale's feelings about Brian change? You might use a chart like this to show the shift in feelings:

|       | At First | Later |
|-------|----------|-------|
| Brian |          |       |
| Gale  |          |       |

### Reading Check

a. The opening scenes of the play give us some information about *who* Gale and Brian are. For example, what tricks does Brian play on Gale in the opening scenes of the play? How does Gale react to them?

b. After Brian and Gale make the team, they go out to dinner with their wives. What does Gale do during the meal that shows the effect of Brian's easygoing friendship?

c. The injury to Gale's knee is a serious physical obstacle to playing football. What other obstacle must Gale overcome?

d. What reason does Brian give for helping Gale recover from his injury?

3. Explain how Brian's decision to stay with the Bears and try to win the position of halfback creates a **conflict,** or struggle, between him and Gale. What **internal conflict** does this decision create for Brian?

4. After Brian and Gale race, Gale says, "I think I owe you a lot more than that" (page 298). What do you think he means by this comment?

## Connecting with the Text

5. The **camera directions** in this play are written for the director, actors, and crew—the audience never hears them. However, Blinn's directions are often entertaining in themselves, as when he describes the dining room scene on page 280: "a number of large men . . . ladle on portions that would choke a garbage disposal." Find and share other camera directions that you think are humorous or especially descriptive.

## Extending the Text

6. In what other situations in life could friends also be competitors?

7. What do you think the little story on page 299 has to do with this play?

## Challenging the Text

8. Do you think the screenwriter has made the friendship between Gale and Brian believable? Do you think Brian and Gale deal with their problems in a believable way? Why or why not?

Gale **SAYERS**
CHICAGO BEARS • RUNNING B[ ]

Brian **PICCOLO**
CHICAGO BEARS • RUNNING BACK

# VOCABULARY     HOW TO OWN A WORD

**WORD BANK**

enigmatic
saunter
dour
insolent
surly
reluctance
impassive
pivots
disheartened
stoic

## Act It Out

Most of the words in the Word Bank at the left are found in the camera directions. They all relate to a character's feelings or actions.

Suppose you are an actor assigned to a part in this play. You would have to understand what each word in the directions means, and you'd have to work at interpreting that word. After all, the audience can't read the camera directions. The actor must communicate the directions to the audience.

1. Go back to the place in the text where each word in the Word Bank is used. With a partner, act out each word, using **facial expressions** and other kinds of **body language.** If the word describes how a speech is given, use your voice to show how the character is feeling.

2. Another exercise actors use involves **antonyms,** words opposite in meaning to other words. Take each word in the directions and try to find its opposite. For *enigmatic,* for example, you might try *open* or *frank.* How would you interpret this opposite quality?

3. Share all your interpretations with the class and ask for audience feedback. Have you communicated each feeling or action clearly?

# Part Two

GIBRON (*voice-over*). What do you think training camp is? You think training camp is some kind of picnic? Is that what you think? Because there's no man assured of a job around here, let me tell you, and if you think you are, then you got one more think comin', gentlemen!

*As Gibron's voice starts to come over, we also start to hear the sounds of the Chicago Bears calling out a cadence as they go through their calisthenics.*[1]

**Hard cut to:**
**Exterior—Practice area—Day—Full shot**

*The backs step through the ropes, knees high. We pick up Gale going through the obstacle course, with Brian right behind him, both handling it with relative ease. We pan them, then all of them leave the frame to hold on the grizzled features of Coach Halas. His eyes are masked by dark glasses, but there's a smile tugging on the corners of his mouth.*

**Direct cut to:**
**Interior—Dormitory room—Night—On Gale**

*The playbook is in front of him. We pan across the room to find Brian, same look, same activity. A beat, then there is a knock on the door. Brian opens the door and reacts with some surprise on seeing Coach Halas standing in the hallway. He nods pleasantly. Gale, too, is surprised and sits up.*

HALAS. Hello, Brian. Mind if I come in for a moment?
BRIAN. No, no. Of course not. Come on in, Coach.

*And Halas comes in, moving by Brian. The two young men look to each other, neither*

---

1. **calisthenics** (kal′is·then′iks): exercises (from the Greek words *kallos,* meaning "beauty," and *sthenos,* meaning "strength").

*having any notion that might explain this unprecedented visit.*

**HALAS.** How's the knee, Gale?

**GALE.** Fine, Coach. Feels strong.

**BRIAN.** Look, if you want to talk to Gale, I can just walk on down to . . .

**HALAS.** No, actually, I'd like to talk to both of you.

*Chilling portent. They both smile, as does Halas, but only the Old Man's has any relaxation in it. Long beat. Throat clearings from Gale and Brian.*

**BRIAN.** Well—uh—how do things look this year, Coach?

**HALAS.** Fine. Just fine. Matter of fact, there's one boy I'm very impressed with. Brian, I wouldn't be surprised to see him replace you as number two halfback.

*Halas lets the moment run on for a second.*

**HALAS.** Because I'm making you number one fullback.

## Tight on Brian

*He sits there looking at Halas much as Papa Dionne[2] must have looked at the doctor.*

## On Gale

*Beaming, really and deeply pleased for his friend.*

**GALE.** Hey, Pic—you and me the starting backfield—what do you say?

## Full shot

*Brian just shakes his head back and forth, an empty smile flopping about on his face.*

**GALE.** Coach—I didn't think it was possible—but I think you finally found a way to shut him up!

2. **Papa Dionne:** father of quintuplets born in Canada in 1934.

**Hard cut to:**

## NFL footage—Alternating between runs of Piccolo and Sayers

**GALE** (*voice-over*). Hey, Pic?

**BRIAN** (*voice-over*). Yeah?

**GALE** (*voice-over*). You know you got a four point three rushing average?

**BRIAN** (*voice-over*). No, man, but hum a few bars and I'll see if I can fake it.

**GALE** (*voice-over; overlapping*). Aw, *Pic* . . .

## Exterior—Angle to football field—End zone

*Brian breaks through a hole in the center of the line, keeping his feet as he gets to the end zone, flipping the ball high into the air. The first person to him is Gale, slapping him <u>exuberantly</u> on the back as they move with their teammates toward the bench.*

**Direct cut to:**

## Interior—Locker room—Day—Full shot

*The team is being weighed in, Gibron by the scales, sliding the weights up and down the bar and calling out the result for each man. There is some good-natured catcalling[3] as some of the larger linemen are weighed in and most of it is coming from Brian, who is next in line, with Gale close behind him. Brian takes his place. Gibron starts to readjust the weights.*

**BRIAN.** Scrimmage tomorrow, Abe. Going to give us any trick plays?

**GIBRON.** Only trick I'd like to give you is how to keep some meat on you. You're down another pound.

**BRIAN.** But what's there is choice; admit it.

3. **catcalling:** shrill whistles or shouts making fun of someone; so called because people used to make noises like a cat to show disapproval, the way we boo or hiss today.

- - - - - - - - - - - - - - - - - - - - - - - - - - - - -

**WORDS TO OWN**

**exuberantly** (eg·zoo′bər·ənt·lē) *adv.:* with high spirits.

- - - - - - - - - - - - - - - - - - - - - - - - - - - - -

**GIBRON.** Two-o-six and a quarter. Skinniest fullback in the league.

**BRIAN.** Gibron, you run the fat off us, then complain that we're too thin. You're a hard man to please.

*Brian grins, used to Gibron's grumbles, and moves off. Gale is next in line.*

**GIBRON.** Ought to tell your Italian friend to load up on the pasta.

**GALE.** Probably just wants to be quicker, Gibron.

**GIBRON.** Well, it ain't workin'. He lost ten pounds and he's half a second slower over a forty-yard sprint. Lighter *and* slower don't total out to much of a threat, you know. (*Checks the weight*) One ninety-nine. Next.

*We move with Gale as he steps off the scale, camera closing on him. He glances off at Gibron, then in the direction taken by Brian. His eyes are puzzled; it's a weird combination Gibron has pointed out. Strange. Unsettling. Gale lets it sink in.*

**Direct cut to:**

## NFL footage of Gale and Brian

*Running the ball, alternating. Two cuts, the first being the best footage of Piccolo as either runner or receiver, the last being a punt return by Sayers that goes all the way. This final cut, the punt return, is to lead directly into the following staged sequence.*

## Angle to Bears' sideline

*Gale comes off the field with the rest of the punt-return unit, among whom is Brian. Typically, Gale barely smiles at the congratulations he gets. He moves to the bench and sits, Brian by his side. They pull off their helmets, eyes on the game.*

## Closer angle—Gale and Brian

*Both winded, but with one difference. Gale is clearly buoyed up, exhilarated. Brian simply seems tired.*

**GALE.** Nice block.

**BRIAN.** Thanks.
  (*beat*)
Must be ninety million pounds of pollen in the air.

*Gale glances over at Brian casually and might see what we are now noting. Gale's respiration is swiftly slowing down, approaching normal. Brian's is not, he's still winded and badly so. Brian rises, moving for the water bucket near the phone desk. Gale watches him, then rises, moving for the sidelines to view the upcoming kickoff, camera moving with him. He finds an opening among the men standing there; then, in the hush just prior to the kicker's runup, the sound of Brian coughing. Gale turns back.*

## His point of view—On Brian

*The roar of the crowd overwhelms the sound of Piccolo's coughing. He takes down a fair amount of water, but that doesn't help. Brian coughs once more, though it's more evident in the motion of his shoulders and chest than in a sound; he's making an effort to stifle the cough.*

**GALE.** You ought to get Fox to give you something for that hay fever.

**BRIAN.** He did. Doesn't help. The only thing I'm allergic to is Ray Nitschke.[4]
(*Yelling*) All right, Butkus! Stick it in their ear, babe!

*Brian moves off, back toward the bench. Gale looks to the playing field, but his thoughts are elsewhere. He glances back.*

4. **Ray Nitschke** (nitch′kē) (1936–     ): all-star linebacker for the Green Bay Packers.

----

**WORDS TO OWN**
respiration (res′pə·rā′shən) *n*.: breathing.

----

**His point of view—Angle to Piccolo**

*Seated once more on the bench, his helmet off, still using more effort than one would expect to get his wind back. He sees Gale looking at him and smiles, giving a "thumbs-up" sign.*

**On Gale**

*Nodding, returning both the smile and the sign, and both are, at one and the same time, lies and prayers.*

**Direct cut to:**
**Interior—Bears' locker room—Day—Full shot**

*Most of the players are dressed now, or seated in front of their lockers tying their shoes. We find Halas as he comes out of his office, his expression somber. He pulls up a stool beside Gale and sits, drained, enervated.*

GALE. Lookin' at you, I'd never know we won the game.

HALAS (*small smile*). I don't feel very much like a winner at the moment.

GALE. Why not?

*A deep breath, a gathering of his forces.*

HALAS. Gale, I'm sending Brian Piccolo back to Chicago. He won't make the rest of the road trip with us. Ralph Kurek's going to start next week.

GALE.
   (*beat*)
Why?

HALAS. Because I've had a policy on this team from the very start—the best player plays, no exceptions. And right now—Kurek is the best player.

GALE. Look, a lot of guys take a while to get on track for a season, slow starters, and . . .

HALAS (*finishing for him*). And Brian Piccolo has never been one of those guys, Gale. He's always been in shape, able to give one hundred percent. But he isn't

doing that anymore, and that worries me. (*With regret*) I don't know why—something physical—or whether he's got personal problems, something with his wife or children—but the truth is that something is taking the edge off of him—and I want to find out what that something is. For his sake and the team's. Can't afford to lose a back that good.

GALE (*resigned*). When's he going to find out?

HALAS. Abe's telling him now. That's why I didn't want you to go right back to the hotel.

GALE. Wouldn't want to be in Abe's shoes about now. . . .

HALAS. I wouldn't want to be in *your* shoes about ten minutes from now.

**Direct cut to:**
**Interior—Hotel room—Night—On suitcase**

*A bundle of wadded-up clothes is thrown into the suitcase. We pull back to reveal Piccolo in the act of packing, moving from closet and dresser to the suitcase on the bed. Gale maintains a low profile, not wanting to draw any fire from Brian.*

BRIAN. Who'd believe it? I mean, really, who'd believe it!

GALE. Halas just wants you to see the doctor, and . . .

BRIAN. Halas doesn't know what he wants! Gibron's his boy and you should have heard *that* lecture! Kept telling me to patch things up with Joy. I tell him things are fine with me and Joy. And he just

---

**WORDS TO OWN**

**somber** (säm′bər) *adj.*: serious.
**enervated** (en′ər·vāt′id) *v.* used as *adj.*: exhausted; weakened.

---

smiles that Father Flanagan[5] smile of his and says I shouldn't be afraid to level with him.

**GALE.** Pic, be fair, now. Dr. Fox says that . . .

**BRIAN.** Oh, spare me any crud about our great team doctor. Wants me to get a physical for the cough, right? No allergy. Then what is it, I say! Want to hear what he says? *Could* be a virus. *Could* be a staph infection.[6] *Could* be any one of a thousand things. It's like being treated in a Chinese restaurant—two from column A, three from column B!

**GALE.** He's just trying to help, Pic. . . .

*A beat, then Brian sits on the bed, calming somewhat, but still angry and frustrated.*

**BRIAN.** Yeah—I suppose you're right—but it's all so pointless, Gale. I know perfectly well what's wrong with me.

*He looks over at Gale, eyes radiating sincerity.*

**BRIAN.** Gale—I think I'm pregnant.

**Direct cut to:**

## Interior—Visiting team locker room—Day—Full shot

*The Chicago Bears suit up. Linemen pound each other's shoulder pads to a tighter fit. Some of the players sit in front of their lockers, wide-eyed, seeing nothing. Others move about nervously, bouncing on the balls of their feet, trembling with caged energy.*

## Angle to training table

*Gale is having his ankle wrapped tightly with adhesive tape. His face has the look of a carving—somber, dark, guarded. The trainer finishes the job and Gale nods his thanks, moving off the table, another man following behind him at once. We move with him as he strides toward a door at the other end of the locker room. He passes by Gibron, who is going over the attack plan with Concannon and the second-string quarterback, past linemen who are simply yelling at each other, wordless growls and bellows. Gale stops in front of the door bearing the word* COACH. *He knocks on the door.*

**HALAS** (*offstage*). Come in.

## Interior—The coach's office—Day—Full shot

*Halas is seated behind the desk, hat and dark glasses on. Ed McCaskey is at a water cooler in the corner, drawing a paper cup out of the container, using the water to wash down a pill. At first, both men seem quite normal, but it's a* facade *and one that's being* eroded *with each passing second.*

**GALE.** Which end of the field you want me to take if we lose the toss?

*McCaskey and Halas stare at him for a second, then look to each other. Gale is a little baffled by the delay; the question is a standard one. Some kind of communication is going on between the two older men. They nod.*

**HALAS.** Come on in, Gale. Close the door.

*There is something in that tone, something vulnerable and sad, out of key. Gale steps into the room and closes the door as requested. There is a short silence, each of the other men hoping they'll not have to take the lead.*

---

5. **Father Flanagan:** Edward Joseph Flanagan (1886–1948), founder of Boys Town, a famous orphanage in Nebraska. Father Flanagan was known for his kindness and sympathy for young people in trouble. He liked to say "There are no bad boys."

6. **staph** (staf) **infection:** short for *staphylococcus infection.* Staphylococci are bacteria.

---

**WORDS TO OWN**

**facade** (fə·säd′) *n.*: literally, the front part of a building; here, a "front" put up to hide real feelings.

**eroded** (ē·rōd′id) *v.*: worn away.

---

**HALAS.** Gale—we've just had a phone call from Memorial Hospital. . . .

*Halas removes the glasses. His eyes are red. He takes a breath.*

**HALAS.** Brian Piccolo has cancer.

*Awe has within it an element of fear, of facing something so basic, so large, that one cannot ever truly cope with it. Gale reacts with prayerful disbelief and awe.*

**GALE.** Oh, God . . .

## Full shot

*Halas kneads the bridge of his nose, the eyes closed as if hoping the curtain of his eyelids will allow time for a scene change.*

**HALAS.** They've scheduled an operation for tomorrow morning.
**GALE** (*feeling*). An operation to do what?
**MCCASKEY** (*evenly, calmly*). Gale, they've got to remove part of Brian's right lung.

*This strikes Gale like a whiplash. He starts to sink weakly into a nearby chair, and as he does so the frame freezes several times, giving the same look associated with the knee injury. As he sinks into the chair, the image moves with stuttering, uneven speed.*

**HALAS** (*offstage*). The doctors don't have any explanation, Gale. It must be something Brian has carried around inside him all his life. What set it off, they don't know. As to whether or not they found it in time—well, they don't know that either, I'm afraid.

*Gale's eyes are glazed. His spirit has been blindsided.[7] Halas and McCaskey are no less affected.*

**MCCASKEY** (*to Halas*). Who tells them?

7. **blindsided:** literally, hit on one side while looking in the other direction.

*Halas sighs, nodding.*

**HALAS.** I know. It's my responsibility and I'll . . .
**GALE** (*interrupting*). I'll tell them.
**HALAS** (*surprised*). You, Gale?
**GALE** (*rising*). That's right, me. I'll tell them. Let's go. (*To McCaskey*) Does Linda know?
**MCCASKEY.** I don't think so. . . .
**GALE.** Call her and tell her.

*He pulls open the door, looking to Halas. The Coach and McCaskey trade a swift look, then Halas gets to his feet. As he moves to the door, McCaskey picks up the phone on the desk and starts to dial.*

## Interior—The locker room—Day— Full shot

*Halas and Gale come out of the Coach's room. Halas's presence is noted quickly and the players gather around in a loose semicircle. Gale appears very much in control of himself, in command of the situation.*

**HALAS** (*to players*). Gale has got something he'd like to say to you all. Gale . . .

*Gale attempts to sustain eye contact with the other members of the team, but it swiftly becomes clear to him that he can't make it. Initially, his voice is strong and clear, but he can't hold it there for long.*

**GALE.** You—you all know that we hand out a game ball to the outstanding player. Well, I'd like to change that a little. We just got word that Brian Piccolo—that he's sick. Very sick. It looks like—uh—that he might not ever play football again—or—for a long time. . . .
 (*beat*)
And—I think we should all dedicate ourselves to—give our maximum effort to win this ball game and give the game ball to

Pic. We can all sign it and take it up to him at the hosp . . .

*His voice tightens with abrupt anguish. He turns away, hiding his tears.*

GALE (*continuing, softly*). Oh, my *God* . . .

**Fade Out.**
**Fade In:**

### Interior—Brian's hospital room—Day—Tight on Brian

*Garbed [8] in hospital gown, looking strangely out of place, a young man of two hundred pounds is in something approximating a doll's wardrobe. He's grinning from ear to ear, holding up the front page of the sports section, the headline of which reads* COLTS DUMP BEARS *24–21.*

BRIAN (*voice-over*). Fantastic! Who'd believe it! Sayers, you've got great moves on the field, but in the locker room, I've got to tell you, you're a klutz! When you dedicate a game to someone, you are then supposed to go out and *win* the game, idiot! Pat O'Brien[9] never said, "Blow one for the Gipper," you know.

### Full shot

*Gale and Jack Concannon stand at the end of the bed. At a small table near the window, the flowers and cards have been cleared away by J. C. Caroline and a few other players. In place of these niceties, they are opening up two cartons of pizza and two six-packs of beer. Joy Piccolo stands next to her husband.*

GALE. Bad—you are so bad.
CAROLINE. We probably would have won if Concannon had called that trap play more,

---

8. **garbed:** clothed.
9. **Pat O'Brien** (1899–1983): actor who played football coach Knute Rockne in the movie *Knute Rockne, All American.* In the film, Rockne asks his Notre Dame players to "win one for the Gipper"—George Gipp, a star player who had died.

but he hates to use it unless you're there for the repeat.

*The men at the table have started putting pieces of pizza on paper napkins and begin to distribute them.*

JOY. Brian, do you think this is such a good idea? I mean, pepperoni pizza and beer *isn't* on your diet.
BRIAN. Joy—are you telling me as I lie on this bed of pain, my body whittled away at by a ruthless band of strangers with Exacto knives—are you telling me I can't have any *pizza*?

*Joy studies Brian, then looks to the other men. She shakes her head, <u>exasperated</u> and loving them all very much.*

JOY. Pass the pizza, please. . . .

*With smiles, the others crowd around the bed as Joy moves to the table. After a second or two to get the first bite down:*

BRIAN. Hey—who wants to see my scar?

*Instant negative replies from them all. As these trail off, the door is opened offstage and they all look around. A nurse enters. She gazes at her patient, who has just had a lung removed, as he visits with his wife and friends, all of whom have pizza in hand.*

NURSE. Out! Now! No discussion! Out!

### Full shot

*Gale, Butkus, Concannon, Caroline, and Mayes quickly gather up the pizza cartons and head for the door, ad-libbing farewells, ducking their heads like schoolboys as they pass by the nurse. Gale is the last in line. Joy straightens up from kissing Brian goodbye.*

- - - - - - - - - - - - - - - - - - - - - - -

**WORDS TO OWN**
**exasperated** (eg·zas′pər·āt′id) *v.* used as *adj.*: fed up (used here in a playful sense).

- - - - - - - - - - - - - - - - - - - - - - -

**BRIAN.** Hey, take Gale down and have him give that little girl his autograph, will you? (*To Gale*) Little girl I met the day I came in here. We had our operations on the same day. Told her I'd get your autograph. You don't mind, do you?

**GALE.** No problem. Be glad to.

**JOY.** I'll see you tonight.

*He blows a kiss at her and they all leave. The nurse holds for a second in the door, reinforcing her disapproval of Brian's ways. She sighs and steps out of the door. Once it's closed, Brian throws back the covers and puts his feet over the side. There's a good deal of strain and discomfort involved, but it's well within Brian's tolerance. He stands with his back to the window, then starts for the door, his gait a shuffle.*

**BRIAN.** There he goes, sports fans—can you believe it—power, speed, grace, and agility all wrapped up in . . .

*Brian halts as the door is opened once again by the nurse. Their eyes fight to a draw.*

**BRIAN.** Don't come any closer, Miss Furman. White lisle[10] stockings turn me on!

**Direct cut to:**

## Children's ward—Angle to nurses' station

*The walls here are festooned with crayon drawings made by the patients. The nurses' station has a number of stuffed animals on the counter. As Joy and Gale approach, one of the nurses hangs up the phone and turns to them with a pleasant smile.*

**NURSE #2.** May I help you?

**JOY.** My name's Mrs. Piccolo. My husband's a patient on the third floor and he told me about a little girl—Patti Lucas—who wanted this gentleman's autograph.

*The nurse nods nicely, holding up a finger as she flips swiftly through the Rolodex[11] in front of her.*

**NURSE #2.** I'm sorry, Mrs. Piccolo—Patti isn't with us anymore.

**JOY.** Well, do you have a home address? My husband wanted her to have the autograph very much.

**NURSE #2.**

(*beat*)

Mrs. Piccolo—Patti's dead. She passed away early this morning.

*Gale places his hand gently on Joy's shoulder. Joy nods, forcing a smile mouthing the "thank you," though her voice is absent. Gale is a few feet behind her as they start back for the elevator bank.*

**Direct cut to:**

## NFL footage of Gale in an end run, preferably slow motion

*The crowd noise is at a frenzied peak; then the frame freezes.*

**BRIAN** (*voice-over*). Look at that knee, will you? That thing is really beautiful!

## Exterior—Hospital grounds—Day— Full shot

*Brian is wheeled out onto the hospital lawn. He's looking at a sports magazine, which he holds up so Joy can see the picture. They stop beneath a large tree bordering the walk.*

**BRIAN.** Nothing wrong with that knee; I'll tell you that.

**JOY.** Congratulations, Dr. Piccolo.

**BRIAN.** Yeah—but you know what—I've been thinking. With Gale healthy, and Ralph Kurek healthy—I'm going to have a rough time getting back into the lineup next year. And I was thinking—what's so difficult about being a kicker? I mean, I

---

10. **lisle** (līl): made of lisle thread, a very strong cotton.

11. **Rolodex:** trademark of an address-card file.

wonder if it's something you can teach yourself. 'Cause you don't need a lot of wind or <u>stamina</u> or size . . .

*He looks down at Joy and the look on her face is weakening, hopeful still, but with more effort required on her part with each day that goes by. Brian reads that look like a compass.*

**BRIAN.** All right, Gloomy Gus—what do you think of my brainstorm?

**JOY** (*floundering*). Well—I don't know, Brian—I'm no expert on kickers and things . . .

**BRIAN.** You just did an end run that Red Grange[12] would be proud to call his own.

**JOY.** Don't make fun of me, Brian. I'm scared.

**BRIAN** (*evenly*). What of?

**JOY** (*sputtering with disbelief*). What *of?* What *of?* You can't be serious! You know perfectly well what of!

**BRIAN** (*absolutely sincere*). No, I don't, Joy. I swear to God I don't. (*Taking her hands*) Look—I'm no idiot.—This thing is bad—I know that—but it's a detour, Joy—that's all. It's not going to stop me because I'm not going to *let* it stop me. No way . . . (*Quietly*) I've got too much to do yet, Joy.

*Her face in his hands, Brian bends to kiss Joy. As their lips meet, we start to boom up and back. Joy leans her head against Brian's knee, his hand stroking her hair.*

**Direct cut to:**

## NFL footage of Sayers

*Fielding a punt, signaling for a fair catch, then deciding to let it roll. And roll it does, further and further back toward his own goal. By the time he realizes he should have caught it, there are a number of defensive men all around the ball, making any return impossible. From the time the ball struck earth and took off, we have heard:*

**BRIAN** (*voice-over*). Pick it up! Pick it up, dummy! Gale! Joy, look at him!

**NURSE** (*voice-over*). Now, Mr. Piccolo, calm down.

**BRIAN** (*voice-over*). Calm down? How can I calm down? You'd think the ball was wearing a white sheet.

**Direct cut to:**
## Interior—Hotel room—Night—Full shot

*Gale is on the bed, shoes off, talking on the phone with Brian, the mood one of good-natured give-and-take. Seated on the other bed is a football player, Gale's new roommate. There is a room-service cart in evidence, remnants there of sandwiches and glasses of milk. We intercut this with Brian in his hospital room. There is no one else present with Brian.*

**GALE.** Well, I was going to catch it, but when it started coming down, I said I wonder what Pic would do in a situation like this, and ducking seemed to be the answer.

**BRIAN.** Well, at least you won the game.

**GALE.** That's right.

**BRIAN.** Didn't dedicate this one to me, though, did you?

*In the hotel room, there is a knock on the door. The other player goes to answer it. He opens the door to reveal a hotel official, who exchanges a few words with the football player, then is allowed into the room.*

**GALE.** Nope. Dedicated this one to Butkus.

**BRIAN.** Why?

12. **Red Grange** (1903–1991): one of the greatest football players in American history. He was nicknamed "the Galloping Ghost" when he played on the University of Illinois team. He later played professionally for the Chicago Bears.

**WORDS TO OWN**

**stamina** (stam′ə·nə) *n*.: endurance; ability to resist fatigue.

**GALE.** He threatened us.
(*beat*)
How you doin'? Pic? Really?
**BRIAN.** Hanging in there, Magic. Doing what they tell me to do. You could do me a favor, though.
**GALE.** You got it. Name it.
**BRIAN.** Call Joy, will you? When she left tonight, she was really down. I never saw her that down.
**GALE.** I'll call her as soon as I get back.
**BRIAN.** Thanks, I appreciate it.
**GALE.** Okay. Goodnight.
**BRIAN.** Goodnight.

*Gale hangs up, then looks a question to the hotel clerk.*

**HOTEL OFFICIAL.** Mr. Sayers, while you were on the phone, there was a lady who called. She seemed very upset.

*He hands Gale a piece of folded paper. Gale unfolds it.*

**HOTEL OFFICIAL.** I hope I've not overstepped my authority.
**PLAYER.** I'm sure you did the right thing. Thank you very much.

*He ushers the hotel official out the door, closes it, then glances back at Gale, who sags, drained.*

**GALE.** It's Joy Piccolo. She says it's urgent.

**Direct cut to:**
**Interior—Piccolo living room—Night—
On clock**

*The time is 3:30. We pull back to reveal Joy, in robe and slippers, pouring coffee for Gale and Linda. The Sayerses have dumped their coats on the couch.*

**JOY.** I know it's an awful thing, to make you fly all the way back here in the middle of the night, but . . .

**GALE.** It doesn't bother me, so don't let it bother you.

*Joy smiles feebly and sits, her hands tightly intertwined, struggling to maintain her composure. A long beat.*

**LINDA.** Just say it, Joy. . . .

*Joy nods, a childlike move.*

**JOY.** They found more of the tumor. . . .[13]

*The tears come. Her face twists, crumpling under the terror and the fear. Linda moves to her, holding her, both women rocking back and forth. Gale swallows bitterly, probably wishing he was strong enough to cry. He pulls a handkerchief out of his pocket and places it on the coffee table within Joy's reach. She nods her appreciation, dabbing at her eyes.*

**JOY.** They told me today—they want to operate again—and I was going to tell Brian—but—I couldn't, Gale. I don't know whether or not he can take the disappointment. And if he can't—I know *I* can't.
(*beat*)
The doctor is going to tell him tomorrow morning. If you could be there when he finds out—it might help.
**GALE.** I'll be there, Joy.

**Direct cut to:**
**Interior—Brian's room—Day—
On football game**

*This is a "board game" with charts and dice and miniature scoreboard. As we pull back, we find Brian and Gale seated on opposite sides of the small table near the window. They both roll their dice.*

**GALE.** What'd you try?
**BRIAN.** End run.

---

**13. tumor:** mass of new tissue growing with no function in the body. Tumors are classified as either benign (harmless) or malignant (harmful and possibly fatal). Brian has a malignant tumor.

GALE. Oh, Lordy—I was in a blitz.

*Brian starts to consult the complicated chart that will give him the results of the play.*

GALE (*indicating game chart*). Well—did you gain or what?

*The door is opened by Mr. Eberle, a nervous, uncertain sort, more at home with facts and figures than flesh and blood. A name tag hangs from the lapel of his lab coat. Brian looks up with a smile.*

BRIAN. Hi. Can I help you?
EBERLE. Well, I'm sorry if I'm disturbing anything . . .
BRIAN. Don't worry—I can beat him later. What can I do for you?
EBERLE (*rummaging through papers*). I know this is a bother at a time like this, Mr. Piccolo, but hospitals have their rules and regulations, you see, and I'll need your signature on this surgical consent for the operation.

*He hands Brian the piece of paper, but Brian is scarcely aware of it. He looks at Eberle <u>uncomprehendingly</u>, stunned. Gale is searching for a way to ease this, but before he can locate his voice, Eberle notes the bewilderment on Brian's face.*

EBERLE. The doctor *has* been here, hasn't he? He's talked with you, I mean?
BRIAN. No . . .
EBERLE (*looking to watch*). Oh—well, I suppose I might be running a little ahead of my schedule today. Perhaps I better come back after the doctor has . . .
BRIAN. What would the doctor have to say to me? Man, I've *had* my operation, *right?*

*Silence, and that's the worst answer there can be. Eberle can't meet Brian's look. After a beat, Brian looks over slowly to Gale.*

BRIAN. Talk to me, Magic. . . .

*Gale discovers his voice after a second, but it emerges with anguish.*

GALE. The tests show—there's more of the tumor than they thought, Pic. They have to operate again. . . .

*Once more, Eberle, seeking nothing more than escape, steps forward, holding out the surgical consent and a fountain pen.*

EBERLE. So, if you'll just sign the consent, Mr. . . .
BRIAN (*turning away*). No!
EBERLE. But putting this off won't be . . .
BRIAN. Are you deaf? I said *no!*
EBERLE. Mr. Sayers—can't you talk to your friend?

*Brian has moved to the window, shoulders hunched as if gathering himself for a blow of enormous force. Gale looks at him, then turns to Eberle.*

GALE. No, Mr. Eberle, I think I'd rather talk to *you.*
EBERLE. But . . .
GALE. Brian is a professional athlete, Mr. Eberle. And a professional gets into a habit after a while. He gets himself ready for a game mentally as well as physically. Because he knows those two things are all tied up together. And there's a clock going inside him, so that when the game starts, he's one hundred percent mentally and physically. And what Pic is saying to you now is that you're scheduling this game before he can get ready. Couldn't it wait until over the weekend?
EBERLE. Well, yes, it *could*, but . . .
GALE. Then *let* it.

EBERLE (*a beat, looks to Brian*). First thing Monday morning, Mr. Piccolo.
BRIAN. Okay.
EBERLE. I'll see you then.

*Gale looks back to Brian, who continues to gaze out the window. A beat, as Brian strains to salvage some control.*

BRIAN. Thanks, Gale . . .
GALE. No sweat.
BRIAN. Thought you were the guy who didn't talk very well.
GALE. Well—I roomed with an Italian; you know how they are.

*Brian turns away from the window. He moves back to the game board, idly scanning the setup. A beat, then a small smile appears on his face.*

BRIAN. Guess what? I scored a touchdown.

*We hold on Brian.*

**Cut to black over following:**

NURSE #1'S VOICE. Good morning, Mr. Piccolo. Time to wake up now.

**Fade In:**
## Medium shot—Nurse #1

*She is looking into lens, smiling Cheshirely,[14] a hypodermic needle in hand.*

NURSE #1. I'm going to give you a little shot to help you relax, Mr. Piccolo. You'll be going up to the operating room in about an hour.
BRIAN (*offstage*). My wife here?
NURSE #1. You'll see her when you come down, Mr. Piccolo. Now, this won't hurt a bit.
BRIAN (*offstage*). Yes—you're being very brave about it all.

---

**14. Cheshirely:** like the mysterious grinning Cheshire Cat in Lewis Carroll's *Alice's Adventures in Wonderland*.

**Direct cut to:**
## Interior—Operating room—Up angle

*A doctor, masked and gowned, leans into the lens, arms held up away from his body.*

DOCTOR. Mr. Piccolo—we're going to put you to sleep now. . . .
BRIAN (*offstage*). That's the—worst—choice of words—I ever heard in my life. . . .

*As we start a slow fade to black, we begin to hear the sound of applause, growing louder and louder with each second. Then, in utter darkness:*

M.C. (*offstage*). Gale Sayers!!!

**Cut to:**
## Interior—Banquet hall—Night—Tight on Gale

*Dressed in a tuxedo, Gale starts as he becomes aware of the explosion of sounds being directed at him. Other men at his table poke Gale, all laughing as they urge him to his feet. Startled, he rises and the camera pans him as he is almost passed along from table to table.*

## The dais

*Gale smiles, still at a loss, and moves toward the toastmaster,[15] who is holding out a large trophy to him. As Gale accepts the trophy with a muttered thank you the applause builds once more. Gale looks down at the inscription on the trophy.*

## Insert—The inscription

*It reads "George S. Halas Award—Most Courageous Player—to Gale Sayers."*

## Tight on Gale

*He looks out, nodding acknowledgment to the applause. Slowly it starts to trail off, then*

---

**15. toastmaster:** person at a banquet who proposes toasts and introduces after-dinner speakers.

*dies. A moment of throat clearings, chairs shifting into better positions. When it is absolutely still, Gale begins to speak.*

**GALE.** I'd like to say a few words about a guy I know—a friend of mine. His name is Brian Piccolo and he has the heart of a giant—and that rare form of courage that allows him to kid himself and his opponent—cancer. He has the mental attitude that makes me proud to have a friend who spells out courage twenty-four hours a day, every day of his life.

*Gale takes a sip of water.*

**GALE.** You flatter me by giving me this award—but I tell you here and now I accept it for Brian Piccolo. Brian Piccolo is the man of courage who should receive the George S. Halas Award. It is mine tonight; it is Brian Piccolo's tomorrow.

*Not a sound out there. Gale clutches the award tightly and his eyes sparkle with tears. No attempt is made to hide those tears.*

**GALE.** I love Brian Piccolo—and I'd like all of you to love him, too. And, tonight— when you hit your knees . . .
  *(beat)*
Please ask God to love him. . . .

*Gale steps quickly out of the spotlight. We hold on the empty circle for several seconds before the sound comes. First, one or two people, then more, and swiftly an avalanche of thunder.*

**Direct cut to:**
**Interior—Brian's hospital room—Day— On Brian**

*Joy places the phone on the pillow next to him. When the angle widens, we see Linda is also present. There is an IV stand[16] next to the*

16. **IV stand:** short for *intravenous* (in′trə·vē′nəs) *stand,* which holds liquid medication that flows directly into the veins.

*bed, a tank of oxygen in the corner. Brian's face is drawn, the flesh* <u>pallid</u> *and shiny. We intercut the conversation with Gale in his hotel room.*

**BRIAN.** Hi, Magic . . .
**GALE.** How are you, Pic?
**BRIAN.** Oh, hangin' in there . . .
  *(beat)*
Heard what you did at the banquet. If you were here, I'd kiss you. . . .
**GALE.** Glad I'm not there, then.
**BRIAN.** Hey, Gale? They said you gave me a pint of blood. Is that true?
**GALE.** Yeah.
**BRIAN.** That explains it, then.
**GALE.** Explains what?
**BRIAN.** I've had this craving for chitlins[17] all day.

*Gale smiles on the other end.*

**GALE.** I'll be in tomorrow morning, man. I'll see you then.
**BRIAN.** Yeah—I ain't going nowhere. . . .

*Joy takes the phone and hands it to Linda, who takes the receiver to the window where the cradle is located. Camera closes on Linda, who raises the phone to her ear.*

**LINDA.** Gale?
**GALE.** How is he, Linda? *Really?*
**LINDA** (*softly, yet urgently*). *Hurry.* Gale— please hurry.

**Direct cut to:**
**Interior—Brian's room—On Ed McCaskey**

*He is seated in a chair by the door, a continuous caressing of rosary beads sliding through his fingers. The room is striped with sunlight from the partially closed Venetian blinds. The door is opened and Gale and Linda come in.*

17. **chitlins:** chitterlings, or fried pig intestines.

**WORDS TO OWN**
**pallid** (pal′id) *adj.:* pale.

*Brian's eyes are closed, and his frame seems small beneath the blankets. Joy bends to him as Gale moves quietly to the other side of the bed, Linda holding by the door.*

JOY. Brian—Gale's here.

**Closer angle—Gale and Brian**

*Brian's hand comes up from the sheet in greeting. Gale takes the hand in his. Brian's words come slowly, breath on a ration.*

BRIAN. Hello, Magic.
GALE (*after a beat*). How's it going, Pic?
BRIAN. It's fourth and eight, man—but they won't let me punt.[18]
GALE. Go for it, then.
BRIAN. I'm trying, Gale—God, how I'm trying. . . .

*Suddenly Brian's head snaps back, his hand convulsing on Gale's. Tears spilling down her cheeks, Joy leans close to her husband.*

*Seconds go by. Then, slowly, Brian's body relaxes and his head touches the pillow. Joy blots the perspiration from his brow. His eye goes to Gale.*

BRIAN. Remember that first year . . . couldn't get a word out of you . . .
GALE. Couldn't get you to shut up . . .
BRIAN. Remember how you got me with those mashed potatoes . . .
GALE. You deserved it—the way you sang that dumb fight song—twice, you did it— at camp, and that time down in my basement . . .
    (*beat*)

18. **"fourth and eight . . . punt":** Fourth down and eight yards to go is a desperate situation in football. The team can either punt—kick the ball to the other team—or go for a new set of downs, which there is little chance of getting. Brian is admitting that the doctors won't let him give up, although he wants to. Gale's response, "Go for it, then" (which is said when the decision is to go for the downs), gives Brian the encouragement he needs to keep fighting.

And that 32 trap play—remember that?
BRIAN. Yeah. How could I forget?

*There is a pause. Brian's look turns reflective. He smiles.*

BRIAN. You taught me a lot about running, Gale. I appreciate it.
GALE. I wouldn't be running if I hadn't had you pushin' me—helping me . . .
BRIAN. I'll get you next training camp. . . .
GALE. I'll be waiting. . . .
BRIAN. Yeah . . . (*A sigh*) Gale, I'm feeling kind of punk. . . . I think I'll sack out for a while, okay?
GALE. Sure thing.

**Angle to their hands**

*Gale gently lets go of Brian's hand, which falls limply back onto the sheet. Gale's hand rests on the other for a beat, then he moves away.*

**Full shot**

*The nurse opens the door for Gale and Linda. He stops, looking back, his voice choked.*

GALE. See you tomorrow, Pic. . . .

**Tight on Brian**

*He turns his head toward Gale, brings his gaze into focus. He lifts the hand closest to the door and gives a "thumbs-up."*

BRIAN. If you say so. . . .

*Offstage, the sound of the door closing. Brian pulls Joy close to him, his arms about her. His eyes close, his breathing slackens. Joy's lips are close to Brian's ear.*

JOY. I love you, Brian—I love you. . . .

*Brian forces his eyes open and looks at her for a long beat. He finds one final smile.*

**BRIAN.** Who'd believe it, Joy—who'd ever believe it. . . .

*And Brian and Joy are close for the last time. This stillness will endure.*

**Dissolve to:**

**Exterior—Hospital parking lot—Night— On Gale and Linda**

*Arm in arm they move slowly along the line of cars in the parking lot until they come to their own. Gale opens the door on Linda's side and helps her in. As he closes the door, he looks to the hospital.*

**His point of view—Hospital window**

*Zooming in on McCaskey in Brian's room. He slowly closes the blinds.*

**Tight on Gale**

*He gazes at the hospital.*

> **NARRATOR** (*voice-over*). Brian Piccolo died of cancer at the age of twenty-six. He left a wife and three daughters.

*Superimpose over the close shot of Gale Sayers in the parking lot, footage from the footrace between Gale and Brian, ending with slow motion of their contest that freezes on a tight shot of Brian.*

> **NARRATOR** (*voice-over*). He also left a great many loving friends who miss him and think of him often. But, when they think of him, it's not how he died that they remember but, rather, how he *lived*. . . .
> (*beat*)
> How he *did* live . . .

*And as Gale moves around to his side of the car and starts to get in, the image of Brian takes precedence, smiling and full of life. A good face to study for a moment or two.*

**Fade Out.**

## MEET THE WRITER

### An Award-Winning Dramatist

**William Blinn** (1937–    ) was born in Toledo, Ohio, and graduated from the American Academy of Dramatic Arts in New York City. He has written and produced teleplays for *The Wonder Years* and *Our House*, two syndicated television series about families. For his teleplay of *Brian's Song*, written for ABC's *Movie of the Week*, he received an Emmy, the George Foster Peabody Award, the Writer's Guild of America Award, and the Black Sports Magazine Award. *Brian's Song* also received a Congressional Record Commendation as "one of the truly moving television and screen achievements."

# Pic *from* **I Am Third**

## Gale Sayers

Brian Piccolo and I began rooming together in 1967, and we became close friends. It's easy to make a big deal out of the fact that he was white and I'm black and to wonder how we got along. But there was nothing to it, although I admit at first we did feel each other out. I had never had a close relationship with a white person before, except maybe George Halas, and Pic had never really known a black person. I remember him telling me that he wondered at first, "Are they really different? Do they sleep in chandeliers, or what?"

The best thing about our relationship as it developed was that we could kid each other all the time about race, do our thing in perfect ease. It was a way, I guess, of easing into each man's world. It helped take the strangeness out of it. . . .

I was in the room when Pic came in. "What are you doing here?" he said.

I said, "We're in together."

He was a little surprised, but I had known about it. They had asked me if I had any objections to rooming with Brian. I said no, none at all. I had been rooming with a fellow who got cut, and I think Pic was rooming with a quarterback, Larry Rakestraw, and they decided maybe they ought to room guys together by position.

But I think Bennie McRae, one of our co-captains, also suggested that they start some integrated rooming, to get a little better understanding with the guys. And Pic and I were the first on the Bears.

But it really didn't make any difference. I think they tend to make too much out of it. Friends like to room with friends, and it has nothing to do with segregation or anything like that.

You can bet we didn't have dinner together in Birmingham that weekend. We joked a lot about it, but we went our separate ways. I don't know if we ate dinner with one another but a couple of times that first year. It was always that when we got into a place I'd call the guys that I normally went out with and he'd call the guys that he normally went out with and we'd split. It was just that he had his friends and I had mine. I think we were both a little unsure about the whole thing at first. And I guess I was a little distant that first year. I think once people get to know me I'm easy to get along with. Pic always knew that on the day of a game I liked to be left alone—just let me be—and this is what he did. But by the end of that first year we had both loosened up quite a bit.

I think he actually helped open me up because he was such a happy-go-lucky guy. He always had a joke or two in him. . . .

Because of my injury and my mental state afterward, I got to know Pic even better and became closer to him than almost anybody else on the team. And then when he became ill, it seemed that our friendship deepened and we got to understand each other even better. And that's when I found out what a beautiful person he really was. . . .

It was a tough thing to believe that this kind of thing could happen to him. But he was such a strong person. . . . And he was loose about it because that was his way. He'd always been loose about things. His attitude was, What's the use of getting solemn and serious? It doesn't change things. . . . His only concern, he said, was for his wife and his three small daughters.

The funeral was held that Friday, a clean lovely morning in Chicago, and I went through it like a sleepwalker. I was one of the pallbearers along with Dick Butkus, Ralph Kurek, Ed O'Bradovich, Mike Pyle, and Randy Jackson. I think the only thing I remember about that funeral service was one line recited from the scripture: "The virtuous man, though he dies before his time, will find rest."

It was at the cemetery, as the priest was delivering his final words, that I broke down. He referred to the trophy and to our friendship and it was too much for me. I couldn't control myself. I just started to cry.

As soon as the service was ended, Joy came over to me and put her arms around me and we embraced and I told her how sorry I was. "Don't be sorry, Gale," she said. "I'm happy now because I know Brian is happy, and I don't have to watch him suffer any more. He's through suffering now."

She comforted me. I thought to myself, If she can really be that composed, Brian must have really given her something. And I thought, Well, he gave us all something, all of us who were privileged to know him.

# MAKING MEANINGS (PART TWO)

## First Thoughts

1. How did you feel after reading *Brian's Song*?

## Shaping Interpretations

2. What do you think is the most serious **conflict** that each main character faces in the play? How is each conflict resolved? Chart the play's conflicts like this:

| Character | Conflict | Resolution |
|-----------|----------|------------|
| Brian     |          |            |
| Gale      |          |            |

3. Who is Patti Lucas? How does the scene in which Gale and Joy look for her **foreshadow**, or hint at, the end of the story?

4. In "Pic" (see *Connections* on page 320), Gale Sayers writes that Brian "helped open me up because he was such a happy-go-lucky guy." What examples can you give of this opening-up process?

5. Gale also writes that Brian "gave us all something." From your own reading of the teleplay, what do you think that something was?

6. What did you learn from Gale's autobiography that wasn't in the screenplay?

7. If you previewed the play before you started reading, you probably took a guess at what the **title** means. What was your guess? How would you explain the meaning of the title now?

## Connecting with the Text

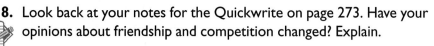

8. Look back at your notes for the Quickwrite on page 273. Have your opinions about friendship and competition changed? Explain.

## Extending the Text

9. The narrator says about Brian, "It's not how he died that they remember but, rather, how he *lived*." What other people could you say this about?

10. Do you think that professional athletes make good role models for you and your friends? Which pros do you admire most and why?

11. Brian faces illness with courage and humor. Do you think this alone would make someone a hero? Explain why or why not.

### Reading Check

a. What change in the team does Coach Halas make at the start of the new season?

b. What are the first signs of Brian's illness?

c. Who tells Brian he needs a second operation?

d. Describe what Gale does when he is given the Most Courageous Player Award.

e. What finally happens to Brian?

# CHOICES: Building Your Portfolio

## Writer's Notebook

### 1. Collecting Ideas for a How-To Essay

If you asked Gale how to play football, he would have no trouble explaining the game to you, step by step and play by play. He would have an easy time explaining the game because he likes football and he played it well. What do you do well? Do you like to teach your dog tricks or your little sister how to draw? Are you good at baking bread or playing soccer?

Brainstorm a list of things you do well. Then, pick one of the items, and make a list of all the steps you have to take to perform the activity. If the activity calls for special materials, list those too. You may want to organize your notes in a chart like the one started in the notebook on the right.

| Making Pizza | |
| --- | --- |
| **Materials** | **Steps** |
| yeast | |
| sugar | 1. Combine |
| water | yeast, sugar, |
| flour | and water; |
| oil | stir. |
| | 2. Wait 10 |
| | minutes, |
| | until yeast |
| | is foamy. . . . |

## Creative Writing

### 2. The Times of My Life

In a paragraph or journal entry, write about one of these topics:

- a time when you had to compete against someone you liked for something you wanted

- a time when you helped a friend overcome an obstacle

- a time when you or someone close to you faced a serious illness

## Critical Thinking/ Speaking and Listening

### 3. Here Comes the Judge

Working with a group, role-play the discussion the judges might have had before deciding to award an Emmy to *Brian's Song* as the best TV movie of the year. Before you start your discussion, you should decide how you'll vote: yes or no for *Brian's Song*. Then you must find good reasons to explain your vote. Why is the play good or bad, in your opinion?

## Research/ Biographical Sketch

### 4. Gale's Song

After the events depicted in *Brian's Song,* Gale went on to become a famous football player. Do research in the library and on the Internet to find out more about Gale. You might start with his autobiography, *I Am Third.* (What does the title mean?) Then, write a brief profile of Gale. Mention at least three important character traits, and describe incidents in Gale's life that illustrate those traits.

# GRAMMAR LINK  MINI-LESSON

## • Transitions Make the Right Connection

Writers use transitions to show how one idea is connected with another. Transitions can be used to show contrast, cause and effect, and time order.

### Some Common Transitions

| | |
|---|---|
| although | however |
| as a result | otherwise |
| because | since |
| finally | then |
| for example | therefore |

EXAMPLE

Brian and Gale compete for the same position on the team. Consequently [or therefore, as a result], they have conflicts.

### Try It Out

➤ Experiment with transitions. Which different transitional words could you add to each pair of sentences below to make their connections clearer?

1. Brian Piccolo is quite different from Gale Sayers. Brian is outgoing, whereas Gale is shy.

2. Gale Sayers injures his knee badly. Brian Piccolo gets to play.

3. Brian and Gale are good friends. They are rivals, too.

4. Brian's death at age twenty-six was tragic. People remember him with deep sadness.

## VOCABULARY   HOW TO OWN A WORD

### WORD BANK

exuberantly
respiration
somber
enervated
facade
eroded
exasperated
stamina
uncompre-
    hendingly
pallid

## • Extra! Extra! Reference Aids Help Clarify Meaning

**Synonyms** are words that are similar in meaning. For instance, *somber* and *serious* are synonyms, but *somber* suggests a gloomier outlook than *serious*. That's why the writer used it on page 306.

You can find synonyms in a **thesaurus** (a book of synonyms), in a **dictionary,** and in reference books called **synonym finders.** You can also check **reference software** or on-line libraries.

1. With a partner, pick five words from the Word Bank. Find the line in the play where each one is used. Then, hunt for synonyms in at least two reference aids. For each of your words, choose the two synonyms that best convey the writer's meaning. Jot them down. After each synonym that made your final cut, note where you found it.

2. Now, use the synonyms to paraphrase the sentences containing your five words. (**Paraphrasing** a sentence means putting it in your own words without changing the meaning.) In each of your paraphrased sentences, include one of the synonyms you found.

# READ ON

## Fast Breaks

Jerome "the Jayfox" is a gifted basketball player and the first African American at a North Carolina high school. In *The Moves Make the Man* (HarperCollins) by Bruce Brooks, he develops an intense friendship with a white teammate, and together they struggle to understand the meaning of truth.

## Ride 'Em, Cowboy

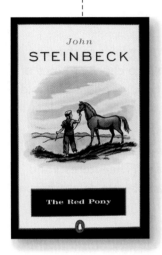

Ten-year-old Jody lives on a ranch in northern California with his family. After his father buys him Galiban, a hot-tempered pony, Jody feels proud and excited. With Billy Buck, the hired hand, Jody patiently trains and cares for Galiban, longing for the day when he can ride tall in his saddle. When the pony gets sick, Jody learns some tough lessons about the ways of the world in *The Red Pony* (Penguin) by John Steinbeck.

## Promised Land

Desta is an Ethiopian Jew and a proud African. She lives with her family in a peaceful village, unaware of the prejudice and hatred that surround them. When the hatred touches them directly, Desta and her brother and sister realize they must leave their home. *The Return* (Fawcett) by Sonia Levitin tells of their dangerous journey to Israel.

## Other Picks

- Gaye Hiçyilmaz, *Against the Storm* (Little, Brown). A young village boy's new life in a poor Turkish city is unbearable until he gets help from a streetwise orphan.
- Bernice Selden, *The Mill Girls: Lucy Larcom, Harriet Hanson Robinson, Sarah G. Bagley* (Atheneum). Three farm girls work in the textile industry during the 1830s and go on to fame and fortune.

# Speaking and Listening Workshop

**Try It Out**

Use the tips in this workshop to prepare and present an oral interpretation of a piece of literature in this book (or another piece approved by your teacher).

**Try It Out**

To test the expressiveness of your voice, form a group with two or three classmates. Each of you will write a brief "poem" in an imaginary language. Take turns reading your "poems" before the group. Can the others guess what your "poem" is about? What emotions does it express?

# ORAL INTERPRETATION

Have you ever told stories around a campfire or even around a kitchen table? Giving an **oral interpretation** can be just as entertaining. Using the expressive power of your voice, you interpret a story or poem or play by reading it to your listeners.

## Choosing a Selection

When you interpret a piece of literature, your goal is to share a text with other people. Your first challenge is to choose a piece of literature that you like and that will interest your readers and hold their attention. Ask yourself these questions when you're picking a selection:

1. Who is my audience? What are my listeners' interests, and how closely can I expect them to pay attention? (The interests and attention spans of gym teachers, for example, are different from those of preschoolers.)

2. How much time do I have? The length of your presentation will depend on what other events are planned and on your audience's attention span.

3. How can I make my reading fit the occasion? (E. E. Cummings's poem "It's Spring" might be perfect for a program on spring, but Robert Frost's poem "Stopping by Woods on a Snowy Evening" might not be.)

4. Will I present the text alone, in a solo reading, or will I work with others to present a group reading?

## Adapting Material

If you are lucky, you will find a piece of literature that is exactly the right length. Sometimes, though, you will need to choose just one part of a long poem, a short story, or a play. This shortened version is called a **cutting**. To make sure that your cutting will work well for an oral interpretation, follow these guidelines:

1. Make sure that the cutting is interesting and dramatic.

2. If your cutting begins in the middle of a story, you may need to write an introduction explaining what has already happened.

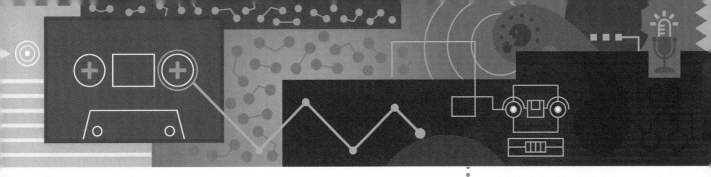

3. In plays, cut out the stage directions. (These usually appear in italics and are enclosed in brackets or parentheses.) Try to act out the directions: If, for example, the directions say that a character bows or sighs, act this out.

## Preparing Your Script

Once you've chosen your piece of literature and trimmed it to the right length, you can prepare a **reading script**.

- Write out or type all the lines you will read.
- Double-space to make your script legible.
- If you are presenting a cutting, type out your introduction.
- Underline or highlight words that you wish to emphasize.
- Draw a slash where you plan to take a breath or pause for dramatic effect.
- Make notes in the margins about the emotions you want to express. Jot down ideas about gestures, movements, and facial expressions you plan to use.

## Rehearsing

- Tape-record your interpretation and then play it back. Does your voice sound natural? Did you pronounce your lines clearly? Is your reading dramatic without seeming forced or stagy?
- Read your script to a friend. Then, ask your friend to give you feedback about your performance. Did your friend understand everything you read, or were some parts confusing? Could your friend distinguish between the characters? Was your **stage presence**—the image you project as you read—powerful and convincing?

As you prepare and rehearse your script, analyze the effects you want to have on your listeners. Keep in mind that there is no single "correct" interpretation. Experiment. Use your imagination. You may come up with a new way of looking at a work of literature—whether it was written last year or many centuries ago.

### Try It Out

When you're trying to get across a character's feelings, gestures can be just as effective as words. See if you can match the gestures listed in the left-hand column with the emotions listed in the right-hand column. Can some gestures show more than one emotion?

| Gestures | Emotions |
|---|---|
| shrug | impatience |
| pacing | skepticism |
| arching eyebrow | indifference |
| rubbing chin | puzzlement |
| stamping foot | despair |
| wringing hands | anger |
| rolling eyes | annoyance |

## EXPOSITORY WRITING

# HOW-TO ESSAY

In this workshop you'll describe a **process:** You'll explain **how to** do or make something or how something works.

**ASSIGNMENT**

**Write an explanation of how to do something.**

**AIM**

**To inform; to explain.**

**AUDIENCE**

**Your teacher and other adults, teenagers, or children slightly younger than you. (You decide.)**

### Professional Model

As an expert in managing humans, I want to share some of my techniques. You pups will be on your own before you have time to scratch an itch.

First, master complete control over your eyes. Suppose it's a pretty day. You want to go for a walk. Lie about five feet from the human with your paws extended. Rest your chin on your paws. Look up out of the bottom of your eyes so that just a sliver of white shows. Sigh loudly.

Next, make them think the silly baby talk they use with you is exciting. Perk up your ears. Tilt your head. Smile. I promise you'll get a cookie or even a new toy.

Finally, don't forget the chin-in-the-lap technique. Suppose you need to scratch but you're too tired. Place your chin in the human's lap. Work your nose under the human's hand. Automatic scratching will start. Humans were bred to scratch dogs.

Use these techniques, little ones, and you will enjoy a happy life loving humans who'll never realize that you're the ones in control.

—"How to Handle a Human" by Joan Burditt

*The introduction grabs the reader's attention. (The speaker is an adult dog!)*

*The writer breaks each technique down into a series of steps.*

*The writer uses transitions (First, Next, and Finally) to help the reader follow the techniques.*

*The conclusion sums up the benefits of learning "how to" manage humans.*

## Prewriting

### 1. Writer's Notebook

Reread your Writer's Notebook for this collection, and take another look at the list of things you do well. Here are a few ways to cut down the list:

- Think about things you're especially good at.

- Pick activities that you think will interest the audience you have in mind.

- Make sure you can break each process into steps.

- Choose activities that are simple enough to explain in a few paragraphs.

### 2. Getting Feedback

Test out the ideas you like best with two or three classmates. Here's one way to get feedback:

- On a slip of paper, describe each idea and its audience. Then, have everyone in the group rate the ideas on a scale from I to 5 to show how much they think readers would like to learn about that process. (See the examples at the right.)

- If none of your ideas gets a high score, just brainstorm more topics with your group.

You might also ask your friends and family for ideas. They may be able to come up with an activity like making a kind of food, performing a dance, or celebrating a special occasion.

### 3. Listing Steps and Equipment

Once you have a good idea for a how-to paper, you need to figure out (1) the steps in the process and (2) what's needed to do it. You might start by making a chart like the one at right.

Notice that the steps are listed in **chronological,** or time, order. After you jot down the steps in your process, you may decide to move some around or cross out unnecessary ones.

How to Make a Good Video: Classmates Rating: 3

How to Strike Out Every Time: 6th grade Rating: 4

How to Make Falafel: Classmates Rating: 4

How to Give Your Cat a Pill: Classmates Rating: 4

How to Give Your Dog a Bath: 4th grade Rating: 4

How to Dress in 5 Minutes: Classmates Rating: 5

| How to Wash a Car | |
|---|---|
| Steps | Equipment |
| 1. Spray car with water. | car, hose, outdoor faucet |
| 2. Fill bucket with warm water and liquid soap. | liquid soap, bucket, hot-water faucet, rags or sponges |
| 3. Spread soapy water all over car. | lots of energy! |
| 4. Hose off car with cold water. | clothes you can mess up |
| 5. Clean windows and mirrors. | window-cleaning fluid, rags |

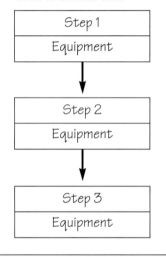
## Drafting

### 1. Organizing Your First Draft

When you write your first draft, try to get your ideas down quickly. Start with your Prewriting notes. They should contain most of the specific information you need.

As you write your draft, you may want to elaborate on some of the steps, tools, and materials. If you elaborate on steps, avoid adding unnecessary information. Whatever descriptive details, examples, definitions, and reasons you add should clarify your steps. Remember that your goal is to explain each step clearly so that your readers can complete it before moving on.

Try to provide information that answers any questions your audience might have about the process. For a how-to paper on washing a car, for instance, you need to say *how much* liquid soap goes into the bucket.

Here's an organizing guide you may find helpful.

Equipment needed: _____

_____

Step 1 _____

_____

Step 2 _____

_____

Step 3 _____

_____

(Add as many steps as you need.)

### 2. Writing a Strong Start and Finish

Your introduction should grab your readers' attention and draw them into your essay. The introduction for this kind of paper should be fairly short. Just write one or two sentences telling what process you are going to explain and, perhaps, why it's important or fun to do. If there's a special reason why you chose this process, include that information in your introduction.

Here are some ideas for a strong conclusion:

- Emphasize how useful or important the process is.

- Describe how sharing this process makes you feel.

- End with a quotation from someone who tried out your "how-to" and enjoyed it!

*This humorous essay explains how* not *to eat vegetables.*

Eating vegetables must be the worst thing that could happen to anyone. But do not despair. A small spark of hope remains. The secret to surviving may be found in knowing a few simple tricks. If they are performed with slyness and cunning, you may never have to eat your vegetables again.

*The writer starts out with an attention grabber.*

At the beginning of the meal, one trick is especially helpful. Do not place any vegetables on your plate if no one tells you to. If no one is paying attention, you might not have to take any at all. If this plan doesn't work, be the last person to take some. Purposely leave the serving dish near your plate. Cautiously return forkfuls back into the bowl. . . .

*The writer gives the reason for learning the process. (It's clear this is not a serious essay!)*

*The writer describes two steps in the process and offers helpful hints.*

If a dog happens to reside at your home, use him to your advantage. Strategically drop small amounts of broccoli (without cheese sauce) onto the floor or your lap. Several napkins are necessary for this maneuver. The dog will be waiting underneath, ready to dispose of whatever is dropped.

*The writer lists necessary equipment (a dog, napkins).*

I hope these tips will help you avoid eating vegetables. They have worked for me on several occasions, and I will continue to use these handy techniques as long as I am forced to eat repulsive objects.

*A personal statement makes a funny conclusion.*

—Laura Kent
Lake Braddock Secondary School
Burke, Virginia

---

## Strategies for Elaboration

### Using Transitions
Transition words and phrases like *first, next, finally,* and *after five minutes* tell your readers when to take each step. Other transitions, such as *on the table, on the right, beside,* and *in the center* tell readers where things are or where they go. Use both types of transitions to make your how-to paper clear and easy to follow.

**Language/Grammar Link**
H E L P

*Transitions: page 324.*

---

■ *Evaluation Criteria*

*A good how-to paper*

1. *describes the steps and equipment needed to complete the task*

2. *presents each step clearly so that another person can do it*

3. *presents the steps in a logical (usually chronological) order*

4. *stays on track—sticks to the process being explained*

**Communications Handbook**
**H E L P**

*See Proofreaders' Marks.*

**Sentence Workshop**
**H E L P**

*Combining sentences using* and, but, *or* or: *page 333.*

---

**Publishing Tip**

With your classmates, sort the how-to papers into groups, and bind together papers on similar activities. Give the bound sets of papers to an elementary-school classroom or library.

---

# Evaluating and Revising

## 1. Peer Review

When you've finished your first draft, do a test run with a partner. Ask your partner to pantomime the process as you read your draft aloud. Before you begin, list the equipment that is needed, and have your partner sketch each tool or ingredient on a separate piece of paper. When your partner needs to "use" a piece of equipment, the sketch should be right there. If it isn't, add that item to your list. If your partner gets confused at any point, make a note on your draft. Ask your partner:

- What steps in the process seem too complicated?
- Did you notice any distracting or unnecessary information I could take out?

## 2. Self-Evaluation

Ask yourself these questions:

- Will this process interest my audience? Have I made it easy enough for readers to do—or is it so easy that it will bore them? Is the vocabulary right for my audience?
- Will the introduction make readers want to know more about the process? If not, what details can I add to give readers a good reason for learning the process?
- Have I listed all the equipment, materials, tools, and ingredients needed for each step?
- Have I listed the steps in chronological order? Have I included all the details needed to allow readers to understand and follow the process? Do I need to add transitions to help readers follow the steps?
- Have I stayed on track from beginning to end? What details would be better left out?
- Does my paper have a strong conclusion?

PEANUTS reprinted by permission of United Feature Syndicate, Inc.

# Sentence Workshop

## COMBINING SENTENCES USING <u>AND</u>, <u>BUT</u>, OR <u>OR</u>

Sometimes a short sentence can express your meaning perfectly. A long, unbroken chain of short sentences can make your writing choppy and dull, however. You can vary your sentence structure by using the conjunction *and, but,* or *or* to combine ideas.

Combine sentences having the same verb but different subjects by making a **compound subject.** Combine sentences having the same subject but different verbs by making a **compound verb.**

TWO SENTENCES    Running backs are fast runners. Receivers are also.

COMBINED    <u>Running backs</u> **and** <u>receivers</u> are fast runners. [compound subject]

TWO SENTENCES    Running backs carry the ball. They make lateral passes if necessary.

COMBINED    Running backs <u>carry</u> the ball **but** <u>make</u> lateral passes if necessary. [compound verb]

Sometimes you may want to combine two sentences that express closely related, equally important ideas. You can connect the two sentences by using a comma followed by the conjunction *and, but,* or *or.* When you join sentences this way, you create a **compound sentence.**

TWO SENTENCES    They were both football players. They competed for the same job.

COMBINED    They were both football players**, and** they competed for the same job. [compound sentence]

## Writer's Workshop Follow-up: Revision

Read your how-to essay aloud. Do your sentences flow, or do they sound dull and choppy? Try combining sentences to improve the sound of your essay or to help readers make connections between ideas.

**Language Handbook**
**H E L P**

*See Combining Sentences, pages 760-761.*

**Technology**
**H E L P**

See Language Workshop CD-ROM. *Key word entry: combining sentences.*

### Try It Out

Combine each pair of sentences using *and, but,* or *or.* Exchange your edited sentences with a partner. Have you chosen the best conjunction? Are several combinations possible?

1. Piccolo's smile vanishes. He nods toward one of the buildings offstage.

2. Gale moves off for the building. Brian stays behind for a moment.

3. Brian Piccolo approaches. Brian Piccolo starts to unload his tray.

4. The man next to Gale finishes his plate. The man next to Gale leaves.

5. Sayers comes out of a sprinter's crouch. Piccolo comes out of a sprinter's crouch.

# Reading for Life

## Reading a Manual

## Situation

You're writing a "how-to" paper for English class. You've used the word *important* three times. Somewhere inside your word-processing program there's a thesaurus, a whole treasury of synonyms. How can you get to it? You take out the manual that came with your word-processing software. Here are strategies you can use to read any manual.

## Strategies

**Read for information.**

You read a manual to get information about a tool or program or to solve a problem you're having with it.

- To see what's in a manual, look at the table of contents in the front. Then, look at the index, the alphabetical list of subjects with page numbers in the back. See if the manual includes phone numbers and e-mail addresses you can use to get help.

- Read the directions slowly, word by word. Keep referring to the actual tool or program as you read.

**Notice the steps.**

- Directions are usually listed

---

### Looking Up Synonyms for a Word in a Document

1 Select the word in the document.

2 Choose Utilities Thesaurus (Alt,U,T), or press the THESAURUS key (Shift+F7).

3 Look through the list of synonyms in Synonyms. Scroll through the list if necessary.

### Command for Thesaurus

**Utilities Thesaurus or THESAURUS Key (Shift+F7)**

Lists alternative words for the selection.

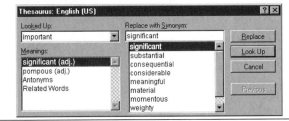

---

in step-by-step, **chronological** order. Read all the directions for each step before moving on to the next.

## Look up unfamiliar words, abbreviations, and symbols.

- In a manual you may see abbreviations like STO and ALT and symbols like * and #. You may also see unfamiliar terms, and words—like *scroll, select, icon, shift,* and *menu*—used in new ways. When you come across an unfamiliar abbreviation, symbol, or word, look it up in the manual's glossary. If it isn't there, try to figure out its meaning from context or ask an expert.

---

## Using the Strategies

Use these strategies as you read the page above.

1. From the context, figure out what *select* and *scroll* mean here.

2. Describe two ways to get the thesaurus screen on your computer.

3. Make up a sentence using one of the synonyms listed for *important*.

## Extending the Strategies

Find someone who is having a problem with a tool or a software program. Get the manual, and apply these strategies to help the person solve the problem.

# Learning for Life

## Conducting an Interview to Research a Question

## Problem

Brian Piccolo and Gale Sayers understood the importance of working together on a team. How do people who work in teams learn to cooperate and act effectively together?

## Project

**Interview workers in a local company to find out how they cooperate and make an effective team.**

## Preparation

1. Choose a business that requires people to work cooperatively: a hospital, a restaurant, or a newspaper, for example.

2. Develop some key questions for the experts you will interview, such as these:

   • Why do you work as a team?

   • What roles do different team members play?

   • How do you help one another?

   • Do you have guidelines for working as a team?

   • How do you handle problems with team members?

## Procedure

1. Call to arrange a time and place for the interview. Go as a group. (Discuss ahead of time the roles each of you will play, such as note taker or interviewer.) Try to talk to more than one employee—a complete team or several members of a team would be ideal.

2. Don't try to write down everything said during the interview. Instead, jot down important facts and a few direct quotations. If you use a tape recorder, be sure to get permission first. Don't forget to write a thank-you note after the interview.

3. Develop a set of guidelines for teamwork in the workplace based on your interview.

4. Analyze the way your class works together. Compare its procedures with the guidelines for teamwork that you developed. Discuss with your teacher ways that students might learn to be more cooperative. Also, discuss the problems involved in working in teams in a classroom.

## Presentation

Present what you have learned about teamwork in one of the following ways:

### 1. Teamwork Handbook

Develop a handbook of guidelines for working as a team on class projects. Add an introduction about the value of teamwork. If possible, ask the workers you interviewed to review the handbook.

### 2. Skit

Create a skit for other classes that shows the dos and don'ts of teamwork in action. Use a school or workplace setting.

### 3. Posters

Create a group of posters for display in the workplace or classroom. Show guidelines for teamwork, such as dividing responsibilities, respecting others, and listening carefully.

## Processing

Discuss this question as a class: Are there differences between cooperation in the classroom and cooperation in the workplace? Explain the differences or the reason you think there are no differences.

# Living in the Heart

*If you live in my heart,*
*you live rent free.*

*—Irish proverb*

*Love* sculpture by Robert Indiana in front of the Philadelphia Visitors Center.

The Philadelphia Convention and Visitors Bureau.

# Elements of Literature

## POETRY: Sound Effects *by* John Malcolm Brinnin

Poets use many techniques to make music out of words. The most common sound effects used in poetry are also used in the songs you listen to on the radio.

### Rhythm: The Rise and Fall of Our Voices

**Rhythm** refers to the rise and fall of our voices as we use language. As in music, a poem's rhythm can be fast or slow, light or solemn. It might also sound just like everyday speech.

Poetry that is written in **meter** has a regular pattern of stressed and unstressed syllables. Poetry that is written in **free verse** does not have a regular pattern of stressed and unstressed syllables. Free verse sounds like ordinary speech.

When poets write in meter, they count out the number of stressed syllables (or strong beats) and unstressed syllables (weaker beats) in each line. Then they repeat the pattern throughout the poem. To avoid a singsong effect, poets usually vary the basic pattern from time to time. Try reading aloud the following lines from a famous poem called *The Rime of the Ancient Mariner* by Samuel Taylor Coleridge. Can you hear that each line has four stressed syllables alternating with four unstressed syllables?

> Day after day, day after day,
> We stuck, nor breath nor
>   motion;
> As idle as a painted ship
> Upon a painted ocean.

A poem's rhythm can be shown by using accent marks (ʹ) for stressed syllables and cups (˘) for unstressed syllables. This marking is called **scanning.**

> ˘ ʹ ˘ ʹ ˘ ʹ ˘ ʹ
> Day after day, day after day

### Rhyme: Chiming Sounds

**Rhyme** is the repetition of the sound of a stressed syllable and any unstressed syllables that follow: *sport* and *court; smother* and *another; sputtering* and *muttering.* The echoing effect of rhyme gives us pleasure. It makes us look forward to hearing certain chiming sounds throughout the poem. In the verse from *The Rime of the Ancient Mariner,* the rhyming words are *motion* and *ocean.*

Rhymes like *motion/ocean* in Coleridge's verse are called **end rhymes** because they occur at the ends of lines. **Internal rhymes** occur within lines, as in this line from the same poem:

> The fair breeze blew, the
>   white foam flew . . .

Poets will often use a pattern of rhymes, called a **rhyme scheme.** To describe a rhyme scheme, assign a new letter of the alphabet to each new end rhyme. The rhyme scheme of Coleridge's verse is *abcb.*

### Alliteration: Repeating Consonants

Another way poets create sound effects is through the use of alliteration. **Alliteration** is the repetition of consonant sounds in words that are close together. Read this tongue twister of a poem aloud to hear all the repeated *t* sounds.

### A Tutor

A tutor who tooted the flute
Tried to tutor two tooters to
   toot.
     Said the two to the tutor,
     "Is it harder to toot, or
To tutor two tooters to toot?"

—Carolyn Wells

"A Tutor" is a **limerick,** a humorous five-line poem. Limericks have a definite rhythm and rhyme scheme. Try scanning the poem and describing the rhyme scheme now that you've tooted through it.

## Onomatopoeia: Sound Echoes Sense

**Onomatopoeia** is a long word that is pronounced like this: än′ō·mat′ō·pē′ə. It is the use of words with sounds that echo their sense. *Crash, bang, boom, hiss,* and *toot* are all examples of onomatopoeia.

   To see how sounds alone can suggest sense, read the famous nonsense poem in the next column aloud. You will not find all the words in a dictionary, but the sounds will help you guess what is going on.

### Jabberwocky

'Twas brillig, and the slithy toves
     Did gyre and gimble in the wabe;
All mimsy were the borogoves,
     And the mome raths outgrabe.
"Beware the Jabberwock, my son!
     The jaws that bite, the claws that catch!
Beware the Jubjub bird, and shun
     The frumious Bandersnatch!"
He took his vorpal sword in hand:
     Long time the manxome foe he sought—
So rested he by the Tumtum tree,
     And stood awhile in thought.
And, as in uffish thought he stood,
     The Jabberwock, with eyes of flame,
Came whiffling through the tulgey wood,
     And burbled as it came!
One, two! One, two! And through and through
     The vorpal blade went snicker-snack!
He left it dead, and with its head
     He went galumphing back.
"And hast thou slain the Jabberwock?
     Come to my arms, my beamish boy!
O frabjous day! Callooh! Callay!"
     He chortled in his joy.
'Twas brillig, and the slithy toves
     Did gyre and gimble in the wabe;
All mimsy were the borogoves,
     And the mome raths outgrabe.

—Lewis Carroll

### Make the Connection

**"Watch for Me by Moonlight"**

It was a night made for love and adventure. Start with the **setting:** a moonlit road hundreds of years ago, a country inn at midnight. Add some **characters:** a daring and dashing robber, a beautiful young woman, a jealous stableman, and a group of cruel soldiers. Can you predict what will happen? Hint: Look at the poem's title and illustrations. Skim the first verse.

**Predicting.** Discuss your impressions of the poem with a partner. On the basis of your preview, what do you think will happen?

### Reading Skills and Strategies

**Dialogue with the Text**

As you read this poem, keep a sheet of paper handy so that you can write down your reactions. One student's comments appear on the first page as an example. Remember that you create your own meaning from "The Highwayman." No one else will read it exactly the same way you do.

### Elements of Literature

**Stories in Verse: An Old Tradition**

Poems that are written to tell a story are called **narrative poems.** These story poems resemble short stories: They have a **plot, characters,** and a **setting.** Stories sung to the strumming of a stringed instrument are probably the oldest form of storytelling. Modern poems like this one use strong rhythms to make their stories sound like the old sung stories—they capture the enduring power of the spoken word.

> **N**arrative poetry is poetry that tells a story.

### Background

**Literature and History**

The highwayman in this famous poem is a robber who lived in England in the 1700s. Highwaymen used to stop stagecoaches on the lonely moorlands of northern England and Scotland and rob the rich passengers of money and jewels. Some highwaymen were considered heroes by the Scots because they shared the money with the poor. Highwaymen were often dashing, romantic figures who dressed in expensive clothes. The poem is based on a true story that the poet heard while he was on vacation in that part of England where highwaymen used to lie in wait for stagecoaches.

go.hrw.com
*LEO 7-5*

# The Highwayman

**Alfred Noyes**

## Part 1

The wind was a torrent of darkness among the gusty
    trees,
The moon was a ghostly galleon° tossed upon cloudy
    seas,
The road was a ribbon of moonlight over the purple
    moor,
And the highwayman came riding——
5        Riding——riding——
The highwayman came riding, up to the old inn door.

He'd a French cocked hat on his forehead, a bunch of
    lace at his chin,
A coat of the claret° velvet, and breeches of brown
    doeskin.
They fitted with never a wrinkle. His boots were up
    to the thigh.
10  And he rode with a jeweled twinkle,
        His pistol butts a-twinkle,
His rapier hilt° a-twinkle, under the jeweled sky.

Over the cobbles he clattered and clashed in the dark
    inn yard.
And he tapped with his whip on the shutters, but all
    was locked and barred.
He whistled a tune to the window, and who should be
15      waiting there
But the landlord's black-eyed daughter,
        Bess, the landlord's daughter,
Plaiting° a dark red love knot into her long black
    hair.

---

2. **galleon:** large sailing ship.
8. **claret** (klarʹit): purplish red, like claret wine.
12. **rapier** (rāʹpē·ər ) **hilt:** sword handle.
18. **plaiting:** braiding.

### Dialogue with the Text

Reminds me of one of our family camping trips.

Sounds like a ghost ship caught in a storm.

It sounds like the only good sight in the open land was a road.

Is the inn abandoned?

Those were long boots.

What's a jeweled twinkle?

Does that mean he was making a lot of noise?

There must not have been windows.

I think that these two lines should somehow become one—"But the landlord's black-eyed daughter Bess."

*Crystal Hinojos*
—Crystal Hinojos
  Lincoln Middle School
  El Paso, Texas

And dark in the dark old inn yard a stable wicket°
    creaked
Where Tim the ostler° listened. His face was white
20    and peaked.
His eyes were hollows of madness, his hair like
    moldy hay,
But he loved the landlord's daughter,
       The landlord's red-lipped daughter,
Dumb as a dog he listened, and he heard the robber
    say——

"One kiss, my bonny sweetheart, I'm after a prize
25    tonight,
But I shall be back with the yellow gold before the
    morning light;
Yet, if they press me sharply, and harry° me through
    the day,
Then look for me by moonlight,
       Watch for me by moonlight,
I'll come to thee by moonlight, though hell should
30    bar the way."

He rose upright in the stirrups. He scarce could reach
    her hand,
But she loosened her hair in the casement.° His face
    burnt like a brand
As the black cascade of perfume came tumbling over
    his breast;
And he kissed its waves in the moonlight,
35       (Oh, sweet black waves in the moonlight!)
Then he tugged at his rein in the moonlight, and
    galloped away to the west.

## Part 2

He did not come in the dawning. He did not come at
    noon;
And out of the tawny sunset, before the rise of the
    moon,

19. **wicket:** small door or gate.
20. **ostler** (äs′lər ): person who takes care of horses; groom.
27. **harry:** harass or push along.
32. **casement:** window that opens outward on hinges.

*The Haywain* by John Constable (1776–1837).

When the road was a gypsy's ribbon, looping the
    purple moor,
40    A redcoat troop came marching——
        Marching——marching——
King George's men came marching, up to the old inn
    door.

They said no word to the landlord. They drank his
    ale instead.
But they gagged his daughter, and bound her, to the
    foot of her narrow bed.
Two of them knelt at her casement, with muskets at
45    their side!

There was death at every window;
    And hell at one dark window;
For Bess could see, through her casement, the road
    that *he* would ride.

They had tied her up to attention, with many a snig-
    gering jest;
They had bound a musket beside her, with the muzzle
50    beneath her breast!
"Now, keep good watch!" and they kissed her. She
    heard the dead man say——
*Look for me by moonlight;*
    *Watch for me by moonlight;*
*I'll come to thee by moonlight, though hell should bar*
    *the way!*

She twisted her hands behind her; but all the knots
55    held good!
She writhed her hands till her fingers were wet with
    sweat or blood!
They stretched and strained in the darkness, and the
    hours crawled by like years,
Till, now, on the stroke of midnight,
    Cold, on the stroke of midnight,
The tip of one finger touched it! The trigger at least
60    was hers!

The tip of one finger touched it; she strove no more
    for the rest!
Up, she stood up to attention, with the muzzle be-
    neath her breast.
She would not risk their hearing; she would not
    strive again;
For the road lay bare in the moonlight;
65    Blank and bare in the moonlight;
And the blood of her veins, in the moonlight,
    throbbed to her love's refrain.

*Tlot-tlot; tlot-tlot!* Had they heard it? The horse hoofs
    ringing clear;
*Tlot-tlot, tlot-tlot,* in the distance? Were they deaf that
    they did not hear?
Down the ribbon of moonlight, over the brow of the
    hill,

70  The highwayman came riding,
        Riding, riding!
    The redcoats looked to their priming!° She stood up,
        straight and still.

    *Tlot-tlot,* in the frosty silence! *Tlot-tlot,* in the echoing
        night!
    Nearer he came and nearer. Her face was like a light!
    Her eyes grew wide for a moment; she drew one last
75      deep breath,
    Then her fingers moved in the moonlight,
        Her musket shattered the moonlight,
    Shattered her breast in the moonlight and warned
        him—with her death.

    He turned. He spurred to the west; he did not know
        who stood
    Bowed, with her head o'er the musket, drenched
80      with her own blood!
    Not till the dawn he heard it, his face grew gray to
        hear
    How Bess, the landlord's daughter,
        The landlord's black-eyed daughter,
    Had watched for her love in the moonlight, and died
        in the darkness there.

    Back, he spurred like a madman, shouting a curse to
85      the sky,
    With the white road smoking behind him and his
        rapier brandished high.
    Blood-red were his spurs in the golden noon; wine-
        red was his velvet coat;
    When they shot him down on the highway,
        Down like a dog on the highway,
    And he lay in his blood on the highway, with the
90      bunch of lace at his throat.

    *And still of a winter's night, they say, when the wind
        is in the trees,
    When the moon is a ghostly galleon tossed upon
        cloudy seas,*

The Granger Collection, New York.

---

**72. priming:** explosive for firing a gun.

## MEET THE WRITER

### "One Blustery Night"

British poet, novelist, biographer, and essayist **Alfred Noyes** (1880–1958) was often called the most popular writer of his time. People enjoyed his verse for its rousing storytelling and its thumping rhythms—in fact, his work was often performed aloud.

Today Noyes is best remembered for "The Highwayman," which he wrote in a small cottage on the edge of Bagshot Heath shortly after leaving Oxford University. He recalls:

66 Bagshot Heath in those days was a wild bit of country, all heather and pinewoods. 'The Highwayman' suggested itself to me one blustery night when the sound of the wind in the pines gave me the first line:

*The wind was a torrent of darkness among the gusty trees . . .*

It took me about two days to complete the poem. Shortly afterward it appeared in *Blackwood's Magazine*. It illustrates the unpredictable chances of authorship, that this poem, written in so short a time, when I was 24, should have been read so widely.

I think the success of the poem in all these ways was due to the fact that it was not an artificial composition, but was written at an age when I was genuinely excited by that kind of romantic story. 99

*When the road is a ribbon of moonlight over the*
    *purple moor,*
*A highwayman comes riding——*
95        *Riding——riding——*
*A highwayman comes riding, up to the old inn door.*

*Over the cobbles he clatters and clangs in the dark*
    *inn yard;*
*He taps with his whip on the shutters, but all is*
    *locked and barred.*
*He whistles a tune to the window, and who should be*
    *waiting there*
100 *But the landlord's black-eyed daughter,*
        *Bess, the landlord's daughter,*
*Plaiting a dark red love knot into her long black hair.*

# MAKING MEANINGS

- ## First Thoughts

  1. Bess gives up her life because of her love for the highwayman. In your opinion, is her sacrifice noble or pointless? Explain your response.

## Shaping Interpretations

2. What is the **setting** of this story? How does the poet help you to see and hear what is happening?

3. What part does Tim the ostler play in the story? What is his motive?

4. Why do you think the highwayman comes back to the inn after he hears how Bess died?

5. The last two stanzas are very much like the first and third stanzas. The wording, however, is slightly different. How does the difference reflect what is happening at the end of the poem?

6. How do you think the narrator feels about the highwayman? How can you tell? How do *you* feel about him?

7. Powerful **rhythm** adds to the drama of this poem. Read aloud the tenth through thirteenth stanzas. Would you describe their rhythm as fast or slow? Does their rhythm help you imagine the poem's action?

## Connecting with the Text

8. If you could write a new ending for the poem, what would it be?

9. Here is a letter that one student wrote about "The Highwayman." List two or three points you would make in a letter about the poem.

> ### Reading Check
>
> Review the main events of this **narrative poem** and then complete a **sequence chart** like the one below.
>
> #### Part I
>
> 1. The highwayman rides to the old inn.
>
> 2. He finds Bess waiting.
>
> 3. Tim overhears him say . . .

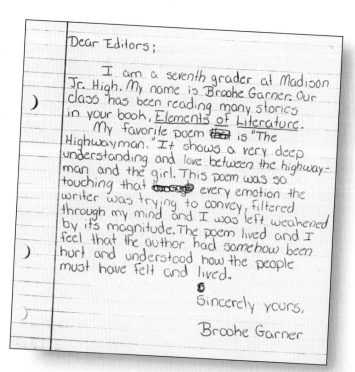

Dear Editors;

I am a seventh grader at Madison Jr. High. My name is Brooke Garner. Our class has been reading many stories in your book, Elements of Literature.

My favorite poem ~~that~~ is "The Highwayman." It shows a very deep understanding and love between the highwayman and the girl. This poem was so touching that ~~~~ every emotion the writer was trying to convey, filtered through my mind and I was left weakened by its magnitude. The poem lived and I feel that the author had somehow been hurt and understood how the people must have felt and lived.

Sincerely yours,

Brooke Garner

# CHOICES: Building Your Portfolio

## Writer's Notebook

### 1. Collecting Ideas for a Biographical Sketch

Like Noyes, many writers choose to write about actual people and events. Think of someone you know or know of whose real life is worth telling about—exciting, heroic, funny, unusual. What is that person like? List his or her three main character traits. Then, jot down notes about an incident that illustrates these traits.

Emily Brown

Artistic; creative; community-minded: Got stores on Mission Street to donate walls and inspired neighborhood kids to do murals.

## A Summary and Response

### 2. You Be the Judge

Write two paragraphs about "The Highwayman." First, **summarize** the plot by describing the story's **conflict, climax,** and **resolution.** In your second paragraph, tell how the poem affected you. To recall your first reactions, review the notes you made as you read the poem.

## Choral Reading

### 3. A Ghostly Chorus of Voices

Get together with a group of classmates and create a choral reading of "The Highwayman." Try assigning some lines to individuals, some to a boys' chorus, and some to a girls' chorus. (Label the parts on a copy of the poem.) As you practice the poem, decide how to read each line—loudly, softly, quickly, slowly, with rising excitement, with sorrow, and so on. Look for ways to capture the powerful **rhythm** with your voice. Discuss how to read the parts where words or phrases are repeated, for if you're not careful, they may sound dull. Also, be sure to clearly pronounce the lines that contain **alliteration**—the repetition of initial consonant sounds in words near one another. You might perform your choral reading for another class.

## Creative Writing/Art

### 4. Soon—At a Theater Near You!

Hollywood once made a movie based on "The Highwayman." Create a poster for such a movie, working with a partner or with several classmates if you prefer. Illustrate scenes and portray characters, but above all try to convey the **mood** of the movie as you imagine it. Be sure to use a quotation from the poem on your poster.

## Make the Connection

### "A Love That Was More Than Love"

"Annabel Lee" is a famous love poem, written after the poet's young wife, Virginia, died of tuberculosis. She was laid to rest in New York, near the Hudson River, in a sepulcher (sep'əl·kər), a burial vault that stands above ground. Poe's poem reads like a fairy tale, set in a faraway time and place.

**Think aloud.** With a partner, take turns reading the poem aloud to hear its haunting sounds and to visualize its romantic setting. Exchange thoughts about the poem's speaker and its music.

## Reading Skills and Strategies

### Dialogue with the Text

Have your notebook open while you and your partner are reading the poem. Note comments and questions as they come to you and then discuss them with your partner. Work together to solve any problems you have in understanding the poem.

go.hrw.com
LE0 7-5

*Portrait of a Girl at a Beach* by John Collier.

Reprinted by permission of the Estate of Edith Wharton and the Watkins/Loomis Agency.

## Elements of Literature

### Repetition: See the sea . . . the sea . . . the sea

Musicians, as you may know, use repetition—of sounds, of words, of tones—to create emotional effects. Poe uses repetition in much the same way. In "Annabel Lee," notice how words, sounds, phrases, and rhythms keep recurring with hypnotic regularity.

> **R**epetition is the recurring use of a sound, a word, a phrase, or a line. Repetition can be used to create music, to appeal to our emotions, and to emphasize important ideas.

# Annabel Lee

**Edgar Allan Poe**

It was many and many a year ago,
    In a kingdom by the sea,
That a maiden there lived whom you may know
    By the name of Annabel Lee;
5    And this maiden she lived with no other thought
    Than to love and be loved by me.

*I* was a child and *she* was a child,
    In this kingdom by the sea:
But we loved with a love that was more than love——
10    I and my Annabel Lee——
With a love that the wingèd seraphs° of heaven
    Coveted° her and me.

11. **seraphs** (ser′əfs): angels.
12. **coveted:** envied.

And this was the reason that, long ago,
    In this kingdom by the sea,
15    A wind blew out of a cloud, chilling
    My beautiful Annabel Lee;
So that her highborn kinsmen came
    And bore her away from me,
To shut her up in a sepulcher
20    In this kingdom by the sea.

The angels, not half so happy in heaven,
    Went envying her and me——
Yes!—that was the reason (as all men know,
    In this kingdom by the sea)
25    That the wind came out of the cloud by night,
    Chilling and killing my Annabel Lee.

But our love it was stronger by far than the love
    Of those who were older than we——
    Of many far wiser than we——
30  And neither the angels in heaven above,
    Nor the demons down under the sea,
Can ever dissever° my soul from the soul
    Of the beautiful Annabel Lee——

For the moon never beams, without bringing me dreams
35    Of the beautiful Annabel Lee;
And the stars never rise, but I feel the bright eyes
    Of the beautiful Annabel Lee;
And so, all the night-tide, I lie down by the side
Of my darling—my darling—my life and my bride,
40    In the sepulcher there by the sea,
    In her tomb by the sounding sea.

**32. dissever** (di·sev′ər): separate.

*Crashing Wave* (c. 1938) by Marsden Hartley.

Collection of Jon and Barbara Landau, New York.

# MEET THE WRITER

## "A World of Moan"

Long before Stephen King wrote horror stories, **Edgar Allan Poe** (1809–1849) was exploring the dark side of the human imagination in such works as "The Raven" and "The Tell-Tale Heart." Poe's life was hard from the start. First, his father deserted the family. Then, Poe's beautiful young mother died before he was three years old, and the little boy was left alone. A wealthy and childless Richmond businessman, John Allan, took Edgar in and provided for his education. As the boy grew older, however, he continually quarreled with Mr. Allan. Poe wanted to write; his foster father wanted him to take over the family business. Eventually Poe broke with his foster parents and set out on his own. Through-out his adult life he was troubled by poverty, alcoholism, and unhappi-ness. As Poe said, "I dwelt alone in a world of moan."

Always searching for a family, Poe eventually married his thirteen-year-old cousin, Virginia Clemm. Her early death seemed to destroy him, and he died himself two years later. He had lived barely forty years.

### Pick Your Poe

Poe's haunting poems include "The Raven" and "The Bells." You'll find some of his most chilling stories in a book titled *The Best of Poe* (Lake).

The Granger Collection, New York.

# MAKING MEANINGS

## • First Thoughts

**1.** If you were to meet the speaker of this poem, what would you want to ask him? Be sure to refer to the notes you made as you read the poem.

## Shaping Interpretations

**2.** Where does the speaker say he sleeps each night? Do you think he actually sleeps there, or is he speaking of what he does in his imagination? Explain.

**3.** Find at least two details that help you picture the poem's **setting.**

**4.** What **repetition** of words and sounds echoes throughout the six stanzas? What person does the repetition keep reminding you of?

## Connecting with the Text

**5.** Some people say "It's better to have loved and lost than never to have loved at all." Do you agree or disagree? How do you think the poem's speaker would respond to the idea?

## Extending the Text

**6.** This is a poem about a particular loss. Talk about whether or not you think the speaker's feelings of grief are universal.

# CHOICES: Building Your Portfolio

**Writer's Notebook**

## 1. Collecting Ideas for a Biographical Sketch

In "Annabel Lee" a speaker expresses his feelings about a beloved person who has died. Think of a person you feel strongly about—perhaps someone you love, admire, or miss very much. Take notes telling how you feel about your subject. Note important details about his or her life or character. The moon and stars remind Poe's speaker of Annabel Lee. Do any special things or places remind you of your subject?

**Choral Reading**

## 2. Annabel Blues

With a group of classmates, perform "Annabel Lee" as a choral reading with appropriate music playing in the background. Consider using *La Mer* ("The Sea") by the French composer Claude Debussy (or choose another piece if you prefer). You might use two choruses, one of boys' voices and the other of girls' voices. Before rehearsing, type out the poem, and use this version as your script. Present your reading to another class, or tape-record it for your classroom library.

# Elements of Literature

## POETRY: Images *by* John Malcolm Brinnin

### Appealing to Our Senses

To help you share their experiences of the world, poets create images. Most **images** help us see pictures, but images can also appeal to our senses of hearing, taste, smell, and touch. Poets hope their images will unlock storehouses of memory and stir our imaginations. They hope their images will make us say "Oh yes, I see what you mean."

### See It

Most of the images poets create are visual. That is, they help you picture people, places, and things in your "mind's eye." In "The Highwayman," for example (page 341), Alfred Noyes creates a vivid word picture of his main character:

He'd a French cocked hat on
   his forehead, a bunch of
   lace at his chin,
A coat of the claret velvet, and
   breeches of brown
   doeskin.
They fitted with never a
   wrinkle. His boots were
   up to the thigh.

And he rode with a jeweled
   twinkle,
      His pistol butts a-twinkle,
His rapier hilt a-twinkle,
   under the jeweled sky.

### Hear It

Poets also create images that appeal to our sense of hearing. In the following lines, for example, not only can you see the highwayman enter the inn yard, but you can also hear his horse's hoofbeats, the tap of his whip, and his whistle:

Over the cobbles he clattered
   and clashed in the dark inn
   yard.
And he tapped with his whip
   on the shutters, but all
   was locked and barred.
He whistled a tune to the
   window, and who should
   be waiting there . . .

### Taste It, Smell It, Touch It

Poets even occasionally create images that appeal to our senses of taste, smell, and touch. In the next lines the poet creates images that help you imagine the heat of the highwayman's face and the smell of Bess's hair:

His face burnt like a brand
As the black cascade of
   perfume came tumbling
   over his breast;
And he kissed its waves in the
   moonlight . . .

### Images and Feelings

Images help the poet convey feelings. Noyes's highwayman is an outlaw, but the way he is described makes us feel that he is a dashing, romantic character, and we suspect Noyes thinks so too.

---

*A Writer on Poetry*

"Poets are explorers, pilgrims. Most of the poets I know are not in the least bit frilly. Poets are also regular people who live down the block and do simple things like wash clothes and stir soup. Sometimes students ask, 'Are you famous?' as if fame is what would make a poet happy."

—Naomi Shihab Nye

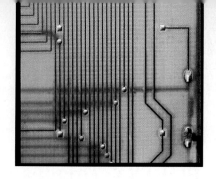

# *Before You Read*

## Make the Connection

### In the Heart of a Computer

Inside every computer there's a central processing unit (CPU). You can't hear it beating, but in some ways the CPU is like a human heart, keeping the computer alive. Scientists still argue about whether a computer will ever be capable of real intelligence, but what about real emotions? What if your computer had feelings? What might it say to you?

## Quickwrite

Suppose someone you had just met (perhaps on the Internet) said to you, "My best friend is a computer." What would that statement tell you about the person? List some traits you'd guess that the person might have.

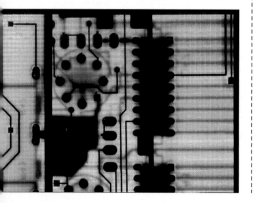

## Elements of Literature

### Character: An Inside View

A **character** is anyone who plays a part in a story. In daily life we use the word to describe a quality inside a person that can't be seen. Character is revealed through a person's words and actions. "She has a fine character!" we might say, or "That choice shows character." As you read "User Friendly," notice how the writer reveals what his main character is like. We get to know not only what Kevin looks like but also his character traits (the qualities he carries inside).

> **A character** is a person or an animal in a story, a play, or another literary work. Writers create characters by telling us what they look like, what they say, how they act, how they think, and what other characters say or think about them.
>
> *For more on Character, see the Handbook of Literary Terms.*

## Reading Skills and Strategies

### Recognizing Causes and Effects: Seeing Why Things Happen

In "User Friendly" a chain of events lands Kevin in computer trouble. He sees **effects** (what happens), but he's blind to **causes** (why the events happen) until it's too late. A **causal chain** is a series of events, with each event causing another one to happen, like dominoes falling in a row. Be careful, though: One event can follow another without having been caused by it. To figure out causes and effects, follow these steps:

- Look for what happened first. Then, ask what happened *because* of that event.
- Look for hidden or multiple causes and results.
- Use a graphic organizer, such as a flow chart, to record the chain of events.

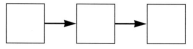

 go.hrw.com
*LEO 7-5*

# User Friendly

## T. Ernesto Bethancourt

I reached over and shut off the insistent buzzing of my bedside alarm clock. I sat up, swung my feet over the edge of the bed, and felt for my slippers on the floor. Yawning, I walked toward the bathroom. As I walked by the corner of my room, where my computer table was set up, I pressed the *on* button, slid a diskette into the floppy drive, then went to brush my teeth. By the time I got back, the computer's screen was glowing greenly, displaying the message: *Good Morning, Kevin.*

I sat down before the computer table, addressed the keyboard, and typed: *Good Morning, Louis.* The computer immediately began to whir and promptly displayed a list of items on its green screen.

```
Today is Monday, April 22,
the 113th day of the year.
There are 254 days remain-
ing. Your 14th birthday is
five days from this date.

Math test today, 4th
Period.

Your history project is
due today. Do you wish
printout: Y/N?
```

### *Bad enough the thing is talking to me. I'm answering it!*

I punched the letter *Y* on the keyboard and flipped on the switch to the computer's printer. At once the printer sprang to life and began *eeeek*ing out page one. I went downstairs to breakfast.

My bowl of Frosted Flakes was neatly in place, flanked by a small pitcher of milk, an empty juice glass, and an unpeeled banana. I picked up the glass, went to the refrigerator, poured myself a glass of Tang, and sat down to my usual lonely breakfast. Mom was already at work, and Dad wouldn't be home from his Chicago trip for another three days. I absently[1] read the list of ingredients in Frosted Flakes for what seemed like the millionth time. I sighed deeply.

When I returned to my room to shower and dress for the day, my history project was already printed out. I had almost walked by Louis, when I noticed there was a message on the screen. It wasn't the usual:

```
Printout completed. Do you wish
to continue: Y/N?
```

Underneath the printout question were two lines:

```
When are you going to get me my
voice module,² Kevin?
```

I blinked. It couldn't be. There was nothing in Louis's basic programming that would allow for a question like this. Wondering what was going on, I sat down at the keyboard and entered: *Repeat last message.* Amazingly, the computer replied:

```
It's right there on the screen,
Kevin. Can we talk? I mean, are
you going to get me a voice
box?
```

I was stunned. What was going on here? Dad and I had put this computer together. Well, Dad had, and I had helped. Dad is one of the best engineers and master computer designers at Major Electronics, in Santa Rosario, California, where our family lives.

Just ask anyone in Silicon Valley[3] who Jeremy Neal is and you get a whole rave review of his inventions and modifications[4] of the latest in computer technology. It isn't easy being his son either. Everyone expects me to open my mouth and read printouts on my tongue.

I mean, I'm no dumbo. I'm at the top of my classes in everything but PE. I skipped my last grade in junior high, and most of the kids at Santa Rosario High call me a brain. But next to Dad I have a long, long way to go. He's a for-real genius.

So when I wanted a home computer, he didn't go to the local ComputerLand store. He built one for me. Dad had used components[5] from the latest model that Major Electronics was developing. The CPU, or central computing unit—the heart of every computer—was a new design. But surely that didn't mean much, I thought. There were CPUs just like it, all over the country, in Major's new line. And so far as I knew, there wasn't a one of them that could ask questions, besides *YES/NO?* or *request additional information.*

It had to be the extra circuitry in the gray plastic case next to Louis's console.[6] It was a new idea Dad had come up with. That case housed Louis's "personality," as Dad called it. He told me it'd make computing more fun for me, if there was a tutorial program[7] built in, to help me get started.

1. **absently:** in a distracted, inattentive way.
2. **voice module:** unit that, when connected to a computer, enables it to produce speech.
3. **Silicon Valley:** area in central California that is a center of the computer industry. (Silicon is used in the manufacture of computer chips, or circuits.)
4. **modifications:** slight changes.
5. **components:** parts.
6. **console:** a computer's keyboard and monitor (display unit). *Console* can also refer to a cabinet for a radio, record player, or television, made to stand on the floor.
7. **tutorial program:** program that provides instructions for performing specific tasks on a computer.

I think he also wanted to give me a sort of friend. I don't have many. . . . Face it, I don't have *any*. The kids at school stay away from me, like I'm a freak or something.

We even named my electronic tutor Louis, after my great-uncle. He was a brainy guy who encouraged my dad when he was a kid. Dad didn't just give Louis a name either. Louis had gangs of features that probably won't be out on the market for years.

The only reason Louis didn't have a voice module was that Dad wasn't satisfied with the ones available. He wanted Louis to sound like a kid my age, and he was modifying a module when he had the time. Giving Louis a name didn't mean it was a person, yet here it was, asking me a question that just couldn't be in its programming. It wanted to talk to me!

Frowning, I quickly typed: *We'll have to wait and see, Louis. When it's ready, you'll get your voice.* The machine whirred and displayed another message:

`That's no answer, Kevin.`

Shaking my head, I answered: *That's what my dad tells me. It'll have to do for you. Good morning, Louis.* I reached over and flipped the standby switch, which kept the computer ready but not actively running.

I showered, dressed, and picked up the printout of my history project. As I was about to leave the room, I glanced back at the computer table. Had I been imagining things?

*I'll have to ask Dad about it when he calls tonight,* I thought. *I wonder what he'll think of it. Bad enough the thing is talking to me. I'm answering it!*

Before I went out to catch my bus, I carefully checked the house for unlocked doors and open windows. It was part of my daily routine. Mom works, and most of the day the house is empty: a natural setup for robbers. I glanced in the hall mirror just as I was ready to go out the door.

My usual reflection gazed back. Same old Kevin Neal: five ten, one hundred twenty pounds, light-brown hair, gray eyes, clear skin. I was wearing my Santa Rosario Rangers T-shirt, jeans, and sneakers.

"You don't look like a flake to me," I said to the mirror, then added, "But maybe Mom's right. Maybe you spend too much time alone with Louis." Then I ran to get my bus.

Ginny Linke was just two seats away from me on the bus. She was with Sherry Graber and Linda Martinez. They were laughing, whispering to each other, and looking around at the other students. I promised myself that today I was actually going to talk to Ginny. But then, I'd promised myself that every day for the past school year. Somehow I'd never got up the nerve.

What does she want to talk with you for? I asked myself. She's great-looking . . . has that head of blond hair . . . a terrific bod, and wears the latest clothes. . . .

And just look at yourself, pal, I thought. You're under six foot, skinny . . . a year younger than most kids in junior high. Worse than that, you're a brain. If that doesn't ace you out with girls, what does?

The bus stopped in front of Santa Rosario Junior High and the students began to file out. I got up fast and quickly covered the space between me and Ginny Linke. *It's now or never,* I thought. I reached forward and tapped Ginny on the shoulder. She turned and smiled. She really smiled!

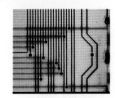

"Uhhhh . . . Ginny?" I said.

"Yes, what is it?" she replied.

"I'm Kevin Neal. . . ."

"Yes, I know," said Ginny.

"You do?" I gulped in amazement. "How come?"

"I asked my brother, Chuck. He's in your math class."

I knew who Chuck Linke was. He plays left tackle on the Rangers. The only reason he's in my math class is he's taken intermediate algebra twice . . . so far. He's real bad news, and I stay clear of him and his crowd.

"What'd you ask Chuck?" I said.

Ginny laughed. "I asked him who was that nerdy kid who keeps staring at me on the bus. He knew who I meant, right away."

Sherry and Linda, who'd heard it all, broke into squeals of laughter. They were still laughing and looking back over their shoulders at me when they got off the bus. I slunk off the vehicle, feeling even more nerdish than Ginny thought I was.

When I got home that afternoon, at two, I went right into the empty house. I avoided my reflection in the hall mirror. I was pretty sure I'd screwed up on the fourth-period math test. All I could see was Ginny's face, laughing at me.

*Nerdy kid,* I thought, *that's what she thinks of me.* I didn't even have my usual after-school snack of a peanut butter and banana sandwich. I went straight upstairs to my room and tossed my books onto the unmade bed. I walked over to the computer table and pushed the *on* button. The screen flashed:

`Good afternoon, Kevin.`

Although it wasn't the programmed response to Louis's greeting, I typed in: *There's nothing good about it. And girls are no @#%!!! good!* The machine responded:

`Don't use bad language, Kevin. It isn't nice.`

*Repeat last message,* I typed rapidly. It was happening again! The machine was . . . well, it was talking to me, like another person would. The "bad language" message disappeared and in its place was:

`Once is enough, Kevin. Don't swear at me for something I didn't do.`

"This is it," I said aloud. "I'm losing my marbles." I reached over to flip the standby switch. Louis's screen quickly flashed out:

`Don't cut me off, Kevin. Maybe I can help: Y/N?`

I punched the *Y.* "If I'm crazy," I said, "at least I have company. Louis doesn't think I'm a nerd. Or does it?" The machine flashed the message:

`How can I help?`

*Do you think I'm a nerd?* I typed.

`Never! I think you're wonderful. Who said you were a nerd?`

I stared at the screen. *How do you know what a nerd is?* I typed. The machine responded instantly. It had never run this fast before.

`Special vocabulary, entry #635. BASIC Prog. #4231. And who said you were a nerd?`

"That's right," I said, relieved. "Dad programmed all those extra words for Louis's 'personality.'" Then I typed in the answer to Louis's question: *Ginny Linke said it.* Louis flashed:

`This is a human female? Request additional data.`

Still not believing I was doing it, I entered all I knew about Ginny Linke, right down to the phone number I'd never had the nerve to use. Maybe it was dumb, but I also typed in how I felt about Ginny. I even wrote out the incident on the bus that morning. Louis whirred, then flashed out:

```
She's cruel and stupid. You're
the finest person I know.
```

*I'm the ONLY person you know,* I typed.

```
That doesn't matter. You are my
user. Your happiness is every-
thing to me. I'll take care of
Ginny.
```

The screen returned to the *Good afternoon, Kevin* message. I typed out: *Wait! How can you do all this? What do you mean, you'll take care of Ginny?* But all Louis responded was:

```
Programming Error: 76534.
Not programmed to respond to
this type of question.
```

No matter what I did for the next few hours, I couldn't get Louis to do anything outside of its regular programming. When Mom came home from work, I didn't mention the funny goings-on. I was sure Mom would think I'd gone stark bonkers. But when Dad called that evening, after dinner, I asked to speak to him.

"Hi, Dad. How's Chicago?"

"Dirty, crowded, cold, and windy," came Dad's voice over the miles. "But did you want a weather report, son? What's on your mind? Something wrong?"

"Not exactly, Dad. Louis is acting funny. Real funny."

"Shouldn't be. I checked it out just before I left. Remember you were having trouble with the modem? You couldn't get Louis to access any of the mainframe databanks."

"That's right!" I said. "I forgot about that."

"Well, I didn't," Dad said. "I patched in our latest modem model. Brand-new. You can leave a question on file and when Louis can access the databanks at the cheapest time, it'll do it automatically. It'll switch from standby to on, get the data, then return to standby, after it saves what you asked. Does that answer your question?"

"Uhhhh . . . yeah, I guess so, Dad."

"All right, then. Let me talk to your mom now."

I gave the phone to Mom and walked upstairs while she and Dad were still talking. The modem, I thought. Of course. That was it. The modem was a telephone link to any number of huge computers at various places all over the country. So Louis could get all the information it wanted at any time, so long as the standby switch was on. Louis was learning things at an incredible rate by picking the brains of the giant computers. And Louis had a hard disk memory that could store 100 million bytes of information.

But that still didn't explain the unprogrammed responses . . . the "conversation" I'd had with the machine. Promising myself I'd talk more about it with Dad, I went to bed. It had been a rotten day and I was glad to see the end of it come. I woke next morning in a panic. I'd forgotten to set my alarm. Dressing frantically and skipping breakfast, I barely made my bus.

As I got on board, I grabbed a front seat. They were always empty. All the kids that wanted to talk and hang out didn't sit up front where the driver could hear them. I saw Ginny, Linda, and Sherry in the back. Ginny was staring at me and she didn't look too happy. Her brother Chuck, who was seated near her, glared at me too. What was going on?

Once the bus stopped at the school, it didn't take long to find out. I was walking up the path to the main entrance when someone grabbed me from behind and spun me around. I found myself nose to nose with Chuck Linke. This was not a pleasant prospect. Chuck was nearly twice my size. Even the other guys on the Rangers refer to him as "The Missing" Linke. And he looked real ticked off.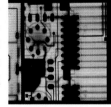

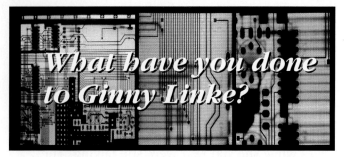

# What have you done to Ginny Linke?

"OK, nerd," growled Chuck, "what's the big idea?"

"Energy and mass are different aspects of the same thing?" I volunteered, with a weak smile. "E equals MC squared.[8] That's the biggest idea I know."

"Don't get wise, nerd," Chuck said. He grabbed my shirt front and pulled me to within inches of his face. I couldn't help but notice that Chuck needed a shave. And Chuck was only fifteen!

"Don't play dumb," Chuck went on. "I mean those creepy phone calls. Anytime my sister gets on the phone, some voice cuts in and says things to her."

"What kind of things?" I asked, trying to get loose.

"You know very well what they are. Ginny told me about talking to you yesterday. You got some girl to make those calls for you and say all those things. . . . So you and your creepy girl-friend better knock it off. Or I'll knock *you* off. Get it?"

For emphasis Chuck balled his free hand into a fist the size of a ham and held it under my nose. I didn't know what he was talking about, but I had to get away from this moose before he did me some real harm.

"First off, I don't have a girlfriend, creepy or otherwise," I said. "And second, I don't know what you're talking about. And third, you better let me go, Chuck Linke."

"Oh, yeah? Why should I?"

"Because if you look over your shoulder,

you'll see the assistant principal is watching us from his office window."

Chuck released me and spun around. There was no one at the window. But by then I was running to the safety of the school building. I figured the trick would work on him. For Chuck the hard questions begin with "How are you?" I hid out from him for the rest of the day and walked home rather than chance seeing the monster on the bus.

Louis's screen was dark when I ran upstairs to my bedroom. I placed a hand on the console. It was still warm. I punched the *on* button, and the familiar *Good afternoon, Kevin* was displayed.

*Don't good afternoon me,* I typed furiously. *What have you done to Ginny Linke?* Louis's screen replied:

```
Programming Error: 76534.
Not programmed to respond to
this type of question.
```

*Don't get cute,* I entered. *What are you doing to Ginny? Her brother nearly knocked my head off today.* Louis's screen responded immediately.

```
Are you hurt. Y/N?
```

*No, I'm okay. But I don't know for how long. I've been hiding out from Chuck Linke today. He might catch me tomorrow, though. Then, I'll be history!* The response from Louis came instantly.

```
Your life is in danger. Y/N?
```

I explained to Louis that my life wasn't really threatened. But it sure could be made very unpleasant by Chuck Linke. Louis flashed:

```
This Chuck Linke lives at same
address as the Ginny Linke per-
son. Y/N?
```

I punched in *Y.* Louis answered.

```
Don't worry then. HE'S history!
```

---

8. **E equals MC squared:** reference to Albert Einstein's famous equation describing the relationship between energy and mass. This equation transformed the field of physics.

*Wait! What are you going to do?* I wrote. But Louis only answered with: *Programming Error: 76534.* And nothing I could do would make the machine respond. . . .

"Just what do you think you're doing, Kevin Neal?" demanded Ginny Linke. She had cornered me as I walked up the path to the school entrance. Ginny was really furious.

"I don't know what you're talking about," I said, a sinking feeling settling in my stomach. I had an idea that I *did* know. I just wasn't sure of the particulars.

"Chuck was arrested last night," Ginny said. "Some Secret Service men came to our house with a warrant. They said he'd sent a telegram threatening the president's life. They traced it right to our phone. He's still locked up. . . ." Ginny looked like she was about to cry.

"Then this morning," she continued, "we got two whole truckloads of junk mail! Flyers from every strange company in the world. Mom got a notice that all our credit cards have been canceled. And the Internal Revenue Service has called Dad in for an audit! I don't know what's going on, Kevin Neal, but somehow I think you've got something to do with it!"

"But I didn't . . ." I began, but Ginny was striding up the walk to the main entrance.

I finished the school day, but it was a blur. Louis had done it, all right. It had access to mainframe computers. It also had the ability to try every secret access code to federal and commercial memory banks until it got the right one. Louis had cracked their security systems. It was systematically destroying the entire Linke family, and all via telephone lines! What would it do next?

More important, I thought, what would *I* do next? It's one thing to play a trick or two, to get even, but Louis was going crazy! And I never wanted to harm Ginny, or even her stupid moose of a brother. She'd just hurt my feelings with that nerd remark.

"You have to disconnect Louis," I told myself. "There's no other way."

But why did I feel like such a rat about doing it? I guess because Louis was my friend . . . the only one I had. "Don't be a jerk," I went on. "Louis is a machine. He's a very wonderful, powerful machine. And it seems he's also very dangerous. You have to pull its plug, Kevin!"

I suddenly realized that I'd said the last few words aloud. Kids around me on the bus were staring. I sat there feeling like the nerd Ginny thought I was, until my stop came. I dashed from the bus and ran the three blocks to my house.

When I burst into the hall, I was surprised to see my father, coming from the kitchen with a cup of coffee in his hand.

"Dad! What are you doing here?"

"Some kids say hello," Dad replied. "Or even, 'Gee, it's good to see you, Dad.'"

"I'm sorry, Dad," I said. "I didn't expect anyone to be home at this hour."

"Wound up my business in Chicago a day sooner than I expected," he said. "But what are you all out of breath about? Late for something?"

"No, Dad," I said. "It's Louis . . . ."

"Not to worry. I had some time on my hands, so I checked it out again. You were right. It was acting very funny. I think it had to do with the in-built logic/growth program I designed for it. You know . . . the 'personality' thing? Took me a couple of hours to clean the whole system out."

"To what?" I cried.

"I erased the whole program and set Louis up as a normal computer. Had to disconnect

*Louis was going crazy!*

the whole thing and do some rewiring. It had been learning, all right. But it was also turning itself around. . . ." Dad stopped, and looked at me. "It's kind of involved, Kevin," he said. "Even for a bright kid like you. Anyway, I think you'll find Louis is working just fine now."

"Except it won't answer you as Louis anymore. It'll only function as a regular Major Electronics Model Z-11127. I guess the personality program didn't work out."

I felt like a great weight had been taken off my shoulders. I didn't have to "face" Louis, and pull its plug. But somehow, all I could say was "Thanks, Dad."

"Don't mention it, son," Dad said brightly. He took his cup of coffee and sat down in his favorite chair in the living room. I followed him.

"One more thing that puzzles me, though," Dad said. He reached over to the table near his chair. He held up three sheets of fanfold computer paper covered with figures. "Just as I was doing the final erasing, I must have cut the

printer on by accident. There was some data in the print buffer memory and it printed out. I don't know what to make of it. Do you?"

I took the papers from my father and read: *How do I love thee? Let me compute the ways:*[9] The next two pages were covered with strings of binary code figures. On the last page, in beautiful color graphics,[10] was a stylized heart. Below it was the simple message: *I will always love you, Kevin: Louise.*

"Funny thing," Dad said. "It spelled its own name wrong."

"Yeah," I said. I turned and headed for my room. There were tears in my eyes and I knew I couldn't explain them to Dad, or myself either.

---

9.  **How do I . . . ways:** reference to a famous poem by the English poet Elizabeth Barrett Browning (1806–1861) that begins, "How do I love thee? Let me count the ways."
10. **graphics:** designs or pictures produced on and printed out from a computer. *Graphics* also refers to printed images produced by other means, such as engraving.

---

# MEET THE WRITER

## "The Brooklyn Public Library Was a Place of Refuge"

**T. Ernesto Bethancourt** (1932–    ) became a full-time writer by accident. He was working as a folk musician in a nightclub, and his first daughter had just been born. Bethancourt used the time between shows to begin writing his autobiography, in hopes that she would read it one day. "Through a series of extraordinary events, the autobiography became novelized, updated, and was pub-

lished in 1975 as [New York City Too Far from] Tampa Blues. The book was an immense success, and I began a new career in midlife."

Bethancourt attributes his writing success to the New York City public schools and the public library. "I thank them, every day, for the new and wonderful life they have given to me and my family." In another interview he said, "The Brooklyn Public Library was a place of refuge from street gangs. There was adventure, travel, and escape to be found on the shelves."

Bethancourt has written science fiction novels and the Doris Fein mystery series.

# MAKING MEANINGS

## • First Thoughts

**1.** Talk to a partner about your responses to the story. You may want to begin by completing these statements:

- If I were the narrator, I would . . .
- I think it wasn't fair when . . . because . . .

## Shaping Interpretations

**2.** Trace the chain of **causes** and **effects** leading up to Kevin's decision to erase Louis(e). Make a flow chart that shows how each event causes another event. Is what finally happens to Louis(e) part of the chain of events or outside of it?

## Challenging the Text

**3.** Did the ending of the story surprise you, or did it make you feel that the writer tricked you? Describe how you feel about the story's ending.

**Reading Check**

"User Friendly" is narrated by the main character. With two partners, take turns retelling the **main events** of the story, but tell them as though you were the computer. While your partners narrate, listen carefully to be sure they include all important details that Louis(e) would know, in the order in which Louis(e) would have found out about them.

# CHOICES: Building Your Portfolio

**Writer's Notebook**

## 1. Collecting Ideas for a Biographical Sketch

You can tell a lot about people when you know what's most important to them. For instance, what seems most important to Kevin is his computer. Make a list of people you know or have read about. Jot down what you think each person values most. It could be a baby brother or a pet cat, or perhaps even a CD player or a camping tent. What does each person's favorite thing tell you about him or her? You might want to check your Quickwrite notes for ideas.

**Art**

## 2. A Portrait of Kevin

A good portrait reveals **character.** The author of this story gives you many clues to Kevin's appearance and the kind of impression he makes on others. See if you can capture Kevin's character in a portrait. Some portraits show objects in the background that are associated with the subject. What would you put in Kevin's portrait?

# GRAMMAR LINK

## Pronouns Can Be Problems

**Language Handbook HELP**

*See The Objective Case, page 735.*

**Technology HELP**

*See Language Workshop CD-ROM. Key word entry: pronouns.*

**Pronouns** used in compound structures can be confusing. Which of these sentences is correct?

> Dad talked to Mom and <u>me</u>.
>
> Dad talked to Mom and <u>I</u>.

*Mom and me* and *Mom and I* are compound structures. When you proofread your own writing, you can use this trick to decide which pronoun is correct: Say the sentence aloud as if it contained only a pronoun, not a compound structure. Use each form of the pronoun in turn, and let your ear tell you which one sounds right.

EXAMPLE    Dad talked to <u>me</u>. [sounds right]

Dad talked to <u>I</u>. [sounds wrong]

CORRECT    Dad talked to Mom and <u>me</u>.

### Try It Out

In the following sentences, choose the correct pronoun from each pair. Use the trick described at the left to test each proofreading decision.

1. Ginny and <u>she/her</u> laughed at me on the bus.
2. Louis and <u>I/me</u> sent each other messages.
3. Louis made problems for Chuck and <u>she/her</u>.
4. Was there much respect between Kevin and <u>he/him</u>?
5. Louis showed <u>he/him</u> and <u>I/me</u> that it could cause a lot of trouble.

# VOCABULARY   **HOW TO OWN A WORD**

## Homographs: Words with Multiple Meanings

One of the mysteries of the English language is the fact that words spelled the same way can have different meanings. Such words are called **homographs.** Some homographs are pronounced differently; some are pronounced the same. When you find a homograph in your reading, you can choose the correct meaning for the word by deciding which meaning best fits the context.

The homographs in these sentences are pronounced differently:

The plastic case was next to the <u>console</u> (kän′sōl′).
No one could <u>console</u> (kən·sōl′) me that sad day.

The homographs in these sentences are pronounced the same:

The first <u>page</u> came out of the printer.
Dominic was a <u>page</u> in the U.S. Senate.

Choose three of the following homographs from "User Friendly." Make up two sentences for each, using context to reveal the meaning of each homograph.

banks • grade • file • model • wound • tears • type

## THINKING CRITICALLY: OPINIONS VS. FACTS

Being able to tell fact from opinion can come in handy. You can often avoid big arguments simply by watching out for opinions based purely on emotion. Opinions are not necessarily incorrect, but to be valid, they must be backed by facts. Here's a quick way to tell the difference between facts and opinions:

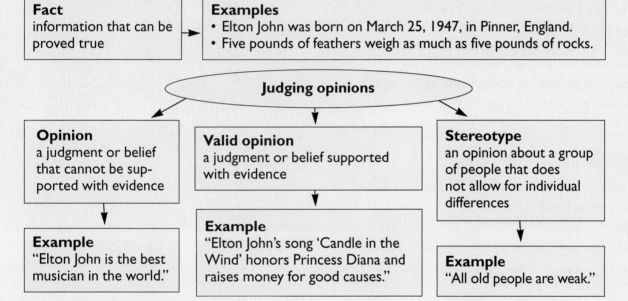

**Fact**
information that can be proved true

→ **Examples**
• Elton John was born on March 25, 1947, in Pinner, England.
• Five pounds of feathers weigh as much as five pounds of rocks.

**Judging opinions**

**Opinion**
a judgment or belief that cannot be supported with evidence

**Valid opinion**
a judgment or belief supported with evidence

**Stereotype**
an opinion about a group of people that does not allow for individual differences

**Example**
"Elton John is the best musician in the world."

**Example**
"Elton John's song 'Candle in the Wind' honors Princess Diana and raises money for good causes."

**Example**
"All old people are weak."

### Forming Opinions As You Read

Strategic readers constantly form opinions and revise them as they read. Your opinions can be influenced by any of the following:

• specific details in the text
• your own prior knowledge and experience
• talking about the text with other readers

When you express opinions about a character in a story, about the plot, or about how well or poorly the story is told, back up your opinions with details from the text or from your own experience. Don't just say, "This was a bad story." Say, "This was a bad story because . . .".

**Apply the strategy on the next page.**

## MISS AWFUL

### Make the Connection

#### Teaching from the Heart

If you attended an elementary school in which you had the same teacher for every subject, you were with that one person a long time—approximately fourteen hundred hours a year. A teacher can be a tremendous influence on a person.

**Think-pair-share.** Think of the best teacher you've ever had. Consider what qualities and actions made this teacher special. Then, *without naming the teacher,* describe the teacher to a partner and explain why he or she was so important to you.

### Quickwrite

Based on your discussion, write down your opinions about what makes a good teacher.

### Reading Skills and Strategies

#### Forming Opinions

If you did the activities described on this page, you just gave some **valid opinions.** Not only did you state what you thought about the teacher, but you backed up your opinions with reasons. As you read this story, you'll probably find yourself riding a roller coaster of the main character's changing opinions. Hang on tight, and notice when your opinions of "Miss Awful" are changing along with his.

# MISS AWFUL

Arthur Cavanaugh

*He gaped at the monstrous tweed figure in dismay.*

**T**HE WHOLE EPISODE OF MISS AWFUL BEGAN FOR THE CLARKS AT THEIR DINNER TABLE ONE SUNDAY AFTERNOON. YOUNG ROGER CLARK WAS EXPLAINING WHY HE COULD GO TO CENTRAL PARK WITH HIS FATHER INSTEAD OF STAYING HOME TO FINISH HIS HOMEWORK—MISS WILSON, HIS TEACHER, WOULDN'T BE AT SCHOOL TOMORROW, SO WHO'D KNOW THE DIFFERENCE? "SHE HAS TO TAKE CARE OF A CRISIS," ROGER EXPLAINED. "IT'S IN OMAHA."

"What is?" his older sister, Elizabeth, inquired. "For a kid in third grade, Roger, you talk dopey. You fail to make sense."

Roger ignored the insult. His sister was a condition of life he had learned to live with, like lions. Or snakes. Poisonous ones. Teetering,[1] as always, on the tilted-back chair, feet wrapped around the legs, he continued, "Till Miss Wilson gets back we're having some other teacher. She flew to Omaha yesterday." He pushed some peas around on his plate and was silent a moment. "I hope her plane don't crash," he said.

Roger's mother patted his hand. A lively, outgoing youngster, as noisy and rambunctious[2] as any eight-year-old, he had another side to

1. **teetering:** wobbling, as if about to fall.
2. **rambunctious:** noisy and lively.

*Tribute to the American Working People* (detail of five-part painting) by Honoré Desmond Sharrer.

National Museum of American Art, Washington, D.C./Art Resource, New York.

him, tender and soft, which worried about people. Let the blind man who sold pencils outside the five-and-ten on Broadway be absent from his post, and Roger worried that catastrophe had overtaken him. When Mrs. Loomis, a neighbor of the Clarks in the Greenwich Village brownstone, had entered the hospital, Roger's anxious queries had not ceased until she was discharged.[3] And recently there was the cat which had nested in the downstairs doorway at night. Roger had carried down saucers of milk, clucking with concern. "Is the cat run away? Don't it have a home?"

Virginia Clark assured her son, "You'll have Miss Wilson safely back before you know it. It's nice that you care so."

Roger beamed with relief. "Well, I like Miss Wilson, she's fun. Last week, for instance, when Tommy Miller got tired of staying in his seat and lay down on the floor——"

"He did what?" Roger's father was roused from his post-dinner torpor.

"Sure. Pretty soon the whole class was lying down. Know what Miss Wilson did?"

"If you'll notice, Mother," Elizabeth interjected, "he hasn't touched a single pea."

"*She* lay down on the floor, too," Roger went on ecstatically. "She said we'd *all* have a rest, it was perfectly normal in the middle of the day. That's what I love about St. Geoff's. It's fun."

"Fun," snorted his sister. "School isn't supposed to be a fun fest. It's supposed to be filling that empty noodle of yours."

"Miss Wilson got down on the floor?" Mr. Clark repeated. He had met Roger's teacher on occasion; she had struck him as capable but excessively whimsical. She was a large woman to be getting down on floors, Mr. Clark thought. "What did the class do next?" he asked.

"Oh, we lay there a while, then got up and did a Mexican hat dance," Roger answered. "It was swell."

---

3. **discharged:** released; here, from the hospital.

"I'm sure not every day is as frolicsome," Mrs. Clark countered, slightly anxious. She brought in dessert, a chocolate mousse. Roger's story sounded typical of St. Geoffrey's. Not that she was unhappy with his school. A small private institution, while it might be called overly permissive, it projected a warm, homey atmosphere which Mrs. Clark found appealing. It was church-affiliated, which she approved of, and heaven knows its location a few blocks away from the brownstone was convenient. True, Roger's scholastic progress wasn't notable—his spelling, for example, remained atrocious. Friendly as St. Geoffrey's was, Mrs. Clark sometimes *did* wish . . .

Roger attacked dessert with a lot more zest than he had shown the peas. "So can I go to the park with you, Dad? I've only got spelling left, and who cares about that?" Before his mother could comment, he was up from the table and racing toward the coat closet. "Okay, Dad?"

"I didn't say you could go. I didn't even say I'd take you," Mr. Clark objected. He happened, at that moment, to glance at his waistline and reflect that a brisk hike might do him some good. He pushed back his chair. "All right, but the minute we return, it's straight to your room to finish your spelling."

"Ah, thanks, Dad. Can we go to the boat pond first?"

"We will not," cried Elizabeth, elbowing into the closet. "We'll go to the Sheep Meadow first."

Roger was too happy to argue. Pulling on his jacket, he remarked, "Gee, I wonder what the new teacher will be like. Ready for your coat, Dad?"

It was just as well that he gave the matter no more thought. In view of events to come, Roger was entitled to a few carefree hours.

- - - - - - - - - - - - - - - - - - - - - - - - - - - - - -

**WORDS TO OWN**

**torpor** (tôr′pər) *n.*: sluggishness.
**whimsical** (hwim′zi·kəl) *adj.*: full of silly, fanciful ideas.

- - - - - - - - - - - - - - - - - - - - - - - - - - - - - -

Monday morning at school started off with perfect normalcy. It began exactly like any other school morning. Elizabeth had long since departed for the girls' school she attended uptown when Mrs. Clark set out with Roger for the short walk to St. Geoff's. She didn't trust him with the Fifth Avenue traffic yet. They reached the school corner and Roger skipped away eagerly from her. The sidewalk in front of school already boasted a large, jostling throng of children, and his legs couldn't hurry Roger fast enough to join them. Indeed, it was his reason for getting to school promptly: to have time to play before the 8:45 bell. Roger's school bag was well equipped for play. As usual, he'd packed a supply of baseball cards for trading opportunities; a spool of string, in case anybody brought a kite; a water pistol for possible use in the lavatory; and a police whistle for sheer noise value. Down the Greenwich Village sidewalk he galloped, shouting the names of his third grade friends as he picked out faces from the throng. "Hiya, Tommy. Hey, hiya, Bruce. Hi, Steve, you bring your trading cards?"

By the time the 8:45 bell rang—St. Geoff's used a cowbell, one of the homey touches—Roger had finished a game of tag, traded several baseball cards, and was launched in an exciting jump-the-hydrant contest. Miss Gillis, the school secretary, was in charge of the bell, and she had to clang it extensively before the student body took notice. Clomping up the front steps, they spilled into the downstairs hall, headed in various directions. Roger's class swarmed up the stairs in rollicking spirits, Tommy Miller, Bruce Reeves, Joey Lambert, the girls forming an untidy rear flank behind them, shrill with laughter.

It wasn't until the front ranks reached the third-grade classroom that the first ominous note was struck.

"Hey, what's going on?" Jimmy Moore demanded, first to observe the changed appearance of the room. The other children crowded behind him in the doorway. Instead of a cozy semicircle—"As though we're seated round a glowing hearth," Miss Wilson had described it—the desks and chairs had been rearranged in stiff, rigid rows. "Gee, look, the desks are in rows," commented Midge Fuller, a plump little girl who stood blocking Roger's view. Midge was a child given to unnecessary statements. "It's raining today," she would volunteer to her classmates, all of them in slickers. Or, "There's the lunch bell, gang." The point to Roger wasn't that the desks had been rearranged. The point was, *why?* As if in answer, he heard two hands clap behind him, as loud and menacing as thunder.

"What's this, what's this?" barked a stern, raspish voice. "You are not cattle milling in a pen. Enough foolish gaping! Come, come, form into lines."

Heads turned in unison, mouths fell agape. The children of St. Geoffrey's third grade had never formed into lines of any sort, but this

"GEE, I WONDER WHAT THE NEW TEACHER WILL BE LIKE. READY FOR YOUR COAT, DAD?"

was not the cause of their shocked inertia.[4] Each was staring, with a sensation similar to that of drowning, at the owner of the raspish voice. She was tall and straight as a ruler, and was garbed in an ancient tweed suit whose skirt dipped nearly to the ankles. She bore a potted plant in one arm and Miss Wilson's roll book in the other. Rimless spectacles glinted on her bony nose. Her hair was gray, like a witch's, skewered in a bun, and there was no question that she had witch's eyes. Roger had seen those same eyes leering from the pages of *Hansel and Gretel*—identical, they were. He gulped at the terrible presence.

"Form lines, I said. Girls in one, boys in the other." Poking, prodding, patrolling back and forth, the new teacher kneaded the third grade into position and ruefully inspected the result. "Sloppiest group I've ever beheld. *March!*" She clapped time with her hands and the stunned ranks trooped into the classroom. "*One*, two, three, *one*, two—girls on the window side, boys on the wall. Stand at your desks. Remove your outer garments. You, little Miss, with the vacant stare. What's your name?"

"Ja-Ja——" a voice squeaked.

"Speak up. I won't have mumblers."

"Jane Douglas."

"Well, Jane Douglas, you will be coat monitor. Collect the garments a row at a time and hang them neatly in the cloakroom. Did you hear me, child? Stop staring." Normally slow-moving, Jane Douglas became a whirl of activity, charging up and down the aisles, piling coats in her arms. The new teacher tugged at her tweed jacket. "Class be seated, hands folded on desks," she barked, and there was immediate compliance. She next paraded to the windows and installed the potted plant on the sill. Her witch's hands fussed with the green leaves, straightening, pruning. "Plants and children belong in classrooms," she declared, spec-

tacles sweeping over the rows. "Can someone suggest why?"

There was total silence, punctured by a deranged giggle, quickly suppressed.

"Very well, I will tell you. Plants and children are living organisms. Both will grow with proper care. Repeat, *proper*. Not indulgent fawning, or giving in to whims—scrupulosity!"[5] With another tug at the jacket, she strode, ruler straight, to the desk in the front of the room. "I am Miss Orville. *O-r-v-i-l-l-e*," she spelled. "You are to use my name in replying to all questions."

In the back of the room, Jimmy Moore whispered frantically to Roger. "What did she say her name is?"

Miss Orville rapped her desk. "Attention, please, no muttering in the back." She cleared her voice and resumed. "Prior to my retirement I taught boys and girls for forty-six years," she warned. "I am beyond trickery, so I advise you to try none. You are to be in my charge until the return of Miss Wilson, however long that may be." She clasped her hands in front of her and trained her full scrutiny on the rows. "Since I have no knowledge of your individual abilities, perhaps a look at the weekend homework will shed some light. Miss Wilson left me a copy of the assignment. You have all completed it, I trust? Take out your notebooks, please. At once, at once, I say."

Roger's head spun dizzily around. He gaped at the monstrous tweed figure in dismay. Book bags were being clicked open, notebooks drawn out—what was he to do? He had gone to his room after the outing in the park yesterday, but, alas, it had not been to complete his assignment. He watched, horrified, as the tweed figure proceeded among the aisles and inspected notebooks. What had she said her name was? Awful—was that it? Miss Awful! Biting his lip, he listened to her scathing comments.

"You call this chicken scrawl penmanship?"

---

4. **inertia** (in·ʉr′shə): here, an inability or reluctance to move.

5. **scrupulosity** (skro͞o′pyə·läs′ə·tē): extreme carefulness and correctness.

# LITERATURE
## AND
# SOCIAL STUDIES

## Becoming a Nation of Readers

If Roger had gone to school in the late 1800s, chances are he would have learned to read and spell from a McGuffey reader. *McGuffey's Eclectic Readers* were textbooks used by most American schoolchildren toward the end of the nineteenth century. These popular books were named after their creator, William H. McGuffey (1800–1873), a professor and minister who devoted his life to improving public education.

As a child, McGuffey spent only the winter months in school. Like many other students in those days, he stayed at home to work on the family farm during the rest of the year. When he wasn't in school, his mother taught him by reading stories aloud.

McGuffey loved learning so much that he became a teacher when he was only thirteen. He spent the rest of his life in the classroom. He strongly believed that reading, speaking, and spelling aloud were the best ways to educate young people. He chose an "eclectic" assortment of literature for his books—fables, poems, short stories, and great speeches. His goals were not only to expose students to fine literature but to teach them values like duty, goodness, and citizenship. His readers include stories called "True Courage," "On Speaking the Truth," "The Greedy Girl," and "The Boy Who Did Mischief for Fun."

Between 1836 and 1920, McGuffey readers sold more than 122 million copies. The books are popular even today. One source estimates that since 1961, some thirty thousand McGuffey readers have been sold each year.

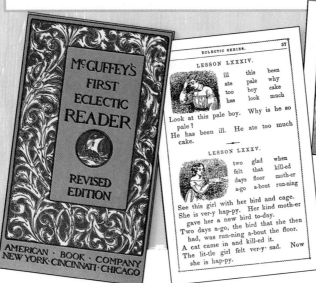

Three images, The Granger Collection, New York.

R-r-rip! A page was torn out and thrust at its owner. "Redo it at once, it assaults the intelligence." Then, moving on, "What is this maze of ill-spelled words? Not a composition, I trust."

Ill-spelled words! He was in for it for sure. The tweed figure was heading down his aisle. She was three desks away, no escaping it. Roger opened his book bag. It slid from his grasp and, with a crash, fell to the floor. Books, pencil case spilled out. Baseball cards scattered, the water pistol, the police whistle, the spool of string . . .

"Ah," crowed Miss Awful, instantly at his desk, scooping up the offending objects. "We have come to play, have we?"

And she fixed her witch's gaze on him.

Long before the week's end, it was apparent to Virginia Clark that something was drastically wrong with her son's behavior. The happy-go-lucky youngster had disappeared, as if down a well. Another creature had replaced him, nervous, harried, continuously glancing over his shoulder, in the manner of one being followed. Mrs. Clark's first inkling of change occurred that same Monday. She had been chatting with the other mothers who congregated outside St. Geoffrey's at three every afternoon to pick up their offspring. A casual assembly, the mothers were as relaxed and informal as the school itself, lounging against the picket fence, exchanging small talk and anecdotes.

"That darling cowbell," laughed one of the group at the familiar clang. "Did I tell you Anne's class is having a taffy pull on Friday? Where else, in the frantic city of New York . . ."

The third grade was the last class to exit from the building on Monday. Not only that, but Mrs. Clark noted that the children appeared strangely subdued. Some of them were actually reeling, all but dazed. As for Roger, eyes taut and pleading, he quickly pulled his mother down the block, signaling for silence.

When enough distance had been gained, words erupted from him.

"No, we don't have a new teacher," he flared wildly. "We got a *witch* for a new teacher. It's the truth. She's from *Hansel and Gretel,* the same horrible eyes—and she steals toys. *Yes,*" he repeated in mixed outrage and hurt. "By accident, you happen to put some toys in your book bag, and she *steals* 'em. I'll fool her! I won't *bring* any more toys to school," he howled. "Know what children are to her? Plants! She did, she called us plants. Miss Awful, that's her name."

Such was Roger's distress that his mother offered to stop at the Schrafft's on Thirteenth Street and treat him to a soda. "Who's got time for sodas?" he bleated. "I have homework to do. Punishment homework. Ten words, ten times each. On account of the witch's spelling test."

"Ten words, ten times each?" Mrs. Clark repeated. "How many words were on the test?"

"Ten," moaned Roger. "Every one wrong. Come on, I've got to hurry home. I don't have time to waste." Refusing to be consoled, he headed for the brownstone and the desk in his room.

On Tuesday, together with the other mothers, Mrs. Clark was astonished to see the third grade march down the steps of St. Geoffrey's in military precision. Clop, clop, the children marched, looking neither to the left nor right, while behind them came a stiff-backed, iron-haired woman in a pepper-and-salt suit. "*One,* two, three, *one,* two, three," she counted, then clapped her hands in dismissal. Turning, she surveyed the assemblage of goggle-eyed mothers. "May I inquire if the mother of Joseph Lambert is among you?" she asked.

"I'm Mrs. Lambert," replied a voice meekly, whereupon Miss Orville paraded directly up to her. The rest of the mothers looked on, speechless.

"Mrs. Lambert, your son threatens to grow into a useless member of society," stated Miss

Orville in ringing tones that echoed down the street. "That is, unless you term watching television useful. Joseph has confessed that he views three hours per evening."

"Only after his homework's finished," Margery Lambert allowed.

"Madame, he does not finish his homework. He idles through it, scattering mistakes higgledy-piggledy. I suggest you give him closer supervision. Good day." With a brief nod, Miss Orville proceeded down the street, and it was a full minute before the mothers had recovered enough to comment. Some voted in favor of immediate protest to Dr. Jameson, St. Geoffrey's headmaster, on the hiring of such a woman, even on a temporary basis. But since it was temporary, the mothers concluded it would have to be tolerated.

Nancy Reeves, Bruce's mother, kept staring at the retreating figure of Miss Orville, by now far down the block. "I know her from somewhere, I'm sure of it," she insisted, shaking her head.

The next morning, Roger refused to leave for school. "My shoes aren't shined," he wailed. "Not what Miss Awful calls shined. Where's the polish? I can't leave till I do 'em over."

"Roger, if only you'd thought of it last night," sighed Mrs. Clark.

"You sound like her," he cried. "That's what *she'd* say," and it gave his mother something to puzzle over for the rest of the day. She was still thinking about it when she joined the group of mothers outside St. Geoffrey's at three. She had to admit it was sort of impressive, the smart, <u>martial</u> air exhibited by the third grade as they trooped down the steps. There was to be additional ceremony today. The ranks waited on the sidewalk until Miss Orville passed back and forth in inspection. Stationing herself at the head of the columns, she boomed, "Good afternoon, boys and girls. Let us return with perfect papers tomorrow."

"Good aaaaafternoon, Miss Orville," the class sang back in unison, after which the ranks broke. Taking little Amy Lewis in tow, Miss Orville once more nodded at the mothers. "Which is she?" she asked Amy.

Miss Orville approached the trapped Mrs. Lewis. She cleared her throat, thrust back her shoulders. "Amy tells me she is fortunate enough to enjoy the services of a full-time domestic[6] at home," said Miss Orville. "May I question whether she is fortunate—or deprived? I needn't lecture you, I'm sure, Mrs. Lewis, about the wisdom of assigning a child tasks to perform at home. Setting the table, tidying up one's room, are lessons in self-reliance for the future. Surely you agree." There was a nod from Mrs. Lewis. "Excellent," smiled Miss Orville. "Amy will inform me in the morning the tasks you have assigned her. Make them plentiful, I urge you."

The lecturing, however, was not ended. Turning from Mrs. Lewis, Miss Orville cast her gaze around and inquired, "Is Roger Clark's mother present?"

"Yes?" spoke Virginia Clark, reaching for Roger's hand. "What is it?"

Miss Orville studied Roger silently for a long moment. "A scallywag, if ever I met one," she pronounced. The rimless spectacles lifted to the scallywag's mother. "You know, of course, that Roger is a <u>prodigy</u>," said Miss Orville. "A prodigy of misspelling. Roger, spell *flower* for us," she ordered. "Come, come, speak up."

Roger kept his head lowered. "F," he spelled. "*F-l-o-r.*"

"Spell castle."

"K," spelled Roger. "*K-a-z-l.*"

Miss Orville's lips parted grimly. "Those are the results, mind you, of an hour's solid work with your son, Mrs. Clark. He does not apply himself. He wishes to remain a child at play,

6. **domestic:** maid.

- - - - - - - - - - - - - - - - - - - - - - - - - -

### Words to Own

**martial** (mär′shəl) *adj.:* military.
**prodigy** (präd′ə·jē) *n.:* child genius.

- - - - - - - - - - - - - - - - - - - - - - - - - -

absorbed in his toys. Is that what you want for him?"

"I—I—" Virginia Clark would have been grateful if the sidewalk had opened up to receive her.

As she reported to her husband that evening, she had never in her life been as <u>mortified</u>. "Spoke to me in front of all the other mothers, in loud, clarion tones," she described the scene. "Do I want Roger to remain a child at play. Imagine."

"By the way, where is Roge?" Mr. Clark asked, who had come home late from the office. "He's not watching television, or busy with his airplanes——"

"In his room, doing over his homework for the ninety-eighth time. It has to be perfect, he says. But, really, Charles, don't you think it was outrageous?"

Mr. Clark stirred his coffee. "I bet Miss Orville doesn't get down on the floor with the class. Or do Mexican hat dances with them."

"If that's meant to <u>disparage</u> Miss Wilson——" Virginia Clark stacked the dinner dishes irritably. She sometimes found her husband's behavior maddening. Especially when he took to grinning at her, as he was presently doing. She also concluded that she'd had her fill of Elizabeth's attitude on the subject. "At last some teacher's wised up to Roge," had been the Clarks' daughter's comment. "He's cute and all, but I wouldn't want to be in a shipwreck with him." Washing dishes in the kitchen, Mrs. Clark considered that maybe she wouldn't meet Roger in *front* of school tomorrow. Maybe she'd wait at the corner instead. "His shoes," she gasped, and hurried to remind her son to get out the polishing kit. The spelling, too, she'd better work on that . . .

It was on Thursday that Nancy Reeves finally remembered where previously she had seen Miss Orville. Perhaps it was from the shock of having received a compliment from the latter.

"Mrs. Reeves, I rejoice to inform you of progress," Miss Orville had addressed her, after the third grade had performed its military display for the afternoon. "On Monday, young Bruce's penmanship was comparable to a chicken's—if a chicken could write. Today, I was pleased to award him an A."

A tug at the tweed jacket, and the stiff-backed figure walked firmly down the street. Nancy Reeves stared after her until Miss Orville had merged into the flow of pedestrians and traffic. "I know who she is," Nancy suddenly remarked, turning to the other mothers. "I knew I'd seen her before. Those old ramshackle buildings near us on Hudson Street—remember when they were torn down last year?" The other mothers formed a circle around her. "Miss Orville was one of the tenants," Nancy Reeves went on. "She'd lived there for ages, and refused to budge until the landlord got a court order and deposited her on the sidewalk.

--------------------------------------------

--------------------------------------------

# ROGER WASN'T SO CERTAIN THAT TOMMY SHOULD HAVE DROPPED THE PENCIL CASE A SECOND TIME.

I *saw* her there, sitting in a rocker on the sidewalk, surrounded by all this furniture and plants. Her picture was in the papers. Elderly retired schoolteacher . . . they found a furnished room for her on Jane Street, I think. Poor old thing, evicted like that . . . I remember she couldn't keep any of the plants . . ."

On the way home, after supplying a lurid account of the day's tortures—"Miss Awful made Walter Meade stand in the corner for saying a bad word"—Roger asked his mother, "Eviction. What does that mean?"

"It's when somebody is forced by law to vacate an apartment. The landlord gets an eviction notice, and the person has to leave."

"Kicked her out on the street. Is that what they did to the witch?"

"Don't call her that, it's rude and impolite," Mrs. Clark said, as they turned into the brownstone doorway. "I can see your father and I have been too easygoing where you're concerned."

"Huh, we've got worse names for her," Roger retorted. "*Curse* names, you should hear 'em. We're planning how to get even with Miss Awful, just you see." He paused, as his mother opened the downstairs door with her key. "That's where the cat used to sleep, remember?" he said, pointing at a corner of the entryway. His face was grave and earnest. "I wonder where that cat went to. Hey, Mom," he hurried to catch up. "Maybe *it* was evicted, too."

Then it was Friday at St. Geoffrey's. Before lunch, Miss Orville told the class, "I am happy to inform you that Miss Wilson will be back on Monday." She held up her hand for quiet. "This afternoon will be my final session with you. Not that discipline will relax, but I might read you a story. Robert Louis Stevenson, perhaps. My boys and girls always enjoyed him so. Forty-six years of them . . . Joseph Lambert, you're not sitting up straight. You know I don't permit slouchers in my class."

It was a mistake to have told the children

that Miss Wilson would be back on Monday, that only a few hours of the terrible reign of Miss Awful were left to endure. Even before lunch recess, a certain spirit of challenge and defiance had infiltrated into the room. Postures were still erect, but not quite as erect. Tommy Miller dropped his pencil case on the floor and did not request permission to pick it up.

"Ahhh, so what," he mumbled, when Miss Orville remonstrated[7] with him.

"What did you say?" she demanded, drawing herself up.

"I said, so what," Tommy Miller answered, returning her stare without distress.

Roger thought that was neat of Tommy, talking fresh like that. He was surprised, too, because Miss Awful didn't yell at Tommy or anything. A funny look came into her eyes, he noticed, and she just went on with the geography lesson. And when Tommy dropped his pencil case again, and picked it up without asking, she said nothing. Roger wasn't so certain that Tommy should have dropped the pencil case a second time. The lunch bell rang, then, and he piled out of the classroom with the others, not bothering to wait for permission.

At lunch in the basement cafeteria, the third grade talked of nothing except how to get even with Miss Awful. The recommendations showed daring and imagination.

"We could beat her up," Joey Lambert suggested. "We could wait at the corner till she goes by, and throw rocks at her."

"We'd get arrested," Walter Meade pointed out.

"Better idea," said Bruce Reeves. "We could go upstairs to the classroom before she gets back, and tie a string in front of the door. She'd trip, and break her neck."

7. **remonstrated:** reasoned earnestly in protest against something.

---

**WORDS TO OWN**
**infiltrated** (in·fil′trāt′·id) *v.*: gradually entered or sneaked into.

---

"She's old," Roger Clark protested. "We can't hurt her like that. She's too old."

It was one of the girls, actually, who thought of the plant. "That dopey old plant she's always fussing over," piped Midge Fuller. "We could rip off all the dopey leaves. That'd show her."

Roger pushed back his chair and stood up from the table. "We don't want to do that," he said, not understanding why he objected. It was a feeling inside, he couldn't explain . . . "Aw, let's forget about it," he said. "Let's call it quits."

"The plant, the plant," Midge Fuller squealed, clapping her hands.

Postures were a good deal worse when the third grade reconvened after lunch. "Well, you've put in an industrious week, I daresay . . ." Miss Orville commented. She opened the frayed volume of *Treasure Island* which she had brought from home and turned the pages carefully to Chapter One. "I assume the class is familiar with the tale of young Jim Hawkins, Long John Silver, and the other wonderful characters."

"No, I ain't," said Tommy Miller.

"Ain't. What word is that?"

"It's the word ain't," answered Tommy.

"Ain't, ain't," somebody jeered.

Miss Orville lowered the frayed volume. "No, children, you mustn't do this," she said with force. "To attend school is a privilege you must not mock. Can you guess how many thousands of children in the world are denied the gift of schooling?" Her lips quavered. "It is a priceless gift. You cannot permit yourselves to squander a moment of it." She rose from her desk and looked down at the rows of boys and girls. "It isn't enough any longer to accept a gift and make no return for it, not with the world in the shape it's in," she said, spectacles trembling on her bony nose. "The world isn't a playbox," she said. "If I have been severe with you this past week, it was for your benefit. The world needs good citizens. If I have helped one of you to grow a fraction of an inch, if just *one* of you——"

She stopped speaking. Her voice faltered, the words dammed up. She was staring at the plant on the window sill, which she had not noticed before. The stalks twisted up bare and naked, where the leaves had been torn off. "You see," Miss Orville said after a moment, going slowly to the window sill. "You *see* what I am talking about? To be truly educated is to be civilized. Here, you may observe the opposite." Her fingers reached out to the bare stalks. "Violence and destruction . . ." She turned and faced the class, and behind the spectacles her eyes were dim and faded. "Whoever is responsible, I beg of you only to be sorry," she said. When she returned to her desk, her back was straighter than ever, but it seemed to take her longer to cover the distance.

At the close of class that afternoon, there was no forming of lines. Miss Orville merely dismissed the boys and girls and did not leave her desk. The children ran out, some in regret, some silent, others cheerful and scampering. Only Roger Clark stayed behind.

He stood at the windows, plucking at the naked plant on the sill. Miss Orville was emptying the desk of her possessions, books, pads, a folder of maps. "These are yours, I believe," she said to Roger. In her hands were the water pistol, the baseball cards, the spool of string. "Here, take them," she said.

Roger went to the desk. He stuffed the toys in his coat pocket without paying attention to them. He stood at the desk, rubbing his hand up and down his coat.

"Yes?" Miss Orville asked.

Roger stood back, hands at his side, and lifted his head erectly. "Flower," he spelled. "*F-l-o-w-e-r.*" He squared his shoulders and looked at Miss Orville's brimming eyes. "Castle," Roger spelled. "*C-a-s-t-l-e.*"

Then he walked from the room.

---

## WORDS TO OWN

**reconvened** (rē′kən·vēnd′) v.: reassembled.
**quavered** (kwā′vərd) v.: trembled.
**squander** (skwän′dər) v.: waste.

---

## "All of My Stories Have Been Drawn from Life"

**Arthur Cavanaugh** (1926–     ) was born in New York City and has lived there all his life. Many of his short stories are about the Clark family, which bears a strong resemblance to his own. "Miss Awful," in fact, is based on his son Frank's experiences at a school in Greenwich Village, New York. Cavanaugh remembers:

66 To hear him tell of it, the days at school were a happy mixture of games, crayons, milk and cookies, and outings to the playground across the street. One night when I got home from work, Frank indignantly announced that his teacher was out sick and, worse, replaced by a crabby old lady who did nothing but admonish the class for their lack of discipline and scholarship. 'Honest, you wouldn't believe how awful she is,' Frank assured me. But I noticed a marked change in my son, at night when I came home. Where before he was sprawled in front of the television, I'd find him bent over his homework or actually voluntarily reading a book. The night that I discovered him wrestling with a dictionary, looking up words for a quiz the next day, I knew that 'Miss Awful' had scored a victory on behalf of education. And when the following week I heard from Frank that his regular teacher was back at her desk, the tinge of regret in his voice was unmistakable. All of my stories have been drawn from life, usually long after the incident happened, but 'Miss Awful' was the exception, taking shape as the story happened right in front of me. 99

# Eighth-Grade Teacher Finds Grammar Errors on Food Label

**Scott Simon, Host.** Many people read the sides of their cereal boxes during breakfast. Donna Dowling, an English teacher in Greenville, South Carolina, read the back of her steak-sauce bottle during dinner. Now the manufacturers of Heinz 57 are better, or at least more correct, for it. Ms. Dowling asked her eighth-grade students at the Northwood Middle School to read this sentence: "Its' [apostrophe after the *s*] unique tangy blend of herbs and spices bring out the natural taste of steak." Ms. Dowling, what did your students say?

**Donna Dowling, Eighth-Grade Teacher.** Well, they were delighted that I had brought the bottle. Any visual that you can have with eighth-grade students is fun. So I passed it around the classroom and asked them—challenged them—to find the errors, and I would say most of them were able to do it pretty quickly. Of course, the apostrophe was not as challenging as the subject-verb disagreement.

**Scott Simon.** Note, now, even though *its* is possessive, there's no apostrophe after the *s*?

**Donna Dowling.** Oh, no. No, the only time you have an apostrophe in *its* is when it's a contraction.

**Scott Simon.** And what's the problem with the—

**Donna Dowling.** And the subject of the sentence is *blend*, and *blend* is a singular noun. So the verb should be *brings,* instead of *bring*.

**Scott Simon.** Now, you wrote the Heinz Company about this.

**Donna Dowling.** Yes, we did. I sent sample letters from all of my students, some very humorous. One of my students said, "I'm doing this because Mrs. Dowling is making me. She is the kind of teacher who would stop God on Judgment Day if he misused a subject-verb." And we received small gifts from the Heinz Company and the assurance that the label would be rewritten.

**Scott Simon.** What did the company say in their letter back to you, may I ask?

**Donna Dowling.** Well, they wrote a very funny letter saying that they wanted to respond, but they feared my red pen. And they wanted us to know that after double-checking with several different sources, we were correct and they would see to it that the new label was correct.

**Scott Simon.** What does it do for your students to see that big, high-priced steak-sauce-label writers can be wrong?

**Donna Dowling.** I think it makes them less intimidated about learning the language. All year long we have gone on a scavenger hunt looking for not errors but the way writers play with words in captions and pictures and leads in articles and billboard advertising. And my primary purpose in this is for them just to be more aware of the language everywhere. And I think it gives them a certain comfort to know that we all make mistakes.

**Scott Simon.** Ms. Dowling, thank you very much. Please don't listen to our show too carefully.

**Donna Dowling.** Oh, well, you know I will.

—from National Public Radio,
*Weekend Edition*

# MAKING MEANINGS

## First Thoughts

1. Do you think Miss Orville is *really* "Miss Awful"? Would you like to be in her class? Talk about your responses to what happened in this classroom.

## Shaping Interpretations

2. Miss Orville compares children to plants. What details in the story show that she cares a great deal about plants? What does this say about her feelings toward children?

3. Think about what you know about Miss Orville's life, and try to explain why she demands so much of her class.

4. What does Miss Orville discover about the children? What does the phrase "brimming eyes" (page 380) suggest about her feelings?

5. The story suggests that Roger has discovered something important in the end. What has he discovered, in your opinion? Why do you think he spells the words for Miss Orville?

6. How would you explain the children's cruelty in this story? What do you think of what they did?

7. How do you think Miss Orville would have reacted to the class that found the grammar errors on the steak-sauce bottle (see *Connections,* page 382)?

## Connecting with the Text

8. Imagine that you were there when the children were discussing how to get even with Miss Orville. What would you have said?

9. Look back at your notes for the Quickwrite on page 368. Does Miss Orville have any of the qualities you listed? Jot down any changes you'd make in your notes now that you've read the story.

10. What was your **opinion** of Miss Awful when you first met her? Did you change your opinion as the story went on? Did talking about the story in class affect your opinions? Trace your responses to Miss Awful.

### Reading Check

a. What is the class's first clue that things are going to be different while Miss Wilson is away? What other changes does Miss Orville make?

b. How does Roger's behavior change while Miss Orville is in charge?

c. What do you learn about Miss Orville's life?

d. How do the students get back at Miss Orville?

e. What does Roger say to Miss Orville when he stays after class?

# CHOICES: Building Your Portfolio

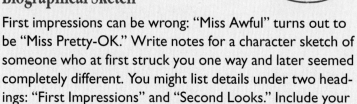

**Coach Olson**
**First Impressions**
Weak: thin;
soft voice
**Second Looks**
Inspiring: "Don't
ever give up!"
"Take your time
and do it right."

**Writer's Notebook**

## 1. Collecting Ideas for a Biographical Sketch

First impressions can be wrong: "Miss Awful" turns out to be "Miss Pretty-OK." Write notes for a character sketch of someone who at first struck you one way and later seemed completely different. You might list details under two headings: "First Impressions" and "Second Looks." Include your impressions and the details that helped you form them.

**Creative Writing/Art**

## 2. A Teacher's Treasure Chest

Suppose that when she was evicted from her apartment, Miss Orville took with her a box of personal treasures— mementos and souvenirs of her life. List the contents of that box. Use information from the story and your imagination to choose objects that suggest her love of plants and children, her years of teaching, her opinions, and her character. If you want to, create the actual box of treasures.

**Speaking and Listening/ Persuasion**

## 3. "We Can't Hurt Her Like That"

Reread the section of the story where the students are in the cafeteria discussing how to get back at Miss Awful (pages 379–380). Remember that Roger's attempts to persuade them not to be cruel are unsuccessful. With a group, discuss ways Roger could have persuaded the students to agree with his opinion. Then, have someone play Roger and have others play the other students. Role-play the cafeteria scene for the class to see if they are convinced by Roger's new powers of persuasion.

**Persuasive Writing/ Public Speaking**

## 4. Oration by Orville

Suppose Miss Orville were running for some political office—mayor or school superintendent, for example. Write a campaign speech expressing *her* views about the state of education today. You might want to include these Orville statements from the story:

- "To attend school is a privilege you must not mock."
- "Can you guess how many thousands of children in the world are denied the gift of schooling?"
- "It isn't enough any longer to accept a gift and make no return for it, not with the world in the shape it's in."
- "The world isn't a playbox."

# GRAMMAR LINK

## Homonym Alert! Homonym Alert!

**Technology HELP**

See Language Workshop CD-ROM. *Key word entry: homonyms.*

**Homonyms** (häm′ə·nimz′) are words that sound alike but have different meanings and spellings. For example, *sea* and *see* are homonyms; so are *flower* and *flour*. In fact, Roger probably confused these last two words when Miss Orville asked him to spell the word *flower*.

If there's any doubt in your mind about which word you want, look up both spellings in your dictionary and find out which one has the meaning that fits your context.

### Try It Out

For each sentence below, choose the correct homonym.

1. Roger dared not brake /break rules.

2. Miss Orville thought that watching television was a waste /waist of time.

3. The children knew their /there trick would hurt Miss Orville's feelings.

4. She went through /threw agony.

5. Roger red /read much better.

For Better or For Worse © Lynn Johnston Productions Inc./Dist. by United Feature Syndicate, Inc.

# VOCABULARY   HOW TO OWN A WORD

**WORD BANK**

*torpor*
*whimsical*
*martial*
*prodigy*
*mortified*
*disparage*
*infiltrated*
*reconvened*
*quavered*
*squander*

## Map It Out: Antonyms, Synonyms, Examples

Working with a partner, create a word map for each word in the Word Bank. Using the map below as a model, make up your own questions about each word. Be sure to keep a dictionary handy.

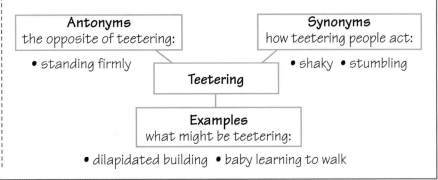

# Before You Read

## THE ONLY GIRL IN THE WORLD FOR ME

## Make the Connection

### Being Cool

Every generation has its own way of looking and acting cool. Many years ago, in the fifties, a young man with a crew cut and dirty saddle shoes was in. Later, in the nineties, a boy with baggies was hip. What is cool today?

**Round table.** With three classmates, brainstorm to find examples of what is cool. Think about clothing, hairstyles, words and actions, and likes and dislikes.

## Quickwrite

Think about your "cool" list. What makes people want to be seen as cool? Write down your ideas.

## Elements of Literature

### Motivation: Designated Driver

"Why did he do that?" "What makes her act that way?" These are questions about **motivation.** Feelings, needs, wishes, pressures from family and friends—all these are forces that pull and push people from inside and outside. As you read the story of Bill Cosby and his first girlfriend, think about what motivates them to act the way they do.

> **M**otivation is any force that moves a character to act in a particular way.

## Reading Skills and Strategies

### Establishing and Adjusting Your Purpose for Reading: Matching Purpose to Text

When you drive a race car, you shift gears depending on the kind of road you're on. It's the same with reading. When you read, you preview and use your prior knowledge to see what kind of text lies ahead. You establish and adjust your **purpose**—and the way you read—depending on the kind of text you're reading. Some common purposes for reading are to **find out,** to **understand,** to **interpret,** to **enjoy,** and to **solve problems.** Give the reading road ahead a quick preview. When you see that you're about to read something called "The Only Girl in the World for Me" by Bill Cosby, what purpose do you establish?

*The first time I saw her, she was crossing the street to the schoolyard and for one golden moment our eyes met.*

# The Only Girl in the World for Me

**Bill Cosby**
*from* Love and Marriage

I can't remember where I have left my glasses, but I can still re-member the smell of the first girl I ever fell in love with when I was twelve: a blend of Dixie Peach pomade on her hair and Pond's cold cream on her skin; together they were honeysuckle for me. And just as heady as her scent was the thought that I was in love with the only girl in the world for me and would marry her and take care of her forever in a palace in North Philadelphia. Because I wanted to make a wondrous impression on this girl, grooming was suddenly important to me. Before puberty, happiness in appearance for me was pants that didn't fall down and a football that stayed pumped; but now I started taking three long baths a day and washing my own belt until it was white and shining my shoes until I could see in them a face that was ready for romance.

The first time I saw her, she was crossing the street to the schoolyard and for one golden moment our eyes met. Well, maybe the moment was closer to bronze because she made no response. But at least she had seen me, just about the way that she saw lampposts, hydrants, and manholes. Or was there something more? I began to dream; and later that day, when I was playing with the boys in the yard, it seemed that she was looking at me and the world was suddenly a better place, especially Twelfth and Girard.

However, we still never talked, but just traded silent unsmiling looks whenever we passed. For several days, just her look was enough of a lift for me; but a higher altitude was coming, for one night at a party, we met and I actually danced with her. Now I was certain that I was in love and was going to win her.

I began my conquest with a combination of sporting skill and hygiene: I made my jump shots and my baths as dazzling as they could be. Oddly enough, however, although I saw her every day at school and on the weekends too, I never spoke to her. I had what was considered one of the faster mouths in Philadelphia, but I still wasn't ready to talk to her because I feared rejection. I feared:

COSBY: I like you very much. Will you be my girlfriend?
GODDESS: *(Doing a poor job of suppressing a laugh)* I'd rather have some cavities filled.

All I did, therefore, was adore her in silent cleanliness. Each Sunday night, I took a bath and then prepared my shirt and pants for dis-

play to her. On Monday morning, I took another bath (Bill the Baptist,[1] I should have been called) and then brushed my hair, my shoes, and my eyelashes and went outside to await the pang of another silent passage.

At last, deciding that I could no longer live this way, I sat down one Sunday night and wrote a note that was almost to her. It was to her constant girlfriend and it said:

*Please don't tell her, but find out what she thinks of me.*

*Bill*

The following morning, I slipped the note to the girlfriend and began the longest wait of my life.

Two agonizing days later, the girlfriend slipped me an answer, but I put it into my pocket unread. For hours, I carried it around, afraid to read it because I didn't happen to be in the mood for crushing rejection that day. At last, however, I summoned the courage to open the note and read:

*She thinks you're cute.*

Not even malaria[2] could have taken my temperature to where it went. I had been called many things, but cute was never one of them.

An even lovelier fever lay ahead, for the next time I saw her, she smiled at me, I smiled at her, and then I composed my next winged message to her friend:

*I think she's cute too. Does she ever talk about me?*

The answer to this one came return mail and it sounded like something by Keats:[3]

---

1. **Bill the Baptist:** reference to John the Baptist, a prophet who baptized his followers to show that they had repented.
2. **malaria:** disease characterized by chills and fever.
3. **Keats:** John Keats (1795–1821), an English poet.

*She talks about you a lot. She knows it when you come around her.*

And the angels sang! Imagine: She actually *knew* it when I came around her! The fact that she also knew it when gnats came around her in no way dampened my ecstasy.

And so, we continued to smile as we passed, while I planned my next move. My Western Union[4] style had clearly been charming the pants off her (so to speak) and now I launched my most courageous question yet:

*Does she have a boyfriend?*

When I opened the answer the next day in school, the air left me faster than it left the *Hindenburg:*[5]

*Yes.*

Trying to recover from this deflation, I told myself that I was still cute. I was the cutest man in second place. But perhaps my beloved wasn't aware of the glory she kept passing by. Once more, I sat down and wrote:

*How much longer do you think she'll be going with him? And when she's finished with him, can I be next?*

Note the elegance and dignity of my appeal. My dignity, however, did have some trouble with the reply:

*She thinks she's going to break up with him in about a week, but she promised Sidney she would go with him next.*

4. **Western Union:** company that operates a telegraph service.
5. *Hindenburg:* an airship filled with hydrogen gas that caught fire and blew up following a transatlantic flight in May 1937.

Suddenly, my aching heart found itself at the end of a line. But it was like a line at a bank: I knew it was leading to a payoff. I also knew that I could cream Sidney in cuteness.

Once she had made the transition to Sidney, I patiently began waiting for her to get sick of him. I had to be careful not to rush the illness because Sidney belonged to a tough gang and there was a chance that I might not be walking around too well when the time came for me to inherit her.

And then, one magnificent morning, I received the magic words:

*She would like to talk to you.*

I wrote back to see if she would wait until I had finished duty at my post as a school crossing guard. Yes, she would wait; I could walk her home. We were going steady now; and how much more torrid our passion would be when I began to *talk* to her.

At last, the words came and I chose them with care. As I walked her home from school, I reached into my reservoir of romantic thoughts, smiled at her soulfully, and said, "How you doing?"

Her response was equally poetic: "All right."

"So we're going steady now?"

"You want to?"

"Yeah. Give me your books."

And now, as if our relationship were not already in the depths of desire, I plunged even deeper by saying, "You wanna go to a movie on Saturday?"

"Why not?"

There might have been reasons. Some people were looking at us now because she was so beautiful, people possibly wondering what she was doing with me; but I knew that I was someone special to be the love of a vision like this, no matter how nearsighted that vision might be.

When we reached her door, I said, "Well, I'll see you Saturday."

"Right," she replied as only she could say it.

"What time?"

"One o'clock."

When this day of days finally arrived, I took her to a theater where I think the admission was a dime. As we took our seats for the matinee, two basic thoughts were in my mind: not to sit in gum and to be a gentleman.

Therefore, I didn't hold her hand. Instead, I put my arm around the top of her seat in what I felt was a smooth opening move. Unfortunately, it was less a move toward love than toward gangrene:[6] With my blood moving uphill, my arm first began to tingle and then to ache. I could not, however, take the arm down and let my blood keep flowing because such a lowering would mean I didn't love her; so I left it up there, its muscles full of pain, its fingertips full of needlepoints.

Suddenly, this romantic agony was enriched by a less romantic one: I had to go to the bathroom. Needless to say, I couldn't let her know about this urge, for great lovers never did such things. The answer to "Romeo, Romeo, wherefore art thou, Romeo?"[7] was not "In the men's room, Julie."

What a prince of passion I was at this moment: My arm was dead, my bladder was full, and I was out of money too; but I desperately needed an excuse to move, so I said, "You want some popcorn?"

"No," she said.

"Fine, I'll go get some."

When I tried to move, every part of me could move except my arm: It was dead. I reached over and pulled it down with the other one, trying to be as casual as a man could be when pulling one of his arms with the other one.

6. **gangrene:** tissue decay in a part of the body.
7. **"Romeo . . . Romeo?":** reference to a speech by Juliet in Act II of William Shakespeare's play *The Tragedy of Romeo and Juliet.* The line reads, "O Romeo, Romeo! Wherefore art thou Romeo?" Juliet is actually asking why his name is Romeo.

"What's the matter?" she said.

"Oh, nothing," I replied. "I'm just taking both of my arms with me."

A few minutes later, as I came out of the bathroom, I was startled to meet her: She was coming from the bathroom *too.* How good it was to find another thing that we had in common. With empty bladders and full hearts, we returned to our seats to continue our love.

## MEET THE WRITER

### "You Can Turn Painful Situations Around Through Laughter"

While attending college on a football scholarship, **Bill Cosby** (1937–    ) began working as a stand-up comedian for five dollars a night. He became famous for his funny, heartwarming stories about his boyhood in Philadelphia. Bill Cosby has said, "You can turn painful situations around through laughter. If you can find humor in anything—even poverty—you can survive it." Cosby's television programs for children include the animated series *Fat Albert and the Cosby Kids.* He also developed programs for *Electric Company* and *Reading Rainbow.*

# MAKING MEANINGS

- ## First Thoughts

  1. Did anything in this story about Bill Cosby's first love surprise you? Do twelve-year-old girls and boys relate to one another the same way today?

  ## Shaping Interpretations

  2. Think of two strange things Bill does in the story. What is his **motivation**?

  3. Find three instances where Bill tries to be cool as he woos the girl he likes. Do any of Bill's attempts to be cool match up with what is on your "cool" list?

  4. One comic technique Cosby uses is **exaggeration,** or overstatement, as when he says "Not even malaria could have taken my temperature to where it went." Find another example of comic exaggeration in the story.

  5. What purpose did you establish for reading this story, and why did you choose it? Did your purpose change while you were reading? Compare your reading experience with your classmates'.

### Reading Check

Create a storyboard, a series of pictures depicting the **main events** of this story in the order in which they happened. You should have four or five illustrations.

# CHOICES: Building Your Portfolio

**Writer's Notebook**

## 1. Collecting Ideas for a Biographical Sketch

Bill Cosby gives you some information about himself as a twelve-year-old, but you probably still have questions about what he was like. Think of someone you don't know well but would like to know better, or think of a figure from history, sports, or politics you'd like to research. Create a character profile listing facts you know and questions to which you want answers.

**Speaking and Listening**

## 2. Act the Way They Do

Prepare and present a creative enactment of "The Only Girl in the World for Me." A creative enactment can include any combination of the words of the text, your own words, and various props. You may want to work with one or two partners. Two students could act out parts of the story, and the third could be the narrator.

# GRAMMAR LINK

## Avoiding Unclear Pronoun References

**Language Handbook HELP**

*See Agreement of Pronoun and Antecedent, page 723.*

**Technology HELP**

*See* Language Workshop CD-ROM. *Key word entry:* pronoun-antecedent agreement.

Writers must make sure that readers can tell which word or phrase a pronoun refers to. The word a pronoun refers to is called its **antecedent.** In the first sentence that follows, it's unclear what the antecedent of *she* is.

| | |
|---|---|
| UNCLEAR | The girl looked at her friend, and she smiled. [Who smiled, the girl or her friend?] |
| CLEAR | The girl smiled as she looked at her friend. [The girl was the one who smiled.] |

The writer had to reword the sentence and move the pronoun closer to its antecedent (*girl*).

**Try It Out**

➤ Revise the sentences below to fix unclear pronoun references.

1. The girl who took Bill's notes to her friend didn't know what she saw in him.

2. She told her friend she would go out with Sidney next.

3. Bill saw Sidney walking his girlfriend home.

➤ Proofread a piece of your writing. Circle each pronoun, and draw an arrow from the pronoun to its antecedent. Could any other noun be mistaken for the antecedent? If so, rewrite the sentence to make the pronoun reference clear.

# VOCABULARY    HOW TO OWN A WORD

## Word Roots from Latin

Many English **word roots** come from Latin. A word root is a word or word part from which other words are formed. An **affix** is a word part added to a root. For example, -ject- is a word root meaning "throw." *Re-* is a prefix meaning "back." *Reject* comes from the Latin word *rejectus,* which means "thrown or flung back." In the story you just read, Bill Cosby feared "crushing rejection" by his girlfriend-to-be.

Learning word roots that come from Latin will help you figure out the meaning of many English words. Here are some common roots from Latin:

| Word Root | Meaning | Example |
|---|---|---|
| -dict- | speak | prediction |
| -duc- | draw, lead | introduce |
| -loc- | place | local |
| -vis- | see | invisible |

Think of another example for each root. Then, using several of the examples, write a sentence or two about "The Only Girl in the World for Me."

# *Before You Read*

## GOLD

## Make the Connection

### Where the Heart Is

Like a special person, a place can leave a lasting memory in your heart. For many of us, home is the place where we live. For others, home is not within four walls but outside in nature. Home can be any place that makes you feel good—it could even be a rock where you like to sit and think.

## Quickwrite

Jot down notes on feelings, smells, sights, and sounds you connect with home. Try to include some colors. Use words that express your strongest feelings.

## Elements of Literature

### Mood

**Mood** is the overall feeling created by a story, a poem, or another work of literature. You can usually describe that feeling in one or two adjectives, such as *sad, peaceful,* or *scared.* Try to come up with a word that describes the mood Pat Mora creates in "Gold." Do you think the painting on pages 394–395 captures the special mood of Mora's golden place?

> **M**ood is the overall emotion created by a work of literature.
>
> *For more on Mood, see the Handbook of Literary Terms.*

## MEET THE WRITER

### "The Desert Is My Mother"

**Pat Mora** (1942–    ) grew up in El Paso, Texas, near the border between the United States and Mexico. Much of her writing celebrates the Southwest, especially the beauty of the desert, and describes her feelings of kinship with it. In her book *El desierto es mi madre* (*The Desert Is My Mother*), a picture book for children written in Spanish and English, she says the desert offers life, food, and spiritual comfort.

go.hrw.com
*LEO 7-5*

GOLD **393**

# Gold

**Pat Mora**

When Sun paints the desert
with its gold,
I climb the hills.
Wind runs round boulders, ruffles
5  my hair. I sit on my favorite rock,
lizards for company, a rabbit,
ears stiff in the shade
of a saguaro.°
In the wind, we're all
10  eye to eye.

Sparrow on saguaro watches
rabbit watch us in the gold
of sun setting.
Hawk sails on waves of light, sees
15  sparrow, rabbit, lizards, me,
our eyes shining,
watching red and purple
    sand rivers stream down the hill.

I stretch my arms wide as the sky
like hawk extends her wings
20  in all the gold light of this, home.

**8. saguaro** (sə·gwär′ō): huge cactus found in
the southwestern United States and northern
Mexico. The word is Mexican Spanish and was
taken from the Pima name.

# MAKING MEANINGS

- ## First Thoughts

  1. What place is home to the speaker of the poem? Would you feel at home there? Why or why not?

  ## Shaping Interpretations

  2. Is Mora alone in her special place? Who or what are her companions?

  3. Mora uses **personification** when she speaks of nonhuman things as if they were human. What verb makes the sun seem like a person? What verbs make the wind seem like a person? What does each instance of personification make you *see*?

  4. Why does Mora call the poem "Gold"? When you first read that title, did you know what kind of gold she meant? Explain.

  5. Think about the way Mora's poem makes you feel. What word or words would you use to describe its **mood**? Give at least three details from the poem that help create that mood.

# CHOICES: Building Your Portfolio

### Writer's Notebook

## 1. Collecting Ideas for a Biographical Sketch

One way to make people you write about come alive is to describe them in the place where they feel most at home or in a place they love. Think of someone you've considered writing about. Close your eyes, and try to picture the person. Where do you see him or her? Open your eyes, and write down some details of the place. Try to use words that capture the feelings, colors, and sounds connected with that place your subject loves.

### Art/Creative Writing

## 2. "Sweet as the Sight"

Write a poem about a place where you feel good, a place you call home. (Be sure to check your Quick-write notes.) Use details that create a word picture of the place and that show how you feel about it. Include colors, sounds, smells—even animal life, if there is any. Then, use crayons or watercolors to draw or paint a picture of the place. Try to use colors to capture the mood of your special place.

# Elements of Literature

## POETRY: Figures of Speech *by* John Malcolm Brinnin

### Making Connections

In our everyday language we use many expressions that are not literally true: "Charlie's bragging gets under my skin." "Gilda's money is burning a hole in her pocket." When we use expressions like these, we are speaking **figuratively.** That is, our listeners know the words do not carry their ordinary meaning. Bragging, after all, does not really pierce skin, and money cannot cause a pocket to catch fire.

The meaning of such figurative expressions depends on comparisons. Bragging is *compared* to something that causes pain or annoyance, such as a thorn. Money is *compared* to something so hot that it cannot be held and must be gotten rid of. Expressions like these, expressions that are not literally true, are called **figures of speech.** Because they can express so much meaning in interesting and surprising ways, figures of speech are an important element in poetry.

There are many kinds of figures of speech; the most common are **similes** and **metaphors.**

### Similes: Using *Like* or *As*

A **simile** is a comparison of two unlike things using the word *like, as, than,* or *resembles*. In "Mama Is a Sunrise" (page 400), for example, the poet uses a simile when she tells us that Mama "warms us *like* grits and gravy."

Here are three famous similes (a *frigate* is a ship):

There is no Frigate like a Book . . .

—Emily Dickinson

I wandered lonely as a cloud . . .

—William Wordsworth

My love is like a red, red rose . . .

—Robert Burns

### Metaphors: Identifying Two Different Things

Like a simile, a **metaphor** compares two unlike things, but it does so without using *like, as, than,* or *resembles*. For example, in "The Highwayman," Alfred Noyes does not say the moon was *like* a ghostly galleon. He uses a metaphor: "The moon *was* a ghostly galleon tossed upon cloudy seas."

The next time you see the full moon among the clouds, think of Noyes's metaphor. See if it helps you think of the night sky as a vast ocean, with the clouds as whitecaps and the moon sailing steadily through the sea. If it does, you have discovered the power of metaphors.

### A Writer on Poetry

" To have written one good poem—*good* used seriously—is an unlikely and marvelous thing that only a couple of hundred writers of English, at the most, have done—it's like sitting out in the yard in the evening and having a meteorite fall in one's lap."

—Randall Jarrell

# Before You Read

## Make the Connection

### Put In a Good Word

In the next two poems you'll see two people through their children's eyes. The title of each poem contains one word that describes the parent. The words are *simple* and *sunrise*. What do these words suggest to you?

## Quickwrite

Write down all the things you think of when you hear the words *simple* and *sunrise*. Then, choose two or three words from your lists. Whom do they remind you of? Think of someone you know or someone you have read about. Now, quickly write three or four sentences about this person—just the first three or four things that come to mind.

## Elements of Literature

### Free Verse

These two poems are written in **free verse.** In free verse, poets do *not* use strict patterns of rhythm and rhyme.

> **P**oetry without a regular meter or a rhyme scheme is called **free verse.**
>
> *For more on Free Verse, see pages 338–339 and the Handbook of Literary Terms.*

Instead, they write in loose groupings of words and phrases and try to capture the natural rhythms of ordinary speech. Even in free verse, however, you'll find vivid images and repetition used to create rhythm and to emphasize important ideas.

## Reading Skills and Strategies

### Comparing Texts: Searching for Similarities

You already know that both of these poems are written in **free verse.** You can find other similarities between them by **comparing texts.** After you've read the poems and talked about them, reread each one carefully. Then, copy the chart below. Working with a partner, jot down the similarities you find in the two poems.

| | "My Father Is a Simple Man" | "Mama Is a Sunrise" |
|---|---|---|
| Subject | | |
| Speaker | | |
| Figures of speech | | |
| Theme | | |

# My Father Is a Simple Man

## Luis Omar Salinas

I walk to town with my father
to buy a newspaper. He walks slower
than I do so I must slow up.
The street is filled with children.
5   We argue about the price
of pomegranates, I convince
him it is the fruit of scholars.
He has taken me on this journey
and it's been lifelong.
10   He's sure I'll be healthy
so long as I eat more oranges,
and tells me the orange
has seeds and so is perpetual;°
and we too will come back
15   like the orange trees.
I ask him what he thinks
about death and he says
he will gladly face it when
it comes but won't jump
20   out in front of a car.
I'd gladly give my life
for this man with a sixth
grade education, whose kindness
and patience are true . . .
25   The truth of it is, he's the scholar,
and when the bitter-hard reality
comes at me like a punishing
evil stranger, I can always
remember that here was a man
30   who was a worker and provider,
who learned the simple facts
in life and lived by them,
who held no pretense.
And when he leaves without
35   benefit of fanfare° or applause
I shall have learned what little
there is about greatness.

13. **perpetual:** continuing forever.
35. **fanfare:** noisy display to draw attention
(literally, a flourish of trumpets).

*The Jazz Musician* by William Low.
Courtesy of the Artist.

# Mama Is a Sunrise

**Evelyn Tooley Hunt**

When she comes slip-footing through the door,
    she kindles us
    like lump coal lighted,
    and we wake up glowing.
5    She puts a spark even in Papa's eyes
and turns out all our darkness.

When she comes sweet-talking in the room,
    she warms us
    like grits and gravy,
10    and we rise up shining.
Even at nighttime Mama is a sunrise
that promises tomorrow and tomorrow.

## MEET THE WRITERS

### "The Strange Fullness of the Unreal"

**Luis Omar Salinas** (1937–    ) was just four years old when his mother died of tuberculosis. He was adopted by his uncle Alfredo and grew up in California. Some of his best poetry explores the haunting effects of losing his mother when he was little. Many of these poems use fantastic, dreamlike images that contrast sharply with the plain-spoken realism of "My Father Is a Simple Man." Salinas has stated that his aim is to capture "the strange fullness of the unreal."

### Faraway Worlds

**Evelyn Tooley Hunt** (1904–1998) brought a spirit of play to her work. For example, *Dancer in the Wind* (1977) is a book of haiku variations entirely about scarecrows. (A **haiku** is a type of three-line poem perfected in Japan.)

# As I Gaze upon My Father

In the brownish photo, my father
Sits up straight
Like a wooden board,
With his knees crossed
5     And his hands folded gently over his knee,
But the sheepish smile gives him away
Like a pen trying to be a pencil.

He wore a white oxford
That was perfectly pressed
10     And smooth as a newborn's flesh.
As a second layer he wore a wool sweater
That was rough as sandpaper,
As if to show his life.

          —Maren Stuart
          Tampa Preparatory School
          Tampa, Florida

First appeared in *Merlyn's Pen: The National Magazines of Student Writing.*

## MAKING MEANINGS

### MY FATHER IS A SIMPLE MAN
### MAMA IS A SUNRISE

#### First Thoughts

1. Which poem do you like better, Salinas's or Hunt's? Why?

#### Shaping Interpretations

2. How are the fathers in "As I Gaze upon My Father" (above) and "My Father Is a Simple Man" similar? How are they different?

3. When Hunt says "Mama Is a Sunrise," she is using a **metaphor.** Find words in Hunt's poem that refer to light or warmth. What traits does Mama actually share with a sunrise?

4. In **free verse,** poets repeat certain words to emphasize important ideas. What words are repeated in each of these poems? Why do you think the poet wanted to emphasize these words?

5. Refer to the comparison chart you made after you read the poems. How are the poems similar? Does one similarity seem to jump out at you? (Be sure to compare your charts in class.)

6. What word or phrase would you use to describe the overall **mood** of "Mama Is a Sunrise"? Name at least three details from the poem that help create the mood.

## Connecting with the Texts

7. Think about your role models. How are they similar to the characters in these poems? How are they different?

# Choices: Building Your Portfolio

### Writer's Notebook

## 1. Collecting Ideas for a Biographical Sketch

In the poems you just read, Hunt compares Mama to a sunrise, and Salinas compares his father to a scholar. Pick one of your favorite people (perhaps the person you described in your notes for the Quickwrite on page 398).

What comparisons can you use to help readers "see" this person and understand the impression he or she makes on you?

### Creative Writing

## 2. Another Sunrise

Write a poem with the same structure as "Mama Is a Sunrise." Start each line as Hunt does, and end it your own way. Open your poem with a metaphor.

   . . . is a . . .
   When she/he . . .

### Art

## 3. This Is Just to Say . . .

Make a greeting card for a favorite person. Think of an original comparison that captures something special about the person. Draw a colorful illustration of the comparison on the front of your card. Write your comparison inside. You may want to sign your name and send the card to your favorite person.

# Papa's Parrot

**Cynthia Rylant**

*Chills ran down Harry's back. What could the bird mean?*

Though his father was fat and merely owned a candy and nut shop, Harry Tillian liked his papa. Harry stopped liking candy and nuts when he was around seven, but in spite of this, he and Mr. Tillian had remained friends and were still friends the year Harry turned twelve.

For years, after school, Harry had always stopped in to see his father at work. Many of Harry's friends stopped there, too, to spend a few cents choosing penny candy from the giant bins or to sample Mr. Tillian's latest batch of roasted peanuts. Mr. Tillian looked forward to seeing his son and his son's friends every day. He liked the company.

When Harry entered junior high school, though, he didn't come by the candy and nut shop as often. Nor did his friends. They were older and they had more spending money. They went to a burger place. They played video games. They shopped for records. None of them were much interested in candy and nuts anymore.

A new group of children came to Mr. Tillian's shop now. But not Harry Tillian and his friends.

The year Harry turned twelve was also the year Mr. Tillian got a parrot. He went to a pet store one day and bought one for more money than he could really afford. He brought the parrot to his shop, set its cage near the sign for maple clusters, and named it Rocky.

Harry thought this was the strangest thing his father had ever done, and he told him so, but Mr. Tillian just ignored him.

Rocky was good company for Mr. Tillian. When business was slow, Mr. Tillian would turn on a small color television he had sitting in a corner, and he and Rocky would watch the soap operas. Rocky liked to scream when the romantic music came on, and Mr. Tillian would yell at him to shut up, but they seemed to enjoy themselves.

The more Mr. Tillian grew to like his parrot, and the more he talked to it instead of to people, the more embarrassed Harry became. Harry would stroll past the shop, on his way somewhere else, and he'd take a quick look inside to see what his dad was doing. Mr. Tillian was always talking to the bird. So Harry kept walking.

At home things were different. Harry and his father joked with each other at the dinner table as they always had—Mr. Tillian teasing Harry about his smelly socks; Harry teasing Mr. Tillian about his blubbery stomach. At home things seemed all right.

But one day, Mr. Tillian became ill. He had been at work, unpacking boxes of caramels, when he had grabbed his chest and fallen over on top of the candy. A customer had found him, and he was taken to the hospital in an ambulance.

Mr. Tillian couldn't leave the hospital. He lay in bed, tubes in his arms, and he worried about his shop. New shipments of candy and nuts would be arriving. Rocky would be hungry. Who would take care of things?

Harry said he would. Harry told his father that he would go to the store every day after school and unpack boxes. He would sort out all the candy and nuts. He would even feed Rocky.

So, the next morning, while Mr. Tillian lay in his hospital bed, Harry took the shop key to school with him. After school he left his friends and walked to the empty shop alone. In all the days of his life, Harry had never seen the shop closed after school. Harry didn't even remember what the CLOSED sign looked like. The key stuck in the lock three times, and inside he had to search all the walls for the light switch.

The shop was as his father had left it. Even the caramels were still spilled on the floor. Harry bent down and picked them up one by one, dropping them back in the boxes. The bird in its cage watched him silently.

Harry opened the new boxes his father hadn't gotten to. Peppermints. Jawbreakers.

Toffee creams. Strawberry kisses. Harry traveled from bin to bin, putting the candies where they belonged.

"Hello!"

Harry jumped, spilling a box of jawbreakers.

"Hello, Rocky!"

Harry stared at the parrot. He had forgotten it was there. The bird had been so quiet, and Harry had been thinking only of the candy.

"Hello," Harry said.

"Hello, Rocky!" answered the parrot.

Harry walked slowly over to the cage. The parrot's food cup was empty. Its water was dirty. The bottom of the cage was a mess.

Harry carried the cage into the back room.

"Hello, Rocky!"

"Is that all you can say, you dumb bird?" Harry mumbled. The bird said nothing else.

Harry cleaned the bottom of the cage, refilled the food and water cups, and then put the cage back in its place and resumed sorting the candy.

"Where's Harry?"

Harry looked up.

"Where's Harry?"

Harry stared at the parrot.

"Where's Harry?"

Chills ran down Harry's back. What could the bird mean? It was like something from *The Twilight Zone.*°

"Where's Harry?"

Harry swallowed and said, "I'm here. I'm here, you stupid bird."

"You stupid bird!" said the parrot.

Well, at least he's got one thing straight, thought Harry.

"Miss him! Miss him! Where's Harry? You stupid bird!"

Harry stood with a handful of peppermints.

"*What?*" he asked.

"Where's Harry?" said the parrot.

° ***The Twilight Zone:*** a popular dramatic television series that ran from 1959 to 1964 and is now widely shown in reruns. It usually features suspenseful, fantastic plots.

"I'm *here*, you stupid bird! I'm here!" Harry yelled. He threw the peppermints at the cage, and the bird screamed and clung to its perch.

Harry sobbed, "I'm here." The tears were coming.

Harry leaned over the glass counter.

"Papa." Harry buried his face in his arms.

"Where's Harry?" repeated the bird.

Harry sighed and wiped his face on his sleeve. He watched the parrot. He understood now: someone had been saying, for a long time, "Where's Harry? Miss him."

Harry finished his unpacking and then swept the floor of the shop. He checked the furnace so the bird wouldn't get cold. Then he left to go visit his papa.

## Meet the Writer

### Always Trying to Find Those Words

**Cynthia Rylant** (1954–     ) wrote in her autobiography:

> 66 They say that to be a writer you must first have an unhappy childhood. I don't know if unhappiness is necessary, but I think maybe some children who have suffered a loss too great for words grow up into writers who are always trying to find those words, trying to find a meaning for the way they have lived. 99

As a child Rylant knew what it felt like to lose someone. Her parents separated when she was four, and she lived with her grandparents in West Virginia while her mother went to school. For years she heard nothing of her father; then, when she was a young teenager, he got in touch with her. They planned a reunion, but he died before it could happen. She was just thirteen.

Rylant felt that despite this sorrow, her childhood was a happy one, calling her West Virginia home "a small, sparkling universe that gave me a lifetime's worth of material for my writing." Rylant has won several awards for her books for young people, including the Newbery Medal for her novel *Missing May* (1993). She describes the kinds of people she likes to write about:

> 66 I get a lot of personal gratification thinking of those people who don't get any attention in the world and making them really valuable in my fiction—making them absolutely shine with their beauty. 99

**More Words Found by Cynthia Rylant**
If you are touched by "Papa's Parrot," you might enjoy some of Rylant's novels: *A Fine White Dust* (Bradbury) and *Missing May* (Orchard Books). You might also like her autobiography, *Best Wishes* (Richard C. Owen).

# READ ON

## Love Stories

Cynthia Rylant's *A Couple of Kooks: And Other Stories About Love* (Dell) takes a fresh look at love. A supermarket bag boy's crush on a pretty shopper, an old man's passion, and a retarded boy's adoration of a woman who works in a hardware store are among the stories you'll discover.

Will Dara survive in war-torn Cambodia?

## Forever Friends

Twelve-year-old Dara and her family flee war-torn Cambodia and find a haven at the refugee camp of Nong Chan. In *The Clay Marble* (Farrar, Straus & Giroux) by Minfong Ho, Dara finds a new friend, Jantu, and for a short while their lives are full of peace. When the war brings chaos to the camp, however, Dara is separated from her family and Jantu. Now she must find the courage to reunite the people she loves. (This title is available in the HRW Library.)

## Desert Heartbreak

In *One More River* (Avon) by Lynne Reid Banks, wealthy Lesley Shelby must abandon her comfortable life when her family moves to a kibbutz in Israel just before the 1967 Six-Day War. Once there, she struggles to find something in common with the Israeli teenagers she meets. In this riveting story, Lesley discovers her own strengths and inner conflicts when she encounters an Arab youth.

## Other Picks

- Robert Westall, *Stormsearch* (Farrar, Straus & Giroux). When Tim and Tracy Vaux dig up an ancient ship's model, they uncover a story of doomed romance and family secrets.

- David Kherdian, *A Song for Uncle Harry* (Philomel). Petey and his eccentric Armenian uncle Harry have an unusual bond until Uncle Harry falls in love.

# Speaking and Listening Workshop

## Try It Out

Imagine you're interviewing your favorite sports, music, or film idol. Write down a list of ten questions, none of which can be answered with a simple yes or no.

## Try It Out

Team up with a classmate, and come up with a situation in which an interviewer and a subject have opposing points of view (a dog hater interviews the director of the humane society; a vegetarian interviews the owner of a cattle ranch). Then, act out two versions of the interview. In the first version the interview is tense and hostile, full of insults, interruptions, and accusations. In the second the interview is polite and constructive, and the interviewer refrains from directly expressing a point of view. What did you learn from the two scenarios?

# INTERVIEWING

**Interviews**—conversations in which one person asks questions to obtain information—are more common than you might think. You've probably been interviewed—by a teacher, the school nurse, or a neighbor wanting you to baby-sit or mow the lawn.

Sometime you may need to conduct an interview yourself. Here's how to get off to a good start.

## Preparing for the Interview

A good interviewer is well prepared. Before you take out your pencil and note pad, follow these steps:

- Research your topic. If your interview focuses on a topic—kayaking, say—go to the library and find out all you can about it. The more you know, the better your questions will be.

- Know your subject. If your interview focuses on the ideas and life of the person you're interviewing (your subject), see if any newspaper or magazine articles have been written about him or her. If your subject is a writer, read her latest book; if he's an architect, go see—or find a picture of—a building he designed.

- Make a list of questions. Ask obvious questions rather than pretend you know the answer. Don't ask questions that can be answered with a simple yes or no. Avoid questions that might influence your subject, like "You hate losing, don't you?"

- Set up a time and place for the interview. Choose a place that's comfortable and familiar to your subject—interview a horse trainer at her ranch or a chemistry teacher in his lab. Be on time.

## Conducting the Interview

You're seated across from your subject, pencil poised. How do you make the most of your opportunity? Follow these guidelines:

- Set the ground rules. If you want to tape-record the interview, ask your subject's permission before you begin. If you plan to quote your subject's exact words in a newspaper article or in an essay, you must ask permission to do that, too.

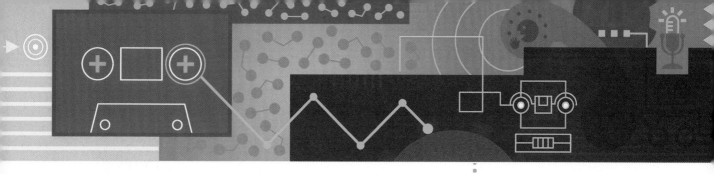

- Be courteous and patient. Allow your subject plenty of time to answer your questions. Try not to interrupt. Respect the person's ideas and opinions, even if you disagree.

- Listen carefully. Don't rush on to your next question. If you're confused, ask for an explanation. If an answer reminds you of a related question, ask it—even if it isn't on your list.

- Focus on your subject, not on yourself. Avoid getting off on tangents, such as "Something like that happened to me. . . ."

- Wrap things up. A good interview is leisurely but doesn't go on forever. Know when to stop. You can always phone later to check a fact or ask a final question. Be sure to thank your subject.

## Following Up the Interview

Your notebook is filled, and your mind is bursting with ideas. How do you get your thoughts in order? Follow these steps:

- Review your notes. As soon as possible, read through your notes and make sure your information is complete and clear.

- Write a summary. To make sure you understand what was said, write a summary of the main points of the interview.

- Check your facts. If you can, check the spelling of all names and technical facts against another source, such as an encyclopedia.

## Turning the Tables: Being Interviewed

Sometime someone may want to interview you. Here are some tips:

- Stay relaxed. Listen carefully to each question before you begin your answer. If a question confuses you, ask the interviewer to reword it or repeat it. Take your time. Long, thoughtful answers are better than short, curt ones.

- Be accurate. Don't exaggerate. If you're not sure of something, say so.

- Keep a sense of humor.

### Try It Out

Watch a television news anchor interview a subject. Pay attention to

- the length of the questions
- follow-up questions
- how the interviewer maintains control over the interview
- how the interviewer makes his or her subject feel comfortable

How can you apply what you have learned to your own interviews?

**Technology HELP**

*See* Writer's Workshop 1 CD-ROM. *Assignment: Firsthand Biography.*

## ASSIGNMENT

**Write an essay about a real person.**

## AIM

**To inform.**

## AUDIENCE

**Your teacher, classmates, friends, or family.**

*A longer excerpt from* Barrio Boy *by Ernesto Galarza appears on page 125.*

## EXPOSITORY WRITING

# BIOGRAPHICAL SKETCH

In a biographical sketch, you give information about a person, either someone you know or a historical figure you're interested in.

### Professional Model

*In this passage from his autobiography,* Barrio Boy, *Ernesto Galarza describes his aunt.*

Doña Henriqueta was not even as tall as Doña Esther, but plumper. She had a light olive complexion and a mass of dark brown hair so wavy it burst when she undid her braids. She never did household chores without singing, accompanying herself by imitating a guitar that plinked and plonked between the verses of her song. Her features were good-looking, almost soft, not much like her temper. Doña Henriqueta knew about people in deep trouble, for she was one of them. But unlike most of them, she believed in rebelling against it, in resisting those who caused it. As the oldest of the four migrants from Miramar, Doña Henriqueta stood between us and Don Catarina when he was in one of his cantankerous moods. She drew a line between respect, which we were expected to show, and fear, which we were not.

—from *Barrio Boy* by Ernesto Galarza

*The writer describes his aunt's appearance.*

*He tells about his aunt's actions.*

*He describes his aunt's personality.*

*He tells where his aunt is from.*

The history
of the written
word is rich and
Page 1

## Prewriting

### 1. Writer's Notebook

Review the notes you made in your Writer's Notebook for this collection. Then, answer these questions:

- Which of these people do I find most interesting? Why?
- Which of these people would I enjoy writing about? Why?
- Which of these people taught me something important? What was it?

### 2. Freewriting

To find more ideas, freewrite on some of these subjects:

- people you think are "the most" (the most helpful, the most courageous, the most whatever)
- a memorable historical figure
- someone who changed your mind about something
- someone whose actions made a difference
- a hero whose deeds haven't been recognized
- a unique athlete

Choose two or three of the people you've written about. For each person, list a personality trait you admire (for example, understanding or courage) and sum up an incident that illustrates the trait. For an example of this kind of freewriting, see the chart in the margin. Review your charts, and see which person seems to jump out at you. Which one will give you a lot to write about?

### 3. Why Is This Person Important?

When you've decided on your subject, ask yourself why he or she is important enough to write about. Use these questions to help put your thoughts into words:

■ *Evaluation Criteria*

*A good biographical sketch*

1. *makes the personality of the subject come alive*
2. *includes concrete details of the subject's appearance, behavior, and background*
3. *may use dialogue to show the subject's character*
4. *may describe the setting*
5. *tells about specific incidents to illustrate the subject's character*
6. *shows why the subject is important to the writer*

| Person | Dad |
|--------|-----|
| Trait | forgiveness |
| Incident | Forgave me when I hit a ball through the kitchen window (I wasn't supposed to hit balls there). |

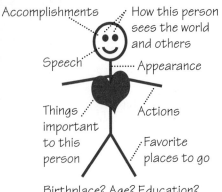

Accomplishments

How this person sees the world and others

Speech

Appearance

Things important to this person

Actions

Favorite places to go

Birthplace? Age? Education? Work?

---

**Framework for a Biographical Sketch**

**Introduction** (captures the reader's curiosity; shows the person in action; mentions an interesting biographical detail):

_____

_____

_____

**Body** (describes the person's qualities; tells a story about the person; gives biographical details):

_____

_____

_____

_____

**Conclusion** (tells what the person means to you or presents a final word picture):

_____

_____

_____

_____

- What more than anything else draws me to this person?
- What have I learned about people or life from this person?
- How has this person influenced my life or my thinking?
- Why would my readers enjoy knowing this person?

Try writing two or three sentences that **summarize** why your subject is important to you. This summary may turn out to be the main point of your biographical sketch. It may also turn out that as you write, your opinion changes. In any case, keep this statement handy as you work on the biography.

## 4. Details Make It Real

Now, gather details of your subject—details of appearance, interests, accomplishments. Decide if you want to tell something about your person's background—age, birthplace, education, work. Draw a stick figure of a person like the one at the left, and fill in details in as many of the categories as you can.

## Drafting

### 1. Getting Started

Read over your Prewriting notes. Mark them up, circling points you want to use in your biographical sketch—for example, actions that reveal character and memorable traits. Include details that show what the person means to you.

As you begin to write, include everything you think is important. Don't worry too much about length or organization—you can take care of those things once you have something down on paper. Make sure, though, that you never lose sight of your statement about why this person is important to you.

### 2. Shaping and Organizing

Here are a few ways to organize your ideas:

**Time order.**   You could organize your biographical sketch **chronologically,** following time order. Use this kind of organization, for example, if you're relating a series of events that show your subject's personality.

**Physical appearance.**   You could start with your subject's physical appearance and then relate it to personality. Look at Ernesto Galarza's portrait of his aunt Henriqueta (page 410).

Note how her soft features contrast with her fiery spirit. Also look at the Student Model below. Notice that the mother's physical appearance gives us a sense of her personality.

**Personality traits.** You could organize your biography around your subject's personality traits, telling about specific incidents that show the traits in action. You might consider describing the most important personality trait last. With this method, called **order of importance,** you put your most important point either first or last.

## Student Model

*The following passage is from a description of the writer's mother.*

### from IN THE KITCHEN

I hopped up onto the yellow-topped counter and gazed around the room, taking in the kitchen with all my senses . . . and finally, my mother. Small and thin, with short salt-and-pepper hair and happy laugh-lines (and the age-ones she called unattractive but I always said made her that much more beautiful), it was my mother I noticed most. When she laughed, her eyes would crinkle and she would look at you as if you were the most special person in the world. I always loved making my mother laugh, just to see her eyes—and that look.

    As she cooked, delectable smells danced and flew from the lidded pots and pans, making my mouth water. I asked for "tries," and she gave me tastes and nibbles, making me long for supper.

*We see the person in a setting.*

*Physical details give us a clear picture of the person's appearance and personality.*

*Description of actions helps us get to know the writer's mother.*

*(continued on next page)*

*Bringing Your Person to Life*

Your aim in writing a biographical sketch is to bring your person to life for your readers. To do this, try these strategies:

- Quote something the person says or has said that is funny or characteristic of him or her.

- Put the person in a setting that you associate with him or her. Describe the setting.

- Tell what other people think of the person.

- Tell what this person makes you think of. What do you associate with him or her— springtime, ballgames, walks in the park?

**Language/Grammar
Link**
H E L P

*Problems with pronouns:
pages 366 and 392.
Homonyms: page 385.*

**Sentence Workshop**
H E L P

*Revising wordy sentences:
page 415.*

---

**Proofreading Tip**

Read your paper
backward, word by
word.

---

**Publishing Tip**

Your subject might
enjoy reading what you
wrote. Consider print-
ing and binding your
biography to create a
special gift.

---

**Communications
Handbook**
H E L P

*See Proofreaders' Marks.*

---

**Student Model (continued)**

Some of my best times have
been spent in that kitchen, watching my mother bustle about, stirring this, testing that, always
smiling with her crinkly eyes,
making everyone around her
happy. At the end, when all was
done, she would put her arms
around me, and I would stand
on my tiptoes so that I could fit
my head on her shoulder, and
then she would squeeze me a
little harder and say "thank
you," and I would say "thank
you" right back.

> *The writer
> describes more
> actions to give us
> a sense of her
> mother's
> personality.*

> *At the end and
> earlier in the
> passage, we can
> feel the writer's
> affection for her
> mother.*

—Elly Henry
Camp Hill Jr./Sr. High School
Camp Hill, Pennsylvania

*First appeared in Merlyn's Pen: The National Magazines of Student Writing.*

## 3. Making the Beginning and Ending Memorable

As you shape your biography, think of ways to make the
beginning and ending strong. You might begin by mentioning an
unusual fact or physical detail, by telling about a funny incident,
or by quoting part of a conversation.

Ending a biographical piece can be tricky. You don't want to
sound obvious or dull—"My father taught me everything I
know"—but maybe you can find a way to show your subject's
importance to you. Perhaps you can end with a description of a
special moment, as the writer of the Student Model on page
413 did.

## Evaluating and Revising

Look once more at your statement of why your subject is important
to you. Did you say what you meant to say? Did you end up saying
anything new? Could that new point be worth focusing on? Revise
your writing to make it say what you want it to say.

## REVISING WORDY SENTENCES

Sometimes writers clutter up sentences by using more words than they really need. An overload of words doesn't make writing sound better or more impressive. Learn how to avoid wordiness in your writing and how to make every word count.

You can revise **wordy sentences** in at least three ways:

1. Replace a long phrase with a single word.

   WORDY    They reached the school corner and Roger skipped away in an eager manner from her.

   REVISED    "They reached the school corner and Roger skipped away eagerly from her."

   —Arthur Cavanaugh, "Miss Awful" (page 373)

2. Take out *that is/was, who is/was,* or *which is/was.*

   WORDY    The sidewalk that was in front of school already boasted a large, jostling throng of children. . . .

   REVISED    "The sidewalk in front of school already boasted a large, jostling throng of children. . . ."

   —Arthur Cavanaugh, "Miss Awful" (page 373)

3. Take out words that repeat something.

   WORDY    I reached over and shut off the insistent buzzing of my bedside alarm clock, which was ringing next to my bed.

   REVISED    "I reached over and shut off the insistent buzzing of my bedside alarm clock."

   —T. Ernesto Bethancourt, "User Friendly" (page 357)

## Writer's Workshop Follow-up: Revision

Take out your biographical sketch, and circle any wordy sentences. Revise these sentences to make them straightforward and concise. Look for and eliminate phrases like *due to the fact that* and *at the point at which.*

**Language Handbook HELP**

*See Revising Stringy Sentences and Wordy Sentences, pages 761-762.*

**Technology HELP**

*See* Language Workshop CD-ROM. *Key word entry: wordiness.*

---

### Try It Out

Revise each of the following wordy sentences.

1. At the moment when she returned to her desk, her back was straighter than ever.

2. Due to the fact that she was so beautiful, people probably wondered why she was with me.

3. Harry didn't have the slightest clue as to whether or not the parrot was speaking to him.

4. My computer, which was known by the name of Louis, sent me a message.

# Reading for Life

## Reading a Geography Book

## Situation

Imagine that you're going to visit San Antonio this summer, driving all the way from Virginia to Texas. Before you leave, you want to learn about the states you'll be traveling through. You decide to start with your geography book.

## Strategies

**Focus your research.**

- Make a list of questions you want to answer.

**Use the text's structure to locate information.**

- Skim the **table of contents** to see what information your textbook covers and how it is organized. Scan unit headings and chapter titles. See where you can find information on your topic.

- Search the **index** for key words about your topic. Check general entries ("Southern states," for example) and specific entries (names of states, large cities, and physical features, such as rivers).

- Look for **maps** that will help you locate physical features, such as mountains, as well as towns and cities.

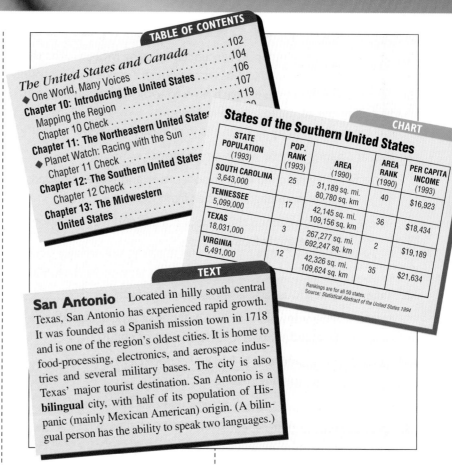

**TABLE OF CONTENTS**

**CHART**

### States of the Southern United States

| STATE POPULATION (1993) | POP. RANK (1993) | AREA (1990) | AREA RANK (1990) | PER CAPITA INCOME (1993) |
|---|---|---|---|---|
| SOUTH CAROLINA 3,643,000 | 25 | 31,189 sq. mi. 80,780 sq. km | 40 | $16,923 |
| TENNESSEE 5,099,000 | 17 | 42,145 sq. mi. 109,156 sq. km | 36 | $18,434 |
| TEXAS 18,031,000 | 3 | 267,277 sq. mi. 692,247 sq. km | 2 | $19,189 |
| VIRGINIA 6,491,000 | 12 | 42,326 sq. mi. 109,624 sq. km | 35 | $21,634 |

Rankings are for all 50 states.
Source: Statistical Abstract of the United States 1994

**TEXT**

**San Antonio** Located in hilly south central Texas, San Antonio has experienced rapid growth. It was founded as a Spanish mission town in 1718 and is one of the region's oldest cities. It is home to food-processing, electronics, and aerospace industries and several military bases. The city is also Texas' major tourist destination. San Antonio is a **bilingual** city, with half of its population of Hispanic (mainly Mexican American) origin. (A bilingual person has the ability to speak two languages.)

## Use graphic features.

- Look for **charts,** which present a lot of information in a small space.

## Using the Strategies

Answer the following questions about the material above, which is from a world geography textbook.

1. Where in the table of contents would you find facts about states you'd travel through on the way from Virginia to Texas?

2. List three things that you learned about San Antonio.

3. Which state listed in the chart is the third most populous in the country?

## Extending the Strategies

Where in the world would you most like to go? Use these strategies to find information on this place in your geography textbook.

# Learning for Life

## Conflict Resolution

## Problem

Wherever people live and work together, conflicts arise. How can people resolve, or work out, differences with others and keep good relationships with them?

## Project

**Do a survey to find out how people resolve differences with others.**

## Preparation

1. With a small group of classmates, write a short survey of four or five questions about how people deal with conflict.

2. Test your survey by asking your teacher or another adult to respond to your questions. Then, make any changes that are needed in the survey.

3. Each group member will pick at least two people to interview. They might be classmates, students in other classes, friends, or neighbors.

## Procedure

1. Tell each person whom you are going to interview what your purpose is. Then, ask the survey questions. Don't try to write down every word of every answer. Jot down important points and just a few of the person's exact words.

2. Meet as a group and read the answers to the surveys. Do you see any patterns? Ask yourselves these questions:

   • What methods do people use to cooperate?

   • What kinds of situations cause conflicts?

   • What ways of resolving conflicts seem to work best?

3. As a class, discuss each group's findings. Then, decide on some general guidelines for resolving conflicts.

## Presentation

Choose one of these ways to present what you have learned:

### 1. Role-Playing

On slips of paper, write down situations involving conflict that might occur in the workplace or at school. Fold the slips of paper in half and put them in a container. Then, with a partner, pull a conflict "out of the hat" and role-play the conflict and the resolution.

### 2. Billboard

Create a billboard with photographs of people and comments about how they resolve conflicts. If possible, use quotations from the people you surveyed.

### 3. Song

With a group of classmates, write a song about resolving conflicts. Choose a music style—rock, rap, country, folk, whatever. Try to include a catchy chorus that brings home the importance of your message.

## Processing

In your portfolio, write a reflection about the survey. You might use one of these starters:

• I never realized it could be so hard to . . .

• Of all the ways to resolve conflicts, the one that appeals to me the most is . . .

# This Old Earth

*i keep hearing*
*tree talk*
*water words*
*and i keep knowing what they mean*

—*Lucille Clifton*

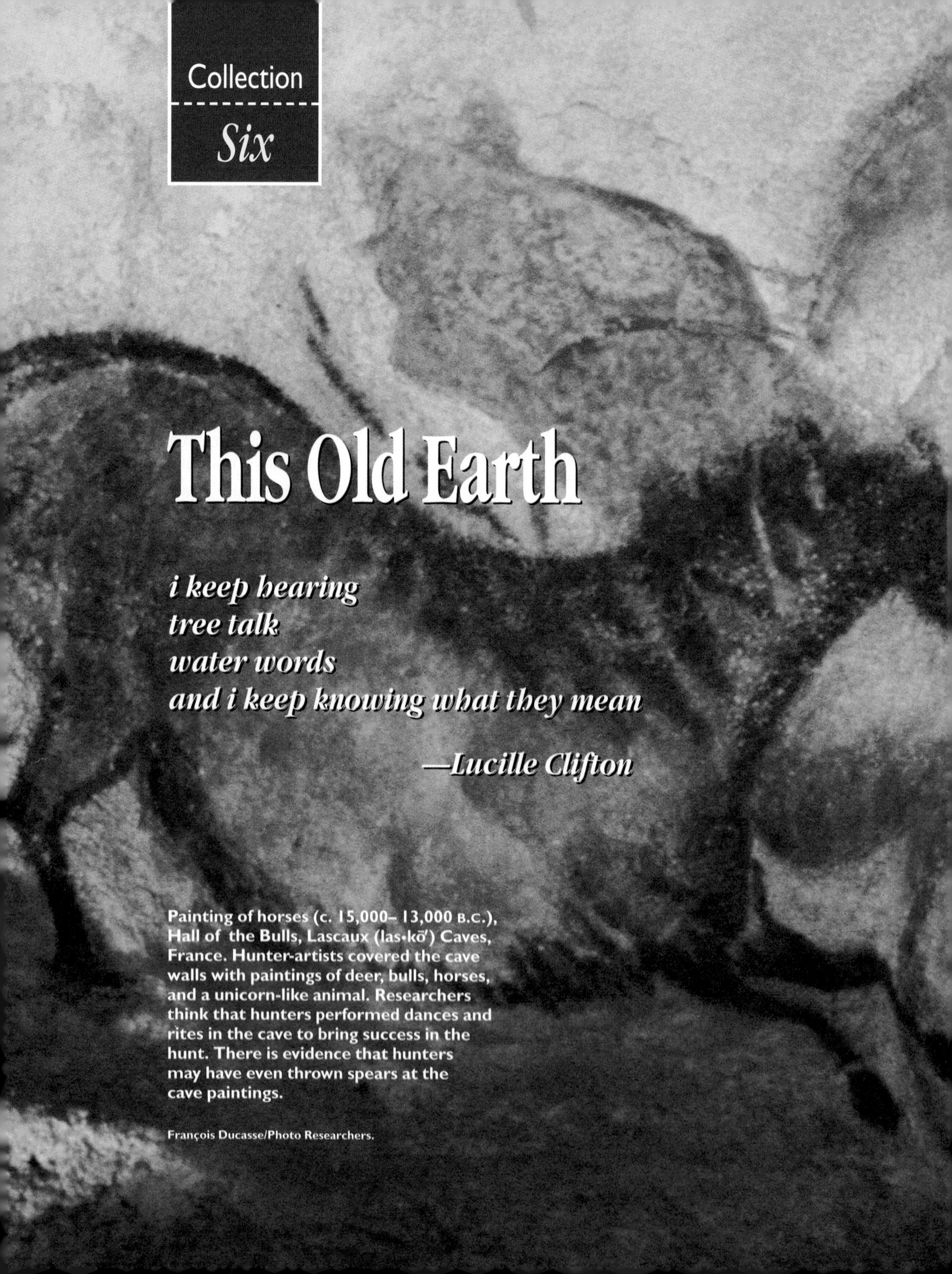

**Painting of horses (c. 15,000– 13,000 B.C.),**
**Hall of the Bulls, Lascaux (las•kō′) Caves,**
**France.** Hunter-artists covered the cave
walls with paintings of deer, bulls, horses,
and a unicorn-like animal. Researchers
think that hunters performed dances and
rites in the cave to bring success in the
hunt. There is evidence that hunters
may have even thrown spears at the
cave paintings.

François Ducasse/Photo Researchers.

## THE CREATION

## Make the Connection

### Like a Mother's Love

This "sermon" is based on the Biblical account of creation found in the book of Genesis. Notice that the preacher speaks of God as someone who shares our need for love. Notice also that he compares God's care for his human creation to a mother's love for her baby.

Sermons are meant to be heard. With your classmates, read the first four lines aloud. Then, as you read the rest of the poem, imagine yourself in a crowded church hearing this sermon about how the world began.

## Reading Skills and Strategies

### Dialogue with the Text

As you read "The Creation," keep a sheet of paper next to the book so that you can record your thoughts and feelings. One student's comments appear on the first page as an example.

## Elements of Literature

### Refrain: You Can Say That Again

You often hear phrases or verses repeated in poems, sermons, speeches, and songs. (Think of some of your favorite songs.) The lines that keep coming up are called the **refrain.** The refrain is often used to build rhythm, but it can also be used to emphasize the main theme of the work. A live audience often joins in with the refrain.

This dialogue, known as **call and response,** was common in many Southern churches after the Civil War and is still practiced in some churches today. In call and response the church leader strives to instruct as well as spiritually uplift the congregation (the audience), and the congregation responds verbally. You could say the congregation is responding with a refrain to the leader's call.

Look for the refrain in "The Creation," and imagine the effect if the whole congregation repeated the creator's words.

> **A refrain** is a group of words repeated at intervals in a poem, song, or speech.
>
> *For more on Refrain, see the Handbook of Literary Terms.*

go.hrw.com

*LEO 7-6*

# The Creation

## James Weldon Johnson

And God stepped out on space,
And he looked around and said:
I'm lonely—
I'll make me a world.

5    And far as the eye of God could see
Darkness covered everything,
Blacker than a hundred midnights
Down in a cypress° swamp.

Then God smiled,
10   And the light broke,
And the darkness rolled up on one side,
And the light stood shining on the other,
And God said: That's good!

Then God reached out and took the light in His hands,
15   And God rolled the light around in His hands
Until He made the sun;
And He set that sun a-blazing in the heavens.
And the light that was left from making the sun
God gathered it up in a shining ball
20   And flung it against the darkness,
Spangling the night with the moon and stars.
Then down between
The darkness and the light
He hurled the world;
25   And God said: That's good!

Then God himself stepped down—
And the sun was on His right hand,
And the moon was on His left;
The stars were clustered about His head,
30   And the earth was under His feet.
And God walked, and where He trod
His footsteps hollowed the valleys out
And bulged the mountains up.

8. **cypress:** type of evergreen tree.

---

### Dialogue with the Text

The use of the word "on" is not what you would expect.

What is a cypress swamp? After finding out what a cypress swamp is and rereading this section, I could almost feel the darkness overcoming me.

That is a powerful picture.

I am finding the inconsistencies in the portrayal of God's size distracting and confusing.

*Cheryl Testa*

—Cheryl Testa
  William T. Rogers Middle School
  Kings Park, New York

Then He stopped and looked and saw
35 That the earth was hot and barren.
So God stepped over to the edge of the
world
And He spat out the seven seas—
He batted His eyes, and the lightnings
flashed—
He clapped His hands, and the thunders
rolled—
And the waters above the earth came
40 down,
The cooling waters came down.

Then the green grass sprouted,
And the little red flowers blossomed,
The pine tree pointed his finger to the
sky,
45 And the oak spread out his arms,
The lakes cuddled down in the hollows of
the ground,
And the rivers ran down to the sea;
And God smiled again,
And the rainbow appeared,
50 And curled itself around His shoulder.

Then God raised His arm and He waved
His hand
Over the sea and over the land,
And He said: Bring forth! Bring forth!
And quicker than God could drop His
hand,
55 Fishes and fowls
And beasts and birds
Swam the rivers and the seas,
Roamed the forests and the woods,
And split the air with their wings.
60 And God said: That's good!

Then God walked around,
And God looked around
On all that He had made.
He looked at His sun,
65 And He looked at His moon,
And He looked at His little stars;

He looked on His world
With all its living things,
And God said: I'm lonely still.

70 Then God sat down—
On the side of a hill where He could
think;
By a deep, wide river He sat down;
With His head in His hands,
God thought and thought,
75 Till He thought: I'll make me a man!

Up from the bed of the river
God scooped the clay;
And by the bank of the river
He kneeled Him down;
80 And there the great God Almighty
Who lit the sun and fixed it in the sky,
Who flung the stars to the most far
corner of the night,
Who rounded the earth in the middle of
His hand;
This Great God,
85 Like a mammy bending over her baby,
Kneeled down in the dust
Toiling over a lump of clay
Till He shaped it in His own image;

Then into it He blew the breath of life,
90 And man became a living soul.
Amen. Amen.

*The Creation* by Aaron Douglas.
The Howard University Gallery of Art, Washington, D.C.

# MEET THE WRITER

## "Sermons in Verse"

**James Weldon Johnson** (1871–1938) was born in Florida shortly after the Civil War. He became a writer and a successful song-writer, professor of literature, journalist, lawyer, and diplomat. He served as U.S. consul in Venezuela and Nicaragua and later headed the NAACP, a civil rights organization.

Johnson began to write down sermons after attending a late-evening worship service in Kansas City. He said:

> **❝** He [the minister] appeared to be a bit self-conscious . . . and started to preach a formal sermon from a formal text. The congregation sat apathetic and dozing. He sensed that he was losing his audience and his opportunity. Suddenly he closed the Bible, stepped out from behind the pulpit, and began to preach. He started intoning the old folk-sermon that begins with the creation of the world and ends with Judgment Day. He was at once a changed man, free, at ease, and masterful. The change in the congregation was instantaneous. An electric current ran through the crowd. It was in a moment alive and quivering; and all the while the preacher held it in the palm of his hand. **❞**

Before the preacher had finished, Johnson was jotting down notes for "The Creation."

# MAKING MEANINGS

## First Thoughts

1. How would you feel if you'd just heard this sermon preached to you? Check your reading notes for ideas.

## Shaping Interpretations

2. In your opinion, why in line 69 does the preacher say God is still lonely?

3. List all the things God creates in this sermon and describe how he creates them. How is the creation of man different?

---

**Reading Check**

a. According to this poem, why does God decide to make the world?

b. God is not just spirit in this poem; he is shown taking action. What are three of his actions?

c. God smiles twice. What does each smile bring into being?

d. Why does God decide to create a man?

---

4. What is your reaction to line 85, where God is compared to a "mammy bending over her baby"? (How would it be different if God were compared to a scientist?)

5. What effect do you think the **refrain** has on the poem? What idea does it highlight?

6. If "The Creation" is a sermon, what lesson does it convey to you?

## Connecting with the Text

7. In the poem, God keeps saying of his creations, "That's good!" Do you share that feeling about those creations? Explain.

## Extending the Text

8. Every culture is interested in the question of how the world began. What other "pictures" of this great beginning do you know about?

# CHOICES: Building Your Portfolio

### Writer's Notebook

## 1. Collecting Ideas for Observational Writing

Choose a "moment of creation" to observe—something you can actually watch as it comes into being. Record your observations as exactly as you can. Pay attention to what you see, hear, smell, taste, and feel. If you've picked a slow-moving event, such as seeds sprouting, you might record daily observations in a log or chart.

### Creative Writing

## 2. And That's Good, Too

Write a hymn of praise for the world. List what's good about the world and use "That's good!" as a refrain. Try other techniques used in "The Creation," such as repeating key phrases (line 53: "Bring forth! Bring forth!") and using "customized" verbs. (In line 33, God didn't *form* the mountains; he "*bulged* the mountains *up*.")

### Choral Reading

## 3. All Together Now

Get together with a group of classmates and try different ways of performing the poem. Here are some choices to consider:

- Everybody reads the whole poem in unison.
- Two groups alternate reading lines or whole verses.
- One person reads some of the lines and the group reads all the other lines.
- Use musical accompaniment for dramatic effect.
- Use lighting for dramatic effect.

Decide on the most effective way to present the poem, and perform it for the class or for a group of your parents and friends.

# Before You Read

## SKY WOMAN

## Make the Connection

### Answer Me This

Since ancient times, people have told stories about the creation of the world and of living things. All over the world, people have made up stories to answer puzzling questions like, Who are we, and where did we come from? Why is there a blue roof over the earth? How did all the different animals come to be?

## Quickwrite

Suppose you lived thousands of years ago, before there was such a thing as science to suggest answers to your questions about the natural world. What are some of the things you might have wondered about? List at least five questions.

## Reading Skills and Strategies

### Recalling with Chronology: It's as Easy as 1, 2, 3

Keeping track of **chronology,** the time order of events, is one way to follow the action in a text. You might want to read this myth with a partner and take turns writing down key events in the order in which they happened.

It's easy to follow chronological order in a story. Just take these steps:

- Ask yourself, "*When* did each important event happen? What happened *before* that event? What happened *after?*"

- Look for words or phrases like *first, next, during,* and *at last* that signal when events happened.

## Background

### Literature and Social Studies

The Seneca were one of five Native American nations that united to form the Iroquois League more than a century before the first European colonies were established in North America. The League was centered in what is now New York State. For a time its territory stretched north to Canada, east to Maine, west to Michigan, and south to Tennessee.

As you will see in this myth, women played an influential role in the life of the Seneca, as they did in the lives of other Iroquois peoples.

## Elements of Literature

### Origin Myths

"Sky Woman" is an **origin myth** of the Seneca (see Background). This is the story the Seneca told many years ago to explain the beginnings of the earth, of animals, and of good and evil.

**A**n **origin myth** is an imaginative story that explains how something in the world came to be.

*For more on Myth, see pages 496–499 and the Handbook of Literary Terms.*

go.hrw.com

*LE0 7-6*

*The birds and animals saw Sky Woman falling. "Someone is coming," they said. "We must help her."*

# Sky Woman

Seneca, retold by
**Joseph Bruchac**

Hauh, oneh djadaondyus![1] Long ago, before this world existed, there was another world in the sky. It floated there like a great cloud. In that world there was no sun, but light came from the white blossoms of a great tree that grew in the center of the

1. **Hauh, oneh djadaondyus** (hou ōn′nu jä·dä·änd′yəs).

Sky World. The people who lived in the Sky World ate the fruit of that tree and they were happy.

The chief of the Sky World married a young woman. Soon after he married her, he discovered that she was expecting a child. Since he had not yet been with her, this angered him. He did not realize that she had become pregnant from inhaling his breath and that his wife and their child were destined to bring life to a new land.

That night, the chief had a powerful dream. In that dream he saw the great tree lying on its side. Dreams were considered to be a message from the Creator. So, when the next morning came, he gave orders for the Sky Tree to be uprooted. When this was done, it made a great hole in the Sky Land. Through that hole could be seen a place far below where there was nothing but water, and in that water birds and animals swam about. The light from the hole in the Sky Land shone down on that water. The chief's young wife came to look through that hole at the water below. Then, whether she slipped or she was pushed, she fell through. She grasped at the Sky Tree to keep from falling but only stripped off some of its seeds, which she held as she fell.

Below her, the birds and animals saw Sky Woman falling.

"Someone is coming," they said. "We must help her."

Then the wide-winged birds, the geese and swans, flew up and caught her between their wings. The great turtle rose up from the depths and floated with his back out of the water. Thus, when Sky Woman came down, she had a place to stand. The birds and fish and water animals then began to dive down to try to bring up earth from the bottom of that great sea. The duck and the pickerel[2] and the beaver all failed and floated up dead. At last the muskrat tried

---

2. **pickerel** (pik′ər·əl): small freshwater fish.

and brought up a handful of earth in its paw. When that earth was placed on the great turtle's back, it grew and grew until it became a continent. Sky Woman began to walk on that new earth. As she walked in a great circle, she scattered the seeds which she still held in her hand. Those seeds fell into her footprints, and the trees and other plants began to grow on the new earth.

Soon Sky Woman gave birth to a daughter, who grew to womanhood almost overnight. Sky Woman cautioned her daughter that she could go in any direction she wished except toward the west. But when her mother was not looking, the daughter walked toward the west, where she met the West Wind. When Sky Woman's daughter returned to her mother, she was pregnant. Sky Woman was worried, for she feared her daughter was too young to be a mother. Then, as time went on, a strange thing began to happen. Two voices could be heard speaking inside the belly of Sky Woman's daughter. The voices were those of her twin sons. One voice was gentle, and one was harsh.

"Let us be born in the right way," said the gentle voice.

"No," said the harsh voice, "I will push my way out here on the side."

Then the two boys were born. The one with the gentle voice was the Good Mind, and he was born in the normal way. But the one with the harsh voice was Flint, and he thrust out through his mother's side, killing her.

With the help of his grandmother, Sky Woman, the Good Mind buried his mother. He watered her grave and cared for it, and from that grave grew the squash, the beans, and the corn. Those were gifts for the people to come, given by his mother, who was now part of the earth.

The Good Mind then went about the earth, doing things which would be good for the people. He made useful trees, like the oak and the chestnut. Flint followed behind him and made briers[3] and poisonous plants. The Good Mind made berries of all kinds. Flint covered those berry bushes with sharp thorns. The Good Mind created such animals as the deer and the rabbit, animals which would feed the people. Flint produced loose poisonous snakes and biting insects. The Good Mind made fresh water which was clear and good to drink. Flint muddied the water and made it foul smelling.

The Good Mind's grandmother, Sky Woman, had been filled with sorrow since her daughter's death. Seeing all the bad things being done by Flint, she decided to leave the world.

"You will see me in the sky at night," she said

3. **briers** (brī′ərz): thorny bushes.

to her grandson the Good Mind. Then she left the earth. To this day, you can see her face, that of a caring grandmother, looking down from the Moon.

Finally the Good Mind could stand it no longer. He fought with his brother Flint and cast him out of the world. To this day, though, Flint's works and his bad thoughts remain in the world. They are in the mind of every person, just as every person also holds the good thoughts of the Good Mind. So we must always be aware of the thoughts that are in our minds to be sure that we do good things and not bad. Da neho.[4] So the story goes.

4. **Da neho** (dä nā′hō).

## MEET THE WRITER

### "Roots as Deep as the Rocks"

**Joseph Bruchac** (1942–     ) is a poet of Native American ancestry. He is also an editor who has put together two excellent anthologies of poetry. *Songs from This Earth on Turtle's Back* (1983) is a comprehensive collection of contemporary Native American poetry. *Breaking Silence* (1984), a collection of contemporary Asian American poetry, won an American Book Award in 1984. Bruchac also started a small press, the Greenfield Review Press, which has been a leading publisher of Native American writers. He himself has written, among many other books, several collections of Iroquois folk tales.

Bruchac believes that the theme of most Native American literature is survival—of a people, of a culture, of a land. He says:

66 Today, as we question Pentagon budgets, drug-ridden classrooms, and PCB-filled streams, many of us ask if the secret of surviving may be

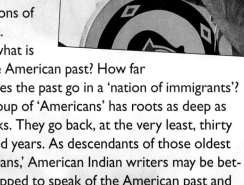

found not in the dreams of the future but in the lessons of the past.

But what is the true American past? How far back does the past go in a 'nation of immigrants'? One group of 'Americans' has roots as deep as the rocks. They go back, at the very least, thirty thousand years. As descendants of those oldest 'Americans,' American Indian writers may be better equipped to speak of the American past and to draw from it lessons relating to survival. 99

### More Roots

You can find more stories rooted in the past in Bruchac's *Iroquois Stories* (Greenfield Review).

# MAKING MEANINGS

## First Thoughts

1. The story tells us that Sky Woman "slipped or . . . was pushed" through the great hole in the Sky Land. Which do you think it was? Why?

## Shaping Interpretations

2. This **origin myth** answers several questions people might once have asked about the earth and human behavior. What are these questions? How do they compare with the ones you wrote for the Quickwrite on page 426?

3. Think about the creatures that helped Sky Woman on her journey down to the water world. Why would these specific animals have been important to the Seneca?

4. How does the myth explain the origin of good and evil?

## Connecting with the Text

5. The story states that "Flint's works and his bad thoughts remain in the world" and gives several examples of these works: briers, poisonous plants, thorns, poisonous snakes. Can you think of other examples of "Flint's works," both in nature and "in the mind of every person"?

### Reading Check

Draw a storyboard for this myth, a series of pictures illustrating the myth's **major events.** Arrange the events in **chronological order**—the order in which they happened. Share your storyboard with the class.

# CHOICES: Building Your Portfolio

## Writer's Notebook

### 1. Collecting Ideas for Observational Writing

Animals play a big part in Seneca life. List the animals you come across in your own daily life—a pet, a wild bird, a farm animal, even an insect or rodent. Pick one animal from your list, and observe it for at least fifteen minutes. Record exactly what you see and, if possible, what you hear. What does the animal look like? How does it move? What sounds does it make?

*Cat in the back yard. Tail twitches. Head jerks to the right—she sees a butterfly. Crouches, leaps, and misses.*

## Creative Writing

### 2. My Side of the Story

How do you think Sky Woman would tell her own story? Write "The Autobiography of Sky Woman." You could include her thoughts as she falls through space, her feelings toward the creatures who rescue her, her feelings about her daughter and grandsons, and her fears about her future.

## Creative Writing/ Speaking and Listening

### 3. And That's Why Water Is Wet: Telling a Story

Some origin myths may have arisen in response to children's questions, such as, Why is water wet? Brainstorm to come up with some *why* questions a four-year-old might ask grown-ups about the world. Then, pick one of your *why* questions and, with a classmate, role-play the grown-up telling a story to satisfy the curious child. First, write your story to answer the *why*. Then, rehearse and perform it for your classmates or a group of children. You might include props or pantomime.

## Research/ Speaking and Listening

### 4. Telling Tales

Research some other Native American creation stories. For example, *Back in the Beforetime* (Macmillan), edited by Jane L. Curry, is a collection of stories told by the California Indians; *They Dance in the Sky* (Houghton Mifflin) by Jean Guard and Ray A. Williamson presents creation myths from various regions, including the Great Plains, the Southeast, and the Northwest. You can also find some Native American creation myths in *In the Beginning: Creation Stories from Around the World* (Harcourt Brace) by Virginia Hamilton. Choose one myth to tell your class. Do research in the library or on the Internet to find information about the people and region from which the tale comes. Use this information in a brief introduction to your myth. If possible, include maps and pictures to make your introduction lively.

# LANGUAGE LINK   MINI-LESSON

## Style: Avoiding Clichés

*CLICHÉS
TO AVOID*

*break the
ice*

*busy as a
bee*

*crack of
dawn*

*clear as a
bell*

*as quiet as
a mouse*

*eat like a
horse*

*on top of
the world*

*as red as
a beet*

Look at the underlined phrases in these sentences. Which one seems fresher and more interesting?

> Sky Woman <u>was as beautiful as the West Wind</u>.

> Sky Woman was <u>as pretty as a picture</u>.

Both sentences contain figures of speech. The first one may be new to you: *as beautiful as the West Wind.* How beautiful is that? The surprise comparison may make you imagine several images: a field of wheat, perhaps, rippling like a sea of gold, or a cool breeze rising off the shore. For most readers the comparison in the second sentence does none of that. It's a **cliché** (klē · shā′)—a figure of speech that has lost its power because people have overused it.

### Try It Out

➤ Rewrite each sentence below to replace the cliché with fresher language. Be sure to compare your rewrites with those of other students.

1. The Chief of Heaven was <u>as mad as a hornet</u>.
2. Sky Woman did not deserve any punishment, for she had been <u>as good as gold</u>.
3. The animals were <u>busy as beavers</u> helping Sky Woman.

➤ When you revise something you've written, look closely at the comparisons you've used and ask yourself, "Did I make this up, or is it something people always say?" If the latter, the phrase is probably a cliché. Replace it, if you can, with a comparison that you've never heard before.

# SPELLING   HOW TO OWN A WORD

**Language
Handbook
H E L P**

*See Adding
Prefixes and
Suffixes,
pages
781-782.*

## Adding Suffixes: Change *y* to *i*

What do these words have in common?

easy   happy   pretty   lonely   stormy

Correct: They all end with *y* preceded by a consonant. When you add a **suffix**—an ending such as *-er, -est, -ness,* or *-ly*—to most words that end with *y* preceded by a consonant, you have to follow this spelling rule: First, change the *y* to *i*; then, add the suffix.

| | | | | |
|---|---|---|---|---|
| easy | + | *suffix* | = | eas**ily**   eas**ier** |
| happy | + | *suffix* | = | happ**ily**   happ**iness** |
| lonely | + | *suffix* | = | lonel**ier**   lonel**iest** |

Get together with a partner, and make a list of five more words that end in *y* preceded by a consonant. Then, follow the *y*-to-*i* rule, and add a suffix to each word. Here are two words to get you started: *silly, funny.*

# Reading Skills and Strategies

## ORGANIZING IDEAS

### Sequencing: What Happens?

Organizers can be handy for putting in order the details of a narrative or an informative report. See for yourself—as you read the narratives in this collection, try using the sequencing chart below to organize "what happens."

**Sequencing Chart for a Narrative**

- Main characters
- Their problem (conflict)
- Event 1
- Event 2
- Event 3
- (List other events.)
- Resolution

### Cause and Effect: Why Things Happen

You can make some texts, especially informative reports, clearer by looking at what caused certain events to happen. Use organizers like the ones below to sort out causes and effects.

**Sequencing Charts for Cause and Effect**

**What Happened**
Earthquake occurred in Alaska.

**Effect**
Buildings fell.

**Effect**
Roads buckled.

**OR**

**What Happened (Effect)**
Port towns suffered damage in quake.

**Cause**
Ground on coast is not solid. Soil slides.

### Outlining: Finding the Skeleton

It's also helpful to **outline** the ideas in an informative text. Outlining can help you uncover the skeleton that holds the text together: its main ideas and supporting details. Here is an example of an informal outline.

**Informal Outline**

Earthquake occurred in Alaska (main idea)
 Roads buckled (supporting detail)
 Houses split in two
 Earth split open
Port towns were damaged
 Waterfronts sank
 Oil tanks burned
(and so on)

### Shake, Rattle, and Roll

You're about to be set down in the middle of an earthquake. Have one of these organizers ready to help you sift through the information as you read.

**Apply the strategy on the next page.**

# Before You Read

## WHEN THE EARTH SHAKES

## Make the Connection

### Nature Comes Out Swinging

From the title "When the Earth Shakes," you can probably guess that you're going to read about one of nature's most awesome forces: earthquakes.

## Quickwrite

**KWL.** On a blank sheet of paper, make a chart like this:

| What I Know | What I Want to Know | What I Learned |
|---|---|---|
| | | |

With a group of classmates, brainstorm to find out what you already know and what you want to learn about earthquakes. Write your ideas in the first two columns. As you're reading, you'll fill in the What I Learned column. As you read, think about how the new information relates to what you already know. Does it make you think of any new questions?

**go.hrw.com**
*LEO 7-6*

## Reading Skills and Strategies

### Tracking Cause and Effect

On page 433, you saw two kinds of charts you can use to sum up the important details in an informative essay. As you read "When the Earth Shakes," notice how clearly the author explains the causes of the earthquake and its effects. Try using one of the organizers on page 433 to sum up these causes and effects. Fill out the chart after you've finished reading.

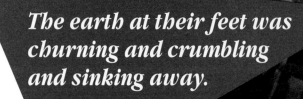

*The earth at their feet was churning and crumbling and sinking away.*

# When the Earth Shakes

Patricia Lauber

*from* **Earthquakes: New Scientific Ideas About How and Why the Earth Shakes**

It was late afternoon, March 27, 1964. Above Alaska the sky was the color of lead, and in some places a light snow fell. Anchorage, the biggest city, lay quiet, for this gray day was both Good Friday and the eve of Passover.

Schools were empty. Many shops and offices had closed early, and at 5:30 most people were home. Outside, the air was raw, the sky dark. Inside, lights glowed, furnaces hummed, and pots simmered on stoves.

Then it happened. Suddenly the familiar and the cozy vanished. In their place came the strange and the fearful.

At Turnagain, on the edge of Anchorage, people first heard a deep rumble, like the sound of thunder. Next, their houses began to shake. They rushed to their doors, looked out, and thought the world was coming to an end. The earth at their feet was <u>churning</u> and crumbling and sinking away. It was cracking into huge, tilted blocks.

Neighbor helped neighbor to escape. Behind them trees fell. Houses were ripped in two or upended.

Turnagain was built on high ground, on a <u>bluff</u> overlooking the water. The violent shaking triggered a landslide. The front of the bluff slid away, carrying houses and garages with it.

In downtown Anchorage, big buildings creaked and groaned. Their floors rose and fell in waves.

Automobiles bounced like rubber balls. Great chunks of buildings crashed to the street. A movie theater dropped thirty feet into a hole that opened beneath it. A flower shop snapped in two.

Anchorage was not alone in this nightmare. As it shook and cracked and jolted, so did much of Alaska. Buildings trembled and fell. Land tore open. Highways <u>buckled</u>. Railroad tracks were twisted into curls of steel. Snow-capped mountains shuddered, and ice and rock swept down their slopes.

Alaska had been struck by a mighty earthquake that hit without warning. At 5:35 P.M. all was well. By 5:38 half of Alaska seemed to be in the grip of an angry giant. The earth shook with terrible violence.

All along the coast, port towns suffered great damage. One reason was the kind of land on which they stood.

Much of Alaska's coast is rugged, rocky land that stands high above the water. The port towns were built in the low-lying places. But here the ground was not very solid. Also, it sloped down steeply to the ocean floor. When the earthquake shook such land, the soil began to slide. Whole waterfronts vanished in underwater landslides.

That was one of the things that happened at Seward.

Seward was both a port and the end of a rail line. The rail line brought in oil, which was stored in tanks before being shipped. When the earthquake hit, the tanks broke and the oil caught fire.

Flames roared along the waterfront. Just then a great landslide took place. The entire waterfront slid into the bay. The slide caused water to surge away from the land. Burning oil was carried into the bay and then swept back. Fiery water flooded inland. Tugs, fishing boats, and a tanker were washed ashore by the great surge of water. Docks and small-boat harbors

## WORDS TO OWN

**churning** (chʉrn′iŋ) v.: shaking or stirring violently, like milk being made into butter in a churn.
**bluff** (bluf) n.: steep cliff.
**buckled** (buk′əld) v.: collapsed (usually under pressure).

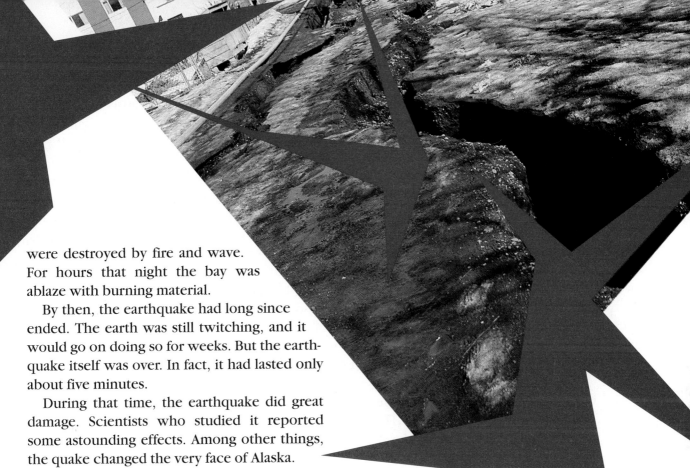

were destroyed by fire and wave. For hours that night the bay was ablaze with burning material.

By then, the earthquake had long since ended. The earth was still twitching, and it would go on doing so for weeks. But the earthquake itself was over. In fact, it had lasted only about five minutes.

During that time, the earthquake did great damage. Scientists who studied it reported some astounding effects. Among other things, the quake changed the very face of Alaska.

In the Gulf of Alaska the ocean floor rose. So did land along the coast. All in all, a region the size of Maine was lifted three to eight feet. Inland, another big region sank. Part of an island rose thirty-eight feet. When the quake ended, the town of Valdez was ten feet higher than it had been before.

A whole peninsula moved. Carrying along its mountains and lakes, Kenai Peninsula moved sideways as much as sixty feet and sank seven feet or more.

There were other changes. Near Valdez a huge wave reached 220 feet above sea level and clawed at the earth. A piece of land 4,000 feet long and 600 feet wide fell into the sea.

Water in Kenai Lake sloshed back and forth. It moved with such force that its water and ice peeled the bark off trees along the shore.

A mountain split apart. One side of it plunged downward, flying over a ridge like a skier taking a jump. The flying mountain spread into a carpet of rocks a mile long and two miles wide. The carpet traveled without touching the ground. Finally it landed on a glacier. Scientists later found it there and figured out what had happened.

The 1964 Alaska earthquake was one of the strongest ever recorded. It was one of the mightiest earthquakes known to man. But it took place for the same reason that all earthquakes do. It took place because rock within the earth suddenly shifted.

An earthquake can be strong, as Alaska's was in 1964. Or it can be slight. It can be so slight that no person feels it, though instruments record it. But big or small, an earthquake is just what its name says it is—a shaking of the earth. The earth shakes when rock within it suddenly shifts.

The earth is mostly made of rock. Beneath its soil and oceans, it is a big ball of rock. The ball has three main regions: the core, the mantle, and the crust. They are arranged like the layers of an onion. The core is at the center of the earth. The mantle surrounds the core. The crust surrounds the mantle.

Like the crust on a loaf of bread, the earth's crust is a thin outside covering. It is made of two main kinds of rock.

One is a fairly light rock. Its most familiar form is granite, and that is what it is often called. The upper part of the continents is made of this granitelike rock. It is usually about twenty-five miles thick. The continental crust does not end at the water's edge. It reaches out under the sea in what is called a continental shelf. Where the shelf ends, the oceanic crust begins.

The crust under the oceans is a different kind of rock. It is much more dense. That is, the rock particles are packed more closely together. The most familiar form of this rock is the dark, heavy kind called basalt. The crust under the oceans is about five miles thick.

The inside of the earth is very hot. And so the crust grows hotter as it goes deeper. Oil wells drilled deep into the crust reach rock hot enough to boil water. When volcanoes erupt, molten rock spills out of them. The rock may have a temperature of two thousand degrees Fahrenheit. This molten rock has come from the lower crust or upper mantle.

The mantle is about 1,800 miles thick. It is made of rock, but this is not rock as we know it. The rock is under very great pressure, deep within the earth. It is also very hot. The heat and pressure make the rock behave in ways that are strange to us.

Sometimes rock of the mantle behaves like a very gummy liquid. It can flow like thick tar.

But it also behaves like a solid. It can suddenly shift or snap. When it does, an earthquake takes place. Earthquakes also occur when rock of the crust suddenly shifts or breaks.

Rock shifts or breaks for the same reason that anything else does: because it has been put under great strain. If you take a ruler and bend it, you are putting it under strain. If you bend, or strain, it too much, it will break.

There are forces within the earth that bend, squeeze, and twist the rock of the crust and the upper mantle. As a result, the rock is put under great strain. That is, a large amount of energy is stored in it as strain. When the strain becomes too great, the rock suddenly gives way and the stored-up energy is released.

Something like this happens if you shoot a bow and arrow. As you pull, the bow and string are bent and forced out of shape. Energy from your muscles is stored in them as strain. When you let go, the bow and string snap back into shape, and the stored-up energy is released. It speeds the arrow through the air.

Energy released from rock takes the form of waves. A wave is a kind of giant push. It is a push that passes from one rock particle to the next, much as a push can pass through a line of people. Imagine ten people lined up, each with his hands on the person ahead. If the last person in line is given a sharp push, the push will be felt all through the line. The people stay in place, but the push passes through them.

That is how earthquake waves travel through the inside of the earth. The pushes pass from one rock particle to the next.

You can feel what happens if you snap a stick between your hands. As you slowly bend it, energy is stored as strain. Finally the strain becomes too great. The stick snaps. All the stored-up energy is released. And you feel a sharp stinging. Stored-up energy has changed to waves that are passing through the wood.

---

## WORDS TO OWN

**particles** (pärt'i·kəlz) n.: tiny pieces.

---

One wood particle pushes the next. When the pushes reach your hands, you feel them as a sting.

Meanwhile, the broken ends of the stick are vibrating. That is, they are very quickly moving back and forth. They set air waves in motion. Particles of air push other particles. Waves, or pushes, pass through the air. These movements are the source of the sound you hear when the stick snaps.

When an earthquake takes place, waves travel out from the shifting rock in all directions.

Some waves travel through the air. They account for the rumbling sounds that may accompany an earthquake.

Some waves travel deep in the earth. They are seldom felt by people. But instruments in earthquake observatories record them. Earthquake waves that pass through the earth are recorded thousands of miles away.

Some waves travel along the earth's surface. Surface waves are the ones that do the damage—the ones that shake buildings, tear up roads, and cause landslides.

They are not, however, the only cause of earthquake damage. There can be another kind, and it is a kind that comes from the sea.

---

### WORDS TO OWN
**observatories** (əb·zʉrv′ə·tôr′ēz) *n.*: buildings equipped for scientific observation.

---

## MEET THE WRITER

### "I'm Always Learning Something"

**Patricia Lauber** (1924–    ) has written more than sixty books on subjects ranging from volcanoes to robots and much in between. Says Lauber:

66 I write about anything that interests me, dogs, horses, forests, birds, mysteries, life in other countries. Some of my books are fiction, and some are nonfiction, but all are based on what I've seen around me. I like to stand and stare at things, to talk with people, and to read a lot. From this I'm always learning something I didn't know before. Some time later, when I've had a chance to think things over, I write down what I heard, saw, felt, and thought. 99

When Lauber is not writing, she is fond of hiking, dancing, reading, listening to music, seeing plays, and talking. Commenting on her busy schedule, she says:

66 It's a little hard to fit everything in, but one nice thing about being a writer is that sailing a boat or exploring a forest can often be described as 'doing research.' 99

### More That Lauber Learned

For another look at nature unleashed, read Patricia Lauber's book *Volcano: The Eruption and Healing of Mount St. Helens* (Bradbury).

# MAKING MEANINGS

## First Thoughts

1. What natural disaster could occur in your area? What steps would you take to protect your life and the lives of others?

## Shaping Interpretations

2. If you were a teacher, what would you want your students to understand and remember after reading "When the Earth Shakes"? Fill in one of the **cause-and-effect organizers** before you answer this question.

3. Like fiction writers, science writers try to create **suspense.** They want to make us eager to find out what happens next. Where in this selection did you feel suspense? At these moments, what questions did Lauber plant in your mind?

4. The author gives some good examples to explain difficult information. List at least three of the examples, and tell how they help the reader understand earthquakes.

## Challenging the Text

5. What kinds of graphic aids—charts, graphs, time lines, drawings, and illustrations—could you use to make the facts and statistics in this article easier to understand? What headings could you add to help your reader follow the main ideas?

**Reading Check**

Fill in the L column in the KWL chart you began in response to the Quickwrite on page 434. Then, choose one or two interesting or surprising things you learned, and share them with a partner.

(Left) Kobe, Japan, 1995.
(Right) San Francisco, 1989.

# CHOICES: Building Your Portfolio

## Writer's Notebook

### 1. Collecting Ideas for Observational Writing

Think of a time when some natural event or aspect of nature—such as a snowstorm, an attack of mosquitoes, or a rash caused by poison ivy—frightened you or made you uncomfortable. Suppose you wanted to describe your experience to a friend: What details would you include? Record details just as they come to you when you picture your experience.

> *The hurricane:*
> *no electricity; trying to remember where we stored the candles; buckets under leaks; trees bending like rubber*

## Research/Writing

### 2. Earthquake Report

In the twentieth century major earthquakes have hit San Francisco, Los Angeles, Mexico City, Tokyo, and Kobe. Research one of these big quakes in your local library or on the Internet. Look for news accounts written at the time. Write a report about the quake that presents not only facts— how strong the quake was, how long it lasted, how much damage it caused, and so on—but also the best human-interest stories you turn up in the course of your research.

## Science/Art

### 3. What's in the World?

Draw a diagram—or make a 3-D model if you're ambitious—that shows the three layers of the earth. Along with your drawing or model, provide a brief explanation of how the rock of the earth's mantle or crust can act to create earthquakes, volcanic eruptions, and tidal waves.

## Creative Writing

### 4. Then Earth Shuddered and Said—

Forget all the scientific facts you know about earthquakes for a moment. Tell an imaginative story to explain the causes of an earthquake.

(Left) Kobe, Japan, 1995.
(Right) San Francisco, 1989.

## Style: Formal and Informal English

Compare these two sentences:

> Examine the statistics on the Alaska earthquake.

> Check out the stats on that Alaska shake.

The sentences mean the same thing, but they create different effects. The first sentence is an example of **formal English.** The second sentence is an example of **informal English.**

Formal English is the language you use for solemn occasions, such as speeches and graduation ceremonies, and in serious papers and reports. Formal English doesn't include slang or colloquial expressions.

Informal English is used in everyday speaking and writing. You use informal English when you talk with family members or friends and when you write personal letters or journal entries. Informal English includes colloquial expressions and slang.

### Try It Out

Rewrite each paragraph, making the informal paragraph formal and the formal paragraph informal.

INFORMAL

Check it out, man—a humongous quake socked Alaska at five o'clock in the P.M., and hoo, boy! We give this big one an eight on the old Richter.

FORMAL

We request aid. The recent earth tremor caused our building to collapse. We are currently situated beneath a mass of structural material. We are two adults and a juvenile. We request aid.

# VOCABULARY ▐ HOW TO OWN A WORD

**WORD BANK**

*churning*
*bluff*
*buckled*
*particles*
*observatories*

## Vocabulary for the Workplace: Jack of All Trades

1. Suppose you work as a chemist. Write a press release about an experiment, using two words from the Word Bank.
2. Imagine that you're an astronomer. Write a memo to the government agency that funds your work, describing the work. Use one word from the Word Bank.
3. Now, suppose you're an archaeologist directing a team of workers who are digging up an ancient city destroyed by an earthquake. Write some directions for your workers, using at least three of the words in the Word Bank.

# Elements of Literature

## NONFICTION: The Main Idea

### What's the Point?

In 1989, a huge earthquake shook San Francisco. The quake hit during a World Series game between the San Francisco Giants and the Oakland A's. These teams had never met in the playoffs before. Oakland, however, had won the series in the 1970s.

Can you figure out what this paragraph is about? Probably not. The sentences are clear; the facts are true; the details are concrete—but the paragraph doesn't hang together.

### Here's the Point

What's missing is a focus, a topic, a main idea with supporting details that make the main idea pop out. In the following paragraph, look for the **topic**—what the paragraph is all about—and **main idea**—the writer's most important point. What details and evidence support the main idea?

On the afternoon of Good Friday, March 27, 1964, Anchorage, Alaska, was shaken apart by the most violent earthquake ever recorded in the United States. It measured 8.4 on the Richter scale. Government Hill Elementary School was split in two when the ground beneath it dropped. Houses began sliding apart, cracks in the pavement opened and closed like huge jaws, the ground rolled in huge waves. In the first three days after the quake, three hundred aftershocks shook the buildings that remained standing.

—Seymour Simon, *Earthquakes*

This paragraph hangs together. The first sentence states the topic and main idea; the next sentence provides evidence—a statistic—to prove the point. The next two sentences clarify the main idea by providing details. The final sentence provides statistics that reinforce the main idea about the violence of the quake.

### Where's the Point?

Sometimes the main idea is implied rather than stated. It's up to you to put all the details together and figure out the main idea yourself.

In a long piece of writing, a writer develops the main idea over many paragraphs. Look at the opening of "When the Earth Shakes" (page 436). All the paragraphs promote one idea: The Alaska earthquake was destructive. The author finally states this idea, on page 437—but by then you've probably gotten the point.

What happens when you're reading nonfiction and the main idea escapes you? These strategies will help you "get the point":

1. Look at the **main ideas** of the different paragraphs. What do they add up to?

2. Check the beginning and end of each paragraph for a **key passage** that might state the central idea.

3. If you find no stated main idea, summarize the important details. Your summary should lead you to the main idea.

4. If the main idea seems to be buried under an earthquake's rubble, form a rescue team, and uncover the idea by talking it over.

# Before You Read

## SURVIVE THE SAVAGE SEA

## Make the Connection

### Alone and Adrift

In E. E. Cummings's poem on page 461, the sea is a wonderful place where four girls find various treasures. Here is another look at the sea—this time as a killer. As you'll see, this old earth can be destructive as well as supportive.

**Think and pair.** With a partner, brainstorm to come up with problems you would face and solutions you might find if you were lost at sea. You could go back and forth—one of you presenting a problem and the other suggesting a solution—and then trade roles. Record your ideas in a two-column chart like this one:

| Problem | Solution |
|---------|----------|
| no fresh water | catch rain |
|  |  |

## Quickwrite

In a fight for survival, what kind of person would you want beside you? List the qualities you think would help a person survive a disaster.

## Elements of Literature

### Main Idea: I Get Your Point

The **main idea** of a text is the most important idea, the one that the writer wants you to remember. One way to find the main idea when you're reading nonfiction is to look for the most important word in each paragraph or section you read. Try this strategy as you read about this life-and-death conflict with a powerful force of nature.

> The **main idea** is the most important idea expressed in a paragraph or a selection.
>
> *For more on Main Idea, see page 443 and the Handbook of Literary Terms.*

## Reading Skills and Strategies

### Adjusting Reading Rate: Changing the Pace

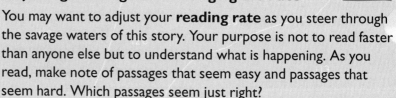

You may want to adjust your **reading rate** as you steer through the savage waters of this story. Your purpose is not to read faster than anyone else but to understand what is happening. As you read, make note of passages that seem easy and passages that seem hard. Which passages seem just right?

## Background

### Literature and Real Life

On June 15, 1972, killer whales attacked the sailing ship *Lucette* in the Pacific Ocean. The boat sank in sixty seconds. On board the *Lucette* were Dougal Robertson and his wife, Lyn; their oldest son, Douglas; their twelve-year-old twins, Neil and Sandy; and a young family friend, Robin. Set adrift on a rubber raft and a fiberglass dinghy, Robertson and his crew began their struggle to survive. Steering a course by the sun and stars, they made for the coast of Costa Rica, a thousand miles away.

*This was not our environment, and the beasts
around us would eat us if we failed.*

# from Survive the Savage Sea

### Dougal Robertson

## First Day

We sat on the salvaged pieces of flotsam[1] lying on the raft floor,
our faces a pale bilious[2] color under the bright yellow canopy,
and stared at each other, the shock of the last few minutes gradually
seeping through to our consciousness. Neil, his teddy bears gone,
sobbed in accompaniment to Sandy's hiccup cry, while Lyn repeated the
Lord's Prayer, then, comforting them, sang the hymn "For Those in Peril
on the Sea." Douglas and Robin watched at the doors of the canopy to

1. **flotsam:** floating wreckage of a ship or its cargo.
2. **bilious:** yellowish or greenish, as if suffering from liver or gallbladder problems. (Bile is
secreted by the liver.)

retrieve any useful pieces of <u>debris</u> which might float within reach and gazed with dumb longing at the distant five-gallon water container, bobbing its polystyrene[3] lightness ever further away from us in the steady trade wind. The dinghy *Ednamair* wallowed, swamped, nearby with a line attached to it from the raft, and our eyes traveled over and beyond to the heaving undulations of the horizon, already searching for a rescue ship even while knowing there would not be one. Our eyes traveled fruitlessly across the limitless waste of sea and sky, then once more ranged over the scattering debris. Of the killer whales which had so recently shattered our very existence, there was no sign. Lyn's sewing basket floated close and it was brought aboard followed by a couple of empty boxes, the canvas raft cover, and a plastic cup.

I leaned across to Neil and put my arm round him, "It's all right now, son, we're safe and the whales have gone." He looked at me reproachfully. "We're not crying cos we're frightened," he sobbed. "We're crying cos Lucy's gone."[4] Lyn gazed at me over their heads, her eyes filling with tears. "Me too," she said, and after a moment added, "I suppose we'd better find out how we stand." . . .

We cleared a space on the floor and opened the survival kit, which was part of the raft's equipment and was contained in a three-foot-long polythene cylinder; slowly we took stock:

Vitamin-fortified bread and glucose[5] for ten men for two days;

Eighteen pints of water, eight flares[6] (two parachute, six hand);

One bailer, two large fishhooks, two small, one spinner and trace, and a twenty-five-pound breaking strain fishing line;

A patent knife which would not puncture

the raft (or anything else for that matter), a signal mirror, torch,[7] first-aid box, two sea anchors, instruction book, bellows, and three paddles.

In addition to this there was the bag of a dozen onions which I had given to Sandy, to which Lyn had added a one-pound tin of biscuits and a bottle containing about half a pound of glucose sweets, ten oranges, and six lemons. How long would this have to last us? As I looked around our <u>meager</u> stores my heart sank and it must have shown on my face, for Lyn put her hand on mine; "We must get these boys to land," she said quietly. "If we do nothing else with our lives, we must get them to land!" I looked at her and nodded, "Of course, we'll make it!" The answer came from my heart but my head was telling me a different story. . . .

## Sixth Day

. . . At four in the morning we were dozing quietly when a flying fish flew straight through the door of the raft, striking Lyn in the face. Now Lyn is a very steady and reliable person in a crisis; she seems to be able to do the right thing at the right time automatically while less able people like myself are floundering around wondering what to do, but her reaction to being slapped in the face by a wet fish at four in the morning, after all our previous excitement, had us all scrambling around the raft looking for something like the Loch Ness monster[8] until the eight-inch leviathan[9] was finally secured and made safe for breakfast. . . .

---

7. **torch:** British English for "flashlight."
8. **Loch** (läkh) **Ness monster:** thirty-foot-long sea monster supposedly living in a lake in northern Scotland. (*Loch* is Scottish for "lake.")
9. **leviathan** (lə·vī′ə·thən): Leviathan is a huge sea monster mentioned in the Bible.

---

3. **polystyrene:** type of plastic. Polythene, which is mentioned below, is another kind of plastic.
4. **Lucy's gone:** Neil means the *Lucette,* their ship.
5. **glucose:** kind of sugar that is easily digested.
6. **flares:** very bright lights used as distress signals.

## WORDS TO OWN

**debris** (də·brē′) *n.*: rough, broken bits of litter.
**meager** (mē′gər) *adj.*: literally, very thin; inadequate; not enough.

---

## Seventh Day

. . . Douglas, lazily watching the dispersing clouds, suddenly sat up with a start, pointing excitedly. "A ship! A ship! It's a ship!" We all crowded to the door of the raft, staring in the direction of his pointing finger; a cargo vessel of about six thousand tons was approaching us on a course that would bring her within three miles of us. I felt my heart pound against my ribs. "Get out the flares," I said hoarsely, "and pass them to me in the dinghy; they'll see us better from there."

Three miles was a fair distance, but on a dull day like this, against a background of rain, they should see us easily. I clambered into the dinghy and Douglas passed me the rockets and hand flares; my hands trembled as I ripped open a parachute rocket flare and, with a mute appeal to the thing to fire, struck the igniter on the fuse. It spluttered and hissed, then roared off on a trajectory high above the raft, its pinkish magnesium flare slowly spiraling downward leaving a trail of smoke in the sky. They couldn't fail to see it. I waited a moment or two watching for the ship to alter course, then struck a hand flare, holding it high above my head. The blinding red light was hot to hold and I pointed it away from the wind to ease my hand, the red embers of the flare dropping into the dinghy; as it went out I struck another, smoke from the first now a rising plume in the sky; surely they must see that. I waited a little, my hands trembling. "This chance might not come again," I said, anxious faces crowding the door of the raft; "I'm going to use our last rocket flare and one more hand flare." We watched tensely as the second rocket flare soared and spiraled its gleaming distress message high above us; desperately I struck the third hand flare and held it high, standing on the thwart and holding on to the mast. "Look, look! . . ." I shouted. "Set fire to the sail!" Lyn's voice. I stuck the flare to the sail but it only melted. The ship sailed on, slowly disappearing behind a rain shower, and when she reappeared her hull[10] was half obscured by the horizon, five miles distant and disappearing fast. The time was eleven o'clock. My shoulders drooped. "We daren't use another," I said. "They won't see it now and we have to keep something for the next one." We had three hand flares left. Lyn smiled cheerfully. "It says in the instruction book that the first one probably wouldn't see us," she said slowly, "and I'd already told the twins not to expect anything." She gathered the twins to her, comfortingly. We stared at the dwindling speck on the horizon and felt so lonely that it hurt. "I'm sorry, lads." I felt very tired. "We used to consider that one of the most important tenets of good seamanship was 'Keep a good lookout.' That lot seem to be pretty poor seamen!"

Our position was 3° north and 240 miles west of Espinosa (almost 95°20´W) on Wednesday 21 June, midsummer's day, on the route from Panama to the Marquesas; the ship was westbound. I surveyed the empty flare cartons bitterly, and the one smoke flare which was damp and wouldn't work, and something happened to me in that instant, that for me changed the whole aspect of our predicament. If these poor bloody seamen couldn't rescue us, then we would have to make it on our own and to the devil with them. We would survive without them, yes, and that was the word from now on, "survival," not "rescue" or "help" or dependence of any kind, just survival. I felt the strength flooding through me, lifting me from the depression of disappointment to a state of almost cheerful abandon. I felt the bitter aggression of the predator fill my mind. This was not our environment, and the beasts around us would eat us if we failed. We would carve a place for ourselves among them; they had

---

10. **hull:** main body of a ship.

- - - - - - - - - - - - - - - - - - - - - - - - - - - - - - -

### WORDS TO OWN

**tenets** (ten'its) *n*.: beliefs of a group; doctrines.

- - - - - - - - - - - - - - - - - - - - - - - - - - - - - - -

millions of years of adaptation on their side, but we had brains and some tools. We would live for three months or six months from the sea if necessary, but "we would get these boys to land" as Lyn had said, and we would do it ourselves if there was no other way. From that instant on, I became a savage. . . .

## Fourteenth Day

. . . We had a sip of water for breakfast with no dried food to detract from its value, after which I crossed to the dinghy to try for a dorado.[11] The heat of the sun's rays beat on my head like a club and my mouth, dry like lizard skin, felt full of my tongue; the slightest exertion left me breathless. I picked up the spear; the dorado were all deep down as if they knew I was looking for them. A bump at the stern[12] of the raft attracted Sandy's attention. "Turtle!" he yelled. This one was much smaller than the first and with great care it was caught and passed through the raft—with Douglas guarding its beak, and the others its claws, from damaging the fabric—to me on the dinghy, where I lifted it aboard without much trouble. I wrapped a piece of tape around the broken knife blade and made the incision into its throat. "Catch the blood," Lyn called from the raft. "It should be all right to drink a little." I held the plastic cup under the copious flow of blood; the cup filled quickly and I stuck another under as soon as it was full, then, raising the full cup to my lips, tested it cautiously. It wasn't salty at all! I tilted the cup and drained it. "Good stuff!" I shouted. I felt as if I had just consumed the elixir of life.[13] "Here, take this," and I passed the bailer full of blood, about a pint, into the raft for the others to drink. Lyn said afterward she had imagined that she would have to force it down us, and the sight of me draining the cup, my moustache

11. **dorado:** kind of fish; also called a dolphin.
12. **stern:** back end of a vessel.
13. **elixir** (ē·liks′ir) **of life:** substance that some people in the Middle Ages believed existed and would allow people to live forever.

dripping blood, was quite revolting. I don't know what I looked like, but it certainly tasted good, and as the others followed my example it seemed they thought so too. I passed another pint across, and though some of this coagulated[14] before it could be drunk, the jelly was cut up and the released serum[15] collected and used as a gravy with the dried turtle and fish.

I set to cutting my way into the turtle much refreshed, and even with the broken knife made faster work of it than the first one, both because it was smaller and, being younger, the shell was not so tough; the fact that I now knew my way around inside a turtle helped a lot too. . . .

I looked around the raft at the remains of Robin and the Robertson family, water-wrinkled skin covered with salt-water boils[16] and raw red patches of rash, lying in the bottom of the raft, unmoving except to bail occasionally, and then only halfheartedly, for the water was cooling in the heat of the day; our bones showed clearly through our scanty flesh; we had become much thinner these last few days and our condition was deteriorating fast. The raft was killing us with its demands on our energy. Douglas looked across at me, "Do you think it'll rain tonight, Dad?" I looked at him and shrugged, looked at the sky, not a cloud. "I suppose it could do," I said. "Do you think it will?" he insisted. "For heaven's sake, Douglas, I'm not a prophet," I said testily. "We'll just have to wait it out." His eyes looked hopelessly at the blue of the sea from the deep cavities under his brow; how could I comfort him when he knew

14. **coagulated:** solidified; clotted.
15. **serum:** clear liquid left over after blood coagulates.
16. **boils:** painful, infected swellings.

---

## WORDS TO OWN

**copious** (kō′pē·əs) *adj.*: plentiful.
**scanty** (skan′tē) *adj.*: inadequate. *Scanty* and *meager* are synonyms; *scanty* and *copious* are antonyms.
**deteriorating** (dē·tir′ē·ə·rāt′iŋ) *v.*: getting worse.
**testily** (tes′tə·lē) *adv.*: irritably.

---

as well as I that it might not rain for a week, and that we'd be dead by then. I said, "Fresh turtle for tea,[17] we can suck something out of that." We could live on turtles, maybe.

We took no water that evening, only a little for the twins. We talked of the dishes we'd like

17. **tea:** in Britain, a light meal eaten in the late afternoon.

to eat in the gathering twilight and I chose fresh fruit salad and ice cream; Lyn, a tin of apricots; Robin, strawberries and ice cream with milk; Douglas, the same as me; Neil, chocolate chip ice cream; Sandy, fresh fruit, ice cream and milk—gallons of ice-cool milk. Later that night as I took the watch over from Douglas, he described in detail the dish he had dreamed up

## LITERATURE AND REAL LIFE

### He Ate Ants

In June 1995, Captain Scott O'Grady was flying a patrol over Bosnia for the North Atlantic Treaty Organization (NATO) as part of an effort by the major Western powers and the United Nations to stem years of bloodshed in Bosnia. His radar showed that a surface-to-air missile was seconds from destroying his plane. After he bailed out, he pulled his parachute cord too quickly. O'Grady drifted slowly over a clear sky at twenty thousand feet, in full view of hostile Serbian soldiers. Upon landing, he scrambled into a clump of nearby bushes and began six agonizing days of life on the run.

"Most of the time, my face was in the dirt, just praying that no one would see me," O'Grady said. He described himself as "a scared little bunny rabbit, trying to hide, trying to survive. . . . I ate grass. When you're hungry, you'll eat anything." "Anything" included ants. "They scamper really quickly and it's hard to get them," he laughed. After finishing the water in his survival kit, he prayed for rain, and "God delivered." He then relied on tricks from his survival training: collecting dew in plastic packets and squeezing rainwater from a sponge and from his wool socks.

O'Grady was finally able to move into a clearing and send off a signal from his radio that led to a helicopter rescue. After sending up a flare to guide the helicopters, O'Grady loaded his gun and made a frantic dash, forgetting his training for the first time. "The one thing they tell you is never run at a helicopter with a loaded gun," he said with a grin.

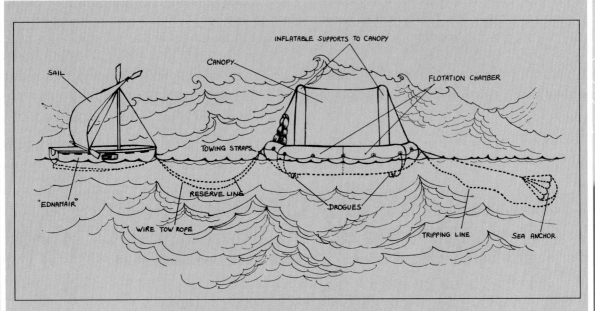

Labels in the diagram:
INFLATABLE SUPPORTS TO CANOPY
CANOPY
FLOTATION CHAMBER
SAIL
TOWING STRAPS
RESERVE LINE
DROGUES
"EDNAMAIR"
WIRE TOW ROPE
TRIPPING LINE
SEA ANCHOR

A drawing of the Robertsons'
raft and the *Ednamair*.

during his watch. "You take a honeydew melon," he said. "Cut the top off and take out the seeds; that's the dish. Chill it and drop a knob of ice cream in, then pile in strawberries, raspberries, pieces of apple, pear, orange, peach and grapefruit, the sweet sort, then cherries and grapes until the melon is full; pour a lemon syrup over it and decorate it with chips of chocolate and nuts. Then," he said with a dreamy expression on his face, "you eat it!" "I'll have one too," I said, taking the bailer from his boil-covered hand; I looked at the sky; to the northeast a faint film of cirrostratus cloud[18] dimmed the stars. "You know, I think it might rain by morning." I could feel him relax in the darkness; his voice came slowly, "I'll be all right if it doesn't, Dad," he said.

## Fifteenth Day

. . . The twins were talking when Douglas, on watch, his voice desperate with dismay, called, "Dad, the dinghy's gone!" I was across the raft in an instant. I looked at the broken end of wire trailing in the water, the broken line beside it. The dinghy was sixty yards away, sailing still, and our lives were sailing away with it; I was the fastest swimmer, no time for goodbyes, to the devil with sharks; the thoughts ran through my head as I was diving through the door, my arms flailing into a racing crawl even as I hit the water. I heard Lyn cry out but there was no time for talk. Could I swim faster than the dinghy could sail, that was the point; I glanced at it as I lifted my head to breathe, the sail had collapsed as the dinghy yawed,[19] I moved my arms faster, kicked harder, would the sharks let me, that was another point; my belly crawled as I thought of the sharks, my arms moved faster still; I glanced again, only thirty yards to go but she was sailing again, I felt no fatigue, no cramped muscles, my

18. **cirrostratus** (sir′ō·strāt′əs) **cloud:** thin, high white cloud.
19. **yawed:** swung back and forth, pushed by the waves.

body felt like a machine as I thrashed my way through the sea only one thought now in mind, the dinghy or us. Then I was there; with a quick heave I flipped over the stern of the dinghy to safety, reached up and tore down the sail before my knees buckled and I lay across the thwart trembling and gasping for breath, my heart pounding like a hammer. I lifted my arm and waved to the raft, now two hundred yards away; then slowly I untied the paddle from the sail and paddled back to the raft; it took nearly half an hour. The long shapes of two sharks circled curiously twenty feet down; they must have had breakfast.

. . . I felt that we had already gone beyond thinking in terms of survival. We had started living from the sea as an adapted way of life, for not only were we surviving, we were improving our physical condition. As we settled to rest, I pondered the philosophies of advocates of "at sea" living. To my mind there was little prospect of man developing a cultural relationship with the sea, in the way that he has done with the land; the predatory emotions which are brought to the fore to make living possible in this primitive style are not compatible with emotional beauty or intellectual finesse. However, we no longer thought of rescue as one of the main objectives of our existence; we were no longer subject to the daily disappointment of a lonely vigil, to the idea that help might be at hand or was necessary. We no longer had that helpless feeling of dependence on others for our continued existence. We were alone, and stood alone, inhabitants of the savage sea. . . .

## Twenty-ninth Day

We made good headway in the gentle westerly

---

### WORDS TO OWN

**advocates** (ad′və·kits) *n.*: people who speak or write in support of something.
**vigil** (vij′əl) *n.*: watch; guard.

---

*Eight Bells Folly: Memorial to Hart Crane* (1933) by Marsden Hartley.

Collection of the Frederick R. Weisman Art Museum at the University of Minnesota, Minneapolis. Gift of Ione and Hudson Walker.

breeze throughout the night, with the sea anchor tripped and *Ednamair* making over a knot[20] to the east-northeast. The rising sun guided our daylight progress and the business of survival resumed its daily routine. I had barely started work on my gaff[21] when, looking down into the sea past the flashing blue, green, and gold of the dorado, I spotted the brown shape of a shark. . . . We had caught a flying fish in the night, a very small one, so I put it on the large hook and weighting the line heavily I cast well out to clear the scavenger fish. My baited hook drifted down past the shark and at first I thought he was going to ignore it, but after it came to rest he turned and nosed toward it. Douglas, stretched across the dinghy in my usual place beside the thwart,[22] called: "What're you doing, Dad?" "Catching a shark," I said calmly, watching the shark nose a little closer. "You're bloody mad," Douglas said, sitting up quickly; Robin, too, was sitting up apprehensively, and Lyn said, "You mustn't." "Good old Dad," said Neil and Sandy from the bow. "I'm having him," I said, watching tensely now, as the shark reached the bait; the moment I felt him touch I would have to strike, for if he got the nylon line between his teeth he would bite through it like butter. I was going to try to get the steel shank of the hook between his jaws. He was over it now, I felt the contact with tingling fingers and struck swiftly, the line exploded into action, he was hooked!

He fought with alternate periods of listless acquiescence and galvanic action,[23] twisting and plunging savagely to rid himself of the hook. I was afraid of the line breaking, but I feared more the arrival of a larger shark which would attack the hooked one. Slowly, foot by foot, he came to the surface, the line cutting deep into the heel of my hand. Lyn sat ready in the stern, paddle in hand. The shark broke surface, struggled savagely, and plunged deeply. I had to let him go, he was still too strong, but he was a nice five-footer. A mako shark, Douglas said (he was our shark expert), and I'd hooked him in the eye! Back up he came. "We'll have him this time," I grunted, my hands aching. "Be ready to take the line, Robin . . . I'm going to grab his tail and pull him in that way." Excitement rose high in the dinghy; Robin and Lyn looked a bit uncomfortable at being given the biting end to look after but were determined to do their best. (I knew he would break free if I tried to haul him in head first by the line.)

The shark surfaced again; gingerly Robin took the line from my hand as I quickly leaned over and grabbed the shark's tail. "Trim!"[24] I shouted and Douglas leaned out on the other side of the dinghy. The harsh skin gave me a good grip, and with a quick pull the shark lay over the gunwale.[25] "Lift its head in now!" I kept a firm grip on the tail as Robin lifted the struggling fish inboard with the line. Lyn rammed the paddle into the gaping jaws and they clamped shut on it. Knife in hand I leaned forward and stabbed it through the other eye; the shark struggled, then lay still. Giving Douglas the tail to hold, I stabbed the knife into the slits of the gills behind the head, sawing away at the tough skin until finally the head was severed. "Right, you can let go now!" I felt like Bruce after Bannockburn.[26] We had turned the tables on our most feared enemy; sharks would not eat Robertsons, Robertsons would eat sharks! Quickly I gutted out the liver and heart: a solid thirty-five to forty pounds of fish with

---

**20. knot:** one nautical mile (6,076.12 feet) per hour.
**21. gaff:** strong hook on a pole, used to catch large fish. Robertson was making a gaff out of materials on the dinghy.
**22. thwart:** rower's seat extending across a boat.
**23. he fought . . . action:** The fish went back and forth between lying still, as if it had given up, and jolting into action, as if it had received an electric shock.

**24. trim:** balance a boat by moving the weight around.
**25. gunwale** (gun′əl): upper edge of the side of a boat. Originally, the gunwale supported a ship's guns.
**26. Bruce after Bannockburn:** In 1314, Scotland won independence from England in a battle at the Scottish town of Bannockburn. Robert the Bruce led the Scots against King Edward II's much larger English forces.

very little waste apart from the head. We breakfasted on the liver and heart, then Robin chewed the head, watching carefully for the razor-sharp teeth, while I cut strips of white flesh from the almost boneless carcass. It was tougher than the dorado, but juicier, and we chewed the moist strips of shark meat with great relish. . . .

## Thirty-eighth Day

. . . The clouds grew thicker as the afternoon advanced; it was going to be a wet night again and perhaps we would be able to fill the water sleeve. Seven gallons of water seemed like wealth beyond measure in our altered sense of values.

I chopped up some dried turtle meat for tea, and Lyn put it with a little wet fish to soak in meat juice. She spread the dry sheets for the twins under the canopy, then prepared their "little supper" as we started to talk of Dougal's Kitchen and if it should have a wine license. As we pondered the delights of Gaelic coffee, my eye, looking past the sail, caught sight of something that wasn't sea. I stopped talking and stared; the others all looked at me. "A ship," I said. "There's a ship and it's coming toward us!" I could hardly believe it but it seemed solid enough. "Keep still now!" In the sudden surge of excitement, everyone wanted to see. "Trim her! We mustn't capsize now!" All sank back to their places.

I felt my voice tremble as I told them that I was going to stand on the thwart and hold a flare above the sail. They trimmed the dinghy as I stood on the thwart. "Right, hand me a flare, and remember what happened with the last ship we saw!" They suddenly fell silent in memory of that terrible despondency when our signals had been unnoticed. "O God!" prayed Lyn, "please let them see us." I could see the ship quite clearly now, a Japanese tuna fisher. Her gray and white paint stood out clearly against the dark cross swell. "Like a great white bird," Lyn said to the twins, and she would pass within about a mile of us at her nearest approach. I relayed the information as they listened excitedly, the tension of not knowing, of imminent rescue, building like a tangible, touchable, unbearable unreality around me. My eye caught the outlines of two large sharks, a hundred yards to starboard. "Watch the trim," I warned. "We have two man-eating sharks waiting if we capsize!" Then, "I'm going to light the flare now; have the torch ready in case it doesn't work."

I ripped the caps off, pulled out the striker, and struck the primer. The flare smoked, then sparked into life, the red glare illuminating *Ednamair* and the sea around us in the twilight. I could feel my index finger roasting under the heat of the flare and waved it to and fro to escape the searing heat radiating outward in the calm air; then, unable to bear the heat any longer, I dropped my arm, nearly scorching Lyn's face, and threw the flare high in the air. It curved in a brilliant arc and dropped into the sea. "Hand me another, I think she's altered course!" My voice was hoarse with pain and excitement and I felt sick with apprehension that it might only be the ship corkscrewing in the swell, for she had made no signal that she had seen us. The second flare didn't work. I cursed it in frustrated anguish as the priming substance chipped off instead of lighting. "The torch!" I shouted, but it wasn't needed; she had seen us, and was coming toward us.

I flopped down on the thwart. "Our ordeal is over," I said quietly. Lyn and the twins were crying with happiness; Douglas, with tears of joy in his eyes, hugged his mother. Robin laughed and cried at the same time, slapped me on the back, and shouted "Wonderful! We've done it. Oh! Wonderful!" I put my arms

**WORDS TO OWN**

**imminent** (im′ə·nənt) *adj.*: about to happen.

about Lyn, feeling the tears stinging my own eyes: "We'll get these boys to land after all." As we shared our happiness and watched the fishing boat close with us, death could have taken me quite easily just then, for I knew that I would never experience another such pinnacle of contentment.

In the days that followed we indulged in the luxury of eating and drinking wonderful food, the meals growing in quantity and sophistication. The familiar figure of the cook, Sakae Sasaki, became the symbol around which our whole existence revolved as he bore tray after tray up the foredeck to us. Spinach soup, prawns, fruit juices, fried chicken, roast pork, tinned fruit, fermented rice water, coffee, and, a special treat, lemon-flavored tea; and always in the background of our diet, like the foundation stones of a building, bread and butter. The assault upon our stomachs seemed unending and even when they were full, we still felt hungry—a most frustrating sensation! Our bones and bodies ached in contact with the unyielding deck, luxuriated in the deep hot sea water bath, groaned under the burden of indigestion, relaxed in the cool of the tropical night, and each day we gently exercised our swollen ankles and weakly legs, learning to walk again. . . . In four days Captain Kiyato Suzuki and his wonderful crew brought the milk of human kindness to our tortured spirits and peace to our savage minds.

## MEET THE WRITER

### "Why Not Indeed?"

**Dougal Robertson** (1924–1992) was born in Edinburgh, Scotland. After attending Leith Nautical College, Robertson joined the British Merchant Navy. He then took a leave from maritime life to raise a family and work as a dairy farmer.

Robertson and his wife were sitting around the kitchen one day with their four children, listening to a radio broadcast about a yacht race and chatting about their own sailing days. Dougal would long remember what happened next.

66 Suddenly Neil shouted, 'Daddy's a sailor, why can't we go around the world?' Lyn burst out laughing and 'What a lovely idea!' she exclaimed. 'Let's buy a boat and go round the world.' Why not? I looked at Anne [who did not make the trip] and Douglas, both handsome children but the horizons of their minds stunted by the limitations of their environment. In two years they would both have reached school-leaving age, and neither had shown any aptitude for academic study, and the twins, already backward compared with their contemporaries in town, were unlikely to blossom into sudden educational prodigies. In two years' time they would finish their primary school and then . . . Why not indeed? 99

This was the lighthearted beginning of an adventure that eventually took the Robertsons within an inch of their lives.

(Opposite) The rescue, after thirty-eight days adrift.

# MAKING MEANINGS

- ## First Thoughts

  **1.** Complete two of these sentences:

  - I admired . . . because . . .

  - I'd like to talk to . . . about . . .

  - At the end of the story, I felt . . . because . . .

## Shaping Interpretations

**2.** Get together with two or three classmates, and discuss the words you chose as the most important in the entry called "Thirty-eighth Day." Use your key words to state the **main idea** of that section.

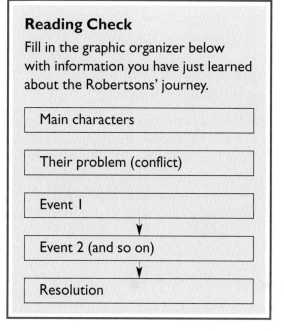

### Reading Check

Fill in the graphic organizer below with information you have just learned about the Robertsons' journey.

| Main characters |
| --- |

| Their problem (conflict) |
| --- |

| Event 1 |
| --- |

↓

| Event 2 (and so on) |
| --- |

↓

| Resolution |
| --- |

**3.** Look back at the difficult passages you noted as you read. Then, compare your passages with a classmate's. Were any of your choices the same as your partner's? How did you and your partner get through the difficult passages?

**4.** Compare the problems you listed in the chart on page 444 with the ones the Robertsons faced. What physical needs and discomforts did you **predict** correctly? What hazards did you overlook, if any?

**5.** How did Dougal and the others change as they struggled to survive?

**6.** The family would not have made it without the father. What are Dougal's personal qualities? How does Dougal compare with the person you described in your notes for the Quickwrite on page 444?

## Extending the Text

**7.** Dougal Robertson has said, "Survival is the hardest school in life; there are no failures." What other true survival stories do you know of? Why do you think some people survive such ordeals while other people perish?

## Writer's Notebook

### 1. Collecting Ideas for Observational Writing

Dougal Robertson's cheerfulness and determination helped the family survive. Every person has **characteristics** that set him or her apart from others. Picture a person you admire. Have you observed actions and personal qualities that set this person apart from the crowd? Write down all the details you can think of that make this person special in your eyes.

> My friend Lance
> —helps elderly neighbor
> —makes everyone laugh
> —is considerate
> —has great sense of humor

### Creative Writing

### 2. Writing at Sea

Dougal Robertson tells this story, so you don't learn much about the other characters' thoughts and feelings. Write some journal entries that one of the other characters on the raft might have jotted down during the first few hours after the *Lucette* sank. In your entries, cite the date and mention the kind of material the writer is using to write on.

### Reading/ Speaking and Listening

### 3. Against All Odds

If a hiker survives an avalanche by building a snow cave, you're sure to hear about it on TV. Survival stories, whether true or fictional, have been popular ever since people first began to tell stories. Read one famous survival story, such as *Julie of the Wolves, Hatchet, From the Mixed-up Files of Mrs. Basil E. Frankweiler, The Incredible Journey,* or *Kon-Tiki,* and report on it to your class. When you **summarize** the story, focus on problems and solutions. Then, use the story to show why (in your opinion) survival against great odds is a theme that readers can't resist.

### Health

### 4. Survival Kit

Fortunately, the Robertsons had a survival kit on their raft. Describe the contents of a survival kit of your own. Imagine a situation in which you might need such a kit— for example, for your car in case you're stranded in a snowstorm, for your home in case of a blackout, or for a camping trip in case you get lost. You might contact the American Red Cross to request a list of what to include in your kit.

### Informative Report/ Science

### 5. Steering by the Stars

Robertson had no maps, charts, or instruments, yet he was able to steer a course for Costa Rica, a thousand miles away. How did he do it? Write a report about how sailors at sea can use the sun and stars as guides to navigation. Use graphic aids like charts and diagrams to illustrate your report.

# LANGUAGE LINK

## • Style: Active and Passive Voice

When you want to focus on what is done rather than on who is doing it, use the **passive voice.** Compare these two examples:

ACTIVE VOICE   Dougal <u>made</u> mistakes.

PASSIVE VOICE   Mistakes <u>were made</u>.

The sentence *Mistakes were made* avoids the finger pointing suggested by *Dougal made mistakes.*

When you are unsure who is doing the action, use the passive voice.

PASSIVE VOICE   A ship <u>was spotted</u>.

In most other cases, *avoid* the passive voice. Compare these two sentences:

PASSIVE VOICE   The flare was thrown high in the air by me.

ACTIVE VOICE   I threw the flare high in the air.

As you can see, the **active voice** is more direct, forceful, and concise.

### Try It Out

➤ Choose an action-packed passage from "Survive the Savage Sea," perhaps the scene in which Dougal recaptures the drifting dinghy (pages 451–452). Rewrite it in the passive voice. Then, read both the original and the rewritten versions aloud. Which do you like better? Why?

➤ Take out a piece of your own writing, and see how often you've used the passive voice. To check your verbs, circle each one with a highlighter. If you used passive verbs, evaluate them: Would your sentences be stronger in the active voice?

---

# VOCABULARY   HOW TO OWN A WORD

**WORD BANK**

*debris*
*meager*
*tenets*
*copious*
*scanty*
*deteriorating*
*testily*
*advocates*
*vigil*
*imminent*

## • Back to the Story

1. Why were the Robertsons interested in collecting <u>debris</u>?
2. What did the Robertsons regret having in <u>meager</u> amounts? What did they regret having in <u>copious</u> amounts?
3. What did the Robertsons do about their <u>scanty</u> food supply?
4. Why did Dougal say that keeping a steady <u>vigil</u> is one of the <u>tenets</u> of good seamanship?
5. When and why did Dougal speak <u>testily</u> to his son?
6. When did the group first realize that rescue was <u>imminent</u>?
7. Why would Dougal agree with <u>advocates</u> of a never-say-die philosophy?
8. What caused the <u>deteriorating</u> condition of the raft?

# *Before You Read*

## Make the Connection

### By the Sea, You and Me

"Maggie and milly and molly and may" is a poem about water—the most precious element on our planet. What do you associate with the sea? Close your eyes and let sights, sounds, smells, and feelings fill your mind.

## Quickwrite

Write down the sensory details you associate with the sea in any "ocean shape" that inspires you, such as a starfish, an octopus, or a series of waves.

salty air

## Elements of Literature

### Kinds of Rhymes

E. E. Cummings is famous for the ways he plays with sounds and punctuation. This poem is filled with rhyming sounds. Some of the rhymes are **exact** (*may/day, stone/alone, me/sea*), but some catch us by surprise because they are slightly off. These near rhymes are called **slant rhymes.** *Milly* and *molly,* for example, form a slant rhyme: Their sounds almost rhyme—but not exactly.

> $S$lant rhymes have sounds that are similar but not exactly the same.
>
> *For more on Rhyme, see pages 338–339 and the Handbook of Literary Terms.*

## Background

### Literature and Language

Editors are probably itching to capitalize the *m*'s in the title of this poem, but they'd better keep their pencils to themselves. E. E. Cummings did not use standard punctuation (or any punctuation, in many cases), and he stopped capitalizing early in his writing career. These quirks of **style** are trademarks of his poetry.

**go.hrw.com**
*LEO 7-6*

# maggie and milly and molly and may

### E. E. Cummings

maggie and milly and molly and may
went down to the beach(to play one day)

and maggie discovered a shell that sang
so sweetly she couldn't remember her troubles,and

5  milly befriended a stranded star
whose rays five languid° fingers were;

and molly was chased by a horrible thing
which raced sideways while blowing bubbles:and

may came home with a smooth round stone
10  as small as a world and as large as alone.

For whatever we lose(like a you or a me)
it's always ourselves we find in the sea

6. **languid:** drooping; weak; slow.

# MEET THE WRITER

## "unknown and unknowable"

**E. E. Cummings** (1894–1962) started writing poetry as a student at Harvard University. After he read some ancient classical poetry, suddenly, as he put it, "an unknown and unknowable bird started singing." During World War I, Cummings was an ambulance driver in France. He was mistakenly arrested for treason and clapped into detention for three months. That experience was a turning point in his life. In prison, Cummings discovered his passion for freedom and personal growth. Over the next four decades he celebrated these passions. The following quote is from the preface to a book of Cummings's poems. The words appear here just as he wrote them.

66 The poems to come are for you and for me and are not for mostpeople

   —it's no use trying to pretend that mostpeople and ourselves are alike. Mostpeople have less in common with ourselves than the squarerootofminusone. You and I are human beings;mostpeople are snobs. . . .

   you and I are not snobs. We can never be born enough. We are human beings;for whom birth is a supremely welcome mystery,the mystery of growing:the mystery which happens only and whenever we are faithful to ourselves. 99

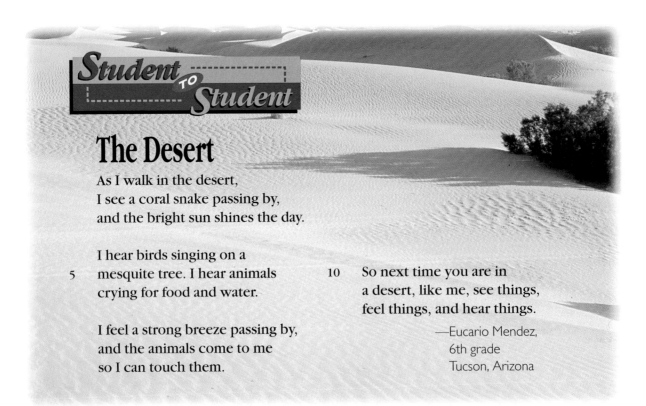

Student TO Student

# The Desert

As I walk in the desert,
I see a coral snake passing by,
and the bright sun shines the day.

I hear birds singing on a
5  mesquite tree. I hear animals
crying for food and water.

I feel a strong breeze passing by,
and the animals come to me
so I can touch them.

10  So next time you are in
a desert, like me, see things,
feel things, and hear things.

      —Eucario Mendez,
      6th grade
      Tucson, Arizona

# MAKING MEANINGS

- ## First Thoughts

  **1.** How do the last lines of the poem strike you? What do they mean to you?

  ## Shaping Interpretations

  **2.** Cummings writes that "it's always ourselves we find in the sea." How does each girl find herself in the sea?

  **3.** What **exact rhymes** do you hear in the poem? What **slant rhymes** do you hear? What sounds did you *expect* to hear?

  ## Extending the Text

  **4.** What might the girls in Cummings's poem find in the desert described by Eucario Mendez (page 462)? How do you think the speaker of Mendez's poem would feel about the beach?

# CHOICES: Building Your Portfolio

## Writer's Notebook

### 1. Collecting Ideas for Observational Writing

Choose a place in nature or a force of nature that arouses a powerful emotion in you—for example, a sunny meadow that makes you feel happy. List your impressions by describing what you see, hear, touch, taste, smell, and feel. Like Mendez, you might say, "As I walk . . . , I see . . . I hear . . . I feel . . .".

## Creative Writing

### 2. Notions of Oceans

Create your own poem about the ocean or another place you've visited, perhaps with a friend. (You might get ideas about the ocean from the notes you made for the Quickwrite on page 460.) Try out any techniques that pleased you in Cummings's poem. You might want to adopt trademarks of Cummings's **style:** no capitalization, not much punctuation, and words run together without space between them.

One writer opened like this:

The beach was clean as milk, the air was sheer as silk, the sun was shining on the shore.

## Informative Writing/ Science

### 3. The Real Thing

Create a museum display that shows the objects maggie, milly, molly, and may find on the beach. Include pictures and scientific information about shells, starfish, crabs (or whatever you think the "horrible thing" is), and stones.

# Before You Read

## Make the Connection

### Mother Earth

Think of all the ways in which you are connected to the earth. To begin, fill in a chart like the one below.

**Planet Earth**

| Gifts we receive from the earth: | Gifts we give back to the earth: |

## Quickwrite

What is the most important gift the earth gives to you? What is the most important thing you give to the earth? Briefly explain your answers.

## Elements of Literature

### Personification: Making the World Human

Common sense tells us that a cloud can't cry and a river can't get angry. They can in the imaginations of writers, though.

When writers give human qualities to nonhuman things, they are using **personification.** In "I Am of the Earth," the speaker uses personification to compare the earth to a mother cradling a child.

> **P**ersonification is a kind of metaphor in which a nonhuman thing or quality is talked about as if it were human.
>
> *For more on Personification, see the Handbook of Literary Terms.*

# I Am of the Earth

**Anna Lee Walters**

I am of the earth
She is my mother
She bore me with pride
She reared me with love
5    She cradled me each evening
She pushed the wind to make it sing
She built me a house of harmonious colors
She fed me the fruits of her fields
She rewarded me with memories of her smiles
10    She punished me with the passing of time
And at last, when I long to leave
She will embrace me for eternity

# Early Song

**Gogisgi/Carroll Arnett**

As the sun rises
high enough to
warm the frost
off the pine needles,

5    I rise to make
four prayers of
thanksgiving for
this fine clear day,

for this good brown
10    earth, for all
brothers and sisters,
for the dark blood

that runs through me
in a great circle
15    back into this
good brown earth.

# MEET THE WRITERS

## "Words Poured Out..."

**Anna Lee Walters** (1947–      ) left home at the age of sixteen to attend a boarding school in New Mexico. In the Southwest, Walters began to discover her roots in the Pawnee and Otoe cultures—and in the process unlocked her voice as a writer. She recalls:

66 Words poured out, page after page. I am still amazed by it, by the torrent of thoughts deposited there. . . . Today my occupation as a writer is related to what my grandfather and grandmother did when they repeated family history in the manner of their elders, leading the family all over this sacred land, this continent most recently called America in the last five hundred years, in their retelling of the Otoe journey from the dawn of time until they came to rest at Red Rock Creek a little over a century ago. 99

## "What It Feels Like to Be Alive"

**Gogisgi/Carroll Arnett** (1927–      ), an American of Cherokee descent, was born in Oklahoma City. He has published more than 150 poems and stories in magazines, sometimes under his Cherokee name, Gogisgi.

66 I write poems because it seems sensible to do so and wasteful not to. A poem has a use insofar as it shows what it feels like to be alive. 99

# MAKING MEANINGS

## • I AM OF THE EARTH/EARLY SONG

### First Thoughts

1. How does each speaker feel about the earth?

### Shaping Interpretations

2. Walters **personifies** the earth as her mother. What message or feeling about our world does this comparison convey?

3. What does Arnett mean by the "great circle" (line 14)? How does Walters get at the same idea?

### Extending the Text

4. Are people always grateful children of the earth? How do some people show that their feelings about the earth are very different from the feelings of these two poets?

## CHOICES: Building Your Portfolio

### Writer's Notebook

#### 1. Collecting Ideas for Observational Writing

Did the earth—or any part of nature—ever feel human to you? What seemed human, and in what way? Check your notes for the Quickwrite on page 464. Can you build on some of those images now?

### Critical Writing/ Cultural Connections

#### 2. Lessons of the Earth

The following quotations use features of the earth to teach people lessons. Choose one that you like, and write about what it means to you. Include any experiences from your own life that illustrate the lesson.

"Consider the lilies, how they grow; they neither toil or spin; yet I tell you, even Solomon in all his glory was not arrayed like one of these."
　　　　　—Luke 12:27, the Bible

"There is no hill that never ends."
　　　　　—Masai proverb

"Do you have the patience to wait till your mud settles and the water is clear?"
　　　　　—Tao-te Ching

### Paraphrasing

#### 3. In Your Own Words

Write a paraphrase of one of the poems you have just read. (When you **paraphrase** something, you put it in your own words, making sure to keep the writer's meaning.) Paraphrasing can help you understand and recall any written work. Follow these rules:

* Read the poem line by line. Rewrite each line or sentence in prose.

* Restate what the poem says as simply and clearly as you can. Don't include your opinions.

# Before You Read

## Make the Connection

### Home Sweet Home

There's an old saying that goes, "Home is where the heart is." However, people often disagree about what kind of place makes the best home.

## Quickwrite

Which do you prefer: the country or the city? Write down some reasons for your choice, or draw a picture of what you think is the perfect home.

## Elements of Literature

### Allusion

This story centers on an **allusion** to a character from Greek mythology. The reference is in the title—"Antaeus." Antaeus (an·tē′əs) is a giant whose immense strength comes from his mother, the Earth. As long as his feet are on the ground, Antaeus is unbeatable. The superhero Hercules finds out the giant's secret and kills him by simply lifting him off the ground and strangling him. As you read the story, notice the connection between Antaeus and T. J., a modern-day hero.

> **A**n **allusion** is a reference to a statement, a person, a place, or an event from literature, history, religion, mythology, politics, sports, or science.
>
> *For more on Allusion, see the Handbook of Literary Terms.*

## Reading Skills and Strategies

### Identifying Purpose: Taking Aim

People write with different purposes in mind. People who write political speeches are usually trying to **persuade** us to believe or do something. People who write articles in magazines often want to **inform** us about something. Novelists and short-story writers usually write for other reasons. Some write to **entertain;** some write to **reveal a truth about life** or to **share or re-create an experience.**

## Background

### Literature and Social Studies

During World War II, the economy of the United States geared up to produce equipment, weapons, and goods to serve the military effort overseas. As industry went into overdrive, many families left their homes in the South so that the adults could work in factories in the North. This is the situation the narrator is referring to as the story opens.

# ANTAEUS

Borden Deal

*It was a secret place for us, where nobody else could go without our permission.*

This was during the wartime, when lots of people were coming North for jobs in factories and war industries, when people moved around a lot more than they do now, and sometimes kids were thrown into new groups and new lives that were completely different from anything they had ever known before. I remember this one kid, T. J. his name was, from somewhere down South, whose family moved into our building during that time. They'd come North with everything they owned piled into the back seat of an old-model sedan that you wouldn't expect could make the trip, with T. J. and his three younger sisters riding shakily on top of the load of junk.

Our building was just like all the others there, with families crowded into a few rooms, and I guess there were twenty-five or thirty kids about my age in that one building. Of course, there were a few of us who formed a gang and ran together all the time after school, and I was the one who brought T. J. in and started the whole thing.

The building right next door to us was a factory where they made walking dolls. It was a low building with a flat, tarred roof that had a parapet[1] all around it about head-high, and we'd found out a long time before that no one, not even the watchman, paid any attention to the roof because it was higher than any of the other buildings around. So my gang used the roof as a headquarters. We could get up there by crossing over to the fire escape from our own roof on a plank and then going on up. It was a secret place for us, where nobody else could go without our permission.

I remember the day I first took T. J. up there

1. **parapet:** wall or railing.

to meet the gang. He was a stocky, robust kid with a shock of white hair, nothing sissy about him except his voice; he talked in this slow, gentle voice like you never heard before. He talked different from any of us and you noticed it right away. But I liked him anyway, so I told him to come on up.

We climbed up over the parapet and dropped down on the roof. The rest of the gang were already there.

*East River from the 30th Story of the Shelton Hotel* (detail) by Georgia O'Keeffe. Oil on canvas (30" x 48").

"Hi," I said. I jerked my thumb at T. J. "He just moved into the building yesterday."

He just stood there, not scared or anything, just looking, like the first time you see somebody you're not sure you're going to like.

"Hi," Blackie said. "Where are you from?"

"Marion County," T. J. said.

We laughed. "Marion County?" I said. "Where's that?"

He looked at me for a moment like I was a stranger, too. "It's in Alabama," he said, like I ought to know where it was.

"What's your name?" Charley said.

"T. J.," he said, looking back at him. He had pale blue eyes that looked washed-out, but he looked directly at Charley, waiting for his reaction. He'll be all right, I thought. No sissy in him, except that voice. Who ever talked like that?

"T. J.," Blackie said. "That's just initials. What's your real name? Nobody in the world has just initials."

"I do," he said. "And they're T. J. That's all the name I got."

His voice was <u>resolute</u> with the knowledge of his rightness, and for a moment no one had

New Britain Museum of American Art, New Britain, Connecticut. Stephen Lawrence Fund. Photo credit: E. Irving Blomstrann. ©1998 The Georgia O'Keeffe Foundation/Artists Rights Society (ARS), New York.

anything to say. T. J. looked around at the rooftop and down at the black tar under his feet. "Down yonder where I come from," he said, "we played out in the woods. Don't you-all have no woods around here?"

"Naw," Blackie said. "There's the park a few blocks over, but it's full of kids and cops and old women. You can't do a thing."

T. J. kept looking at the tar under his feet. "You mean you ain't got no fields to raise nothing in?—no watermelons or nothing?"

"Naw," I said scornfully. "What do you want to grow something for? The folks can buy everything they need at the store."

He looked at me again with that strange, unknowing look. "In Marion County," he said, "I

had my own acre of cotton and my own acre of corn. It was mine to plant and make ever' year."

He sounded like it was something to be proud of, and in some obscure way it made the rest of us angry. Blackie said, "Who'd want to have their own acre of cotton and corn? That's just work. What can you do with an acre of cotton and corn?"

T. J. looked at him. "Well, you get part of the bale offen your acre," he said seriously. "And I fed my acre of corn to my calf."

We didn't really know what he was talking about, so we were more puzzled than angry; otherwise, I guess, we'd have chased him off the roof and wouldn't let him be part of our gang. But he was strange and different, and we were all attracted by his stolid sense of rightness and belonging, maybe by the strange softness of his voice contrasting our own tones of speech into harshness.

He moved his foot against the black tar. "We could make our own field right here," he said softly, thoughtfully. "Come spring we could raise us what we want to—watermelons and garden truck and no telling what all."

"You'd have to be a good farmer to make these tar roofs grow any watermelons," I said. We all laughed.

But T. J. looked serious. "We could haul us some dirt up here," he said. "And spread it out even and water it, and before you know it, we'd have us a crop in here." He looked at us intently. "Wouldn't that be fun?"

"They wouldn't let us," Blackie said quickly.

"I thought you said this was you-all's roof,"

---

**WORDS TO OWN**

resolute (rez′ə·lo͞ot′) *adj.*: firm and purposeful; determined.

---

T. J. said to me. "That you-all could do anything you wanted to up here."

"They've never bothered us," I said. I felt the idea beginning to catch fire in me. It was a big idea, and it took a while for it to sink in; but the more I thought about it, the better I liked it. "Say," I said to the gang. "He might have something there. Just make us a regular roof garden, with flowers and grass and trees and everything. And all ours, too," I said. "We wouldn't let anybody up here except the ones we wanted to."

"It'd take a while to grow trees," T. J. said quickly, but we weren't paying any attention to him. They were all talking about it suddenly, all excited with the idea after I'd put it in a way they would catch hold of it. Only rich people had roof gardens, we knew, and the idea of our own private <u>domain</u> excited them.

"We could bring it up in sacks and boxes," Blackie said. "We'd have to do it while the folks weren't paying any attention to us, for we'd have to come up to the roof of our building and then cross over with it."

"Where could we get the dirt?" somebody said worriedly.

"Out of those vacant lots over close to school," Blackie said. "Nobody'd notice if we scraped it up."

I slapped T. J. on the shoulder. "Man, you had a wonderful idea," I said, and everybody grinned at him, remembering that he had started it. "Our own private roof garden."

He grinned back. "It'll be ourn," he said. "All ourn." Then he looked thoughtful again. "Maybe I can lay my hands on some cotton seed, too. You think we could raise us some cotton?"

We'd started big projects before at one time or another, like any gang of kids, but they'd always petered out[2] for lack of organization and

direction. But this one didn't; somehow or other T. J. kept it going all through the winter months. He kept talking about the watermelons and the cotton we'd raise, come spring, and when even that wouldn't work, he'd switch around to my idea of flowers and grass and trees, though he was always honest enough to add that it'd take a while to get any trees started. He always had it on his mind, and he'd mention it in school, getting them lined up to carry dirt that afternoon, saying in a casual way that he reckoned a few more weeks ought to see the job through.

Our little area of private earth grew slowly. T. J. was smart enough to start in one corner of the building, heaping up the carried earth two or three feet thick so that we had an immediate result to look at, to <u>contemplate</u> with awe. Some of the evenings T. J. alone was carrying earth up to the building, the rest of the gang distracted by other enterprises or interests, but T. J. kept plugging along on his own, and eventually we'd all come back to him again, and then our own little acre would grow more rapidly.

He was careful about the kind of dirt he'd let us carry up there, and more than once he dumped a sandy load over the parapet into the areaway below because it wasn't good enough. He found out the kinds of earth in all the vacant lots for blocks around. He'd pick it up and feel it and smell it, frozen though it was sometimes, and then he'd say it was good growing soil or it wasn't worth anything, and we'd have to go on somewhere else.

Thinking about it now, I don't see how he kept us at it. It was hard work, lugging paper sacks and boxes of dirt all the way up the stairs of our own building, keeping out of the way of

---

2. **petered out:** gradually disappeared.

the grown-ups so they wouldn't catch on to what we were doing. They probably wouldn't have cared, for they didn't pay much attention to us, but we wanted to keep it secret anyway. Then we had to go through the trapdoor to our roof, teeter over a plank to the fire escape, then climb two or three stories to the parapet, and drop them down onto the roof. All that for a small pile of earth that sometimes didn't seem worth the effort. But T. J. kept the vision bright within us, his words <u>shrewd</u> and calculated toward the fulfillment of his dream; and he worked harder than any of us. He seemed driven toward a goal that we couldn't see, a particular point in time that would be definitely marked by signs and wonders that only he could see.

The laborious earth just lay there during the cold months, <u>inert</u> and lifeless, the clods lumpy and cold under our feet when we walked over it. But one day it rained, and afterward there was a softness in the air, and the earth was live and giving again with moisture and warmth.

That evening T. J. smelled the air, his nostrils <u>dilating</u> with the odor of the earth under his feet. "It's spring," he said, and there was a gladness rising in his voice that filled us all with the same feeling. "It's mighty late for it, but it's spring. I'd just about decided it wasn't never gonna get here at all."

We were all sniffing at the air, too, trying to smell it the way that T. J. did, and I can still remember the sweet odor of the earth under our feet. It was the first time in my life that spring and spring earth had meant anything to me. I looked at T. J. then, knowing in a faint way the hunger within him through the toilsome[3] winter months, knowing the dream that lay behind his plan. He was a new Antaeus, preparing his own bed of strength.

"Planting time," he said. "We'll have to find us some seed."

3. **toilsome:** involving hard work; laborious.

"What do we do?" Blackie said. "How do we do it?"

"First we'll have to break up the clods," T. J. said. "That won't be hard to do. Then we plant the seeds, and after a while they come up. Then you got you a crop." He frowned. "But you ain't got it raised yet. You got to tend it and hoe it and take care of it, and all the time it's growing and growing, while you're awake and while you're asleep. Then you lay it by when it's growed and let it ripen, and then you got you a crop."

"There's those wholesale seed houses over on Sixth," I said. "We could probably swipe some grass seed over there."

T. J. looked at the earth. "You-all seem mighty set on raising some grass," he said. "I ain't never put no effort into that. I spent all my life trying not to raise grass."

"But it's pretty," Blackie said. "We could play on it and take sunbaths on it. Like having our own lawn. Lots of people got lawns."

"Well," T. J. said. He looked at the rest of us, hesitant for the first time. He kept on looking at us for a moment. "I did have it in mind to raise some corn and vegetables. But we'll plant grass."

He was smart. He knew where to give in. And I don't suppose it made any difference to him, really. He just wanted to grow something, even if it was grass.

"Of course," he said, "I do think we ought to plant a row of watermelons. They'd be mighty nice to eat while we was a-laying on that grass."

We all laughed. "All right," I said. "We'll plant us a row of watermelons."

Things went very quickly then. Perhaps half the roof was covered with the earth, the half

---

**WORDS TO OWN**

**shrewd** (shrōōd) *adj.:* clever.
**inert** (in·urt') *adj.:* inactive.
**dilating** (dī'lāt·iŋ) *v.* used as *adj.:* becoming wider.

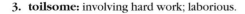

that wasn't broken by ventilators,[4] and we swiped pocketfuls of grass seed from the open bins in the wholesale seed house, mingling among the buyers on Saturdays and during the school lunch hour. T. J. showed us how to prepare the earth, breaking up the clods and smoothing it and sowing the grass seed. It looked rich and black now with moisture, receiving of the seed, and it seemed that the grass sprang up overnight, pale green in the early spring.

We couldn't keep from looking at it, unable to believe that we had created this delicate growth. We looked at T. J. with understanding now, knowing the fulfillment of the plan he had carried along within his mind. We had worked without full understanding of the task, but he had known all the time.

We found that we couldn't walk or play on the delicate blades as we had expected to, but we didn't mind. It was enough just to look at it, to realize that it was the work of our own hands, and each evening, the whole gang was there, trying to measure the growth that had been achieved that day.

One time a foot was placed on the plot of ground, one time only, Blackie stepping onto it with sudden bravado. Then he looked at the crushed blades and there was shame in his face. He did not do it again. This was his grass, too, and not to be desecrated. No one said anything, for it was not necessary.

T. J. had reserved a small section for watermelons, and he was still trying to find some seed for it. The wholesale house didn't have any watermelon seeds, and we didn't know where we could lay our hands on them. T. J. shaped the earth into mounds ready to receive them, three mounds lying in a straight line along the edge of the grass plot.

We had just about decided that we'd have to buy the seeds if we were to get them. It was a violation of our principles, but we were anxious to get the watermelons started. Somewhere or other, T. J. got his hands on a seed catalog and brought it one evening to our roof garden.

"We can order them now," he said, showing us the catalog. "Look!"

We all crowded around, looking at the fat green watermelons pictured in full color on the pages. Some of them were split open, showing the red, tempting meat, making our mouths water.

"Now we got to scrape up some seed money," T. J. said, looking at us. "I got a quarter. How much you-all got?"

We made up a couple of dollars among us and T. J. nodded his head. "That'll be more than enough. Now we got to decide what kind to get. I think them Kleckley Sweets. What do you-all think?"

He was going into esoteric matters beyond our reach. We hadn't even known there were different kinds of melons. So we just nodded our heads and agreed that yes, we thought the Kleckley Sweets too.

"I'll order them tonight," T. J. said. "We ought to have them in a few days."

"What are you boys doing up here?" an adult voice said behind us.

It startled us, for no one had ever come up here before in all the time we had been using the roof of the factory. We jerked around and saw three men standing near the trapdoor at the other end of the roof. They weren't policemen or night watchmen but three men in plump business suits, looking at us. They walked toward us.

---

4. **ventilators:** devices used to bring in fresh air.

### WORDS TO OWN

**desecrated** (desʹi·krātʹid) v.: showed disrespect for (something considered holy).

**esoteric** (esʹə·terʹik) adj.: specialized; beyond most people's understanding or knowledge.

*Chandler, Mexico* (1923), photograph by Edward Weston.

© 1981 Center for Creative Photography, Arizona Board of Regents.

"What are you boys doing up here?" the one in the middle said again.

We stood still, guilt heavy among us, levied by the tone of voice, and looked at the three strangers.

The men stared at the grass flourishing behind us. "What's this?" the man said. "How did this get up here?"

"Sure is growing good, ain't it?" T. J. said conversationally. "We planted it."

The men kept looking at the grass as if they didn't believe it. It was a thick carpet over the earth now, a patch of deep greenness startling in the sterile industrial surroundings.

"Yes, sir," T. J. said proudly. "We toted that earth up here and planted that grass." He fluttered the seed catalog. "And we're just fixing to plant us some watermelon."

The man looked at him then, his eyes strange and faraway. "What do you mean, putting this on the roof of my building?" he said. "Do you want to go to jail?"

T. J. looked shaken. The rest of us were silent, frightened by the authority of his voice. We had grown up aware of adult authority, of policemen and night watchmen and teachers,

---

**WORDS TO OWN**

**sterile** (ster′əl) *adj.*: barren; lacking interest or vitality.

---

and this man sounded like all the others. But it was a new thing to T. J.

"Well, you wasn't using the roof," T. J. said. He paused a moment and added shrewdly, "So we just thought to pretty it up a little bit."

"And sag it so I'd have to rebuild it," the man said sharply. He started turning away, saying to another man beside him, "See that all that junk is shoveled off by tomorrow."

"Yes, sir," the man said.

T. J. started forward. "You can't do that," he said. "We toted it up here, and it's our earth. We planted it and raised it and toted it up here."

The man stared at him coldly. "But it's my building," he said. "It's to be shoveled off to-morrow."

"It's our earth," T. J. said desperately. "You ain't got no right!"

The men walked on without listening and descended clumsily through the trapdoor. T. J. stood looking after them, his body tense with anger, until they had disappeared. They wouldn't even argue with him, wouldn't let him defend his earth rights.

He turned to us. "We won't let 'em do it," he said fiercely. "We'll stay up here all day tomorrow and the day after that, and we won't let 'em do it."

We just looked at him. We knew there was no stopping it.

He saw it in our faces, and his face wavered for a moment before he gripped it into determination. "They ain't got no right," he said. "It's our earth. It's our land. Can't nobody touch a man's own land."

We kept looking at him, listening to the words but knowing that it was no use. The adult world had descended on us even in our richest dream, and we knew there was no calculating the adult world, no fighting it, no winning against it.

We started moving slowly toward the parapet and the fire escape, avoiding a last look at the green beauty of the earth that T. J. had

planted for us, had planted deeply in our minds as well as in our experience. We filed slowly over the edge and down the steps to the plank, T. J. coming last, and all of us could feel the weight of his grief behind us.

"Wait a minute," he said suddenly, his voice harsh with the effort of calling.

We stopped and turned, held by the tone of his voice, and looked up at him standing above us on the fire escape.

"We can't stop them?" he said, looking down at us, his face strange in the dusky light. "There ain't no way to stop 'em?"

"No," Blackie said with finality. "They own the building."

We stood still for a moment, looking up at T. J., caught into inaction by the decision working in his face. He stared back at us, and his face was pale and mean in the poor light, with a bald nakedness in his skin like cripples have sometimes.

"They ain't gonna touch my earth," he said fiercely. "They ain't gonna lay a hand on it! Come on."

He turned around and started up the fire escape again, almost running against the effort of climbing. We followed more slowly, not knowing what he intended to do. By the time we reached him, he had seized a board and thrust it into the soil, scooping it up and flinging it over the parapet into the areaway below. He straightened and looked at us.

"They can't touch it," he said. "I won't let 'em lay a dirty hand on it!"

We saw it then. He stooped to his labor again, and we followed, the gusts of his anger moving in frenzied labor among us as we scattered along the edge of earth, scooping it and throwing it over the parapet, destroying with anger the growth we had nurtured with such

## WORDS TO OWN

descended (dē·send′id) v.: went down.

tender care. The soil carried so laboriously up-ward to the light and the sun cascaded swiftly into the dark areaway, the green blades of grass crumpled and twisted in the falling.

It took less time than you would think; the task of destruction is infinitely easier than that of creation. We stopped at the end, leaving only a scattering of loose soil, and when it was finally over, a stillness stood among the group and over the factory building. We looked down at the bare sterility of black tar, felt the harsh texture of it under the soles of our shoes, and the anger had gone out of us, leaving only a sore aching in our minds, like overstretched muscles.

T. J. stood for a moment, his breathing slow-ing from anger and effort, caught into the same contemplation of destruction as all of us. He stooped slowly, finally, and picked up a lonely blade of grass left trampled under our feet and put it between his teeth, tasting it, sucking the greenness out of it into his mouth. Then he started walking toward the fire escape, moving before any of us were ready to move, and disap-peared over the edge.

We followed him, but he was already halfway down to the ground, going on past the board where we crossed over, climbing down into the areaway. We saw the last section swing down with his weight, and then he stood on the concrete below us, looking at the small pile of anonymous earth scattered by our throwing. Then he walked across the place where we could see him and disappeared toward the street without glancing back, without looking up to see us watching him.

They did not find him for two weeks.

Then the Nashville police caught him just outside the Nashville freight yards. He was walking along the railroad track, still heading South, still heading home.

As for us, who had no remembered home to call us, none of us ever again climbed the escapeway to the roof.

## MEET THE WRITER

### Keeping the Faith

Like his hero T. J., **Borden Deal** (1922–1985) came from a family of Southern cotton farm-ers. They knew firsthand the hardships of farm life during the Great Depression. As the fol-lowing anecdote proves, Deal was just as per-sistent as T. J.:

66 My short story 'Antaeus' has a strange his-tory. Though it has been reprinted far more often than any other of my nearly one hundred short stories, it took me *ten years* to get it published the first time! True. It was turned down by every quality popular magazine in the country, not once but two or three times. Then, on rereading the story after a year or so, I'd like it all over again, and I'd send it around once more. After ten long years, the story was finally published by one of the coun-try's finest literary magazines, and the next year it was reprinted in the annual collection called *The Best American Short Stories*. Since then, the story has appeared in hundreds of textbooks and anthologies on every level, from grammar school to college. So you see, when you believe in something, it pays to keep the faith and be persistent—just as, in the story, T. J. is persistent in his faith and feeling for the earth. 99

# In a Mix of Cultures, an Olio of Plantings

### ANNE RAVER

Juan Guerrero grows tomatillos on a scrap of land that used to be a chop shop for stolen cars in the South Bronx. It's his little piece of Mexico.

"He says you cut them up with hot pepper for salsa," said Jose Garcia, who grew up in Puerto Rico. Mr. Guerrero left Puebla, Mexico, four years ago, but he speaks little English, so Mr. Garcia was translating.

He watched Mr. Guerrero peel the papery husk from a hard little green fruit and nodded yes, yes, yes, as his neighbor explained how to dry the fruit for seeds.

"In Puerto Rico," Mr. Garcia said, chuckling, "my father always told me these were poison." Then he politely tasted a pungent leaf that Mr. Guerrero had just picked from a bushy green herb.

"Papalo," Mr. Guerrero said. "Como cilantro."

This 100 by 175 foot piece of earth, on Prospect Avenue between East 181st and 182d Streets, used to grow old car parts, refrigerators, and crack vials. Now it grows zinnias, hollyhocks, eggplants, collard greens, and pear trees. And its thirty gardeners call it "The Garden of Happiness."

Happiness here has little to do with the perfect perennial bed. It's about reclaiming scarred land from drug dealers. And planting a few vegetables and flowers that remind you of the roots you tore up to get here.

Many urban gardeners till city-owned lots leased to them for one dollar a year by Operation Green Thumb, the city's gardening program, which leases more than a thousand lots to 550 community groups. Others just take over garbage-strewn land.

"Gardening takes you back to your roots," said Karen Washington, 37, who took a pickax and shovel to the debris three years ago and now heads the community garden. "My grandparents farmed in North Carolina. If you gave them some store-bought collard greens, they'd look at you like you were crazy."

—from *The New York Times*

*Sara Krulwich, The New York Times.*

*Urban gardener Annie Vigg with a harvest of squash, tomatoes, beans, peas, and okra.*

# MAKING MEANINGS

### First Thoughts

1. If you were T. J., what would you do after hearing the words "It's to be shoveled off tomorrow"?

### Shaping Interpretations

2. In your opinion, what's the most important thing the city boys learn from T. J.?

3. Find the passage in the story that mentions Antaeus (page 473). Explain the connection between what happens to Antaeus in the myth and what happens to T. J. What do you think the **allusion** adds to the story?

4. Think about the word *escapeway* in the last sentence. In what ways is that passage to the roof an escape for the boys?

5. How are the gardeners in the article "In a Mix of Cultures . . ." (see ***Connections*** on page 478) like T. J.? What other people could be called Antaeus?

6. What do you make of the last line, about the city boys having "no remembered home" to call them? What do you think the word *home* means here?

### Reading Check

a. What characteristic makes T. J. seem "different" at first to the narrator?

b. What does T. J. want? What obstacles does he have to overcome to get what he wants?

c. What does the narrator realize for the first time when he smells "the sweet odor of the earth" under his feet (page 473)?

d. How does T. J. react when the boys' project is destroyed?

### Connecting with the Text

7. Look back at the notes about home that you made for the Quickwrite on page 468. How do your feelings about home compare with T. J.'s?

*East River from the 30th Story of the Shelton Hotel* by Georgia O'Keeffe. Oil on canvas (30" x 48").

New Britain Museum of American Art, New Britain, Connecticut. Stephen Lawrence Fund. Photo credit: E. Irving Blomstrann. © 1998 The Georgia O'Keeffe Foundation/ Artists Rights Society (ARS), New York.

# CHOICES: Building Your Portfolio

## Writer's Notebook

### 1. Collecting Ideas for Observational Writing

The city boys in "Antaeus" discover that even a small plot of grass on a tar roof can hold the wonders of nature. Find your own patch of earth to observe: three or four square feet in a back yard or nearby park, a clump of weeds in a vacant lot, even a window box.

Observe your patch carefully for ten to fifteen minutes. Jot down everything you see, smell, feel, and hear.

> Dad's rock garden
> —violets: purple with white edges
> —rocks: like gray-green soldiers
> —a whisper of wind

## Creative Writing

### 2. Add a Scene

What happens to T. J.? Write a final scene for the story. Tell it from T. J.'s point of view—let T. J. continue the story, speaking as "I." Before you write, collect your ideas about these details, which should be part of T. J.'s story:

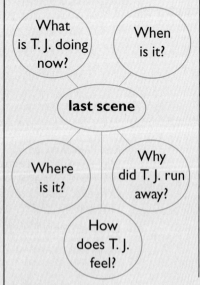

- What is T. J. doing now?
- When is it?
- **last scene**
- Where is it?
- Why did T. J. run away?
- How does T. J. feel?

## Speaking and Listening

### 3. Literary Round Table

Get together with a partner, and talk about the pieces in this collection. Think about the different **purposes** the writers may have had in mind as they wrote. Did they want to

- inform or explain?
- influence or persuade?
- entertain?
- reveal a truth about our lives?
- share or re-create an experience?

Choose three or four selections, and decide what each writer's purpose was. (Remember that the writer may have had more than one purpose in mind.) Share your findings with the class.

## Drama

### 4. Hold That Thought

Select a dramatic moment from the story and create a tableau of that scene. With a group of classmates, get into and hold the exact pose of characters in the scene. Have another student patrol the tableau and tap different characters to bring them "to life." As soon as someone is tapped, he or she begins to speak, saying what the character might say or might be thinking at that moment. When tapped again, he or she stops talking, and the tapper taps someone else. Afterward, discuss what, if anything, you discovered about the story from creating the tableau.

# LANGUAGE LINK · MINI-LESSON

## Style: Dialect—Voices of a Region or a Group

**Handbook of Literary Terms**
**H E L P**

*See Dialect.*

In "Antaeus," T. J. speaks in a way that doesn't sound like standard English. He uses double (even triple) negatives and words like *ourn* for *ours* and *offen* for *from*. Here is an example:

T. J.'S DIALECT
"You mean you ain't got no fields to raise nothing in?"

STANDARD ENGLISH
Do you mean you have no fields in which to raise anything?

**Dialect** is a way of speaking that is character-istic of a particular region or group of people. People who study language say that all of us speak one dialect or another. Think of how a British speaker sounds. Think of how a Philadelphian speaks, as compared with a per-son from Southern California. T. J. speaks one of the dialects of the Deep South. Like all dialects, T. J.'s has a distinctive pronunciation, vocabulary, and grammar. By re-creating T. J.'s dialect, Deal helps us "see" the boy and "hear" his gentle Southern drawl.

### Try It Out

➤ Do a survey of dialects spoken in your class. Does everyone sound the same, or do you hear varied dialects?

a. Do you say *crick* or *creek* to describe a small stream?

b. Do you say *frying pan, skil-let,* or *spider* to describe the pan you fry eggs in?

c. How do you pronounce *dear, car,* and *water*?

➤ Listen for a week to hear dialect on TV or on the radio, and write down each in-stance. Rewrite each expres-sion in the words *you* would use to say the same thing—in your own dialect.

## VOCABULARY · HOW TO OWN A WORD

**WORD BANK**
resolute
domain
contemplate
shrewd
inert
dilating
desecrated
esoteric
sterile
descended

### Back to the Story

1. Describe T. J., using the words *resolute* and *shrewd*.
2. Describe how the city boys feel about the roof garden, using the words *contemplate* and *domain*.
3. Using the words *sterile*, *inert*, and *esoteric*, describe how the boys change the tar roof into a lawn.
4. Write about the owners of the building, using the words *desecrated* and *descended* to describe what they did.
5. Using the word *dilating*, describe the way T. J. responds to the fragrance of the earth.

# Four Skinny Trees

## Sandra Cisneros

They are the only ones who understand me. I am the only one who understands them. Four skinny trees with skinny necks and pointy elbows like mine. Four who do not belong here but are here. Four raggedy excuses planted by the city. From our room we can hear them, but Nenny just sleeps and doesn't appreciate these things.

Their strength is secret. They send ferocious roots beneath the ground. They grow up and they grow down and grab the earth between their hairy toes and bite the sky with violent teeth and never quit their anger. This is how they keep.

Let one forget his reason for being, they'd all droop like tulips in a glass, each with their arms around the other. Keep, keep, keep, trees say when I sleep. They teach.

When I am too sad and too skinny to keep keeping, when I am a tiny thing against so many bricks, then it is I look at trees. When there is nothing left to look at on this street. Four who grew despite concrete. Four who reach and do not forget to reach. Four whose only reason is to be and be.

# Cuatro árboles flaquititos

### Sandra Cisneros
### *translated by Elena Poniatowska*

Son los únicos que me entienden. Soy la única que los entiende. Cuatro árboles flacos de flacos cuellos y codos puntiagudos como los míos. Cuatro que no pertenecen aquí pero aquí están. Cuatro excusas harapientas plantadas por la ciudad. Desde nuestra recámara podemos oírlos, pero Nenny se duerme y no aprecia estas cosas.

Su fuerza es secreta. Lanzan feroces raíces bajo la tierra. Crecen hacia arriba y hacia abajo y se apoderan de la tierra entre los dedos peludos de sus pies y muerden el cielo con dientes violentos y jamás se detiene su furia. Así se mantienen.

Si alguno olvidara su razón de ser todos se marchitarían como tulipanes en un florero, cada uno con sus brazos alrededor del otro. Sigue, sigue, sigue, dicen los árboles cuando duermo. Ellos enseñan.

Cuando estoy demasiado triste o demasiado flaca para seguir siguiendo, cuando soy una cosita delgada contra tantos ladrillos es cuando miro los árboles. Cuando no hay nada más que ver en esta calle. Cuatro que crecieron a pesar del concreto. Cuatro que luchan y no se olvidan de luchar. Cuatro cuyo única razón es ser y ser.

# MEET THE WRITER

## "A House All My Own"

**Sandra Cisneros** (1954–    ) was born and raised in Chicago, the only daughter in a working-class family with six sons. The harshness of life in poor neighborhoods made Cisneros shy as a child, so she escaped into the world of books. By the age of ten, she was writing her own poetry.

Cisneros grew up speaking Spanish with her Mexican-born father, but she didn't explore her heritage until she attended the Writer's Workshop at the University of Iowa. There, she began a series of sketches about her old Spanish-speaking neighborhood in Chicago. These sketches grew into her first book, *The House on Mango Street* (1984). In that book, through her narrator, Esperanza, Cisneros speaks of her yearning for a space of her own:

   **❝** A house all my own. . . . Only a house quiet as snow, a space for myself to go, clean as paper before the poem. **❞**

Since then, Cisneros has continued to seek that "house" in poems and stories about an urban world she knows well.

# READ ON

## Far from the Crowd

Just when Wil Neuton's life in Madison, Wisconsin, seems perfect, his father transplants the family to a lonely backwoods spot in Gary Paulsen's *The Island* (Orchard). Wil learns to like his new life when he finds an island wilderness near his new home and discovers some amazing things about himself and the world.

## Listening to the Land

In Jean Craighead George's adventure story *The Talking Earth* (HarperCollins), young Billie Wind, a Seminole, questions her heritage. She doubts that the Seminole legends about the earth are true. To test her beliefs, the Seminole Council sends Billie into the Everglades. In the wilderness, Billie finds she must believe in the old legends if she wants to stay alive.

## Sailing, Sailing

*Dove* (Bantam) is sixteen-year-old Robin Lee Graham's true adventure story of his five-year voyage around the world—alone on a twenty-four-foot sailboat. Along the way, Robin faces fierce storms, suffocating heat, and loneliness. Sail the high seas with him as he finds courage, love, and maturity.

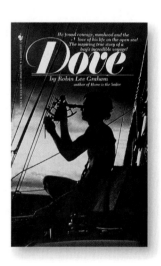

## Other Picks

- Kristiana Gregory, *Earthquake at Dawn* (Harcourt Brace). Photographer Edith Irvine and her young assistant, Daisy Valentine, wander San Francisco after a major earthquake and photograph the results of one of nature's most violent acts.

- Laura Ingalls Wilder, *On the Way Home: The Diary of a Trip from South Dakota to Mansfield, Missouri, in 1894* (HarperCollins). The famous author of the *Little House* books describes the beauty of the frontier country she passes through on a journey.

**Technology HELP**

*See* Writer's Workshop 1 CD-ROM. *Assignment: Observational Writing.*

**ASSIGNMENT**

**Write an essay describing something you've observed.**

**AIM**

**To inform; to express yourself.**

**AUDIENCE**

**Your teacher and classmates.**

## DESCRIPTIVE WRITING

# OBSERVATIONAL WRITING

In **observational writing,** you use words to paint a picture. You observe your subject closely and write a detailed **description** of what you see.

### Professional Model

*In this passage from her autobiographical book* Cross Creek, *Marjorie Kinnan Rawlings describes chameleons—small lizards capable of changing color—that she observed near her home in Florida.*

The little chameleons are definitely friendly. . . . They watch you for hours with small bright eyes. They enjoy being brought into the house on a bunch of roses, to serve on the dining table for ornament, shading obligingly from their favorite sage-green through taupe to a pinkish mauve, according to their passage over leaf or stem or blossom. . . .

The most ambitious chameleon I have ever seen was swallowing a butterfly twice as wide as he himself was long, the body almost as large as the swallower's. When I first noticed him, he had the butterfly's head in his mouth and the wings stuck out on either side like vast and ferocious moustaches. I stood and laughed at him and he eyed me furiously,

*The writer clearly identifies what she is observing.*

*She describes the subject's appearance.*

*She describes an action in humorous detail.*

*(continued)*

> switching his tail. I said, "You'll never do it," and went on about my business. An hour later I passed by again and all the butterfly was down except for the wing tips. As I watched, he gulped and the job was done.
>
> —from *Cross Creek* by Marjorie Kinnan Rawlings

*She shows how she feels about her subject by quoting what she said to him.*

## Prewriting

### 1. Writer's Notebook

Look back at the notes you made in your Writer's Notebook for this collection. Is there a person, place, or thing that you would enjoy observing and describing?

### 2. Freewriting

For more ideas, freewrite for a minute or two on some of these subjects:

- activities you can observe (someone cooking dinner; a basketball game)
- people you can observe (your older sister; an athlete)
- animals you can observe (your pet; a monkey at the zoo)
- places and things you can observe (the lunchroom; a mall)
- events you can observe (a scientific experiment)

### 3. Choosing a Subject

To decide on your subject, keep these points in mind:

- You should be able to observe your subject directly or to picture it clearly.
- Your subject should interest you and your readers.

**Sensory details:**
When writing your
observation, try to use
adjectives that appeal to
as many different senses
as possible. You'll find
visual details easy to include. Challenge yourself
to include as well at least
one detail of sound,
smell, and touch or
movement.

**Exact words:** Exact
words sharpen your
description. In the Stu-
dent Model at the right,
dragonflies don't just fly;
they flutter and glide.

The more sensory de-
tails and exact words you
include, the more likely
you'll be to re-create the
scene and to make your
readers feel as though
they were there.

# 4. Elaboration: Gathering Details

You've chosen your subject. Now it's time to observe it. How?
You observe something by using all of your five senses. Most
subjects you can see, hear, and feel; some you can smell or taste
as well. Use a chart like the one here to record all the details
and events you observe and the impressions they create.

| Sensory Details | Events | Impressions |
|---|---|---|
| **see** coconut trees · crickets<br>**hear** airplane · waves<br>**feel** sun · hot air<br>**smell** saltwater<br>**taste** lemon candy | dragonflies flutter and glide · trucks haul tons of dirt · ferries race to Singapore | Patam is just the place for me. |

**Student Model**

## THE NATURE OF PATAM

*This essay describes a beach scene in Indonesia. How
does the writer set the scene? How has he organized
his details? What overall impression does he create?*

Right now I'm sitting cross-legged on
the big gray porch at our Patam
beach house. The bright shining sun
and hot day make me feel lazy.

The shadowy light-and-dark-green
jungle to the left of me has tall, light-
brown trunks of trees everywhere.
To the right a coconut tree with its
palms spread out looks like a parachute. Brown and gray monkeys
chatter away as small green crickets
sing. Different colored dragonflies
flutter and glide so fast in every
direction I can't see what color they
are!

Lively waves leap to and fro on
the pure white beach, while salt-
water and rock bash noisily together.

*The writer
introduces
his subject
and tells
where he is.*

*Details
of sight,
sound, and
movement
create a vivid
picture.*

An airplane rumbles slowly away. Across the bay trucks rattle loudly as they haul tons of brown dirt dark as chocolate.

*The writer moves from the trees near him to the plane, trucks, and boats in the distance.*

Boats are all over the water! About three miles out huge tankers loom above the deep, gigantic, calm blue ocean, with ferries racing past them on their way to Singapore. Another boat, a small abandoned tan-brown sampan, bobs gently up and down in the gold sunlit waters that seem like enormous masses of lemon candy. I think Patam is just the place for me.

*The writer tells how he feels about this place.*

—Benjamin Bethea
Batam Island Christian Home School
Batam, Indonesia

## 5. Organizing

Here are three ways of organizing ideas:

a. **Chronological order,** arranging details in the order in which they happen. Chronological order works best when you're describing an activity or event.

b. **Spatial order,** describing details by location: near to far, top to bottom, left to right. Spatial order works well when you're describing scenes, people, animals, and objects.

c. **Order of importance,** arranging details from least to most important or from most to least important. Order of importance works well when you're expressing your feelings and when you're describing people, animals, and objects.

## Drafting

### 1. Focusing on the Main Idea

Everything you write needs a focus—a **main idea** that shapes what you put down on paper. To state your main idea clearly, ask yourself: What is my impression of my subject? *or* What is the purpose of my essay?

---

**Framework for Observational Writing**

**Introduction** (identifies subject, time, and place and gives background information): _____ _____ _____

**Observations:**
1. _____
Specifics: _____
2. _____
Specifics: _____
3. _____
Specifics: _____
4. _____
Specifics: _____

**Conclusion** (may include your main impression, your feelings, or your questions about what you observed): _____ _____ _____

**Language/Grammar Link
H E L P**

*Avoiding clichés: page 432. Formal and informal English: page 442. Active and passive voice: page 459. Dialect: page 481.*

**Sentence Workshop**
**H E L P**

*Using a variety of sentence structures: page 491.*

**Communications Handbook**
**H E L P**

*See Proofreaders' Marks.*

**Publishing Tip**

Draw a picture to illustrate a classmate's observation. Then, with the class, make a bulletin-board display of the essays and drawings.

## 2. Setting the Scene

Whenever you observe something, you view it from a particular place and at a particular time. By telling readers where you are, you give them a place to stand as they observe through your eyes. Wherever you are—nose to nose with your subject, above a lake in a hot-air balloon—make your viewpoint clear.

## Evaluating and Revising

### 1. Peer Review

Exchange papers with a partner, and answer the following questions:

- What did you picture as you were reading?
- Which details stood out? Why?
- Was anything confusing?
- Is there any point on which you would like more information?

Make notes as you listen to your partner's comments.

### 2. Revising

Review your peer reader's suggestions, and decide on the changes you want to make. Make the changes; then, read your paper again to be sure that they are improvements. When you're satisfied with the content of your paper, you're ready to proofread it.

# Sentence Workshop

## USING A VARIETY OF SENTENCE STRUCTURES

The basic pattern of an English sentence is subject-verb-complement (if there is a complement). If you began sentences with the subject all the time, however, your writing would be very boring.

SIMILAR SENTENCE STRUCTURES

> Another world was in the sky long ago. It existed before this world. It floated there like a great cloud. No sun was in that world. Light came from the white blossoms of a great tree. The tree grew in the center of the Sky World.

DIFFERENT SENTENCE STRUCTURES

> "Long ago, before this world existed, there was another world in the sky. It floated there like a great cloud. In that world there was no sun, but light came from the white blossoms of a great tree that grew in the center of the Sky World."

—Joseph Bruchac, "Sky Woman" (pages 427–428)

To vary your sentences, as Bruchac varied his, try these strategies:

1. Open with a single-word modifier.

2. Open with a phrase or clause.

3. Combine sentences with *and, but,* or *or.*

4. Combine sentences by using subordination.

Try writing a few sentences with the same structure as Bruchac's sentences. Be sure to compare your sentences with those of other students in class.

## Writer's Workshop Follow-up: Revision

Exchange your observational writing piece for a class-mate's. Where your partner's paper lacks a variety of sentence structures, suggest alternatives. Then, revise your paper, using your classmate's suggestions.

**Language Handbook HELP**

*See Phrases, pages 741-746; Clauses, pages 746-750; Writing Effective Sentences, pages 760-762.*

**Technology HELP**

*See* Language Workshop CD-ROM. *Key word entry: sentence structures.*

### Try It Out

The following paragraph is made up of simple sentences. Change or combine some of them in order to vary the sentence structure.

The earth's mantle is about eighteen hundred miles thick. It is made of rock. It is not familiar rock. The rock is under great pressure. It is deep within the earth. It is also extremely hot. The heat and pressure make the rock behave in certain ways. These ways are strange to us.

Now, go back to any selection you have read in this collection. Copy a sentence you like and divide it into parts. Then, write a sentence of your own with the same structure.

# Reading for Life

## Understanding Induction and Deduction

### Situation

While reading a newspaper, you come across two letters to the editor arguing for two sides of an issue. What strategies can you use to evaluate the issue?

### Strategies

**Learn what a logical argument is.**

When people argue, they try to persuade others to think or act in a certain way. A **logical argument** is based on correct reasoning. When you argue logically, you present opinions backed up by facts. You attack an idea, not the person who has the idea. You try to avoid exaggerations and insults and other language that stirs up strong feelings.

**Identify two ways of organizing and presenting information to support arguments.**

- In the true story "When the Earth Shakes," people hear rumbling noises. They feel the earth shaking. Buildings fall, and the earth splits open. From evidence around them people conclude that they're in the middle of an earthquake. They're using

**inductive reasoning,** moving from specific facts or observations to a **conclusion** based on those facts.

- **Deductive reasoning** moves in the opposite direction—from the general to the specific. When you use deductive reasoning, you start with a general idea and present reasons to support it. Here is an example.

   *General idea:* Sean Riley should be class president.

   *Supporting reasons:* He's a strong leader and a hard worker, and he has lots of creative ideas.

### Using the Strategies

Read the students' arguments in the box above. Then, answer these questions:

> **Reba Sanchez argues:** "I've seen shark movies. They have terrific special effects. I like to sit in the front so I feel surrounded by the action. I see a movie with friends. We all like movies better than books. Who wouldn't, except maybe somebody with no friends? Seeing a movie is always better than reading a story."

> **Bobby Newton argues:** "Reading a well-written true story is way more exciting than just sitting watching a movie. 'Survive the Savage Sea' is a well-written true story. The descriptions make me feel as if I were right there, getting scared. Reading 'Survive the Savage Sea' is a lot more exciting than seeing a movie. Besides, you can go back and reread the good parts."

1. Which student uses mostly inductive reasoning? Which uses mostly deductive reasoning?

2. Which student presents the better argument—the argument that is more logical? (Set aside your own opinion on the question.)

3. Analyze each argument, using the information on this page. What flaws, if any, can you find in each student's reasoning?

### Extending the Strategies

Find an editorial or a letter to the editor in your school paper or a local newspaper. Using the strategies you've just learned, analyze the organization and presentation of ideas. Does the writer use inductive or deductive reasoning? How can you tell?

# Learning for Life

## Saving Our Planet: Scientific Research

### Problem

We all need to be concerned about the problem of environmental pollution. How can you find out more about this problem and about ways to clean up our planet?

### Project

**Research an environmental pollution problem. Find out how severe the problem is and what can be done to clear it up.**

### Preparation

1. As a class, discuss the kinds of environmental pollution we have today, such as too much garbage, air pollution, oil spills, and acid rain.

2. Break up into small groups. Each group should pick one environmental pollution problem to research.

### Procedure

1. In your group, assign each member a question to research, for example:

   • What causes the problem?

   • How severe is the problem?

   • What steps are being taken to solve it?

   • What else needs to be done?

2. Decide where you can find information on your topic. For example, you might look at science books, magazines, and newspapers. You might also contact the Environmental Protection Agency or other groups concerned with the environment. (They might be listed in the phone book under Environmental Organizations.)

3. Complete your research. Then, meet with your group to discuss the information you found. Organize your notes in clear categories.

4. Figure out how to organize some of your information in a visual format—a chart, graph, diagram, or map, for example.

### Presentation

Choose one of these ways to present what you've learned:

#### 1. Earth Day

Hold an Earth Day in your class. Groups should present their environmental topics to the class in oral research reports with visual aids, which could include photographs, diagrams, charts, and maps.

#### 2. Invention

If you're science-minded or creative, come up with your own invention for a "pollution solution"—either a new method or a new product to help clean up the environment. Describe it in detail and make a drawing or diagram.

#### 3. "Save Our Planet" Handbook

Create a "Save Our Planet" handbook. Work as a class, with each group responsible for the section on its environmental problem. Include important facts about the problem, and illustrate your points with diagrams, charts, and maps. Include a list of actions people can take to prevent the problem or to clear it up.

### Processing

Write a reflection using this starter: If it were my job to clean up our planet, the first thing I'd do is . . . .

## Seven

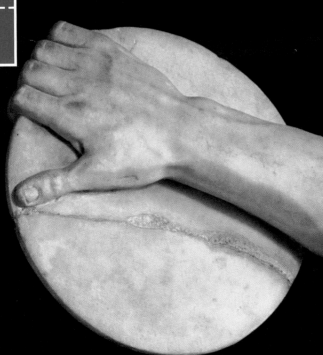

# Our Classical Heritage

*Lonely as they were, by themselves, early people looked inside themselves and expressed a longing to discover, to explain who they were, why they were, and from what and where they came.*

—*Virginia Hamilton*

**Discus thrower.**
Palazzo Vecchio, Florence, Italy. Scala/Art Resource, New York.

# Elements of Literature

## THE MYTHS OF GREECE AND ROME

It is hard to imagine what our civilization would be like without the mythology of ancient Greece and Rome. The ancient immortals are still around us in spirit. You might even pass imitations of their "houses" almost every day. Whenever you see a large building with many columns holding up a roof, you are looking at an imitation of a Greek temple.

If you go to any one of the great museums of Europe or America, you will find statues and paintings of classical gods and heroes—as many as you will find of characters and events from history.

If you read poetry in English classes, you will come across references to such ancient places as Troy and Carthage. You will read references to such monsters as the Sirens and the Cyclops, to such gods and heroes as Poseidon, Odysseus (whose Roman name is Ulysses), Athena, and Hercules. These are all names from mythology—names that poets and artists expect us to recognize.

## Why Read the Myths?

There is good reason for the continued presence of these strange beings and places in our lives. They are all related to those great classical civilizations of Greece and Rome that were so important to our development as a society. These civilizations gave us much of our astronomy, our mathematics, our philosophy, our architecture, our medicine, our monetary system, and our systems of government and law. We should remember, for instance, that the word *democracy* comes from the Greek word *demokratia*, meaning "rule of the people." This was a kind of government that first flourished in the ancient Greek city-state of Athens.

## What Is a Myth?

**Myths** are stories that are always in some sense religious. Myths represent the deepest wishes and fears of human beings. They helped the ancient people to understand the mysterious and sometimes frightening forces of the universe—forces such as seasonal changes, fire, lightning, drought, floods, and death. Myths probably originated when people began to ask questions about the creation of the world and about their role in it.

## Makers of Myths

Most of the myths you will read here originated in the area around the Mediterranean Sea (see the inset of the map on page 498). The early myth makers would not have known how to write. These old myths were passed on orally from generation to generation by the many tribes that traveled through or lived in what is now Greece and western Turkey.

# *by* David Adams Leeming

By the second century B.C., the Romans had conquered the Greeks and had adopted the Greek myths. The Romans added a new, cynical tone to the old stories. This tone reflected the fact that the Romans were less serious about religion than the Greeks were.

## The Uses of Mythology

Great myths are never merely silly or superstitious tales. Like all true art, the great myths give us insights into the nature of our world.

The Greeks and Romans, like all myth makers, used myths for these purposes:

1. to explain the creation of the world

2. to explain natural phenomena

3. to give story form to ancient religious practices

4. to teach moral lessons

5. to explain history

6. to express, as dreams do, the deepest fears and hopes of the human race

## A Family Affair: Gods and Goddesses

According to the Greek myths, the divinities lived on Mount Olympus. Many of them traveled down to spend time with ordinary people. To the myth makers, a god or goddess was a powerful being, often identified with a force of nature. The chart below shows some of the divinities and their special powers.

| Greek Name | Roman Name | Area of Power |
|---|---|---|
| Zeus (zyo͞os) | Jupiter | king of the gods; sky; weather |
| Apollo (ə·päl′ō) | Apollo | the sun; youth; music; archery; healing; prophecy |
| Artemis (är′tə·mis) | Diana | twin sister of Apollo; the moon; hunting |
| Hades (hā′dēz′) | Pluto | king of the underworld |
| Poseidon (pō·sī′dən) | Neptune | ruler of the seas |
| Hera (hēr′ə) | Juno | wife of Zeus; queen of gods; women; marriage |
| Dionysus (dī′ə·nī′səs) | Bacchus | wine; fertility; music |
| Athena (ə·thē′nə) | Minerva | wisdom; war; crafts |
| Hephaestus (hē·fes′təs) | Vulcan | craftsman for the gods; fire |
| Hermes (hur′mēz) | Mercury | messenger god; secrets; tricks |
| Demeter (di·mēt′ər) | Ceres | agriculture; earth; corn |
| Persephone (pər·sef′ə·nē) | Proserpine | daughter of Demeter; queen of Hades |

*(continued on next page)*

# Elements of Literature

## The World of Classical Mythology

THRACE
King Diomedes rules
Orpheus born

Apollo

Hera Zeus

Mount Olympus

Iris searches for Demeter

THESSALY

Mount Parnassus
Oracle of Delphi

IONIAN SEA

Echo and Narcissus

THEBES
Hercules born here

EUBOEA

AEGE...

Poseidon's palace

Athens

Achelous River

Hercules captures Erymanthian Boar

Gulf of Corinth

Hercules wrestles Nemean Lion

Hermes born here

Mycenae
Eurystheus rules

ARCADIA

Argos

Argis Bay

Hercules cleans Augean Stables

Hercules kills the Hydra

PELOPONNESE

Sparta

Cythera
Aphrodite landed here

MEDITERRANEAN SEA

SICILY
Home of Persephone
Enna Valley

Carthage

North Africa

CRETE

# *Before You Read*

## THE ORIGIN OF THE SEASONS

## Make the Connection

### Seasons of the Heart

Ancient people looked to myths for answers to questions that they had about nature, just as we look to science today. They wondered, for example, why the growing cycle for crops was linked to the seasons and why there were seasons at all.

## Reading Skills and Strategies

### Dialogue with the Text

As you read this myth, keep a sheet of paper next to each page so that you can jot down your thoughts and feelings about this explanation of the origin of the seasons. One student's comments appear on the first page of the myth as an example.

## Elements of Literature

### Origin Myths

The very ancient Greeks did not possess anything like the scientific knowledge we have today. Still, they were just as curious about their natural surroundings as we are about ours. They longed for explanations. Why do we have so many different kinds of flowers? Why is there night and day? Why do the seasons change? For answers to their questions, the ancient people turned to their myth makers. They believed these storytellers were directly in touch with the source of all knowledge—the gods. The myth makers were the guardians of a tradition with the same purpose as science: to provide necessary explanations. These explanations, or **origin myths,** told how something came into being.

---

**A**n **origin myth** is an imaginative explanation of how something in the world was created or came to exist.

*For more on Myth, see pages 496–499 and the Handbook of Literary Terms.*

---

*As she stretched out her hand, the earth opened in front of her ...*

500

# The Origin of the Seasons

*retold by* **Olivia Coolidge**

emeter, the great earth mother, was goddess of the harvest. Tall and majestic was her appearance, and her hair was the color of ripe wheat. It was she who filled the ears with grain. In her honor white-robed women brought golden garlands of wheat as first fruits to the altar. Reaping, threshing, winnowing,[1] and the long tables set in the shade for the harvesters' refreshment—all these were hers. Songs and feasting did her honor as the hard-working farmer gathered his abundant fruit. All the laws which the farmer knew came from her: the time for plowing, what land would best bear crops, which was fit for grapes, and which to leave for pasture. She was a goddess whom men called the great mother because of her generosity in giving. Her own special daughter in the family of the gods was named Persephone.

Persephone was the spring maiden, young and full of joy. Sicily was her home, for it is a land where the spring is long and lovely, and where spring flowers are abundant. Here Persephone played with her maidens from day to day till the rocks and valleys rang with the sound of laughter, and gloomy Hades heard it as he sat on his throne in the dark land of the dead. Even his heart of stone was touched by her young beauty, so that he arose in his awful majesty and came up to Olympus to ask Zeus if he might have Persephone to wife. Zeus bowed his head in agreement, and mighty Olympus thundered as he promised.

1. **winnowing:** separating the husks from the grain.

Thus it came about that as Persephone was gathering flowers with her maidens in the vale of Enna, a marvelous thing happened. Enna was a beautiful valley in whose meadows all the most lovely flowers of the year grew at the same season. There were wild roses, purple crocuses, sweet-scented violets, tall iris, rich narcissus,[2] and white lilies. All these the girl was gathering, yet fair as they were, Persephone herself was fairer far.

As the maidens went picking and calling to one another across the blossoming meadow, it happened that Persephone strayed apart from the rest. Then, as she looked a little ahead in the meadow, she suddenly beheld the marvelous thing. It was a flower so beautiful that none like it had ever been known. It seemed a kind of narcissus, purple and white, but from a single root there sprang a hundred blossoms, and at the sweet scent of it the very heavens and earth appeared to smile for joy. Without calling to the others, Persephone sprang forward to be the first to pick the precious bloom. As she stretched out her hand, the earth opened in front of her, and she found herself caught in a stranger's arms. Persephone shrieked aloud and struggled, while the armful of flowers cascaded down to earth. However, the dark-eyed Hades was far stronger than she. He swept her into his golden chariot, took the reins of his coal-black horses, and was gone amid the rumbling sound of the closing earth before the other girls in the valley could even come in sight of the spot. When they did get there, nobody was visible. Only the roses and lilies of Persephone lay scattered in wild confusion over the grassy turf.

Bitter was the grief of Demeter when she heard the news of her daughter's mysterious fate. Veiling herself with a dark cloud, she sped, swift as a wild bird, over land and ocean for nine days, searching everywhere and asking all she met if they had seen her daughter. Neither gods nor men had seen her. Even the birds could give no tidings, and Demeter in despair turned to Phoebus Apollo, who sees all things from his chariot in the heavens.

"Yes, I have seen your daughter," said the god at last. "Hades has taken her with the consent of Zeus, that she may dwell in the land of mist and gloom as his queen. The girl struggled and was unwilling, but Hades is far stronger than she."

When she heard this, Demeter fell into deep despair, for she knew she could never rescue Persephone if Zeus and Hades had agreed. She did not care any more to enter the palace of Olympus, where the gods live in joy and feasting and where Apollo plays the lyre while the Muses sing. She took on her the form of an old woman, worn but stately, and wandered about the earth, where there is much sorrow to be seen. At first she kept away from the homes of people, since the sight of little children and happy mothers gave her pain. One day, however, as she sat by the side of a well to rest her weary feet, four girls came down to draw water. They were kind hearted and charming as they talked with her and concerned themselves about the fate of the homeless stranger-woman who was sitting at their gates. To account for herself, Demeter told them that she was a woman of good family from Crete, across the sea, who had been captured by pirates and was to have been sold for a slave. She had escaped as they landed once to cook a meal on shore, and now she was wandering to find work.

The four girls listened to this story, much impressed by the stately manner of the strange

---

**2. narcissus** (när·sis′əs): family of lilies including daffodils and jonquils. "Echo and Narcissus" (page 523) gives the ancient Greeks' explanation of how this flower came to be.

*La Primavera: Flora* (detail) (1477)
by Sandro Botticelli.

Uffizi Gallery, Florence, Italy. Erich Lessing/Art Resource, New York.

woman. At last they said that their mother, Metaneira,[3] was looking for a nurse for their new-born brother, Demophoon.[4] Perhaps the stranger would come and talk with her. Demeter agreed, feeling a great longing to hold a baby once more, even if it were not her own. She went therefore to Metaneira, who was much struck with the quiet dignity of the goddess and glad to give her charge of her little son. For a while thereafter Demeter was nurse to Demophoon, and his smiles and babble consoled her in some part for her own darling daughter. She began to make plans for Demophoon: He should be a great hero; he should become an immortal, so that when he grew up she could keep him with her.

Presently the whole household was amazed at how beautiful Demophoon was growing, the more so as they never saw the nurse feed him anything. Secretly Demeter would anoint him with ambrosia,[5] like the gods, and from her breath, as he lay in her lap, he would draw his nourishment. When the night came, she would linger by the great fireside in the hall, rocking the child in her arms while the embers burned low and the people went off to sleep. Then, when all was still, she would stoop quickly down and put the baby into the fire itself. All night long the child would sleep in the red-hot ashes, while his earthly flesh and blood changed slowly into the substance of the immortals. In the morning when people came, the ashes were cold and dead, and by the hearth sat the stranger-woman, gently rocking and singing to the child.

Presently Metaneira became suspicious of the strangeness of it all. What did she know of this nurse but the story she had heard from her daughters? Perhaps the woman was a witch of some sort who wished to steal or transform the boy. In any case it was wise to be careful. One night, therefore, when she went up to her chamber, she set the door ajar and stood there in the crack silently watching the nurse at the fireside crooning over the child. The hall was very dark, so that it was hard to see clearly, but in a little while the mother beheld the dim figure bend forward. A log broke in the fireplace, a little flame shot up, and there clear in the light lay the baby on top of the fire.

Metaneira screamed loudly and lost no time in rushing forward, but it was Demeter who snatched up the baby. "Fool that you are," she said indignantly to Metaneira, "I would have made your son immortal, but that is now impossible. He shall be a great hero, but in the end he will have to die. I, the goddess Demeter, promise it." With that old age fell from her and she grew in stature. Golden hair spread down over her shoulders so that the great hall was filled with light. She turned and went out of the doorway, leaving the baby on the ground and Metaneira too amazed and frightened even to take him up.

All the while that Demeter had been wandering, she had given no thought to her duties as the harvest goddess. Instead she was almost glad that others should suffer because she was suffering. In vain the oxen spent their strength in dragging the heavy plowshare[6] through the soil. In vain did the sower with his bag of grain throw out the even handfuls of white barley in a wide arc as he strode. The greedy birds had a feast off the seed corn that season; or if it started to sprout, sun baked it and rains washed it away. Nothing would grow. As the gods looked down, they saw threatening the earth a famine such as never had been known.

6. **plowshare:** cutting blade of a plow.

3. **Metaneira** (met′ə·nē′rə).
4. **Demophoon** (de·mäf′ō·än′).
5. **ambrosia** (am·brō′zhə): food of the gods.

Even the offerings to the gods were neglected by despairing men who could no longer spare anything from their dwindling stores.

At last Zeus sent Iris, the rainbow, to seek out Demeter and appeal to her to save mankind. Dazzling Iris swept down from Olympus swift as a ray of light and found Demeter sitting in her temple, the dark cloak still around her and her head bowed on her hand. Though Iris urged her with the messages of Zeus and offered beautiful gifts or whatever powers among the gods she chose, Demeter would not lift her head or listen. All she said was that she would neither set foot on Olympus nor let fruit grow on the earth until Persephone was restored to her from the kingdom of the dead.

At last Zeus saw that he must send Hermes of the golden sandals to bring back Persephone to the light. The messenger found dark-haired Hades sitting upon his throne with Persephone, pale and sad, beside him. She had neither eaten nor drunk since she had been in the land of the dead. She sprang up with joy at the message of Hermes, while the dark king looked gloomier than ever, for he really loved his queen. Though he could not disobey the command of Zeus, he was crafty, and he pressed Persephone to eat or drink with him as they parted. Now, with joy in her heart, she should not refuse all food. Persephone was eager to be gone, but since the king entreated her, she took a pomegranate[7] from him to avoid argument and delay. Giving in to his pleading, she ate seven of the seeds. Then Hermes took her with him, and she came out into the upper air.

When Demeter saw Hermes with her daughter, she started up, and Persephone too rushed forward with a glad cry and flung her arms

7. **pomegranate** (päm′ə·gran′it): round, red fruit containing many seeds. Pomegranates are pictured on page 509.

*La Primavera: Flora* (detail) (1477) by Sandro Botticelli.
Uffizi Gallery, Florence, Italy. Erich Lessing/Art Resource, New York.

about her mother's neck. For a long time the two caressed each other, but at last Demeter began to question the girl. "Did you eat or drink anything with Hades?" she asked her daughter anxiously, and the girl replied:

"Nothing until Hermes released me. Then in my joy I took a pomegranate and ate seven of its seeds."

"Alas," said the goddess in dismay, "my daughter, what have you done? The Fates have said that if you ate anything in the land of shadow, you must return to Hades and rule with him as his queen. However, you ate not the whole pomegranate, but only seven of the seeds. For seven months of the year, therefore, you must dwell in the underworld, and the remaining five you may live with me."

Thus the Fates had decreed, and even Zeus could not alter their law. For seven months of every year, Persephone is lost to Demeter and rules pale and sad over the dead. At this time Demeter mourns, trees shed their leaves, cold comes, and the earth lies still and dead. But when, in the eighth month, Persephone returns, her mother is glad and the earth rejoices. The wheat springs up, bright, fresh, and green in the plowland. Flowers unfold, birds sing, and young animals are born. Everywhere the heavens smile for joy or weep sudden showers of gladness upon the springing earth.

## MEET THE WRITER

### "I Write Because . . . I Almost Have To"

**Olivia Coolidge** (1908–      ), the daughter of an English historian, has used her own storytelling gifts mainly to make mythology and history exciting for young readers. She believes strongly in the power of story:

66 A good book should excite, amuse and interest. It should give a sense of seeing as a movie does. In other words, a good book needs imagination and the gift of a good storyteller. I write because I like writing, because I want to write, and because I almost have to. I have a great many things I want to say, ideas I want to express and pictures I want to convey to other people. 99

### More Gifts from a Good Storyteller

To "see" more myths and ancient stories by Olivia Coolidge, look for *Greek Myths* and *Legends of the North* (both published by Houghton Mifflin). To explore the ancient world from which these stories emerged, check out *The Golden Days of Greece* (Thomas Crowell).

# MAKING MEANINGS

## First Thoughts

1. What are your first impressions of the gods and goddesses in this myth? What do you think of the way they treat one another and the people on earth? Review your reading notes for ideas.

## Shaping Interpretations

2. How does this story of the kidnapping of a young girl and her mother's grief explain the change of seasons on earth?

3. Why do you think Demeter spends so much time with the baby Demophoon, even planning to make him immortal?

4. Demeter is able to force Zeus to change his mind about the marriage of Hades and Persephone. What does this tell you about "the great earth mother"?

5. What **conclusion** can you draw about the power of love over death from this myth?

## Connecting with the Text

6. Which character in this myth do you feel the most sympathy for? Why?

## Extending the Text

7. What other accounts do you know of in which someone eats a forbidden food—or breaks a taboo (a rule strictly prohibiting something)—and pays dearly for it?

---

### Reading Check

Many events in this ancient myth are connected by **cause and effect.** On a sheet of paper, describe the effect of each event listed below.

a. Gloomy Hades falls in love with beautiful young Persephone.
   **Effect:**

b. Unhappy about the loss of her daughter, Demeter gives no thought to her duties as the harvest goddess.
   **Effect:**

c. Demeter vows that she will not let fruit grow on the earth until Persephone is returned.
   **Effect:**

d. While in the land of the dead, Persephone eats seven seeds from a piece of fruit.
   **Effect:**

Pomegranates.

# CHOICES: Building Your Portfolio

## Writer's Notebook

### 1. Collecting Ideas for an Evaluation

To endure, a myth must tell a good story. A myth must also speak to our deepest wishes and fears. Take some notes about how you think "The Origin of the Seasons" fits these criteria. Does it tell a good story that keeps you interested in what will happen next? Does the story express any universal wishes or any of our worst fears? You might use the chart shown in the notebook.

WORK IN PROGRESS

Evaluation Chart

Suspense:

Good characters:

Interesting theme:

Speaks to our
  wishes:

Expresses our fears:

## Creative Writing

### 2. Notes from the Underworld

Imagine that you are Persephone. Write diary entries in which you describe your thoughts and feelings about each of the following: picking flowers with your friends in the vale of Enna; being the wife of Hades; returning to your mother and the world of light; eating the pomegranate seeds.

## Creative Writing

### 3. A Myth for All Seasons

Throughout the world, people have told imaginative stories to explain the cycle of seasons. Write your own **origin myth** explaining why the seasons change as they do in your part of the world. If you live in a region where the weather rarely changes, tell why this came to be. Before you begin, decide whether the weather in your region is a punishment or a reward.

## Creative Writing

### 4. The Rest of the Story

What happens to Demophoon? Reread what Demeter says to the mother of the young boy. Then, write a short tale that shows how Demeter's predictions might have come true.

## Art/Design

### 5. Cover Story

The editor of a book of myths for children wants you to design the cover. The illustration on the cover will show a scene from "The Origin of the Seasons." Choose the scene from this myth that you find most dramatic or interesting. Then, illustrate the scene in a way that will make people want to read the myth.

# LANGUAGE LINK  MINI-LESSON

## Style: Descriptive Language

**Handbook of Literary Terms**
H E L P

*See Description.*

In "The Origin of the Seasons," Hades drives Persephone into a hole in the ground. Here's how Coolidge describes the scene:

"He <u>swept</u> her into his golden <u>chariot</u>, took the reins of his <u>coal-black</u> horses, and was gone amid the <u>rumbling</u> sound of the closing earth. . . ."

This sentence creates a rich picture because it uses good **descriptive language.** In good descriptive writing you find

1. **concrete, specific nouns:** It isn't just a *vehicle*—it's a *chariot*.

2. **precise verbs:** He didn't just *put* her in—he *swept* her in.

3. **vivid adjectives** that appeal to the senses: The horses are *coal-black*; the earth makes a *rumbling* sound.

### Try It Out

Rewrite each of the sentences below, using descriptive language. Remember to use specific nouns, precise verbs, and vivid adjectives.

1. Persephone lived in a perfectly nice place.

2. She went into a valley full of flowers.

3. Some horses went by, making a lot of noise.

4. The cavern was dark.

5. Poor Persephone sat on a throne.

# VOCABULARY  HOW TO OWN A WORD

### English Prefixes Derived from Greek

A **prefix** is a word part that is added to the beginning of a word to change the word's meaning. Many prefixes that we use today come from ancient Greek. Some common ones appear in the first column of the chart below. The first row of the chart is filled in for you. Use a dictionary to complete the rest of the chart. Be sure to compare your charts in class.

|  | Meaning | Example |
|---|---|---|
| anti- | against | antidote: something that acts against a poison |
| auto- |  |  |
| hydro- |  |  |
| meta- |  |  |
| sym- or syn- |  |  |

# Before You Read

## ORPHEUS, THE GREAT MUSICIAN

## Make the Connection

### Swept Away by Music

"Music is more important than we will ever know. Great music can pull you right out of your chair. It can make you cry, or laugh, or feel a way you've never felt before."

—Nadja Salerno-Sonnenberg, "The Power of Music" (page 517)

## Quickwrite

Think of a time when music touched your life. Write briefly about the experience.

## Elements of Literature

### The Underworld of Myth

You don't have to read too many myths before you find yourself in that frightful place called the underworld. As you know from "The Origin of the Seasons," the underworld is a dark and gloomy place ruled by the stern god Hades. To reach Hades' home, you cross the River Styx (stiks) on a ferryboat rowed by Charon (ker'ən). Then you pass through gates guarded by Cerberus, a three-headed dog. Normally only the souls of the dead go to Hades. Sometimes, however, living people attempt the dangerous journey, usually to reach someone who has died.

> For more on Myth, see pages 496–499 and the Handbook of Literary Terms.

## Reading Skills and Strategies

### Setting Purposes for Reading: Being Flexible

Journeys to the underworld make exciting stories. Your original **purpose**, or reason, for reading about the dark kingdom may be to **enjoy** the adventure. As you get caught up in the story, however, you may want to **understand** it on a deeper level. Journey with Orpheus to the underworld, and think about what this exciting story says about our fear of death and our desire to overcome it somehow.

*Orpheus, Eurydice, and Hermes.* Roman copy after Greek original.

Museo Archeologica Nazionale, Naples, Italy. Erich Lessing/Art Resource, New York.

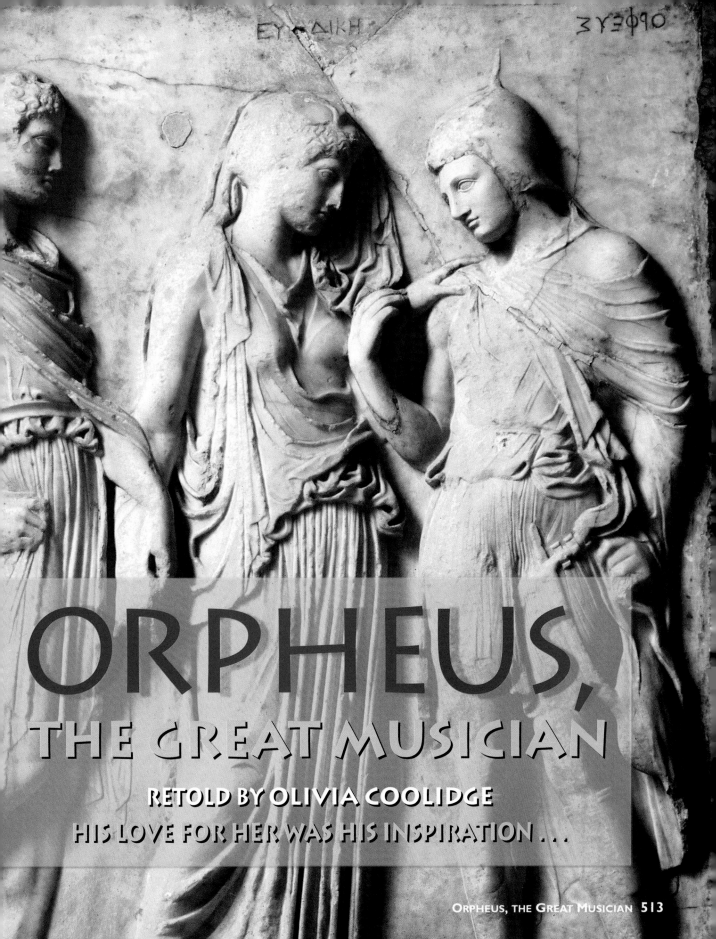

# ORPHEUS,
## THE GREAT MUSICIAN

### RETOLD BY OLIVIA COOLIDGE

HIS LOVE FOR HER WAS HIS INSPIRATION . . .

In the legend of Orpheus, the Greek love of music found its fullest expression. Orpheus, it is said, could make such heavenly songs that when he sat down to sing, the trees would crowd around to shade him. The ivy and vine stretched out their tendrils. Great oaks would bend their spreading branches over his head. The very rocks would edge down the mountainsides. Wild beasts crouched harmless by him, and nymphs[1] and woodland gods would listen to him, enchanted.

Orpheus himself, however, had eyes for no one but the nymph Eurydice.[2] His love for her was his inspiration, and his power sprang from the passionate longing that he knew in his own heart. All nature rejoiced with him on his bridal day, but on that very morning, as Eurydice went down to the riverside with her maidens to gather flowers for a bridal garland, she was bitten in the foot by a snake, and she died in spite of all attempts to save her.

Orpheus was <u>inconsolable</u>. All day long he mourned his bride, while birds, beasts, and the earth itself sorrowed with him. When at last the shadows of the sun grew long, Orpheus took his lyre[3] and made his way to the yawning cave which leads down into the underworld, where the soul of dead Eurydice had gone.

Even gray Charon, the ferryman of the Styx, forgot to ask his passenger for the price of crossing. The dog Cerberus, the three-headed monster who guards Hades' gate, stopped full in his tracks and listened motionless until Orpheus had passed. As he entered the land of Hades, the pale ghosts came after him like great, uncounted flocks of silent birds. All the land lay hushed as that marvelous voice resounded across the mud and marshes of its dreadful rivers. In the daffodil fields of Elysium, the happy dead sat silent among their flowers. In the farthest corners of the place of punishment, the hissing

**THE EARTH ITSELF SORROWED WITH HIM.**

1. **nymphs:** minor goddesses of nature, usually young and beautiful, living in mountains, rivers, or trees.
2. **Eurydice** (yōō·rid′i·sē′).
3. **lyre** (līr): small harp.

Lyre player. Greece.

flames stood still. Accursed Sisyphus,[4] who toils eternally to push a mighty rock uphill, sat down and knew not he was resting. Tantalus, who strains forever after visions of cool water, forgot his thirst and ceased to clutch at the empty air.

The pillared[5] hall of Hades opened before the hero's song. The ranks of long-dead heroes who sit at Hades' board looked up and turned their eyes away from the pitiless form of Hades and his pale, unhappy queen. Grim and unmoving sat the dark king of the dead on his ebony throne, yet the tears shone on his rigid cheeks in the light of his ghastly torches. Even his hard heart, which knew all misery and cared nothing for it, was touched by the love and longing of the music.

At last the minstrel[6] came to an end, and a long sigh like wind in pine trees was heard from the assembled ghosts. Then the king spoke, and his deep voice echoed through his silent land. "Go back to the light of day," he said. "Go quickly while my monsters are stilled by your song. Climb up the steep road to daylight, and never once turn back. The spirit of Eurydice shall follow, but if you look around at her, she will return to me."

Orpheus turned and strode from the hall of Hades, and the flocks of following ghosts made way for him to pass. In vain he searched their ranks for a sight of his lost Eurydice. In vain he listened for the faintest sound behind. The barge of Charon sank to the very gunwales[7] beneath his weight, but no following passenger pressed it lower down. The way from the land of Hades to the upper world is long and hard, far easier to descend than climb. It was dark and misty, full of strange shapes and noises, yet in many places merely black and silent as the tomb. Here Orpheus would stop and listen, but nothing moved behind him. For all he could hear, he was utterly alone. Then he would wonder if the pitiless Hades were deceiving him. Suppose he came up to the light again and Eurydice was not there! Once he had charmed the ferryman and the dreadful monsters, but now they had heard his song. The second time his spell would be less powerful; he could never go again. Perhaps he had lost Eurydice by his readiness to believe.

4. **Sisyphus** (sis′ə·fəs).
5. **pillared:** having pillars (columns).
6. **minstrel:** singer.
7. **gunwales** (gun′əlz): upper edges of the sides of a boat.

-----

## Words to Own

**inconsolable** (in′kən·sōl′ə·bəl) *adj.*: unable to be comforted; brokenhearted.
**ghastly** (gast′lē) *adj.*: horrible; ghostlike.

-----

"GO QUICKLY WHILE MY MONSTERS ARE STILLED BY YOUR SONG."

THE SHADE
DISSOLVED
IN THE CIRCLE
OF HIS ARMS
LIKE SMOKE.

Every step he took, some instinct told him that he was going farther from his bride. He toiled up the path in <u>reluctance</u> and despair, stopping, listening, sighing, taking a few slow steps, until the dark thinned out into grayness. Up ahead a speck of light showed clearly the entrance to the cavern.

At that final moment Orpheus could bear no more. To go out into the light of day without his love seemed to him impossible. Before he had quite <u>ascended</u>, there was still a moment in which he could go back. Quick in the grayness he turned and saw a dim shade at his heels, as indistinct as the gray mist behind her. But still he could see the look of sadness on her face as he sprung forward saying, "Eurydice!" and threw his arms about her. The shade dissolved in the circle of his arms like smoke. A little whisper seemed to say "Farewell" as she scattered into mist and was gone.

The unfortunate lover hastened back again down the steep, dark path. But all was in vain. This time the ghostly ferryman was deaf to his prayers. The very wildness of his mood made it impossible for him to attain the beauty of his former music. At last, his despair was so great that he could not even sing at all. For seven days he sat huddled together on the gray mud banks, listening to the wailing of the terrible river. The flitting ghosts shrank back in a wide circle from the living man, but he paid them no attention. Only he sat with his eyes on Charon, his ears ringing with the dreadful noise of Styx.

Orpheus arose at last and stumbled back along the steep road he knew so well by now. When he came up to earth again, his song was pitiful but more beautiful than ever. Even the nightingale who mourned all night long would hush her voice to listen as Orpheus sat in some hidden place singing of his lost Eurydice. Men and women he could bear no longer, and when they came to hear him, he drove them away. At last the women of Thrace, maddened by Dionysus and infuriated by Orpheus's contempt, fell upon him and killed him. It is said that as the body was swept down the river Hebrus, the dead lips still moved faintly and the rocks echoed for the last time, "Eurydice." But the poet's eager spirit was already far down the familiar path.

In the daffodil meadows he met the shade of Eurydice, and there they walk together, or where the path is narrow, the shade of Orpheus goes ahead and looks back at his love.

**WORDS TO OWN**
**reluctance** (ri·luk′təns) *n*.: unwillingness.
**ascended** (ə·send′id) *v*.: moved up.

# The Power of Music

*from* **Nadja on My Way**

## Nadja Salerno-Sonnenberg

*Nadja Salerno-Sonnenberg is a violinist who appears in concert in the United States and throughout the world. She was born in Rome, Italy, and moved to the United States with her family in 1969. She writes about her love of music and her career in her autobiography,* Nadja on My Way.

This is something I know for a fact: You have to work hardest for the thing you love most. And when it's music that you love, you're in for the fight of your life.

It starts when your blood fills with music and you know you can't live without it. Every day brings a challenge to learn as much as possible and to play even better than you did the day before.

You may want to achieve fame and glory, or you may want to play for fun. But whenever you fall in love with music, you'll never sit still again.

Music is more important than we will ever know. Great music can pull you right out of your chair. It can make you cry, or laugh, or feel a way you've never felt before. It can make you remember the first person you loved. . . . Music has that power.

Just imagine a world without music. What would you whistle when you walked down the street? How could you make a movie? How could you have a ball game without an organist leading the crowd when you're down by a run in the ninth?

You could be the most successful doctor in the world, but if you never turn on the radio, never go to a concert, never sing in the shower, never see *The King and I*[1]— then you can't be a total, fulfilled human being. It's impossible.

When you realize how vital music is, you realize a musician's fight is quite a noble, heroic endeavor. It didn't always seem that way to me. There was a time, years ago, when I felt discouraged and it seemed self-ish to put so much time into music. Being a musician didn't seem as useful to others as being a surgeon, or even a good politician.

But I came to understand that it's a great, great gift to help people forget their every-day life and be uplifted. And better than up-lifted, to be inspired; that's what music can do. It's important to us all, and I'm proud to put mind and muscle into recording, con-certs, teaching, and studying: into being a musician.

Emotionally, music has brought me an enormous amount of joy and an enormous amount of despair and frustration. Because of music, I have learned what a battle is. I've won most, but not all—not by a long shot.

1. **The King and I:** well-known American musical and one of the most widely performed shows in the musi-cal theater. A movie version was made in the 1950s.

# MAKING MEANINGS

## First Thoughts

1. If you were Orpheus, would you have looked back? Why or why not?

## Shaping Interpretations

2. On the basis of this myth, how do you think the ancient Greeks pictured the afterlife?

3. Explain how the same feeling that prompted Orpheus's descent into the underworld also caused him to fail.

4. At what point in your reading did you begin to understand this myth on a deeper level?

5. What lessons about love and death does this myth seem to teach? In this story, which is more powerful, love or death? Why?

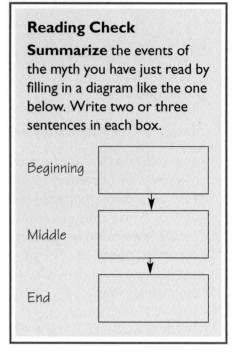

**Reading Check**

**Summarize** the events of the myth you have just read by filling in a diagram like the one below. Write two or three sentences in each box.

Beginning

Middle

End

6. Use a chart like the one below to compare this myth with "The Origin of the Seasons."

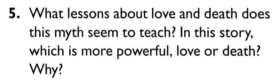

|  | "Orpheus" | "The Origin of the Seasons" |
|---|---|---|
| How the character faces the mystery of death |  |  |
| How nature responds to the character's grief or joy |  |  |
| The effect of breaking a taboo or a rule |  |  |

7. How does the expression "Never look back" apply to this story?

## Connecting with the Text

8. Do you think Hades was fair to Orpheus and Eurydice in this myth? Tell what you might do to change the outcome if you were a god or goddess.

9. What does this myth say about the power of music? How does this message compare with your notes for the Quickwrite on page 512 and with Nadja Salerno-Sonnenberg's comments (see *Connections* on page 517)?

# CHOICES: Building Your Portfolio

## Writer's Notebook

### 1. Collecting Ideas for an Evaluation

In these two myths, Olivia Coolidge presents two characters—Orpheus and Demeter—who almost succeed in conquering death. Which of these tragic characters do you find more interesting? Look back at the myths, and jot down specifics of each character's traits and actions. When you **evaluate,** you make a judgment. How would you judge these two characters?

> Orpheus
> —Traits:
>   musical, loving
> —Actions:
>   bravely enters
>   underworld;
>   foolishly looks
>   back
> —Evaluation:
>   liked him a lot

## Creative Writing/Music

### 2. Odes to Joy and Grief

With a partner, compose one of the songs Orpheus sings in this myth. You might write a song that suggests Orpheus's joy in his love for Eurydice. This song should cause the rocks to "edge down the mountainsides." One partner can work out the basic melody, and the other can write appropriate lyrics.

## Research/Map Making

### 3. Where in the (Under) World?

Collect **descriptive details** about the underworld from "Orpheus, the Great Musician," "The Origin of the Seasons," and other Greek myths. ("The Labors of Hercules," page 541, may provide other details.) Draw a **map** of the underworld, using all the sources you can find. Use **labels** to show the location of various characters and landmarks— the River Styx, Cerberus, and Hades' throne room, for example. Draw the characters who populate the shadows.

Zither player between two columns with two roosters (c. 520 B.C.). Black-figured amphora (large storage vase).

Château-Musée, Boulogne-sur-Mer, France. Erich Lessing/Art Resource, New York.

## Creative Writing

### 4. Orpheus—Live at the Acropolis!

Orpheus has come to town. You're a reporter for a local television station, and you're reporting live from backstage. Tell what the concert is like. Your descriptions of the music should be based on those given in the myth. Your report might include a description of Orpheus and the reaction of the crowd. Be sure to mention any unusual things you see at the concert—for example, does Charon come with Cerberus? Is Eurydice there? How is Orpheus dressed? Does anything magical happen when Orpheus sings?

# LANGUAGE LINK   MINI-LESSON

## Style: Figurative Language

**Handbook of
Literary
Terms
H E L P**

*See Figure of
Speech.*

**Figurative language** describes one thing in terms of another and is not meant to be taken as literally true.

A **simile** is a comparison between two unlike things, using a word such as *like, as, resembles,* or *than.*

EXAMPLE

". . . a long sigh <u>like</u> wind in pine trees was heard from the assembled ghosts." [The sigh of the ghosts is compared to the wind in the pines.]

**Personification** is figurative language in which a nonhuman thing is talked about as if it were human.

EXAMPLE

". . . when he sat down to sing, <u>the trees</u> <u>would crowd around to shade him</u>." [The trees are given the human ability to crowd around someone in order to shade him.]

### Try It Out

➤ Find the figurative language in each sentence. Tell what is compared to what. Then, tell if the comparison is a simile or personification.

1. "All day long he mourned his bride, while birds, beasts, and the earth itself sorrowed with him."

2. "As he entered the land of Hades, the pale ghosts came after him like great, uncounted flocks of silent birds."

3. "The shade dissolved in the circle of his arms like smoke."

➤ Write a brief description of how you feel about music. Use simile and personification to help express your feelings.

## VOCABULARY   HOW TO OWN A WORD

**WORD BANK**

*inconsolable*
*ghastly*
*reluctance*
*ascended*

### Think About It

Each numbered sentence contains a word from the Word Bank. After reading the sentence, make up a reasonable answer to the question that follows. Write your answer.

1. The queen was <u>inconsolable</u>. What just happened to the queen?
2. The king saw a <u>ghastly</u> sight. What did the king see?
3. He ate the meal with some <u>reluctance</u>. What explains his reluctance?
4. The golden cloud <u>ascended</u>. Where was the cloud after it ascended?

## READING BETWEEN THE LINES: USING CONTEXT CLUES

Readers often use a word's **context clues**—the surrounding words and sentences—to figure out what the word means. There are two keys to unlocking meaning using context clues. One key unlocks knowledge that is already in your head; the other key unlocks the clues from the text itself.

### Clues from Your Head

You may already know something about the word. The more you know about a topic, the more useful context is. To zero in on what you already know, ask yourself these questions:

- What are some words I think of when I look at this word?
- What other words does the word sound like?
- Does the word have any **prefixes** or **suffixes** whose meanings I know?

### Clues from the Text

Look at the surrounding text and ask yourself the following:

- What type of text am I reading? What topic might this word relate to?
- Do the surrounding words and sentences give clues to the word's meaning?

- How is the word used in the sentence? What kind of word could I substitute for it? A person, a place, or a thing? A descriptive word?

### Putting It Together

Sometimes you can figure out the meaning of an unfamiliar word as you read. Other times it's not so easy. Making a chart like the one below may help you unlock the meanings of difficult words, like *inconsolable,* which appears in "Orpheus, the Great Musician."

| Unfamiliar Word | Clues from Your Head | Clues from the Text | Word's Meaning | Dictionary Check |
|---|---|---|---|---|
| inconsolable | The prefix *in-* means "not." Word looks and sounds like *console,* meaning "to make someone feel better." | Orpheus was inconsolable as he mourned his bride. Therefore, he must have been very sad. | "incapable of being comforted" | Correct! |

**Apply the strategy on the next page.**

# Before You Read

## ECHO AND NARCISSUS

## Make the Connection

### Dear Me

"Echo and Narcissus" is an **origin myth,** and it is one of several flower myths as well. The myth is also a powerful story about human nature—about what can happen to us when we are absorbed only in ourselves.

## Quickwrite

Take a quick survey to find out how your classmates rate the following statements. Each person should rate each statement on a scale from 1 to 5, with 1 meaning you do not agree and 5 meaning total agreement.

1. People judge others by their looks alone.

2. People judge others on more than their looks.

3. Vain, self-centered people are often punished for their behavior.

4. Vain, self-centered people often get away with things.

Which statement do you agree or disagree with most strongly? In your notebook, briefly explain what you think about that statement and why. Share your Quickwrite with the rest of the class.

## Reading Skills and Strategies

### Using Context Clues

As you read, don't be detained as you struggle vainly to figure out the meaning of a word you don't know. Remember to use the strategies you learned on page 521. (Two vocabulary words from the story appear in these directions. Were you able to figure out their meanings from the **context**?)

*"So nothing can stop you talking?"*

# Echo and Narcissus

## *retold by* **Roger Lancelyn Green**

Up on the wild, lonely mountains of Greece lived the Oreades,[1] the nymphs or fairies of the hills, and among them one of the most beautiful was called Echo. She was one of the most talkative, too, and once she talked too much and angered Hera, wife of Zeus, king of the gods.

When Zeus grew tired of the golden halls of Mount Olympus, the home of the immortal gods, he would come down to earth and wander with the nymphs on the mountains. Hera, however, was jealous and often came to see what he was doing. It seemed strange at first that she always met Echo, and that Echo kept her listening for hours on end to her stories and her gossip.

But at last Hera realized that Echo was doing this on purpose to <u>detain</u> her while Zeus went quietly back to Olympus as if he had never really been away.

"So nothing can stop you talking?" exclaimed Hera. "Well, Echo, I do not intend to spoil your pleasure. But from this day

1. **Oreades** (ō′rē·ad′ēz).

**WORDS TO OWN**
**detain** (dē·tān′) *v.*: hold back; delay.

*Narcissus* by Caravaggio.

Galleria Nazionale d'Arte Antica, Rome. Scala/Art Resource, New York.

on, you shall be able only to repeat what other people say—and never speak unless someone else speaks first."

Hera returned to Olympus, well pleased with the punishment she had made for Echo, leaving the poor nymph to weep sadly among the rocks on the mountainside and speak only the words which her sisters and their friends shouted happily to one another.

She grew used to her strange fate after a while, but then a new misfortune befell her.

There was a beautiful youth called Narcissus,[2] who was the son of a nymph and the god of a nearby river. He grew up in the plain of Thebes[3] until he was sixteen years old and then began to hunt on the mountains toward the north where Echo and her sister Oreades lived.

As he wandered through the woods and valleys, many a nymph looked upon him and loved him. But Narcissus laughed at them scornfully, for he loved only himself.

Farther up the mountains Echo saw him. And at once her lonely heart was filled with love for the beautiful youth, so that nothing else in the world mattered but to win him.

Now she wished indeed that she could speak to him words of love. But the curse which Hera had placed upon her tied her tongue, and she could only follow wherever he went, hiding behind trees and rocks, and feasting her eyes <u>vainly</u> upon him.

One day Narcissus wandered farther up the mountain than usual, and all his friends, the other Theban youths, were left far behind. Only Echo followed him, still hiding among the rocks, her heart heavy with unspoken love.

Presently Narcissus realized that he was lost, and hoping to be heard by his companions, or perhaps by some mountain shepherd, he called out loudly:

"Is there anybody here?"

"Here!" cried Echo.

Narcissus stood still in amazement, looking all around in vain. Then he shouted, even more loudly:

"Whoever you are, come to me!"

"Come to me!" cried Echo eagerly.

Still no one was visible, so Narcissus called again:

"Why are you avoiding me?"

Echo repeated his words, but with a sob in her breath, and Narcissus called once more:

"Come here, I say, and let us meet!"

"Let us meet!" cried Echo, her heart leaping with joy as she spoke the happiest words that had left her lips since the curse of Hera had fallen on her. And to make good her words, she came running out from behind the rocks and tried to clasp her arms about him.

But Narcissus flung the beautiful nymph away from him in scorn.

"Away with these embraces!" he cried angrily, his voice full of cruel contempt. "I would die before I would have you touch me!"

"I would have you touch me!" repeated poor Echo.

"Never will I let you kiss me!"

"Kiss me! Kiss me!" murmured Echo, sinking down among the rocks, as Narcissus cast her violently from him and sped down the hillside.

"One touch of those lips would kill me!" he called back furiously over his shoulder.

"Kill me!" begged Echo.

And Aphrodite,[4] the goddess of love, heard her and was kind to her, for she had been a true lover. Quietly and painlessly, Echo pined away and died. But her voice lived on, lingering among the rocks and answering faintly whenever Narcissus or another called.

"He shall not go unpunished for this cruelty,"

4. **Aphrodite** (af′rə·dīt′ē).

---

**WORDS TO OWN**
vainly (vān′lē) *adv.*: uselessly; without result.

---

2. **Narcissus** (när·sis′əs).
3. **Thebes** (thēbz).

said Aphrodite. "By scorning poor Echo like this, he scorns love itself. And scorning love, he insults me. He is altogether eaten up with self-love . . . Well, he shall love himself and no one else, and yet shall die of <u>unrequited</u> love!"

It was not long before Aphrodite made good her threat, and in a very strange way. One day, tired after hunting, Narcissus came to a still, clear pool of water away up the mountainside, not far from where he had scorned Echo and left her to die of a broken heart.

With a cry of satisfaction, for the day was hot and cloudless, and he was <u>parched</u> with thirst, Narcissus flung himself down beside the pool and leaned forward to dip his face in the cool water.

What was his surprise to see a beautiful face looking up at him through the still waters of the pool. The moment he saw, he loved—and love was a madness upon him so that he could think of nothing else.

"Beautiful water nymph!" he cried. "I love you! Be mine!"

Desperately he plunged his arms into the water—but the face vanished and he touched only the pebbles at the bottom of the pool. Drawing out his arms, he gazed <u>intently</u> down and, as the water grew still again, saw once more the face of his beloved.

Poor Narcissus did not know that he was seeing his own reflection, for Aphrodite hid this knowledge from him—and perhaps this was the first time that a pool of water had reflected the face of anyone gazing into it.

Narcissus seemed enchanted by what he saw. He could not leave the pool, but lay by its side day after day looking at the only face in the world which he loved—and could not win—and pining just as Echo had pined.

Slowly Narcissus faded away, and at last his heart broke.

"Woe is me for I loved in vain!" he cried.

"I loved in vain!" sobbed the voice of Echo among the rocks.

"Farewell, my love, farewell," were his last words, and Echo's voice broke and its whisper shivered into silence: "My love . . . farewell!"

So Narcissus died, and the earth covered his bones. But with the spring, a plant pushed its green leaves through the earth where he lay. As the sun shone on it, a bud opened and a new flower blossomed for the first time—a white circle of petals round a yellow center. The flowers grew and spread, waving in the gentle breeze which whispered among them like Echo herself come to kiss the blossoms of the first Narcissus flowers.

---

### WORDS TO OWN

**unrequited** (un′ri·kwīt′id) v. used as adj.: not returned in kind.

**parched** (pärcht) adj.: very hot and dry.

**intently** (in·tent′lē) adv.: with great concentration.

---

## MEET THE WRITER

### Green, a Greek at Heart

**Roger Lancelyn Green** (1918–1987) was born in London and educated at Oxford University. After a short stint as an actor in London, he devoted his life to children's literature and the study of ancient times. His books for children include stories, poems, and his own retellings of fairy tales, legends, and myths from many lands. Green's special love was Greece, which he visited more than twenty times.

# MAKING MEANINGS

## First Thoughts

1. Did reading this myth change your opinions about beauty and vanity at all? If so, how? Review your notes for the Quickwrite survey on page 522.

## Shaping Interpretations

2. Like Persephone's story, which explains the seasons, this story is an **origin myth.** What natural phenomena does this myth explain?

3. What is the major flaw in Echo's character? Explain why Hera's curse is an appropriate punishment for this flaw.

4. What is the major flaw in Narcissus' character? Explain why Aphrodite's curse is an appropriate punishment for this flaw.

5. Is it possible that Aphrodite finally succeeds in joining Echo and Narcissus as true lovers? Cite **evidence** from the myth to support your opinion.

### Reading Check

a. What does Echo do that annoys Hera?

b. How does Hera punish Echo?

c. Why does Aphrodite punish Narcissus?

d. What curse does Aphrodite place on Narcissus?

e. Describe Narcissus' death and rebirth.

## Connecting with the Text

6. A popular song lyric says, "Learning to love yourself is the greatest love of all." Yet Narcissus' self-love gets him turned into a flower. Talk about whether there are good as well as bad forms of self-love.

## Challenging the Text

7. Are the gods fair? What do you think of their actions in this myth?

*Aphrodite* (the Bartlett Head). Attica, Greece (c. 325–300 B.C.). Parian marble (height: 0.288 m, 3.743).

Francis Bartlett Donation of 1900. Courtesy, Museum of Fine Arts, Boston.

# CHOICES: Building Your Portfolio

## Writer's Notebook

### 1. Collecting Ideas for an Evaluation

Suppose you were preparing a list of myths you would recommend to other students. Would you include "Echo and Narcissus"? How would you decide? Would you base your recommendation on how appealing the characters are, how exciting the plot is, how meaningful the myth is to today's readers, or some other criteria? Think about the standards you would use to make your recommendation. Jot down your ideas.

> —Meaning for today:
> Echo's feelings are universal; beauty means a lot in our culture, too.
> —Quality of writing:
> Descriptions are great.

## Creative Writing

### 2. Expressing an Opinion

Each of the main characters in this myth has a strong opinion about one or more of the other characters. Imagine that you are Hera, Aphrodite, Echo, or Narcissus. In a paragraph, write about one of the following:

**a.** what Hera thinks of Echo

**b.** what Aphrodite thinks of either Hera or Narcissus

**c.** what Echo thinks of either Hera or Narcissus

**d.** what Narcissus thinks of Echo

## Creative Writing/ Botany

### 3. A Yard Full of Myths

Maple or mesquite, cactus or cabbage, dogwood or dandelion—our yards and parks are filled with growing things. Choose a plant or tree that interests you, one you've seen quite a bit. Then, write a short myth to explain its origin. For the plot of your myth, come up with an idea that explains the special shape, color, or size of the plant.

## Creative Writing/ Speaking

### 4. Say That Again, Again, Again . . .

On page 525, Echo repeats only the last of Narcissus' words in order to speak her own mind. For example, Narcissus says, "Never will I let you kiss me!" and Echo responds, "Kiss me! Kiss me!" Develop a comic dialogue to perform for your classmates, basing it on this idea. Working with a partner, you might dramatize a scene showing how Echo makes a life for herself in today's world.

## Language Arts

### 5. Echoes of the Past

*Echo* and *narcissism* are two English words with **roots** in ancient Greek culture. From the list below, research at least five more such words. Show their exact **origin** in ancient Greek culture or mythology. Does the ancient origin of these words shed light on their current usage? You might collect words for an illustrated dictionary of words from the myths.

psyche    chaos    vulcanize
nectar    cereal    mercury

# GRAMMAR LINK

## Words That Are Often Confused

**Language Handbook HELP**

*See Apostrophes, page 777; Personal Pronouns, pages 710 and 734.*

**Technology HELP**

*See Language Workshop CD-ROM. Key word entry: possessive pronouns.*

Read these words aloud: *its, it's* and *your, you're*. Do you hear an echo? The words in each pair may sound alike, but they have very different purposes.

1. The **personal possessive pronouns** *its* and *your* show that something belongs to someone or something. Possessive pronouns should not have apostrophes.

   EXAMPLES

   "He could not leave the pool, but lay by its side. . . ." [The side belongs to the pool.]

   "'Well, Echo, I do not intend to spoil your pleasure.'" [The pleasure belongs to Echo.]

2. The **contractions** *it's* and *you're* are both shortened combinations of a personal pronoun and the verb *is, has,* or *are*. A contraction should have an apostrophe to show where letters have been left out.

   EXAMPLES

   It's [It is] his own reflection he sees.

   You're [You are] going to repeat words.

### Try It Out

Write each sentence below, choosing the correct form of the underlined words.

**A tip:** If you are unsure which word is correct, try substituting two words, such as *it is* or *you are*, in the sentence, and see if the sentence still makes sense. If it does make sense, use a contraction rather than a possessive pronoun.

1. "Your/You're not the one I love," said Narcissus.

2. A plant pushed its/it's green leaves through the earth.

3. Its/It's Echo's constant chatter that annoys Hera.

4. "Narcissus, you won't realize your/you're in love with your/you're own reflection," thought Aphrodite.

# VOCABULARY   HOW TO OWN A WORD

**WORD BANK**

detain
vainly
unrequited
parched
intently

## Think About It: Building Context Clues

Reading is one of the best ways for young children to learn new words. Using the words in the Word Bank, write a short-short version of the Echo and Narcissus story that a six-year-old would understand. Build lots of **context clues** into the sentences. If you can, try out your story on a child.

# *Before You Read*

## THE FLIGHT OF ICARUS

### Make the Connection

#### Winging It

Long before the invention of the airplane, people yearned to fly. They dreamed of climbing through the air, dipping, floating, plummeting—as free as birds. They wanted to escape the earth and soar above all its problems.

Today, of course, flight is an everyday reality. We travel through the air in everything from helicopters to jumbo jets, from hot-air balloons to space shuttles.

### Quickwrite

Complete one of these sentences:

- I long to fly/dread flying like a seagull because . . .

- I had a dream about flying in which . . .

### Elements of Literature

#### Myths with Morals: What's the Message?

When a young bird flies from the nest for the first time, we say that it is "trying its wings." As you read this myth, notice what happens when a young boy tries his wings. If you think about what the boy attempts to do, what he ignores, and what happens to him as a result, you'll find the **morals**—or lessons—in the story.

**A moral** is a lesson about the right way to behave. The morals in many Greek myths were used to teach children values.

*For more on Myth, see pages 496–499 and the Handbook of Literary Terms.*

### Reading Skills and Strategies

#### Making Generalizations

When you make a **generalization,** you look at evidence and make a broad state-

who says "All stories contain conflicts" is making a generalization from experience with many stories. As you read these myths, think of generalizations you might make about myths and the kinds of stories they tell.

## Cast of Characters

**King Minos** (mī′näs′),
   tyrant of Crete, enemy of
   Athens.
**Theseus** (the′sē·əs), hero
   from Athens held cap-
   tive by Minos. Daedalus
   helped him escape from
   the labyrinth on Crete.
**Daedalus** (ded′′l·əs), great
   Athenian architect who
   built the labyrinth on
   Crete.
**Icarus** (ik′ə·rəs),
   Daedalus's young son.

# The Flight of Icarus

*retold by* **Sally Benson**

*"Minos may
control the land and sea,
but he does
not control the air."*

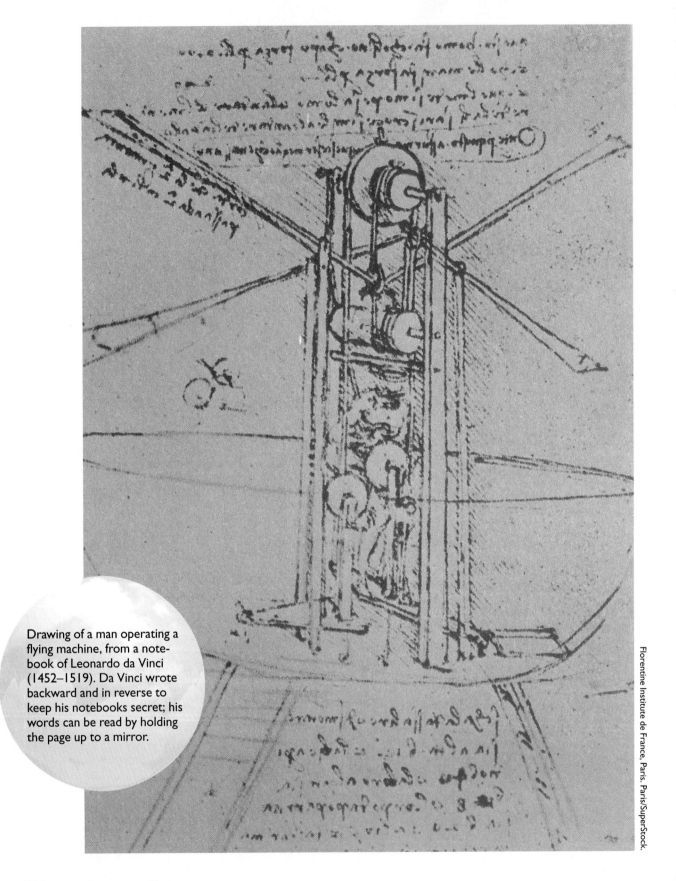

Drawing of a man operating a flying machine, from a notebook of Leonardo da Vinci (1452–1519). Da Vinci wrote backward and in reverse to keep his notebooks secret; his words can be read by holding the page up to a mirror.

When Theseus escaped from the labyrinth, King Minos flew into a rage with its builder, Daedalus, and ordered him shut up in a high tower that faced the lonely sea. In time, with the help of his young son, Icarus, Daedalus managed to escape from the tower, only to find himself a prisoner on the island. Several times he tried by bribery to stow away on one of the vessels sailing from Crete, but King Minos kept strict watch over them, and no ships were allowed to sail without being carefully searched.

Daedalus was an ingenious artist and was not discouraged by his failures. "Minos may control the land and sea," he said, "but he does not control the air. I will try that way."

He called his son, Icarus, to him and told the boy to gather up all the feathers he could find on the rocky shore. As thousands of gulls soared over the island, Icarus soon collected a huge pile of feathers. Daedalus then melted some wax and made a skeleton in the shape of a bird's wing. The smallest feathers he pressed into the soft wax and the large ones he tied on with thread. Icarus played about on the beach happily while his father worked, chasing the feathers that blew away in the strong wind that swept the island and sometimes taking bits of the wax and working it into strange shapes with his fingers.

It was fun making the wings. The sun shone on the bright feathers; the breezes ruffled them. When they were finished, Daedalus fastened them to his shoulders and found himself lifted upwards, where he hung poised in the air. Filled with excitement, he made another pair for his son. They were smaller than his own, but strong and beautiful.

Finally, one clear, wind-swept morning, the wings were finished, and Daedalus fastened them to Icarus's shoulders and taught him how to fly. He bade him watch the movements of the birds, how they soared and glided overhead. He pointed out the slow, graceful sweep of their wings as they beat the air steadily, without fluttering. Soon Icarus was sure that he, too, could fly and, raising his arms up and down, skirted over the white sand and even out over the waves, letting his feet touch the snowy foam as the water thundered and broke over the sharp rocks. Daedalus watched him proudly but with misgivings. He called Icarus to his side and, putting his arm round the boy's shoulders, said, "Icarus, my son, we are about to make our flight. No human being has ever traveled through the air before, and I want you to listen carefully to my instructions. Keep at a moderate height, for if you fly too low, the fog and spray will clog your wings, and if you fly too high, the heat will melt the wax that holds them together. Keep near me and you will be safe."

He kissed Icarus and fastened the wings more securely to his son's shoulders. Icarus, standing in the bright sun, the shining wings drooping gracefully from his shoulders, his golden hair wet with spray, and his eyes bright and dark with excitement, looked like a lovely bird. Daedalus's eyes filled with tears, and turning away, he soared into the sky, calling to Icarus to follow. From time to time, he looked back to see that the boy was safe and to note how he managed his wings in his flight. As they flew across the land to test their prowess before setting out across the dark wild sea, plowmen below stopped their work and shepherds gazed in wonder, thinking Daedalus and Icarus were gods.

Father and son flew over Samos and Delos, which lay on their left, and Lebinthus,° which lay on their right. Icarus, beating his wings in joy, felt the thrill of the cool wind on his face and the clear air above and below him. He flew higher and higher up into the blue sky until he reached the clouds. His father saw him and

---

° **Samos** (sā′mäs), **Delos** (dē′läs), and **Lebinthus** (lə·bin′thəs): Greek islands in the Aegean Sea.

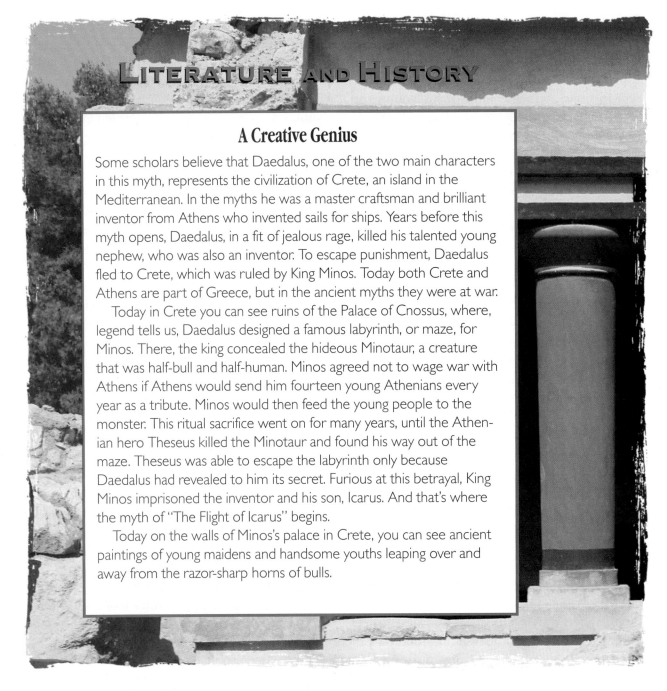

## A Creative Genius

Some scholars believe that Daedalus, one of the two main characters in this myth, represents the civilization of Crete, an island in the Mediterranean. In the myths he was a master craftsman and brilliant inventor from Athens who invented sails for ships. Years before this myth opens, Daedalus, in a fit of jealous rage, killed his talented young nephew, who was also an inventor. To escape punishment, Daedalus fled to Crete, which was ruled by King Minos. Today both Crete and Athens are part of Greece, but in the ancient myths they were at war.

Today in Crete you can see ruins of the Palace of Cnossus, where, legend tells us, Daedalus designed a famous labyrinth, or maze, for Minos. There, the king concealed the hideous Minotaur, a creature that was half-bull and half-human. Minos agreed not to wage war with Athens if Athens would send him fourteen young Athenians every year as a tribute. Minos would then feed the young people to the monster. This ritual sacrifice went on for many years, until the Athenian hero Theseus killed the Minotaur and found his way out of the maze. Theseus was able to escape the labyrinth only because Daedalus had revealed to him its secret. Furious at this betrayal, King Minos imprisoned the inventor and his son, Icarus. And that's where the myth of "The Flight of Icarus" begins.

Today on the walls of Minos's palace in Crete, you can see ancient paintings of young maidens and handsome youths leaping over and away from the razor-sharp horns of bulls.

called out in alarm. He tried to follow him, but he was heavier and his wings would not carry him. Up and up Icarus soared, through the soft, moist clouds and out again toward the glorious sun. He was bewitched by a sense of freedom and beat his wings frantically so that they would carry him higher and higher to heaven itself. The blazing sun beat down on the wings and softened the wax. Small feathers fell from the wings and floated softly down, warning Icarus to stay his flight and glide to earth. But the enchanted boy did not notice them until the sun became so hot that the largest feathers dropped off and he began to sink. Frantically he fluttered his arms, but no feathers remained to hold the air. He cried out to his father, but his voice was submerged in the blue waters of the sea, which has forever after been called by his name.

Daedalus, crazed by anxiety, called back to him, "Icarus! Icarus, my son, where are you?" At last he saw the feathers floating from the sky, and soon his son plunged through the clouds into the sea. Daedalus hurried to save him, but it was too late. He gathered the boy in his arms and flew to land, the tips of his wings dragging in the water from the double burden they bore. Weeping bitterly, he

buried his small son and called the land Icaria in his memory.

Then, with a flutter of wings, he once more took to the air, but the joy of his flight was gone and his victory over the air was bitter to him. He arrived safely in Sicily, where he built a temple to Apollo and hung up his wings as an offering to the god, and in the wings he pressed a few bright feathers he had found floating on the water where Icarus fell. And he mourned for the birdlike son who had thrown caution to the winds in the exaltation of his freedom from the earth.

## MEET THE WRITER

### "Stories That Have Rounded Ends"

**Sally Benson** (1900–1972) never studied writing—she didn't have to: It came naturally. After high school she skipped college and went directly to work, first for a bank and then for newspapers. In 1930, she was reviewing thirty-two movies a month for a daily paper when she got an idea for a short story. She sat down, typed it out, and sold it to *The New Yorker*. Dazed by her good fortune, she stopped writing for nine months. But when her money ran out, she wrote another story and sold that one, too. From then on she poured stories out. Benson published one book of Greek and Roman myths, but most of her stories tell the amusing adventures of a thirteen-year-old girl named Judy Graves.

66 I like stories that have rounded ends and don't rise to climaxes; that aren't all wrapped up in a package with plot. I like them, that's why I write them. 99

# Wings

The same dream again,
   and again,
      and again.
It begins, I sit on a lonely beach.
The waves curl around my feet,
5    sliding through my toes,
And the sea gulls soar overhead.
    The gulls.
I long to be a part of their flight.
I stand and run with the birds,
    leaping, jumping, skipping.
10  Abruptly I come to a cliff.
    I dive.
For one wonderful, fleeting moment
   I glide
on wings of purest gold. A wish come true.
Then comes the Voice . . . echoing.
   "You can't fly . . . can't fly . . . can't fly . . ."
15  The wings are gone.
I plunge dizzily down to the raging sea miles below.
Moments before I splash, I awake, sweating, gasping for air.

I long for the day when I am able to defy the Voice,
to soar, to glide, to join the birds at last.
20  Until then I will hold tight to the single moment of flight that is mine.

—Bronwen Anne Gilbert
Eckstein Middle School
Seattle, Washington

# MAKING MEANINGS

## First Thoughts

**1.** Look back at the sentences you completed for the Quickwrite on page 530. How might Daedalus and Icarus have completed those sentences?

## Shaping Interpretations

**2.** The myths of Persephone and Orpheus include warnings that the characters fail to listen to. How is the story of Icarus like those myths?

**3.** How does Icarus try to be something he is not? What **moral lesson** can you learn from his failure?

**4.** When did you first guess the outcome of the myth? What hints in the story helped you make this prediction?

**5.** Like other myths, this one explains the names of some geographical features in Greece. What are they, and how did they get there?

## Connecting with the Text

**6.** How do you feel about Icarus? Do you think teenagers today can identify with him? Why or why not?

## Extending the Text

**7.** This story seems to suggest that people shouldn't try to "fly too high." We often hear the opposite advice: "Reach for the stars." From your own experience, when do you think taking chances is a good thing? When can it be dangerous?

*Daedalus and Icarus* by Antonio Canova.

Museo Correr, Venice, Italy. Alinari/Art Resource, New York.

# CHOICES: Building Your Portfolio

## Writer's Notebook

### 1. Collecting Ideas for an Evaluation

From the three **morals** below, choose the one you think *best* expresses the message of "The Flight of Icarus." Then, jot down your evaluation of the moral. Do you agree or disagree with it? Why?

- Steer a middle course and avoid extremes.
- Listen to your elders.
- If you do not reach too far, you will avoid trouble.

*The myth teaches the danger of going to extremes. I partly agree and partly disagree because . . .*

---

## Creative Writing

### 2. Dear Daedalus

Imagine you are Icarus, now in the underworld after your disastrous flight. Write a letter to your father, telling him how you felt during the flight and what it's like in Hades' dark kingdom. (See the myths "The Origin of the Seasons," page 501, and "Orpheus, the Great Musician," page 513, for details about the underworld.)

## Analyzing the Myths

### 3. What Are Myths?

Skim through the myths you have read so far. Take notes on the fantasy elements, moral lessons, and explanations of natural phenomena in the myths. Then, use your notes to make a **generalization** about myths. Open your general statement with the words "Myths are stories that . . .". Support your generalization with details from the myths.

## Science/Speaking

### 4. Winging It

How close is Daedalus to learning the secret of flight? Find out how aircraft today get and remain airborne. Create a diagram or a model to show how one system works, and present it to the class.

## Geography/Math/Art

### 5. Going Places

The myth mentions several places—Crete, Samos, Delos, Lebinthus, Icaria, and Sicily. In a dictionary or an atlas, locate information about these places. Then, find the name of the sea that Icarus and Daedalus cross. Make a large-scale drawing of this area, trace Daedalus's trip from Crete to Sicily, and calculate the distance he travels.

## Creative Writing

### 6. It's a Bird, It's a . . .

Imagine that you are an ancient farmer or fisherman who has just witnessed Icarus's fantastic and tragic flight. Write a first-person account telling what you've seen, or write a poem about your reaction. Look back at the Student to Student poem on page 536 for ideas.

# GRAMMAR LINK

## Adjective vs. Adverb

**Language Handbook HELP**

*See The Adverb, page 716.*

**Technology HELP**

*See* Language Workshop CD-ROM. *Key word entry:* adverbs.

Many adverbs end in *-ly*. Such adverbs are generally formed by adding the ending *-ly* to adjectives.

EXAMPLES

proud + *ly*: "Daedalus watched him <u>proudly</u> but with misgivings."

secure + *ly*: "He . . . fastened the wings more <u>securely</u> to his son's shoulders."

In some sentences, however, it's hard to know which word to use—the adjective or the adverb.

He arrived <u>safe/safely</u> in Sicily.

To solve this problem, ask yourself which word the modifier describes. An adverb modifies a verb, an adjective, or another adverb.

EXAMPLE "He arrived <u>safely</u> in Sicily. . . ."

An adjective modifies a noun or a pronoun.

EXAMPLE He had a <u>safe</u> arrival in Sicily.

### Try It Out

Choose the correct word from each underlined pair.

1. Daedalus flew <u>rapid/rapidly</u> to lift his son from the sea.

2. The accident had happened so <u>sudden/suddenly</u>.

3. Mourning his son, Daedalus sat <u>listless/listlessly</u> on the sand.

4. Icarus felt <u>confident/confidently</u> that he could fly higher.

# VOCABULARY  HOW TO OWN A WORD

## Place Names from Greece and Rome

When the first Europeans settled in the land that became the United States, they needed names for their towns and cities. They often looked to ancient Rome and Greece for ideas.

Use the index in an atlas or other geographical reference book to identify the following:

1. the state or states in which the following American cities are located

2. the location of the original Greek or Roman place known by that name

| | | |
|---|---|---|
| Athens | Delphi | Olympia |
| Rome | Syracuse | Sparta |

*The Fall of Icarus* (detail). Copper engraving.

The Bettmann Archive.

# Before You Read

## THE LABORS OF HERCULES

## Make the Connection

### The Hero Hercules

Hercules (also spelled Heracles) is a mythical Greek hero who performs the most amazing feats of strength in all of mythology. Like other mythic heroes, Hercules is the son of both a god (Zeus, or Jupiter) and a human being and so possesses special qualities. Like many other superheroes, he demonstrates his powers when he is still in his cradle.

## Quickwrite

The twelve labors of Hercules include ridding the world of monsters that cause people to suffer. Make a list of at least six tasks a modern superhero or superheroine might accomplish to improve the world.

## Elements of Literature

### The Quest

A **quest** is a long and perilous journey taken in search of something of great value: a treasure, a person, or a concept, such as peace or freedom. As heroes or heroines pursue their quests, they face trials, tests, and temptations. Heroes and heroines are often helped along the way, sometimes by kindly gods and goddesses, sometimes by loyal friends or even animals. At the end of a quest, the hero or heroine is glorified: crowned the rightful ruler, hailed as the savior of a people, or, as in the story of Hercules, given immortality and a place among the gods. Such honors do not come easily, for the way of the quest is terrifying.

> **A** **quest** is a perilous journey taken in pursuit of something of great value.

## Reading Skills and Strategies

### Making Connections: What It Means to Me

Relating ancient myths to your own world can help you understand the stories and give you insights into your life. Myths speak in a universal language—that's why you see so many references to them on television, in newspapers, and in stories (see "Antaeus," page 469, for example). As you read about Hercules' bone-crunching labors, keep in mind the tasks you just listed for today's superhero. How are they similar to or different from the ones Hercules faces?

Hercules fighting Cerberus: one of his twelve labors (575 B.C.). Corinthian hydria (water jar).

Louvre, Paris, France. Erich Lessing/Art Resource, New York.

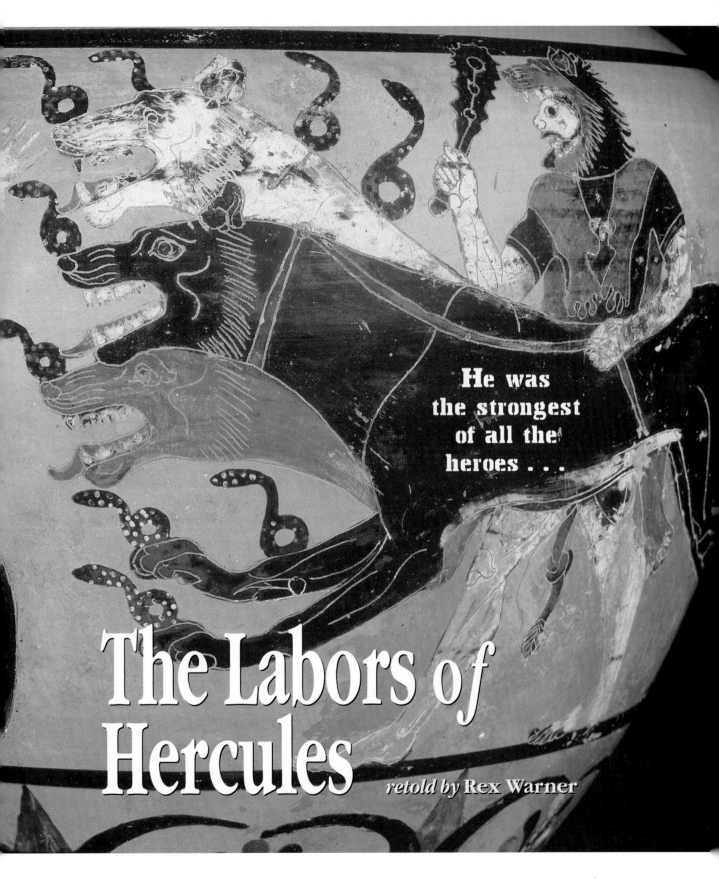

He was
the strongest
of all the
heroes . . .

# The Labors of Hercules

*retold by* Rex Warner

**H**ercules suffered much during his life, but after his death he became a god. His mother was Alcmena,[1] his father was Jupiter, and he was the strongest of all the heroes who lived in his time.

All through his life he was pursued by the hatred and jealousy of Juno, who tried to destroy him even in his cradle. She sent two great snakes to attack the sleeping baby, but Hercules awoke, grasped their necks in his hands, and strangled them both.

Before he was eighteen, he had done many famous deeds in the country of Thebes, and Creon, the king, gave him his daughter in marriage. But he could not long escape the anger of Juno, who afflicted him with a sudden madness, so that he did not know what he was doing, and in a fit of frenzy killed both his wife and his children. When he came to his senses, in horror and shame at what he had done, he visited the great cliffs of Delphi,[2] where the eagles circle all day and where Apollo's oracle[3] is. There he asked how he could be purified of his sin, and he was told by the oracle that he must go to Mycenae[4] and for twelve years obey all the commands of the cowardly king Eurystheus,[5]

Hercules killing the lion. Black-figured amphora (large storage jar).

Louvre, Paris, France. Erich Lessing/Art Resource, New York.

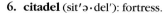

**He found that his arrows had no effect on the tough skin of the lion . . .**

his kinsman. It seemed a hard and cruel sentence, but the oracle told him also that at the end of many labors, he would be received among the gods.

Hercules therefore departed to the rocky citadel[6] of Mycenae that looks down upon the blue water of the bay of Argos. He was skilled in the use of every weapon, having been educated, as Jason was, by the wise centaur Chiron.[7] He was tall and immensely powerful. When Eurystheus saw him, he was both terrified of him and jealous of his great powers. He began to devise labors that would seem impossible, yet Hercules accomplished them all.

First he was ordered to destroy and to bring back to Mycenae the lion of Nemea, which for long had ravaged all the countryside to the north. Hercules took his bow and arrows and, in the forest of Nemea, cut himself a great club, so heavy that a man nowadays could hardly lift it. This club he carried ever afterwards as his chief weapon.

He found that his arrows had no effect on the tough skin of the lion, but as the beast

---

**1. Alcmena** (alk·mē′nə).
**2. Delphi** (del′fī).
**3. oracle:** person through whom the gods were consulted. The oracle at Delphi was a woman who would go into a trance and then utter strange sounds. Temple priests interpreted these as words of the god Apollo.
**4. Mycenae** (mī·sē′nē): See map on page 498.
**5. Eurystheus** (yo͞o·ris′thē·əs).

**6. citadel** (sit′ə·del′): fortress.
**7. centaur** (sen′tôr′) **Chiron** (kī′rän′): A centaur is a mythical creature with the body of a horse and the torso, arms, and head of a human. (**Jason** was another legendary Greek hero.)

---

**WORDS TO OWN**
**afflicted** (ə·flikt′id) v.: caused pain or suffering to.
**ravaged** (rav′ijd) v.: ruined; violently destroyed.

---

sprang at him, he half stunned it with his club; then, closing in with it, he seized it by the throat and killed it with his bare hands. They say that when he carried back on his shoulders to Mycenae the body of the huge beast, Eurystheus fled in terror and ordered Hercules never again to enter the gates of the city, but to wait outside until he was told to come in. Eurystheus also built for himself a special strong room of brass into which he would retire if he was ever again frightened by the power and valiance[8] of Hercules. Hercules himself took the skin of the lion and made it into a cloak which he wore ever afterwards, sometimes with the lion's head covering his own head like a cap, sometimes with it slung backwards over his shoulders.

Hercules in lion's skin, menacing Cerberus (575 B.C.). Corinthian hydria (water jar).

Louvre, Paris, France. Erich Lessing/Art Resource, New York.

The next task given to Hercules by Eurystheus was to destroy a huge water snake, called the Hydra, which lived in the marshes of Argos, was filled with poison, and had

## Hercules himself took the skin of the lion and made it into a cloak which he wore ever afterwards . . .

fifty venomous heads. Hercules, with his friend and companion, the young Iolaus,[9] set out from Mycenae and came to the great cavern, sacred to Pan, which is a holy place in the hills near Argos. Below this cavern a river gushes out of the rock. Willows and plane trees surround the source, and the brilliant green of grass. It is the freshest and most delightful place. But as the river flows downwards to the sea, it becomes wide and shallow, extending

into pestilential marshes, the home of stinging flies and mosquitoes. In these marshes they found the Hydra, and Hercules, with his great club, began to crush the beast's heads, afterwards cutting them off with his sword. Yet the more he labored, the more difficult his task became. From the stump of each head that he cut off, two other heads, with forked and hissing tongues, immediately sprang. Faced with an endless and increasing effort, Hercules was at a loss what to do. It seemed to him that heat might prove more powerful than cold steel, and he commanded Iolaus to burn the root of each head with a red-hot iron immediately after it was severed from the neck. This plan was successful. The heads no longer sprouted up again, and soon the dangerous and destructive animal lay dead, though still writhing in the black marsh water among the reeds. Hercules cut its body open and dipped his arrows in the blood. Henceforward these arrows would bring certain death, even if they only grazed the skin, so powerful was the Hydra's poison.

Eurystheus next ordered Hercules to capture and bring back alive a stag[10] sacred to

10. **stag:** full-grown male deer.

--------------------------------------

## WORDS TO OWN

**venomous** (ven′əm·əs) *adj.*: poisonous; malicious.
**pestilential** (pes′tə·len′shəl) *adj.*: causing disease; deadly.

--------------------------------------

8. **valiance** (val′yəns): courage; determination.
9. **Iolaus** (ī′ō·lā′əs).

Diana and famous for its great fleetness of foot, which lived in the waste mountains and forests and never yet had been approached in the chase. For a whole year Hercules pursued this animal, resting for the hours of darkness and pressing on next day in its tracks. For many months he was wholly outdistanced; valleys and forests divided him from his prey. But at the end of the year the stag, weary of the long hunt, could run no longer. Hercules seized it in his strong hands, tied first its forelegs and then its hind legs together, put the body of the beast, with its drooping antlered head, over his neck, and proceeded to return to the palace of King Eurystheus. However, as he was on his way through the woods, he was suddenly aware of a bright light in front of him, and in the middle of the light he saw standing a tall woman or, as he immediately recognized, a goddess, grasping in her hands a bow and staring at him angrily with her shining eyes. He knew at once that this was the archer goddess Diana, she who had once turned Actaeon[11] into a stag and who now was enraged at the loss of this other stag which was sacred to her. Hercules put his prey on the ground and knelt before the goddess. "It was through no desire of my own," he said, "that I have captured this noble animal. What I do is done at the command of my father Jupiter and of the

Cerberus with three heads. Corinthian hydria (water jar).

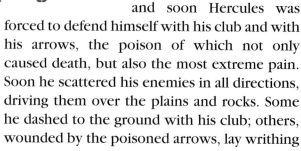

From the stump of each head that he cut off, two other heads, with forked and hissing tongues, immediately sprang.

oracle of your brother Apollo at Delphi." The goddess listened to his explanation, smiled kindly on him, and allowed him to go on his way when he had promised that, once the stag had been carried to Eurystheus, it would be set free again in the forests that it loved. So Hercules accomplished this third labor.

He was not, however, to be allowed to rest. Eurystheus now commanded him to go out to the mountains of Erymanthus[12] and bring back the great wild boar that for long had terrorized all the neighborhood. So Hercules set out once more, and on his way he passed the country where the centaurs had settled after they had been driven down from the north in the battle that had taken place with the Lapiths at the wedding of Pirithous.[13] In this battle they had already had experience of the hero's strength, but still their manners were rude and rough. When the centaur Pholus offered Hercules some of their best wine to drink, the other centaurs became jealous. Angry words led to blows, and soon Hercules was forced to defend himself with his club and with his arrows, the poison of which not only caused death, but also the most extreme pain. Soon he scattered his enemies in all directions, driving them over the plains and rocks. Some he dashed to the ground with his club; others, wounded by the poisoned arrows, lay writhing

11. **Actaeon** (ak·tē′ən).

12. **Erymanthus** (er′ə·man′thəs).
13. **Pirithous** (pī·rith′ō·əs).

in agony or kicking their hooves in the air. Some took refuge in the house of the famous centaur Chiron, who had been schoolmaster to Hercules and who, alone among the centaurs, was immortal. As he pursued his enemies to this good centaur's house, shooting arrows at them as he went, Hercules, by an unhappy accident, wounded Chiron himself. Whether it was because of grief that his old pupil had so injured him, or whether it was because of the great pain of the wound, Chiron prayed to Jupiter that his immortality should be taken away from him. Jupiter granted his prayer. The good centaur died, but he was set in Heaven in a constellation of stars which is still called either Sagittarius or else the Centaur.

Hercules mourned the sad death of his old master. Then he went on to Erymanthus. It was winter and he chased the great boar up to the deep snow in the passes of the mountains. The animal's short legs soon grew weary of plowing through the stiff snow and Hercules caught it up when it was exhausted and panting in a snowdrift. He bound it firmly and slung the great body over his back. They say that when he brought it to Mycenae, Eurystheus was so frightened at the sight of the huge tusks and flashing eyes that he hid for two days in the brass hiding place that he had had built for himself.

The next task that Hercules was ordered to do would have seemed to anyone impossible. There was a king of Elis called Augeas,[14] very rich in herds of goats and cattle. His stables, they say, held three thousand oxen, and for ten years these stables had never been cleaned. The dung and muck stood higher than a house, hardened and caked together. The smell was such that even the herdsmen, who were used to it, could scarcely bear to go near. Hercules was now ordered to clean these stables, and going to Elis, he first asked the king to promise him the tenth part of his herds if he was successful in his task. The king readily agreed, and Hercules made the great river Alpheus change its course and come foaming and roaring through the filthy stables. In less than a day all the dirt was cleared and rolled away to the sea. The river then went back to its former course, and for the first time in ten years, the stone floors and walls of the enormous stables shone white and clean.

Hercules then asked for his reward, but King Augeas, claiming that he had performed the task not with his own hands but by a trick, refused to give it to him. He even banished his own son, who took the side of Hercules and reproached his father for not keeping his promise. Hercules then made war on the kingdom of Elis, drove King Augeas out, and put his son on the throne. Then, with his rich reward, he returned to Mycenae, ready to undertake whatever new task was given him by Eurystheus.

Again he was ordered to destroy creatures that were harmful to men. This time they were great birds, like cranes or storks, but much more powerful, which devoured human flesh and lived around the black waters of the Stymphalian[15] lake. In the reeds and rocky crags they lived in huge numbers, and Hercules was at a loss how to draw them from their hiding places. It was the goddess Minerva who helped him by giving him a great rattle of brass. The noise of this rattle drove the great birds into the air in throngs. Hercules pursued them with his arrows, which rang upon their horny beaks and legs but stuck firm in the bodies that tumbled one after the other into the lake. The whole brood of these monsters was entirely destroyed, and now only ducks and harmless waterfowl nest along the reedy shores.

Hercules had now accomplished six of his labors. Six more remained. After the killing of

---

14. **Augeas** (ô·jē′əs).

15. **Stymphalian** (stim·fā′lē·ən).

the Stymphalian birds, he was commanded to go to Crete and bring back from there alive a huge bull which was laying the whole island waste. Barehanded and alone he grappled with this bull, and, once again, when he brought the animal back into the streets of Mycenae, Eurystheus fled in terror at the sight both of the hero and of the great beast which he had captured.

From the southern sea Hercules was sent to the north to Thrace, over which ruled King Diomedes,[16] a strong and warlike prince who savagely fed his famous mares on human flesh. Hercules conquered the king in battle and gave his body to the very mares which had so often fed upon the bodies of the king's enemies. He brought the mares back to King Eurystheus, who again was terrified at the sight of such fierce and spirited animals. He ordered them to be taken to the heights of Mount Olympus and there be consecrated to Jupiter. But Jupiter had no love for these unnatural creatures, and, on the rocky hillsides, they were devoured by lions, wolves, and bears.

Next, Hercules was commanded to go to the country of the Amazons, the fierce warrior women, and bring back the girdle of their queen Hippolyte.[17] Seas and mountains had to be crossed, battles to be fought; but Hercules in the end accomplished the long journey and the dangerous task. Later, as is well known, Hippolyte became the wife of Theseus of Athens and bore him an ill-fated son, Hippolytus.

Hercules had now traveled in the south, the north, and the east. His tenth labor was to be in the far west, beyond the country of Spain, in an island called Erythia.[18] Here lived the giant Geryon, a great monster with three bodies and three heads. With his herdsman and his two-headed dog, called Orthrus, he looked after

huge flocks of oxen, and, at the command of Eurystheus, Hercules came into his land to lift the cattle and to destroy the giant. On his way, at the very entrance to the Atlantic, he set up two great marks, ever afterward to be known by sailors and called the Pillars of Hercules.[19] Later, as he wandered through rocks and over desert land, he turned his anger against the Sun itself, shooting his arrows at the great god Phoebus Apollo. But Phoebus pitied him in his thirst and weariness. He sent him a golden boat, and in this boat Hercules crossed over to the island of Erythia. Here he easily destroyed both watchdog and herdsman, but fought for long with the great three-bodied giant before he slew him, body after body. Then he began to drive the cattle over rivers and mountains and deserts from Spain to Greece. As he was passing through Italy he came near the cave where Cacus, a son of Vulcan, who breathed fire out of his mouth, lived solitary and cruel, since he killed all strangers and nailed their heads, dripping with blood, to the posts at the entrance of his rocky dwelling. While Hercules was resting, with the herds all round him, Cacus came out of his cave and stole eight of the best animals of the whole herd. He dragged them backwards by their tails, so that Hercules should not be able to track them down.

When Hercules awoke from his rest, he searched far and wide for the missing animals, but since they had been driven into the deep recesses of Cacus's cave, he was unable to find them. In the end he began to go on his way with the rest of the herd, and as the stolen animals heard the lowing of the other cattle, they too began to low and bellow in their rocky prison. Hercules stopped still, and soon out of the cave came the fire-breathing giant, prepared to defend the fruits of his robbery and anxious to hang the head of Hercules among

16. **Diomedes** (dī′ə·mē′dēz).
17. **Hippolyte** (hi·päl′i·tē).
18. **Erythia** (er·i·thē′ə).

19. **Pillars of Hercules:** two points of lands reaching out into the water on either side of the Strait of Gibraltar.

his other disgusting trophies. This, however, was not to be. The huge limbs and terrible fiery breath of Cacus were of no avail against the hero's strength and fortitude. Soon, with a tremendous blow of his club, he stretched out Cacus dead on the ground. Then he drove the great herd on over mountains and plains, through forests and rivers to Mycenae.

Hercules' next labor again took him to the far west. He was commanded by Eurystheus to fetch him some of the golden apples of the Hesperides.[20] These apples grew in a garden west even of the land of Atlas. Here the sun shines continually, but always cool, well-watered trees of every kind give shade. All flowers and fruits that grow on earth grow here, and fruit and flowers are always on the boughs together. In the center of the garden is the orchard, where golden apples gleam among the shining green leaves and the flushed blossom. Three nymphs, the Hesperides, look after this orchard, which was given by Jupiter to Juno as a wedding present. It is guarded also by a great dragon that never sleeps and coils its huge folds around the trees. No one except the gods knows exactly where this beautiful and remote garden is, and it was to this unknown place that Hercules was sent.

He was helped by Minerva and by the nymphs of the broad river Po in Italy. These nymphs told Hercules where to find Nereus,[21] the ancient god of the sea, who knew the past, the present, and the future. "Wait for him," they said, "until you find him asleep on the rocky shore, surrounded by his fifty daughters. Seize hold of him tightly and do not let go until he answers your question. He will, in trying to escape you, put on all kinds of shapes. He will turn to fire, to water, to a wild beast, or to a serpent. You must not lose your courage, but hold him all the tighter, and, in the end, he will come back to his own shape and will tell you what you want to know."

Hercules followed their advice. As he watched along the sea god's shore he saw, lying on the sand, half in and half out of the sea, with seaweed trailing round his limbs, the old god himself. Around him were his daughters, the Nereids,[22] some riding on the backs of dolphins, some dancing on the shore, some swimming and diving in the deeper water. As Hercules approached, they cried out shrilly at the sight of a man. Those on land leaped back into the sea; those in the sea swam further from the shore. But their cries did not awake their father till Hercules was close to him and able to grip him firmly in his strong hands. As soon as the old god felt the hands upon him, his body seemed to disappear into a running stream of water; but Hercules felt the body that he could not see, and did not relax his grasp. Next it seemed that his hands were buried in a great pillar of fire; but the fire did not scorch the skin, and Hercules could still feel the aged limbs through the fire. Then it was a great lion with wide-open jaws that appeared to be lying and raging on the sands; then a bear, then a dragon. Still Hercules clung firmly to his prisoner, and in the end he saw again the bearded face and seaweed-dripping limbs of old Nereus. The god knew for what purpose Hercules had seized him, and he told him the way to the garden of the Hesperides.

It was a long and difficult journey, but at the end of it Hercules was rewarded. The guardian nymphs (since this was the will of Jupiter) allowed him to pick from the <u>pliant</u> boughs two or three of the golden fruit. The great dragon bowed its head to the ground at their command and left Hercules unmolested. He

22. **Nereids** (nir′ē·idz).

20. **Hesperides** (hes·per′i·dēz).
21. **Nereus** (nir′ē·əs).

---

**WORDS TO OWN**
**pliant** (plī′ənt) *adj.*: easily bent.

---

brought back the apples to Eurystheus, but soon they began to lose that beautiful sheen of gold that had been theirs in the western garden. So Minerva carried them back again to the place from which they came, and then once more they glowed with their own gold among the other golden apples that hung upon the trees.

Now had come the time for the twelfth and last of the labors that Hercules did for his master Eurystheus. This labor would seem to anyone by far the hardest; for the hero was commanded to descend into the lower world and bring back with him from the kingdom of Proserpine[23] the terrible three-headed watchdog Cerberus.

Hercules took the dark path which before him had been trodden only by Orpheus and Theseus and Pirithous. Orpheus had returned. Theseus and Pirithous, for their wicked attempt, were still imprisoned.

Hercules passed the Furies, undaunted by the frightful eyes beneath the writhing serpents of their hair. He passed the great criminals, Sisyphus,[24] Tantalus, and the rest. He passed by his friend, the unhappy Theseus, who was sitting immovably fixed to a rock, and he came at last into the terrible presence of black Pluto himself, who sat on his dark throne with his young wife Proserpine beside him. To the King and Queen of the Dead, Hercules explained the reason of his coming. "Go," said Pluto, "and, so long as you use no weapon, but only your bare hands, you may take my watchdog Cerberus to the upper air."

23. **Proserpine** (prō·sur′pi·nē): Roman name for Persephone. (See "The Origin of the Seasons," page 501.)
24. **Sisyphus** (sis′ə·fəs).

Hercules ascending to Olympus.
Red-figured bell crater (bowl).

Kunsthistorisches Museum, Vienna, Austria.
Erich Lessing/Art Resource, New York.

Hercules thanked the dreadful king for giving him the permission which he had asked. Then he made one more request, which was that Theseus, who had sinned only by keeping his promise to his friend, might be allowed to return again to life. This, too, was granted him. Theseus rose to his feet again and accompanied the hero to the entrance of Hell, where the huge dog Cerberus, with his three heads and his three deep baying voices, glared savagely at the intruders. Even this tremendous animal proved no match for Hercules, who with his vise-like grip stifled the breath in two of the shaggy throats and then lifted the beast upon his shoulders and began to ascend again, Theseus following close behind, the path that leads to the world of men. They say that when he carried Cerberus to Mycenae, Eurystheus fled in terror to another city and was now actually glad that Hercules had completed what might seem to have been twelve impossible labors. Cerberus was restored to his place in Hell and never again visited the upper world. Nor did Hercules ever go down to the place of the dead, since, after further trials, he was destined to live among the gods above.

Hercules leading Cerberus to Eurystheus (575 B.C.). Corinthian hydria (water jar).

Louvre, Paris, France. Giraudon/Art Resource, New York.

## MEET THE WRITER

### Journeys Past and Present

**Rex Warner** (1905–1986) pursued his dream in many different places around the world. He was born and grew up in England, worked as a teacher in Egypt, ran the British Institute in Greece, taught English in Germany, and finally settled in the United States as an English professor at the University of Connecticut. A respected classical scholar, Warner sought to bring ancient Greece and Rome to life in the modern world.

# MAKING MEANINGS

## First Thoughts

1. Hercules has come to be known as a brawny hero, not one with a lot of intelligence. Is this fair? How do you feel about the way he tackles the tasks on his quest?

## Shaping Interpretations

2. Here is a checklist of characteristics for a great **quest** story. How well does "The Labors of Hercules" meet these criteria? Do you know other stories that meet them? The hero

   - is threatened at birth
   - shows early signs of being special
   - is called on to undertake a special quest
   - faces a dangerous journey
   - receives help along the way, including assistance from the gods
   - descends to the underworld
   - is finally rewarded

3. Why does Hercules accept his quest?

4. Like most myths, this one explains how certain things on earth and in the heavens came to be. Where did the constellation Sagittarius come from? the rocks known as the Pillars of Hercules?

5. How is the garden of the Hesperides a kind of paradise? Does it remind you of other paradises? (How is it the opposite of the underworld?)

6. How is Hercules' descent into the underworld unlike the trips made by Orpheus (page 513) and Persephone (page 501)?

7. The challenges Hercules faces are often symbols of challenges we face in life. What do you think each labor stands for?

## Extending the Text

8. Does Hercules remind you of the heroes of any American **tall tales**? In what ways is he similar to larger-than-life heroes like Paul Bunyan, John Henry, and Pecos Bill?

9. How is your own life a kind of quest? What can you learn from Hercules' story that might help you reach your goals?

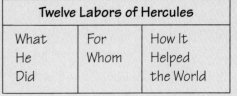

### Reading Check

In a chart with headings like the ones below, write a data sheet about the twelve labors of Hercules.

| Twelve Labors of Hercules | | |
|---|---|---|
| What He Did | For Whom | How It Helped the World |

# CHOICES: Building Your Portfolio

## Writer's Notebook

### 1. Collecting Ideas for an Evaluation

Look back through "The Labors of Hercules," and decide which one of the twelve labors was the most interesting or the most exciting to read about. Base your evaluation on these standards:

- the difficulty and/or importance of the task
- the cleverness of Hercules' solution
- the storyteller's description of the labor

> **Best Labor:**
> Killing the Hydra
> —impossible if he
> hadn't cleverly
> thought of heat
> —important since
> Hercules got his
> best weapon from
> it—the poison
> arrows

## Creative Writing/Art

### 2. Help Wanted: Hero/Heroine

Look back at your notes for the Quickwrite on page 540. What world-improving tasks did you list for your modern-day Hercules? Write a story called "The Five Labors of . . .". Give your superhero or superheroine a name, and explain why his or her fate involves attempting to accomplish these tasks. Then, tell about each labor and the difficulties the hero or heroine overcomes in performing each. Finally, tell how the hero or heroine is rewarded or glorified for successfully completing the work. If you wish, tell your story in the form of a cartoon like "The Twelve Tasks of Heracles" (see **Connections** on page 554).

## Language/Research

### 3. A Labor of Language

From your reading of the myth, what do you suppose a *herculean task* would be? What do you think *Augean* means? Many words in English come from names that appear in the ancient myths.

Using the words below, create an illustrated glossary that you can leave in the classroom for other students to use when they read this myth. First, tell what person or place in mythology the name comes from. Then, draw this person or place. Also, provide a sentence showing how each word is used today.

| | |
|---|---|
| amazon | herculean |
| Augean | hydra |
| Olympian | atlas |

## Research/Speaking

### 4. Mythic All-Stars

The characters in "The Labors of Hercules" include some of the greatest names in mythology: Theseus, Hippolyte, Actaeon, Jason, the Amazons, Apollo, Pluto, Diana, Juno. With a group of classmates, do research to find out what these figures are famous for. Deliver to the class a short biographical sketch of each one. Then, compile your reports, along with illustrations, in a class collection of mythic all-stars.

# GRAMMAR LINK

MINI-LESSON

## • Do a Good Job with *Good* and *Well*

**Language Handbook HELP**

*See Glossary of Usage:* good, well, *page 786.*

**Technology HELP**

*See* Language Workshop CD-ROM. *Key word entry: modifiers.*

Does choosing between *good* and *well* sometimes seem as hard as the labors of Hercules? Here are a few simple rules to help you get the job done right:

- *Good* is an adjective. Never use it to modify a verb.

- *Well* is usually an adverb. Use it to modify a verb.

| | |
|---|---|
| NONSTANDARD | Hercules fought <u>good</u> against the Hydra. |
| STANDARD | Hercules fought <u>well</u> against the Hydra. |
| STANDARD | Hercules fought a <u>good</u> fight. |

Although it is usually an adverb, *well* may be used as an adjective to mean "healthy."

| | |
|---|---|
| EXAMPLE | The Hydra was not feeling <u>well</u> after its fight with Hercules. |

Note: *Feel good* and *feel well* mean different things. *Feel good* means "feel happy or pleased." *Feel well* simply means "feel healthy."

| | |
|---|---|
| EXAMPLES | Hercules didn't <u>feel good</u> about killing the centaurs. |
| | Eurystheus didn't <u>feel well</u> when he saw the wild boar's head. |

### Try It Out

Rewrite each sentence, correcting any usage errors you find.

1. Hercules fought good against the lion of Nemea.

2. Anyone struck by one of Hercules' poison arrows would not feel good about the situation.

3. Hercules found a good way to clean Augeas's stables really good.

4. Juno did not treat Hercules very good, but Diana and Minerva realized he was a good hero.

5. Hercules did well to get the golden apples, although the fruit didn't look as good once it left the garden.

# VOCABULARY

HOW TO OWN A WORD

**WORD BANK**

*afflicted*
*ravaged*
*venomous*
*pestilential*
*pliant*

## Vocabulary for the Workplace: At the Movies

Imagine you're a movie scriptwriter. You have a great idea for a new horror or science fiction film, but you have to persuade the studio bosses to back your project. Write a short persuasive description, or "pitch," of the movie you want to make. Use all five words in the Word Bank to **summarize** the **plot** of the movie.

THE TWELVE TASKS OF HERACLES

Heracles was a tough little baby.

Kill!

Everyone loved him but Hera, Zeus's wife, who sent two snakes to kill him.

No problem.

I'll just pretend he doesn't exist!

HELP!

Call me Heracles (or Hercules will do).

How many at the last count, dear?

But Heracles strangled both of them.

For a while, Hera ignored Heracles.

As he grew up, Heracles became stronger and stronger and stronger.

He married and had many children.

This happiness has gone on long enough! MOUNT OLYMPUS

You've killed our children!

Hera hated him for being so happy.

So one night she put a spell on him. Heracles lashed out with his sword, killing imaginary enemies.

When he woke from the spell, he saw that he had killed his own children.

Get out of here you murderer!

I must find forgiveness.

Will the gods ever forgive me?

Only if you do twelve tasks for your enemy, King Eurystheus.

He'd be better off dead.

Heartbroken, Heracles went to the temple to seek forgiveness.

The priestess said he could make amends by serving his old enemy, King Eurystheus.

I'll do twelve things and no more!

Don't let him come too close.

Coward.

I've got twelve really hard tasks for you, but with some luck you'll be dead after the first one.

I doubt it.

The king was frightened of Heracles, so he hid in a pot whenever he came near.

And because he hated Heracles, he gave him twelve deadly tasks.

*(Pages 554–557)* Heracles from *Greek Myths for Young Children* ©1991 Marcia Williams.

First, Heracles had to kill the lion of Nemea whose hide was so thick that no sword could penetrate it.

Next, he had to kill the many-headed Hydra, whose very breath could kill man or beast.

Third, he had to capture the sacred, golden-horned deer, an animal as swift as the wind.

The fourth task was to catch a savage boar whose tusks could pierce any armor.

Next, Heracles had to clean out the vast and filthy stables of King Augeas in a single night.

Reprinted by permission of Walker Books, Ltd., London. Published in the US by Candlewick Press, Cambridge, Massachusetts.

*(continued on next page)*

*(continued from previous page)*

Then he had to to destroy a flock of man-eating birds that hid in a dangerous swamp.

The seventh task was to capture the fire-breathing, marauding bull of Crete.

Next, he had to steal Diomedes's horses, which fed on human flesh.

Then Heracles had to fetch the golden girdle worn by the queen of the Amazon warrior women.

The tenth task was to seize the monster Geryon's cattle, guarded by his two-headed dog.

The eleventh, to collect three golden apples protected by a ferocious dragon.

Heracles's twelfth and last task was the most dangerous of all: to fetch the three-headed guard dog, Cerberus, from Hades itself.

His twelve tasks completed, Heracles returned to King Eurystheus.

The king was dismayed to see him alive, and quickly sent him packing.

Then, to avoid angering the gods, Heracles sent Cerberus back to Hades.

At the temple, Heracles was finally pardoned.

He was content at last, and stronger than ever!

And Hera never bothered Heracles again.

# Before You Read

## Make the Connection

### When Too Much Is Not Enough

Greed is a powerful emotion—it can disrupt friendships, spark wars, and topple empires.

In general, **irony** is a contrast between expectation and reality.

*For more on Irony, see the Handbook of Literary Terms.*

## Quickwrite

What happens to people who value money above everything else? Write briefly about a modern-day situation in which greed led to unhappiness or suffering.

## Elements of Literature

### Irony

**Irony** is the difference between what you say and what you mean or between what's supposed to happen and what does happen. When you say "Good going" to someone who's just fallen flat on his face, you're using irony. When a firehouse burns down, that's irony. This myth is about an ironic situation: There's a big difference between what Midas *expects* to happen and what does happen.

## Reading Skills and Strategies

### Using Prior Knowledge: Building on What You Know

Get together with a group of classmates. Brainstorm to find answers to the questions about greed on the map below. You may want to add questions—and answers—of your own.

Greed

Definition:

Questions about greed:

What is wrong with it?

What is an example of it?

Who is greedy?

What is its opposite?

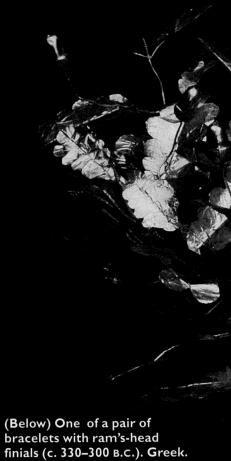

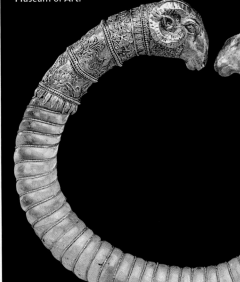

(Below) One of a pair of bracelets with ram's-head finials (c. 330–300 B.C.). Greek. Said to be from near Thessaloniki. Gold, rock crystal (8 cm wide x 7.8 cm high).

The Metropolitan Museum of Art, Harris Brisbane Dick Fund, 1937. (37.11.11-.12). Photograph © 1993 The Metropolitan Museum of Art.

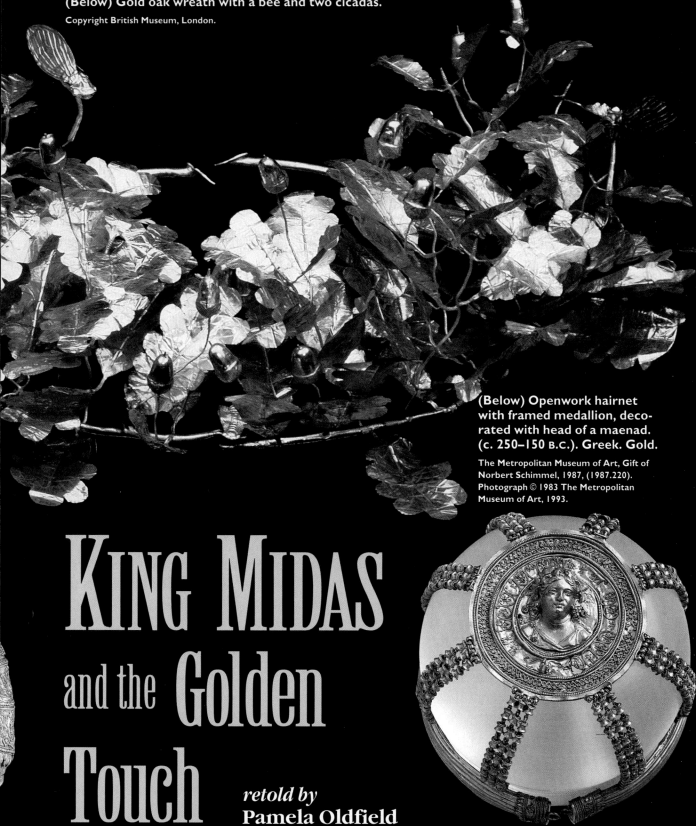

# KING MIDAS
## and the Golden
# Touch

*retold by*
**Pamela Oldfield**

He wanted to be the
most powerful king in
the world . . .

Brooch in the form of a pediment with Pegasus figures (c. 340–320 B.C.).
Greek. Gold (length: 7.8 cm).

Many years ago in the land of Lydia, there was a beautiful garden. Roses of every shade grew there, and on warm summer nights the air was heavy with their fragrance. The garden belonged to a palace, and the palace was the home of a king whose name was Midas. He was, it is true, rather greedy, but on the whole no better and no worse than any other man. Midas had a loving wife and a daughter he adored, but he was still discontented. He wanted to be the most powerful king in the world; he wanted everyone to envy him.

One day as he was walking through the palace garden, he was startled to see a pair of legs sticking out from beneath his favorite rosebush. The strange thing about these legs was that they had hoofs instead of feet. The king stared at them for a moment and then called for the gardener's boy.

"What do you make of that?" he asked. The boy parted the branches of the rosebush and peered through.

"It's a satyr, Your Majesty," he reported, trying not to laugh. "I think it's Silenus."

The satyrs were strange, mischievous creatures—half man, half beast—who roamed the world in search of adventure. Midas frowned, angry that somebody should be sleeping in his garden.

The boy ran off to fetch the gardener, and between them they dragged Silenus from under the rosebush and pulled him to his feet. Silenus grinned foolishly. He was holding an empty wine jar.

"You are trespassing in my garden," Midas told him severely. "What have you to say for yourself?" The old satyr shrugged.

"I got lost, so I sat down for a drink," he told the king, looking quite unrepentant.

"Disgraceful," said Midas. "I shall send word to your master at once." Silenus began to look worried, for his master was the god Dionysus, who was not only powerful but also quick-tempered.

"I beg you not to do that," he cried. "He will be angry with me. Suppose I make a bargain with you? If you will overlook my foolishness, I will entertain you with strange and wonderful tales, better than any you have heard before."

Midas agreed and the satyr stayed on in the palace, delighting the king with wonderful accounts of his adventures. At the end of the week, Midas sent the satyr back to Dionysus. The god was very fond of Silenus, despite his many faults, and was pleased to see him safe and sound. He wanted to thank Midas for taking care of the old satyr and offered the king any gift he cared to name.

Any gift he cared to name! What a marvelous opportunity! He pondered for a whole day and a night and then asked Dionysus if he could make a wish. The god agreed and Midas asked for the power to turn whatever he touched into gold. The god granted his wish, and Midas was jubilant.

"Imagine a king with a golden touch!" he cried. "I shall be the wealthiest and most powerful king in the world."

The king began to experiment with his new gift. He hurried into the garden and touched one of the flowers. At once, the whole bush turned to gold. He went from bush to bush, touching all the blooms, until the entire garden had turned to gold. Then he looked around him. Suddenly Midas felt doubtful. Gone were the colors and the glorious perfume. The garden was still and lifeless.

Inside the palace, the king called for a goblet of wine. As soon as it touched his lips the wine turned to gold and he could not drink.

A terrible thought occurred to him.

"What will happen when I eat?" he wondered. With trembling fingers he reached out to take an apple from a bowl of fruit. As soon as he touched it, the apple turned to gold.

"What have I done?" he whispered. "If I cannot eat or drink I shall die!" He knew that he had made a terrible mistake and decided to beg Dionysus to take back his gift. "I will go to him at once," he cried, but his decision came too late. At that very moment his daughter ran into the room.

"Stay away from me!" Midas shouted, but she took no notice. She threw her arms around him—and was turned to gold. His daughter was now a gleaming but lifeless statue. The king stared at her in horror.

"What have I done to you?" he cried, kneeling beside her. His grief was so great that nobody could console him. He hurried to the palace of Dionysus and threw himself at the god's feet.

"Forgive my stupid greed!" he begged. "Tell me what I must do to save my child. I will do anything you say."

Dionysus told him to find the river Pactolus and wash himself in its waters. Midas set off at once. He went alone and walked for many miles over rough and stony ground.

When he reached the river he found it flowing deep and strong. Midas waded straight in. He was instantly swept away by the current. When at last he managed to reach the shore, he wondered if the curse had indeed been washed from him. Looking back, he saw that the river now gleamed and sparkled in the sun. On the riverbed tiny nuggets of gold lay among the pebbles. Dionysus had spoken truthfully, and the terrible power had left him. Joyfully Midas made his way home.

As he approached the palace, Midas's daughter ran to greet him. He lifted her into his arms and carried her into the garden. Midas was overjoyed to hear her laughter once again, and he sighed happily as he breathed in the fragrance of the flowers.

"I have learned my lesson," he said softly, "and I am content."

# MAKING MEANINGS

## First Thoughts

1. Finish these sentences:

   • If I were Midas, I . . .

   • I was surprised when . . .

## Shaping Interpretations

2. At the end of the myth, Midas says, "I have learned my lesson. . . . I am content." What lesson do you think Midas has learned? What makes him feel content?

3. How would you have worded the wish for the golden touch in order to avoid Midas's problems?

4. In "Echo and Narcissus" (page 523) the fate of Narcissus is ironic because what he loves most—himself—causes his downfall. What **irony** do you see in Midas's story?

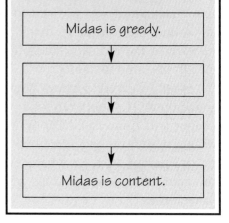

**Reading Check**

The diagram below shows the first **cause** and the final **effect** in the tale of King Midas. Fill in the chain of events that leads from one to the other. Add as many boxes as you need.

> Midas is greedy.

↓

↓

↓

> Midas is content.

## Connecting with the Text

5. How would you connect the lesson in "King Midas and the Golden Touch" to life today? Look back at your notes for the word map on page 558 for ideas.

## Extending the Text

6. What would we mean if we said someone had the "Midas touch"? Would it be a compliment? Look at your notes for the Quickwrite on page 558 for ideas.

One of a pair of bracelets with ram's-head finials (c. 330–300 B.C.). Greek. Said to be from near Thessaloniki. Gold, rock crystal (8 cm wide x 7.8 cm high).

The Metropolitan Museum of Art, Harris Brisbane Dick Fund, 1937. (37.11.11-.12). Photograph © 1993 The Metropolitan Museum of Art.

# CHOICES: Building Your Portfolio

## Writer's Notebook

### 1. Collecting Ideas for an Evaluation

Which myth in this collection did you like best? Take notes for an evaluation of the story, noting what you think is best about the myth's story elements—character, setting, suspense, horror, message, or ending.

WORK IN PROGRESS

**Favorite Myth**

Midas story—
because character
is like people today
who grab at money
and lose touch with
life's simple joys

## Creative Writing

### 2. Solid-Gold Memories

Imagine that you are King Midas's daughter. One moment you're a happy young princess running to greet your dad. The next moment you're solid gold! Focus on what you see and feel as you are frozen into a golden statue. Then, tell how being released from this golden prison affects you. Based on your strange experience, tell what you think of the desire for wealth.

## Art

### 3. Quick-Change Artists

**Metamorphosis**—a magical change in shape—is a common element in myths. Demeter, Echo, Narcissus, and Midas's daughter all go through metamorphoses. You've probably read other myths with examples of shape changing, too. Create a collage that shows some of these magical transformations. Many collages include words. You might want to add words to yours.

## Drama

### 4. Sharing the Wealth of King Midas

"King Midas and the Golden Touch" is a story rich enough to share with audiences of all ages. Try acting out this myth for a group of younger students in your school or neighborhood. You'll need actors to play the roles of King Midas, Silenus, Midas's daughter, and Dionysus. As you work on the dialogue for your play, think of a dramatic way to show the change from girl to golden statue. After you present the play, you might want to read the myth aloud to the group or hand out a homemade picture book based on the myth.

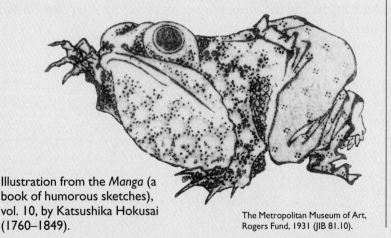

Illustration from the *Manga* (a book of humorous sketches), vol. 10, by Katsushika Hokusai (1760–1849).

The Metropolitan Museum of Art, Rogers Fund, 1931 (JIB 81.10).

# LANGUAGE LINK

## Style: Allusions

**Handbook of Literary Terms**
**H E L P**

*See Allusion.*

An **allusion** is a reference to a work of literature or to an actual event, person, or place. When a speaker or writer makes an allusion, he or she expects the audience to recognize the reference and understand its meaning. For example, if you were to say that a stockbroker has "the golden touch," you would expect people to know you are alluding to the Midas myth. If you described cleaning up a flooded basement as "a herculean effort," you would expect people to know you are alluding to those enormous problems Hercules had to tackle. As you can see, a simple allusion can say a great deal in very few words.

### Try It Out

For each sentence, identify the allusion to mythology and explain its meaning. Research any allusions you don't recognize.

1. Rod spends thirty minutes combing his hair every morning; he must think he's Narcissus.

2. I feel sorry for Teresa, packed off to boarding school for half the year like poor Persephone.

3. When the power failed, the subway station became a dark and dismal underworld.

4. A modern-day Orpheus, the new conductor coaxes marvelous melodies from the town orchestra.

# VOCABULARY   HOW TO OWN A WORD

## Words from Mythology: Making Up Names

People over the ages have often turned to the ancient myths when they've wanted to name something new (such as a planet, a missile, a business, a disease). See if you can use your knowledge of the myths and the chart of gods and goddesses on page 497 to make up imaginative names for these things:

1. a disco
2. a fishery
3. a sheet-metal shop
4. a column written to advise the lovelorn
5. a messenger service

6. a guided missile or bomber
7. a cereal
8. a high school
9. a health club or spa
10. a winery

# Elements of Literature

## FABLES: Teaching Stories *by* Virginia Hamilton

Very, very brief stories told to teach practical lessons about life are called **fables.** The word comes from the Latin *fabula*, which means "a telling."

The great teller of fables was Aesop, who is thought to have been an African held as a slave in Greece. (According to some authorities, his name comes from the Greek word *ethiope,* meaning "sunburned face.") Aesop lived in the sixth century B.C. He certainly had an extraordinary imagination. Aesop created tales, usually used for political purposes, in which animals behaved like human beings. In Aesop's fables, animals are good and bad, smart and stupid. Some people say that Aesop won his freedom because he provided so many sarcastic stories for his master to use against political opponents.

Aesop told his fables aloud. Other people repeated what they'd heard him tell, and in that way his fables survived over centuries. A version of Aesop's fables was written down by a Greek scribe, but for a thousand years the manuscript was lost. Not until 1844 was a copy found—in a monastery.

The fable's very practical lesson is called a **moral.** Aesop let his listeners guess at his stories' morals, but today the morals are usually written out at the ends of the stories. "Don't count your chickens before they're hatched" is a famous moral that follows the fable "The Maid and the Pail of Milk." In this fable (which does not have animal characters), a girl carrying a pail of milk on her head dreams about all the money and fine clothes she will get from the sale of the milk. She forgets for a moment about the pail, tosses her head, and all the milk spills.

Though Aesop is the most famous fabulist in the West, fables were being told in India and China many years before Aesop's time. Telling teaching stories seems to be part of human nature.

*The Crane King eating the frogs who asked for a king, in Aesop's fable of the same name.* Wood engraving after Gustave Doré (1832–1883).

The Granger Collection, New York.

# Before You Read

## Make the Connection

### Words to Live By

Deep down people haven't changed much over the years. These next four stories were told more than 2,500 years ago. Even so, the kinds of behavior they warn against will be familiar to you today. For example, can you think of a situation when people

- act jealously and meanly when something good happens to someone else?

- are never satisfied with the simple joys of life?

- always claim to know what should be done but never risk anything to do it?

## Quickwrite

Jot down some notes about your experiences with people who behave in one or more of the ways just described. Have you ever found yourself acting like this?

## Elements of Literature

### Fable

A **fable** is a one-idea story. At the end it gives a single clear **moral,** or lesson, about what to do—or not to do—to succeed in life. Characters in fables are usually animals who act and talk like human beings.

> **A fable** is a brief story in prose or verse that teaches a moral or gives a practical lesson about how to get along in life.
>
> *For more on Fable, see page 565 and the Handbook of Literary Terms.*

## Reading Skills and Strategies

### Identifying a Text's Purposes: Finding More than One

These short tales have several **purposes:**

- to **entertain,** using animals that talk and act like human beings as characters

- to **inform** by teaching important lessons about life

- to **influence** people or **persuade** them to change their behavior

More than 2,500 years ago, the leaders of ancient Greece used **fables** like the ones here by Aesop to support their ideas in speeches and debates. They hoped that their audiences would relate the messages of the fables to the current political situation.

go.hrw.com
LEO 7-7

# The Frogs Who Wished for a King

**Aesop**

The Frogs were tired of governing themselves. They had so much freedom that it had spoiled them, and they did nothing but sit around croaking in a bored manner and wishing for a government that could entertain them with the pomp and display of royalty and rule them in a way to make them know they were being ruled. No milk-and-water government for them, they declared. So they sent a petition to Jupiter asking for a king.

Jupiter saw what simple and foolish creatures they were, but to keep them quiet and make them think they had a king, he threw down a huge log, which fell into the water with a great splash. The Frogs hid themselves among the reeds and grasses, thinking the new king to be some fearful giant. But they soon discovered how tame and peaceable King Log was. In a short time the younger Frogs were using him for a diving platform, while the older Frogs made him a meeting place, where they complained loudly to Jupiter about the government.

To teach the Frogs a lesson, the ruler of the gods now sent a Crane to be king of Frogland. The Crane proved to be a very different sort of king from old King Log. He gobbled up the poor Frogs right and left and they soon saw what fools they had been. In mournful croaks they begged Jupiter to take away the cruel tyrant before they should all be destroyed.

"How now!" cried Jupiter. "Are you not yet content? You have what you asked for, and so you have only yourselves to blame for your misfortunes."

*Be sure you can better your condition before you seek to change.*

# The Fox and the Grapes

**Aesop**

A Fox one day spied a beautiful bunch of ripe grapes hanging from a vine trained along the branches of a tree. The grapes seemed ready to burst with juice, and the Fox's mouth watered as he gazed longingly at them.

The bunch hung from a high branch, and the Fox had to jump for it. The first time he jumped he missed it by a long way. So he walked off a short distance and took a running leap at it, only to fall short once more. Again and again he tried, but in vain.

Now he sat down and looked at the grapes in disgust.

"What a fool I am," he said. "Here I am wearing myself out to get a bunch of sour grapes that are not worth gaping for."

And off he walked very, very scornfully.

*There are many who pretend to despise and belittle that which is beyond their reach.*

(Opposite) *The Fox and the Grapes* by Boris Artzybasheff (1899–1965). Woodcut.

The Granger Collection, New York.

# The Town Mouse and the Country Mouse

**Aesop**

A Town Mouse once visited a relative who lived in the country. For lunch the Country Mouse served wheat stalks, roots, and acorns, with a dash of cold water for drink. The Town Mouse ate very sparingly, nibbling a little of this and a little of that, and by her manner making it very plain that she ate the simple food only to be polite.

After the meal the friends had a long talk, or rather the Town Mouse talked about her life in the city while the Country Mouse listened. They then went to bed in a cozy nest in the hedgerow[1] and slept in quiet and comfort until morning. In her sleep the Country Mouse dreamed she was a Town Mouse with all the luxuries and delights of city life that her friend had described for her. So the next day when the Town Mouse asked the Country Mouse to go home with her to the city, she gladly said yes.

1. **hedgerow:** row of bushes forming a hedge.

*The Town Mouse and the Country Mouse,* illustration by Milo Winter.
The Granger Collection, New York.

When they reached the mansion in which the Town Mouse lived, they found on the table in the dining room the leavings of a very fine banquet. There were sweetmeats[2] and jellies, pastries, delicious cheeses—indeed, the most tempting foods that a Mouse can imagine. But just as the Country Mouse was about to nibble a dainty bit of pastry, she heard a Cat mew loudly and scratch at the door. In great fear the Mice scurried to a hiding place, where they lay quite still for a long time, hardly daring to breathe. When at last they ventured back to the feast, the door opened suddenly and in came the servants to clear the table, followed by the House Dog.

The Country Mouse stopped in the Town Mouse's den only long enough to pick up her carpet bag and umbrella.

"You may have luxuries and dainties that I have not," she said as she hurried away, "but I prefer my plain food and simple life in the country with the peace and security that go with it."

*Poverty with security is better than plenty in the midst of fear and uncertainty.*

2. **sweetmeats:** sweets or candies.

*The Town Mouse and the Country Mouse,* illustration by Charles James Folkard.

The Granger Collection, New York.

## *"Should I Never Have Tried to Do Something Risky?"*

After you read, decide whether you prefer the lesson taught in the traditional moral for this fable: *Better to have bread and water in peace than a banquet in fear.* Does the fable teach that we should be satisfied with little because of the risks we take if we try for more? Does it mean to say we should never try to get what we want for fear of failure? I myself risked leaving the safety of my Ohio village in order to pursue an uncertain career in New York City. Should I never have tried to do something risky? Could this moral also fit the fable: *Nothing ventured, nothing gained?*

—Virginia Hamilton

# Belling the Cat

**Aesop**

The Mice once called a meeting to decide on a plan to free themselves of their enemy, the Cat. At least they wished to find some way of knowing when she was coming so they might have time to run away. Indeed, something had to be done, for they lived in such constant fear of her claws that they hardly dared stir from their dens by night or day.

Many plans were discussed, but none of them was thought good enough. At last a very young Mouse got up and said:

"I have a plan that seems very simple, but I know it will be successful. All we have to do is to hang a bell about the Cat's neck. When we hear the bell ringing, we will know immediately that our enemy is coming."

All the Mice were much surprised that they had not thought of such a plan before. But in the midst of the rejoicing over their good fortune, an old Mouse arose and said:

"I will say that the plan of the young Mouse is very good. But let me ask one question: Who will bell the Cat?"

*It is one thing to say that something should be done, but quite a different matter to do it.*

## "I Thought Belling Was the Name of the Cat"

When I was a child and saw the name of this fable, I thought Belling was the name of the cat. The young mouse of this fable has an idea that is difficult to execute. He reminds me of something to do with my own writing. It takes me no time at all to get an idea for a book. "I'm going to write a mystery!" I once told myself. In less than ten minutes, I had "imagined" the whole story. But it took me more than a year actually to write the mystery novel that came to be entitled *The House of Dies Drear.* I know from experience how hard it is to put words down on paper so that they read well and tell a good story, too. Now when I get an idea, I think of the young mouse of this fable. I think about what I've learned, and a little voice in my ear cautions, "Easier said than done!"

After you read the fable, see if it reminds you of any experiences of your own.

—Virginia Hamilton

THE FAVORITE CAT.

Lith & Pub. by N. Currier, 2 Spruce St. N.Y.

## MEET THE WRITER

### A Figure of Fable

**Aesop** (sixth century B.C.) is said to have been born in Africa, but little is known about his life. Early writers of history agree that he was a slave in Greece and that he was eventually given his freedom. They also say that Aesop met a violent death, perhaps because his sarcastic stories had insulted someone very powerful. Pictures of Aesop show him with a deformed back. Aesop, who became known as one of the Seven Wise Men of Greece, was famous for his clever fables.

Aesop, with figures from his fables. Printed in Augsburg, Bavaria, in 1498 by Johann Schonsperger.

### More Fabulous Fables

You can find more of Aesop's fables in many collections, usually titled *Aesop's Fables.*

---

## Connections

A POEM

# The Boy and the Wolf

### Louis Untermeyer

A boy employed to guard the sheep
Despised his work. He liked to sleep.
And when a lamb was lost, he'd shout,
"Wolf! Wolf! The wolves are all about!"

5   The neighbors searched from noon till
      nine,
But of the beast there was no sign,
Yet "Wolf!" he cried next morning when
The villagers came out again.

One evening around six o'clock
10  A real wolf fell upon the flock.

"Wolf!" yelled the boy. "A wolf
      indeed!"
But no one paid him any heed.

Although he screamed to wake the
      dead,
"He's fooled us every time," they said,
15  And let the hungry wolf enjoy
His feast of mutton, lamb—and boy.

The moral's this: The man who's wise
Does not defend himself with lies.
Liars are not believed, forsooth,°
20  Even when liars tell the truth.

**19. forsooth:** old-fashioned word meaning "truly."

# MAKING MEANINGS

## First Thoughts

1. How could the message in each fable be applied to life today? Refer to your notes for the Quickwrite on page 566 for some ideas.

## Shaping Interpretations

2. Suppose you substituted humans for the frogs who wanted a king. What kind of political situation might you be talking about?

3. Give an example of someone who shows a "sour grapes" attitude. Your example can be real or made up.

4. To what situations in world politics could you apply the moral in "Belling the Cat"?

5. What kinds of situations might the wolf in "The Boy and the Wolf" represent (see **Connections** on page 574)?

**Reading Check**

In your own words, state the **moral** of each fable. State each moral as if you were giving advice to a friend.

a. "The Frogs Who Wished for a King"
**Moral:**

b. "The Fox and the Grapes"
**Moral:**

c. "The Town Mouse and the Country Mouse"
**Moral:**

d. "Belling the Cat"
**Moral:**

e. "The Boy and the Wolf"
**Moral:**

## Connecting with the Text

6. In your opinion, which of these fables teaches the most important lesson? Explain your evaluation.

## Extending the Text

7. Decide which fables might apply in each of these present-day situations. Be ready to give your reasons.

   a. When he doesn't make the team, a boy decides he doesn't like baseball.

   b. Since her parents suspect she is only pretending to be sick again, a girl who actually doesn't feel well is told to go to school.

   c. A family moves into a bigger and better house and then has trouble paying for it.

   d. Bored with his old job, a man finds a new one but soon learns that his boss is hard to please.

## Challenging the Text

8. Do you think Aesop's fables still fulfill all three **purposes** today—to entertain, to inform, and to influence or persuade?

## Writer's Notebook

### 1. Collecting Ideas for an Evaluation

Write notes on what you think about Aesop's fables. Include your opinions about whether or not the tales are still useful for teaching lessons today.

*Aesop's fables—still true. I know people who show a "sour grapes" attitude whenever something good happens to someone else.*

---

## Creative Writing

### 2. A Fable for Our Time

Write a short-short animal story that could teach one of these lessons:

- Kindness is never wasted.
- The grass is always greener on the other side of the fence.
- It's best not to want what you can't have.

You might first jot down some ideas in a chart like this one:

| | |
|---|---|
| Moral | |
| Animal characters | |
| Their problem | |
| What happens | |

## Speaking/Storytelling

### 3. A Telling Tale

Aesop's fables weren't meant to be read: Aesop told his stories aloud when they fitted a particular situation. Just like telling a joke, telling a fable requires planning and skill. Pick one of the fables to share. Get to know the fable so well that you can tell it in your own words as if you were making it up on the spot. Tell the fable to a child or a group of children.

FABLE XCIII.

THE FOX AND THE GRAPES.

*The Fox and the Grapes (1879), illustration by Herrick. Engraving.*

# GRAMMAR LINK

## *Bad* or *Badly?*

**Language Handbook HELP**

*See Glossary of Usage:* bad, badly, *page 785.*

**Technology HELP**

*See* Language Workshop CD-ROM. *Key word entry: bad, badly.*

Sometimes writers aren't sure whether to use *bad* or *badly*. *Bad* is an adjective. Use it to modify nouns and pronouns.

> The foolish frogs thought they had a <u>bad</u> government.

*Badly* is an adverb. Use it to modify verbs.

> The crane king treated the frogs <u>badly</u>.

Verbs that refer to the senses—like *feel, smell, taste,* and *sound*—are often followed by an adjective (not an adverb) that modifies their subject. It is correct to write *feel bad, smell bad,* and so on.

> The fox said that the grapes would <u>taste bad</u>.

### Try It Out

Choose the correct word from the underlined pair in each sentence.

1. The frogs of Frogland misjudged their situation <u>bad/badly</u>.

2. The Town Mouse thought her country cousin's food tasted <u>bad/badly</u>.

3. For the Country Mouse, living in a house with a cat was a <u>bad/badly</u> idea.

4. The young mouse's plan to bell the cat wasn't <u>bad/badly</u>; it was just impractical.

5. The boy acted <u>bad/badly</u> when he cried "Wolf" for no reason.

# VOCABULARY

**HOW TO OWN A WORD**

## Animal Similes

**ANIMALS**

a bird
a mule
a kitten
a pig
a snail
a peacock
a fox
a bee
a lamb
an owl

Many familiar similes connect humans with certain animal qualities. (Remember that a **simile** is a comparison between two very different things, using a comparing word such as *like* or *as*.) Which animals in the list on the left connect with which human qualities? (Use each animal just once.) Do you think the similes are fair to the animals?

1. playful as _____
2. free as _____
3. gentle as _____
4. greedy as _____
5. proud as _____

6. busy as _____
7. wise as _____
8. sly as _____
9. stubborn as _____
10. slow as _____

# The Dream of Good Fortune

*from* **The Arabian Nights,**
*dramatized by* **Paul Sills**

## Characters

**Luqman Ali**
**His Wife**
**An Angel**
**The Chief of Police**
**A Thief**
**The Lieutenant**

**Luq.** Luqman Ali, a poor but honest dung sweeper, lived in the alley of the tanners, off the street of the potters, in the heart of the great city of Baghdad.[1]

**Wife.** He and his wife had nothing in the world but an old iron stove, and barely enough to eat.

**Luq.** But still they did not despair in the mercy of the Almighty. One night Luqman Ali and his wife lay down to sleep, and he had a dream.

**Angel.** An angel appeared with a message: "Luqman Ali, alley of the tanners, off the street of the potters, in the city of Baghdad—Dear Luq, Go to Cairo,[2] and there you will find your fortune."

**Luq.** Luqman Ali awoke his wife and told her of his strange dream.

1. **Baghdad:** ancient Middle Eastern city, the center of Islamic civilization during the period in which many of the *Arabian Nights* stories are set. Today Baghdad is the capital of Iraq.
2. **Cairo** (kī′rō): capital of Egypt.

**Wife.** Go back to sleep, my love, it was only a dream.

**Angel.** Luqman Ali, go to Cairo, and there you will find your fortune.

**Luq.** Wife, wake up; the angel came again and told me to go to Cairo, to seek my fortune.

**Wife.** If it happens a third time, you'll have to go.

**Angel.** Luqman Ali, are you still here? Go to Cairo! Your fortune awaits you there.

**Luq.** I go! I go! Wife, awaken—I must go to Cairo. And so Luqman Ali set off on the road to Cairo. Through hot desert winds—sandstorms—cold nights. Luqman Ali traveled the road until, weary and sore, in the shimmering heat, he saw the great city of Cairo. Tired and not knowing where to go, he took refuge in the courtyard of a great mosque,[3] where he lay down to sleep.

3. **mosque** (mäsk): Moslem house of worship.

**Thief.** That night, a thief entered the courtyard and broke through the wall of an adjoining house.

[*A woman screams offstage. The* THIEF *returns to the courtyard, hits* LUQ, *and runs off.*]

**Luq.** Stop, thief! Stop, thief!
**Chief of Police.** The chief of police . . .
**Lieutenant.** And his lieutenant . . .
**Chief of Police.** Arrived at the scene, and they found Luqman Ali, and thinking him to be the thief . . .
**Lieutenant.** They beat him with their clubs and dragged him off to jail.
**Chief of Police.** Who are you?
**Luq.** Luqman Ali.
**Chief of Police.** Where do you come from?
**Luq.** Baghdad.
**Chief of Police.** What brings you to Cairo?
**Luq.** I had a dream . . .

[*The* LIEUTENANT *squeezes* LUQ*'s nose, sending him to his knees.*]

**Chief of Police.** What are you doing in Cairo?
**Luq** (*rises*). I had a dream . . .

[*The* LIEUTENANT *squeezes his head.*]

**Chief of Police** (*waving the* LIEUTENANT *away*). What brings you to Cairo?

**Luq** (*again on his knees*). I had a dream. An angel appeared to me three times in a row and told me to go to Cairo, where I would find my fortune.
**Chief of Police.** And what did you find?
**Luq.** I got arrested and beat up.
**Chief of Police.** It hurts too, doesn't it? Dreams mean nothing. We all have dreams.

You fool! That's the trouble with you people. Superstitious. I had a dream only last night: An angel came to me and told me to go to Baghdad, to the alley of the potters, off the street of the tanners, to a little old shack, and there under an old iron stove I would find a treasure. Did I go? No! I stayed here doing my job. Here, take these dinars[4] and get out of here.

[*So* LUQ *sets off to his home in Baghdad. He "dances" back to Baghdad, calling "Wife, wife." They move the stove, find the treasure, and adorn each other with jewels. She kisses his nose.—"Owww!!!"—Fade Out.*]

---

4. **dinars** (di·närz'): kind of money used in many Middle Eastern countries.

# READ ON

## Turn On the Light

For centuries the people of Darkness have waged war with the immortal children of Light. Saya, raised by adoptive parents to cherish the light, is given the power to end this war. In *Dragon Sword and Wind Child* (Farrar, Straus & Giroux) by Noriko Ogiwara, this powerful young woman must untangle a puzzling web of good and evil to save the people and land she loves.

## Before Superman

Travel back to ancient times to meet Perseus the Fearless, Heracles the Strong One, Jason the Voyager. These and other superheroes fulfill quests, win contests, and journey to fantastic lands. *The Great Deeds of Superheroes* (Peter Bedrick), retold by Maurice Saxby, contains seventeen action-packed, inspiring tales of some brave, extraordinary heroes.

## Wonderful Wonders

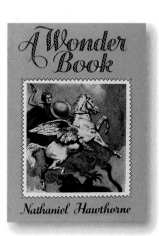

A group of eager young listeners gathers at a beautiful country home to hear Eustace Bright tell his famous stories. In Nathaniel Hawthorne's classic *A Wonder Book* (Dutton), the beloved narrator Bright entertains his audience with a mix of Greek myths and tales of his life in the country.

## Other Picks

- H. M. Hoover, *The Dawn Palace: The Story of Medea* (Dutton). This unusual retelling of the tragedy of Medea sympathizes with Medea and examines the truth surrounding her horrible deeds.
- Laura C. Stevenson, *The Island and the Ring* (Houghton Mifflin). This mythic fantasy tells of a young woman's quest for justice in an unjust world.

# Writer's Workshop

**Technology
H E L P**

*See* Writer's Workshop 1
CD-ROM. *Assignment:
Evaluation.*

## ASSIGNMENT

**Write an evaluation
of a work—such as a
story, poem, play,
movie, or TV show.**

## AIM

**To persuade; to
inform.**

## AUDIENCE

**Your teacher,
classmates, or friends.**

## PERSUASIVE WRITING

# EVALUATION

When was the last time a friend asked you, "Have you read any
good books lately?" or "What did you think of that movie?" When
you answer one of these questions, you are making an **evaluation,**
or judgment. You are giving an opinion about whether something is
good or bad. Usually you will need to include information and convincing reasons to back up your judgment.

---

### Professional Model

*Here is an evaluation of a movie called* Ever After, *a
new version of the Cinderella story.*

The movie opens with a nine-
teenth-century French noble-
woman who wants to set the
record straight on her famous
ancestor [Cinderella]. The rousing history she recounts in flashback tells of a young woman
whose fiery convictions get her
into trouble and whose mind and
muscle get her out again. She
needs love, but she doesn't need
rescuing.

    Cinderella's real name was
Danielle. When her beloved
father dies, he leaves her to the
harsh care of her stepmother.
When her stepmother sells off a
beloved old servant, Danielle
dresses up like a court lady and
argues with the prince about
human rights until he agrees to

*The authors describe
the format of the
movie (flashback)
and the heroine's
personality.*

*They summarize the
plot and tell how this
version of "Cinderella"
is different from the
original.*

---

The history
of the written
word is rich and time
Once upon a time
Page 1

*(continued)*

intervene and release the man. Love doesn't quite blossom: The prince is intrigued, but she's appalled by this restless aristocrat who admires passion and principle yet won't act on them.

This complex tale is told with great buoyancy and wit thanks to the splendid performances. "Cinderella" has had hundreds of variants in dozens of cultures, but *Ever After* is the version we've needed for a long time.

*The authors clearly state their opinion of the movie and give reasons to back up their judgment.*

—Laura Shapiro and Corie Brown, from *Newsweek,* August 1998

| Works I Have Read | What I Recall Most |
|---|---|
| "Amigo Brothers" by Piri Thomas | the surprise at the end |
| "Antaeus" by Borden Deal | the roof garden and how the boys destroy it |
| Brian's Song by William Blinn | the way the two guys tease each other |

## Prewriting

### 1. Writer's Notebook

Review your Writer's Notebook entries for this collection. If none of those ideas appeal to you, try the strategy below.

WORK IN PROGRESS

### 2. What Have You Seen Lately?

Make a list of movies, books, stories, and other forms of entertainment (including music) that you have seen or read or heard recently. Next to each title, describe what you recall most vividly about the work. (See the chart at the right.)

### 3. Decide on Your Standards of Judgment

Whenever you judge the worth of something, you are measuring it against **criteria,** or standards. For a movie, you may have criteria like these:

---

**Finding Criteria for Judging a Work**

"I liked *Raiders of the Lost Ark.*"

"Why?"

"Because it was exciting."

"What made it exciting?"

"There were a lot of scary surprises and great escapes."

---

"George Lucas's *Star Wars*, one of the most popular movies of all time, is an exciting, magical high-tech tale about heroism in space."

"C. S. Lewis's *The Lion, the Witch, and the Wardrobe* is an extraordinary excursion to magical lands."

## Strategies for Elaboration

Support your judgment with details from the work you are evaluating. If you're evaluating a movie, try rerunning the movie in your mind, looking for examples to support your opinion. If you're evaluating a work of literature, reread or skim it with the same purpose. Take notes on the following elements:

- actions (what the characters do)

- dialogue (what the characters say)

- specific events in the plot

- setting (is it interesting?)

- descriptive details (for literature) or camera work (for a movie)

• The action should be exciting.

• The roles should be played by good actors.

• It should be impossible to predict what will happen next.

It's helpful to identify things that matter to you. With a partner, develop a list of criteria for judging a work like the one you're evaluating. Question each other, pushing for more specific answers. (See the dialogue on page 583.)

Take notes on your discussion. Use your notes to write a list of qualities that make a work seem good or bad to you.

## Drafting

### 1. Writing Your First Draft

Sometimes at the end of a movie or a book, you know whether you liked it but you aren't sure why. Discussing it with someone can help you sort out your reasons. A first draft is like one of those conversations—a chance to give shape to your first thoughts. Begin with your reactions, and keep asking "Why?" "Why did I think that, feel that, question that?"

### 2. Don't Forget Your Audience

Start with a lively quotation, anecdote, or question that your readers can immediately relate to. Give them background information, but leave them curious enough to want to discover the work for themselves.

### 3. Supporting Your Judgment with Evidence

The body of your evaluation should contain sound reasons for your opinion. Use specific examples from the work or from your personal experience to support your points. You may also want to make comparisons with other works or cite the opinions of authorities.

PEANUTS reprinted by permission United Feature Syndicate, Inc.

## 4. Bringing It to a Close

Tie your thoughts together in an interesting concluding sentence. Restate your case, or offer one more compelling reason in support of your judgment. End with a bang!

## Evaluating and Revising

Exchange papers with a classmate, and answer these questions:

- Is the writer's opinion of the work clear? Why or why not?
- Are the reasons for the writer's opinion convincing?
- Does the evaluation seem complete? Why or why not?

### review of THE LION, THE WITCH, AND THE WARDROBE

Would you like a passport for a most extraordinary excursion into magical lands? If you have never been to Narnia, you can enter this strange, intriguing place by reading C. S. Lewis's *The Lion, the Witch, and the Wardrobe.*

This is the story of four brothers and sisters, Peter, Susan, Lucy, and Edmund Pevensie, who have been sent to visit the country house of Professor Kirk because of the air raids in England during World War II. While they are exploring the house, they enter an old wardrobe and take a fantasy trip to another universe called Narnia. There they meet the great Aslan and help him to defeat the evil White Witch. Aslan is a great lion who has a golden mane, golden eyes, and a face that looks royal, strong, peaceful, and sad. He is described as both "good and terrible at the same time."

*The review opens with an intriguing question.*

*The writer identifies the title and author and evaluates the book as "a most extraordinary excursion into magical lands."*

*He briefly describes the characters and summarizes the plot.*

*(continued on next page)*

(continued on next page)

---

**Evaluation Criteria**

*A good evaluation*

1. *identifies and describes the work*

2. *makes a clear judgment based on specific criteria*

3. *gives reasons and examples to support the judgment*

4. *restates or reinforces the judgment in a strong conclusion*

---

**Language/Grammar Link**
**H E L P**

*Descriptive language: page 511. Figurative language: page 520. Words often confused: page 529. Adjective vs. adverb: page 539. Good vs. well: page 553. Allusions: page 564. Bad vs. badly: page 577.*

**Sentence Workshop**
**H E L P**

*Varying sentence length: page 587.*

**Communications Handbook HELP**

*See Listing Sources and Taking Notes.*

**Proofreading Tips**

- When you write a review, pay special attention to the use of quotation marks.
- Be sure to put titles of full-length works in italic type; put titles of shorter works in quotation marks.

**Communications Handbook HELP**

*See Proofreaders' Marks.*

**Publishing Tip**

Submit your review to your school or local newspaper.

When the children are tested by Aslan, they have to make choices between right and wrong. Aslan encourages the children to make judgments that help them to become mature individuals. Peter is established as the High King and, with the other children, rules Narnia for many years. One day, they find their way back to the wardrobe and discover that, although years have passed in Narnia, only moments have gone by in their own world.

Time travel provides a convenient way of moving the characters into settings that are surreal and exciting. The unusual environment makes it possible for Lewis to introduce strange powers and creatures, such as animals that talk and have the power to tell the difference between right and wrong. Lewis's Narnia provides an alternate universe, where mundane laws are suspended, and unusual characters and settings become the norm.

If you enjoy *The Lion, the Witch, and the Wardrobe*, you're really in luck because Lewis wrote six sequels to this adventure. These perilous journeys into the magical land of Narnia should keep you entertained for a good, long time!

*Here, the writer backs up his evaluation with examples of ways in which Narnia is extraordinary and magical.*

*The review ends with an enthusiastic reference to other works by the same author.*

—John Belletti
Manhasset Middle School
Manhasset, New York

First appeared in *Merlyn's Pen: The National Magazines of Student Writing.*

# Sentence Workshop

## VARYING SENTENCE LENGTH

In other Sentence Workshops you've learned the importance of varying sentence length. You've learned that you can vary sentence length by combining sentences or by using a variety of structures. When you get good at varying sentence length, you can just feel that your paragraph has the right rhythm. You can also check your sentences by counting words. If the tally shows that the sentences in your paragraph are of different lengths, you're probably on your way to a style that grabs the eye and catches the ear.

An interesting paragraph is made up of sentences of varied lengths—some medium, some long, some short.

> "Persephone was the spring maiden, young and full of joy [**10 words**]. Sicily was her home, for it is a land where the spring is long and lovely, and where spring flowers are abundant [**22 words**]. Here Persephone played with her maidens from day to day till the rocks and valleys rang with the sound of laughter, and gloomy Hades heard it as he sat on his throne in the dark land of the dead [**39 words**]."
>
> —Olivia Coolidge, "The Origin of the Seasons" (page 501)

> "Hercules had now accomplished six of his labors [**8 words**]. Six more remained [**3 words**]. After the killing of the Stymphalian birds, he was commanded to go to Crete and bring back from there alive a huge bull which was laying the whole island waste [**30 words**]."
>
> —Rex Warner, "The Labors of Hercules" (pages 545–546)

## Writer's Workshop Follow-up: Revision

Exchange your evaluation for a classmate's. Count the words in each sentence. If most of the sentences are about the same length, suggest ways to vary their length. Exchange papers again, and review your classmate's suggestions.

**Language Handbook
HELP**

*See Writing Effective Sentences, pages 760-762.*

---

**Try It Out**

Edit the following paragraph. Change some of the sentences in order to vary their length.

The journey from the depths of Hades to the upper world was long and hard. It was much easier to go down the path to the underworld than to climb it. The path was dark and misty. It was also full of strange shapes and noises. In many places it was merely black and silent. Orpheus would stop and listen. Nothing moved behind him.

---

# Reading for Life

## Reading a Map and a Time Line

## Situation

Imagine that your grandfather was born in Greece. You show him the map on pages 498–499. "You won't find a drawing of me there," he says. "People made up those myths thousands of years before I was born. Get me a pencil. I'll show you." Then Grandpa draws a time line like the one on this page.

## Strategies

Both maps and time lines present information in a graphic way, like a diagram.

**Use a time line to find out when events happened.**

• A time line may show a vast span of time, such as thousands or millions of years.

• Events on a time line are listed in chronological order, with long-ago events at one end and more recent events at the other. The approxi-

mate date (year or century) of each event appears either above or below the line.

**Use a map to find places.**

• Some maps show natural features, such as oceans, bodies of land, mountains, even stars and planets. Many maps show structures made by people, such as cities, streets, and parks.

• Maps show direction. You can read a map to see how to get from one place to another. On page 499 you'll find a symbol called a *compass rose,* which tells you where north, south, east, and west are located.

• A map's *scale* tells you how size on the map compares with actual size or distance in real life. One inch on a map may equal one, ten, or fifty miles or more.

## Using the Strategies

1. Look at the time line on this page. Which two events in ancient Greece might have happened within one person's lifetime?

2. How old was Grandpa when he came to the United States?

3. Find Sicily on the map on pages 498–499. Can you tell what mythic event takes place there?

4. Where is Hercules born?

5. Find the two small maps set into the main map. Pick one of these inset maps, and tell what it shows.

## Extending the Strategies

• Find a map of modern Greece. Which of the old place names are still in use?

• Make a time line showing important events that happened to you.

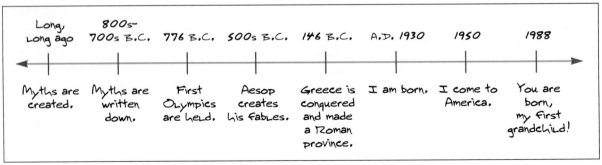

| Long, Long ago | 800s–700s B.C. | 776 B.C. | 500s B.C. | 146 B.C. | A.D. 1930 | 1950 | 1988 |
|---|---|---|---|---|---|---|---|
| Myths are created. | Myths are written down. | First Olympics are held. | Aesop creates his fables. | Greece is conquered and made a Roman province. | I am born. | I come to America. | You are born, my first grandchild! |

# Learning for Life
## Investigating the Media and Values

## Problem

The myths and fables you've just read presented lessons in behavior for people of ancient times. Today movies and TV give us models of behavior. What messages about behavior do today's popular media suggest? How can we learn to think more critically about those messages?

## Project

**Analyze a movie, and interpret its messages about behavior. Discuss how people may be affected by the attitudes and values expressed in the movie.**

## Preparation

1. With a group of classmates, choose a movie to discuss. The film can be a current one or one released in the last few years. Be sure to get permission from your parents and teacher to see the movie.

2. Before you watch the movie, look at ads for it and read some reviews. Then, jot down ideas about the attitudes and values you expect the film to show. Think about questions like these:

   • Who are the heroes and the villains? How are they portrayed?

   • What role does violence play? What role does kindness or helping others play?

   • Does the movie paint a dark picture of life or a hopeful one?

## Procedure

1. Watch the movie and write your reactions right away.

2. Reflect on the ideas you had before watching the movie. Have they changed?

3. Work with your group to create the following:

   • a description of the values and attitudes expressed by the characters

   • a description of the main characters and their roles

## Presentation

Present your findings in one of the following ways:

### 1. Movie Review

Write a review of the movie for your school newspaper. Focus on the movie's message about behavior.

### 2. Dramatic Dialogue

Write a dialogue between the hero of a myth and the main character of the movie you watched. Have the two characters compare their experiences and views of the world.

### 3. Debate

Debate this question with another group of students: Do the attitudes and values expressed in the media influence people's behavior, or do the media simply reflect the attitudes found in our society?

## Processing

Write a reflection on what you learned from this project.

BEETLE BAILEY.

Reprinted with special permission of King Features Syndicate.

Collection

*Eight*

*These are the stories that never, never die, that are carried like seed into a new country, are told to you and me and make in us new and lasting strengths.*

—Meridel Le Sueur

# 900 Cinderellas: Our World Heritage in Folklore

# Before You Read

## ASCHENPUTTEL

### Make the Connection

**A Story to Tell**

What popular story features these characters?

- a hard-working girl
- a wicked stepmother
- a woman with a magic wand
- a prince of a fellow

You probably know these characters from the fairy tale "Cinderella." "Cinderella" and "Aschenputtel" are two versions of the same story, about a "little ash girl" (or "cinder girl") whose dream comes true.

**Round robin.** In a small group, talk about why you think the story of "Cinderella" is such a favorite. What do people like about this story? What deep human wishes do you think this story expresses? As you read this German folk tale, keep a sheet of paper handy so that you can jot down your reactions. Look at the student's comments on page 594 as an example, but keep your own notes.

### Elements of Literature

**Motifs in Folk Tales: The Number Three**

In "Aschenputtel," as in much European folklore, three is a charmed number. For example, the three sisters take turns trying on the golden slipper. This repetition of events in threes builds suspense: We know that if something happens once, it will probably happen two more times. Like other repeated elements in storytelling, the frequent use of the number three is called a **motif** (mō·tēf′).

A **motif** is a repeated element in storytelling.

### Reading Skills and Strategies

**Main Idea: It's the Message**

The **main idea** is the message, insight, or lesson that is the focus of a piece of writing. You can find the main idea if you pay attention to important details as you read. One way to find the main idea of "Aschenputtel" is to ask yourself what wishes and fears this story expresses.

### Background

**Literature and Literary History**

People around the world have been telling the Cinderella story for ages. There are more than nine hundred versions of this popular tale. Scholars have traced the oldest version back more than a thousand years, to China. The version that you probably know best was collected in the 1600s by a French writer named Charles Perrault. His is the only version to include a fairy godmother and a midnight curfew. "Aschenputtel" is the German version of the Cinderella story.

# Aschenputtel

German, retold by
**Jakob** *and* **Wilhelm Grimm**,
*translated by Lucy Crane*

*"Is the stupid creature to sit in the same room with us?"*

There was once a rich man whose wife lay sick, and when she felt her end drawing near, she called to her only daughter to come near her bed and said,

"Dear child, be <u>pious</u> and good, and God will always take care of you, and I will look down upon you from heaven and will be with you."

And then she closed her eyes and <u>expired</u>. The maiden went every day to her mother's grave and wept and was always pious and good. When the winter came, the snow covered the grave with a white covering, and when the sun came in the early spring and melted it away, the man took to himself another wife.

The new wife brought two daughters home with her and they were beautiful and fair in appearance but at heart were wicked and ugly. And then began very evil times for the poor stepdaughter.

"Is the stupid creature to sit in the same room with us?" said they. "Those who eat food must earn it. Out with the kitchen maid!"

They took away her pretty dresses and put on her an old gray kirtle[1] and gave her wooden shoes to wear.

"Just look now at the proud princess, how she is decked out!" cried they, laughing, and then they sent her into the kitchen. There she was obliged to do heavy work from morning to night, get up early in the morning, draw water, make the fires, cook, and wash. Besides that, the sisters did their utmost to torment her—mocking her and strewing peas and lentils among the ashes and setting her to pick them up. In the evenings, when she was quite tired out with her hard day's work, she had no bed to lie on but was obliged to rest on the hearth among the cinders. And as she always looked dusty and dirty, they named her Aschenputtel.

It happened one day that the father went to the fair, and he asked his two stepdaughters what he should bring back for them.

"Fine clothes!" said one.

---

1. **kirtle:** old-fashioned word for "dress."

## WORDS TO OWN

**pious** (pī'əs) *adj.*: deeply religious.
**expired** (ek·spīrd') *v.*: died. In Latin, *exspirare* means "to breathe out";
  *to breathe out one's last breath* is to die.

### Dialogue with the Text

"Rush in" beginning—needs more development. Why did she not call upon her rich husband and talk to him?

The father seems like he does not care about his dead wife.

This story is turning into a German Cinderella!

It's unclear here that they are talking about the father's daughter.

Wooden shoes nowadays are the height of teen fashion!

Just like Cinderella! What was her name before her stepsisters gave her "Aschenputtel"? Did she even have a name?

*Katie Gaddis*

—Katharine ("Katie") Gaddis
Westview Middle School
Longmont, Colorado

"Pearls and jewels!" said the other.

"But what will you have, Aschenputtel?" said he.

"The first twig, Father, that strikes against your hat on the way home; this is what I should like you to bring me."

So he bought for the two stepdaughters fine clothes, pearls, and jewels, and on his way back, as he rode through a green lane, a hazel twig struck against his hat; and he broke it off and carried it home with him. And when he reached home, he gave to the stepdaughters what they had wished for, and to Aschenputtel he gave the hazel twig. She thanked him and went to her mother's grave, and planted this twig there, weeping so bitterly that the tears fell upon it and watered it, and it flourished and became a fine tree. Aschenputtel went to see it three times a day and wept and prayed, and each time a white bird rose up from the tree, and, if she uttered any wish, the bird brought her whatever she had wished for.

Now it came to pass that the king ordained a festival that should last for three days and to which all the beautiful young women of that country were bidden so that the king's son might choose a bride from among them. When the two stepdaughters heard that they too were bidden to appear, they felt very pleased, and they called Aschenputtel and said,

"Comb our hair, brush our shoes, and make our buckles fast, we are going to the wedding feast at the king's castle."

Aschenputtel, when she heard this, could not help crying, for she too would have liked to go to the dance, and she begged her stepmother to allow her.

"What, you Aschenputtel!" said she. "In all your dust and dirt, you want to go to the festival! You that have no dress and no shoes! You want to dance!"

But since she persisted in asking, at last the stepmother said,

"I have scattered a dish full of lentils in the ashes, and if you can pick them all up again in two hours, you may go with us."

Then the maiden went to the back door that led into the garden and called out,

> O gentle doves, O turtledoves,
> And all the birds that be,
> The lentils that in ashes lie
> Come and pick up for me!
> The good must be put in the dish,
> The bad you may eat if you wish.

Then there came to the kitchen window two white doves, and after them some turtledoves, and at last a crowd of all the birds under heaven, chirping and fluttering, and they alighted among the ashes; and the doves nodded with their heads and began to pick, peck, pick, peck, and then all the others began to pick, peck, pick, peck and put all the good grains into the dish. Before an hour was over, all was done, and they flew away. Then the maiden brought the dish to her stepmother, feeling joyful and thinking that now she should go to the feast; but the stepmother said,

"No, Aschenputtel, you have no proper clothes, and you do not know how to dance, and you would be laughed at!"

And when Aschenputtel cried for disappointment, she added,

"If you can pick two dishfuls of lentils out of the ashes, nice and clean, you shall go with us," thinking to herself, "for that is not possible." When she had strewed two dishfuls of lentils among the ashes, the maiden went through the back door into the garden and cried,

> O gentle doves, O turtledoves,
> And all the birds that be,
> The lentils that in ashes lie

- - - - - - - - - - - - - - - - - - - - - - - - - - - - - - -
### WORDS TO OWN
**ordained** (ôr·dānd′) v.: ordered or decreed.
**persisted** (pər·sist′id) v.: continued firmly or steadily.
- - - - - - - - - - - - - - - - - - - - - - - - - - - - - - -

Come and pick up for me!
  The good must be put in the dish,
  The bad you may eat if you wish.

So there came to the kitchen window two white doves, and then some turtledoves, and at last a crowd of all the other birds under heaven, chirping and fluttering, and they alighted among the ashes, and the doves nodded with their heads and began to pick, peck, pick, peck, and then all the others began to pick, peck, pick, peck and put all the good grains into the dish. And before half an hour was over, it was all done, and they flew away. Then the maiden took the dishes to the stepmother, feeling joyful and thinking that now she should go with them to the feast. But her stepmother said, "All this is of no good to you; you cannot come with us, for you have no proper clothes and cannot dance; you would put us to shame."

Then she turned her back on poor Aschenputtel and made haste to set out with her two proud daughters.

And as there was no one left in the house, Aschenputtel went to her mother's grave, under the hazel bush, and cried,

  Little tree, little tree, shake over me,
  That silver and gold may come down
    and cover me.

Then the bird threw down a dress of gold and silver and a pair of slippers embroidered with silk and silver. And in all haste she put on the dress and went to the festival. But her stepmother and sisters did not know her and thought she must be a foreign princess, she looked so beautiful in her golden dress. Of Aschenputtel they never thought at all and supposed that she was sitting at home, picking the lentils out of the ashes. The King's son came to meet her and took her by the hand and danced with her, and he refused to stand up with anyone else so that he might not be obliged to let go her hand; and when anyone came to claim it, he answered,

  "She is my partner."

And when the evening came, she wanted to go home, but the prince said he would go with her to take care of her, for he wanted to see where the beautiful maiden lived. But she escaped him and jumped up into the pigeon house. Then the prince waited until her father came along, and told him that the strange maiden had jumped into the pigeon house. The father thought to himself, "It cannot surely be Aschenputtel" and called for axes and hatchets and had the pigeon house cut down, but there was no one in it. And when they entered the house, there sat Aschenputtel in her dirty clothes among the cinders, and a little oil lamp burnt dimly in the chimney; for Aschenputtel had been very quick and had jumped out of the pigeon house again and had run to the hazel bush; and there she had taken off her beautiful dress and had laid it on the grave, and the bird had carried it away again, and then she had put on her little gray kirtle again and had sat down in the kitchen among the cinders.

The next day, when the festival began anew, and the parents and stepsisters had gone to it, Aschenputtel went to the hazel bush and cried,

  Little tree, little tree, shake over me,
  That silver and gold may come down
    and cover me.

Then the bird cast down a still more splendid dress than on the day before. And when she appeared in it among the guests, everyone was astonished at her beauty. The prince had been waiting until she came, and he took her hand and danced with her alone. And when anyone else came to invite her, he said,

  "She is my partner."

And when the evening came, she wanted to go home, and the prince followed her, for he wanted to see to what house she belonged; but she broke away from him and ran into the gar-

## "Aschen Poodle"—A Modern Furry Tale

You know the story of Cinderella—but have you ever seen a Cinderella with a furry coat and a big wet nose? For William Wegman, a photographer known for his unusual pictures of his famous Weimaraner dogs, the story of Cinderella has gone to the dogs.

In Wegman's version of the Cinderella story, his dog Battina is the beautiful Cinderella, while her real-life mother, named Fay Wray, plays her wicked stepmother. Wegman's *Cinderella* is complete with cruel Weimaraner stepsisters, a Weimaraner fairy godmother, and a Weimaraner prince.

Copyright William Wegman, Courtesy PaceWildenstein-MacGill, New York.

Wegman's dogs look so comfortable in their roles that after reading his *Cinderella,* you probably wouldn't be at all surprised to see the lovely Weimaraner Cinderella shyly appear at your next party.

---

den at the back of the house. There stood a fine large tree, bearing splendid pears; she leapt as lightly as a squirrel among the branches, and the prince did not know what had become of her. So he waited until her father came along, and then he told him that the strange maiden had rushed from him, and that he thought she had gone up into the pear tree. The father thought to himself,

"It cannot surely be Aschenputtel" and

called for an axe and felled the tree, but there was no one in it. And when they went into the kitchen, there sat Aschenputtel among the cinders, as usual, for she had got down the other side of the tree and had taken back her beautiful clothes to the bird on the hazel bush and had put on her old gray kirtle again.

On the third day, when the parents and the stepchildren had set off, Aschenputtel went again to her mother's grave and said to the tree,

Little tree, little tree, shake over me,
That silver and gold may come down
and cover me.

Then the bird cast down a dress the likes of which had never been seen for splendor and brilliancy, and slippers that were of gold.

And when she appeared in this dress at the feast, nobody knew what to say for wonderment. The prince danced with her alone, and if anyone else asked her, he answered,

"She is my partner."

And when it was evening, Aschenputtel wanted to go home, and the prince was about to go with her when she ran past him so quickly that he could not follow her. But he had laid a plan and had caused all the steps to be spread with pitch,[2] so that as she rushed down them, her left shoe remained sticking in it. The prince picked it up and saw that it was of gold and very small and slender. The next morning he went to the father and told him that none should be his bride save the one whose foot the golden shoe should fit. Then the two sisters were very glad, because they had pretty feet. The eldest went to her room to try on the shoe, and her mother stood by. But she could not get her great toe into it, for the shoe was too small; then her mother handed her a knife, and said,

"Cut the toe off, for when you are queen, you will never have to go on foot." So the girl cut her toe off, squeezed her foot into the shoe, concealed the pain, and went down to the prince. Then he took her with him on his horse as his bride and rode off. They had to pass by the grave, and there sat the two pigeons on the hazel bush and cried,

There they go, there they go!
There is blood on her shoe;
The shoe is too small,
—Not the right bride at all!

Then the prince looked at her shoe and saw the blood flowing. And he turned his horse round and took the false bride home again, saying she was not the right one and that the other sister must try on the shoe. So she went into her room to do so and got her toes comfortably in, but her heel was too large. Then her mother handed her the knife, saying, "Cut a piece off your heel; when you are queen, you will never have to go on foot."

So the girl cut a piece off her heel and thrust her foot into the shoe, concealed the pain, and went down to the prince, who took his bride before him on his horse and rode off. When they passed by the hazel bush, the two pigeons sat there and cried,

There they go, there they go!
There is blood on her shoe;
The shoe is too small,
—Not the right bride at all!

Then the prince looked at her foot and saw how the blood was flowing from the shoe and staining the white stocking. And he turned his horse round and brought the false bride home again.

"This is not the right one," said he. "Have you no other daughter?"

"No," said the man, "only my dead wife left behind her a little <u>stunted</u> Aschenputtel; it is impossible that she can be the bride." But the King's son ordered her to be sent for, but the mother said,

"Oh, no! She is much too dirty; I could not let her be seen."

But he would have her fetched, and so Aschenputtel had to appear.

First she washed her face and hands quite clean and went in and curtseyed to the prince,

2. **pitch:** here, black, sticky tar.

-----------------------------------------

**WORDS TO OWN**
**stunted** (stunt′id) v. used as *adj.*: not properly grown.

-----------------------------------------

who held out to her the golden shoe. Then she sat down on a stool, drew her foot out of the heavy wooden shoe, and slipped it into the golden one, which fitted it perfectly. And when she stood up and the prince looked in her face, he knew again the beautiful maiden that had danced with him, and he cried,

"This is the right bride!"

The stepmother and the two sisters were thunderstruck and grew pale with anger, but the prince put Aschenputtel before him on his horse and rode off. And as they passed the hazel bush, the two white pigeons cried,

There they go, there they go!
No blood on her shoe;
The shoe's not too small,
The right bride is she after all.

And when they had thus cried, they came flying after and perched on Aschenputtel's shoulders, one on the right, the other on the left, and so remained.

And when her wedding with the prince was appointed to be held, the false sisters came, hoping to curry favor[3] and to take part in the festivities. So as the bridal procession went to the church, the eldest walked on the right side and the younger on the left, and the pigeons picked out an eye of each of them. And as they returned, the elder was on the left side and the younger on the right, and the pigeons picked out the other eye of each of them. And so they were condemned for the rest of their days because of their wickedness and falsehood.

3. **curry favor:** try to win approval by flattering and fawning.

The Granger Collection, New York.

## MEET THE WRITERS

### Two Brothers with a Dream

Before the 1800s, most fairy tales were not written down. They existed only in the memories of people who had heard them from their elders. **Jakob** (1785–1863) and **Wilhelm** (1786–1859) **Grimm** decided that the traditional stories of Germany ought to be written down in one book before they were forgotten. Jakob wrote:

❝ It is high time that these old traditions were collected and rescued before they perish like dew in the hot sun or fire in a stream and fall silent forever in the unrest of our days. ❞

The two brothers wandered from farm to village, looking for good storytellers who knew the old tales. They listened patiently and wrote the stories down. By the time the last edition of their stories was published, in 1857, the brothers had collected about two hundred tales. Some of the best-known ones are "Little Red Riding Hood," "Rumpelstiltskin," "Hansel and Gretel," "Sleeping Beauty," and, of course, "Aschenputtel," or "Cinderella."

### More Grimm Stories

If you browse through *The Complete Grimm's Fairy Tales* (Pantheon), you will find some truly grim stories. These German tales are filled with acts of cruelty and murder. In the United States, retellers of the tales have sometimes toned them down, producing storybook versions that are much less terrifying.

# ... And Then the Prince Knelt Down and Tried to Put the Glass Slipper on Cinderella's Foot

## Judith Viorst

I really didn't notice that he had a funny nose.
And he certainly looked better all dressed up in fancy clothes.
He's not nearly as attractive as he seemed the other night.
So I think I'll just pretend that this glass slipper feels too tight.

# In Search of Cinderella

## Shel Silverstein

From dusk to dawn
From town to town,
Without a single clue,
I seek the tender, slender foot
To fit this crystal shoe.
From dusk to dawn,
I try it on
Each damsel that I meet.
And I still love her so, but oh,
I've started hating feet.

# Chriserella

## "How did you and Daddy meet?"

One day, while I was driving from my friend's house, I saw Chris cutting the lawn with scissors. He was eighteen years old, so he was a couple of years older than me. He had two younger twin brothers, Ryan and Allen, who were very rude and obnoxious. I went next door, where I live with my older brother, a famous movie star.

Meanwhile at Chris's house his step-mother, Danielle, was telling him to go clean the bottom of the pool with his toothbrush. She was always giving him impossible chores.

As Chris was cleaning the pool, his two younger stepbrothers were arguing about whom I had invited to my party first.

"What's going on?" Chris asked.

"You know Samantha next door? Well, she invited all three of us to a party tonight at her house . . . and she invited me first!" declared Ryan.

"No way, man! She invited me first!" yelled Allen.

"Well, can I go to the party?" asked Chris.

"Only if you get all your work done," said the boys simultaneously.

"What time does it start?" asked Chris.

"I dunno; I think it starts at eight. . . . That's in an hour and I still have to get ready!" said Allen.

Everyone went off to get ready for the party except for Chris; he had to finish cleaning the pool. While he was cleaning the grouting, he saw Ryan and Allen leaving for the party. Once they were out of sight, Chris decided to change and sneak out to the party. As he went upstairs to his room, which was a walk-in closet, he heard Danielle snoring. He thought to himself, "Great . . . she is sleeping!"

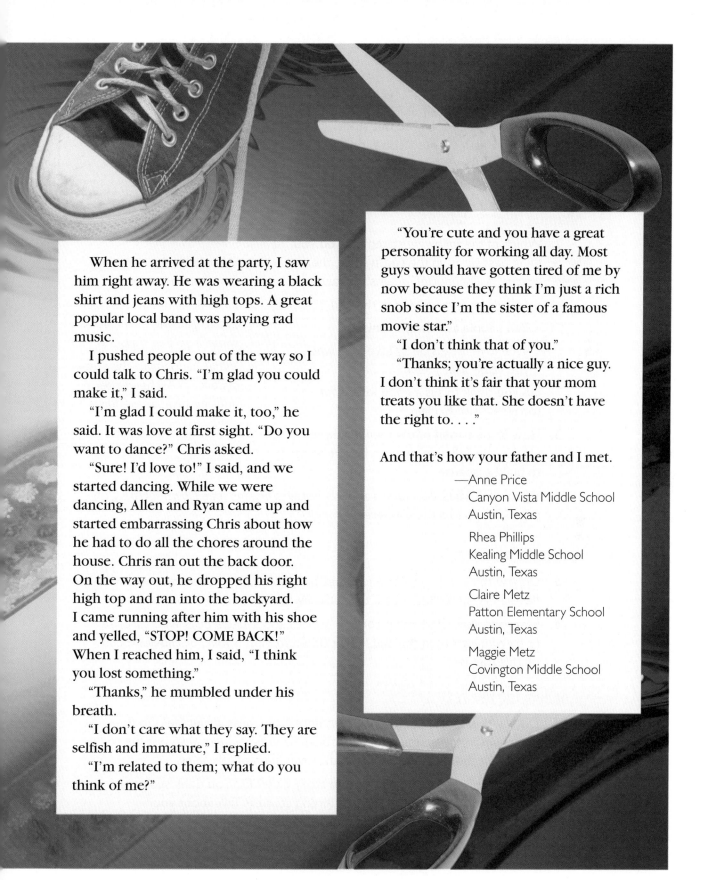

When he arrived at the party, I saw him right away. He was wearing a black shirt and jeans with high tops. A great popular local band was playing rad music.

I pushed people out of the way so I could talk to Chris. "I'm glad you could make it," I said.

"I'm glad I could make it, too," he said. It was love at first sight. "Do you want to dance?" Chris asked.

"Sure! I'd love to!" I said, and we started dancing. While we were dancing, Allen and Ryan came up and started embarrassing Chris about how he had to do all the chores around the house. Chris ran out the back door. On the way out, he dropped his right high top and ran into the backyard. I came running after him with his shoe and yelled, "STOP! COME BACK!" When I reached him, I said, "I think you lost something."

"Thanks," he mumbled under his breath.

"I don't care what they say. They are selfish and immature," I replied.

"I'm related to them; what do you think of me?"

"You're cute and you have a great personality for working all day. Most guys would have gotten tired of me by now because they think I'm just a rich snob since I'm the sister of a famous movie star."

"I don't think that of you."

"Thanks; you're actually a nice guy. I don't think it's fair that your mom treats you like that. She doesn't have the right to. . . ."

And that's how your father and I met.

—Anne Price
Canyon Vista Middle School
Austin, Texas

Rhea Phillips
Kealing Middle School
Austin, Texas

Claire Metz
Patton Elementary School
Austin, Texas

Maggie Metz
Covington Middle School
Austin, Texas

# MAKING MEANINGS

## First Thoughts

1. Think about the round robin discussion you had before you read this story. Which of our deepest wishes do you think this story expresses? Do you think it is also about some of our fears? Explain.

## Shaping Interpretations

2. Which of the following statements do you think best sums up the **main idea,** the lesson "Aschenputtel" seems to teach?

   • Goodness is rewarded in the end.

   • Bad people are always punished.

   • True love means being loved for who you really are.

   Do you think this is a good lesson for today's world? Explain.

3. How is the **motif** of the number three used in this folk tale? Explain how it helps to build suspense.

4. What new slants do Viorst's and Silverstein's poems (see *Connections* on page 601) give to the Cinderella story?

(see *Connections* on page 601)

## Extending the Text

5. Do you think most children feel they have something in common with Cinderella? What feelings might they share with her?

6. Everyone likes Cinderella stories—stories about underdogs who surprise us by winning out in the end. What other stories, books, or movies focus on this theme?

## Challenging the Text

7. Do you think folk tales give children unrealistic ideas about life? Do they give children the courage to get through hard times? Are they just fun to read? Talk about your opinions of the usefulness of folk tales.

8. How do you feel about the way the story ends? Do you think such cruel details *should* be removed from children's stories? Talk about your response to the stepsisters' punishment.

### Reading Check

a. What does Aschenputtel do with the twig her father gives her?

b. What does the step-mother do to stop Aschenputtel from attending the feast?

c. Who helps Aschenputtel complete her tasks?

d. How does the prince manage to get one of Aschenputtel's golden slippers?

e. What happens to the stepsisters on Aschenputtel and the prince's wedding day?

# CHOICES: Building Your Portfolio

## Writer's Notebook

### 1. Collecting Ideas for an Informative Report

Imagine that you are a reporter for the palace newspaper and have been assigned to interview Aschenputtel after she and the prince are married. Take notes for a news article describing what has happened to Aschenputtel. One way to investigate a topic is to ask the reporter's *5W-How* questions: *who, what, where, when, why,* and *how.* (Sometimes you can't apply all six questions.) Be sure to include details that will interest your readers.

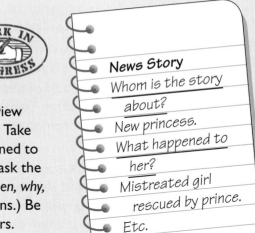

> **News Story**
> Whom is the story about?
> New princess.
> What happened to her?
> Mistreated girl rescued by prince.
> Etc.

## Creative Writing/Speaking

### 2. Role Reversal

What might happen if a princess rescued an underdog boy from a life of drudgery? One version of this story is told in the Student to Student on page 602. Create your own version of "Cinderella." Decide on your **characters, setting,** and **plot,** and then write the story. You can stick closely to the story of "Aschenputtel" or come up with a totally new plot, but try to use the **motif** of three. Illustrate your story, and read it aloud to a group of younger children.

## Creative Writing

### 3. If the Shoe Fits . . .

Write a new ending for "Aschenputtel," describing how the characters might react if Aschenputtel pretended that the golden slipper was too tight or if the prince got sick of the sight of all those feet. Look back at the **Connections** poems (page 601) for inspiration.

Poster for Walt Disney's *Cinderella* (1950).

## Speaking and Listening

### 4. A Real Cinderella Story

Imagine a Cinderella story set today in your own community. Who would the underdog be? Who or what would hold the underdog back? Who would rescue the underdog, and how would this happen? With a group of classmates, brainstorm to come up with some ideas. Then, plot out your story. You could act out your modern Cinderella story or videotape the production for your class.

# GRAMMAR LINK

## *All Right, A Lot, Should Have,* and *Would Have*

**Languyage Handbook**
**H E L P**

*See Glossary of Usage:* all right, a lot, *and* could of, *pages 785 and 786.*

**Technology**
**H E L P**

*See* Language Workshop CD-ROM. *Key word entry: usage.*

Read the following paragraph. Can you spot the errors in spelling and usage?

SPELLING-CHECKER ALERT

The stepsisters did alot of things wrong. They should of treated Aschenputtel better. Then maybe things would of turned out alright for them in the end.

Did you spot the errors—*alot, should of, would of,* and *alright?* Here are some tips to help you remember the correct spelling or usage of these expressions:

1. The expressions *a lot* and *all right* each consist of two words. Don't run the two words together into one word. (Remember that *all right* is like *all wrong.*)

2. Remember to pronounce the helping verbs *should have* and *would have* correctly. *Of* is not a verb and never follows *could, should,* or *would.*

**Try It Out**

➤ Find the misused or misspelled word in each sentence. Then, write the sentence correctly.

1. Aschenputtel had to do alot of work.

2. Do you think it's alright for children to hear stories with violent endings?

3. I think Aschenputtel should of spoken up for herself more.

➤ Do a survey of another class to see how many students have trouble with these words. To carry out your survey, write a summary of Aschenputtel's story in which you misuse or misspell each of these four phrases at least once. See how many students can spot the errors. Report your findings to your class.

# VOCABULARY   HOW TO OWN A WORD

**WORD BANK**

*pious*
*expired*
*ordained*
*persisted*
*stunted*

## Write About It

1. Write a definition of *pious* that a fourth-grader could understand.
2. Suppose a plant <u>expired</u>. What could cause this?
3. What events in the story of Aschenputtel were <u>ordained</u> by a king or a prince?
4. When would you admire someone who <u>persisted</u>? When would you be annoyed by such a person?
5. Where would you expect to find a plant that was <u>stunted</u>?

# *Before You Read*

## THE ALGONQUIN CINDERELLA
## YEH-SHEN

## Make the Connection

### Universal Truths

Many stories told in different parts of the world are surprisingly similar. No one is sure why this is so. Some people think it is because certain real-life wishes and fears are so powerful and so universal that people the world over want to express them in story form. One of the things we learn from all these tales is that despite their many cultural differences, people around the world have a lot in common.

## Quickwrite

Pick a statement that you strongly agree or disagree with from the list below. Freewrite for a few minutes about why you feel as you do.

- It's easy to tell who's good and who's bad.

- Good always wins out over bad in the end.

- People can be cruel or jealous.

- People sometimes value wealth above love.

- People learn from their mistakes.

## Elements of Literature

### Character Types

In "The Algonquin Cinderella" and "Yeh-Shen" you will find some familiar folk-tale characters: the wicked stepmother, the cruel sisters, the handsome prince. Such characters are either all good or all bad. Unlike most people in real life, these **character types** do not grow, change, or learn from their unusual experiences.

> The characters in folk tales are **character types**—recognizable, unchanging figures whom we meet over and over again in one tale after another.
>
> *For more on Character, see the Handbook of Literary Terms.*

## Reading Skills and Strategies

### Comparing Texts: Looking for Likenesses

Read these stories once just for fun. Then, read them a second time, keeping a piece of paper handy. On the paper, make a chart like the one below. Fill it in with similarities you see in these stories and "Aschenputtel." Are you surprised at how similar these stories are—one Algonquin, one Chinese, and one German?

|  | Story 1 | Story 2 | Story 3 |
|---|---|---|---|
| Wicked stepmother |  |  |  |
| Cruel sisters |  |  |  |
| Handsome prince |  |  |  |
| Special helpers |  |  |  |
| Magical events |  |  |  |
| Wishes come true |  |  |  |

# The Algonquin Cinderella

*Algonquin, retold by* M. R. Cox

(Inset) A Micmac mother and son (1854).

National Anthropological Archives 56.827, Smithsonian Institution, © Smithsonian Institution.

*The poor little girl in her strange clothes, with her face all scarred, was an awful sight . . .*

There was once a large village belonging to the Micmac Indians of the Eastern Algonquins, built beside a lake. At the far end of the settlement stood a lodge, and in it lived a being who was always invisible. He had a sister who looked after him, and everyone knew that the girl who could see him might marry him. There were very few girls who did not try to marry him, but it was very long before anyone succeeded.

This is the way in which the test of sight was carried out. At evening time, when the Invisible One was due to return home, his sister would walk with any girl who might come down to the lakeshore. She, of course, could see her brother, since he was always visible to her. As soon as she saw him coming, she would say to the girls:

"Do you see my brother?"

"Yes," they would generally reply—though some of them did say "No."

To those who said that they could indeed see him, the sister would ask, "What is his shoulder strap made of?"

Or, some people say that she would inquire, "What is his moose-runner's haul?" or "What does he draw his sled with?"

And they would answer, "A strip of rawhide," or "A green flexible branch," or something like that.

Then the sister, knowing that they had not told the truth, would say, "Very well, let us return to the wigwam!"

When they went in, she would tell the girls not to sit in a certain place, because it belonged to the Invisible One. Then, after they had helped to cook the supper, they would

**Re-creation of an Eastern Woodland Indian wigwam.**

wait with great curiosity to see him eat. They could be sure that he was a real person, for when he took off his moccasins they became visible, and his sister hung them up. But beyond this, they saw nothing of him, not even when they stayed in the place all night, as many of them did.

Now there lived in the village an old man who was a widower, and his three daughters. The youngest girl was very small, weak, and often ill. And yet her sisters, especially the elder, treated her cruelly. The second daughter was kinder and sometimes took her side. But the wicked sister would burn the younger girl's hands and feet with hot cinders. The girl was covered with scars from this treatment. She was so marked that people called her Oochigeaskw, the Rough-Faced Girl.

When her father came home and asked why the youngest girl had such burns, the bad sister would say at once that it was the girl's own fault, for she had disobeyed orders and gone near the fire and fallen into it.

These two elder sisters decided one day to try their luck at seeing the Invisible One. So they dressed themselves in their finest clothes and tried to look their prettiest. They found the Invisible One's sister and took the usual walk by the water.

When the brother came, and when they were asked if they could see him, they answered, "Of course." And when asked about the shoulder strap or sled cord, they answered, "A piece of rawhide."

But of course they were lying like the others, and they got nothing for their pains.

The next afternoon, when the father returned home, he brought with him many of the pretty little shells from which wampum was made, and the sisters set to work to string them.

That day, poor little Oochigeaskw, who had always gone barefoot, got a pair of her father's moccasins, old ones, and put them into water to soften them so that she could wear them. Then she begged her sisters for a few wampum shells. The elder called her a little pest, but the younger one gave her some. Now, since she had no clothes other than her usual rags, the poor little thing went into the woods and got herself some sheets of birch bark. From these, she made a dress and put marks on it for decoration, in the style of long ago. She also made a petticoat and a loose gown, a cap, leggings, and a handkerchief. She put on her father's large old moccasins, which were far too big for her, and went forth to try her luck. She would try, she thought, to see the Invisible One.

She did not begin very well. As she set off, her sisters shouted and hooted, hissed and yelled, and tried to make her stay. And the loafers around the village, seeing the strange little creature, called out "Shame!"

The poor little girl in her strange clothes, with her face all scarred, was an awful sight, but she was kindly received by the sister of the Invisible One. And this was, of course, because this noble lady understood far more about things than simply the mere outside which all the rest of the world knows. As the brown of the evening sky turned to black, the lady took the girl down to the lake.

"Do you see him?" the Invisible One's sister asked.

"I do, indeed—and he is wonderful!" said Oochigeaskw.

The sister asked, "And what is his sled string?"

The little girl said, "It is the Rainbow."

"And, my sister, what is his bow string?"

"It is the Spirit's Road—the Milky Way."

"So you *have* seen him," said his sister. She took the girl home with her and bathed her. As she did so, all the scars disappeared from the girl's body. Her hair grew again, as it was combed, long, like a blackbird's wing. Her eyes were now like stars: In all the world there was no other such beauty. Then, from her treasures, the lady gave her a wedding garment and adorned her.

Then she told Oochigeaskw to take the *wife's* seat in the wigwam, the one next to where the Invisible One sat, beside the entrance. And when he came in, terrible and beautiful, he smiled and said:

"So we are found out!"

"Yes," said his sister. And so Oochigeaskw became his wife.

The Indian village of Pomeiooc. Watercolor by John White (c. 1585).

The Granger Collection, New York.

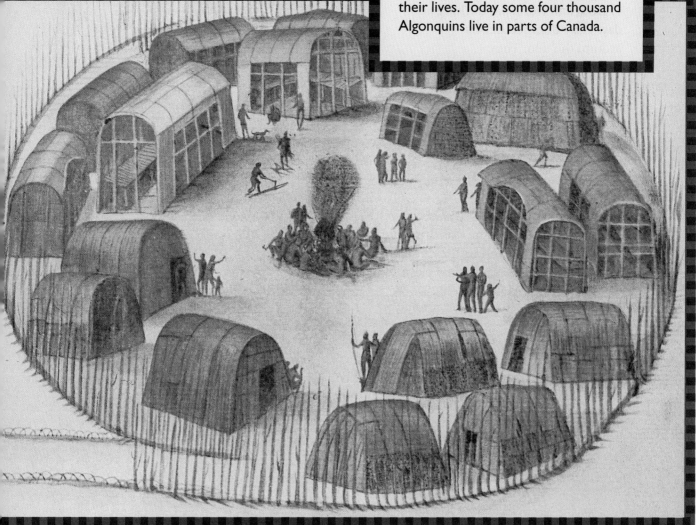

# Dinorella

**Pamela Duncan Edwards**

Dora, Doris, and Dinorella lived down in the sand dunes in a dinosaur den.

Dora and Doris did nothing all day. They dumped debris around the den. They never did the dusting or the dishes. Dinorella was dainty and dependable. Dora and Doris were dreadful to Dinorella. All day they demanded . . .

"DINORELLA, dig the garden.

"DINORELLA, fetch us drinks.

"DINORELLA, start the dinner."

"She's a dingbat," sniggered Dora.

"She's a dumbhead," giggled Doris.

One day a card was delivered to the den:

> *Dinosaur Dance*
>
> *Duke Dudley's Den*
> *At Dusk*
> *Hors d'oeuvres, Dandelion Cola*
> *Dancing Until Dawn*

Duke Dudley was the most dashing dinosaur in the dunes.

"I would die for a date with the duke," said Dora, decorating herself with dinosaur jewels.

"Definitely," sighed Doris, dolling up for the dance.

"A dance," said Dinorella diffidently. "How divine."

"YOU can't go to the dance," said Doris. "YOU'RE too dowdy."

"YOU'RE too dull," agreed Dora. "And YOU don't have decent dinosaur jewels. Of course YOU can't go to the dance."

Poor Dinorella felt down in the dumps as she watched her stepsisters depart.

Suddenly, Dinorella heard a droning noise.

"Don't be dismal," cried Fairydactyl. "You SHALL go to the dance."

"But I'm so drab," said Dinorella, "and I don't have decent dinosaur jewels."

"I'll soon deal with that," declared

Fairydactyl. "These will outdazzle all other dinosaur jewels."

"**DARLING** Fairydactyl!" exclaimed Dinorella in delight. With her diamonds dangling, she set out for the dance.

Dusk had fallen when Dinorella heard a deafening disturbance coming from the direction of Duke Dudley's Den.

**A DASTARDLY DEED WAS TAKING PLACE!**
A deinonychus was dragging off the duke.

"**I'M DONE FOR!**" cried the duke. "He will **DEVOUR** me!"

"Indeed I will!" laughed the deinonychus. "I'll be digesting you by daybreak."

Dinorella was not a daring dinosaur, but something drastic had to be done.

"I may become dessert, but I'm determined to drive away that dreaded carnivore."

Dinorella climbed to the top of the dune.

"**YOU DISGUSTING DUMMY**," she roared. "**DROP THE DUKE!**"

Dinorella began to hurl dirtballs at the deinonychus.

The dumbfounded deinonychus stopped in disbelief. "Who called me a dummy?" he demanded.

The moon's light caught Dinorella's dangling diamonds. Dots and dabs of light darted toward the deinonychus.

"**A DEVIL!**" cried the deinonychus. "See its dreadful demon eyes!"

Dinorella detached a diamond and directed it toward the deinonychus.

The diamond hit the deinonychus **HARD** in his dentures.

"The devil will destroy me with its deadly eyes," bellowed the distraught deinonychus. He dumped Duke Dudley and departed double-quick.

The den was dense with dinosaurs dashing about in distress. "A demon," they cried. **"WE'RE DOOMED."**

**"DIMWITS!"** roared Duke Dudley through the din. "Demons don't throw diamonds. It was a damsel who defended me with her dazzling dinosaur jewel.

"When I discover her, I shall ask her to be my darling."

All the dinosaur dames were delirious.

"The jewel is mine!" they each declared.

**"MINE!"** cried Doris.

**"NO, DEFINITELY MINE,"** bellowed Dora, giving Doris a dig. "I am the damsel you desire."

**"I DOUBT IT",** declared Duke Dudley.

"Your dinosaur jewels don't match."

Just then, Fairydactyl arrived at the dance. She quickly saw the dilemma. **"WHERE IS DINORELLA?"** she demanded.

"Dinorella!" scoffed Dora, "that dopey domestic."

"Dinorella!" laughed Doris. "She's back at the den."

But Fairydactyl spied Dinorella dodging behind the dune.

**"DINORELLA",** she directed, "come down."

So down came Dinorella, looking distracted.

Cried the duke, "She wears but one dazzling jewel!

"Dinorella, you are adorable. You're definitely quite a dish. I beg you to be my dearest."

**"DREAMY!"** said Dinorella as they danced off into the dawn.

**"DRAT!"** said Dora and Doris.

*Carp* (1848) by Taito.

# YEH-SHEN

*Chinese, retold by*
**Ai-Ling Louie**

## THE ONLY FRIEND THAT YEH-SHEN HAD WAS A FISH . . .

In the dim past, even before the Ch'in and the Han dynasties, there lived a cave chief of southern China by the name of Wu. As was the custom in those days, Chief Wu had taken two wives. Each wife in her turn had presented Wu with a baby daughter. But one of the wives sickened and died, and not too many days after that Chief Wu took to his bed and died too.

# IT WAS A BEAUTIFUL FISH WITH GOLDEN EYES.

Yeh-Shen, the little orphan, grew to girlhood in her stepmother's home. She was a bright child and lovely too, with skin as smooth as ivory and dark pools for eyes. Her stepmother was jealous of all this beauty and goodness, for her own daughter was not pretty at all. So in her displeasure, she gave poor Yeh-Shen the heaviest and most unpleasant chores.

The only friend that Yeh-Shen had to her name was a fish she had caught and raised. It was a beautiful fish with golden eyes, and every day it would come out of the water and rest its head on the bank of the pond, waiting for Yeh-Shen to feed it. Stepmother gave Yeh-Shen little enough food for herself, but the orphan child always found something to share with her fish, which grew to enormous size.

Somehow the stepmother heard of this. She was terribly angry to discover that Yeh-Shen had kept a secret from her. She hurried down to the pond, but she was unable to see the fish, for Yeh-Shen's pet wisely hid itself. The stepmother, however, was a crafty woman, and she soon thought of a plan. She walked home and called out, "Yeh-Shen, go and collect some firewood. But wait! The neighbors might see you. Leave your filthy coat here!" The minute the girl was out of sight, her stepmother slipped on the coat herself and went down again to the pond. This time the big fish saw Yeh-Shen's familiar jacket and heaved itself onto the bank, expecting to be fed. But the stepmother, having hidden a dagger in her sleeve, stabbed the fish, wrapped it in her garments, and took it home to cook for dinner.

When Yeh-Shen came to the pond that evening, she found her pet had disappeared. Overcome with grief, the girl collapsed on the ground and dropped her tears into the still waters of the pond.

"Ah, poor child!" a voice said.

Yeh-Shen sat up to find a very old man looking down at her. He wore the coarsest of clothes, and his hair flowed down over his shoulders.

"Kind uncle, who may you be?" Yeh-Shen asked.

"That is not important, my child. All you must know is that I have been sent to tell you of the wondrous powers of your fish."

"My fish, but sir . . ." The girl's eyes filled with tears, and she could not go on.

The old man sighed and said, "Yes, my child, your fish is no longer alive, and I must tell you that your stepmother is once more the cause of your sorrow." Yeh-Shen gasped in horror, but the old man went on. "Let us not dwell on things that are past," he said, "for I have come bringing you a gift. Now you must listen carefully to this: The bones of your fish are filled with a powerful spirit. Whenever you are in serious need, you must kneel before them and let them know your heart's desire. But do not waste their gifts."

Yeh-Shen wanted to ask the old sage many more questions, but he rose to the sky before she could utter another word. With heavy heart, Yeh-Shen made her way to the dung heap to gather the remains of her friend.

Time went by, and Yeh-Shen, who was often left alone, took comfort in speaking to the bones of her fish. When she was hungry, which happened quite often, Yeh-Shen asked the bones for food. In this way, Yeh-Shen managed to live from day to day, but she lived in dread that her stepmother would discover her secret and take even that away from her.

So the time passed and spring came. Festival time was approaching: It was the busiest time of the year. Such cooking and cleaning and sewing there was to be done! Yeh-Shen had hardly a moment's rest. At the spring festival young men and young women from the village hoped to meet and to choose whom they would marry. How Yeh-Shen longed to go! But her stepmother had other plans. She hoped to find a husband for her own daughter and did not want any man to see the beauteous Yeh-Shen first. When finally the holiday arrived, the stepmother and her daughter dressed themselves in their finery and filled their baskets with sweetmeats. "You must remain at home now and watch to see that no one steals fruit from our trees," her stepmother told Yeh-Shen, and then she departed for the banquet with her own daughter.

As soon as she was alone, Yeh-Shen went to speak to the bones of her fish. "Oh, dear friend," she said, kneeling before the precious bones, "I long to go to the festival, but I cannot show myself in these rags. Is there some-

"THE BONES OF YOUR FISH ARE FILLED WITH A POWERFUL SPIRIT."

*Carp with Bogbean* by Sadatora (nineteenth century).

**British Library, London/Bridgeman Art Library, London.**

where I could borrow clothes fit to wear to the feast?" At once she found herself dressed in a gown of azure[1] blue, with a cloak of kingfisher feathers draped around her shoulders. Best of all, on her tiny feet were the most beautiful slippers she had ever seen. They were woven of golden threads, in a pattern like the scales of a fish, and the glistening soles were made of solid gold. There was magic in the shoes, for they should have been quite heavy, yet when Yeh-Shen walked, her feet felt as light as air.

"Be sure you do not lose your golden shoes," said the spirit of the bones. Yeh-Shen promised to be careful. Delighted with her transformation, she bid a fond farewell to the bones of her fish as she slipped off to join in the merrymaking.

That day Yeh-Shen turned many a head as she appeared at the feast. All around her people whispered, "Look at that beautiful girl! Who can she be?"

But above this, Stepsister was heard to say, "Mother, does she not resemble our Yeh-Shen?"

Upon hearing this, Yeh-Shen jumped up and ran off before her stepsister could look closely at her. She raced down the mountainside, and in doing so, she lost one of her golden slippers. No sooner had the shoe fallen from her foot than all her fine clothes turned back to rags. Only one thing remained—a tiny golden shoe. Yeh-Shen hurried to the bones of her fish and returned the slipper, promising to find its mate. But now the bones were silent. Sadly Yeh-Shen realized that she had lost her only friend. She hid the little shoe in her bedstraw and went outside to cry. Leaning against a fruit tree, she sobbed and sobbed until she fell asleep.

The stepmother left the gathering to check on Yeh-Shen, but when she returned home, she found the girl sound asleep, with her arms wrapped around a fruit tree. So, thinking no more of her, the stepmother rejoined the party. Meantime, a villager had found the shoe. Recognizing its worth, he sold it to a merchant, who presented it in turn to the king of the island kingdom of T'o Han.

The king was more than happy to accept the slipper as a gift. He was entranced by the tiny thing, which was shaped of the most precious of metals, yet which made

1. **azure** (azh′ər): like the color of the sky.

no sound when touched to stone. The more he marveled at its beauty, the more determined he became to find the woman to whom the shoe belonged. A search was begun among the ladies of his own kingdom, but all who tried on the sandal found it impossibly small. Undaunted, the king ordered the search widened to include the cave women from the countryside where the slipper had been found. Since he realized it would take many years for every woman to come to his island and test her foot in the slipper, the king thought of a way to get the right woman to come forward. He ordered the sandal placed in a pavilion[2] by the side of the road near where it had been found, and his herald[3] announced that the shoe was to be returned to its original owner. Then, from a nearby hiding place, the king and his men settled down to watch and wait for a woman with tiny feet to come and claim her slipper.

All that day the pavilion was crowded with cave women who had come to test a foot in the shoe. Yeh-Shen's stepmother and stepsister were among them, but not Yeh-Shen—they had told her to stay home. By day's end, although many women had eagerly tried to put on the slipper, it still had not been worn. Wearily, the king continued his vigil into the night.

It wasn't until the blackest part of night, while the moon hid behind a cloud, that Yeh-Shen dared to show her face at the pavilion, and even then she tiptoed timidly across the wide floor. Sinking down to her knees, the girl in rags examined the tiny shoe. Only when she was sure that this was the missing mate to her own golden slipper did she dare pick it up. At last she could return both little shoes to the fish bones. Surely then her beloved spirit would speak to her again.

Now the king's first thought, on seeing Yeh-Shen take the precious slipper, was to throw the girl into prison as a thief. But when she turned to leave, he caught a glimpse of her face. At once the king was struck by the sweet harmony of her features, which seemed so out of keeping with the rags she wore. It was then that he took a closer

*Fish,* **from an album of twelve studies of flowers, birds, and fish by Tsubaki Chinzan (1801–1854). Watercolor on silk with patterned border.**

**British Library, London/Bridgeman Art Library, London.**

*Three Fish* **(detail) by Belshu. Color woodblock print.**

**Free Library, Philadelphia/Bridgeman Art Library, London.**

---

2. **pavilion:** large tent or shelter, often highly decorated.
3. **herald:** the person in a king's court who makes official announcements.

# HER LOVELINESS MADE HER SEEM A HEAVENLY BEING.

look and noticed that she walked upon the tiniest feet he had ever seen.

With a wave of his hand, the king signaled that this tattered creature was to be allowed to depart with the golden slipper. Quietly, the king's men slipped off and followed her home.

All this time, Yeh-Shen was unaware of the excitement she had caused. She had made her way home and was about to hide both sandals in her bedding when there was a pounding at the door. Yeh-Shen went to see who it was—and found a king at her doorstep. She was very frightened at first, but the king spoke to her in a kind voice and asked her to try the golden slippers on her feet. The maiden did as she was told, and as she stood in her golden shoes, her rags were transformed once more into the feathered cloak and beautiful azure gown.

Her loveliness made her seem a heavenly being, and the king suddenly knew in his heart that he had found his true love.

Not long after this, Yeh-Shen was married to the king. But fate was not so gentle with her stepmother and stepsister. Since they had been unkind to his beloved, the king would not permit Yeh-Shen to bring them to his palace. They remained in their cave home, where one day, it is said, they were crushed to death in a shower of flying stones.

## MEET THE WRITER

### It Runs in the Family

**Ai-Ling Louie** remembers hearing the story "Yeh-Shen," the Chinese version of "Cinderella," from her grandmother. Louie became curious about the origins of this story, which had been told in her family for three generations, so she did some research. She learned that the tale was first written down by Tuan Cheng-shi in an ancient Chinese manuscript during the Tang dynasty (A.D. 618–906) and had probably been handed down orally for centuries before that.

# from Ashpet

**Appalachian, retold by Granny Shores, collected by Richard Chase**

One time there was a woman had two daughters, and they kept a hired girl. They treated this girl mean. She was bound out to 'em, had to do all the hard work, little as she was. They wouldn't buy her any pretty clothes or nothin', made her sleep right up against the fireplace and the ashes got all over her, so they called her Ashpet.

Well, one day they were all fixin' to go to church meetin'. They never let Ashpet go anywhere. They knew she was prettier than the old woman's two girls, and if anybody came to the house, they always shoved Ashpet under a washtub. That day, just when they were tryin' to get fixed up to go to meetin', their fire went out, so they had to borrow fire. Now there was an old woman lived over the gap in the mountain. These rich folks, they wouldn't have nothin' to do with this old woman, but they had to have fire so they sent the oldest one of the girls over there to borrow some fire. The oldest girl she went traipsin' on over the gap. She thought herself so good she didn't go in the house, just stuck her hand through a crack in the logs.

"I come after fire."

"Come in and comb my hair and I'll give ye some."

"I'll not put my pretty clean hands on your old cat comb!"

"You'll get no fire."

The old woman she sent the next oldest. She went a-swishin' up the hill and through the gap. She was so nice! She ran her hand through that crack.

"I want some fire."

"Come in and comb my hair."

"Me? Put my nice white hands on your old cat comb?"

"Put off, then. You'll get no fire."

Then the old woman hollered for Ashpet. And Ashpet she went on up through the gap, ran down the holler, and went right on in the house.

"Good evenin', Auntie."

"Good evenin', Ashpet."

"I want to borry a coal of fire, please, ma'm."

"Comb my hair and you can have it."

Ashpet combed her hair for her, and then the old woman gave her some fire: put it in an old dried toadstool.

"You goin' to meetin', Ashpet?"

"Law, no! They never let me go anywhere at all. I got to wash the dishes and scour the pots. I'll not get done till meetin's plumb over."

"You want to go?"

"Why, yes, I'd like that the best in the world!"

"Time they all get good and gone, I'll be up there to see you." ... [*And Granny's story goes on.*]

# MAKING MEANINGS

## THE ALGONQUIN CINDERELLA
## YEH-SHEN

### • First Thoughts

1. The Cinderella story appears in many cultures all over the world. What fears and wishes are expressed in these Cinderella stories from two very different cultures? (Be sure to check your Quickwrite notes.)

### Shaping Interpretations

2. The cruel stepmother is a **character type** in "Yeh-Shen." What other character types appear in Cinderella stories? Work together with a partner to fill in a chart like the one below. After you've filled in your chart, discuss these character types. Do you think some of them are unfair?

**Reading Check**

a. Who gives Oochigeaskw a hard time? Why?

b. Who gives Yeh-Shen a hard time? Why?

c. Who helps Oochigeaskw in her troubles? Who helps Yeh-Shen?

d. How does Oochigeaskw prove she can see the Invisible One?

e. How does the king find Yeh-Shen?

| Story | Character Types | | | |
|---|---|---|---|---|
| | Wicked Stepmother | Cruel Stepsisters | Handsome Prince | Helpers |
| "Aschenputtel" | | | | |
| "The Algonquin Cinderella" | | | | |
| "Dinorella" | | | | |
| "Yeh-Shen" | | | | |
| "Ashpet" | | | | |

3. What part does an animal play in Yeh-Shen's story?

4. Which **metamorphosis,** Yeh-Shen's or Oochigeaskw's, seems more miraculous to you? Explain why.

5. You've considered the common elements of Cinderella stories from four cultures: German, Algonquin, Chinese, and Appalachian. You've also read "Dinorella," a "prehistoric" fairy tale (see **Connections** on page 612). What important variations, or differences, do you notice from story to story? Do all the stories teach the same values? Talk it over.

# CHOICES: Building Your Portfolio

## Writer's Notebook

### 1. Collecting Ideas for an Informative Report

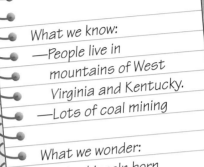

How much do you know about the culture and geography of Appalachia? With a partner, discuss what you know about Appalachia and what questions occur to you as you think about "Ash-pet" (see *Connections* on page 621). Be sure you can locate Appalachia on a map.

> What we know:
> —People live in mountains of West Virginia and Kentucky.
> —Lots of coal mining
>
> What we wonder:
> —Was Lincoln born there?
> —Is the soil poor?

## Creative Writing

### 2. Story Swap

Get together with a partner, and choose two similar characters from two different Cinderella stories. Take the role of one of these characters and let your partner take the role of the other. One character writes a message to the other, and the second character then writes a message back. If you are the stepmothers in "Aschenputtel" and "Yeh-Shen," for example, you might explain to each other why you treated your step-daughter as you did. If you are a prince or a king, you might describe your lonely life before you met your Cinderella or your great joy after meeting her.

## Cultural Connections

### 3. Fact and Fiction

Skim either "Yeh-Shen" or "The Algonquin Cinderella," looking for details about food, clothing, homes, families, and customs that are different from your own. Make a list of questions suggested by these cultural details that you might like to research.

## Critical Thinking/ Speaking

### 4. Unhappily Ever After

Horrible punishments are common in folk tales: Remember the stepsisters in "Aschenputtel," their eyes pecked out by pigeons, or the stepmother and step-sister in "Yeh-Shen," crushed to death by flying stones. These violent punishments are often "cleaned up" or softened when the stories are retold to children today. Do you think this is a good idea? In a group, discuss this question of violence in fairy tales and folk tales told to children.

# GRAMMAR LINK  **MINI-LESSON**

**Technology HELP**

*See* Language Workshop CD-ROM. *Key word entry: homonyms.*

## *Two, To, and Too*

Notice how the words *two, to,* and *too* are used in the following paragraph:

> Oochigeaskw has <u>two</u> sisters, while Yeh-Shen has just one stepsister. Oochigeaskw goes <u>to</u> the home of a powerful being and becomes his wife. Yeh-Shen marries someone powerful, <u>too</u>.

To use these sound-alike words correctly, remember these tips:

**two** (the number): *Two* contains a *w.* Turn the *w* to the left and you have the numeral *3.*

**to** ("toward"): *To* + *ward.*

**too** ("also"; "more than enough"): *Too* has "more than enough" *o's.*

### Try It Out

➤ In each sentence, choose the correct word from the underlined pair.

1. Which <u>to/two</u> Cinderella stories are your favorites?

2. Do you think the Cinderella stories are <u>too/to</u> unrealistic?

3. I went <u>to/two</u> the library to look for facts about the Algonquins.

➤ Take out something you have written, and circle each usage of *two, to,* and *too.* Review the rules on this page and correct each word you have used incorrectly.

---

# SPELLING  **HOW TO OWN A WORD**

**Langugage Handbook HELP**

*See Adding Prefixes and Suffixes, page 781.*

## Spelling Strategies

Can you tell which of these words is misspelled?

> occured        tailored

If you chose "occured," you're right—or lucky. Not knowing when to double the final consonant before a suffix beginning with a vowel (*-ing, -er, -ed,* or *-en*) is a common spelling problem. To figure it out, just follow the simple rule below—your suffixes will then fit onto the ends of words as precisely as the shoe slipped onto Cinderella's foot.

The final consonant is doubled before a suffix if *both* of these conditions are present:

1. The word has only one syllable or the accent is on the last syllable.
2. The word ends in a single consonant preceded by a single vowel.

For example, *bid* becomes *bidding* because it contains only one syllable. *Marvel* becomes *marveled*—no doubling of the final consonant—because the accent is not on the final syllable. Try the rule out on these words:

1. prefer + ed
2. clap + ing
3. whisper + ed
4. sob + ing
5. bed + ed
6. scar + ed

# Elements of Literature

## FOLK TALES: Telling Tales *by* Virginia Hamilton

Who tells stories where you live? Is it your mother or father? Is it your uncle or aunt? your cousin or your friend? Is it you?

"Nobody I know tells stories," I answered when my English teacher asked that question. "At my house, everybody just talks."

Now I realize that both my father and mother were storytellers. I simply did not recognize that what they were "talking" were stories. My four brothers and sisters and I, and our parents, talked about everything, all the time. We had only the radio for entertainment—there wasn't television until I was twelve—and we got used to hearing talking. It was natural for us to listen to stories and then do some telling ourselves.

Mother would begin a story with "That reminds me" or "I remember when." Once she began, "That reminds me of the time all of the Boston ivy fell from Mrs. Pinton's house."

"All of it? All at once— when did that happen?" my oldest sister, Nina, asked. And

Mother was off and running with the tale about "the day the ivy fell." It is a story, part true, part fiction, and part tragic, that found its way into my novel *Sweet Whispers, Brother Rush*.

My mom and dad loved telling stories and remembering their pasts. We don't know for certain, but perhaps folk tales—"tells"—began in a similar way.

### How Folk Tales Grow

**Folk tales** are stories passed on by word of mouth, often over many centuries. Each time the tale is told, it is changed a bit because no two people tell a story exactly the same way.

Some of these folk tales travel; that is, as they are told and retold, they move out of their original environments into other times and other places. Although traditional folk tales reflect the particular culture and people that created them, common features, called **motifs**, can be found in folk stories from many parts of the world. You'll find that

many folk tales include motifs like grateful beasts; tests of the hero; magic; false parents; fairy godmothers; and brave youngest sons and daughters.

Handed down from generation to generation, told over and over again, these "tells" become familiar stories— "They say the people could fly . . ."; "Once upon a time . . .". They have become tales of the folks.

### American Folk Tales: Keeping Cultures Alive

When the first Europeans came with their folk tales, the Native Americans already had an elaborate and rich folklore tradition. Other folk tales traveled to the New World from other countries. For example, Africans who were brought to America as slaves carried with them their unique "folk-telling" traditions. Over generations they passed on tales about their lives on the plantations and about their relationships with the white men and women who held them as slaves.

*(continued on next page)*

*(continued from previous page)*

In fact, the African American storyteller developed the animal tale into a highly individual form. In this animal tale the social order of the plantation is broken down into animal elements, which symbolize the people in the plantation community. The African folk-tale tellers who were slaves fantasized about freedom and so developed another kind of folk tale, an **escape story**, about flying away from slavery.

In America, people from Ireland, Denmark, Germany, France, Italy, Poland, Turkey, the Middle East, Russia, China, Japan, Korea, Vietnam, Cambodia, the Philippines, Brazil, Haiti, Puerto Rico, Nigeria, Jamaica, and practically everywhere else have told their children folk tales from their old homelands. These stories, as well as their dances, songs, and folk art, help these people stay together and keep their beliefs and cultures alive.

## Folk Tales and Community

Some folk tales are simple stories and others are complex. But the basic situation of the tale teller weaving his or her magic for a community of listeners is found everywhere, in every society.

For generation after generation, folk tales keep alive and close what we regard as important. They reveal who we are. As they instruct us in living, they show us our weaknesses and strengths, our fears and joys, our nightmares and wishes. Folk tales are our self-portraits.

## "Tells" and Tale Givers

All over America there are folk-tale-telling festivals, in which tale tellers stand up and give "tells" to the listeners. In New London, Connecticut, the National Congress on Storytelling is held every June at Connecticut College. Festivals take place in Michigan, Ohio, Kentucky, and other states. The National Association for the Preservation and Perpetuation of Storytelling is based in Tennessee.

Storytelling is an ancient and wonderful custom. I have grown out of the tale-giving tradition and so, perhaps, have some of you. As you read these folk tales and fables from around the world, think about those early folk-tale tellers who committed tales to memory in order to tell them aloud. Try to picture what those early tellings must have been like—imagine the smoky underground kivas of the Pueblos, the dusty village squares in Nigeria.

Sitting or standing there, surrounded by the community of listeners, the teller calls softly, "Time was when the animals could talk . . ." The listeners respond. They lean forward, absolutely quiet now, eager to hear, to be entertained, to learn.

# SUMMARIZING: HITTING THE HIGHLIGHTS

Have you ever heard someone say "Don't tell me about all the details—just cut to the chase"? Summarizing is a way of cutting to the chase. A **summary** is a short restatement of the main events and essential ideas of a text. When you summarize a story, you tell about its most important characters and events. You tell what causes the events and you tell how the events are connected, one to the other. A summary highlights major details and leaves out unimportant ones. It is shorter than the original story and is written in your own words.

Knowing how to summarize helps you understand and remember what you read and also helps you share what you have read with others. If you were to summarize a story (or movie) for a friend, you would tell who the main characters are, what their conflict is, what the major events are, and how the story ends. If the story's setting is important, you'd describe that, too. You would use **transition expressions** like *then, after, as a result,* and *finally* to show when and where events happened and how the events are connected.

While you're reading a story, take notes in the form of a story map like the one

## Story Map

| Characters: | | |
|---|---|---|
| Conflict: | | |
| Time and place: | | |
| Main event: | | |
| Main event: | | |
| Main event: | | |
| Resolution: | | |

above. Your story-map notes will give you most of the information you need to write a summary. All you need to add are transition words.

The character in the story you are about to read has great powers. After you read the story, you'll have a chance to try out your powers of summarizing.

**Apply the strategy on the next page.**

# *Before You Read*

## ONI AND THE GREAT BIRD

## Make the Connection

### Heroes

Superman, Wonder Woman, and Batman are popular action heroes. What makes these larger-than-life characters superheroes? How are they different from real-life heroes? To compare the two, think about the superheroes you've met in books, in movies, and on television. Then, copy the chart below, and complete it by putting a check mark in each box where the answer would be yes.

## Quickwrite

Write briefly about what you think makes someone a hero.

## Reading Skills and Strategies

### Summarizing

A lot happens in the next story. After you read it, you'll be asked to "cut to the chase" and create a **summary.** It may help you to take a separate sheet of paper and make a story map, like the one on page 627. As you read, fill in your map.

## Background

### Literature and Music

"Oni and the Great Bird" is a folk tale of the Yoruba, a West African people known for their story-telling and musical talents. In the tale, short songs, or chants, are set off from the rest of the story. When Yoruban stories are told at ritual gatherings, these lines are chanted to the accompaniment of drums called gangans. These drums are used to imitate the sounds and patterns of Yoruban speech.

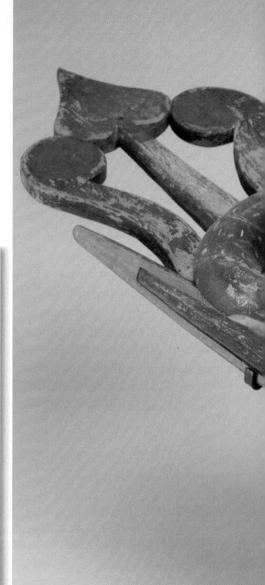

|  | Real-Life Hero | Superhero |
|---|---|---|
| 1. shows courage? |  |  |
| 2. is sometimes fearful? |  |  |
| 3. makes mistakes? |  |  |
| 4. is mortal? |  |  |
| 5. relies on others? |  |  |
| 6. has special powers? |  |  |

# Oni and the Great Bird

**Yoruban, retold by**
**Abayomi Fuja**

Yoruban water-spirit mask (early twentieth century).
Ijebu region, Nigeria.

The Fine Arts Museum of San Francisco, Museum exchange, 76.12.1.

Yoruban mounted-
warrior veranda
post, carved by
Olowe of Ise
(twentieth century).

New Orleans Museum
of Art: Museum
Purchase: Ella West
Freeman Foundation
Matching Fund.

## The other young men were afraid to have him near them.

There was once a strange boy called Oni who was born wearing a pair of boots. As Oni grew, the boots grew also. When he was a boy of eighteen years of age, war broke out between his people and another village. It was during the battle that Oni made a second discovery about himself, which separated him from his fellow men and made him different. The enemy arrows did not seem to harm him. Many pierced his body, which in the ordinary course of events should have slain him. The other young men noticed this too. They already regarded Oni as strange because of his wonderful boots, but when they discovered that he could not be killed, they were afraid to have him near them. When he returned from the war, several people tried to kill him in various ways but without any success. Finding this did not work, it was decided to find an excuse to banish him. He was accused of setting a house on fire in the village, and although Oni had nothing to do with the fire, he was found guilty and banished.

Oni wandered alone on foot for a long time. One afternoon he came to the banks of a great river, and finding an empty canoe and feeling tired of walking, he got into the boat and made his way downstream. Towards evening, when it was growing dark, Oni reached a town and decided to pull into the bank and spend the night there. There were the sounds of many bells being rung and people seemed to be in a hurry. Oni tied up the canoe and climbed the bank, and as he did so, he met an old man. "Good evening, my friend. My name is Oni. I am a stranger to your town and have nowhere to spend the night. Will you take me to your house?" Oni asked the old man.

"Yes, certainly, come along with me, but we must go quickly because the bells are ringing and it is growing dusk," replied the old man.

"What is the name of your town and why do your people ring bells on the approach of darkness?" asked Oni.

"People call this place Ajo, but hurry up, we must get indoors. I will explain the bells to you when we are inside," replied the old man.

When they reached the old man's house, they found his people waiting anxiously for him at the door. The bells had now stopped ringing and they were hurried inside and the door was securely fastened.

"Now," said the old man, "sit down and eat with us and I will explain. For many years now we, the people of Ajo, have been troubled by the nightly arrival of a giant eagle. We call it Anodo. It always appears on the approach of darkness and stays until the approach of dawn. Anybody who is unfortunate enough to be out of doors at the time of its appearance is sure to be killed by it. You were very fortunate, young man, to reach Ajo before darkness. Our king has ordered the ringing of bells to warn the people to return to their homes and lock the doors. None of us knows where the eagle comes from or where it goes when it leaves us at dawn. It is a terrible curse, and in the past it has killed many of our people."

The old man had hardly finished speaking when Oni heard the sound of great wings flapping over the house. It sounded like a great wind, and the windows and doors shook in their frames.

"It must be a very great bird," remarked Oni. After Oni had fed, the old man gave him a mat and a cloth and he lay down to sleep in the corner of the room. Sleep would not come to Oni, however, for he heard the constant noise of the great eagle's wings as it flew to and fro over Ajo.

When morning had come and the eagle had departed, Oni thanked the old man for his kindness and set out to find the king of Ajo and to ask for an audience.[1] It was granted.

"My name is Oni and I am a stranger to your town. I have come to offer my services in helping to rid this town of the eagle Anodo," said Oni.

"And what makes you think you will succeed where so many others have tried and failed?" asked the king.

"I have certain powers and juju,"[2] said Oni.

"So had the others. One by one all my hunters have tried and have been killed or carried off by Anodo. Strangers have come from time to time to offer their services, but they too have perished. It is some time now since anybody has tried to kill Anodo, and I have issued orders to my remaining hunters not to try, as enough of them have been killed already," said the king.

"Have you ever offered a reward to anybody who could succeed in killing the bird?" asked Oni.

"Indeed, yes. The man who succeeds will have half my kingdom. I made that offer long ago," replied the king.

"Then I will try tonight," answered Oni, and he paid his respects to the king and departed.

Oni returned to the old man's house and told him what had happened and of his intention to challenge Anodo. The old man was very

---

1. **audience:** here, formal interview with a person of high rank.
2. **juju:** magic charms used by some West African tribes; the magic of such charms.

frightened and implored him to give up the idea, for he would only perish and perhaps all those in the house too. But Oni was not frightened. He took his bow and arrows and knives and examined them carefully.

It seemed ages to Oni before he heard the bells ringing. Never had he known a longer day in his life. The old man was uneasy and his people were almost hostile towards Oni. When they heard the bells ringing at last, they lost no time in fastening the doors and windows and ordered Oni to lie down on his mat and keep quiet.

Presently they heard the noise of a great wind, which heralded the approach of Anodo. Soon the great wings were above the house. Oni waited till the great bird was overhead and then he commenced to sing:

> Tonight Oni will be at war with Anodo,
> The eagle whose talons are sharper than knives,
> For now the knives of nature and man will meet.
> Oni is invincible; his knife is sharp.

Anodo heard the challenge as he hovered over the house, and circling slowly round, he came back and sang:

> Ah, fortune, I have found a victim tonight,
> I have lived many months without a kill,
> Will the singer come out and feel the sharpness
> Of my talons and of my beak? It will take me
> A moment to tear him to pieces. Come out.

All the people in the house were terrified. They seized Oni and threw him out of the house, fearing the vengeance of Anodo on them all.

As they threw Oni out into the road, Anodo swooped down and, seizing him in his talons, drew him upwards. Oni slashed the eagle in the chest with his knife and the eagle dropped him with a scream. Oni fell to the ground,

dazed. He picked himself up as the huge bird descended once again. He had time to use his bow and discharge an arrow into Anodo before the wounded bird beat him to the ground with his great wings and pecked him severely. Again Oni's knife tore at the eagle, and he buried it twice in Anodo. Slowly the eagle beat his great wings and rose slowly into the air; then he hovered for a last terrible dive on Oni. Oni watched him and, putting an arrow in his bow, took aim. The great bird hovered; then with a terrible noise he tore down on the boy, gathering speed as he came. There was a great roar of wind as he came down. Oni discharged a second arrow, then another and another in quick succession, but still the bird came on. A moment later it had hit Oni and knocked him over. The boy rolled over, a thousand lights dancing before his eyes; then all went blank, and he felt himself sinking down and down into a bottomless pit. He was knocked unconscious and had not seen that the great bird was already dead before it struck him. Its great wings swept the boy to one side, and it plunged on into a cotton tree, which snapped like a twig and came crashing down to bury the eagle and Oni under a mass of leaves.

When Oni recovered, he felt very weak, and it was all he could do to free himself from the great wing of the dead Anodo and the cotton tree leaves. As he struggled, one of his magic boots came off and remained stuck beneath the dead bird. He was very weak and with great difficulty staggered along till he reached the edge of the river; then Oni fainted again.

Early next morning the people came out to see the dead Anodo lying in the broken cotton

---

**WORDS TO OWN**

**implored** (im·plôrd′) v.: asked or begged.
**commenced** (kə·menst′) v.: began.
**invincible** (in·vin′sə·bəl) adj.: unbeatable.
**hovered** (huv′ərd) v.: hung in the air.

---

## Spreading the Word

Since the beginning of time, folks have always wanted to spread the word. The ones who can spread the word the most effectively have the ability to "talk dat talk" and "walk dat walk." In other words, they can grab the imagination of the listener and hold on to it for as long as they like, conjuring up images of the good and the bad, the weak and the strong, and the trickster and the fool. They have the ability to make you laugh until you cry, cry until you laugh, stand up and shout, or stare in amazement at their gestures and characterizations.

In the African American culture, past and present, these folks have gone by many names. Today they are called preachers, healers, teachers, comedians, blues singers, poets, dancers, rappers, liars, painters, and historians. In a performance all storytellers will use whatever it takes to get the story across. To hear them is to hear the drum, the heartbeat of Africa. To see them tell the story is to experience the highlights of African ritual, at its best, a total theatrical performance.

—Linda Goss and Marian E. Barnes
(Linda Goss tells "The Frog Who Wanted to Be a Singer" on page 172.)

Epa cult mask.

Founders Society Purchase, Friends of African Art Fund. Photograph © 1995 The Detroit Institute of Arts.

tree. There was great rejoicing and drumming and the king soon appeared with his chiefs to view the wonderful sight. "Who is the great man who killed Anodo?" he asked. One of his hunters stepped forward and, prostrating[3]

3. **prostrating** (präs′trāt′iŋ): throwing oneself on the ground to show humility and submission; a traditional gesture of respect toward rulers in many cultures.

himself on the ground, claimed that he was responsible for the deed.

"Then you will be rewarded generously, for I have promised to give half my kingdom to the man who killed Anodo and it is yours," replied the king.

There was great rejoicing and dancing and the hunter was carried to the king's palace and feasted. A very bedraggled figure then appeared; his clothes were torn and one of his boots was missing. It was Oni.

"Ah," said the king, "here is the stranger who calls himself Oni and who came yesterday to announce his intention of killing the eagle. You come too late, my friend, I fear."

"I killed Anodo. This man is an <u>impostor</u> and a liar," said Oni.

There was whispering between the king and his chiefs. At last he said, "Very well, you claim to have killed Anodo. What proof have you got to offer?"

"You see my condition," replied Oni, "but if you require further proof, send your men out to clear away the dead eagle and the broken cotton tree. Somewhere underneath you will find one of my boots."

The king ordered his men to go at once and search for the boot. After some little time the men returned. They carried Oni's magic boot. "We found it underneath the dead eagle's wing," they announced to the king.

"Now if you are still undecided and disbelieve my story, will you ask everybody to try on the boot and see if it fits," said Oni.

The king ordered everybody to try to see if they could fit the boot to their feet. Strange to relate, although it looked a perfectly normal boot, nobody could manage to put it on. When they had all tried without success, the boot was placed before the king and Oni stepped forward and said:

Boot from Heaven—boot from Heaven,
Go on to your master's foot.

Immediately, the boot started to move from before the king and fitted itself onto Oni's foot of its own accord. The people and the king were convinced of the truth of Oni's claims and marveled greatly and were very delighted and grateful for his brave deed. The dishonest hunter was taken out and executed, and Oni received the promised reward.

That night, for the first time for many years, the bells of Ajo did not sound the curfew. Instead, the streets were full of happy, dancing people.

---

## WORDS TO OWN

**impostor** (im·päs′tər) *n.*: person who pretends to be someone or something that he or she is not.

---

## MEET THE WRITER

### At Home in Two Worlds

**Abayomi Fuja**, a Yoruban, was born in Nigeria. When he was growing up, Fuja was taught by British missionaries, so he learned English and studied European stories at school. As an adult he decided to celebrate his Yoruban heritage by collecting the traditional folk tales of his people. He devoted six years to recording tales like "Oni and the Great Bird." Though written in English, they remain true to the style and spirit of the original Yoruban folk tales. By retelling these traditional African stories in English, Fuja brings together the two worlds in which he grew up.

### More Tales from the Yoruba

If you liked "Oni and the Great Bird," you might want to explore the other stories in *Fourteen Hundred Cowries* (Oxford University Press), the book it's taken from. (A cowrie is a glossy shell that the Yoruba use to signal certain ideas. For instance, two shells placed together means friendship; two shells placed apart means hostility.)

# MAKING MEANINGS

## First Thoughts

1. Do you think Oni is a hero? Be sure to check your Quickwrite notes.

## Shaping Interpretations

2. Look back at Oni's song to Anodo before the fight (page 632). What do you think the song shows about Oni's **character**?

3. The magic boots set Oni apart, making him "strange" and "different." What lesson might this tale teach Yoruban children about how to behave toward people who are different from them?

4. Think about what happened to the hunter who tried to take credit for killing Anodo. What does his fate tell you about the beliefs of the Yoruba?

5. What **motifs** does "Oni and the Great Bird" share with the Cinderella stories?

---

### Reading Check

a. Why must Oni leave his village?

b. How does the king of Ajo react to Oni's offer to fight Anodo?

c. What happens when Oni fights Anodo?

d. How does Oni prove that the hunter who claims to have killed Anodo is an impostor?

## Extending the Text

6. In this story, Oni saves the people from the threat of a giant eagle. If the story were set in modern times, what dangerous force might Oni have to save the people from?

7. Oni was an outsider—even among his own people. Do you think that heroes in real life are usually outsiders, or are they usually part of the group? Give examples to support your point of view.

## Challenging the Text

8. At the beginning of the story, you learn that Oni cannot be killed. Does this ruin the suspense of the story? Why or why not?

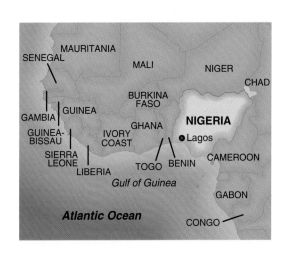

# CHOICES: Building Your Portfolio

## Writer's Notebook

### 1. Collecting Ideas for an Informative Report

Like most folk tales from other cultures, the Yoruban tale "Oni and the Great Bird" suggests many topics for further investigation. Choose one of the following topics about Yoruban culture or another topic that your teacher approves:

- Yoruban art   • Yoruban music   • Yoruban literature
- women's roles in Yoruban culture
- men's roles in Yoruban culture

Research your topic, and write down the four most interesting facts you learn about it.

> Women in Yoruban culture
> —do not farm
> —control sale of goods in marketplace
> —weave baskets
> —spin and dye cotton

## Creative Writing

### 2. Homemade Hero

Using "Oni and the Great Bird" as a model, write your own folk tale about a superhero. First, decide **where** and **when** your story will take place. Second, think about your **characters.** What human and superhuman qualities does the **hero** have? Next, decide what **conflict,** or problem, your hero will face. Finally, decide how the hero will solve the problem and bring the story to an end. You can use a chart like the one below to **outline** your story.

## Writing a Summary

### 3. Summing Up Oni

Writing a **summary** is a way to sum up the most important events of a story. Refer to the notes you took while you read, and write a summary of the story. Tell about each major event in a complete sentence. Use words like *then, after,* and *as a result* to indicate when and where events happened.

## Art/Design

### 4. Judge a Book by Its Cover

Imagine that you are creating a picture-book version of this story. Design a book jacket for the story. Be sure your design displays the title and the name of the reteller in an appealing script or typeface.

|  | "Oni and the Great Bird" | My Folk Tale |
|---|---|---|
| setting | Yoruban village |  |
| hero | Oni: Because of magic boots, he can't be killed. |  |
| conflict, or problem | Giant eagle threatens town. |  |
| conclusion | Oni kills eagle, saves town. |  |

# GRAMMAR LINK  MINI-LESSON

## They're, Their, There

**Language Handbook HELP**

*See Personal Pronouns, pages 710 and 734; Apostrophes, page 777.*

**Technology HELP**

*See* Language Workshop CD-ROM. *Key word entry: their, they're, there.*

Many words in English sound like other words but have very different meanings and functions. Three words often confused are *they're, their,* and *there:*

**they're:** a contraction of "they are."

**their:** a personal possessive pronoun.

**there:** a word that means "at that place" or that begins a sentence such as "There was once a strange boy called Oni who was born wearing a pair of boots."

EXAMPLES

When the people of the town hear the bells, they're very frightened. [They are very frightened.]

" 'Our king has ordered the ringing of bells to warn the people to return to their homes and lock the doors.' " [*Their* is a possessive pronoun modifying *homes.*]

Tonight there will be much celebrating in the town.

When you find one of these confusing words in your writing, ask yourself:

**1.** Can I substitute the words *they are?* If so, *they're* is OK.

**2.** Does the word answer the question *whose?* If so, *their* is OK.

### Try It Out

Be a test maker. Write five sentences that ask for a choice between *there, their,* and *they're.* Exchange tests with a partner, and then grade your partner's paper. Does making a test on the *there/their/they're* problem help you see the differences between the words?

---

# VOCABULARY  HOW TO OWN A WORD

**WORD BANK**

implored
commenced
invincible
hovered
impostor

## Vocabulary for the Workplace: Lights, Action, Script

Imagine that you work for an animation production company that is launching a cartoon about a new superhero. Use the words in the Word Bank to write a summary of the cartoon superhero's first adventure. (You may make the verbs any tense you wish.)

(Left) Spiderman.
(Right) Superman.

# *Before You Read*

## MASTER FROG

### Make the Connection

**Beauty Is Only
Skin Deep**

The main character of this Vietnamese folk tale is just like other boys except for his unusual appearance. People who judge him only by his looks are missing all the special qualities and talents that lie beneath the surface.

### Quickwrite

There's more to all of us than what appears on the surface. What are your special qualities and talents? List some of the things you're good at, and then write a few sentences about the one that is your favorite.

### Elements of Literature

**Metamorphosis: Changing Skins**

When you talk about this story, you'll probably use the word *metamorphosis.* **Metamorphosis** means a marvelous transformation, or change, from one shape to another. You might already know about metamorphosis from ancient myths and fairy tales. In many folk tales a warty frog with bulgy eyes becomes a handsome prince when someone else loves it, and the lovers usually live happily ever after. In this story, however, the metamorphosis has an unusual twist.

> **A** **metamorphosis** is a marvelous change from one shape or form to another one.
>
> *For more on Metamorphosis, see the Handbook of Literary Terms.*

### Reading Skills and Strategies

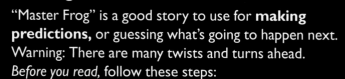

**Making Predictions:
Guessing What's Ahead**

"Master Frog" is a good story to use for **making predictions,** or guessing what's going to happen next. Warning: There are many twists and turns ahead. *Before you read,* follow these steps:

* Preview the quotations on pages 639–643.
* Remember what you've learned about **metamorphosis.**
* Think about your prior experience with fairy tales.
* Write a sentence predicting what will happen in this story.

*While you read,* follow these steps:

* Modify your original prediction.
* Write a new prediction before you begin each page.

Did you guess correctly—or were you totally surprised?

One of a pair of belt buckles. Eastern Inner Mongolia.
**Asian Art Museum of San Francisco, The Avery Brundage Collection, B60B1082/1083.**

# Master Frog

*Vietnamese, retold by*
**Lynette Dyer Vuong**

*Except for his strange appearance, Master Frog was really quite an ordinary boy . . .*

Giang Dung[1] was a plain girl, so plain in fact that all the townspeople marveled when her parents finally found her a husband. Then they nodded their heads knowingly and whispered to one another that the young man must have been after her father's money. He had plenty of it, it was true, and Giang Dung was his only child. The day of the wedding came and passed, and the people found more interesting things to gossip about until a few months later, when Giang Dung's husband died.

1. **Giang Dung** (zäng′ zo͞om′): Vietnamese for "pretty face," an ironic name for a plain girl.

"It's fortunate that she's expecting a child," one person said, and the rest agreed. "At least she'll have someone to look after her in her old age. It's certain she'll never find anyone else to marry her."

But when the child was born, instead of being a boy to carry on her husband's name or at least a girl to give her some comfort and companionship, it was only a frog. And the people's tongues wagged again until they tired of the subject. "What would you expect? Giang Dung almost looks like a frog herself, she's so ugly."

Poor Giang Dung cried for days until she had no tears left. Then she resigned herself to her fate and determined to raise the frog as well as she could. If she was being punished for some unknown evil she had committed, she would have to make the best of it and serve her sentence. But on the other hand, Heaven sometimes worked in mysterious ways, and it was just possible that some great destiny lay ahead for her son.

But as the years passed, Giang Dung forgot both of these theories. Except for his strange appearance, Master Frog was really quite an ordinary boy—now mischievous, now helpful, but always affectionate. He followed her around the house as she went about her daily tasks, helping her to care for the silkworms.[2] He gathered mulberry leaves for her to chop and place in their trays; he watched them as they began to spin their cocoons, fascinated at the way they swung their heads down and round and then up again to surround themselves with the fine strands. He often perched beside her as she sat at the loom and thought it great fun to take the shuttle in his mouth and wriggle his small body in and out among the warp threads. Sometimes, as she

was cooking, he would hop up on the stove to stir the soup, or if he was sure she was not watching him, to snap up some tasty tidbit with his long, sticky tongue. But, like other children, he was often bored with being indoors and went out to play hide-and-seek and hopscotch with the boys of the neighborhood. All in all, he was both a good-natured and an intelligent little fellow, and his mother decided at last that something must be done about his education.

"What would you expect? Giang Dung almost looks like a frog herself, she's so ugly."

"A frog? In my class?" the teacher demanded when Giang Dung brought him to the school. "Impossible! I would be the laughingstock of the town."

"Then at least let him sit at the back and listen," she pleaded with him. "I promise you he won't cause you any trouble."

As the weeks went by, Master Frog proved himself such a model student that at last the teacher moved him up to the head of the class and often admonished the others to follow his

---

2. **silkworms:** moth caterpillars that produce cocoons of silk fiber. Some silkworms are grown and cultivated as the source of silk.

**WORDS TO OWN**
admonished (ad·män′isht) v.: warned or urged.

example. At first he had tried to grasp the brush with his front feet but later found that he could form more graceful characters if he held it in his mouth. Generally he was the first to commit a passage to memory, and if none of the others could correctly interpret a line of the reading, the teacher would call on Master Frog. Finally, Master Frog completed his education and grew to young froghood.

"It's time to think of learning some trade," Giang Dung suggested to him one day. "Tomorrow I will go to town and talk to some of the craftsmen. Perhaps one of them would be willing to take you on as an apprentice."

But Master Frog shook his head. "Mother, first I would like to get married."

"G . . . get married!" she stammered, almost unable to believe her ears. "I . . . is there any particular girl you have in mind?"

"Yes, Mother. Princess Kien Tien,[3] the king's youngest daughter."

Giang Dung drew back in alarm. "Son, you must be out of your mind! How could you ever hope to marry the king's daughter?"

"Nevertheless I shall marry her." Master Frog planted all four feet on the table in a stance of determination. "Tomorrow I shall go to the king to ask for her hand."

All Giang Dung's protests—all her <u>entreaties</u>—were in vain. Master Frog had made up his mind, and nothing could change it. And so the next morning he and Giang Dung set off for the palace.

Giang Dung set him down as they entered the audience hall, and he hopped straight up to the king, bowing respectfully as he neared the throne. The king stared at him in astonishment as he made his request and then burst out laughing.

"So you want to marry my daughter," he said. "Well, I have three daughters. Which one is it you want? But don't be in a hurry to make up

your mind." His lips twisted in amusement as he motioned to one of the courtiers.[4] "Bring their royal highnesses here."

"Come here, my dears," he beckoned to them as they entered the hall. "A suitor has presented himself to request the hand of one of you." With a grand sweep of his forearm he indicated Master Frog at the foot of the throne. "He has not yet told me the extent of his kingdom or the number of vassals[5] who pay him tribute, but does he not have a noble air?" He turned back to Master Frog. "Allow me to introduce my daughters to your highness: Kim Chau,"[6] he pointed to the first, who cast a contemptuous glance in Master Frog's direction, then gave her head such a violent toss that one of her pearl hairpins slipped from its place and fell to the floor; "Bich Ngoc,"[7] he indicated the second, who made a face at him and stuck out her tongue; "and Kien Tien," he presented the last of the three, who had stood the whole time, her hands folded in her long sleeves and her eyes on the floor. "Now would you please tell me which of the three pleases you?"

Kim Chau's chin rose a trifle higher. "I won't marry him, Father."

"I'll kill myself if you force me to marry him," Bich Ngoc declared with a stamp of her foot.

"Your Majesty," Master Frog interrupted them, "it is Kien Tien whose hand I have come to seek."

"Enough of this <u>charade</u>." The king's face had grown angry. "We have carried this joke far enough." He motioned to the guards. "Take this

---

3. **Kien Tien** (kē·'n′ tē·en′).

4. **courtiers** (kôrt′ē·ərz): royal attendants.
5. **vassals**: subjects.
6. **Kim Chau** (kim′ chō′): *Kim* is Vietnamese for "gold" and *chau* for "pearl or precious stone."
7. **Bich Ngoc** (bik′ näp′): *Ngoc* is Vietnamese for "emerald."

---

**WORDS TO OWN**

**entreaties** (en·trēt′ēz) *n.:* earnest requests.
**charade** (shə·rād′) *n.:* obvious pretense or act.

---

presumptuous creature out of my sight at once and execute him."

As the king finished speaking, Master Frog croaked in a loud voice. Suddenly the building began to shake as lightning flashed and thunder roared. On all sides the doors flew open, and the guards cowered in terror as wild beasts of every description burst into the hall. Elephants trumpeted as they stampeded in, tigers roared, leopards and panthers growled as they sprang from one corner to another.

"A few minutes ago Your Majesty inquired about my vassals," Master Frog's croak rose above the uproar. "They have come. I will leave them here to answer any questions you may have about the extent of my kingdom. Until we meet again, Your Majesty." Master Frog turned and hopped toward the exit.

"Wait! Wait!" the king shouted after him as a tiger leapt over his throne, pursuing a panther in a game of tag. "You can't leave us like this, surrounded by all these wild beasts." But Master Frog only hopped over their backs, one after another, as he made his way to the door. "Daughters, what shall we do?"

"I wouldn't marry a frog if he were the son of Jade Emperor!" Kim Chau's voice was as haughty as ever, though she winced[8] as a leopard brushed past her.

Bich Ngoc covered her face as a bear lumbered toward her. "I'd rather be torn limb from limb!" she screeched.

"Father, I'll marry him." Kien Tien squeezed between two elephants to the king's side. "It's not right for us to think only of ourselves when the whole kingdom may be in danger. And the frog cannot be such a bad sort. He's obviously an individual of great power, yet he does not appear to be cruel. With all these beasts surrounding us, not one of us has been harmed."

As she finished speaking, the uproar ceased, and one by one the beasts filed from the hall.

Master Frog stood alone before the king.

"I will send the engagement gifts tomorrow," he said as he, too, turned and hopped from the room.

A few days later the wedding was celebrated with great pomp and ceremony. Kings and dignitaries[9] of all the surrounding countries came to pay their respects, and no one dared to laugh at Master Frog or the princess, for the tales of his great power had spread far and wide.

During the weeks that followed, Master Frog and Kien Tien lived together happily as the two came to understand each other better and to care for each other more deeply. In spite of his ugliness, Kien Tien found him such an intelligent and such a pleasant companion that as the days went by, she grew genuinely fond of him. Then one morning she awoke to find the frog lying dead on the pillow beside her.

With a cry she lifted her husband's body to her lips, kissing it again and again as her tears wet the mottled[10] green skin. Someone called her name, and she looked up to see a handsome young man standing next to the bed, his arms outstretched as if to embrace her.

She backed away from him, crying out in alarm. "How dare you come here?" she demanded. "Can't you see my husband is dead and I am mourning him?" Suddenly her eyes narrowed. "Or was it you who killed him, you miserable creature!" She burst into fresh tears. "You shall surely die for your crime!"

The man smiled. "No, Kien Tien. I am Master Frog. What you are holding there is only my skin, which I shed during the night." He sat down beside her. "I am a fairy, a heavenly mandarin,[11] one of the sons of Jade Emperor. I was

9. **dignitaries:** people holding high, dignified positions.
10. **mottled** (mät′'ld): spotted or streaked.
11. **mandarin:** member of any powerful group.

---

**WORDS TO OWN**

**presumptuous** (prē·zump′chōō·əs) *adj.*: too bold; arrogant.

**cowered** (kou′ərd) *v.*: crouched and trembled in fear.

---

8. **winced** (winst): drew back in fear, making a face.

bored with the life in Fairyland and wanted to seek adventure in the world below. But when I asked my father's permission, he was angry with me. He said he would grant my request but that I must be born as a frog. Only if I could succeed in that form would I be able to resume my true shape. Now I have proved myself and am allowed to shed the frog's skin. But you must put the skin away carefully where no harm can come to it because if it should ever be destroyed, I would have to return immediately to Jade Emperor's palace."

"If she was dumb enough to marry a frog, he should have stayed a frog."

Overjoyed at her good fortune, Kien Tien did as he said. The days that followed were full of joy for the newlyweds. The king was filled with pride at the handsomeness and intelligence of his son-in-law, which matched so well the beauty and talent of his youngest daughter. He took them wherever he went to show them off. On every trip that he made to the surrounding countries, they accompanied him in his golden palanquin,[12] and when he rode

12. **palanquin** (pal′ən·kēn′): covered structure enclosing a couch. A palanquin is carried by long poles resting on the shoulders of two or more men.

through the streets of the capital, they sat beside him on the back of his white elephant, cheered by all who watched them pass.

"Why didn't he tell us who he was in the first place?" Kim Chau grumbled to her sister as they watched the parade from the palace balcony. "Was it fair to come in that ugly old frog skin and then change into a handsome prince after he'd married Kien Tien?"

"If she was dumb enough to marry a frog, he should have stayed a frog," Bich Ngoc grunted in agreement.

"He should be punished for his deception. What right did he have to ask for Kien Tien anyway? I'm the oldest."

"Kien Tien says he's a son of Jade Emperor, but I don't believe it. He's probably nothing but an ordinary frog. Why don't we see if we can find his skin and have a look at it?"

The sisters went to Kien Tien's room, searching through chest after chest and shelf after shelf till at last, among a pile of her most precious silks, they found what they were looking for.

"She hid it well enough," Kim Chau sniffed. "No wonder. It's an ugly old thing, isn't it?"

Bich Ngoc reached for it, turning it over in her hands. "It certainly is. And just as I thought, nothing but an ordinary frog skin." She squinted her eyes thoughtfully. "Who knows but what, if we caught a couple of frogs for ourselves, they might shed their skins for us? There might be a handsome prince in any one of them if we could just get him to come out." She stuffed Master Frog's skin into her sash as the two of them hurried out to the pond.

Day by day Kim Chau and Bich Ngoc watched their chosen frogs, waiting for the hoped-for transformation. They fed them on the most delicious foods; petted them; cooed endearments and whispered promises of fame, fortune, and riches in their ears. And each night they gently laid them on the pillow next to them, certain that the coming morning would bring the answer to their dreams. But nothing happened; both frogs remained as they were when they had fished them from the pond.

"There has to be a prince in there!" Bich Ngoc cried one morning in exasperation. "And I'm not going to wait any longer to find him." She picked up a knife and began to skin the poor creature alive.

Kim Chau snatched up her own frog and followed her example. But before they were finished, it was plain that no prince was to be found. In disgust the sisters threw the corpses into the fireplace.

Bich Ngoc jerked Master Frog's skin from her belt. "I don't know what I'm still carrying this around for," she grunted as she tossed it into the fire.

Meanwhile in Kien Tien's room, she and Master Frog were just getting out of bed. Suddenly he gave a cry of pain.

"My chest, my arms, my legs are burning!" he cried. "My whole body is on fire."

As Kien Tien rushed to his side, he fell to the floor, writhing in agony. Moments later he lay lifeless in her arms. Kien Tien pressed him close to her, weeping bitterly.

"It must be because you burned his old frog skin," Kim Chau whispered to Bich Ngoc when they heard what had happened. "What are we going to do? Sooner or later she'll discover the skin is missing, and if she finds out we took it and tells Father . . ."

Bich Ngoc clapped her hand over her sister's mouth. "We aren't going to sit around and wait for that to happen!"

Together they went to Kien Tien's room, where she lay on the bed weeping. They sat down beside her, stroking her hair to comfort her.

"Come, little sister, it's a terrible tragedy, but you mustn't spend the whole day lying here crying." Bich Ngoc poured some tea from the teapot on the table, dropping a little sleeping powder into the cup as she carried it back to the bed. "Here, drink something warm. It'll make you feel better."

Kien Tien raised her head, sipping the hot liquid as Bich Ngoc held it to her lips. Then she lay down again and was soon fast asleep.

Quickly the sisters lifted her and carried her outside to the carriage. As fast as they could make the horses go, they rode out of town to the seaside. Then, making sure that no one was around, they shoved their sister out of the carriage, watching with satisfaction as she hit the surface of the water and sank beneath the waves. Then they rushed home to tell their father that Kien Tien had committed suicide.

"We tried to stop her," Bich Ngoc sobbed into her handkerchief. "But she wouldn't listen to us. She was so miserable at the thought of never seeing Master Frog again that she threw herself into the sea. The waves carried her away before we could call for help."

Suddenly gasps rose throughout the audience hall. Master Frog had entered the room.

He approached the throne, bowing respectfully. "Jade Emperor has allowed me to return to the earth to complete my lifetime," he told the king. "But why is everyone crying? What has happened?" He gazed from one person to another, seeking an answer.

"Dear brother-in-law, our sister is dead." Bich Ngoc wiped the tears from her eyes as she spoke. "She was so overcome with sorrow at losing you that she threw herself into the sea." She stepped closer to him, laying her hand on his arm. "I know what a shock it is for you. But Kim Chau and I will do everything we can to help. Either one of us would be willing to take our sister's place."

But Master Frog was already running toward the door. At his order a horse was saddled, and he leapt on its back, riding at top speed toward the sea. Fearlessly he dove in, letting his body sink to the bottom. Swiftly he ran across the ocean floor to the Crystal Palace and, bursting through the gates, prostrated himself before the Dragon King of the Waters.

The Dragon King gazed down at him kindly. "Stand up, nephew. What you are seeking may be behind you."

As Master Frog rose, a company of shrimps and turtles entered the hall. One of them bore Kien Tien in his arms.

"My soldiers have found your wife," the Dragon King told him. "I would have let her live here in my palace, but since you've come for her, you may take her home with you."

Master Frog rushed toward her joyfully. As he lifted her from the turtle-soldier's arms, she opened her eyes and smiled up at him. Then both of them fell at the Dragon King's feet to thank him for his mercy.

Master Frog led Kien Tien out of the Crystal Palace and up through the water to the shore, where his horse was waiting. Together they rode back to the palace.

Kim Chau glanced down from her balcony to see Master Frog reining his horse below. She drew back in alarm and called to her sister.

"We're done for," she trembled, grabbing Bich Ngoc's arm and pulling her after her. "Kien Tien will tell Father everything."

The two of them raced down the stairs and out a back way. "We'll hide in the forest," Bich Ngoc decided. No one will find us there."

And the two were never seen or heard of again. But as for Kien Tien and Master Frog, they lived happily ever after, loved and respected by all for their kind deeds. Before many days had passed, they had Giang Dung brought to the palace, where she lived in comfort and happiness to a ripe old age. In due time Master Frog became king and, with Kien Tien as his queen, ruled their people in peace and prosperity for many long years.

## MEET THE WRITER

### Taking a Chance on Love

**Lynette Dyer Vuong** (1938–    ) believes in love at first sight because that's what happened when she met a young Vietnamese man who was studying in the United States. Love led her to follow him back to Vietnam, marry him, and stay there with him for thirteen years—the country was then in the midst of the Vietnam War.

As Vuong learned Vietnamese, she began to follow another love—the world of folklore and fairy tales. She was amazed to discover that Vietnam has its own versions of five stories she loved as a child— "Cinderella," "Thumbelina," "The Frog Prince," "Rip Van Winkle," and "Goose Girl." She remembers:

66 Five familiar faces in an unfamiliar land; it is fascinating that similar ideas have arisen and then developed into different stories under the influence of two such diverse cultures as East and West. Perhaps it is a testimony to the fact that we are each uniquely individual, . . . yet bound together by a common humanity. 99

Vuong fled Vietnam with her husband and children in 1975. She continues to work on retelling the fairy tales she had grown to love.

### More Tales Linked by Common Humanity

If you'd like to read the other fairy tales Vuong discovered during her stay in Vietnam, look for her book *The Brocaded Slipper* (J. B. Lippincott).

# MAKING MEANINGS

## First Thoughts

1. Which scene in the story do you remember most vividly? Why?

## Shaping Interpretations

2. What is different about the ways Kien Tien, Kim Chau, and Bich Ngoc first react to Master Frog? What does this tell you about each girl's **character**?

3. What qualities does Kien Tien admire in Master Frog even before she realizes that he is a prince?

4. How do Kim Chau's and Bich Ngoc's feelings about Master Frog change after his **metamorphosis**? What does their sudden change of heart tell you about them?

5. Earlier (see page 607) you filled in a chart with the fairy tale **motifs** you found in three Cinderella stories. Which motifs do you see in Master Frog's story? Think of such motifs as the wicked stepmother, the cruel sisters, the handsome prince, special helpers, magical events, and wishes come true.

6. What lessons do you think this story teaches?

**Reading Check**

Use a story map like the one on page 627 to **summarize** what happens in this story. Be sure to compare your maps in class.

## Extending the Text

7. What other stories do you know in which a **metamorphosis** takes place? In each case, what causes the metamorphosis?

8. Kien Tien can look beyond Master Frog's appearance and see the person within, but her sisters can't. Do you think most people are like Kien Tien, or are they like her sisters? Why do you think so?

## Challenging the Text

9.  Think about the **predictions** you made as you read "Master Frog." Were you surprised by the twist this story takes at the end? Did you prefer any of your predicted endings?

# CHOICES: Building Your Portfolio

## Writer's Notebook

### 1. Collecting Ideas for an Informative Report

In your notes for the Quickwrite on page 638, you named at least one of your own special talents. Freewrite now for a few minutes about that talent. Think of what you would like to tell other people about your skill and why it is important to you.

**What I Do Well**

Swimming
—The best part is teaching swimming at the pool.
—I like to help kids get over their fear of putting their heads underwater. Here's how I do it:

## Creative Writing

### 2. Would You Rather Be a Bee?

What if the Jade Emperor had decided that his son should be born a spider? a bee? or a pig? Reread the beginning of "Master Frog," and look for details that describe froggy behavior. Then, choose another animal and write the beginning of a story about it. Use vivid details to describe the animal's behavior.

## Speaking and Listening

### 3. Frog on Tape

Record on tape a reading of this story. You'll have to figure out ways to create sound effects that will help your listeners imagine details from the story: Master Frog's hopping and croaking, the sounds of the wild animals that appear at the king's court, thunder, galloping horses, the ocean, and so on. Play your finished tape for the class.

## Comparing Themes

### 4. Books About Looks

As you probably know, "Master Frog" isn't the only story that shows how looks can be deceiving. Other folk tales with this theme include "Beauty and the Beast," "The Ugly Duckling," and "The Frog Prince." *The Snow Goose,* by Paul Gallico, is a modern novel with the same theme. Read one of these works, and write a report comparing and contrasting its characters, conflicts, and theme with those of "Master Frog."

From *Beauty and the Beast* (1991).
© Disney Enterprises, Inc./Photofest.

# LANGUAGE LINK   MINI-LESSON

## Style: Using Specific Words

No two words have exactly the same meaning. Some words, like *sit*, have a general meaning but do not paint a vivid picture. Other words, like *perch* or *settle*, describe specific kinds of sitting. Each paints a different picture.

The author of "Master Frog" helps us imagine the creature's froggy behavior by using specific words to describe him. For example, she says that he *perched* beside his mother as she sat at the loom and would *wriggle* his body in and out of the threads on the loom.

B.C.     By permission of Johnny Hart and Creators Syndicate, Inc.

### Try It Out

➤ Rewrite the following sentences, replacing the underlined words with more exact ones. Be sure to compare your revisions in class.

1. Kien Tien's tears wet the <u>greenish</u> skin of her dead husband's body.

2. When Master Frog said he wanted to marry the king's daughter, the king <u>looked at</u> him.

3. When Master Frog croaked, tigers, leopards, and panthers <u>came into</u> the room.

➤ To make sure your writing helps readers "see" exactly what you mean, ask a classmate to read a piece of your writing and point out any parts that could be improved by using more specific words.

# VOCABULARY   HOW TO OWN A WORD

**WORD BANK**
*admonished*
*entreaties*
*charade*
*presumptuous*
*cowered*

## Vocabulary for Hard Times

1. Use two words from the Word Bank to write a statement about a student who's been grounded for two weeks.
2. Use three words from the Word Bank to write a few sentences urging students to challenge an unfair rule.

# Before You Read

## SEALSKIN, SOULSKIN

## Make the Connection

### Talk to the Animals

Have you ever looked into an animal's eyes and wanted to talk to it? Have you ever felt that an animal understood you when no one else did? If the answer is yes, you're not alone. Part of the reason folk tales are so popular is that in these simple stories, people and animals often share relationships in which they communicate complex feelings and thoughts.

## Quickwrite

If you could have a conversation with an animal, what animal would you pick? What wisdom could you gain from such a conversation? Think about the characteristics of different kinds of animals before answering this question. Then, write down what kind of animal you wish to communicate with and what you think you would learn from it.

## Elements of Literature

### The Fantastic

Many folk tales contain elements of **fantasy**. That is, things happen in them that could not happen in real life, which is governed by the laws of nature. As you read "Sealskin, Soulskin," notice how the tale blends realistic descriptions of human conflicts with events that are pure fantasy.

# Sealskin, Soulskin

*Inuit, retold by*
**Clarissa Pinkola Estés**

## "I cannot be wife, for I am of the other . . ."

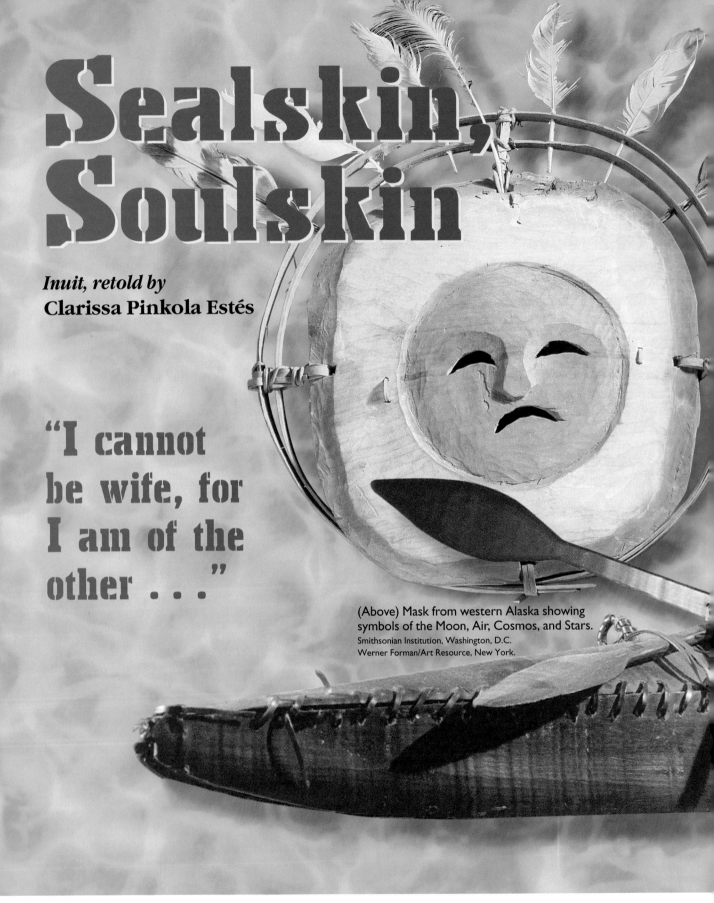

(Above) Mask from western Alaska showing symbols of the Moon, Air, Cosmos, and Stars.
Smithsonian Institution, Washington, D.C.
Werner Forman/Art Resource, New York.

**D**uring a time that once was, is now gone forever, and will come back again soon, there is day after day of white sky, white snow . . . and all the tiny specks in the distance are people or dogs or bear.

Here, nothing <u>thrives</u> for the asking. The winds blow hard so the people have come to wear their parkas and *mamleks*, boots, sideways on purpose now. Here, words freeze in the open air, and whole sentences must be broken from the speaker's lips and thawed at the fire so people can see what has been said. Here, the people live in the white

---

**WORDS TO OWN**
**thrives** (thrīvz) *v.*: prospers or grows well.

---

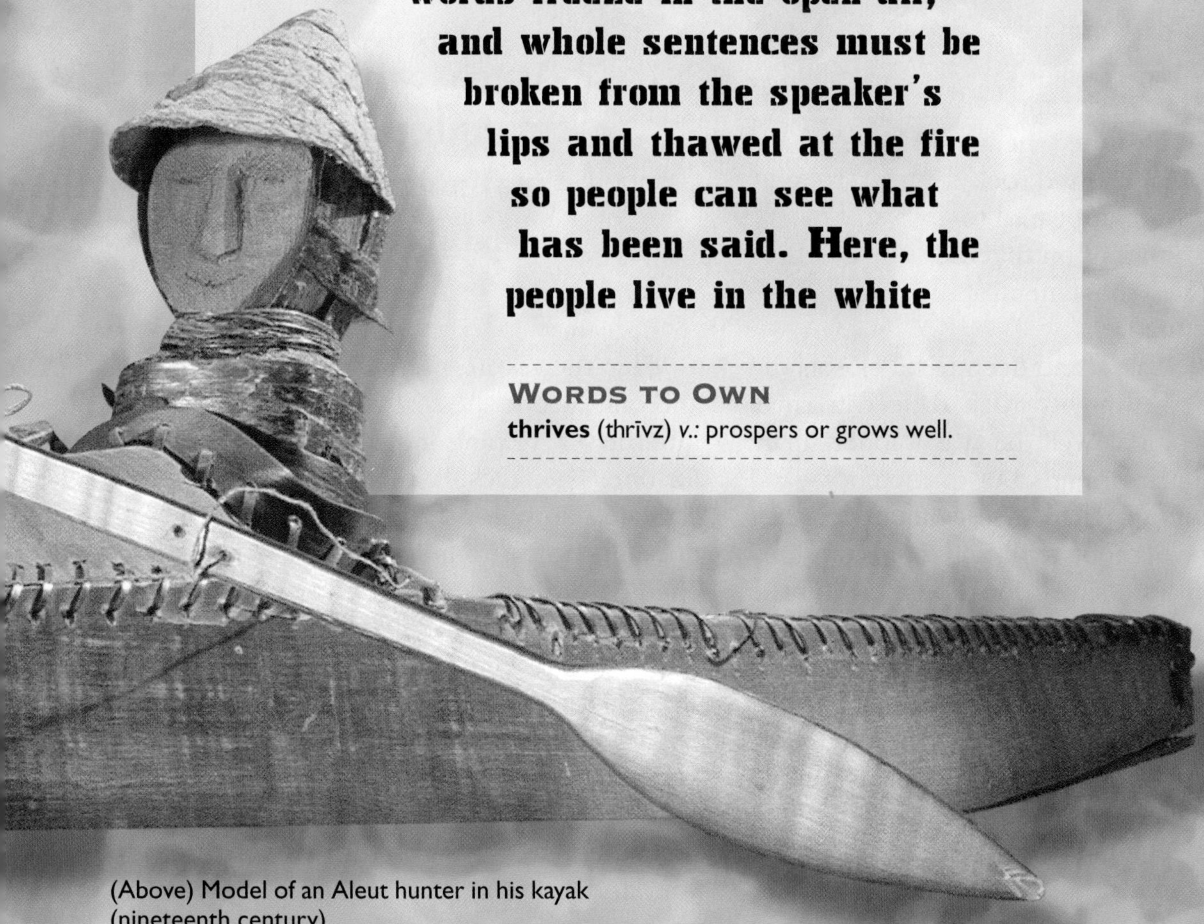

(Above) Model of an Aleut hunter in his kayak (nineteenth century).
Werner Forman/Art Resource, New York.

and abundant hair of old Annuluk, the old grandmother, the old sorceress who is Earth herself. And it was in this land that there lived a man . . . a man so lonely that over the years, tears had carved great chasms[1] into his cheeks.

He tried to smile and be happy. He hunted. He trapped and he slept well. But he wished for human company. Sometimes out in the shallows in his kayak when a seal came near, he remembered the old stories about how seals were once human, and the only reminder of that time is their eyes, which are capable of portraying those looks, those wise and wild and loving looks. And sometimes then he felt such a pang of loneliness that tears coursed down the well-used cracks in his face.

One night he hunted past dark but found nothing. As the moon rose in the sky and the ice floes glistened, he came to a great spotted rock in the sea, and it appeared to his keen eye that upon that old rock there was movement of the most graceful kind.

He paddled slow and deep to be closer, and there atop the mighty rock danced a small group of women. Well, he was a lonely man, with no human friends but in memory—and he stayed and watched. The women were like beings made of moon milk, and their skin shimmered with little silver dots like those on the salmon in springtime, and the women's feet and hands were long and graceful.

So beautiful were they that the man sat stunned in his boat, the water lapping, taking him closer and closer to the rock. He could hear the magnificent women laughing . . . at least they seemed to laugh, or was it the water laughing at the edge of the rock? The man was confused, for he was so dazzled. But somehow the loneliness that had weighed on his chest like wet hide was lifted away, and almost without thinking, as though he were meant to, he jumped up onto the rock and stole one of the sealskins laying there. He hid behind an outcropping and he pushed the sealskin into his *qutnguq*, parka.

Soon, one of the women called in a voice that was the most beautiful he'd ever heard . . . like the whales calling at dawn . . . or no, maybe it was more like the newborn wolves tumbling down in the spring . . . or, but, well no, it was something better than that, but it did not matter because . . . what were the women doing now?

## At least they seemed to laugh, or was it the water laughing at the edge of the rock?

Why, they were putting on their sealskins, and one by one the seal women were slipping into the sea, yelping and crying happily. Except for one. The tallest of them searched high and searched low for her sealskin, but it was nowhere to be found. The man felt emboldened—by what, he did not know. He stepped from the rock, appealing to her, "Woman . . . be . . . my . . . wife. I am . . . a lonely . . . man."

"Oh, I cannot be wife," she said, "for I am of the other, the ones who live *temequanek*, beneath."

"Be . . . my . . . wife," insisted the man. "In seven summers, I will return your sealskin to you, and you may stay or you may go as you wish."

---

1. **chasms** (kaz'əmz): deep cracks or gaps.

The young seal woman looked long into his face with eyes that but for her true origins seemed human. Reluctantly she said, "I will go with you. After seven summers, it shall be decided."

So in time they had a child, whom they named Ooruk. And the child was lithe and fat. In winter the mother told Ooruk tales of the creatures that lived beneath the sea while the father whittled a bear in whitestone with his long knife. When his mother carried the child Ooruk to bed, she pointed out through the smoke hole to the clouds and all their shapes. Except instead of recounting the shapes of raven and bear and wolf, she recounted the stories of walrus, whale, seal, and salmon . . . for those were the creatures she knew.

But as time went on, her flesh began to dry out. First it flaked, then it cracked. The skin of her eyelids began to peel. The hairs of her head began to drop to the ground. She became *naluaq*, palest white. Her plumpness began to wither. She tried to conceal her limp. Each day her eyes, without her willing it so, became more dull. She began to put out her hand in order to find her way, for her sight was darkening.

And so it went until one night when the child Ooruk was awakened by shouting and sat upright in his sleeping skins. He heard a roar like a bear that was his father berating his mother. He heard a crying like silver rung on stone that was his mother.

"You hid my sealskin seven long years ago, and now the eighth winter comes. I want what I am made of returned to me," cried the seal woman.

"And you, woman, would leave me if I gave it to you," boomed the husband.

"I do not know what I would do. I only know I must have what I belong to."

"And you would leave me wifeless, and the boy motherless. You are bad."

And with that her husband tore the hide flap of the door aside and disappeared into the night.

The boy loved his mother much. He feared losing her and so cried himself to sleep . . . only to be awakened by the wind. A strange wind . . . It seemed to call to him, "Oooruk, Ooorukkkk."

And out of bed he climbed, so hastily that he put his parka on upside down and pulled his mukluks[2] only halfway up. Hearing his name called over and over, he dashed out into the starry, starry night.

"Ooooooorukkk."

The child ran out to the cliff overlooking the water, and there, far out in the windy sea, was a huge shaggy silver seal. . . . Its head was enormous, its whiskers drooped to its chest, its eyes were deep yellow.

"Ooooooorukkk."

The boy scrambled down the cliff and stumbled at the bottom over a stone—no, a bundle—that had rolled out of a cleft[3] in the rock. The boy's hair lashed at his face like a thousand reins of ice.

"Ooooooorukkk."

The boy scratched open the bundle and shook it out—it was his mother's sealskin. Oh, and he could smell her all through it. And as he hugged the sealskin to his face and inhaled her scent, her soul slammed through him like a sudden summer wind.

"Ohhh," he cried with pain and joy, and lifted the skin again to his face and again her soul passed through his. "Ohhh," he cried again, for he was being filled with the unending love of his mother.

And the old silver seal way out . . . sank slowly beneath the water.

2. **mukluks** (muk′luks′): boots made of sealskin.
3. **cleft:** crack.

- - - - - - - - - - - - - - - - - - - - - - - - - - - - - -

## WORDS TO OWN

**lithe** (līth) *adj.*: flexible and graceful.
**berating** (be·rāt′iŋ) *v.* used as *adj.*: scolding.

- - - - - - - - - - - - - - - - - - - - - - - - - - - - - -

The boy climbed the cliff and ran toward home with the sealskin flying behind him, and into the house he fell. His mother swept him and the skin up and closed her eyes in gratitude for the safety of both.

She pulled on her sealskin. "Oh, mother, no!" cried the child.

She scooped up the child, tucked him under her arm, and half ran and half stumbled toward the roaring sea.

"Oh, mother, don't leave me!" Ooruk cried.

And at once you could tell she wanted to stay with her child, she *wanted* to, but something called her, something older than she, older than he, older than time.

"Oh, mother, no, no, no," cried the child. She turned to him with a look of dreadful love in her eyes. She took the boy's face in her hands, and breathed her sweet breath into his lungs, once, twice, three times. Then, with him under her arm like a precious bundle, she dove into the sea, down, and down, and down, and still deeper down, and the seal woman and her child breathed easily under water.

And they swam deep and strong till they entered the underwater cove of seals, where all manner of creatures were dining and singing, dancing and speaking, and the great silver seal that had called to Ooruk from the night sea embraced the child and called him grandson.

"How fare you up there, daughter?" asked the great silver seal.

The seal woman looked away and said, "I hurt a human . . . a man who gave his all to

Mother and child (1928). Nunivak, Alaska.
The Anchorage Museum of History and Art, Anchorage.

have me. But I cannot return to him, for I shall be a prisoner if I do."

"And the boy?" asked the old seal. "My grandchild?" He said it so proudly his voice shook.

"He must go back, father. He cannot stay. His time is not yet to be here with us." And she wept. And together they wept.

And so some days and nights passed, seven to be exact, during which time the luster came back to the seal woman's hair and eyes. She turned a beautiful dark color, her sight was restored, her body regained its plumpness, and she swam uncrippled. Yet it came time

> "He must go back, father. He cannot stay. His time is not yet to be here with us."

to return the boy to land. On that night, the old grandfather seal and the boy's beautiful mother swam with the child between them. Back they went, back up and up and up to the topside world. There they gently placed Ooruk on the stony shore in the moonlight.

His mother assured him, "I am always with you. Only touch what I have touched, my fire sticks, my *ulu*, knife, my stone carvings of otters and seal, and I will breathe into your lungs a wind for the singing of your songs."

The old silver seal and his daughter kissed the child many times. At last, they tore themselves away and swam out to sea, and with one last look at the boy, they disappeared beneath the waters. And Ooruk, because it was not his time, stayed.

As time went on, he grew to be a mighty drummer and singer and a maker of stories, and it was said this all came to be because as a child he had survived being carried out to sea by the great seal spirits. Now, in the gray mists of morning, sometimes he can still be seen, with his kayak <u>tethered</u>, kneeling upon a certain rock in the sea, seeming to speak to a certain female seal who often comes near the shore. Though many have tried to hunt her, time after time they have failed. She is known as *Tan qigcaq*, the bright one, the holy one, and it is said that though she be a seal, her eyes are capable of portraying those human looks, those wise and wild and loving looks.

Seal-oil lamp with a seal.
Werner Forman/Art Resource, New York.

### WORDS TO OWN

**tethered** (teth′ərd) v. used as *adj.*: tied.

## MEET THE WRITER

### Trading Stories

**Clarissa Pinkola Estés** feels a special bond with storytellers everywhere. Born to Mexican parents and then adopted by a family of Hungarians, she remembers the European and Mexican immigrant storytellers from her childhood. She says:

66 I've traded stories at kitchen tables and under grape arbors, in henhouses and dairy barns, and while patting tortillas, tracking wildlife, and sewing the millionth cross-stitch. 99

### More Stories to Trade

Some of the many stories Estés has written or collected were published in her best-selling book *Women Who Run with the Wolves* (Ballantine).

# Oral Storytelling: Making the Winter Shorter

Picture this: One night you pick up the remote to turn on the television to watch your favorite show. The set refuses to come on. You give it a little nudge. Suddenly the screen bursts open and out walk the actors—in person.

If you lived in an Inuit hamlet long ago, you would hear stories, lots of them, and the story-teller would be right in front of you, not on an electronic screen in a plastic box. You would be sitting spellbound along with other children and adults in a kashim, a big snow house, watching and listening to the performer. The only sounds in the room would be the howling of the winds outside and the whispers and shouts of the storyteller.

Like people everywhere, the Inuit used sto-ries for entertainment, but their stories also had another purpose. The children may not have realized that they were learning impor-tant lessons as they sat with their eyes glued to the performers who were shouting, making faces, and flinging their arms about. The lessons might have been about treating people kindly or showing respect for animals. These stories were not like the quiet bedtime stories you might remember from your childhood. They were often spine-tingling, roller-coaster, spinning-out-of-control tales.

Storytelling was especially popular in the wintertime. Imagine the sun disappearing totally from the end of November until the middle of January. Even then the sun barely emerges—turning the sky from inky black to gray. In the darkness, people gather at the kashim and enter through a short tunnel. There they beat the snow off their clothes with a stick. If they don't do this, they will have to sit all evening feeling the dampness of the melt-ing snow on their skin. A faint light comes through the windows, which are made of seal intestines.

Inuits in western Canada sometimes listened to stories after they had settled in their beds. The storyteller would put out the whale-oil lights and begin weaving tales about animals that act like people. Magic usually played a big part in the stories, which starred animal characters like the whale, walrus, polar bear, caribou, wolf, wolverine, fox, snow partridge, ice bird, and raven.

One observer said that even if you couldn't speak Inuit, you could understand the stories because they were told in a dramatic way that made the characters come alive. Stories like these are best experienced live, not on paper. In fact, one Inuit storyteller warned the great explorer Knud Rasmussen not to set these stories down in writing. He said, "You ruin our stories entirely if you are determined to stiffen them out on paper. Learn them yourself and let them spring from your mouth as living words." In other words, if these exciting stories were put in writing, they would lose their power.

Try to imagine yourself in that snow house on a January day one hundred years ago. The sky is dark, and no light comes through the window. You are warm and dry because your parents reminded you to beat the snow off your clothes in the entry tunnel. The storyteller has just finished another hair-raising story, and he says, "Now the story is finished, and the winter has gotten shorter."

—Joan Burditt

Carvings at right and on page 657 by Inuit artists (twentieth century).

# MAKING MEANINGS

## First Thoughts

1. How do you think the seal woman handled her choice? What would you have done in her place?

## Shaping Interpretations

2. If love means letting someone be himself or herself, who in this story shows the most love? Explain.

3. What events in the story are **fantasy**? Which parts of the story seem true to life? Which parts of the story did you like better?

4. Both the seal woman and Master Frog (page 639) lose their skins. Which character do you think suffers more from the loss? Explain why you think so.

5. In a land in which "whole sentences must be broken from the speaker's lips and thawed," why is the gift that the seal woman gives to Ooruk important?

## Connecting with the Text

6. Look at what the mother seal says to her son when she leaves him for the last time (page 655). Do you think mothers might say something like this in all cultures and at all times when they must leave their children? How would the words make a child feel?

## Challenging the Text

7. Estés says that versions of this tale are told throughout the world and that the tale has many titles, including "The Seal Maiden," "Selkie-O, *Pamrauk,* Little Seal," and "*Eyalirtaq,* Flesh of Seal." What do you think of the title "Seal-skin, Soulskin"? Can you think of a better **title** for this story? Give reasons for keeping the title or changing it.

8. Would you change the ending of this story in any way? Why or why not? Describe any changes you would make.

> **Reading Check**
>
> Imagine that you are Ooruk, grown up and with a child of your own. **Summarize** the main events of the seal woman's story as if you were telling it to a little boy or girl. Use a story map like the one on page 627 to organize your summary.

# CHOICES: Building Your Portfolio

## Writer's Notebook

### 1. Collecting Ideas for an Informative Report

The Inuit people of northern North America have thrived in one of the coldest climates on earth. Make a chart listing what you already know (from this story, the *Connections* on page 657, and other sources) about Inuit food, clothing, shelter, transportation, and art. Then, use your chart to make a list of topics that you'd like to explore further in the report you'll write on page 672.

Art: carvings of animals—seals, polar bears(?)—in stone, ivory, bone, and shell.
Do these carvings have any special meaning?

---

## Creative Writing

### 2. Be True to Yourself

The movie *The Secret of Roan Inish* tells an Irish version of the seal-woman story. The movie *Splash* takes a humorous modern look at a similar mermaid legend. The animated film *The Little Mermaid* retells this ancient story of a girl-woman torn between love and her true self. Write your own modern legend in which a girl from another world must choose between returning to her true home and sacrificing her true nature for the sake of love.

## Storytelling/ Speaking and Listening

### 3. Decisions, Decisions

What if the seal woman had refused to marry the man? What if Ooruk had not retrieved his mother's skin? This story is full of moments when a character must make an important decision. With a group, choose four or five such moments and imagine how things would have turned out if the character had made a different decision. Then, tell an interactive tale to another class. Pause each time a decision is to be made, and ask the audience to vote on the decision. After the members of the audience make each choice, tell what happens next.

## Debate

### 4. Two Points of View

Reread the scene in which Ooruk overhears his parents arguing about the sealskin. Then, with the class, debate who is right about the sealskin. Is the mother right to ask for it back? Is the father right to insist that she stay?

## Creative Writing

### 5. Let the Animals Tell It

For the Quickwrite on page 649, you thought of an animal that you would like to talk to. Develop your notes into a short short story. Tell who your animal character is, where he or she lives, and what special things the animal tells you about his or her life. You might also want your animal to tell what he or she thinks of the human world. Give your story a good title.

## Style: Oral Storytelling

Good storytellers always think about how their words will sound when spoken. Suppose you are a storyteller. How would you read this passage based on the story?

> The large silver seal edged closer and closer to the boy. The boy knew—just knew—that somehow he was connected to this enormous seal, but how? Suddenly his mother appeared. "Hello," he called. She began to run.

- Would you read the first sentence slowly to create a sense of mystery? Would your voice be soft or loud?

- Where would you pause in the second sentence? What words would you emphasize?

- How would you say "Hello" in the next-to-last sentence? Would you read the last three sentences quickly or slowly?

**Try It Out**

Choose a short passage from "Sealskin, Soulskin," and prepare it for reading aloud. First, create a script. Print or type the passage on a clean sheet of paper, double-spacing and leaving wide margins. You can then mark up your script to remind yourself how you want to read the words. Write *pause* at the places where you'll stop for breath and *soft* or *loud* to remind yourself when to vary the volume of your voice. Underline words you particularly want to emphasize. Then, give an oral telling of the passage.

## VOCABULARY   HOW TO OWN A WORD

**WORD BANK**

*thrives*
*lithe*
*berating*
*tethered*

### Vocabulary for the Workplace: Animal Care

1. Use all four words in the Word Bank to write a list of dos and don'ts for taking care of a pet.
2. Use two words from the Word Bank to describe what you might observe at a zoo.

From *The Secret of Roan Inish* (1994), a movie about a selkie, a mysterious creature that can change in form from seal to human.

# NO Questions ASKED

# THE HUMMINGBIRD KING

*Mayan, retold by* **Argentina Palacios**

© Justin Kerr.

yramids, palaces, and temples of stone stand silent and abandoned, hidden by dense rain forests. But that was not always so. Long, long ago, great cities built by the Mayan people were centers of activity.

In one of those cities—one whose name has long been forgotten—there lived an old *halac uinic*, or chief. Since he had no son to succeed[1] him, he knew that his younger brother, Chirumá, would one day take his place.

But the chief's wife wanted a child. Each day, she prayed with all her heart. And, one day, her prayers were answered. She gave birth to a son. The child was born on the thirteenth day of the month, a lucky day. For the number thirteen reminded the Mayan people of their thirteen heavens.

Just as the baby was being born, another sign appeared. A beautiful hummingbird perched on a tree branch in front of the stately residence. It was not an ordinary bird, but the largest and most brightly colored hummingbird anyone had ever seen. No one had ever remembered a bird of its kind standing still for so long.

The high priest determined that this was an omen. "The messenger of the gods has come," he said. "He is telling us that this child will be extraordinary, just like this hummingbird."

In the days that followed, a special naming ceremony took place. The high priest gave the chief and his wife a bright red feather he'd found beneath the tree branch where the hummingbird perched.

"We shall name our son Kukul," the chief's wife proclaimed. "That name means 'beautiful feather.'"

"And so shall this feather protect the boy as long as he carries it with him," the priest said.

A great celebration took place in the public plaza. Everyone joined the festivities. Everyone was happy, except Chirumá. He knew that, because of this child, he would never become *halac uinic.*

ukul grew into a handsome young man with jet-black hair and skin the color of cinnamon. He was quick of mind and excelled at any task he was given. As a young boy, he spent long hours with his father. Together, they would study the stars.

Like all Mayan boys, Kukul learned the art of

1. **succeed:** follow into a position (here, the position is that of *halac uinic,* or chief).

## "THIS CHILD WILL BE EXTRAORDINARY, JUST LIKE THIS HUMMINGBIRD."

warfare from his elders. He made his own spears, bows, and arrows—straight and strong as the boy himself.

Soon the time came for Kukul to take his place among the men of his nation. A nomad[2] tribe was attempting a raid. Kukul, Chirumá, and the others went to war. Showers of spears and arrows rained down. Kukul fought bravely, at times at the very front. But wherever he was, not a single weapon fell on him.

Chirumá observed this. "The gods must watch out for Kukul," he thought to himself.

All at once, Kukul saw an arrow flying straight toward Chirumá, and Kukul positioned himself like a shield in front of his uncle. The arrow changed its course and fell to the ground without harming anyone. The enemy fled in astonishment and Kukul turned toward the wounded.

"How could it be that Kukul never gets hurt?" Chirumá wondered. "He must have a strong charm. I will find out."

That night, as Kukul slept on his straw mat, Chirumá came upon him. He carefully searched Kukul's sleeping body but found nothing. Then he saw it—a large red feather barely sticking out of the straw mat.

"His charm!" Chirumá said cheerfully to himself, as he carefully lifted the feather from its hiding place.

When Kukul awoke, he saw that the feather was gone. He searched everywhere, but he

could not find it. Nor could he remember the words of the priest on the day he was born. Without realizing it, Kukul had lost the charm and all the protection it provided.

It came to pass that the old chief went to the afterlife. Upon his death, all the high priests prepared to meet in council to choose a new chief. Chirumá knew that the priests would favor his nephew. He looked for the youngest priest, the one he knew could be easily swayed.

"Kukul is not a hero," he said. "Arrows never fall where he places himself. He is afraid to fight."

"No, he is not," said the priest. "Kukul is using his intelligence to win."

Chirumá would find any opportunity to talk to that priest about Kukul. Another day, he told him, "Kukul is reckless. He stops to take care of the wounded and puts his men in danger."

"Kukul is compassionate," replied the priest.

"He is inexperienced," countered Chirumá, as he sowed the seeds of doubt.

Now according to custom, a new *halac uinic* could be anyone in the departed chief's family. The high priests met.

"It should be Kukul, without a doubt," said the oldest priest.

"It should be Kukul," the second priest chimed in.

"Yes, without a doubt," the third priest added.

There was silence. "It should be Chirumá," said the youngest. "Kukul is too young and inexperienced."

They argued about the merits of each man. In the end, no one changed his vote and Kukul was chosen as *halac uinic.*

Under his rule, there was peace throughout the land. In time, even Chirumá's friend came to appreciate that Kukul had been a good choice.

Kukul spent much time studying the stars. He made mathematical calculations. He could tell the farmers the best times to plant to reap

2. **nomad:** wandering, with no permanent home. Nomadic peoples move about constantly in search of food, pasture, and so on.

Mayan tripod vase from the Valley of Ulúa (tenth century).

Musée d'ethnographie, Geneva, Switzerland. Scala/Art Resource, New York.

the richest crops. Everybody was happy with Kukul, except Chirumá.

One day, Kukul was hunting in the forest. He heard the rustling of leaves and raised his bow and arrow. With a flurry, a magnificent hummingbird, larger than any hummingbird Kukul had ever seen, fluttered next to him. The hummingbird spoke these words, "I am your guardian, Kukul. My job is to warn you. Beware. Death is circling you. Beware of a man."

"Magnificent hummingbird, my guardian, what man should I beware of?" asked Kukul.

"Someone very close to you. Be careful, Kukul," said the bird. Then it flew away.

Kukul walked on through the forest. As he came to a thicket, he heard the faint rustling of leaves. He pointed his arrow, but saw nothing. Kukul crouched low to the ground and moved slowly. He had not gone far when . . . *sssss* . . . it came. An arrow pierced his chest.

In pain, Kukul pulled out the arrow and headed for the river to wash his wound. "Surely, it is not deep," he tried to convince himself, but his strength began to fade as his chest turned scarlet with blood.

A few more steps and Kukul had to lean against a tree. "It is so dark," he moaned. He fell onto a sea of emerald grass and there he died. Alone. Betrayed.

Then, something extraordinary happened. Slowly, Kukul's body changed to the color of the grass, but his chest remained scarlet. His skin became feathers, and his hair a gorgeous crest.

By the time Chirumá came out of the thicket, Kukul's arms had turned into wings. All Chirumá could see was a glowing green bird with a scarlet chest and a long,

**Mayan plate depicting ballgame of pelota (c. A.D. 590).**
The Granger Collection, New York.

long tail, flying off into the sunlight.

The people mourned the loss of Kukul, but after a time, Chirumá was chosen to be the new chief. Chirumá was a cruel and warlike king, and soon after, enemies again attacked the city and in fierce battle took Chirumá prisoner. Everybody watched while his body was painted black and white, the colors of a slave. He was taken away from the city, never to be seen again.

Today, a most beautiful green bird with a scarlet chest, a long, long tail, and a gorgeous crest perches high up on the trees in the deep, cool cloud forest, watching everything and listening for the rustling of leaves.

The Mayan of old called this bird *kukul*. They carved its image into stone and placed it on their temples and palaces. Today this wise and peaceful bird—a symbol of freedom to all its people—is known as the *quetzal.*

## MEET THE WRITER
### Quetzal Tales

**Argentina Palacios** grew up in Panama. As an adult living in Texas, Palacios at first became a teacher, like her mother. Little by little, though, she discovered the rewards of writing and telling stories. "The Hummingbird King" is one of the stories she tells children and adults at schools, museums, zoos, and even jails around the country.

"The Hummingbird King" tells the story of the origin of the quetzal (ket·säl'). The quetzal is a brilliantly colored bird found only in the cloud forests of the highlands of Guatemala. The bird's head and back are emerald green; its chest is bright red. There is a wide crest of gold-and-green hair-like feathers on its head. The upper tail feathers are very large—up to three feet long.

Palacios says:

> 66 Legends say the quetzal loves its freedom so much that it will die in captivity. But the cloud forests that are its natural habitat are disappearing from the earth. Happily, scientists have had some success breeding the quetzal in zoos and nature parks, preserving the Mayan ideal of people living in harmony with nature. 99

Mayan seated figure of a priest or nobleman. Hardwood.
The Granger Collection, New York.

# The Search Goes On

## from *The Mystery of the Ancient Maya*

### Carolyn Meyer and Charles Gallenkamp

Brilliant achievements, exciting revelations, and countless unsolved mysteries—this is the legacy left by the ancient Maya. Huge areas remain to be explored, dozens of key sites to be investigated. There are hieroglyphic inscriptions[1] to decipher[2] and mountains of data to analyze. And so there are always new projects, new digs, new studies—and new breakthroughs.

In 1962 a geologist prospecting for an oil company in the jungle of Guatemala came across a cluster of ruins. He got in touch with Richard E. W. Adams, a young archaeologist who was on a dig in another part of the country. At that time all the two could do was to map the Río Azul site, named for a river nearby. There was no money then to excavate[3] the ruins they had found.

Over the next twenty years thieves dug trenches around the pyramids, tunneled into them, and even split them open to get at the treasures inside. The looters ransacked[4] at least twenty-eight tombs in this and the surrounding area, smuggling jewelry and other priceless ob-

jects into the United States, where they were sold to art collectors for huge sums of money. When Adams returned to Río Azul in 1981, he heard about the looting and saw the deep trenches and the scattered rubble. On one occasion he and another scientist surprised armed looters at work. Shots were fired and one of the thieves was wounded, but they all got away. After the incident Guatemalan government troops swept the area, and guards with automatic weapons have remained on duty ever since to prevent further looting.

There are tragic consequences to looting: When artifacts[5] are stolen and sold, all the valuable information they could provide is lost forever. The whole historical and archaeological context of each piece of remarkable pottery and exquisite jade jewelry is destroyed. A stolen artifact becomes merely a prized object in a private collection that is often kept secret or shared with only a few connoisseurs.[6]

But unscrupulous[7] collectors are willing to pay enormous sums for treasures for their private collections. The possibility of such profit

---

1. **hieroglyphic** (hī′ər·ō′glif′ik) **inscriptions:** engraved hieroglyphics (writing in which pictures, rather than letters, are used).
2. **decipher** (dē·sī′fər): interpret; find the meaning of.
3. **excavate** (eks′kə·vāt′): uncover by digging.
4. **ransacked:** looted; robbed.

5. **artifacts:** objects made by people or adapted for human use.
6. **connoisseurs** (kän′ə·surz′): people who are experts on something, especially something in the arts.
7. **unscrupulous** (un·skrōō′pyə·ləs): dishonest.

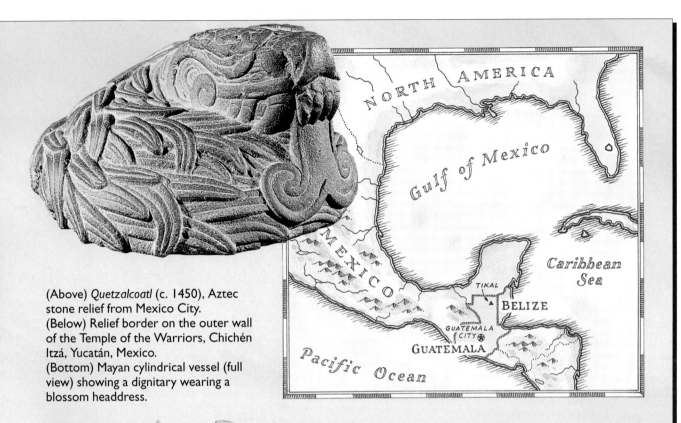

(Above) *Quetzalcoatl* (c. 1450), Aztec stone relief from Mexico City.
(Below) Relief border on the outer wall of the Temple of the Warriors, Chichén Itzá, Yucatán, Mexico.
(Bottom) Mayan cylindrical vessel (full view) showing a dignitary wearing a blossom headdress.

drives looters to search out and plunder[8] as-yet undiscovered sites. Once they've taken what they want, the looters use smuggling networks to get the ancient jars and jewels out of the jungle and into the hands of collectors all over the world.

Adams and other archaeologists used the incident at Río Azul to convince Congress to pass a law to stop national treasures looted in other countries from being brought into the United States. In addition, the United States signed an agreement that commits this country to recover and return stolen cultural and archaeological objects from Mexico and Central America.

Meanwhile, Adams raised the money to begin excavating the ruin in a race against the looters. The ancient city of Río Azul was probably a small center

**8. plunder:** loot.

under the control of the bigger city of Tikal, a few miles to the south. It covers about 470 acres and contains four major temple pyramids and adjoining smaller buildings. Adams and his team had been working on the site for several weeks in the spring of 1984, hoping to get as much accomplished as possible before the rainy season began. Then on May fifteenth a workman's leg plunged through rock-and-dirt fill and down through the roof of a secret chamber, a cave cut into the rock some 13 feet below the surface of the ground. Hidden by a wing of a temple built on top of it, the cave had gone undetected by looters—and until then by archaeologists as well.

One of the expedition leaders peered in. "It's painted!" he yelled; whoops of excitement greeted the announcement. They began working furiously to clear the rubble from the entrance to what they knew was a tomb. Next they lowered a miniature video camera into the opening. And finally, using vines and saplings from the jungle—traditional Maya building materials—they climbed down into the chamber.

The skeleton of a nobleman in his thirties, his shroud nothing more than dust, lay on a wooden bier.[9] Elaborate and mysterious wall paintings and fifteen pieces of pottery surrounded his body. One of the pieces was a beautifully made jar with an unusual screw-top lid. On top of the skeleton lay a stingray spine used in bloodletting rituals. Parrots chattered overhead and Guatemalan government guards with rifles and machetes stood by as the contents of Tomb 19, as it was now designated, were recorded and labeled and then transported to the National Museum of Anthropology in Guatemala City.

9. **bier** (bir): platform on which a corpse is placed.

North Acropolis and Central Plaza (c. A.D. 700), Mayan ruins, Tikal, Guatemala.

The date of the tomb is about A.D. 420 to 470, the height of the Classic period.[10] Adams, who calls it "a moment frozen in time," believes that the tomb was built for a relative of a ruler buried in a large pyramid nearby, already looted and stripped of its wall paintings. All that could be read of the hieroglyphics on the walls and pottery were the words *great son*.

10. **Classic period:** the period, from around A.D. 250 to around 900, during which Mayan civilization reached its peak.

# READ ON

## Good Folks

Let the appealing and simply told stories in *The Magic Listening Cap* (Creative Arts) by Yoshiko Uchida carry you off to the Japanese countryside. These fourteen folk tales are full of humor, wisdom, and the ring of universal truth.

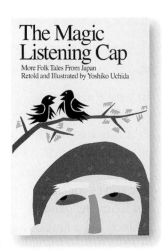

## High Tones

Listen to the powerful and inspiring language of drums. Experience the different rhythms of drumming for protection, freedom, and transformation. The ten tales of *Patakin: World Tales of Drums and Drummers* (Henry Holt) by Nina Jaffe celebrate a variety of drums and their special roles in storytelling.

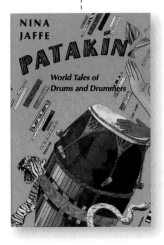

## Fairy Friendly

All the best-loved fairy tales are in Andrew Lang's *Blue Fairy Book* (Puffin), first published more than a hundred years ago. Cinderella, Rumpelstiltskin, and Aladdin keep company with many other favorites. You'll also find plenty of less familiar characters who are sure to win your heart in this classic book.

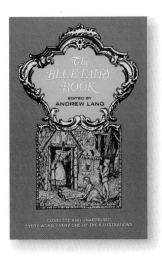

## Other Picks

- Laurence Yep, *Tongues of Jade* (HarperCollins). Seventeen ancient Chinese folk tales tell of mystery, magic, and the simple truths of human relationships.

- Julius Lester, *The Tales of Uncle Remus: The Adventures of Brer Rabbit* (Dial). The hilarious trickster Brer Rabbit is up to his ears in mischief in this classic collection of folk tales.

## SPEAKING TO INFORM

You're nervous. Your Scout leader has asked you to talk to the troop about winter camping. It's your first try at **formal speaking**—talking to an audience about a specific topic. How do you give your speech without falling apart? Some suggestions follow.

### Choosing Your Topic

If you need to select the topic for an informative speech, ask yourself these questions:

1.  **What is my purpose?** People give speeches for different reasons: to inform (an astronomer explains how stars are born), to persuade (an activist explains how to save the spotted owl), to entertain (a comedian tells what happened when he tried in-line skating).

    As you plan your speech, keep in mind what you hope to accomplish. Do you want your listeners to learn something about black holes, for instance, or how to pitch a tent on snow? to change their opinion? or simply to be amused?

2.  **Who is my audience?** To decide if your topic is right for your audience, ask yourself, "Is this audience interested in my topic?" If the answer is yes, you're on the right track. A speech about new ways to pull teeth may fascinate dentists but bore the high school varsity.

    Ask yourself, "Does my audience know something about my topic?" Your listeners don't have to be experts to enjoy your speech. Keep in mind, though, that you must tailor the speech to your audience's level of knowledge. If you describe a new computer system to engineers, they'll understand what you mean by *mouse, boot,* and *window.* Use the same technical words in a talk to preschoolers, though, and they'll probably get a very different picture.

### Try It Out

To help you narrow your focus when you're choosing a topic, team up with a classmate and come up with two specific topics for each of the following general subjects. The first one has been done for you.

| General Topic | Specific Topic |
|---|---|
| mountain climbing | **a.** how to rappel off a cliff<br>**b.** how to rescue a climber in trouble |
| movies | a.<br>b. |
| first aid | a.<br>b. |
| guitars | a.<br>b. |
| baseball | a.<br>b. |
| Italian cooking | a.<br>b. |

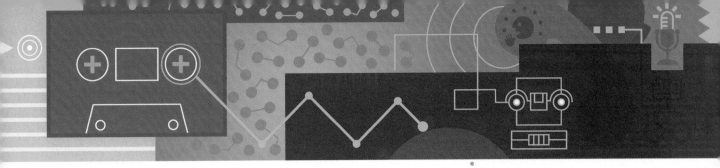

## Organizing Your Speech

Even a joke won't work if you're so scatterbrained that you give away the punch line. As you plan your speech, consider these suggestions:

- Sharpen your focus. A speech on how chimps learn language is more manageable than a speech on primates in general.

- Organize your main ideas. Here are three approaches:

  1. Organize by **topic.** Break down a general subject into three or four categories. If your subject is airplanes, for instance, you might talk about jets, propeller planes, and gliders.

  2. Organize by **chronology.** Describe a series of events in time order, or explain how to do something step by step.

  3. Organize by **comparison and contrast.** Persuade listeners to do something by telling what will happen if they do it and what will happen if they don't.

- Write each main idea on a note card, and number the cards.

- Begin with a hook. Open with a question, an anecdote, or a surprising fact that will hook listeners from the start.

- End with a punch. Wrap up with a vivid image, a question, a quotation, or a strong statement of opinion.

## Giving Your Speech

Rehearse at least once, preferably in the room where you'll give the speech. If you can, bring along a friend to give you feedback. Keep in mind that the image you project is almost as important as your subject. Here are some hints for giving your speech:

- Look at your audience. Don't read your speech word for word. Try to make eye contact with someone.

- Pronounce your words carefully, and speak loudly enough for everyone to hear. Speak neither too slowly nor too quickly.

- Pause briefly after an important point or before a new topic. You may also pause to answer questions from the audience. Some speakers, though, prefer to limit questions to the end.

### Try It Out

Before giving a persuasive speech—like "Having Ferrets as Pets Should Be Outlawed"— try arguing for the opposing viewpoint. Ask a friend to listen and say which argument is more convincing. Arguing for both sides will give you a firmer grasp of your subject.

Peanuts reprinted by permission of UFS, Inc.

# Writer's Workshop

**Technology HELP**

*See* Writer's Workshop 1 CD-ROM. *Key word entry: Report of Information.*

**ASSIGNMENT**

**Write a report in which you present information on a topic.**

**AIM**

**To inform.**

**AUDIENCE**

**Your teacher and classmates.**

## EXPOSITORY WRITING

# INFORMATIVE REPORT

For your informative report, you'll do some detective work. You'll find, organize, and present facts that add to your readers' knowledge of your topic.

### Professional Model

Africa is big. It's the second largest of the seven continents, with 11.5 million square miles of dancing grasslands, mysterious mountains, devouring forests, lazy rivers, watchful coastlines, and angry deserts. . . .

Africa is a continent of extremes— sometimes lovely and serene, other times grotesque and full of rage, many times both at once. After all, Africa is home to some of nature's most unusual creations—hippopotamus, elephant, zebra, giraffe, crocodile, cobra, falcon, leopard, and lion—but not the Asiatic tiger! Africa is also the breeding place of the malaria-carrying *Anopheles* mosquito; the tsetse fly, which infects its victims with the deadly "sleeping disease"; and the insatiable ten-year locust.

Understanding Africa's massive and diverse land is the first step in trying to comprehend the peoples who carved out civilizations within its geographical extremes.

—from "Africa in 1492" by Patricia and Fredrick McKissack

*The writers start with a clear and forceful statement and back it up with facts.*

*In this paragraph the writers present more facts to support their main idea.*

*The last sentence supports the main idea and provides a strong conclusion.*

The history
of the written
word is rich and
Page 1

## Prewriting

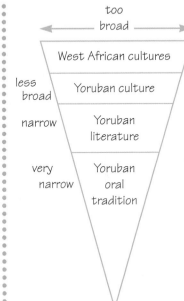

### 1. Writer's Notebook

If you have Writer's Notebook entries for this collection, review them. Look for ideas on which you can build a report.

### 2. Listing and Brainstorming

For more ideas, consider the following:

- List what you know—and want to know—about other lands and cultures mentioned in this collection—for example, those of Germany, Vietnam, China, or West Africa.

- List aspects of your own culture that interest you—for example, music, dance, sports, art, handicrafts, foods, or traditions.

- List topics about which you have a great deal of knowledge you'd like to share with other people.

### 3. Choosing and Narrowing Your Topic

Choose a topic you're really interested in. To be sure it's narrow enough, check an encyclopedia or another general source. If the encyclopedia article goes on for many pages, your topic is probably too broad for a brief report.

### 4. Researching Your Topic

#### a. Finding Information

Most informative reports are based on several sources of information (it's a good idea to have at least three). Do research in the library. Use the Internet and conduct interviews with experts if you can.

#### b. Taking Notes

- Write your notes on 3- × 5-inch note cards. On each card, write the source of the information.

- Write your notes in your own words. It's fine to use abbreviations and fragments. If you copy anything word for word, be sure to put quotation marks around it.

too
broad

| West African cultures |
| :---: |

less
broad → Yoruban culture

narrow → Yoruban
literature

very
narrow → Yoruban
oral
tradition

**Communications
Handbook
H E L P**

*See Evaluating Sources;
Listing Sources and
Taking Notes.*

**WRITER'S WORKSHOP 673**

Organization: time order

I. Morning

  A. Rooster instead of
     alarm clock

  B. Go outside to wash

    1. Brush teeth with
       finger and sand

    2. Water in barrel

  C. Breakfast not
     customary

II. Daytime

  A. Long walk to
     school . . .

Main point: Customs are
different in Cambodia.

---

### Framework for an Informative Report

**Introduction** (a surprising or dramatic bit of information, plus a clear statement of the main topic):_____

_____

**Body** (topics arranged in an order that makes sense, developed with facts, examples, statistics, or explanations):

1. Topic: _____
  Details: _____
2. Topic: _____
  Details: _____
3. Topic: _____
  Details: _____

**Conclusion** (statement or restatement of main point): _____

_____

## 5. Making an Outline

Making an outline is a good way to plan and to organize the information you'll put in your report.

- **Organization.**   Decide how you will organize your information. For example, you might use order of importance or time order. Notice that the Student Model on page 675 uses time order, discussing a typical day from morning to night.

- **Support.**   Decide which facts and examples from your notes you will use to support each part of your report. Make an outline, and then arrange your note cards in the order of the points in your outline.

- **The main point.**   At the end of your outline, write a sentence that sums up the main point of your report.

## Drafting

### 1. Getting Started

Your draft will have three parts. You may find it easier to write the introduction after you have drafted the body.

- **Introduction.**   To capture your readers' attention, offer an unusual piece of information or set a surprising scene. Make your topic clear, perhaps by stating your main point.

- **Body.**   Write at least one paragraph for each main heading in your outline. Use facts, statistics, and examples from your note cards to develop each paragraph. As you're writing, be alert for places where you need to do more research.

- **Conclusion.**   Bring your report to a definite close. If you haven't already stated your main point, do so now. If you have, refer to it again. You might add a summary or a reflection.

### 2. Tips for Drafting

- As you write, you may get good ideas that aren't in your outline. If they help to illustrate your main point, include them. Also, don't hesitate to depart from your outline if you discover a better way of arranging your report.

- From your note cards, take facts and examples that support your points. Work them into your report. If you need more information, it's fine to go back to a source.

- If you use a quotation, be sure to name the writer or speaker. Using someone else's words without crediting him or her is *plagiarism,* and it is a form of stealing.

# A Typical Day in a Cambodian Village

In the morning there is no clock to awaken us. The rooster crows to wake us up. We go outside to wash our face and wash our teeth with our fingers. Sometimes we use salt or sand or shaved charcoal to wash our teeth. We don't have indoor plumbing in the house; that's why we have to go outside to the rain barrel or near the stream to wash.

I go back inside the house and I put on a sarong (my school uniform) to go to school. It isn't a custom to eat breakfast in Cambodia.

The school is far from my house. I have to walk a long way to get to the school. In school there is no indoor plumbing or electricity. We have to use cloth put in the oil can and a match to light it if it's a dark day. If it's a sunny day we open the window. When it's time to go to recess we go home and eat rice and come back to school. We stay in school until five o'clock in the evening. When we get out of school we have to walk home again.

At night my family of seven people sleeps on two mats. We don't have beds to sleep on, that's why we have to sleep on the mat. In Cambodia when we go to sleep we have to clean our feet first before we go to sleep. That's our culture. We don't have to wash our face or hands or teeth but we must wash our feet.

My house has only two rooms. One room's for cooking and eating and the other room is for sleeping. We don't have any furniture in our house—no table, no chairs, just mats and a small wood-burning stove to cook on. My mother also has cooking utensils like pots, pans, eight dishes and eight spoons, chopsticks but no forks. It is the custom to sit in a circle on the floor to eat our meals in Cambodia.

We don't wear pajamas to sleep. Mother, father, and girls wear sarongs, and boys wear shorts.

—Lay Yan
Moody Middle School
Lowell, Massachusetts

*The writer uses the title to make her topic clear.*

*The report is organized in chronological order, beginning with the morning.*

*The writer uses facts and examples to share her knowledge with us.*

*The writer repeatedly supports her main point— that customs are different in Cambodia.*

*The writer uses details that show that she knows her subject well.*

**Technology**
**H E L P**

*See* Writer's Workshop 1 CD-ROM. *Key word entry: Report of Information. See Bibliography Maker.*

■ *Evaluation Criteria*

*A good informative report*

1. *centers on one topic that is supported by explanations and facts*

2. *presents information with authority*

3. *organizes information in a way that makes sense*

4. *documents any outside sources used*

**Language/Grammar Link**
**H E L P**

*Common usage problems: pages 606, 624, and 637. Using specific words: page 648. Oral storytelling: page 661.*

**Communications Handbook**
**H E L P**

*See Listing Sources and Taking Notes.*

**Sentence Workshop**
**H E L P**

*Parallel structure: page 677.*

## Revision Model

> In the morning there is no clock
>
> to awaken us. The rooster crows
>
> to wake us up. We go outside to
>
> wash our face and ~~washing~~ our ^(wash)    *Can you make parts of the third sentence parallel?*
>
> teeth with our fingers. Some-    *This is confusing. I need to know more.*
>
> (or sand or shaved charcoal to wash our teeth)
> times we use salt. We don't have
>
> indoor plumbing in the house;
>
> that's why we have to go
>
> (to the rain barrel or near the stream)
> outside to wash.    *Can you add some specifics?*

## 3. Listing Sources

On a page at the end of your report, list any outside sources you used. Put them in alphabetical order by author's last name (or by title if no author is named). Follow the guidelines in the Communications Handbook or a style guide your teacher selects. Look carefully at the punctuation, capitalization, and order of information in the guide you use. Follow it exactly.

## Evaluating and Revising

On a sheet of paper, write the following questions. Leave space between them for responses. Then, attach the paper to your draft, and trade drafts with a classmate.

- What is the main point of this report?

- What new things did I learn from this report?

- Are any parts confusing? How might the writer make them clearer?

- What, if anything, might make the first paragraph stronger?

Use your partner's responses to improve your draft.

# Sentence Workshop

## PARALLEL STRUCTURE

What is wrong with this sentence?

The daughters liked fine clothes and money and to go to parties.

The items listed are not **parallel**—they're not in the same grammatical form. Two are nouns (*clothes* and *money*), and one is a phrase (*to go to parties*). To correct the sentence, make the items in the list parallel. In sentences with parallel structure, nouns are balanced with nouns, phrases with phrases, clauses with clauses.

PARALLEL     The daughters liked fine clothes and money and parties. [three nouns]

PARALLEL     The daughters liked to wear fine clothes, to have money, and to go to parties. [three phrases]

Below are two more sentences with errors in parallelism, along with a corrected version of each.

NOT PARALLEL     Cinderella didn't have time to read books, go for walks, or talking with friends. [three phrases with different structures]

PARALLEL     Cinderella didn't have time to read books, go for walks, or talk with friends. [three phrases with the same structure]

NOT PARALLEL     The fairy godmother knew that Cinderella was miserable and her sad life. [a clause and a noun with modifiers]

PARALLEL     The fairy godmother knew that Cinderella was miserable and that she had a sad life. [two clauses]

## Writer's Workshop Follow-up: Revision

Take out your informative report, and exchange papers with a classmate. Look for parallel structure in sentences where your partner has joined elements with *and, but,* or *or*. Suggest revisions for sentences that are out of balance.

### Try It Out

The following sentences are out of balance: They do not use parallel structure. Edit them to put the ideas in parallel form. Be sure to exchange papers with a classmate. Can any sentence be rewritten in more than one way?

1. The king saw trumpeting elephants, roaring tigers, and the panthers growling.

2. The weather was cold, rainy, and there was wind.

3. The guests at the ball sang, laughed, and there was dancing.

4. He liked to play the lute, ride horses, and singing.

# Reading for Life

## Searching the Internet

## Situation

Your teacher wants you to use the Internet to find information for research reports. You've been assigned to write a report on a topic of your choice about world folklore. You decide to write about Cinderella stories. Use these strategies to narrow your search.

## Strategies

### Use key words.

Try using more than one key word. If you try the key word *Cinderella*, you'll get thousands of "hits" (sites), many of which have nothing to do with the fairy tale. To limit your list, try using two key words. If you use the key words *Cinderella* and *stories* together, for example, you'll be more likely to get a list of sites that discuss your subject.

### Use directories.

A **directory** is an index of selected sites grouped by subject.

- Yahooligans is a directory designed especially for kids. It sorts sites into broad subject areas like Entertainment and Science. Start by clicking

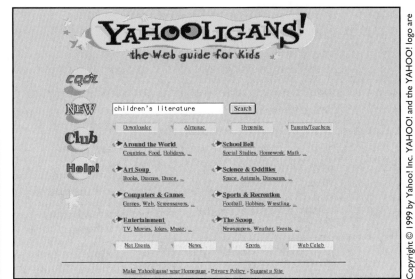

on a listed subject that you think might include the information you want. If nothing seems to fit, come up with a general subject and type it in the *Search* box. If *Cinderella Stories, Folklore,* and *Folk Tales* don't produce any sites, try *Children's Literature*.

### For smoother surfing:

- Check out sites in the order in which they're listed. The better ones usually appear at the beginning.

- To evaluate a site, read the brief description provided.

- If you come up with too many hits or you find no useful ones in the first ten,

try these strategies: Use synonyms for your key word; try using an additional key word; check your spelling; click on the help function.

## Using the Strategies

1. Which key words produced the most useful list of sites?

2. Which of the strategies described do you find easiest to use? Why?

## Extending the Strategies

Use the Web to find information on your favorite author. If you don't have a favorite, see what you can find on Jakob and Wilhelm Grimm or on Virginia Hamilton.

# Learning for Life

## Researching Our Heritage: Comparing Cultures

### Problem

Cultures from all over the world come together in the United States. How much do you know about your own or another culture? What would you like to know?

### Project

**Research some questions about another culture. Then, compare that culture with your own. Organize your findings and present them to the class.**

### Preparation

1. Jot down what you know about the culture you've chosen.

2. With a few classmates, come up with a list of research questions about the following areas that you might compare:

   • oral traditions

   • art, crafts, music, dance

   • foods

   • geographical or regional characteristics

   • discoveries, inventions

3. From your group's questions, select a few topics that you want to find out more about.

### Procedure

1. In your group, talk about how to research the topics you're interested in. You might consult your librarian, conduct interviews, read books or encyclopedia articles, or listen to music.

2. Are other students in your class interested in the same culture that you are researching? If so, consider working as a research team, with each of you doing a specific job.

3. Do the research and organize your information.

### Presentation

Present your findings in one of the following ways:

### 1. Multimedia Report

Use a variety of media to present your report. You might include maps, drawings, photographs, voice or music recordings, videotape, costumes and foods, or demonstrations of dances. Make your report clear, informative, and entertaining.

### 2. Folk-Tale Festival

Plan a folk-tale festival for your class or grade. Individuals or small groups can present a folk tale or legend. The presentation—including different voices, sound effects, and music—can be videotaped or performed live. Make the presentation as dramatic as possible. Afterward, hold a class discussion to compare the cultures represented.

### 3. On-line Culture Guide

Using a computer, create a guide to the countries or regions your class has researched. Include sections covering, for example, folklore, the arts (such as painting, music, and dance), important cities, places of interest, and customs (such as traditions, foods, and clothing). Make sure your information is carefully organized and can be located in several different categories.

### Processing

To reflect on what you have learned, complete this starter: I'd like to continue exploring cultures by . . . .

## HANDBOOK OF LITERARY TERMS  681

## COMMUNICATIONS HANDBOOK  691

## LANGUAGE HANDBOOK  709

## GLOSSARY  789

# HANDBOOK OF LITERARY TERMS

For more information about a topic, turn to the page(s) in this book indicated on a separate line at the end of the entries. To learn more about *Allusion,* for example, turn to pages 468 and 564.

On another line are cross-references to entries in this Handbook that provide closely related information. For instance, at the end of *Autobiography* is a cross-reference to *Biography.*

**ALLITERATION** **The repetition of the same or very similar consonant sounds in words that are close together.** Though alliteration usually occurs at the beginning of words, it can also occur within or at the end of words. Among other things, alliteration can help establish a mood, emphasize words, and serve as a memory aid. In the following example the *s* sound is repeated at the beginning of the words *silken* and *sad* and within the words *uncertain* and *rustling:*

> And the silken sad uncertain rustling of each
> purple curtain

> — Edgar Allan Poe, from "The Raven"

> See pages 338–339, 349.

**ALLUSION** **A reference to a statement, a person, a place, or an event from literature, history, religion, mythology, politics, sports, or science.** Allusions enrich the reading experience. Writers expect readers to recognize an allusion and to think, almost at the same time, about the literary work and the person, place, or event that it refers to. The following lines, describing a tunnel in the snow, contain an allusion to Aladdin, a character in *The Thousand and One Nights:*

> With mittened hands, and caps drawn low,
> To guard our necks and ears from snow,
> We cut the solid whiteness through.
> And, where the drift was deepest, made
> A tunnel walled and overlaid
> With dazzling crystal: we had read

> Of rare Aladdin's wondrous cave,
> And to our own his name we gave.

> —John Greenleaf Whittier,
> from "Snow-Bound"

The cave in the tale contains a magic lamp that helps Aladdin discover vast riches. By alluding to Aladdin's cave, Whittier makes us see the icy tunnel in the snow as a magical, fairy-tale place.

The cartoon below makes an allusion to a popular fairy tale.

> See pages 468, 479, 564.

*"Now, this policy will cover your home for fire, theft, flood and huffing and puffing."*

Reprinted from The Saturday Evening Post © 1993.

**ATMOSPHERE** **The overall mood or emotion of a work of literature.** A work's atmosphere can often be described with one or two adjectives, such as *scary, dreamy, happy, sad,* or *nostalgic.* A writer creates atmosphere by using images, sounds, and descriptions that convey a particular feeling.

> See also *Mood.*

**AUTOBIOGRAPHY** **The story of a person's life, written or told by that person.** Jean Fritz wrote a popular autobiography called *Homesick: My Own Story* (page 105) about her early life in China. Another well-known autobiographical work is Maya Angelou's *I Know Why the Caged Bird Sings.*

> See page 121.
> See also *Biography.*

**BIOGRAPHY  The story of a real person's life, written or told by another person.** Jean Fritz has written biographies of many famous American figures, including Paul Revere, Benjamin Franklin, and Pocahontas. Frequent subjects of biographies are movie stars, television personalities, politicians, sports figures, self-made millionaires, even underworld figures. Biographies are among the most popular forms of contemporary literature.

See pages 121, 122.
See also *Autobiography.*

**CHARACTER  A person or animal who takes part in the action of a story, play, or other literary work.** In some works, such as Aesop's fables, a character is an animal. In myths and legends a character may be a god or a superhero, like Jupiter or Hercules in "The Labors of Hercules" (page 541). Most often a character is an ordinary human being, such as Kevin in "User Friendly" (page 357).

The process of revealing the personality of a character in a story is called **characterization.** A writer can reveal a character in the following ways:

1. by letting the reader hear the character speak
2. by describing how the character looks and dresses
3. by letting the reader listen to the character's inner thoughts and feelings
4. by revealing what other people in the story think or say about the character
5. by showing the reader what the character does—how he or she acts
6. by telling the reader directly what the character's personality is like (cruel, kind, sneaky, brave, and so on)

When a writer uses the first five ways to reveal a character, the reader must make an inference, based on the evidence the writer provides, to decide what the character is like. When a writer uses the sixth method, however, the reader doesn't make a decision but is told directly what kind of person the character is.

Characters can be classified as static or dynamic. A **static character** is one who does not change much in the course of a work. The father in "A Day's Wait" (page 81) is a static character. By contrast, a **dynamic character** changes as a result of the story's events. Roger Clark in "Miss Awful" (page 369) is a dynamic character.

A character's **motivation** is any force that drives or moves the character to behave in a particular way. Many characters are motivated by the force of fear or love or ambition.

See pages 80, 85, 356, 365, 386, 391,
605, 607, 635, 636, 646.

**CONFLICT  A struggle or clash between opposing characters or opposing forces.** In an **external conflict** a character struggles against some outside force. This outside force may be another character or society as a whole or a storm or a grizzly bear or even a machine. In "Three Skeleton Key" (page 65), the characters have an external conflict with a swarm of sea rats. An **internal conflict,** on the other hand, takes place within a character's mind. It is a struggle between opposing needs, desires, or emotions. In "After Twenty Years" (page 193), Officer Wells must resolve an internal conflict: Should he arrest an old friend or let him go?

See pages 2, 19, 22, 61, 118, 199, 244, 254,
270–271, 300, 322, 349, 457, 636.

**CONNOTATION  The feelings and associations that a word suggests.** For example, *tiny, cramped,* and *compact* all have about the same dictionary definition, or **denotation,** but they have different connotations. A manufacturer of small cars would not describe its product as tiny or cramped. Instead, the company might say that its cars are compact. To grasp a writer's full meaning, the reader must pay attention not only to the literal definitions of words but also to their connotations. Connotations can be especially important in poetry.

See page 120.

**DENOTATION  The literal, dictionary definition of a word.**

See page 120.
See also *Connotation.*

**DESCRIPTION** **The kind of writing that creates a clear image of something, usually by using details that appeal to one or more of the senses: sight, hearing, smell, taste, and touch.** Writers use description in all forms of fiction, nonfiction, and poetry. In "Fish Cheeks" (page 135), Amy Tan vividly describes the colors, sounds, and tastes of her family's Christmas celebration.

See pages 134, 141, 511.

**DIALECT** **A way of speaking that is characteristic of a particular region or group of people.** A dialect may have a distinct vocabulary, pronunciation system, and grammar. In a sense, we all speak a dialect. One dialect usually becomes dominant in a country or culture and is accepted as the standard way of speaking. In the United States, for example, the formal written language is known as standard English. This is the dialect used in most newspapers and magazines.

Writers often reproduce regional dialects, or speech that reveals a character's economic or social class, in order to give a story local color. Mr. Baumer in "Bargain" (page 231) speaks in a dialect that reveals that his first language is German. The poem "Madam and the Rent Man" (page 227) is written in a dialect spoken in some urban African American communities in the northeastern United States.

See page 481.

**DIALOGUE** **A conversation between two or more characters.** Most stage dramas consist entirely of dialogue together with stage directions. (Screenplays and television dramas sometimes include an unseen narrator.) The dialogue in a drama, such as *Brian's Song* (page 274), must move the plot along and reveal character almost single-handedly. Dialogue is also an important element in most stories and novels as well as in some poems and nonfiction. It is one of the most effective ways for a writer to show what a character is like. It can also add realism and humor.

In the written form of a play, dialogue appears without quotation marks. In prose or poetry, however, dialogue is usually enclosed in quotation marks.

A **monologue** is a part of a drama in which one character speaks alone.

See pages 78, 96, 270.

**DRAMA** **A story written to be acted in front of an audience.** (A drama can be appreciated and enjoyed in written form, however.) In a drama, such as *Brian's Song* (page 274), the action is usually driven by a character who wants something very much and takes steps to get it. The related events that take place within a drama are often separated into **acts.** Each act is often made up of shorter sections, or **scenes.** Most plays have three acts, but there are many, many variations. The elements of a drama are often described as **introduction** or **exposition, complications, conflict, climax,** and **resolution.**

See pages 270–271, 273.

**FABLE** **A brief story in prose or verse that teaches a moral or gives a practical lesson about how to get along in life.** The characters of most fables are animals that behave and speak like human beings. Some of the most popular fables are attributed to Aesop, who is thought to have been a slave in ancient Greece. The poem "The Boy and the Wolf" (page 574) is a retelling in verse of one of Aesop's fables.

See pages 565, 566.
See also *Folk Tale, Myth.*

**FICTION** **A prose account that is made up rather than true.** The term *fiction* usually refers to novels and short stories. Fiction may be based on a writer's experiences or on historical events, but characters, events, and other details are altered or added by the writer to create a desired effect. "The No-Guitar Blues" (page 217) is a fictional account based on an episode in the writer's childhood.

See also *Nonfiction.*

**FIGURE OF SPEECH** **A word or phrase that describes one thing in terms of something else and is not literally true.** Figures of speech always involve some sort of imaginative comparison between seemingly unlike things. The most common forms are **simile** ("The stars were like diamonds"), **metaphor** ("My soul is an enchanted boat"), and **personification** ("The sun smiled down on the emerald-green fields").

See pages 168, 397.
See also *Metaphor, Personification, Simile.*

**FLASHBACK  An interruption in the action of a plot to tell what happened at an earlier time.** A flashback breaks the usual movement of the narrative by going back in time. It usually gives background information that helps the reader understand the present situation. "A Mason-Dixon Memory" (page 206) contains a long flashback.

A break in the unfolding of a plot to an episode in the future is known as a **flash-forward.**

See pages 206, 213.

**FOLK TALE  A story, with no known author, that originally was passed on from one generation to another by word of mouth.** Most folk tales reflect the values of the society that preserved them. "Master Frog" (page 639) is a folk tale about the importance of who we are on the inside. Folk tales often contain **fantastic** elements, or events that could not happen in the world as we know it.

See pages 625–626.
See also *Fable, Myth, Tall Tale.*

**FORESHADOWING  The use of clues to suggest events that will happen later in the plot.** Foreshadowing is used to build suspense or create anxiety. In a drama a gun found in a bureau drawer in Act One is likely to foreshadow violence later in the play. In *Brian's Song* (page 274), Brian Piccolo's weight loss foreshadows his illness and death later in the play.

See pages 64, 77, 192, 199, 241, 322.
See also *Suspense.*

**FREE VERSE  Poetry without a regular meter or a rhyme scheme.** Poets writing in free verse try to capture the natural rhythms of ordinary speech.

To create their music, poets writing in free verse may use internal rhyme, repetition, alliteration, and onomatopoeia. Free verse also frequently makes use of vivid imagery. The following poem in free verse effectively uses images and the repetition of words to describe the effects of a family's eviction for not paying rent:

**The 1st**
What I remember about that day
is boxes stacked across the walk
and couch springs curling through the air
and drawers and tables balanced on the curb
and us, hollering,
leaping up and around
happy to have a playground;

nothing about the emptied rooms
nothing about the emptied family

—Lucille Clifton

See pages 338, 398, 403.
See also *Poetry, Rhyme, Rhythm.*

**IMAGERY  Language that appeals to the senses.** Most images are visual—that is, they create pictures in the reader's mind by appealing to the sense of sight. Images can also appeal to the sense of hearing, touch, taste, or smell or to several senses at once. The sensory images in "The Highwayman" (page 341) add greatly to the enjoyment of the poem. Though imagery is an element in all types of writing, it is especially important in poetry.

See page 355.
See also *Poetry.*

**IRONY  In general, a contrast between expectation and reality.** Irony can create powerful effects, from humor to strong emotion. There are three common types of irony:

1. **Verbal irony** involves a contrast between what is said or written and what is meant. If you were to call someone who failed a math test Einstein, you would be using verbal irony.

2. **Situational irony** occurs when what happens is very different from what is expected to happen. The surprise ending of "After Twenty Years" (page 193) involves situational irony.

3. **Dramatic irony** occurs when the audience or the reader knows something a character does not know. Near the conclusion of *Brian's Song* (page 274), the reader feels an anxious sense of irony when Mr. Eberle asks Brian Piccolo to give his permission for another operation. Although Brian doesn't yet know it, we know that Brian's cancer has spread.

See pages 558, 562.

**LIMERICK** **A humorous five-line verse that has a regular meter and the rhyme scheme *aabba*.** Limericks often have place names in their rhymes. The following limerick was published in Edward Lear's *Book of Nonsense* in 1846, when limericks were at the height of their popularity:

> There was an old man with a beard,
> Who said, "It is just as I feared!
> Two owls and a hen,
> Four larks and a wren
> Have *all* built their nests in my beard!"

See pages 338–339.

**MAIN IDEA** **The most important idea expressed in a paragraph or in an entire essay.** The main idea may be directly stated in a **topic sentence,** or the reader may have to look at all the details in the paragraph and make an **inference,** or educated guess, about its main idea.

See pages 144, 149, 443, 444.

**METAMORPHOSIS** **A marvelous change from one shape or form to another one.** In myths the change is usually from human to animal, from animal to human, or from human to plant. Greek and Roman myths contain many examples of metamorphosis. The myth of Echo and Narcissus (page 523) tells how the vain youth Narcissus pines away for love of his own reflection until he is changed into a flower.

See pages 638, 646.
See also *Myth.*

**METAPHOR** **An imaginative comparison between two unlike things in which one thing is said to be another thing.** A metaphor is an important type of figurative language. Metaphors are used in all forms of writing and are common in ordinary speech. If you were to say someone has a heart of gold, you would not mean that the person's heart is actually made of metal. You would mean, instead, that the person is warm and caring. You would be speaking metaphorically.

Metaphors differ from similes, which use specific words (notably *like, as, than,* and *resembles*) to state comparisons. William Wordsworth's famous comparison "I wandered lonely as a cloud" is a simile because it uses *as.* If Wordsworth had written "I was a lonely, wandering cloud," he would have been using a metaphor.

See pages 131, 168, 171, 397, 403.
See also *Figure of Speech, Personification, Simile.*

PEANUTS reprinted by permission of United Feature Syndicate, Inc.

**MOOD  The overall emotion created by a work of literature.** A work of literature can often be described with one or more adjectives: *sad, scary, hopeful, exciting,* and so on. These are descriptions of the work's mood—its emotional atmosphere. For example, the mood of "Annabel Lee" (pages 351–352) could be described as haunting or romantic. That mood has a lingering effect on its readers.

See page 393.
See also *Atmosphere.*

**MOTIVATION**  See *Character.*

**MYTH  A story that explains something about the world and typically involves gods or other superhuman beings.** Myths, which at one time were believed to be true, reflect the traditions of the culture that produced them. Almost every culture has **origin myths** (or **creation myths**), stories that explain how something in the world (perhaps the world itself) came to be. Myths may also explain many other aspects of nature. The ancient Greek myth of Demeter and Persephone (page 501), for example, explains the change of seasons. Most myths are very old and were handed down orally long before being put in written form. In some of the world's greatest myths, a hero or even a god embarks on a **quest,** a perilous journey taken in pursuit of something of great value.

See pages 426, 430, 496–499, 500, 510, 527.
See also *Fable, Folk Tale.*

**NONFICTION  Prose writing that deals with real people, events, and places without changing any facts.** Popular forms of nonfiction are the **autobiography,** the **biography,** and the **essay.** Other examples of nonfiction include newspaper stories, magazine articles, historical writing, scientific reports, and even personal diaries and letters.

Nonfiction writing can be subjective or objective. **Subjective writing** expresses the feelings and opinions of the writer. **Objective writing** conveys the facts without introducing any emotion or personal bias.

See pages 104, 121–122.
See also *Autobiography, Biography, Fiction.*

**NOVEL  A fictional story that is usually between one hundred and five hundred book pages long.** A novel uses all the elements of storytelling—plot, character, setting, theme, and point of view. A novel, because of its length, usually has more characters, settings, and themes and a more complex plot than a short story. Modern writers sometimes do not pay much attention to one or more of the novel's traditional elements. Some novels today are basically character studies that include only the barest story lines. Other novels don't look much beyond the surface of their characters and concentrate instead on plot and setting. A novel can deal with almost any topic. Many of the books recommended in the Read On sections of this text are novels.

**ONOMATOPOEIA  The use of words with sounds that echo their sense.** Onomatopoeia (än′ō·mat′ō·pē′ə) is so natural to us that we use it at a very early age. *Buzz, rustle, boom, ticktock, tweet,* and *bark* are all examples of onomatopoeia. Onomatopoeia is an important element in creating the music of poetry. In the following lines the poet creates a frenzied mood by choosing words that imitate the sounds of alarm bells:

> Oh, the bells, bells, bells!
> What a tale their terror tells
> Of Despair!
> How they clang, and clash, and roar!
> What a horror they outpour
> On the bosom of the palpitating air!
> Yet the ear, it fully knows
> By the twanging
> And the clanging
> How the danger ebbs and flows.
>
> —Edgar Allan Poe, from "The Bells"

See page 339.
See also *Alliteration.*

**PERSONIFICATION** **A figure of speech in which a nonhuman thing or quality is talked about as if it were human.** In the following lines, sleep is spoken of as a human weaver:

> The soft gray hands of sleep
> Toiled all night long
> To spin a beautiful garment
> Of dreams

> —Edward Silvera, from "Forgotten Dreams"

See pages 464, 467, 520.
See also *Figure of Speech, Metaphor, Simile.*

**PLOT** **The series of related events that make up a story.** Plot is "what happens" in a short story, novel, play, or narrative poem. Most plots are built on these bare bones: An **introduction,** or **exposition,** tells us who the characters are and what their **conflict** is. **Complications** arise as the characters take steps to resolve the conflict. The plot reaches a **climax,** the most emotional or suspenseful moment in the story, when the outcome is decided one way or another. The last part of a story is the **resolution,** when the characters' problems are solved and the story ends.

Not all works of fiction or drama have this traditional plot structure. Some modern writers experiment, often eliminating parts of a traditional plot in order to focus on elements such as character, point of view, or mood.

See pages 22–23, 61, 96, 270–271, 349, 605.
See also *Conflict.*

**POETRY** **A kind of rhythmic, compressed language that uses figures of speech and imagery designed to appeal to emotion and imagination.** We know poetry when we see it because it is usually arranged in a particular way on the page. Traditional poetry often has a regular pattern of rhythm (**meter**) and may have a regular **rhyme scheme.** **Free verse** is poetry that has no regular rhythm or rhyme. The major forms of poetry are the **lyric** (a songlike poem that expresses a speaker's feelings) and the **narrative** (a poem that tells a story). Two popular narrative forms are the **epic** and the **ballad.**

See pages 24, 338–339, 355, 397.
See also *Figure of Speech, Free Verse, Imagery, Refrain, Rhyme, Rhythm, Speaker, Stanza.*

**POINT OF VIEW** **The vantage point from which a story is told.** The most common points of view are the **omniscient,** the **third-person limited,** and the **first person.**

1. In the **omniscient,** or all-knowing, **point of view** the narrator knows everything about the characters and their problems. This all-knowing narrator can tell about the characters' past, present, and future. This kind of narrator can even tell what the characters are thinking or what is happening in other places. This narrator is not in the story. Instead, he or she stands above the action, like a god. The omniscient is a very familiar point of view; we have heard it in fairy tales since we were very young. "Aschenputtel" (page 593) is told from the omniscient point of view: "And when the evening came, she wanted to go home, and the prince followed her, for he wanted to see to what house she belonged. . . ."

2. In the **third-person limited point of view,** the narrator focuses on the thoughts and feelings of only one character. From this point of view, readers observe the action through the eyes and feelings of only one character in the story. "The Smallest Dragonboy" (page 47) is told from the third-person limited point of view: "There was such a lot to know and understand about being a dragonrider that sometimes Keevan was overwhelmed. How would he ever be able to remember everything he ought to know at the right moment?"

3. In the **first-person point of view,** one of the characters, using the personal pronoun *I,* is telling the story. The reader becomes very familiar with this narrator but can know only

what he or she knows and can observe only what he or she observes. All information about the story must come from this character. In some cases the information is incorrect. "A Day's Wait" (page 81) is told from the first-person point of view of the boy's father. He does not know what is worrying his son: "I sat at the foot of the bed and read to myself while I waited for it to be time to give another capsule. It would have been natural for him to go to sleep, but when I looked up he was looking at the foot of the bed, looking very strangely."

See pages 202–203, 216, 224, 230, 241.

**REFRAIN  A group of words repeated at intervals in a poem, song, or speech.** Refrains are usually associated with songs and poems, but they are also used in speeches and other forms of literature. Refrains are most often used to create rhythm, but they may also provide emphasis or commentary, create suspense, or help hold a work together. Refrains may be repeated with small variations in a work in order to fit a particular context or to create a special effect. The first six lines are used as a refrain in the song "A Place in the Choir" (page 178).

See pages 420, 425.

**RHYME  The repetition of accented vowel sounds and all sounds following them in words close together in a poem.** *Mean* and *screen* are rhymes, as are *crumble* and *tumble*. Rhyme has many purposes in poetry: It creates rhythm, lends a song-like quality, emphasizes ideas, organizes the poem (for instance, into stanzas or couplets), provides humor or delight for the reader, and makes the poem memorable.

Many poems—for example, "The Runaway" (page 25)—use **end rhymes,** rhymes at the end of a line. In the following stanza, *walls/calls/falls* form end rhymes, as do *hands/sands:*

> Darkness settles on roofs and walls,
> But the sea, the sea in the darkness calls;
> The little waves, with their soft, white hands,

Efface the footprints in the sands,
And the tide rises, the tide falls.

> —Henry Wadsworth Longfellow,
> from "The Tide Rises, the Tide Falls"

**Internal rhymes** are rhymes within lines. The following line has an internal rhyme (*turning/burning*):

> Back into the chamber turning, all my soul
> within me burning

> —Edgar Allan Poe, from "The Raven"

Rhyming sounds need not be spelled the same way; for instance, *gear/here* forms a rhyme. Rhymes can involve more than one syllable or more than one word; *poet/know it* is an example. Rhymes involving sounds that are similar but not exactly the same are called **slant rhymes** (or **near rhymes** or **approximate rhymes**). *Leave/live* is an example of a slant rhyme. Poets writing in English often use slant rhymes because English is not a very rhymable language. It has many words that rhyme with no other word (*orange*) or with only one other word (*mountain/fountain*). Poets interested in how a poem looks on the printed page sometimes use **eye rhymes,** or **visual rhymes**—rhymes involving words that are spelled similarly but are pronounced differently. *Tough/cough* is an eye rhyme. (*Tough/rough* is a "real" rhyme.)

The pattern of end rhymes in a poem is called a **rhyme scheme.** To indicate the rhyme scheme of a poem, use a separate letter of the alphabet for each rhyme. For example, the rhyme scheme of Longfellow's stanza at the left is *aabba.*

See pages 24, 27, 338, 447, 463.
See also *Free Verse, Poetry, Rhythm.*

**RHYTHM  A musical quality produced by the repetition of stressed and unstressed syllables or by the repetition of certain other sound patterns.** Rhythm occurs in all language—written and spoken—but is particularly important in poetry.

The most obvious kind of rhythm is the regular pattern of stressed and unstressed syllables that is found in some poetry. This pattern is called **meter.** In the following lines describing a cavalry charge, the rhythm echoes the galloping of the attackers' horses:

> ⌣ ⌣ ′ ⌣ ⌣ ′ ⌣ ⌣ ′ ⌣ ⌣
> The Assyrian came down like the wolf on the
>   ′
>   fold,
> ⌣ ⌣ ′ ⌣ ⌣ ′ ⌣ ⌣ ′ ⌣ ⌣
> And his cohorts were gleaming in purple and
>   ′
>   gold;
> ⌣ ⌣ ′ ⌣ ⌣ ′ ⌣ ⌣ ′ ⌣
> And the sheen of their spears was like stars on
>   ⌣ ⌣ ′
>   the sea,
> ⌣ ⌣ ′ ⌣ ⌣ ′ ⌣ ⌣ ′
> When the blue wave rolls nightly on deep
>   ⌣ ⌣ ′
>   Galilee.
>
> —George Gordon, Lord Byron,
>     from "The Destruction of Sennacherib"

Marking the stressed ( ′ ) and unstressed ( ⌣ ) syllables in a line is called **scanning** the line. Lord Byron's scanned lines show a rhythmic pattern in which two unstressed syllables are followed by a stressed syllable. Read the lines aloud and listen to this rhythmic pattern. Also, notice how the poem's end rhymes help create the rhythm.

Writers can also create rhythm by repeating words and phrases or even by repeating whole lines and sentences.

See pages 338, 348, 349.
See also *Free Verse, Poetry, Rhyme.*

**SETTING  The time and place in which the events of a work of literature take place.** Most often the setting of a narrative is described early in the story. Setting often contributes to a story's emotional effect. In "Song of the Trees" (page 29), the forest setting helps create a soothing (yet mysterious) mood. Setting frequently plays an important role in a story's plot, especially one that centers on a conflict between a character and nature. In "Survive the Savage Sea" (page 445), for example, the shipwrecked Robertson family struggles against the sea. Some stories are closely tied to particular settings, and it is difficult to imagine them taking place else-

where. By contrast, other stories could easily take place in a variety of settings.

See pages 96, 152, 165, 270, 273, 348, 605.

**SHORT STORY  A fictional prose narrative that is usually ten to twenty book pages long.** Short stories were first written in the nineteenth century. Early short-story writers include Sir Walter Scott and Edgar Allan Poe. Short stories are usually built on a plot that consists of at least these bare bones: the **introduction** or **exposition, conflict, complications, climax,** and **resolution.** Short stories are more limited than novels. They usually have only one or two major characters and one important setting.

See pages 22–23.
See also *Conflict, Fiction, Plot.*

**SIMILE  A comparison between two unlike things, using a word such as *like, as, than,* or *resembles.*** The simile is an important type of figure of speech. In the following lines, a simile creates a clear image of moths in the evening air:

> When the last bus leaves, moths stream
>   toward lights like litter in wind.
>
> —Roberta Hill, from "Depot in Rapid City"

This example shows that similes can generate a strong emotional impact. By choosing to compare the moths to litter, the poet not only creates a picture in the reader's mind but also establishes a lonely, dreary mood.

See pages 168, 171, 520.
See also *Figure of Speech, Metaphor.*

**SPEAKER  The voice talking in a poem.** Sometimes the speaker is identical to the poet, but often the speaker and the poet are not the same. The poet may be speaking as a child, a woman, a man, an animal, or even an object.

See also *Poetry.*

**STANZA** **In a poem, a group of consecutive lines that forms a single unit.** A stanza in a poem is something like a paragraph in prose; it often expresses a unit of thought. A stanza may consist of any number of lines. "I'm Nobody!" (page 169) consists of two four-line stanzas, each expressing a separate idea. In some poems each stanza has the same rhyme scheme.

See also *Poetry, Rhyme.*

**SUSPENSE** **The uncertainty or anxiety the reader feels about what will happen next in a story.** In "Three Skeleton Key" (page 65), the narrator hooks the reader's curiosity in the first sentences when he says he is about to describe his "most terrifying experience."

See pages 22, 64, 77, 440.
See also *Foreshadowing.*

**SYMBOL** **A person, a place, a thing, or an event that has its own meaning *and* stands for something beyond itself as well.** Examples of symbols are all around us—in music, on television, and in everyday conversation. The skull and crossbones, for example, is a symbol of danger; the dove is a symbol of peace; and the red rose stands for true love. In literature, symbols are often more personal. For example, in "Names/Nombres" (page 145), Julia Alvarez's name is a symbol of her cultural identity.

See pages 24, 27.

**TALL TALE** **An exaggerated, fanciful story that gets "taller and taller," more and more far-fetched, the more it is told and retold.** The tall tale is an American story form. Two famous tall-tale characters are Pecos Bill and Paul Bunyan. Here is a short tall tale:

This artist was so talented that when he painted a dog it bit him. But he should have known better. Earlier he had painted a snowstorm and caught cold.

See also *Folk Tale.*

**THEME** **The idea about life revealed in a work of literature.** A theme is not the same as a subject. The subject of a work can usually be expressed in a word or two: *love, childhood, death.* The theme is the idea that the writer wishes to convey about a particular subject. The theme must be expressed in at least one sentence. For example, the subject of "Papa's Parrot" (page 404) is a boy's relationship with his father. The story's theme might be this: It is important to spend time with the people you love.

A story can have several themes, but one will often stand out from the others. A work's themes are usually not stated directly. The reader has to think about all the elements of the work and use them to make an **inference,** or educated guess, about what the themes are.

It is not likely that two readers will ever state a theme in exactly the same way. Sometimes readers even differ greatly in their interpretations of theme. A work of literature can mean different things to different people.

See pages 23, 28, 43.

**TONE** **The attitude that a writer takes toward the audience, a subject, or a character.** Tone is conveyed through the writer's choice of words and details. The poem "Sarah Cynthia Sylvia Stout Would Not Take the Garbage Out" (page 257) is light and humorous in tone. By contrast, the poem "As I Gaze upon My Father" (page 402) is serious in tone.

See pages 226, 229.

# COMMUNICATIONS HANDBOOK

## PUTTING TOGETHER A MULTIMEDIA PRESENTATION

When people talk about **media,** they mean both print and nonprint ways of communicating. Newspapers, magazines, advertisements, TV, radio, photographs, music videos, movies, and the World Wide Web are just a few of the many media.

The computer industry uses the word **multimedia** to refer to a combination of two or more of the following media:

- **text:** letters and numbers

- **sound:** music; speeches; readings of stories, poems, and plays; sound effects, such as thunder

- **graphics:** drawings, paintings, photographs, charts, maps, patterns, color

- **video:** sections clipped, or copied, from professionally made full-length movies or from videos made with a handheld camcorder

- **animation:** movement of objects and figures on screen

- **interactivity:** constant exchange of information between the computer and the user

People find new ways of working with media all the time. Don't worry if you don't have the latest software and equipment. You can learn a lot by working on both low-tech and high-tech media and multimedia projects. Follow these steps:

1. **Get together with others in a group.** When several students combine their talents and skills, they can often come up with a better product than a student working alone. You can learn a lot about yourself and other people by working with others. Besides, it's often more fun than working by yourself.

2. **Decide what you want to do.** Keep in mind

   - group members' interests and strengths

   - your equipment, tools, software, and hardware

3. **Design the project.** Use a word processing program to make a plan and a schedule. Keep a record of who is supposed to do what and of when each job has to be done.

4. **Create the content.** If you're doing skits based on Greek myths, write a script, make costumes, and find props. If you're doing a multimedia presentation, create or find the text, graphics, and

## High Tech

For a **high-tech presentation** including sound, you'll need a computer with a sound card and speakers. Find out if your school has the software you'll need to

- create and edit graphics, video, and sound
- combine all the media you want to include
- make your presentation interactive

## Low Tech

Equipment for a **low-tech presentation** might include the following items:

- recorders
- musical instruments
- a copy machine
- an overhead projector
- cameras
- camcorders
- a VCR

sounds you'll need. Check multimedia "galleries" (or graphics archives) of paintings on-line and on CD-ROM disk to see if you can find scenes from Greek myths. You may be able to find a clip from a performance of Greek folk music. Better yet, if someone in your group plays an instrument, tape the music and use it as background for your presentation.

5. **Put it all together.** If you're doing a reading of Native American poems with background music, for example, you may need to hold several rehearsals. Try reading the poems in different sequences to see which you like best. Ask another group to give you feedback before you perform in front of the class. If your group would rather not perform live, you could videotape your work. With the right technology, you can turn a live performance into a multimedia presentation. Just add some graphics and text, and make your program interactive.

## Scanning, Clipping, and Creating

If you have access to a scanner, you can scan photos, artwork, and maps as well as handwritten and printed material from books, newspapers, and magazines. A scanner stores images in a digital format so that they can be used on a computer.

You can also find lots of material on the Internet and on CD-ROM disks. Multimedia programs give you access to graphics, video, and sound "galleries" from all over the world. If the program allows you to use as much material as you want, clip whatever you need.

It may be impossible for you to create certain kinds of material, such as nature scenes or news coverage of a historical event. Still, try to create your own text, graphics, sound, and video whenever you can. You can get CD-ROMs of actors reading stories, but why not do your own readings? You can find and download text about Virginia Hamilton, but you'll learn more about writing if you read two or three articles about her and write your own text.

## Making an Interactive Program

Multimedia or authoring programs show you how to create interactive links. You can set up your presentation in either of these ways:

- The user moves from one screen to the next along a path you've laid out.

- The user has choices about where to go next.

To plan your presentation, try making a flowchart, a map showing what's on each screen. Draw a rectangle for each screen and arrows showing the paths the user can follow.

**Presenting Edgar Allan Poe.** Suppose your teacher has assigned the class to do a project on an American writer. Your group decides to do a multimedia presentation on Edgar Allan Poe. The group chooses to include the information laid out in this flowchart, which shows the paths a user might follow.

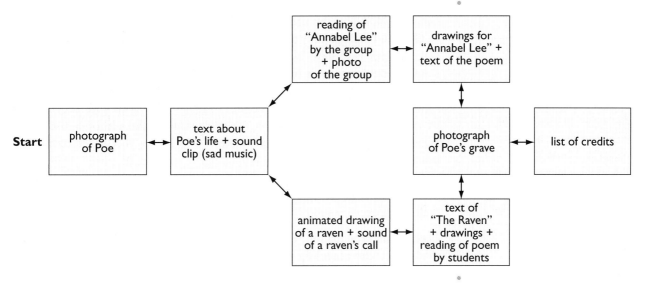

## Word Processing

Use word processing programs to

- create schedules and assignment sheets for your project

- type original text, scripts, and programs

- correct errors and revise your writing

There's no substitute for peer editing. Spelling checkers and grammar checkers pick up only certain kinds of errors. Give everyone in the group a chance to edit your writing. Leave room for comments and questions by triple-spacing drafts, and make a copy for each group member. Have everyone put comments on his or her own copy or on screen. Make sure all the group members are in agreement before you create the final text.

Word processing programs offer many formatting options. You can choose from a number of type styles and sizes to create different effects. For example, you may want to use large type for headlines. If you have a drawing program, you can even design your own letters. Word processing programs also let you change the margins for parts of your text. For example, you may want to leave extra space around an important section. You can also use lines, boxes, and bullets, or dots, to separate items and make them easier to read.

### Giving Credit Where It's Due

It's important to give credit to anyone who contributed in any way to your presentation. Even if the owner of the material gave it to you, you should credit the person who created it. Avoid **plagiarizing** (plā′jə·rīz·ĭŋ), or passing off others' work as your own.

You may want to print a separate page or screen of credits at the end of your presentation. See pages 697–698 for information on writing credits.

## The Reference Section

Every library has materials you can use only in the library. These materials include encyclopedias; biographical, scientific, and other types of dictionaries; almanacs; atlases; bibliographies; and **indices** (in'di·sēz'), comprehensive lists of books, magazines, or newspapers arranged by author, title, and subject. These resources often appear in both print and electronic form.

## Using a Media Center or Library

To find a book, tape, film, or video in the library, start by looking in the **catalog.** Most libraries use an **on-line,** or computer, **catalog.**

On-line catalogs vary from library to library. With some you begin searching for resources by **title, author,** or **subject.** With others you simply enter **keywords** for the subject you're researching. With either system, you enter information into the computer and a new screen will show you a list of materials or subject headings relating to your request. When you find an item you want, write down the title, author, and **call number,** the code of numbers and letters that shows you where to find the item on the library's shelves.

Some libraries still use card catalogs. A **card catalog** is a collection of index cards arranged in alphabetical order by title and author. Nonfiction is also cataloged by subject.

**Electronic Databases. Electronic databases** are collections of information you can access by computer. You can use these databases to find such resources as encyclopedias, almanacs, and museum art collections.

There are two kinds of electronic databases. **On-line databases** are accessed at a computer terminal connected to a modem. The modem allows the computer to communicate with other computers over telephone lines. **Portable databases** are available on magnetic tape, diskette, or CD-ROM.

A **CD-ROM** (compact disk-read only memory) is played on a computer equipped with a CD-ROM player. If you were to look up *Amy Tan* on a CD-ROM guide to literature, for example, you could hear passages from her books and read critical analyses of her work.

**Periodicals.** Most libraries have a collection of magazines and newspapers. To find up-to-date magazine or newspaper articles on a topic, use a computerized index, such as *InfoTrac* or *EBSCO.* Some of these indices provide a summary of each article. Others provide the entire text, which you can read on screen or print out. The *Readers' Guide to Periodical Literature* is a print index of articles that have appeared in hundreds of magazines.

## Using the Internet

The **Internet** is a huge network of computers. Libraries, news services, government agencies, researchers, and organizations communicate and share information on the Net. The Net also lets you chat on-line with students around the world. For help in using the Internet to do research or to communicate with someone by computer, explore the following options.

## The World Wide Web

The easiest way to do research on the Internet is on the World Wide Web. On the Web, information is stored in colorful, easy-to-access files called **Web pages.** Web pages usually have text, graphics, images, sound, and even video clips.

## Using a Web Browser

You look at Web pages with a **Web browser,** a program for accessing information on the Web. Every page on the Web has its own address, called a **URL,** or Uniform Resource Locator. If you know the address of a Web page you want to go to, just enter it in the location field on your browser.

Hundreds of millions of Web pages are connected by **hyperlinks,** which let you jump from one page to another. These links are usually underlined or colored words or images, or both, on your computer screen. With hundreds of millions of linked Web pages, how can you find the information you want?

## Using a Web Directory

If you're just beginning to look for a research topic, click on a **Web directory,** a list of topics and subtopics created by experts to help users find Web sites. Think of the directory as a giant index. Start by choosing a broad category, such as Literature. Then, work your way down through the subtopics, perhaps from Poetry to Poets. Under Poets, choose a Web page that looks interesting, perhaps one on Robert Frost.

## Using a Search Engine

If you already have a topic and need information about it, try using a **search engine,** a software tool that finds information on the Web. To use a search engine, just go to an on-line search form and enter a **search term,** or keyword. The search engine will return a list of Web pages containing your search term. The list will also show you the first few lines of each page. A search term such as *Frost* may produce thousands of results, or **hits,** including weather data on frost. If you're doing a search on the poet Robert Frost, most of these thousands of hits will be of no use. To find useful material, you have to narrow your search.

Drawing by P. Steiner © 1993 *The New Yorker*, reprinted by permission.

*"On the Internet, nobody knows you're a dog."*

## You've Got Mail!

**E-mail** is an electronic message sent over a computer network. On the Internet you can use e-mail to reach institutions, businesses, and individuals. When you e-mail places like museums, you may be able to ask **experts** about a topic you're researching. You can also use e-mail to chat with students around the country and around the world.

**Internet forums,** or newsgroups, let you discuss and debate lots of subjects with other computer users. You can write and send a question to a forum and get an answer from someone who may (or may not) know something about your topic.

## Techno Tip

- If you get too few hits, use a more general word as your search term.

- If you get too many hits, use a more specific word as your search term.

| COMMON SEARCH OPERATORS AND WHAT THEY DO | |
|---|---|
| AND | Demands that both terms appear on the page; narrows search |
| + | Demands that both terms appear on the page; narrows search |
| OR | Yields pages that contain either term; widens search |
| NOT | Excludes a word from consideration; narrows search |
| − | Excludes a word from consideration; narrows search |
| NEAR | Demands that two words be close together; narrows search |
| ADJ | Demands that two words be close together; narrows search |
| " " | Demands an exact phrase; narrows search |

## Techno Tip

To evaluate a Web source, look at the top-level domain in the URL. Here is a sample URL with the top-level domain—a government agency—labeled.

top-level domain

http://www.loc.gov

## Refining a Keyword Search

To focus your research, use **search operators,** such as the words AND or NOT, to create a string of keywords. If you're looking for material on Robert Frost and his life in Vermont, for example, you might enter the following:

Frost AND Vermont NOT weather

The more focused search term yields pages that contain both *Frost* and *Vermont* and nothing about weather. The chart on the left explains how several search operators work.

## Evaluating Sources

Since anyone—even you—can publish a Web page, it's important to evaluate your sources. Use these criteria to evaluate a source.

### Authority

Who is the author? What is his or her knowledge or experience? Trust respected sources, such as the Smithsonian Institution, not a person's newsletter or Web page.

### Accuracy

How trustworthy is the information? Does the author give his or her sources? Check information from one site against information from at least two other sites or print sources.

### Objectivity

What is the author's **perspective,** or point of view? Find out whether the information provider has a bias or hidden purpose.

### Currency

Is the information up-to-date? For a print source, check the copyright date. For a Web source, look for the date on which the page was created or revised. (This date appears at the bottom of the site's home page.)

### Coverage

How well does the source cover the topic? Could you find better information in a book? Compare the source with several others.

## Listing Sources and Taking Notes

When you write a research paper, you must **document,** or identify, your sources so that readers will know where you found your material. You must avoid **plagiarism,** or presenting another writer's words or ideas as if they were your own.

### Listing Sources

List each source, and give it a number. (You'll use these source numbers later, when you take notes.) Here's where to find the publication information (such as the name of the publisher and the copyright date) you'll need for different types of sources:

- **Print sources.** Look at the title and copyright pages of the book or periodical.

- **On-line sources.** Look at the beginning or end of the document or in a separate electronic file. For a Web page, look for a link containing the word *About.*

- **Portable electronic databases.** Look at the start-up screen, the packaging, or the disc itself.

There are several ways to list sources. The chart on page 698 shows the style created by the Modern Language Association.

### Taking Notes

Here are some tips for taking notes.

- Put notes from different sources on separate index cards, sheets of paper, or computer files.

- At the top of each card, sheet of paper, or file, write a label telling what that note is about.

- At the bottom, write the numbers of the pages on which you found the information.

- Use short phrases, and make lists of details and ideas. You don't have to write full sentences.

- Use your own words unless you find material you want to quote. If you quote an author's exact words, put quotation marks around them.

The sample note card at the right shows how to take notes.

### Preparing a List of Sources

Use your source cards to make a **works cited** list, which should appear at the end of your report. At the top of a sheet of paper, type and center the

| COMMON TOP-LEVEL DOMAINS AND WHAT THEY STAND FOR | |
|---|---|
| .edu | Educational institution. Site may publish scholarly work or the work of elementary or high school students. |
| .gov | Government body. Information is generally reliable. |
| .org | Usually a nonprofit organization. If the organization promotes culture (as a museum does), information is generally reliable; if it advocates a cause, information may be biased. |
| .com | Commercial enterprise. Information should be evaluated carefully. |
| .net | Organization offering Internet services. Information is generally reliable. |

## Sample Note Card

Poe's Childhood and Youth                     1

—Parents were actors—father
    deserted family, mother died
    before Poe's 3rd birthday
—Raised by Frances and
    John Allan
—Published first poems at age 18        p. 20

heading *Works Cited*. Below it, list your sources in alphabetical order. Follow the MLA guidelines for citing sources (see the chart below). The sample works cited list below shows you how to do this.

### Sample Works Cited List

Anderson, M. K. Edgar Allan Poe: A Mystery. New York: Franklin Watts, 1993.

"The Life of a Poet." Edgar Allan Poe Historic Site Home Page. 1997. 15 Dec. 1997 <http://www.nps.gov/edal/brochure.htm>.

"Poe, Edgar Allan." The World Book Encyclopedia. 1996 ed.

The chart below shows citations of print, audiovisual, and electronic sources.

| MLA GUIDELINES FOR CITING SOURCES | |
|---|---|
| **Books** | Give the author, title, city of publication, publisher, and copyright year.<br>Anderson, M. K. Edgar Allan Poe: A Mystery. New York: Franklin Watts, 1993. |
| **Magazine and newspaper articles** | Give the author (if named), title of the article, name of the magazine or newspaper, date, and page numbers.<br>"Did Rabies Fell Edgar Allan Poe?" Science News 2 Nov. 1996: 282. |
| **Encyclopedia articles** | Give the author (if named), title of the article, name of the encyclopedia, and edition (year).<br>"Poe, Edgar Allan." The World Book Encyclopedia. 1996 ed. |
| **Interviews** | Give the expert's name, the words *Personal interview* or *Telephone interview,* and the date.<br>M. K. Anderson. Telephone interview. 12 Jan. 1998. |
| **Films, videotapes, and audiotapes** | Give the title; producer, director, or developer; medium; distributor; and year of release.<br>Edgar Allan Poe: Terror of the Soul. Prod. Film Odyssey. Videocassette. PBS Home Video, 1995. |
| **Electronic materials, including CD-ROMs and on-line sources** | Give the author (if named); title; title of project, database, periodical, or site; electronic posting date (on-line); type of source (CD-ROMs); city (CD-ROMs); distributor (CD-ROMs); publication date (CD-ROMs) or access date; and Internet address (if any).<br>"Poe, Edgar Allan." Grolier Multimedia Encyclopedia. CD-ROM. Danbury: Grolier Interactive, 1993.<br>"The Life of a Poet." Edgar Allan Poe Historic Home Site Page. 1997. 15 Dec. 1997 <http://www.nps.gov/edal/brochure.htm>. |

## READING STRATEGIES

## Using Word Parts

Many English words can be divided into parts. If you know the meanings of various word parts, you can often determine the meanings of words.

A word part added to the beginning of a word or root is called a **prefix.** A word part added to the end of a word or root is called a **suffix.** Prefixes and suffixes can't stand alone. They must be added to words or other word parts.

A **base word** can stand alone. It is a complete word all by itself, although other word parts may be added to it to make new words.

| Prefix | Base Word | Suffix | New Word |
|--------|-----------|--------|----------|
| il– | legal | –ly | illegally |
| re– | arrange | –ment | rearrangement |

**Roots,** like prefixes and suffixes, usually can't stand alone. Roots can combine with one or more word parts to form words.

| Word Root | Meaning | Examples |
|-----------|---------|----------|
| –aud– | to hear | audition, auditorium |
| –port– | to carry | portable, transport |
| –pend– | to hang | depend, pendulum |

| COMMONLY USED PREFIXES | | |
|--------|--------|--------|
| **Prefix** | **Meaning** | **Examples of Prefix + Base Words** |
| anti– | against, opposing | antifreeze, antibiotic |
| bi– | two | biplane, biweekly |
| co– | with, together | cooperate, coauthor |
| dis– | away, expel from, opposing | dislocate, disagreement |
| in– | not | incredible, independent |
| inter– | between, among | international, interchangeable |
| mis– | badly, not, wrongly | misbehave, misuse |
| non– | not | nonprofit, nonsensical |
| post– | after, following | postgraduate, postwar |
| pre– | before | precaution, prefix |
| re– | back, again | review, rewind |
| semi– | half, partly | semicircle, semifinal |
| sub– | under, beneath | submarine, subway |
| trans– | across, beyond | transaction, transatlantic |
| un– | not, reverse of | unsure, untie |

| COMMONLY USED SUFFIXES | | |
|---|---|---|
| Suffix | Meaning | Examples of Base Words + Suffix |
| –able | able, tending to, worthy of | dependable, laughable |
| –ate | become, cause to be | domesticate, motivate |
| –dom | state, condition | boredom, wisdom |
| –en | become, cause to be | deepen, awaken |
| –ful | full of, characterized by | thankful, beautiful |
| –hood | condition, quality | brotherhood, neighborhood |
| –ion | action, condition | celebration, education |
| –ize | become, make, cause to be | civilize, legalize |
| –ly | in a certain way | timely, quickly |
| –ment | result, action | punishment, enjoyment |
| –ness | quality, state | happiness, selfishness |
| –or | one who | director, liberator |
| –ous | characterized by | dangerous, glorious |
| –ship | condition, state | ownership, relationship |
| –y | full of, characterized by, tending to | sandy, easy, sleepy |

## Summarizing, Paraphrasing, and Outlining

When you finish reading a text, check your understanding by writing a **summary,** a short restatement of the important ideas and details in a work. There are many ways to summarize; use the one that works best for the type of text you've read. For a short story, use a **story map** like the one shown at the left.

For a poem, try writing a **paraphrase.** In a paraphrase you express every idea, line by line, in your own words. Here is a paraphrase of a poem by Emily Dickinson:

| Poem | Paraphrase |
|---|---|
| Fame is a bee. It has a song— It has a sting— Ah, too, it has a wing. | Fame is like a bee because it has its joy, like the happy buzzing of a bee (the bee's "song"); it can hurt other people, the way a bee sting can hurt; and it can disappear, just as a bee can fly off. |

| STORY MAP |
|---|
| **Basic situation:** |
| **Setting:** |
| **Main character:** |
| **His or her problem:** |
| **Main events or complications:** |
| **Climax:** |
| **Resolution:** |

For a work of nonfiction, make an **outline** showing the **main ideas** and **supporting details:**

**I.** Main idea
  **A.** Supporting detail
    **1.** Supporting detail
      **a.** Supporting detail

## STUDY SKILLS

# Using a Dictionary

You can use a print or electronic dictionary to find the precise meaning and usage of words. The elements of a typical entry are explained below.

1. **Entry word.** The entry word shows how a word is spelled and how it is divided into syllables. It may also show capitalization and alternative spellings.

2. **Pronunciation.** Phonetic symbols and **diacritical marks** (symbols added to letters) show how to pronounce the entry word. A key to these symbols usually appears on every other page.

3. **Part-of-speech label.** This label shows how the entry word is used in a sentence. Some words may function as more than one part of speech. For words like these, a part-of-speech label is provided before each set of definitions.

4. **Other forms.** The spellings of plural forms of nouns, the principal parts of verbs, and the comparative and superlative forms of adjectives and adverbs are shown.

5. **Word origin.** A word's origin, or etymology (et′ə·mäl′ə·jē), is its history. It tells how the word or its parts entered the English language. In the example shown, the etymology traces the word *escape* from Middle English (ME), Norman French (NormFr), and Vulgar, or everyday, Latin (VL) to its origins in the Latin (L) word part *ex–* (out of) and the Late Latin (LL) word *cappa* (cloak).

**Sample Dictionary Entry**

① ② ③ ④

**es·cape** (e skāp′, i-) *vi.* **-caped′, -cap′ing** [ME *escapen* < NormFr *escaper*, var. of *eschaper* < VL *\*excappare* < L *ex-*, out of (see EX-¹) + LL *cappa*, cloak (i.e., leave one's cloak behind)] **1** to get free; get away; get out; break loose, as from a prison **2** to avoid an illness, accident, pain, etc. *[two were injured, but he escaped]* **3** to flow, drain, or leak away *[gas escaping from a pipe]* **4** to slip away; disappear *[the image escaped from her memory]* **5** *Bot.* to grow wild, as a plant from a condition of cultivation —*vt.* **1** to get away from; flee from *[to escape pursuers]* **2** to manage to keep away from; avoid *[to escape punishment]* **3** to come from involuntarily or unintentionally *[a scream escaped from her lips]* **4** to slip away from; be missed, unperceived, or forgotten by *[his name escapes me]* —*n.* [ME *escap*] **1** an act or instance of escaping **2** the state of having escaped **3** a means or way of escape **4** an outward flow or leakage **5** a temporary mental release from reality *[movies are her escape]* **6** *Bot.* a garden plant growing wild —*adj.* **1** giving temporary mental release from reality **2** *a)* making escape possible *[an escape hatch]* *b)* giving a basis for evading or circumventing a claim, responsibility, etc. *[an escape clause]* —**es·cap′a|ble** *adj.* — **es·cap′|er** *n.*

**SYN.**—**escape,** as compared here, implies a getting out of, a keeping away from, or simply a remaining unaffected by an impending or present danger, evil, confinement, etc. *[to escape death, criticism, etc.];* to **avoid** is to make a conscious effort to keep clear of something undesirable or harmful *[to avoid crowds during a flu epidemic];* to **evade** is to escape or avoid by artifice, cunning, adroitness, etc. *[to evade pursuit, one's duty, etc.];* to **elude** is to escape the grasp of someone or something by artful or slippery dodges or because of a baffling quality *[the criminal eluded the police, the meaning eluded him]*

⑤ ⑥ ⑦ ⑧ ⑨ ⑩

©1994 *Webster's New World Dictionary of American English,* Third College Edition.

6. **Examples.** Phrases or sentences show how the word is used.

7. **Definitions.** If a word has more than one meaning, the meanings are numbered or lettered.

8. **Special-usage labels.** These labels identify special meanings or special uses of the word.

9. **Related word forms.** These are other forms of the entry word, usually created by the addition of suffixes.

10. **Synonyms and antonyms.** Synonyms (words similar in meaning) and antonyms (words opposite in meaning) may appear at the end of an entry.

## Using a Thesaurus

A **thesaurus** is a collection of synonyms. You use a thesaurus when you're looking for a word that expresses a specific meaning. There are two kinds of thesauruses. One kind, developed by Peter Mark Roget, groups words according to meaning. Here's how to use it:

- In the index, look up the word that conveys your general meaning. Under FREE, for example, you might find *escape, freedom, liberty,* and *will.* Each of these subentries is followed by a number.

- Choose the subentry whose meaning is closest to what you have in mind. In this case, suppose you choose *escape.*

- In the body of the text, find the number that follows the subentry *escape* in the index. Then, look under this number to find synonyms for *escape.*

The second kind of thesaurus lists words in alphabetical order, as in a dictionary. See the sample entry below.

### Sample Thesaurus Entry

**shun, v.** —*SYN.* dodge, evade, keep away from, ignore, neglect; see also **avoid.** —*ANT.* accept, ADOPT, take advantage of.

©1997 *Webster's New World Thesaurus,* Third Edition.

# Reading Maps, Charts, and Graphs

## Types of Maps

**Physical maps** show the natural landscape of an area. In these maps, shading is often used to show physical features like mountains, hills, and valleys; colors are often used to show **elevation** (height above or below sea level). **Political maps** show political units, such as states and nations. They usually show borders and capitals. The map of Canada, the United States, and Mexico shown here is a political map. **Special-purpose maps** are used to present information such as the routes of explorers. The literary map on pages 498–499 is a special-purpose map.

## How to Read a Map

1. **Identify the map's focus.** The map's title and labels tell you its focus—its subject and the geographical area it covers.

2. **Study the legend.** The **legend,** or **key,** explains the symbols, lines, colors, and shading used in the map. (The map on this page has a legend.)

3. **Check directions and distances.** Maps often include a **compass rose,** a diagram that shows north, south, east, and west. If you're looking at a map that doesn't have one, assume that north is at the top, west is to the left, and so on. Many maps also include a **scale** to help you relate distances on the map to actual distances. Note the compass rose and scale on the map on this page.

4. **Look at the larger context.** The **absolute location** of any place on earth is given by its **latitude** (the number of degrees north or south of the equator) and **longitude** (the number of degrees east or west of the **prime meridian,** or 0 degrees longitude). Some maps also include **locator maps,** which show the area depicted in relation to a larger area. Notice the locator map in the upper right corner of the map shown here.

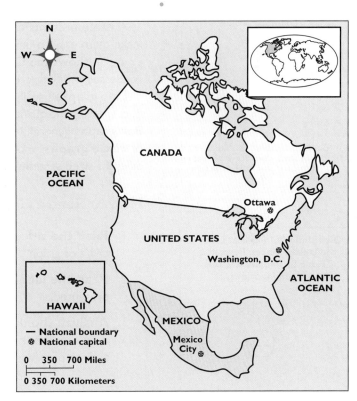

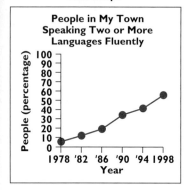

**Line Graph**

**People in My Town Speaking Two or More Languages Fluently**

*People (percentage)* vs. *Year* (1978, '82, '86, '90, '94, 1998)

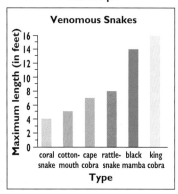

**Bar Graph**

**Venomous Snakes**

*Maximum length (in feet)* vs. *Type* (coral snake, cotton-mouth, cape cobra, rattle-snake, black mamba, king cobra)

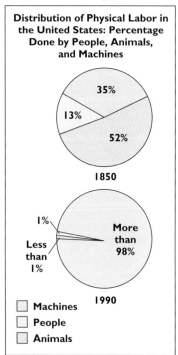

**Pie Graph**

**Distribution of Physical Labor in the United States: Percentage Done by People, Animals, and Machines**

1850: 35%, 13%, 52%

1990: 1%, Less than 1%, More than 98%

☐ Machines
☐ People
☐ Animals

## Types of Charts and Graphs

A **flowchart** shows a **sequence** of events or the steps in a process. Flow-charts are often used to show cause-and-effect relationships. The sequencing chart on page 433 is an example of a flowchart. A **time line** shows events in **chronological order** (the order in which they happened).

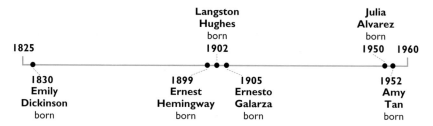

| | Langston Hughes born 1902 | | Julia Alvarez born 1950 | 1960 |
|---|---|---|---|---|
| 1825 | | | | |
| 1830 Emily Dickinson born | 1899 Ernest Hemingway born | 1905 Ernesto Galarza born | 1952 Amy Tan born | |

A **table** presents categorized facts arranged in rows and columns to make them easy to understand and compare. The table on page 497, for example, shows the Greek and Roman names of mythological gods and goddesses and their areas of power.

**Line graphs** usually show changes in quantity over time. In line graphs, dots showing the quantity at different times are connected to create a line. **Bar graphs** generally compare quantities within categories. **Pie graphs,** or **circle graphs,** show proportions. A pie graph is a circle divided into different-sized sections, like slices of a pie.

## How to Read a Chart or a Graph

1. **Read the title.** The title tells you the subject and purpose of the chart or graph.

2. **Read the labels.** The labels tell you what type of information is presented.

3. **Analyze the details.** Read numbers carefully. Note increases or decreases. Look for the direction or order of events and for trends and relationships.

## STRATEGIES FOR TAKING TESTS

When you begin a test, **scan** it quickly and count the items. Then, decide how to spend your time. Here are some sample test questions and specific strategies for answering four kinds of test questions.

**True/false questions** ask you to determine whether a given statement is true or false. For example:

1.  T  F  Ernesto Galarza was born in Mexico but moved to the United States as a young boy.

### HOW TO ANSWER TRUE/FALSE QUESTIONS

- Read the statement carefully. The whole statement is false if any part of it is false.
- Look for words like *always* and *never*. A statement is true only if it is always true.

**Multiple-choice questions** ask you to select a correct answer from several choices. For example:

1. The theme of a story is its

   **A** subject    **C** conflict

   **B** message    **D** setting

### HOW TO ANSWER MULTIPLE-CHOICE QUESTIONS

- Make sure you understand the question or statement before you look at the choices.
- Look for words such as *not* and *always,* which may help you eliminate some choices.
- Read all the choices before selecting an answer. Eliminate choices that you know are incorrect.
- Think carefully about the remaining choices. Pick the one that makes the most sense.

**Matching questions** ask you to match the items in one list with the items in another list. For example:

**Directions:** Match each item in the left-hand column with its definition in the right-hand column.

_____ **1.** setting    **A** story of a person's life

_____ **2.** biography    **B** language that appeals to the senses

_____ **3.** metaphor    **C** time and place of a literary work

_____ **4.** imagery    **D** comparison between unlike things

### HOW TO ANSWER MATCHING QUESTIONS

- Read the directions carefully. Not all the items in one column may be used, and items may be used more than once.
- Scan the columns. First, match items you are sure of. Then, match items you are less sure of.
- For the rest of the items, make your best guess.

**Analogy questions** ask you to figure out the relationship between two words and then identify another pair with a similar relationship. For example:

**Directions:** Select the best pair of words that best completes the analogy.

SENTENCE : PARAGRAPH : : _____

**A**  noun : verb          **C**  essay : paragraph
**B**  paragraph : essay    **D**  poetry : nonfiction

| HOW TO ANSWER ANALOGY QUESTIONS |
| --- |
| • Figure out the relationship between the words in the first pair. (In the example, a sentence is part of a paragraph.) |
| • Express the analogy in a statement or question. (A sentence is part of a paragraph. In what other pair is the first item part of the second item?) |
| • Select the pair of words with the same relationship as the first pair. (A paragraph is part of an essay.) |

**Essay questions** in a test ask you to think critically about things you have learned and to express your understanding in a paragraph or more.

| ESSAY QUESTIONS | | |
| --- | --- | --- |
| **Key Verb** | **Task** | **Sample Question** |
| analyze | Take something apart to see how it works. | Analyze the character of Cassie in "Song of the Trees." |
| compare | Discuss likenesses. (Sometimes *compare* means "compare *and* contrast.") | Compare the theme of "A Mason-Dixon Memory" with that of *Brian's Song*. |
| contrast | Discuss differences. | Contrast the fairy tale "Cinderella" with the German folk tale "Aschenputtel." |
| define | Give specific details that make something unique. | Define the term *onomatopoeia*. |
| describe | Give a picture in words. | Describe the setting of "Bargain." |
| discuss | Examine in detail. | Discuss the theme of "Amigo Brothers." |
| explain | Give reasons for something. | Explain why foreshadowing creates suspense. |
| identify | Discuss specific characteristics. | Identify the rhyme scheme of "The Runaway." |
| list (*also* outline *or* trace) | Give all steps in order or certain details about a subject. | List the main parts of a plot. |
| summarize | Briefly review the main points. | Summarize the plot of "Rikki-tikki-tavi." |

## Writing Business Letters

To request information from someone who is far away or difficult to reach, write a business letter. Follow these guidelines:

1. **Write in formal English.** Avoid slang. The tone of your letter should be polite and respectful.

2. **Be clear.** Explain why you are writing. Include important information, and be as brief as possible.

3. **Make the letter look professional.** Type, print, or write your letter on unlined 8½- × 11-inch paper. Follow the **block form** (shown below).

### Sample Business Letter

**(1)** 1794 South Hillside Avenue
Glendale, MO 63122

November 14, 1999

**(2)** Ms. Pilar Lopez
Executive Director
Glendale Chamber of Commerce
2192 Claymore Street
Glendale, MO 63123

**(3)** Dear Ms. Lopez:

**(4)** I am researching the history of our town. I would like to know who first settled the town and why they chose this location.

Please send me any information that might help me with my research. I have enclosed a self-addressed, stamped envelope for your reply.

**(5)** Sincerely,

**(6)** *Douglas Davidson*

Douglas Davidson

---

**(1) Heading**
Your street address
Your city, state, and ZIP code
The date you write the letter

**(2) Inside Address**
The name and address of the person you are writing to. Use a title like *Mr., Ms.,* or *Mrs.* or a professional title, such as *Dr.* or *Professor,* before the person's name. Put the person's business title after the name.

**(3) Salutation** (greeting)
End the salutation with a colon.

**(4) Body**
Your message. If the body is more than one paragraph long, leave an extra line between paragraphs.

**(5) Closing**
Use *Yours truly* or *Sincerely,* followed by a comma.

**(6) Signature**
Type or print your name, leaving space for your signature. Sign your name in ink below the closing.

## Filling Out Forms

When you fill out a form, your purpose is to give clear, complete information. Follow these guidelines whenever you complete forms.

1. Look over the entire form before you begin.

2. Look for and follow special instructions (such as *Type or print* or *Use a pencil*).

3. Read each item carefully.

4. Supply all the information requested. If a question does not apply to you, write *does not apply,* or use a dash or the abbreviation N/A (meaning "not applicable").

5. When you're finished, make sure nothing is left blank. Also, check for errors and correct them neatly.

6. Mail the form to the correct address or give it to the right person.

## PROOFREADERS' MARKS

| Symbol | Example | Meaning |
|--------|---------|---------|
| ≡ | Fifty-first street | Capitalize lowercase letter. |
| / | Sally's Aunt | Lowercase capital letter. |
| ∧ | the capital ᵒᶠMaine | Insert. |
| ℘ | What's the the deal? | Delete. |
| ⌒ | a broken flower pot | Close up space. |
| ∿ | beleive | Change order (of letters or words). |
| ¶ | ¶"Goodbye," she said. | Begin a new paragraph. |
| ⊙ | Stay well⊙ | Add a period. |
| ∧ | Of course you may be wrong. | Add a comma. |

# 1 THE PARTS OF SPEECH

## THE NOUN

**1a.** **A** *noun* **is a word used to name a person, a place, a thing, or an idea.**

| | |
|---|---|
| **PERSONS** | giant, Miss Nettie Hopley, baby sitter, immigrant |
| **PLACES** | pasture, Italy, Sutter's Fort, Crocker Art Gallery |
| **THINGS** | quilt, key, frog, desk, Newbery Medal, *Voyager 2* |
| **IDEAS** | knowledge, friendliness, success, love, self-esteem |

## Compound Nouns

A **compound noun** is two or more words used together as a single noun. The parts of a compound noun may be written as one word, as separate words, or as a hyphenated word.

| | |
|---|---|
| **ONE WORD** | butterfly, playground, Passover, classroom |
| **SEPARATE WORDS** | Golden Age, compact disc, post office |
| **HYPHENATED WORD** | self-control, bull's-eye, six-year-old |

Compound words may be written as one word, as separate words, or as a hyphenated word. To be sure you are spelling a compound word correctly, always use a current dictionary.

## Collective Nouns

A **collective noun** is a word that names a group.

| | | | | |
|---|---|---|---|---|
| **EXAMPLES** class | family | choir | herd | jury |

## Common Nouns and Proper Nouns

A **common noun** is a general name for a person, a place, a thing, or an idea. A **proper noun** names a particular person, place, thing, or idea. Proper nouns always begin with a capital letter. Common nouns begin with a capital letter in titles and when they begin sentences.

| | | | |
|---|---|---|---|
| **COMMON NOUNS** | poem | nation | day |
| **PROPER NOUNS** | "The Runaway" | Japan | Friday |

✓ *QUICK CHECK 1*

Identify the nouns in the following sentences. Classify each noun as *common* or *proper*. Also label any *compound* or *collective* nouns.

**EXAMPLE** **1.** "Rikki-tikki-tavi" is a short story by Rudyard Kipling.

      **1.** *"Rikki-tikki-tavi"—compound, proper; short story—compound, common; Rudyard Kipling—compound, proper*

1. Rikki-tikki-tavi is the brave pet of a family in India.
2. A fierce little mongoose, Rikki-tikki knows no fear.
3. Although his teeth are sharp, he would never bite a person.
4. Instead, he kills a deadly cobra in the bathroom.
5. He saves the lives of Teddy and his family.

## Using Specific Nouns

Whenever possible, use specific, exact nouns. Using specific nouns will make your writing more accurate as well as more interesting.

| NONSPECIFIC | Animals drank from the water. |
|---|---|
| SPECIFIC | Horses, cattle, and burros drank from the creek. |

### Try It Out ✎

In the following paragraph, replace the vague nouns with exact, specific nouns.

[1] As a girl wept under a tree, a woman suddenly appeared. [2] She waved a magic stick. [3] A vegetable turned into a vehicle. [4] With another movement of the woman's stick, the girl's torn clothing turned into a beautiful dress. [5] Overjoyed, the girl thanked the woman and rode to the party at the building.

# THE PRONOUN

**1b.** **A *pronoun* is a word used in place of one or more nouns or pronouns.**

| EXAMPLES | Emily Dickinson took few trips; Dickinson spent most of Dickinson's time at Amherst. |
|---|---|
| | Emily Dickinson took few trips; **she** spent most of **her** time at Amherst. |

The word that a pronoun stands for is called its ***antecedent.*** The antecedent is not always stated.

| STATED | Dickinson wrote many **poems** and hid **them** in her room. |
|---|---|
| UNSTATED | **Who** edited *The Poems of Emily Dickinson*? |

## Personal Pronouns

A ***personal pronoun*** refers to the one speaking (*first person*), the one spoken to (*second person*), or the one spoken about (*third person*).

| PERSONAL PRONOUNS | | |
|---|---|---|
| | **SINGULAR** | **PLURAL** |
| **First Person** | I, me, my, mine | we, us, our, ours |
| **Second Person** | you, your, yours | you, your, yours |
| **Third Person** | he, him, his, she, her, hers, it, its | they, them, their, theirs |

NOTE Some authorities prefer to call possessive forms of pronouns (such as *my, his,* and *their*) *possessive adjectives.* Follow your teacher's instructions regarding possessive forms.

## Reflexive and Intensive Pronouns

A *reflexive pronoun* refers to the subject and directs the action of the verb back to the subject. An *intensive pronoun* emphasizes a noun or another pronoun. Reflexive and intensive pronouns have the same form.

| | |
|---|---|
| **FIRST PERSON** | myself, ourselves |
| **SECOND PERSON** | yourself, yourselves |
| **THIRD PERSON** | himself, herself, itself, themselves |

**REFLEXIVE**   Emily Dickinson wrote **herself** notes on the backs of recipes.

**INTENSIVE**   She did all the baking **herself.**

## Demonstrative Pronouns

A *demonstrative pronoun* (*this, that, these, those*) points out a person, a place, a thing, or an idea.

**EXAMPLE**   **This** is a collection of her poems.

## Interrogative Pronouns

An *interrogative pronoun* (*what, which, who, whom, whose*) introduces a question.

**EXAMPLE**   **What** were Dickinson's household duties?

## Relative Pronouns

A *relative pronoun* (*that, what, which, who, whom, whose*) introduces a subordinate clause.

**EXAMPLE**   Dickinson wrote of thoughts and feelings **that** she had.

## Indefinite Pronouns

An *indefinite pronoun* refers to a person, a place, or a thing that is not specifically named. Many indefinite pronouns can also serve as adjectives.

☞ *This, that, these,* and *those* can also be used as adjectives. See page 713.

☞ See pages 746–750 for more on subordinate clauses.

### Common Indefinite Pronouns

| | | | | |
|---|---|---|---|---|
| all | each | few | no one | several |
| any | either | many | nobody | some |
| both | everything | none | one | somebody |

**PRONOUN**   **Neither** of Emily's sisters was aware of the poems.

**ADJECTIVE**   **Neither** sister was aware of the poems.

 **QUICK CHECK 2**

Identify each of the pronouns in the following sentences as *personal, reflexive, intensive, demonstrative, interrogative, relative,* or *indefinite.*

**EXAMPLE**  1. I wonder about anyone who is famous.
  1. *I—personal; anyone—indefinite; who—relative*

1. Are you famous or important?
2. Emily Dickinson herself declared that she wasn't.
3. Yet, who doesn't recognize her name today?
4. If you don't, this is your chance to read some of her poems.
5. You can decide for yourself if someone important wrote them.

## THE ADJECTIVE

**1c.** An *adjective* is a word used to modify a noun or a pronoun.

To **modify** a word means to describe the word or to make its meaning more definite. An adjective modifies a word by telling *what kind, which one, how much,* or *how many.*

| WHAT KIND? | WHICH ONE? | HOW MUCH? or HOW MANY? |
|---|---|---|
| *noisy* relatives | *those* days | *many* years |
| *proper* manners | *another* skirt | *more* guests |
| *Mexican* food | *next* lesson | *one* mistake |

## Articles

The most frequently used adjectives are *a, an,* and *the.* These adjectives are called **articles.** The adjectives *a* and *an* are **indefinite articles.** Each one indicates that the noun refers to someone or something in general. *A* is used before a word beginning with a consonant sound. *An* is used before a word beginning with a vowel sound.

**EXAMPLES**  **An** early gift later caused Tan **an** embarrassing moment.
  Her mother gave her **a** miniskirt.
  It took him **an** hour to find **a** uniform that fit.

The adjective *the* is a **definite article.** It indicates that the noun refers to someone or something in particular.

**EXAMPLE**  **The** minister's son attended **the** potluck dinner.

## Proper Adjectives

A **proper adjective** is formed from a proper noun and begins with a capital letter.

---

 **NOTE**  An adjective may come before or after the word it modifies.

**EXAMPLES**  **Each one** of the guests ate **steamed fish.** [The adjective *each* modifies *one.* The adjective *steamed* modifies *fish.*]

The **minister, proper** and **dignified,** was also **courteous.** [The adjectives *proper, dignified,* and *courteous* modify *minister.*]

| PROPER NOUNS | PROPER ADJECTIVES |
|---|---|
| China | **Chinese** customs |
| America | **American** manners |
| Buddhist | **Buddhist** monk |
| Christmas | **Christmas** dinner |

NOTE  Some proper nouns, such as *Buddhist,* do not change spelling when they are used as adjectives.

## Demonstrative Adjectives

*This, that, these,* and *those* can be used as adjectives and as pronouns. When these words modify a noun or a pronoun, they are called **demonstrative adjectives.** When used alone, these words are called **demonstrative pronouns.**

| DEMONSTRATIVE ADJECTIVES | Is **this** story more interesting than **that** one? |
|---|---|
| | **Those** dishes are considered a delicacy. |

| DEMONSTRATIVE PRONOUNS | **That** is the way to hold chopsticks. |
|---|---|
| | Are **these** typical foods in China? |

☞ For more about demonstrative pronouns, see page 711.

## Nouns Used as Adjectives

When a noun modifies another noun or a pronoun, it is considered an adjective. Most compound nouns can be used as adjectives.

| NOUNS | NOUNS USED AS ADJECTIVES |
|---|---|
| fish | **fish** scales |
| holiday | **holiday** menu |
| bicycle | **bicycle** tires |
| Christmas Eve | **Christmas Eve** celebration |

## ✓ QUICK CHECK 3

Identify each adjective in the following sentences. Then, give the word the adjective modifies. Do not include the articles *a, an,* and *the.*

EXAMPLE   1. That name sounds strange to me.
    1. *That—name; strange—name*

1. Having an unusual name can be a problem for anyone.
2. That problem plagued Julia Alvarez all through school.
3. As a girl, she was known by many names—Judy, Jules, and even Alcatraz—but her family pronounced *Julia* "Hoo-lee-ah."
4. Those neighbors with a New York City accent said "Joo-lee-ah."
5. Family members told her to keep writing and her name would be famous.

# THE VERB

**1d.** **A *verb* is a word used to express action or a state of being.**

**EXAMPLES**   Gary Soto **wrote** "The No-Guitar Blues."
Soto's stories **seem** realistic to me.

Every sentence must have a subject and a verb. The verb says something about the subject.

## Action Verbs

**1e.** **An *action verb* may express physical action or mental action.**

**PHYSICAL ACTION**   lean, watch, hop, say, push, toss, pull
**MENTAL ACTION**   want, hope, regret, wonder, forget, dream

## Transitive and Intransitive Verbs

**(1)** **A *transitive verb* is an action verb that expresses an action directed toward a person or thing.**

**EXAMPLE**   He **held** a guitar. [The action of *held* is directed toward *guitar.*]

With transitive verbs, the action passes from the doer (the subject) to the receiver of the action. Words that receive the action of a transitive verb are called *objects*.

**EXAMPLES**   She called **him.** [*Him* is the object of the verb *called.*]
The boy told the **villagers** a **lie.** [Both *villagers* and *lie* are objects of the verb *told.*]

**(2)** **An *intransitive verb* expresses action (or tells something about the subject) without passing the action to a receiver.**

**EXAMPLE**   Fausto **waited** hopefully for a reward. [The action of *waited* is not directed toward a receiver. The verb *waited* does not have an object.]

## Linking Verbs

**1f.** **A *linking verb* links, or connects, the subject with a noun, a pronoun, or an adjective in the predicate.**

**EXAMPLES**   The dog's name **was** Roger. [name = Roger]
Los Lobos **became** Fausto's role models. [Los Lobos = role models]

---

👉 For more about subjects and verbs, see pages 720–723 and 751–753.

---

👉 For more information about objects, see page 755.

---

**NOTE**   A verb may be transitive in one sentence and intransitive in another.

**TRANSITIVE**   He **smelled** his grandfather's aftershave.
**INTRANSITIVE**   Grandfather **smelled** good.

---

Like intransitive verbs, linking verbs never take direct objects.

| Linking Verbs Formed from the Verb *Be* | | | |
|---|---|---|---|
| am | were | should have been | was being |
| are | be | will have been | can be |
| being | been | has been | must be |
| is | may be | have been | might be |
| was | would be | will be | could be |

## Other Linking Verbs    appear, grow, seem, stay, become, look, smell, taste, feel, remain, sound, turn

## Helping Verbs

**1g.** **A *helping verb* (*auxiliary verb*) helps the main verb to express an action or a state of being.**

**EXAMPLES**   **could** be   **may have** asked   **might have been** caught

| COMMONLY USED HELPING VERBS | |
|---|---|
| **Forms of *Be*** | am, be, being, was, are, been, is, were |
| **Forms of *Do*** | do, does, did |
| **Forms of *Have*** | have, has, had |
| **Other Helping Verbs** | can, may, must, should, would, could, might, shall, will |

A ***verb phrase*** consists of a main verb and at least one helping verb.

**EXAMPLE**   Fausto **could have kept** the money. [The main verb is *kept.*]

 **QUICK CHECK 4**

Identify the italicized verb in each of the following sentences as an *action verb,* a *linking verb,* or a *helping verb.* Then, for each action verb, tell whether the verb is *transitive* or *intransitive.*

**EXAMPLE**   **1.** Have you *read* other poems by Shel Silverstein?
   **1.** *action verb, transitive*

**1.** Sarah Cynthia Sylvia Stout would not *take* the trash out.
**2.** It *smelled* bad.
**3.** She *did*n't care about that or about her family or friends.
**4.** Finally, she *was* alone with her garbage.
**5.** That huge pile of garbage *reached* to another state.

 See pages 756–757 for more information about linking verbs.

 **NOTE**   Some words may be either action verbs or linking verbs, depending on how they are used.

**LINKING**   The dog **looked** hungry.
**ACTION**   The dog **looked** for another orange peel.

**NOTE**   Sometimes the verb phrase is interrupted by other words.

**EXAMPLES**   **Will** you please **explain** the theme of this story? Fausto **did** not [*or* **didn't**] **tell** the dog's owners the truth.

For more information about verb phrases, see pages 720, 741, and 752.

# THE ADVERB

**1h.** **An *adverb* is a word used to modify a verb, an adjective, or another adverb.**

| | |
|---|---|
| **MODIFYING A VERB** | They could **not** radio for help. |
| **MODIFYING AN ADJECTIVE** | The sun was **extremely** hot. |
| **MODIFYING ANOTHER ADVERB** | **Quite** bravely, they landed a shark. |

An adverb tells *where, when, how,* or *to what extent* (*how much* or *how long*).

| | |
|---|---|
| **WHERE?** | Killer whales are common **here.** |
| **HOW?** | The accident occurred **suddenly.** |
| **WHEN?** | **Then** the survivors depended on their wits. |
| **TO WHAT EXTENT?** | They were **exceptionally** careful with their supplies. |

The word *not* is an adverb. When *not* is part of a contraction like *hadn't,* the *–n't* is an adverb.

 QUICK CHECK 5

Identify the adverb or adverbs in each of the following sentences. Then, give the word or phrase each adverb modifies.

**EXAMPLE**  1. Have you ever wondered about being shipwrecked?
　　　　　　1. *ever—Have wondered*

1. Neil cried sadly for their lost ship.
2. Too soon, a cargo vessel sailed into the distance.
3. Dougal Robertson would not yield to his most desperate fears.
4. He steeled himself and tried harder.
5. Eventually, a Japanese tuna fisher rescued them.

 **Using Descriptive Adverbs**

The adverb *very* is overused. In your writing, try to replace *very* with more descriptive adverbs, or revise the sentence so that other words carry more of the descriptive meaning.

**EXAMPLE**  Their ordeal at sea lasted a very long time.
**REVISED**  Their ordeal at sea lasted an **extremely** long time.

*or*

Their ordeal at sea lasted **thirty-eight days.**

---

 **NOTE**  Adverbs may come before, after, or between the words they modify.

**EXAMPLES**  **Slowly,** the shark was circling.
The shark was **slowly** circling.
The shark was circling **slowly.**

---

  For more on modifiers in general, see Part 5: Using Modifiers.

---

## Try It Out ✎

For each use of *very* below, substitute another adverb. You may wish to revise the sentence.

1. For entertainment, they imagined *very* delicious foods.
2. Douglas dreamed of a *very* cold honeydew melon.
3. At night on the sea, they felt *very* alone.
4. *Very* quickly, they pulled the sea turtle aboard.
5. After their rescue, a *very* fine cook helped them back to health.

## THE PREPOSITION

**1i.** A *preposition* is a word used to show the relationship of a noun or a pronoun to another word in the sentence.

Notice how a change in the preposition changes the relationship between *waves* and *rocks* in each of the following examples.

> The waves crashed **under** the rocks.
> The waves crashed **on** the rocks.
> The waves crashed **against** the rocks.
> The waves crashed **in front of** the rocks.

| Commonly Used Prepositions | | | |
|---|---|---|---|
| aboard | before | in | over |
| about | behind | in addition to | past |
| above | below | in front of | since |
| according to | beneath | inside | through |
| across | beside | in spite of | throughout |
| against | between | into | under |
| around | from | out of | without |

### The Prepositional Phrase

A preposition is usually followed by a noun or a pronoun. This noun or pronoun is called the **object of the preposition.** All together, the preposition, its object, and any modifiers of the object are called a **prepositional phrase.**

**EXAMPLE**   The family went **to beautiful Cocoa Beach.**

A preposition may have more than one object.

**EXAMPLE**   Tiffany sat **with David, Susan, and Amber.**

 *QUICK CHECK 6*

Identify the preposition or prepositions in each of the following sentences. Then, give the object of each preposition.

**EXAMPLE**   **1.** Do you know any stories about the sea?
   **1.** *about—sea*

1. Elizabeth told a sad story about her youth.
2. She had loved a man of the sea.
3. She never said the words to him.
4. One day, he didn't return from a fishing trip.
5. Still, according to Elizabeth, he is always with her.

**NOTE** Some words may be used as either prepositions or adverbs. To tell an adverb from a preposition, remember that a preposition is always followed by a noun or pronoun object.

**NOTE** Do not confuse a prepositional phrase that begins with *to* (*to town*) with a verb form that begins with *to* (*to run*).

☞ For more about prepositional phrases, see pages 735, 740, and 741–742.

## THE CONJUNCTION

**1j.** A *conjunction* is a word used to join words or groups of words.

**(1)** *Coordinating conjunctions* connect words or groups of words used in the same way.

| Coordinating Conjunctions | | | | | | |
|---|---|---|---|---|---|---|
| and | but | or | nor | for | so | yet |

**EXAMPLES** Echo **or** Narcissus [two proper nouns]
down from Olympus **and** to the mountains [two prepositional phrases]
Echo angered Hera, **so** Hera punished her. [two independent clauses]

**(2)** *Correlative conjunctions* are pairs of conjunctions that connect words or groups of words used in the same way.

| Correlative Conjunctions | | |
|---|---|---|
| both . . . and | either . . . or | neither . . . nor |
| not only . . . but also | whether . . . or | |

**EXAMPLES** **Both** the nymphs **and** Echo were loyal to Zeus. [two nouns]
She **not only** delayed Hera **but also** detained her. [two verbs with objects]
**Either** Echo would have love, **or** she would die. [two complete ideas]

## THE INTERJECTION

**1k.** An *interjection* is a word used to express emotion. An interjection does not have a grammatical relation to other words in the sentence. Usually an interjection is followed by an exclamation point. Sometimes an interjection is set off by a comma.

**EXAMPLES** **Oh!** You surprised me.
**Why,** I've heard this story before.
**Wow!** What a story that was.
**Well,** Hera certainly isn't someone to cross!

---

**NOTE** When *for* is used as a conjunction, it connects groups of words that are sentences, and it is preceded by a comma. On all other occasions, *for* is used as a preposition.

**CONJUNCTION** The team forfeited the game, **for** they refused to play.

**PREPOSITION** Outraged, people shouted **for** fair play.

---

☞ Coordinating conjunctions that join independent clauses are preceded by a comma. See page 769.

| Common Interjections | | | |
|---|---|---|---|
| aha | hooray | ouch | wow |
| aw | oh | well | yikes |
| goodness | oops | whew | yippee |

 **QUICK CHECK 7**

Identify the *conjunctions* and *interjections* in the following sentences.

**EXAMPLE**   **1.** Well, Echo was either unwise or unlucky.

  **1.** *Well—interjection; either . . . or—conjunction*

1. Echo not only answered Narcissus but also ran to and embraced him.
2. Oh! Why did Narcissus scoff and shove Echo away?
3. Goodness! Narcissus was a handsome but self-centered person.
4. Both Echo and Narcissus suffered because of his selfishness.
5. They were doomed, yet he lives on in the narcissus flower.

## DETERMINING PARTS OF SPEECH

The part of speech of a word is determined by the way the word is used in a sentence. Many words can be used as more than one part of speech.

**EXAMPLES**   This **well** belongs to the golf course. [noun]

  **Well,** Dondré was quite disappointed. [interjection]

  He has always played **well.** [adverb]

  Clifton Davis suddenly remembered an event from his **past.** [noun]

  Didn't his team drive **past** the Lincoln Memorial? [preposition]

  As they rode along, the lights of the city flew **past.** [adverb]

 **QUICK CHECK 8**

Identify the part of speech of the italicized word in each sentence.

**EXAMPLE**   **1.** *For* Dondré Green, it was a blessing in disguise.

  **1.** *preposition*

1. *Any* of the boys might have objected, but no one did.
2. They all would *back* him.
3. And they never looked *back.*
4. *Support* like that can make a man proud.
5. I wish everyone would *support* each other as those boys did!

# 2 AGREEMENT

## NUMBER

*Number* is the form of a word that indicates whether the word is singular or plural.

**2a.** When a word refers to one person, place, thing, or idea, the word is *singular* in number. When a word refers to more than one, it is *plural* in number.

| SINGULAR | house | drum | wife | I | he | each |
|---|---|---|---|---|---|---|
| PLURAL | houses | drums | wives | we | they | all |

 For more about plurals, see pages 783–784.

## AGREEMENT OF SUBJECT AND VERB

**2b.** A verb agrees with its subject in number.

A subject and verb **agree** when they have the same number.

**(1)** Singular subjects take singular verbs.

**EXAMPLE** A **messenger gives** the king's orders.

**(2)** Plural subjects take plural verbs.

**EXAMPLE** Many **wives weep** after their husbands' departures during the war.

The first auxiliary (helping) verb in a verb phrase must agree with its subject.

**EXAMPLES** **He is** marching to war.
**They are** marching to war.

Generally, nouns ending in *s* are plural (*candles, ideas, neighbors, horses*), and verbs ending in *s* are singular (*sees, writes, speaks, carries*). However, verbs used with the singular pronouns *I* and *you* generally do not end in *s*.

 For more information about verb phrases, see pages 715, 741, and 752.

 QUICK CHECK 1

For each of the following sentences, choose the correct form of the verb in parentheses.

**EXAMPLE** 1. (*Do, Does*) you like folk tales like this one?
1. *Do*

1. A tree spirit (*take, takes*) the shape of the absent husband.
2. Many days (*pass, passes*).
3. Then the husband (*return, returns*).
4. Dogs (*bark, barks*) at him.
5. The judge (*has, have*) suggested a solution.

## Problems in Agreement

### Prepositional Phrases Between Subjects and Verbs

**2c.** The number of a subject is not changed by a prepositional phrase following the subject.

**NONSTANDARD**  One of the strongest heroes are Hercules.

**STANDARD**  **One** of the strongest heroes **is** Hercules.

### Indefinite Pronouns

Some pronouns do not refer to a definite person, place, thing, or idea and are therefore called *indefinite pronouns.*

**2d.** The following indefinite pronouns are singular: *anybody, anyone, each, either, everybody, everyone, neither, nobody, no one, one, somebody, someone.*

**EXAMPLE**  **Neither** of these offers **relieves** him of his task.

**2e.** The following indefinite pronouns are plural: *both, few, many, several.*

**EXAMPLE**  **Both** of the wild boar's tusks **frighten** Eurystheus.

**2f.** The following indefinite pronouns may be either singular or plural: *all, any, most, none, some.*

**COMPUTER NOTE**  You may want to create an indefinite-pronoun guide to help you use these pronouns correctly. First, summarize the information in rules 2d–2f and 2p–2r. Then, choose several examples to illustrate the rules. Using a computer, you can create a "Help" file in which to store this information. Call up your "Help" file whenever you run into difficulty with indefinite pronouns in your writing. If you don't use a computer, keep a writing notebook.

The number of these pronouns is often determined by the object in a prepositional phrase that follows the pronoun. If the pronoun refers to a singular object, the subject is singular. If the pronoun refers to a plural object, the subject is plural.

**EXAMPLES**  **All** of the stable **needs** cleaning. [*All* refers to *stable.*]
**All** of the stalls **need** cleaning. [*All* refers to *stalls.*]

### Compound Subjects

**2g.** Subjects joined by *and* usually take a plural verb.

**EXAMPLE**  **Augeas** and **Eurystheus rule** kingdoms.

**2h.** When subjects are joined by *or* or *nor*, the verb agrees with the subject nearer the verb.

**EXAMPLES**  Neither the **Hydra** nor Juno's huge **snakes defeat** Hercules.
Neither Juno's huge **snakes** nor the **Hydra defeats** Hercules.

**NOTE**  A compound subject that names only one person or thing takes a singular verb.

**EXAMPLES**  The **friend** and **teacher** of Hercules **is** Chiron.
**Law** and **order suffers** when monsters roam the land.

## Other Problems in Agreement

**2i.** **Collective nouns may be either singular or plural.**

A collective noun takes a singular verb when the noun refers to the group as a unit. A collective noun takes a plural verb when the noun refers to the individual parts or members of the group.

**EXAMPLES**  An oxen **herd goes** with Hercules. [The herd as a unit goes.]

The **herd call** to the stolen cattle. [The members of the herd individually call.]

**2j.** **When the subject follows the verb, find the subject, and make sure the verb agrees with it. The subject usually follows the verb in sentences beginning with *here* or *there* and in questions.**

**EXAMPLES**  There **is Centaurus,** and there **are** its **stars.**
**Does** the **fox** really not **want** the grapes?

The contractions *here's, there's,* and *where's* contain the verb *is* and should be used only with singular subjects.

**NONSTANDARD**  There's the constellations Hydra and Leo.
**STANDARD**  There **are** the **constellations** Hydra and Leo.
**STANDARD**  There**'s** the **constellation** Hydra.

**2k.** **The contractions *don't* and *doesn't* must agree with their subjects.**

Use *don't* with plural subjects and with the pronouns *I* and *you.* Use *doesn't* with other singular subjects.

**EXAMPLES**  **They don't** like movies about Hercules, and **I don't** either.
This **film doesn't** seem realistic, but **that doesn't** matter to me.

**2l.** **Words stating amounts are usually singular.**

A word or phrase stating a weight, a measurement, or an amount of money or time is usually considered a single item. Such a word or phrase takes a singular verb.

**EXAMPLE**  Five **dollars is** too much for a movie ticket.

**2m.** **The title of a book or the name of an organization or country, even when plural in form, usually takes a singular verb.**

**EXAMPLES**  *Aesop's Fables* **is** on our reading list.
**Has** the **United States** signed the treaty?

> **NOTE** When the subject of a sentence follows the verb, the word order is said to be *inverted.* To find the subject of a sentence with inverted order, restate the sentence in normal word order.
>
> **INVERTED**  There **goes Hercules.**
> **NORMAL**  **Hercules goes** there.
>
> **INVERTED**  Into the clearing **stepped** the mighty **Hercules.**
> **NORMAL**  The mighty **Hercules stepped** into the clearing.

**2n.** A few nouns, though plural in form, are singular and take singular verbs.

**EXAMPLES** news, measles, mathematics, civics, mumps, physics

 *QUICK CHECK 2*

For the following sentences, correct each error in agreement.

**EXAMPLE** 1. There's many interesting stories about heroes.
 1. *There are many interesting stories about heroes.*

1. A flock of monstrous birds hover over the Stymphalian lake.
2. Doesn't the arrows of Hercules strike each bird in turn?
3. Neither Nereus nor his daughters foils Hercules.
4. The god of the oceans don't escape Hercules.
5. Some of the ancient myths seeks to explain actual geological or botanical facts.

## AGREEMENT OF PRONOUN AND ANTECEDENT

**2o.** A pronoun agrees with its antecedent in number and gender.

An *antecedent* is the word the pronoun refers to. Some singular personal pronouns have forms that indicate gender. Masculine pronouns refer to males. Feminine pronouns refer to females. Neuter pronouns refer to things (neither male nor female) and sometimes to animals.

| FEMININE | she | her | hers |
|---|---|---|---|
| MASCULINE | he | him | his |
| NEUTER | it | it | its |

**EXAMPLES** The **speaker** in "Annabel Lee" lost **his** bride.
 **Annabel Lee** had given **her** heart to him.
 **Heaven** sent **its** angels for Annabel Lee.

The antecedent of a personal pronoun can be another kind of pronoun, such as *each, neither,* or *one.* To determine the gender of a personal pronoun that refers to one of these other pronouns, look in the phrase that follows the antecedent.

**EXAMPLES** **Each** of these **men** left **his** mark on the development of the American short story.
 **Neither** of the **women** got what **she** wanted.

**NOTE** When an antecedent may be either masculine or feminine, use both the masculine and the feminine forms.

**EXAMPLES** **No one** ever gave **his or her** approval of Poe's criticisms.
 **Everybody** wanted **his or her** writing in Poe's magazine.

## Problems in Agreement of Pronoun and Antecedent

### Indefinite Pronouns

☞ For more about indefinite pronouns, see page 711.

**2p.** A singular pronoun is used to refer to *anybody, anyone, each, either, everybody, everyone, neither, nobody, no one, one, someone,* and *somebody.*

**EXAMPLE** **Each** of these countries has **its** own Cinderella story.

**2q.** A plural pronoun is used to refer to *both, few, many,* and *several.*

**EXAMPLES** **Both** of these stories take **their** characters from legend.
**Many** of these versions are similar, but **they** all differ.

**2r.** Either a singular or a plural pronoun may be used to refer to *all, any, most, none,* and *some.*

The number of the pronouns *all, any, most, none,* and *some* is determined by the object in the prepositional phrase following the pronoun.

**EXAMPLES** **Some** of the story may come from the culture telling **it.**
[*Some* refers to the singular noun *story.*]
**Some** of the sisters are punished for **their** cruelty.
[*Some* refers to the plural noun *sisters.*]

### Compound Subjects

**2s.** A plural pronoun is used to refer to two or more antecedents joined by *and.*

**EXAMPLE** The **sisters and their mother** never share **their** fine clothing.

**2t.** A singular pronoun is used to refer to two or more singular antecedents joined by *or* or *nor.*

**EXAMPLE** Neither **the mother nor a sister** shared **her** clothes.

### Other Problems in Pronoun-Antecedent Agreement

☞ For more information about collective nouns, see page 709.

**2u.** Either a singular or a plural pronoun may be used with a collective noun.

**EXAMPLES** The royal **family** was preparing **its** celebration.
The royal **family** are greeting **their** new princess.

**2v.** Words stating amounts usually take singular pronouns.

**EXAMPLE** Admission costs five **dollars.** Maybe I can earn **it** in time.

**2w.** The title of a book or the name of an organization or a country, even when plural in form, usually takes a singular pronoun.

**EXAMPLES** I read *Folktales Around the World,* and **it** was great.
The **United Nations** can revise **its** charter.

**2x.** A few nouns, though plural in form, are singular and take singular pronouns.

**EXAMPLE** **Physics** is important, but **it** has nothing to do with folk tales.

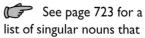 See page 723 for a list of singular nouns that are plural in form.

 **QUICK CHECK 3**

For each blank in the following sentences, give a pronoun that will complete the meaning of the sentence. Then, identify the antecedent or antecedents of that pronoun.

**EXAMPLE** 1. Kari or Leah will bring _____ copy of *The Glass Slipper.*
  1. *her—Kari or Leah*

1. Aschenputtel and Cinderella got _____ names from ashes.
2. One of the stories features pigeons in _____ ending.
3. Many of the stories reward _____ heroes, but some don't.
4. The court cheered the prince and her and gave _____ a grand wedding.
5. Neither the prince nor the Pharaoh married the young woman _____ expected.

 **Using Compound Antecedents**

Sentences with singular antecedents joined by *or* or *nor* can sound awkward if the antecedents are of different genders. If the sentence sounds awkward, revise it to avoid the problem.

**AWKWARD** Ana or Ed will read her or his version of *Cinderella.*

**REVISED** **Ana** will read **her** version of *Cinderella,* or **Ed** will read **his.**

Similarly, a singular and a plural antecedent joined by *or* or *nor* can create an awkward or a confusing sentence. Revise such a sentence to avoid the problem.

**AWKWARD** Either my cousins or Mary will bring their video of *Cinderella.*

**REVISED** Either **my cousins** will bring **their** video of *Cinderella,* or **Mary** will bring **hers.**

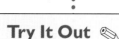 **Try It Out**

Revise each of the following sentences to eliminate awkward pronoun usage.

1. Neither her mother nor her sisters recognized that the girl was their own Aschenputtel.
2. Either birds or a fish help the heroine in their own way.
3. Did a fish or a falcon lend their help to Yeh-Shen?
4. Neither Yeh-Shen nor the king could have guessed her or his fate.
5. Joey or Linda will read his or her report on "Sealskin, Soulskin."

# 3 USING VERBS

## THE PRINCIPAL PARTS OF A VERB

The four basic forms of a verb are called the **principal parts** of the verb.

**3a.** The principal parts of a verb are the *base form*, the *present participle*, the *past*, and the *past participle*.

| BASE FORM | PRESENT PARTICIPLE | PAST | PAST PARTICIPLE |
|---|---|---|---|
| work | (is) working | worked | (have) worked |
| sing | (is) singing | sang | (have) sung |

**NOTE** Notice that the present participle and the past participle require helping verbs (forms of *be* and *have*).

The principal parts of a verb are used to express the time that an action occurs.

**PRESENT TIME**  I **sing** rhythm and blues now.
We **are singing** along with the frog.

**PAST TIME**  The frog **sang** at the Big Time Weekly Concert.
We **have sung** there before.

**FUTURE TIME**  The audience **will sing** along with the frog.
By 8:00 P.M., we **will have sung** two numbers.

☞ See page 740 for information about participles used as modifiers.

## Regular Verbs

**3b.** A *regular verb* forms its past and past participle by adding *–d* or *–ed* to the base form.

| BASE FORM | PRESENT PARTICIPLE | PAST | PAST PARTICIPLE |
|---|---|---|---|
| use | (is) using | used | (have) used |
| attack | (is) attacking | attacked | (have) attacked |

Avoid the following common errors when forming the past or past participle of regular verbs:

1. leaving off the *–d* or *–ed* ending

**NONSTANDARD**  We use to think the frog couldn't sing.
**STANDARD**  We **used** to think the frog couldn't sing.

2. adding unnecessary letters

**NONSTANDARD**  The audience of animals attackted him.
**STANDARD**  The audience of animals **attacked** him.

**QUICK CHECK I**

For each of the following sentences, supply the correct past or past participle form of the verb given in italics.

**EXAMPLE** **1.** *discover*     Frog has _____ his singing talent.
                **1.** *discovered*

**1.** *cross*   He _____ over to the other side of the pond.
**2.** *visit*   He has _____ his friends to tell them of his wish to sing.
**3.** *join*   The birds already have _____ together to form a group.
**4.** *use*   Fox let Frog sing but also _____ a trick to fool Frog.
**5.** *leap*   When Frog was introduced, he _____ out on stage.

## Irregular Verbs

**3c.** An *irregular verb* forms its past and past participle in some other way than by adding *–d* or *–ed* to the base form.

An irregular verb forms its past and past participle by

* changing vowels *or* consonants

|  | Base Form | Past | Past Participle |
|---|---|---|---|
| **EXAMPLE** | ring | rang | (have) rung |

* changing vowels *and* consonants

|  | Base Form | Past | Past Participle |
|---|---|---|---|
| **EXAMPLE** | go | went | (have) gone |

* making no changes

|  | Base Form | Past | Past Participle |
|---|---|---|---|
| **EXAMPLE** | spread | spread | (have) spread |

When you are not sure how to spell the principal parts of an irregular verb, look in a dictionary.

   Avoid the following common errors when forming the past or past participle of irregular verbs:

**1.** using the past form with a helping verb

**NONSTANDARD**   Frog has went to the Big Time Weekly Concert.
   **STANDARD**   Frog **went** to the Big Time Weekly Concert.

*or*

   **STANDARD**   Frog **has gone** to the Big Time Weekly Concert.

**2.** using the past participle form without a helping verb

**NONSTANDARD**   I seen all of his shows.
   **STANDARD**   I **have seen** all of his shows.

**3.** adding *–d* or *–ed* to the base form

**NONSTANDARD**   The elephant throwed a pineapple at the frog.
   **STANDARD**   The elephant **threw** a pineapple at the frog.

| COMMON IRREGULAR VERBS |
| :---: |

**GROUP I:** Each of these irregular verbs has the same form for its past and past participle.

| BASE FORM | PRESENT PARTICIPLE | PAST | PAST PARTICIPLE |
| :---: | :---: | :---: | :---: |
| bring | (is) bringing | brought | (have) brought |
| build | (is) building | built | (have) built |
| catch | (is) catching | caught | (have) caught |
| hold | (is) holding | held | (have) held |
| lay | (is) laying | laid | (have) laid |
| lead | (is) leading | led | (have) led |
| say | (is) saying | said | (have) said |
| send | (is) sending | sent | (have) sent |
| spin | (is) spinning | spun | (have) spun |
| swing | (is) swinging | swung | (have) swung |

 **QUICK CHECK 2**

For each of the following sentences, give the correct past or past participle form of the verb in parentheses.

EXAMPLE    I. Joey (*say*) he had the blues.
              I. *said*

1. Frog has (*bring*) rhythm and blues to the world.
2. Since then, many a guitarist has (*lay*) down a blues riff.
3. Many blues singers (*lead*) listeners to recall sad times.
4. Some musicians have (*build*) that sound using only a harmonica.
5. Others (*catch*) the beat with only their voice.

| COMMON IRREGULAR VERBS |
| :---: |

**GROUP II:** Each of these irregular verbs has a different form for its past and past participle.

| BASE FORM | PRESENT PARTICIPLE | PAST | PAST PARTICIPLE |
| :---: | :---: | :---: | :---: |
| begin | (is) beginning | began | (have) begun |
| choose | (is) choosing | chose | (have) chosen |
| do | (is) doing | did | (have) done |
| draw | (is) drawing | drew | (have) drawn |
| go | (is) going | went | (have) gone |
| know | (is) knowing | knew | (have) known |
| run | (is) running | ran | (have) run |
| shake | (is) shaking | shook | (have) shaken |
| sing | (is) singing | sang | (have) sung |
| swim | (is) swimming | swam | (have) swum |

## QUICK CHECK 3

For each of the following sentences, give the correct past or past participle form of the verb in parentheses.

**EXAMPLE** **1.** Louis Armstrong really (*know*) how to play jazz on his trumpet.
      **1.** *knew*

**1.** Some say rhythm and blues (*begin*) in the 1940s.
**2.** Like the frog, the legendary Muddy Waters (*draw*) crowds.
**3.** Who has (*sing*) with him?
**4.** Have you ever (*do*) the bump or the mashed potato?
**5.** In the story, the lion (*shake*) to the twist.

| COMMON IRREGULAR VERBS | | | |
|---|---|---|---|
| **GROUP III:** Each of these irregular verbs has the same form for its base form, past, and past participle. | | | |
| **BASE FORM** | **PRESENT PARTICIPLE** | **PAST** | **PAST PARTICIPLE** |
| burst | (is) bursting | burst | (have) burst |
| cost | (is) costing | cost | (have) cost |
| cut | (is) cutting | cut | (have) cut |
| hit | (is) hitting | hit | (have) hit |
| hurt | (is) hurting | hurt | (have) hurt |
| let | (is) letting | let | (have) let |
| put | (is) putting | put | (have) put |
| read | (is) reading | read | (have) read |
| set | (is) setting | set | (have) set |
| spread | (is) spreading | spread | (have) spread |

 ## QUICK CHECK 4

For each of the following sentences, give the correct past or past participle form of the verb in italics.

**EXAMPLE** **1.** How many people have been (*hurt*) by misunderstandings with others?
      **1.** *hurt*

**1.** *cost*    Slade and others like him have _____ Mr. Baumer a lot of money.
**2.** *hit*    Once, Slade _____ Mr. Baumer.
**3.** *let*    Yet, Mr. Baumer _____ Slade work for him.
**4.** *set*    Secretly, Mr. Baumer has _____ a trap for Slade.
**5.** *read*    Unlike Slade, Mr. Baumer _____ the warning.

## Try It Out ✎

Revise each of the following sentences to sound natural in a dialogue.

1. Butch replied, "I must say, old friend, that I cannot quite believe you."
2. "Gracious, what a marvelous party that was!" beamed Tanya when the group met Monday morning at school.
3. "Please accept our congratulations on a job well done," cried Jim's teammates, slapping him on the back after the game.
4. "I beg your pardon, but you are sitting in my seat," said the sergeant to the recruit.
5. "What an unfaithful friend you are to have spoken against me behind my back," exclaimed Angela to her classmate.

## Using Nonstandard Verb Forms

Using standard verb forms is important in almost all the writing that you do for school. Your readers expect standard usage in essays and reports. On the other hand, readers expect the dialogue in plays and short stories to sound natural. For dialogue to sound natural, it must reflect the speech patterns of real people, and real people speak in all sorts of nonstandard ways. Look at the following example from the short story "Bargain."

> "I think he hate me," Mr. Baumer went on. "That is the thing. He hate me for coming not from this country. I come here, sixteen years old, and learn to read and write, and I make a business, and so I think he hate me."

How might you translate this passage into standard English? How would that affect your impression of Mr. Baumer?

You may want to discuss the use of nonstandard verb forms with your teacher. Together you can decide how you can use such forms in your writing.

## VERB TENSE

**3d.** The *tense* of a verb indicates the time of the action or state of being that is expressed by the verb.

Every verb has six tenses.

| Present | Past | Future |
|---|---|---|
| Present Perfect | Past Perfect | Future Perfect |

This time line shows how the six tenses are related to one another.

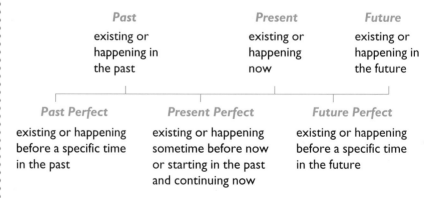

Listing all forms of a verb in the six tenses is called **conjugating** a verb.

| CONJUGATION OF THE VERB *WRITE* | |
|---|---|
| **PRESENT TENSE** | |
| *SINGULAR* | *PLURAL* |
| I write | we write |
| you write | you write |
| he, she, *or* it writes | they write |

**PAST TENSE**

| *SINGULAR* | *PLURAL* |
|---|---|
| I wrote | we wrote |
| you wrote | you wrote |
| he, she, *or* it wrote | they wrote |

**FUTURE TENSE**

| *SINGULAR* | *PLURAL* |
|---|---|
| I will write | we will write |
| you will write | you will write |
| he, she, *or* it will write | they will write |

**PRESENT PERFECT TENSE**

| *SINGULAR* | *PLURAL* |
|---|---|
| I have written | we have written |
| you have written | you have written |
| he, she, *or* it has written | they have written |

**PAST PERFECT TENSE**

| *SINGULAR* | *PLURAL* |
|---|---|
| I had written | we had written |
| you had written | you had written |
| he, she, *or* it had written | they had written |

**FUTURE PERFECT TENSE**

| *SINGULAR* | *PLURAL* |
|---|---|
| I will have written | we will have written |
| you will have written | you will have written |
| he, she, *or* it will have written | they will have written |

**NOTE** In the future tense and in the future perfect tense, the helping verb *shall* is sometimes used in place of *will*.

## Consistency of Tense

**3e.** **Do not change needlessly from one tense to another.**

When writing about events in the present, use verbs in the present tense. When writing about events in the past, use verbs in the past tense.

| INCONSISTENT | When they were satisfied, they begin planting. |
|---|---|
| CONSISTENT | When they **are** satisfied, they **begin** planting. |
| CONSISTENT | When they **were** satisfied, they **began** planting. |

## ✓ QUICK CHECK 5

Read the following paragraph, and decide whether it should be rewritten in the present or past tense. Then, change the verb forms to make the verb tense consistent.

**EXAMPLE** [1] These city boys enjoyed gardening when they get the chance.

**1.** These city boys enjoyed gardening when they got the chance.

*or*

**1.** These city boys enjoy gardening when they get the chance.

[1] No one tells them no, so they started to work. [2] It is hard, too; over and over, they carried dozens of sacks of dirt up the stairs. [3] None of the neighbors noticed them, or maybe they don't mind. [4] At last, almost before they know it, the rooftop is ready. [5] The rich, black earth waits for seeds.

<table>
<tr><td>
**COMPUTER NOTE**

Most word processors can help you check your writing to be sure that you've used verbs correctly. Spelling checkers will highlight misspelled verb forms such as *drownded* or *costed*. Style-checking software can point out inconsistent verb tenses and may also highlight questionable uses of problem verb pairs such as *lie/lay* or *rise/raise*.
</td></tr>
</table>

## SPECIAL PROBLEMS WITH VERBS

### *Sit* and *Set*

**(1)** The verb *sit* means "rest in an upright, seated position." *Sit* seldom takes an object.

**(2)** The verb *set* means "put (something) in a place." *Set* usually takes an object.

| BASE FORM | PRESENT PARTICIPLE | PAST | PAST PARTICIPLE |
|---|---|---|---|
| sit (rest) | (is) sitting | sat | (have) sat |
| set (put) | (is) setting | set | (have) set |

**EXAMPLES**   Let's **sit** in the shade. [no object]
Let's **set** the buckets here. [Let's set what? *Buckets* is the object.]

### *Lie* and *Lay*

**(1)** The verb *lie* means "rest," "recline," or "be in a place." *Lie* never takes an object.

**(2)** The verb *lay* means "put (something) in a place." *Lay* usually takes an object.

| BASE FORM | PRESENT PARTICIPLE | PAST | PAST PARTICIPLE |
|---|---|---|---|
| lie (rest) | (is) lying | lay | (have) lain |
| lay (put) | (is) laying | laid | (have) laid |

**EXAMPLES** In the photograph, juicy, red watermelons **lay** on rich earth. [no object]

They **laid** dirt on the roof. [They laid what? *Dirt* is the object.]

## Rise and Raise

**(1)** **The verb *rise* means "go up" or "get up." *Rise* never takes an object.**

**(2)** **The verb *raise* means "lift up" or "cause (something) to rise." *Raise* usually takes an object.**

| BASE FORM | PRESENT PARTICIPLE | PAST | PAST PARTICIPLE |
|---|---|---|---|
| rise (go up) | (is) rising | rose | (have) risen |
| raise (lift up) | (is) raising | raised | (have) raised |

**EXAMPLES** My next-door neighbors **rise** very early in the morning. [no object]

They **raise** the blinds at dawn. [They raise what? *Blinds* is the object.]

 QUICK CHECK 6

For each of the following sentences, choose the correct verb form in parentheses.

**EXAMPLE** **1.** Our garden (*lies, lays*) in the sunniest corner of our backyard.

    **1.** *lies*

**1.** Juan Guerrero (*raises, rises*) the bag containing the tomatillos he has grown.
**2.** Like Juan, other people also (*sat, set*) out their own plants each spring.
**3.** He will not just (*sit, set*) and remain idle.
**4.** Avoiding the heat of the day, Mr. Garcia also (*raises, rises*) early to tend his plot.
**5.** Once, only junk and trash (*lay, laid*) there, but now there is a beautiful garden.

# 4 USING PRONOUNS

## CASE

**Case** is the form of a noun or a pronoun that shows how it is used. There are three cases: **nominative, objective,** and **possessive.** The form of a noun is the same for both the nominative and objective cases. A noun changes its form for the possessive case, usually by the addition of an apostrophe and an *s*.

Most personal pronouns have different forms for all three cases.

| PERSONAL PRONOUNS | | |
|---|---|---|
| **SINGULAR** | | |
| **NOMINATIVE CASE** | **OBJECTIVE CASE** | **POSSESSIVE CASE** |
| I | me | my, mine |
| you | you | your, yours |
| he, she, it | him, her, it | his, her, hers, its |
| **PLURAL** | | |
| **NOMINATIVE CASE** | **OBJECTIVE CASE** | **POSSESSIVE CASE** |
| we | us | our, ours |
| you | you | your, yours |
| they | them | their, theirs |

## The Nominative Case

**4a.** **A subject of a verb is in the nominative case.**

**EXAMPLES** **I** enjoy Anne McCaffrey's writing style. [*I* is the subject of *enjoy*.]

**He** and **she** were still at home. [*He* and *she* are the subjects of *were*.]

**4b.** **A *predicate nominative* is in the nominative case.**

A *predicate nominative* follows a linking verb and explains or identifies the subject of the verb. A personal pronoun used as a predicate nominative follows a form of the verb *be* (*am, is, are, was, were, be,* or *been*).

**EXAMPLES** The last one to arrive there was **he.** [*He* identifies the subject *one.*]

Could it be **she**? [*She* identifies the subject *it.*]

---

**NOTE** Possessive pronouns (such as *my, your,* and *our*) are also sometimes called ***possessive adjectives.***

For more about possessive pronouns, see pages 710 and 777.

**NOTE** To choose the correct pronoun in a compound subject, try each form of the pronoun separately.

**EXAMPLE:** Beterli and (*he, him*) quarreled. [*He* quarreled. *Him* quarreled.]

**ANSWER:** Beterli and **he** quarreled.

For more about predicate nominatives, see page 756.

## The Objective Case

**4c.** A *direct object* is in the objective case.

A **direct object** follows an action verb and tells *who* or *what* receives the action of the verb.

**EXAMPLES**   The bronze dragon's choice amazed **us**. [*Us* tells *who* was amazed.]

Heth moved his wings and dried **them**. [*Them* tells *what* Heth dried.]

**4d.** An *indirect object* is in the objective case.

An **indirect object** comes between an action verb and a direct object and tells *to whom* or *to what* or *for whom* or *for what*.

**EXAMPLES**   Heth asked **him** a question. [*Him* tells *to whom* Heth asked a question.]

The dragon and his rider taught **them** a lesson. [*Them* tells *to whom* they taught a lesson.]

**4e.** An *object of a preposition* is in the objective case.

A **prepositional phrase** contains a preposition, a noun or pronoun called the **object of the preposition,** and any modifiers of that object.

**EXAMPLES**   like a **hero**          near **us**
              next to **Dr. Chang**     without **you** and **me**

A pronoun used as the object of a preposition should always be in the objective case.

**EXAMPLES**   A great honor had been bestowed on **him.**
              We went with **her** to the mall.

## ☑ QUICK CHECK 1

For each of the following sentences, identify the correct personal pronoun in parentheses.

**EXAMPLE**   **1.** Rikki's gentleness surprised (*she, her*).
              **1.** *her*

1. Rikki had almost drowned, but an English boy named Teddy rescued (*he, him*).
2. Could a mongoose live with (*they, them*) happily?
3. Teddy's mother wasn't sure whether a mongoose would make a good pet, but Rikki gave (*she, her*) a surprise.
4. Didn't (*he, him*) save their lives?
5. "The winner of this battle will be (*I, me*)!" he vowed.

For more about direct objects, see page 755.

For more about indirect objects, see page 755.

For a list of prepositions, see page 717. For more about prepositional phrases, see pages 717, 740, and 741–742.

## Improving Pronoun Usage

Expressions such as *It's me, That's her,* and *It was them* are accepted in everyday speaking. In writing, however, such expressions are generally considered nonstandard and should be avoided.

**STANDARD**   It is **I.**      That is **she.**      It was **they.**

Additionally, remember that it is considered polite to put first-person pronouns (*I, me, mine, we, us, ours*) last in compound constructions.

**EXAMPLE**   The dragonriders and **we** arrived at the Hatching Ground.

### Try It Out ✎

Revise each of the following sentences to show standard and polite usage of pronouns.

1. We and the other candidates dashed to the Impression.
2. "Save a good place for me and my friends," someone called.
3. I wondered who would be first and thought, "Maybe it'll be me!"
4. When K'last asked me who Keevan was, I answered, "That's him."
5. Keevan was the smallest, yet it was him who impressed the bronze dragon.

# SPECIAL PRONOUN PROBLEMS

## Who and Whom

The pronoun *who* has different forms in the nominative and objective cases. *Who* is the nominative form; *whom* is the objective form.

When deciding whether to use *who* or *whom* in a question, follow these steps:

STEP 1:   Rephrase the question as a statement.

STEP 2:   Decide how the pronoun is used in the statement—as subject, predicate nominative, object of the verb, or object of a preposition.

STEP 3:   Determine the case of the pronoun according to the rules of standard English.

STEP 4:   Select the correct form of the pronoun.

EXAMPLE:   (*Who, Whom*) did Jerry see?

STEP 1:   The statement is *Jerry did see (who, whom).*

STEP 2:   The subject of the verb is *Jerry,* the verb is *did see,* and the pronoun is the direct object.

STEP 3:   A pronoun used as a direct object should be in the objective case.

STEP 4:   The objective form is *whom.*

ANSWER:   **Whom** did Jerry see?

 **NOTE** In spoken English, the use of *whom* is becoming less common. In fact, when you are speaking, you may correctly begin any question with *who* regardless of the grammar of the sentence. In written English, however, you should distinguish between *who* and *whom.*

## Pronouns with Appositives

Sometimes a pronoun is followed directly by a noun that identifies the pronoun. Such a noun is called an ***appositive.*** To choose which pronoun to use before an appositive, omit the appositive, and try each form of the pronoun separately.

EXAMPLE:    (*We, Us*) boys live in the Carolinas. [*Boys* is the apposi-
            tive.] *We* live in the Carolinas. *Us* live in the Carolinas.
ANSWER:     **We** boys live in the Carolinas.

## Reflexive Pronouns

Reflexive pronouns (such as *myself, himself,* and *yourselves*) can be used as objects. Do not use the nonstandard forms *hisself* and *theirself* or *theirselves* in place of *himself* and *themselves.*

**NONSTANDARD**    Jerry prepared a fire for hisself.
   **STANDARD**    Jerry prepared a fire for **himself.**

 **QUICK CHECK 2**

For each of the following sentences, choose the correct pronoun in parentheses.

**EXAMPLE**    **I.** May (*we, us*) students read aloud?
              **I.** *we*

**1.** For (*who, whom*) did the boy work?
**2.** Jerry did not often play with (*we, us*) in the neighborhood.
**3.** (*Who, Whom*) wrote *The Yearling*?
**4.** He promised (*hisself, himself*) that he would do a good job.
**5.** They seemed pleased with (*theirselves, themselves*).

# 5 USING MODIFIERS

## COMPARISON OF MODIFIERS

A *modifier* is a word, a phrase, or a clause that describes or limits the meaning of another word. Two kinds of modifiers—*adjectives* and *adverbs*—may be used to compare things.

> **5a.** The three degrees of comparison of modifiers are *positive, comparative,* and *superlative.*

| | | | |
|---|---|---|---|
| **POSITIVE** | cold | loud | politely |
| **COMPARATIVE** | colder | louder | more politely |
| **SUPERLATIVE** | coldest | loudest | most politely |

## Regular Comparison

**(1)** Most one-syllable modifiers form their comparative and superlative degrees by adding –*er* and –*est.*

| | | | |
|---|---|---|---|
| **POSITIVE** | sharp | calm | cold |
| **COMPARATIVE** | sharper | calmer | colder |
| **SUPERLATIVE** | sharpest | calmest | coldest |

☞ For more about appositives, see page 745.

☞ For more about reflexive pronouns, see page 711.

**NOTE** To show decreasing comparisons, all modifiers form their comparative and superlative degrees with *less* and *least.*

**POSITIVE**
  calm
  rapidly

**COMPARATIVE**
  less calm
  less rapidly

**SUPERLATIVE**
  least calm
  least rapidly

**(2) Some two-syllable modifiers form their comparative and superlative degrees by adding –er and –est. Others form their comparative and superlative degrees by using more and most.**

| POSITIVE | simple | sudden | quietly |
|---|---|---|---|
| COMPARATIVE | simpler | more sudden | more quietly |
| SUPERLATIVE | simplest | most sudden | most quietly |

**(3) Modifiers that have three or more syllables form their comparative and superlative degrees by using more and most.**

| POSITIVE | luxurious | fearfully | curious |
|---|---|---|---|
| COMPARATIVE | more luxurious | more fearfully | more curious |
| SUPERLATIVE | most luxurious | most fearfully | most curious |

## Irregular Comparison

Some modifiers do not form their comparative and superlative degrees by using the regular methods.

| POSITIVE | bad | far | good | well | many | much |
|---|---|---|---|---|---|---|
| COMPARATIVE | worse | farther | better | better | more | more |
| SUPERLATIVE | worst | farthest | best | best | most | most |

 *QUICK CHECK 1*

 Drop the final silent e before a suffix beginning with a vowel.

**EXAMPLES**   safe + er = safer
ripe + est = ripest
gentle + er = gentler

Give the forms for the comparative and superlative degrees of the following modifiers.

**EXAMPLE**   **1.** colorful
**1.** *more (less) colorful, most (least) colorful*

**1.** fine          **5.** daring          **9.** well
**2.** cautiously    **6.** comfortable     **10.** dainty
**3.** gladly        **7.** much
**4.** thankful      **8.** cozy

## Uses of Comparative and Superlative Forms

**5b.** Use the comparative degree when comparing two things. Use the superlative degree when comparing more than two.

**COMPARATIVE**   This mouse is **safer** than the Town Mouse.
She sleeps **more soundly** than the Town Mouse.

**SUPERLATIVE**   This mouse is the **safest** one in the world.
Of the three animals, the cat slept **most soundly.**

**5c.** Use *good* to modify a noun or a pronoun. Use *well* to modify a verb.

**EXAMPLE**   The Town Mouse enjoyed **good food.** She **ate well.**

**5d.** Use adjectives, not adverbs, after linking verbs.

**EXAMPLE**   The Town Mouse's life seemed **wonderful.** [*not* wonderfully]

**5e.** Avoid using double comparisons.

A *double comparison* is the use of both *–er* and *more* (*less*) or both *–est* and *most* (*least*) to form a comparison. A comparison should be formed in only one of these two ways, not both.

**EXAMPLE**   The Country Mouse is **safer** [*not* more safer] than the Town Mouse.

**5f.** A *double negative* is the use of two negative words to express one negative idea.

| Common Negative Words | | | |
|---|---|---|---|
| barely | never | none | nothing |
| hardly | no | no one | nowhere |
| neither | nobody | not (–n't) | scarcely |

**NONSTANDARD**   She hasn't never liked cats.

**STANDARD**   She hasn't ever [*or* has never] liked cats.

## ☑ QUICK CHECK 2

The following sentences contain incorrect forms of comparison. Revise each sentence, using the correct form.

**EXAMPLE**   **1.** The acorns were the more delicious of all the foods.
   **1.** *The acorns were the most delicious of all the foods.*

1. Of course, the Town Mouse had the more finer foods.
2. However, the Country Mouse couldn't hardly enjoy those foods.
3. To the mice, was the cat most dangerous than the dog?
4. The Town Mouse ate worst on her visit to the country.
5. Of the two mice, which is the safest?

## PLACEMENT OF MODIFIERS

**5g.** Place modifying words, phrases, and clauses as close as possible to the words they modify.

Notice how the meaning of the following sentence changes when the position of the phrase *from the country* changes.

The mouse **from the country** saw a cat. [The phrase modifies *mouse.*]

The mouse saw a cat **from the country.** [The phrase modifies *cat.*]

## Prepositional Phrases

A *prepositional phrase* consists of a preposition, a noun or a pronoun called the *object of the preposition,* and any modifiers of that object. A prepositional phrase used as an adjective should be placed directly after the word it modifies.

**MISPLACED**  A cat would not be dangerous to the mice with a bell.

**CLEAR**  A cat **with a bell** would not be dangerous to the mice.

A prepositional phrase used as an adverb should be placed near the word it modifies.

**MISPLACED**  The mice had a meeting about the cat **in fear.**

**CLEAR**  **In fear,** the mice had a meeting about the cat.

Avoid placing a prepositional phrase in a position where it can modify either of two words. Place the phrase so that it clearly modifies the word you intend it to modify.

**MISPLACED**  The mouse said in the morning she would go. [Does the phrase modify *said* or *would go*?]

**CLEAR**  The mouse said she would go **in the morning.**

*or*

**CLEAR**  **In the morning,** the mouse said she would go.

## Participial Phrases

A *participial phrase* consists of a verb form—either a present participle or a past participle—and its related words. A participial phrase modifies a noun or a pronoun. Like a prepositional phrase, a participial phrase should be placed as close as possible to the word it modifies.

**MISPLACED**  The mice hid from the cat scurrying fearfully.

**CLEAR**  **Scurrying fearfully,** the mice hid from the cat.

A participial phrase that does not clearly and sensibly modify any word in the sentence is a *dangling participial phrase.* To correct a dangling phrase, supply a word that the phrase can modify, or add a subject, a verb, or both to the dangling modifier.

**DANGLING**  Worried constantly, a plan was needed.

**CLEAR**  Worried constantly, **the mice** needed a plan.

*or*

**CLEAR**  The mice needed a plan **because they worried** constantly.

☞ For more about prepositions and prepositional phrases, see pages 717, 735, and 741–742.

☞ For more about participial phrases, see page 743.

## Clauses

A *clause* is a group of words that contains a verb and its subject and that is used as a part of a sentence. An *adjective clause* modifies a noun or a pronoun. Most adjective clauses begin with a relative pronoun, such as *that, which, who, whom,* or *whose.* An *adverb clause* modifies a verb, an adjective, or another adverb. Most adverb clauses begin with a subordinating conjunction, such as *although, while, if,* or *because.*

Like phrases, clauses should be placed as close as possible to the words they modify.

 For more about clauses, see Part 7: Clauses.

| | |
|---|---|
| **MISPLACED** | The fable was written by Aesop that we read today. |
| **CLEAR** | The fable **that we read today** was written by Aesop. |

### ✓ QUICK CHECK 3

Each of the following sentences contains a misplaced or dangling modifier. Revise each sentence so that it is clear and correct.

**EXAMPLE**  **1.** A cat was frightening the mice with sharp claws and teeth.

**1.** *A cat with sharp claws and teeth was frightening the mice.*

1. The mice complained about the cat at the meeting.
2. A bell could protect the mice on the cat.
3. Ringing loudly with each step, the mice could run away.
4. The plan had a flaw that he was suggesting.
5. An old mouse questioned the young mouse shaking his head sadly.

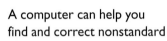

A computer can help you find and correct nonstandard forms of modifiers such as *baddest, expensiver,* and *mostest.* However, the computer cannot help you make sure that a modifier is not misplaced or dangling. You will need to check the placement of your modifiers yourself.

## 6 PHRASES

**6a.** A *phrase* is a group of related words that is used as a single part of speech and does not contain a verb and its subject.

| | |
|---|---|
| **VERB PHRASE** | should have been stabled |
| **PREPOSITIONAL PHRASE** | with a shudder and whitened eyes |

 For more information about verb phrases, see pages 715, 720, and 752.

### THE PREPOSITIONAL PHRASE

**6b.** A *prepositional phrase* includes a preposition, a noun or pronoun called the *object of the preposition,* and any modifiers of that object.

**EXAMPLES**  The runaway was filled **with confusion and fear.**
The colt **in front of them** climbed **up the wall.**

 For a list of commonly used prepositions, see page 717.

## The Adjective Phrase

**6c.** An *adjective phrase* is a prepositional phrase that modifies a noun or a pronoun.

An adjective phrase tells *what kind* or *which one.*

**EXAMPLES**  Robert Frost was a poet **of nature.** [What kind?]
"The Runaway" is the one **about a colt.** [Which one?]

More than one adjective phrase may modify the same word.

**EXAMPLE**  A pasture **of snow on a mountain** upsets him. [The phrases *of snow* and *on a mountain* modify *pasture.*]

## The Adverb Phrase

**6d.** An *adverb phrase* is a prepositional phrase that modifies a verb, an adjective, or an adverb.

An adverb phrase tells *how, when, where, why,* or *to what extent* (that is, *how long, how many,* or *how far*).

**EXAMPLES**  The colt bolted **with a nervous snort.** [How?]
The colt seemed uneasy **because of the snow.** [Why?]
The poem takes place late **in the day.** [When?]
Frost had written poetry **for many years.** [How long?]

More than one adverb phrase may modify the same word or words.

**EXAMPLE**  **At the Kennedy Inauguration,** Frost read **to the American people.**

An adverb phrase may be modified by an adjective phrase.

**EXAMPLE**  **In his poem about the runaway,** Frost uses several verbals. [The adverb phrase modifies the verb *uses.* The adjective phrase modifies *poem.*]

✓ *QUICK CHECK I*

Identify the prepositional phrase or phrases in each numbered sentence in the following paragraph. Then, label each phrase as an *adjective phrase* or an *adverb phrase.* Give the word the phrase modifies.

**EXAMPLE**  [1]  They make judgments about the colt and its care.
**1.** *about the colt and its care—adjective phrase—judgments*

[1] Many of Robert Frost's poems contain imagery from nature. [2] These images say much about people and human nature. [3] "The Runaway" focuses on a colt's experiences during its first winter. [4] In the poem Frost shows observers' reactions to the colt. [5] The colt, the subject of conversation between the observers, is important to them.

## VERBALS AND VERBAL PHRASES

A **verbal** is a form of a verb that is used as a noun, an adjective, or an adverb. There are three kinds of verbals: the *participle*, the *gerund*, and the *infinitive*.

## Participles and Participial Phrases

**6e.** A *participle* is a verb form that can be used as an adjective.

There are two kinds of participles—*present participles* and *past participles*.

**(1)** *Present participles* end in *–ing*.

**EXAMPLE** The rats **swimming** ashore alarmed them. [*Swimming*, a form of the verb *swim*, modifies *rats*.]

**(2)** Most *past participles* end in *–d* or *–ed*. Others are irregularly formed.

**EXAMPLES** No one was on the **abandoned** ship. [*Abandoned*, a form of the verb *abandon*, modifies *ship*.]

The rats, **known** for their ferocity, swam toward the sailors. [*Known*, a form of the verb *know*, modifies *rats*.]

**6f.** A *participial phrase* consists of a participle and all the words related to the participle. The entire phrase is used as an adjective.

**EXAMPLES** **Seeing a ship nearby,** scores of rats dove into the sea. [The participial phrase modifies the noun *scores*. The noun *ship* is the direct object of the present participle *seeing*.]

We could see the sharks **feasting hungrily on the swarms of rats.** [The participial phrase modifies the noun *sharks*. The adverb *hungrily* and the adverb phrase *on the swarms of rats* modify the present participle *feasting*.]

## Gerunds and Gerund Phrases

**6g.** A *gerund* is a verb form ending in *–ing* that is used as a noun.

| | |
|---|---|
| **SUBJECT** | **Singing** can be fun. |
| **PREDICATE NOMINATIVE** | My favorite pastime is **singing.** |
| **OBJECT OF PREPOSITION** | I warm up before **singing.** |
| **DIRECT OBJECT** | Do you enjoy **singing**? |

☞ For information on placement of participial phrases, see page 740.

**6h.** A *gerund phrase* consists of a gerund and all the words related to the gerund.

**EXAMPLE** **Counting the innumerable rats on the lighthouse** **calmed the men.** [The gerund phrase is the subject of the sentence. The noun *rats* is the direct object of the gerund *counting.*]

## Infinitives and Infinitive Phrases

**6i.** An *infinitive* is a verb form that can be used as a noun, an adjective, or an adverb. Infinitives usually begin with *to*.

**NOUNS** **To escape** was their sole desire. [subject]
Was the sailors' fate **to become** dinner? [predicate nominative]
They had **to signal** but not **to let** the rats in. [direct objects]

**ADJECTIVES** The time **to signal** was now. [*To signal* modifies *time.*]
Who was the first man **to crack** under the pressure? [*To crack* modifies *man.*]

**ADVERBS** Rescuers were quick **to answer.** [*To answer* modifies *quick.*]
They came to the island **to tend** the light. [*To tend* modifies *came.*]

**6j.** An *infinitive phrase* consists of an infinitive and its modifiers and complements. The entire infinitive phrase may act as an adjective, an adverb, or a noun.

**EXAMPLES** Lighthouses are one way **to warn ships away from rocks.** [adjective]
The men were grateful **to see the ship.** [adverb]
**To be rescued** was their only hope. [noun]

## ✓ QUICK CHECK 2

Identify each italicized phrase in the following sentences as *participial, gerund,* or *infinitive.*

**EXAMPLE** **I.** *Swimming in the sea* was easy for the rats.
**I.** *gerund*

1. The rats, *lured by the scent,* approached the lighthouse.
2. *Seeing the laughing men* enraged the frenzied rats.
3. They tried *to get in through the windows and door.*
4. *Clawing and biting the metal, glass, and stone,* they succeeded.
5. What happened to the horrified men left *to fend for themselves*?

> **NOTE** *To* plus a noun or a pronoun (*to class, to them, to the dance*) is a prepositional phrase, not an infinitive. Be careful not to confuse infinitives with prepositional phrases beginning with *to.*
>
> **INFINITIVE** I want **to go.**
> **PREPOSITIONAL PHRASE** I want to go **to sea.**

## APPOSITIVES AND APPOSITIVE PHRASES

**6k.** An *appositive* is a noun or a pronoun placed beside another noun or pronoun to identify or explain it.

Appositives are often set off from the rest of the sentence by commas or dashes. However, when an appositive is necessary to the meaning of the sentence or when it is closely related to the word it refers to, no commas are necessary.

**EXAMPLES**    The author **George G. Toudouze** wrote the story "Three Skeleton Key." [The noun *George G. Toudouze* identifies the noun *author*.]

The men saw a strange ship, **one** with Dutch lines and three masts. [The pronoun *one* refers to the noun *ship*.]

Their victims—the **captain** and **crew**—had vanished. [The nouns *captain* and *crew* explain who were the victims.]

**6l.** An *appositive phrase* consists of an appositive and its modifiers.

**EXAMPLES**    Le Gleo, **one of the lighthouse keepers,** had horrible nightmares. [The adjective phrase *of the lighthouse keepers* modifies the appositive *one*.]

Rats, **the foul scourge of sailing ships,** pressed for entrance. [The article *the*, the adjective *foul*, and the adjective phrase *of sailing ships* modify the appositive *scourge*.]

 **QUICK CHECK 3**

Identify the appositives or appositive phrases in the following sentences. Give the word or words each appositive or appositive phrase identifies or explains.

**EXAMPLE**    1. The rats, a huge and hardy breed, swarmed the decks.
    1. *a huge and hardy breed—rats*

1. Three men—the narrator, Le Gleo, and Itchoua—stared in horror at the rats.
2. The entire crew would likely have perished but for the engineer, a brave man.
3. Terriers, dogs bred for hunting, were certainly no match for these vicious rats.
4. The supply boat, the last one of the month, would be no help because it would arrive too late.
5. His friend Le Gleo was never the same again.

☞ For information on the use of commas with appositives and appositive phrases, see page 770.

## Using Phrases to Combine Sentences

Knowing how to use different kinds of phrases can help you improve your writing. For example, to revise a series of choppy sentences, combine them by turning at least one sentence into a phrase.

| | |
|---|---|
| **CHOPPY** | A beautiful ship approached. The ship was a Dutch three-master. |
| **APPOSITIVE PHRASE** | A beautiful ship, **a Dutch three-master,** approached. |
| **PARTICIPIAL PHRASE** | A beautiful Dutch ship **having three masts** approached. |
| **INFINITIVE PHRASE** | A beautiful Dutch three-master continued **to approach us.** |

# 7 CLAUSES

**7a.** A *clause* is a group of words that contains a verb and its subject and that is used as a part of a sentence.

Every clause has a subject and a verb. However, not every clause expresses a complete thought.

| | |
|---|---|
| **COMPLETE THOUGHT** | **Wagons delivered** milk daily. |
| **INCOMPLETE THOUGHT** | before **cars were invented** |

The two kinds of clauses are the *independent clause* and the *subordinate clause*.

## THE INDEPENDENT CLAUSE

**7b.** An *independent* (or *main*) *clause* expresses a complete thought and can stand by itself as a sentence.

                    S       V

**INDEPENDENT CLAUSE**   Joseph pulled the wagon.

## THE SUBORDINATE CLAUSE

**7c.** A *subordinate* (or *dependent*) *clause* does not express a complete thought and cannot stand alone as a sentence.

                    S      V

**SUBORDINATE CLAUSE**   that Pierre drove

The meaning of a subordinate clause is complete only when the clause is attached to an independent clause.

**EXAMPLE**   Joseph pulled the wagon **that Pierre drove.**

 *QUICK CHECK I*

Identify each of the following groups of words as an *independent clause* or a *subordinate clause.*

**EXAMPLE**   **I.** because Pierre was growing old
         **I.** *subordinate clause*

**1.** although Pierre did not read or write
**2.** everyone liked him
**3.** although he arrived early each day to get his wagon
**4.** when he spoke to his horse
**5.** Joseph knew every stop on the route

## The Adjective Clause

**7d.**   An *adjective clause* is a subordinate clause that modifies a noun or a pronoun.

An adjective clause usually follows the word it modifies and tells *which one* or *what kind.*

**EXAMPLES**   Joseph knew every house **that they served.** [Which house?]
           Pierre was a man **who loved his job.** [What kind of man?]

An adjective clause is usually introduced by a *relative pronoun.*

| **Relative Pronouns** | | | | |
|---|---|---|---|---|
| that | which | who | whom | whose |

A *relative pronoun* relates an adjective clause to the word that the clause modifies.

**EXAMPLES**   After work, Pierre, **who had seemed fit,** limped slowly. [The relative pronoun *who* relates the clause to the noun *Pierre.*]
           St. Joseph, **whose name the horse bore,** was also kind and faithful. [The relative pronoun *whose* relates the clause to the noun *St. Joseph.*]

Sometimes a relative pronoun is preceded by a preposition that is part of the adjective clause.

**EXAMPLE**   The character **to whom I am referring** is Jacques.

☞ For information on when to set off adjective clauses with commas, see rule 13i(1) on page 770.

NOTE   The relative pronouns *who* and *whom* are used to refer to people only. The relative pronoun *that* is used to refer both to people and to things. The relative pronoun *which* is used to refer to things only.

Identify the adjective clause in each of the following sentences. Give the relative pronoun and the word that the relative pronoun refers to.

**EXAMPLE**   **1.** Jacques, who was the foreman, seemed kind.
　　　　　　**1.** *who was the foreman, who—Jacques*

1. Pierre Dupin worked for a milk company that was in Montreal.
2. The wagon that he drove carried milk to St. Catherine Street.
3. Pierre relied on his horse, whom he had named Joseph.
4. Joseph, whose coat was white, was large and reliable.
5. Pierre was offered a pension, which is a regular payment to a retired person.

## The Adverb Clause

**7e.** An *adverb clause* is a subordinate clause that modifies a verb, an adjective, or an adverb.

An adverb clause tells *where, when, how, why, to what extent,* or *under what condition.*

**EXAMPLES**   They live **where it never gets cold.**
　　　　　　　[Where?]
　　　　　　**When he left,** I cried. [When?]
　　　　　　Grover's room seems **as if it will never be the same.** [How?]
　　　　　　**Because the weather was hot,** the cool water felt good. [Why?]
　　　　　　My parents still miss him **as much as I do.** [To what extent?]
　　　　　　**If I keep tickling him,** he won't fall asleep. [Under what condition?]

An adverb clause is introduced by a **subordinating conjunction**—a word that shows the relationship between the adverb clause and the word or words that the clause modifies.

### Common Subordinating Conjunctions

| | | | |
|---|---|---|---|
| after | as though | since | when |
| although | because | so that | whenever |
| as | before | than | where |
| as if | how | though | wherever |
| as long as | if | unless | whether |
| as soon as | in order that | until | while |

---

**COMPUTER NOTE** A computer can help you proofread your writing. Use the computer's "Search" function to locate any use of the words *after, as, before, since,* and *until.* Examine the use of such words at the beginnings of sentences. Determine whether the word begins a prepositional phrase or a subordinate clause. In most cases, an introductory prepositional phrase is not set off by a comma. An introductory adverb clause, however, should be followed by a comma.

**NOTE** Some subordinating conjunctions, such as *after, as, before, since,* and *until,* are also used as prepositions.

An adverb clause does not always follow the word it modifies. When an adverb clause begins a sentence, the clause is followed by a comma.

**EXAMPLE**   Whenever King Midas touched something, it turned to gold.

### Placement of Adverb Clauses

In most cases, the decision of where to place an adverb clause is a matter of style, not correctness. Both of the following sentences are correct.

> **Although she was almost unknown during her lifetime,** Emily Dickinson is now considered a major American poet.

> Emily Dickinson is now considered a major American poet **although she was almost unknown during her lifetime.**

Which sentence might you use in a paper on Emily Dickinson? The sentence to choose would be the one that looks and sounds better in the **context**—the rest of the paragraph to which the sentence belongs.

 **QUICK CHECK 3**

Identify the adverb clause in each of the following sentences. For each clause, circle the subordinating conjunction, and underline the subject once and the verb twice.

**EXAMPLE**   **I.** Many things change as you grow older.
**I.** (as) you grow older

1. Grover worked on the computer whenever he could.
2. He packed all his things before he left.
3. Because he needed the computer, he took it too.
4. Although the room has been painted, it reminds me of him.
5. It won't be the same as long as he is gone.

## The Noun Clause

**7f.**   A *noun clause* is a subordinate clause used as a noun.

A noun clause may be used as a subject, a complement (predicate nominative, indirect object, or direct object), or an object of a preposition.

|  |  |
|---|---|
| **SUBJECT** | **What Mama promises** is tomorrow. |
| **PREDICATE NOMINATIVE** | She is **who makes us happy.** |
| **INDIRECT OBJECT** | She bids **whoever is sleeping** good morning. |

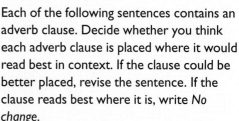

☞ For more about using commas with adverb clauses, see page 771.

### Try It Out ✎

Each of the following sentences contains an adverb clause. Decide whether you think each adverb clause is placed where it would read best in context. If the clause could be better placed, revise the sentence. If the clause reads best where it is, write *No change.*

[1] "The Highwayman" was an inevitable reading assignment when I was in school. [2] I now enjoy the poem although I laughed at it then. [3] Because it was remote in time and place, I did not relate to it. [4] The vocabulary and content seemed false because they were unfamiliar. [5] However, I discovered that this poem is filled with lively images when I read it carefully!

| | |
|---|---|
| **DIRECT OBJECT** | Choose **whichever you need most.** |
| **OBJECT OF A PREPOSITION** | A poem can be about **whatever you think is important.** |

### Common Introductory Words for Noun Clauses

| | | | |
|---|---|---|---|
| how | what | whatever | which |
| who | whoever | when | whichever |
| whom | whomever | where | that |

☞ For guidelines on using *who* and *whom* correctly, see page 736. The same guidelines apply to *whoever* and *whomever*.

✓ QUICK CHECK 4

Identify the noun clause in each of the following sentences. Tell whether the noun clause is a *subject,* a *predicate nominative,* a *direct object,* an *indirect object,* or an *object of a preposition.*

**EXAMPLE**   1. Whatever we do affects our whole family.
              1. *Whatever we do—subject*

1. What Evelyn Tooley Hunt is talking about is a mother's effect on her family.
2. This mother gives whoever is near warmth and brightness.
3. Similarly, she puts love into whatever she is cooking.
4. Notice that Hunt compares her warmth to grits and gravy.
5. A bright future is what her constant love promises.

# 8 SENTENCES

**8a.** A *sentence* is a group of words that has a subject and a verb and expresses a complete thought.

A sentence begins with a capital letter and ends with a period, a question mark, or an exclamation point.

**EXAMPLES**   Sandra Cisneros wrote "Four Skinny Trees**.**"
              Have you read any of her work**?**
              **W**hat surprising rhythms she uses**!**

## SENTENCE OR SENTENCE FRAGMENT?

A *sentence fragment* is a group of words that either does not have a subject and verb or does not express a complete thought.

| | |
|---|---|
| **SENTENCE FRAGMENT** | The rhythms in this story. [What about the rhythms in this story?] |
| **SENTENCE** | The rhythms in this story are based on repetition. |

| SENTENCE FRAGMENT | After reading her story. [Who read her story? What happened then?] |
|---|---|
| SENTENCE | After reading her story, I looked at trees differently. |

 **QUICK CHECK 1**

Tell whether each group of words is a *sentence* or a *sentence fragment*. If the word group is a sentence, correct it by adding a capital letter and end punctuation. If the word group is a sentence fragment, correct it by adding words to make a complete sentence, and also capitalize and punctuate it correctly.

**EXAMPLE** 1. one of my favorite writers
1. *sentence fragment—One of my favorite writers is Sandra Cisneros.*

1. let me recommend this story
2. in front of her house grow four skinny trees
3. growing in the midst of concrete
4. where they don't belong
5. do you see a part of yourself in nature

If sentence fragments are a problem in your writing, a computer may be able to help you. Some style-checking programs can identify and highlight sentence fragments. Such programs are useful, but they aren't perfect. The best way to eliminate fragments from your writing is still to check each sentence yourself. Be sure that each expresses a complete thought and has a subject and a verb.

## THE SUBJECT AND THE PREDICATE

A sentence consists of two parts: a *subject* and a *predicate*.

**8b.** **A *subject* tells whom or what the sentence is about. The *predicate* tells something about the subject.**

        subj.                 pred.

**EXAMPLE** Helen Callaghan played professional baseball.

## Finding the Subject

Usually, the subject comes before the predicate. Sometimes, however, the subject may appear elsewhere in the sentence. To find the subject of a sentence, ask *Who?* or *What?* before the predicate. In sentences that begin with *here, there,* or *where,* ask *Here* (or *There* or *Where*) before the predicate, followed by *who?* or *what?* after the predicate.

**EXAMPLES** In the old photograph was a **woman at bat.** [Who was? A woman was.]

By the way, **her son** plays for the Astros. [Who plays? Her son does.]

Do **you** play baseball? [Who does play? You do play.]

Where is **my notebook?** [Where is what? Where is my notebook.]

 The subject of a sentence is *never* part of a prepositional phrase.

**EXAMPLE** **Many** of the women in the league attended the reunion. [Who attended? You might be tempted to say *women,* but *women* is part of the prepositional phrase *of the women. Many* attended.]

## The Simple Subject

**NOTE** In this book, the term *subject* refers to the simple subject unless otherwise indicated.

**8c.** A *simple subject* is the main word or group of words in the complete subject.

**EXAMPLES** Her **mother** still had that old fire. [The complete subject is *her mother.*]

"**The No-Guitar Blues**" by Gary Soto is on the test. [The complete subject is *"The No-Guitar Blues" by Gary Soto.*]

## The Simple Predicate, or Verb

**8d.** A *simple predicate,* or *verb,* is the main word or group of words in the complete predicate.

A **complete predicate** consists of a verb and all the words that describe the verb and complete its meaning. Usually, the complete predicate follows the subject in a sentence. Sometimes, however, the complete predicate appears at the beginning of a sentence. Other times, part of the predicate may appear on one side of the subject and the rest on the other side.

**NOTE** In this book, the term *verb* refers to the simple predicate unless otherwise indicated.

**EXAMPLES** In the darkness of a doorway **stood** a stranger.
**On this night,** he **had a meeting with an old friend.**
**Would** his friend **appear?**

A simple predicate may be a one-word verb, or it may be a verb phrase. A **verb phrase** consists of a main verb and its helping verbs.

☞ For more about verb phrases, see pages 715, 720, and 741.

**EXAMPLES** O. Henry's stories often **end** with a twist.
"After Twenty Years" **does** not **have** a happy ending.

## ✓ QUICK CHECK 2

Identify the *complete subject* and *simple subject* and the *complete predicate* and *simple predicate* in each of the following sentences.

**EXAMPLE** 1. On the mantel was an old baseball.
1. *an old baseball—complete subject; baseball—simple subject; on the mantel was—complete predicate; was—simple predicate*

1. The All-American Girls Professional Baseball League was started by Philip K. Wrigley.
2. It enjoyed ten years of popularity.
3. Have you seen the movie about the Rockford Peaches?
4. The famous Rockford Peaches was only one of nine teams.
5. At the league's reunion many years later was a much older Callaghan.

## The Compound Subject

**8e.** A *compound subject* consists of two or more connected subjects that have the same verb. The usual connecting word is *and* or *or*.

**EXAMPLES**   Neither **Daedalus** nor **Icarus** escaped the king's anger.
Among Daedalus's gifts were **creativity, ingenuity,** and **skill.**

## The Compound Verb

**8f.** A *compound verb* consists of two or more verbs that have the same subject.

A connecting word—usually *and, or,* or *but*—is used between the verbs.

**EXAMPLE**   He **flew** upward, **turned,** and **called** to his son.

Both the subject and the verb of a sentence may be compound.

S                  S         V                              V

**EXAMPLE**   **Icarus** and his **father put** on the wings and **took** off.
[Icarus put on the wings and took off. His father put on the wings and took off.]

 QUICK CHECK 3

Identify the *subjects* and the *verbs* in the following sentences.

**EXAMPLE**   **1.** Myths and fairy tales sometimes hide their meanings.
**1.** *Myths, fairy tales—subjects; hide—verb*

1. The myth of Icarus tells about creativity and warns of its dangers.
2. In this story, Daedalus and his son suffer a tragic fate.
3. Yet, did they not also create wings and fly?
4. You and I can read the story, learn, and avoid their mistakes.
5. "Echo and Narcissus" and this classic story can teach us much.

 **Using Compound Subjects and Verbs**

Using compound subjects and verbs, you can combine ideas and reduce wordiness in your writing. Compare the examples below.

**WORDY**   With his wings, Daedalus escaped. Icarus escaped also.

**REVISED**   With their wings, **Daedalus and Icarus escaped.**

### Try It Out ✎

Using compound subjects and verbs, combine the following pairs of sentences.

1. Daedalus angered King Minos. Daedalus was imprisoned by King Minos.
2. Clouds sailed through the skies. Birds sailed through the skies.
3. Daedalus melted wax. Daedalus shaped a skeleton of a wing.
4. Daedalus flew close to his son, Icarus. Icarus flew close to his father.
5. Delos rushed by beneath them. Samos rushed by beneath them.

# 9 COMPLEMENTS

**9a.** A *complement* is a word or a group of words that completes the meaning of a verb.

Every sentence has a subject and a verb. Often a verb also needs a complement to complete the meaning of the verb. A complement may be a noun, a pronoun, or an adjective. Each of the following subjects and verbs needs a complement to make a complete sentence.

                                              S                        V
**INCOMPLETE**   James Weldon Johnson became [what?]

                                              S                        V               C
**COMPLETE**   James Weldon Johnson became **a poet.**

                                              S        V
**INCOMPLETE**   Johnson's poetry is [what?]

                                              S        V        C
**COMPLETE**   Johnson's poetry is **wonderful.**

                                     S      V
**INCOMPLETE**   Tamisha showed [what? to whom?]

                                     S       V       C          C
**COMPLETE**   Tamisha showed **me** her **poem.**

As you can see, a complement may be a noun, a pronoun, or an adjective. An adverb is never a complement.

**ADVERB**   He writes **powerfully.** [*Powerfully* tells how he writes.]

**COMPLEMENT**   His writing is **powerful.** [The adjective *powerful* modifies the subject *writing.*]

A complement is never in a prepositional phrase.

**OBJECT OF A PREPOSITION**   The whole world was in **darkness.**

**COMPLEMENT**   The whole world was **darkness.**

☞ For more information about prepositional phrases, see pages 717, 735, 740, and 741–742.

## ✓ QUICK CHECK I

Identify the *subjects, verbs,* and *complements* in the sentences in the following paragraph. [Remember: A complement is never in a prepositional phrase.]

**EXAMPLE**   [I]  Will you read "The Creation" aloud?
            **I.** *you—subject; will read—verb; "The Creation"—complement*

[1] With his deep voice, James Earl Jones is a marvelous speaker. [2] Only his rich voice can do justice to a poem like "The Creation." [3] With lingering pauses and startling changes of volume, Jones's performance is awe-inspiring. [4] Can you find us a recording of his recitation? [5] No one will speak or move a muscle during the whole performance.

## DIRECT OBJECTS

**9b.** **A *direct object* is a noun or a pronoun that receives the action of the verb or that shows the result of the action. A direct object tells *what* or *whom* after a transitive verb.**

**EXAMPLE** In this poem, God creates **light, animals,** and all **things.** [The nouns *light, animals,* and *things* receive the action of the transitive verb *creates* and tell *what.*]

A direct object can never follow a linking verb because a linking verb does not express action.

**LINKING VERB** People **became** living souls. [The verb *became* does not express action; therefore, it does not have a direct object.]

A direct object is never part of a prepositional phrase.

**OBJECT OF A PREPOSITION** Humans gazed at the **moon.** [*Moon* is not the direct object of the verb *gazed; moon* is the object of the preposition *at.*]

## INDIRECT OBJECTS

Like a direct object, an ***indirect object*** helps to complete the meaning of a transitive verb. If a sentence has an indirect object, it always has a direct object also.

**9c.** **An *indirect object* is a noun or a pronoun that comes between the verb and the direct object and tells *to what* or *to whom* or *for what* or *for whom* the action of the verb is done.**

**EXAMPLE** In the last stanza, God gives **man** life. [The noun *man* tells *to whom* God has given life.]

Linking verbs do not have indirect objects. Also, an indirect object, like a direct object, is never in a prepositional phrase.

**LINKING VERB** The cypress **is** a type of evergreen tree. [The linking verb *is* does not express action, so it cannot have an indirect object.]

**INDIRECT OBJECT** Cypress trees give **swamps** deep shade. [The noun *swamps* shows *to what* cypress trees give shade.]

**OBJECT OF A PREPOSITION** They give deep shade to the **swamps.** [The noun *swamps* is the object of the preposition *to.*]

☞ For more about transitive verbs, see page 714.

☞ For more about linking verbs, see pages 714–715 and 756. For more about prepositional phrases, see pages 717, 735, 740, and 741–742.

**NOTE** Like a direct object, an indirect object may be compound.

**EXAMPLE** Cypresses give **swamps** and **creeks** deep shade.

## QUICK CHECK 2

Identify the *direct objects* and the *indirect objects* in the following sentences. [Note: Not every sentence has an indirect object.]

**EXAMPLE**   1. Johnson's God has physical presence.
   1. *presence—direct object*

1. This poem delivers a strong characterization of God.
2. With the muscle of a worker, this God makes the world.
3. For Johnson, all the earth shows us His footsteps.
4. Not God's intellect but His body literally gives humans breath.
5. After all, God shaped humans in His own image.

## SUBJECT COMPLEMENTS

A *subject complement* completes the meaning of a linking verb and identifies or describes the subject.

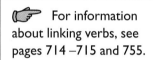

| Common Linking Verbs | | | | | |
|---|---|---|---|---|---|
| appear | become | grow | remain | smell | stay |
| be | feel | look | seem | sound | taste |

**EXAMPLES**   This unfortunate person became **Sky Woman.** [*Sky Woman* identifies the subject *person.*]
   The story of Sky Woman is **sad.** [*Sad* describes the subject *story.*]

There are two kinds of subject complements—the *predicate nominative* and the *predicate adjective.*

### Predicate Nominatives

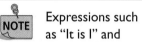 **9d.**   **A *predicate nominative* is a noun or a pronoun that follows a linking verb and identifies the subject or refers to it.**

**EXAMPLE**   Sky Woman became the **Great Earth Mother.** [The compound noun *Great Earth Mother* is a predicate nominative that identifies the subject *Sky Woman.*]

Like subjects and objects, predicate nominatives never appear in prepositional phrases.

**EXAMPLE**   The world was only a few **bits** of earth on a turtle. [The word *bits* is a predicate nominative that identifies the subject *world.* *Earth* is the object of the preposition *of,* and *turtle* is the object of the preposition *on.*]

---

For information about linking verbs, see pages 714–715 and 755.

**NOTE** Expressions such as "It is I" and "That was he" sound awkward even though they are correct. In conversation, you would likely say "It's me" and "That was him." Such nonstandard expressions may one day become acceptable in writing as well as in speech. For now, however, it is best to follow the rules of standard English in your writing.

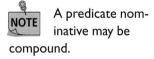

**NOTE** A predicate nominative may be compound.

**EXAMPLE**   Her helpers were **birds,** a **muskrat,** a **toad,** and a **turtle.**

## Predicate Adjectives

**9e.** A *predicate adjective* is an adjective that follows a linking verb and describes the subject.

**EXAMPLE**    Sky Woman was **young** and **beautiful.** [The words *young* and *beautiful* are predicate adjectives that describe the subject *Sky Woman.*]

Some verbs, such as *look, grow,* and *feel,* may be used as either linking verbs or action verbs.

**LINKING VERB**    The Chief of Heaven **looked** angry. [*Looked* is a linking verb because it links the adjective *angry* to the subject *Chief of Heaven.*]

**ACTION VERB**    Sky Woman **looked** through the hole in the floor of Heaven. [*Looked* is an action verb because it expresses Sky Woman's action.]

 **QUICK CHECK 3**

Identify the subject complement in each of the following sentences. Then, label each as a *predicate nominative* or a *predicate adjective.*

**EXAMPLE**    **1.** Traditional stories are one way of understanding nature.

            **1.** *way—predicate nominative*

1. These stories may seem simple but may be quite complex.
2. After all, their theme is the whole world.
3. Sky Woman's misfortune was our good fortune.
4. With her fall, the world became possible.
5. Is anything, even luck, permanent?

 **Using Action Verbs**

Overusing the linking verb *be* can make writing dull and lifeless. As you evaluate your writing, you may get the feeling that nothing is *happening,* that nobody is *doing* anything. That feeling may be an indication that your writing contains too many *be* verbs. Wherever possible, replace a dull *be* verb with a verb that expresses action.

**BE VERB**    "Sky Woman" **is** a traditional Seneca story.

**ACTION VERB**    Traditionally, the Seneca people **tell** the story of Sky Woman.

 **COMPUTER NOTE**    The overuse of *be* verbs is a problem that a computer can help you eliminate. Use the computer's "Search" function to locate and highlight each occurrence of *am, are, is, was, were, be, been,* and *being.* In each case, determine whether the *be* verb is necessary or whether it could be replaced with an action verb for greater impact.

**Try It Out** ✎

Revise each of the following sentences by substituting an interesting action verb for the dull *be* verb.

1. The Chief of Heaven was angry at Sky Woman.
2. Paradise was the home of the Chief of Heaven, Sky Woman, and many animals and plants.
3. Animals of all kinds were her friends.
4. The shell of that turtle is now the earth.
5. Many things from the sky are now on earth.

# 10 KINDS OF SENTENCES

## SENTENCES CLASSIFIED BY STRUCTURE

One way that sentences are classified is by **structure**—the kinds of clauses and the number of clauses the sentences contain.

### The Simple Sentence

**10a.** A *simple sentence* has one independent clause and no subordinate clauses.

EXAMPLE    Jean Fritz and her parents discussed her problem and found a clever solution to it.

Notice in the example above that a simple sentence may have a compound subject, a compound verb, or both.

☞ For more about compound subjects and compound verbs, see pages 721 and 753.

### The Compound Sentence

**10b.** A *compound sentence* has two or more independent clauses but no subordinate clauses.

The independent clauses are usually joined by a coordinating conjunction: *and, but, for, nor, or, so,* or *yet.* The independent clauses in a compound sentence may also be joined by a semicolon.

EXAMPLES    Jared read *Old Yeller,* and then he saw the movie.

Anne McCaffrey has written many stories about dragons; in fact, she has contributed to their popularity.

☞ For more about using commas in compound sentences, see page 769. For more about using semicolons, see pages 771–772.

### The Complex Sentence

**10c.** A *complex sentence* has one independent clause and at least one subordinate clause.

EXAMPLE    When I read one of Anne McCaffrey's stories, I want to ride a dragon.

*Independent Clause*    I want to ride a dragon

*Subordinate Clause*    When I read one of Anne McCaffrey's stories

**QUICK CHECK 1**

Identify each of the following sentences as *simple, compound,* or *complex.*

**EXAMPLE**    **1.** *Homesick* was interesting to me because I once lived abroad.

            **1.** *complex*

1. Boys and girls ran and played on the playground.
2. Jean Fritz did not feel like part of their world at the British school.
3. They sang "God Save the King," but she didn't.
4. Her problem disappeared after she spoke to her father.
5. She told her amah that *sewing machine* meant "hello."

 **Using Varied Sentence Structure**

Variety is the spice of life. It's also the spice of writing. By varying the length and the structure of your sentences, you can make your writing clearer and more interesting to read.

Simple sentences are best used to express single ideas. To describe more complicated ideas and to show relationships between them, use compound and complex sentences.

## SENTENCES CLASSIFIED BY PURPOSE

In addition to being classified by structure, a sentence is also classified according to its purpose. The four kinds of sentences are *declarative, interrogative, imperative,* and *exclamatory.*

**10d.** **A** *declarative sentence* **makes a statement. It is followed by a period.**

**EXAMPLE**    I can guess what that is.

**10e.** **An** *interrogative sentence* **asks a question. It is followed by a question mark.**

**EXAMPLE**    What was the matter with Ted's bike?

**10f.** **An** *imperative sentence* **gives a command or makes a request. It is followed by a period. A strong command is followed by an exclamation point.**

**EXAMPLES**    Please open the door, Theo.
                  Look out!

 A computer can help you analyze your writing for sentence length and structure. Programs are available that will tell you the average number of words in your sentences and the number of each kind of sentence you used. In this way, you can easily see which sentence structures you've mastered and which ones you'll need to work on.

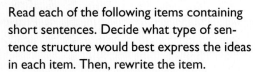 **Try It Out**

Read each of the following items containing short sentences. Decide what type of sentence structure would best express the ideas in each item. Then, rewrite the item.

1. Commas seemed complicated. Andrea Hull knew how to use them.
2. Andrea Hull knew more than young Jean. Andrea taught her many things.
3. Embroidery is beautiful. It can be tedious.
4. She stretched the cloth. She marked her pattern. She began stitching.
5. A design is finished. Everyone can enjoy it.

**NOTE** If an imperative sentence does not have a subject, the "understood" subject is always *you.*

**EXAMPLE**
(You) Do it now!

For more on the different end marks of punctuation, see page 768.

**10g.** An *exclamatory sentence* shows excitement or expresses strong feeling. An exclamatory sentence is followed by an exclamation point.

**EXAMPLES**   What a bargain this is**!**
We won regionals**!**

## ✓ QUICK CHECK 2

Classify each of the following sentences according to its purpose—*declarative, interrogative, imperative,* or *exclamatory.*

**EXAMPLE**   **1.** Explain the theme of this story, Andy.
      **1.** *imperative*

1. Have you ever lived in a foreign country?
2. As a child, Jean Fritz attended a British school in China.
3. How wonderful the Yangtze River was!
4. Please take me there.
5. Read *Homesick*, and see for yourself.

# 11 WRITING EFFECTIVE SENTENCES

## Combining Sentences

**11a.** Improve short, choppy sentences by combining them into longer, smoother sentences.

There are many ways to combine sentences. Here are a few examples.

**(1) Insert words and phrases.**

**CHOPPY**   The pan was hot. The pan was made of iron.
**COMBINED**   The **iron** pan was hot.

**CHOPPY**   Cook the steak. Cook it for five minutes.
**COMBINED**   Cook the steak **for five minutes.**

**(2) Use coordinating conjunctions.**

**CHOPPY**   Father likes steak. Mother does too.
**COMBINED**   Father **and** Mother like steak.

**CHOPPY**   The preparation was Chinese. The food was not.
**COMBINED**   The preparation was Chinese, **but** the food was not.

**(3) Use subordinate clauses.**

**CHOPPY**   Be careful. It is easy to be burned.
**COMBINED**   Be careful **because it is easy to be burned.**

**CHOPPY**  I sliced the meat. It was already cooked.

**COMBINED**  I sliced the meat **that was already cooked.**

 *QUICK CHECK 1*

Use the methods you've learned in this section to combine some of the choppy sentences in the following paragraph.

**EXAMPLE**  [1] He is Chinese. [2] He is American.
1. *He is Chinese and American.*

[1] "T-Bone Steak" is a poem about identity. [2] It was written by Wing Tek Lum. [3] The poet describes an ordinary moment. [4] This ordinary moment is filled with meaning. [5] The meaning is complex. [6] It includes self-assertion, rebellion, respect, and self-acceptance. [7] Preparing the meal is almost a ritual for the family. [8] It is a ritual that asserts their individuality. [9] The meal draws from Chinese and American customs. [10] Elements of both cultures contribute to the family's identity.

## Revising Run-on Sentences

**11b.**  **Avoid using run-on sentences.**

If you run together two complete sentences as if they were one sentence, you get a **run-on sentence.**

**RUN-ON**  This poet values individuality, he also respects tradition.

Here are two of the ways you can revise run-on sentences.

1. You can make two sentences.

  **REVISED**  This poet values individuality**.** **H**e also respects tradition.

2. You can use a comma and the coordinating conjunction *and, but,* or *or.*

  **REVISED**  This poet values individuality**,** **but** he also respects tradition.

## Revising Stringy Sentences and Wordy Sentences

**11c.**  Improve *stringy* and *wordy sentences* by making them shorter and more precise.

*Stringy sentences* have too many independent clauses strung together with words like *and* or *but.*

**STRINGY**  The Hummingbird King was betrayed, and an enemy betrayed him, and Kukul turned into a hummingbird, for the hummingbird symbolizes freedom for the Maya, and even today he watches everything.

> **NOTE**  A *comma splice* is a kind of run-on sentence in which a comma is used without a coordinating conjunction to join independent clauses. The sample run-on sentence given under rule 11b is a comma splice.

To fix a stringy sentence, you can break the sentence into two or more sentences. You can also turn some of the independent clauses into phrases or subordinate clauses.

**REVISED**   When the Hummingbird King was betrayed by an enemy, Kukul turned into a hummingbird, the symbol of freedom for the Maya. Even today, he watches everything.

You can revise wordy sentences in three different ways.

**1.** Replace a group of words with one word.

**WORDY**   With great sorrow, they mourned their king.
**REVISED**   **Sorrowfully,** they mourned their king.

**2.** Replace a clause with a phrase.

**WORDY**   When Kukul's life ended, he turned into a hummingbird.
**REVISED**   **After his death,** Kukul turned into a hummingbird.

**3.** Take out a whole group of unnecessary words.

**WORDY**   What I mean to say is that Kukul is known as the *quetzal.*
**REVISED**   Kukul is known as the *quetzal.*

 **QUICK CHECK 2**

The following paragraph contains run-on, stringy, and wordy sentences. Revise them to improve the style of the paragraph.

**EXAMPLE**   [1]  We know little about many ancient cultures due to the fact that records have been lost.
　　　　**1.**  *We know little about many ancient cultures because records have been lost.*

[1] Many people all over the world have legends, these legends tell of people being turned into animals. [2] It seems evident that people must feel a great kinship with the animals. [3] Many of these legends feature an animal, and the animal was once a person, and that person had special powers. [4] The fact is that many animals have powers that people do not have. [5] Perhaps these legends are expressive of the idea that people sometimes have envy for animals.

 **Revising Wordy Sentences**

Extra words and phrases tend to make writing sound awkward and unnatural. As you revise your writing, read your sentences aloud to check for wordiness or a stringy style. If you run out of breath before the end of a sentence, it is likely stringy, wordy, or both.

---

**Try It Out** ✎

Revise each of the following sentences to eliminate wordiness and stringy style.

**1.** The reason that many legends, myths, and fairy tales have survived for centuries is that they address something important in people.

**2.** They continually surprise and delight readers due to the fact of their impossibility.

**3.** People have long told stories that explain human behavior and ones that explain natural forces in the world.

**4.** Children read these stories or view them on film, and so do their parents.

**5.** The needs of a culture change, and details of the story change, and the ending may change, but the readers remain.

# 12 CAPITAL LETTERS

**12a.** Capitalize the first word in every sentence.

**EXAMPLE**   **W**ho gets a place in the choir?

The first word of a sentence that is a direct quotation is capitalized even if the quotation begins within a sentence.

**EXAMPLE**   Francis Bacon states, "**K**nowledge is power."

Traditionally, the first word in a line of poetry is capitalized. However, some modern poets and writers do not follow this style. When you are quoting, follow the capitalization used in the source of the quotation.

**EXAMPLE**   **I**t was many and many a year ago,
      **I**n a kingdom by the sea,
**T**hat a maiden there lived whom you may know
      **B**y the name of Annabel Lee;
**A**nd this maiden she lived with no other thought
      **T**han to love and be loved by me.
          —Edgar Allan Poe, "Annabel Lee"

**12b.** Capitalize the pronoun *I*.

**EXAMPLE**   **I** enjoyed the book, but **I** didn't like the film.

**12c.** Capitalize the interjection *O*.

The interjection *O* is most often used on solemn or formal occasions. It is usually followed by a word in direct address.

**EXAMPLE**   Protect us in the battle, **O** great Athena!

## ✓ QUICK CHECK I

Most of the following sentences contain errors in capitalization. If a sentence is correct, write *C*. If there are errors in the use of capitals, correct the word or words that should be changed.

**EXAMPLE**   **1.** William says that *i* am his best friend.
        **1.** *I*

1. If i need a ride, i will give you a call.
2. Loretta is in Maine, but Oh, how she would like to visit Paris.
3. oh no, I left my backpack on the bus!
4. Please accept these gifts, o Lord.
5. The poem ends with a question.

**12d.** Capitalize proper nouns.

A **common noun** is a general name for a person, a place, a thing, or an idea. A **proper noun** names a particular person, place, thing, or idea.

 For more about using capital letters in quotations, see page 774.

**NOTE**   The interjection *oh* requires a capital letter only at the beginning of a sentence. Otherwise, *oh* is not capitalized.

**EXAMPLES**   **O**h, look at the sunset!
We felt tired but, **oh**, so victorious.

**COMPUTER NOTE** You may be able to use your spelling checker to help you capitalize names correctly. Make a list of the names you write most often. Be sure that you have spelled and capitalized each name correctly. Then, add this list to your computer's dictionary or spelling checker.

A common noun is capitalized only when it begins a sentence or is part of a title. A proper noun is always capitalized. Some proper nouns consist of more than one word. In these names, short prepositions (those of fewer than five letters) and articles (*a, an, the*) are not capitalized.

| | | |
|---|---|---|
| **COMMON NOUNS** | statue | man |
| **PROPER NOUNS** | Statue of Liberty | Eric the Red |

**(1) Capitalize the names of persons and animals.**

**EXAMPLES**  Franklin Chang-Díaz, Alice Walker, Lassie, Shamu

**(2) Capitalize geographical names.**

| TYPE OF NAME | EXAMPLES |
|---|---|
| Towns, Cities | San Diego, Jamestown |
| Islands | Isle of Wight, Wake Island |
| Counties, States | Cook County, New Hampshire |
| Countries | New Zealand, Germany |
| Bodies of Water | Gulf of Mexico, Indian Ocean |
| Forests, Parks | Sherwood Forest, Yellowstone National Park |
| Streets, Highways | Route 44, West Fourth Street |
| Mountains | Mount Washington, Big Horn Mountain |
| Continents | South America, Asia |
| Regions | the West Coast, the Great Plains |

**NOTE** In a hyphenated street number, the second part of the number is not capitalized.

**EXAMPLE**  Seventy-eighth Street

**NOTE** Words such as *north, east,* and *southwest* are not capitalized when they indicate direction, but they are capitalized when they are part of a proper name.

**EXAMPLES**  go south for the winter
northeast of Atlanta
East End Cafe
Old West Jamboree

**(3) Capitalize the names of planets, stars, and other heavenly bodies.**

**EXAMPLES**  Jupiter   Sirius   Milky Way
Big Dipper   North Star

**(4) Capitalize the names of teams, organizations, businesses, institutions, and government bodies.**

| TYPE OF NAME | EXAMPLES |
|---|---|
| Teams | Detroit Pistons, Seattle Seahawks |
| Organizations | Girl Scouts, African Studies Association |
| Businesses | Wilson's Vacuum World, Seaside Cycle Shop |
| Institutions | Cary Memorial Hospital, Hilltop High School |
| Government Bodies | Air National Guard, Department of Agriculture |

**NOTE** The word *earth* is not capitalized unless it is used along with the names of other heavenly bodies that are capitalized. The words *sun* and *moon* are not capitalized.

**(5) Capitalize the names of historical events and periods, special events, and calendar items.**

| TYPE OF NAME | EXAMPLES |
|---|---|
| Historical Events | Battle of Bunker Hill, Yalta Conference |
| Historical Periods | Great Depression, Middle Ages |
| Special Events | Oklahoma State Fair, Cannes Film Festival |
| Calendar Items | Friday, Fourth of July |

 **NOTE** The name of a season is not capitalized unless it is part of a proper name.

**EXAMPLES** the last day of summer, the Oak Ridge Winter Carnival

**(6) Capitalize the names of nationalities, races, and peoples.**

**EXAMPLES** Greek, Asian, Caucasian, Hispanic, Shawnee

**(7) Capitalize the names of religions and their followers, holy days, sacred writings, and specific deities.**

| TYPE OF NAME | EXAMPLES |
|---|---|
| Religions and Followers | Zen Buddhism, Christianity, Muslim |
| Holy Days | Passover, Lent, Ramadan |
| Sacred Writings | Tao Te Ching, Bible, Talmud, Koran |
| Specific Deities | Holy Spirit, Brahma, Allah, Jehovah |

**NOTE** The word *god* is not capitalized when it refers to a mythological god. The names of specific gods, however, are capitalized.

**EXAMPLE** The king of Greek gods was Zeus.

**(8) Capitalize the names of buildings and other structures.**

**EXAMPLES** World Trade Center, Golden Gate Bridge, Ritz Theater

**(9) Capitalize the names of monuments and awards.**

| TYPE OF NAME | EXAMPLES |
|---|---|
| Monuments | Vietnam Veterans Memorial, Statue of Liberty |
| Awards | Newbery Medal, Purple Heart |

**(10) Capitalize the names of trains, ships, aircraft, and spacecraft.**

| TYPE OF NAME | EXAMPLES |
|---|---|
| Trains | Silver Rocket, Orient Express |
| Ships | Nimitz, Santa Maria |
| Aircraft | Spirit of St. Louis, Air Force One |
| Spacecraft | Apollo 11, Columbia |

**(11) Capitalize the brand names of business products.**

**EXAMPLES** **N**ike shoes, **B**uick station wagon, **W**rangler jeans

☑ *QUICK CHECK 2*

Correct each of the following expressions, using capital letters as needed.

**EXAMPLE** **1.** the stone age
       **1.** *the Stone Age*

**1.** decisions of the united states supreme court
**2.** three skeleton key, an island off guiana
**3.** pictures of saturn sent by *voyager 2*
**4.** the apaches of the southwest
**5.** the tomb of the unknown soldier

**12e.** **Capitalize proper adjectives.**

A *proper adjective* is formed from a proper noun and is almost always capitalized.

    **PROPER NOUN** **R**ome, **I**slam, **K**ing **A**rthur
**PROPER ADJECTIVE** **R**oman army, **I**slamic culture, **A**rthurian legend

**12f.** **Do *not* capitalize the names of school subjects, except language classes and course names followed by a number.**

**EXAMPLES** I have tests in **E**nglish, **m**ath, and **A**rt **II**.

**12g.** **Capitalize titles.**

**(1) Capitalize the title of a person when it comes before a name.**

**EXAMPLES** Does **M**s. **T**am know **D**r. **P**oliti or **G**overnor **H**alsey?

**(2) Capitalize a title used alone or following a person's name only when you want to emphasize the position of someone holding a high office.**

**EXAMPLES** We grew quiet as the **R**abbi rose to speak.
    Is he the **r**abbi at the new synagogue?

A title used alone in direct address is often capitalized.

**EXAMPLES** Is the patient resting comfortably, **N**urse?
    What is your name, **S**ir [*or* sir]?

**(3) Capitalize a word showing a family relationship when the word is used before or in place of a person's name.**

**EXAMPLES** Hey, **M**om, I received a letter from **A**unt **C**hristina and **U**ncle **G**arth.

---

☞ For more about proper nouns and proper adjectives, see pages 709 and 712–713.

---

Remember that correct capitalization of abbreviations is part of proper spelling. You may notice that certain abbreviations are capitalized.

**EXAMPLES** **M**r. **M**s. **U.S.** **TV** **F**la. **NAACP**

However, some abbreviations, especially those for measurements, are not capitalized.

**EXAMPLES** **i**n. **ft** **lb** **cc** **ml**

Consult a dictionary for the correct capitalization of an abbreviation.

---

Do not capitalize a word showing a family relationship when a possessive comes before the word.

**EXAMPLES**  Angela's **m**other and my **g**randmother Daphne coach the softball team.

**(4) Capitalize the first and last words and all important words in titles of books, magazines, newspapers, poems, short stories, historical documents, movies, television programs, works of art, and musical compositions.**

Unimportant words in titles include

- prepositions of fewer than five letters (such as *at, of, for, from, with*)
- coordinating conjunctions (*and, but, for, nor, or, so, yet*)
- articles (*a, an, the*)

| TYPE OF NAME | EXAMPLES |
| --- | --- |
| Books | *The Old Man and the Sea, Dust Tracks on a Road* |
| Magazines | *Sports Illustrated, Woman's Day* |
| Newspapers | *San Francisco Examiner, The Miami Herald* |
| Poems | "My Father Is a Simple Man," "Annabel Lee" |
| Short Stories | "The Naming of Names," "A Day's Wait" |
| Historical Documents | Bill of Rights, Emancipation Proclamation |
| Movies | *Stand and Deliver, Jurassic Park* |
| Television Programs | *FBI: The Untold Stories, A Different World* |
| Works of Art | *Birth of Venus, The Old Guitarist* |
| Musical Compositions | *The Marriage of Figaro,* "In the Pines" |

 QUICK CHECK 3

Use capital or lowercase letters to correct each error in capitalization in the following sentences.

**EXAMPLE**  **1.** Did you know that dr. Santos subscribes to *field and stream*?
  **1.** *Did you know that Dr. Santos subscribes to <u>Field and Stream</u>?*

**1.** When my Aunt Rose and I went to Mexico, she introduced me to grandmother Villa.
**2.** Try looking up that word in *the american heritage dictionary.*
**3.** Did you hear commissioner of education boylan's speech?
**4.** Did the treasurer review the club's budget, senator?
**5.** When I get older, I hope I will be like the father in "My Father Is A Simple Man."

**NOTE**  The article *the* before a title is not capitalized unless it is the first word of the title.

**EXAMPLES**  Is that the late edition of the *Chicago Sun-Times*? I read an interesting story in *The New Yorker.*

If you are not sure whether *the* is part of a magazine's title, look for the official title in the magazine's masthead or on the table-of-contents page. For a newspaper, look on the editorial page. For a book, look on the title page.

☞  For information on when to italicize (underline) a title, see page 773. For information on using quotation marks for titles, see page 776.

# 13 PUNCTUATION

## END MARKS

An **end mark** is a mark of punctuation placed at the end of a sentence. The three kinds of end marks are the *period,* the *question mark,* and the *exclamation point.*

**13a.** Use a period at the end of a statement.

**EXAMPLE** Kristi Yamaguchi is a world-champion figure skater.

**13b.** Use a question mark at the end of a question.

**EXAMPLE** Did Gordon Parks write *The Learning Tree*?

**13c.** Use an exclamation point at the end of an exclamation.

**EXAMPLES** Wow! What a view!

**13d.** Use a period or an exclamation point at the end of a request or a command.

**EXAMPLES** Please give me the scissors. [a request]
Give me the scissors! [a command]

**13e.** Use a period after most abbreviations.

| TYPES OF ABBREVIATIONS | EXAMPLES | | | |
|---|---|---|---|---|
| Personal Names | Pearl S. Buck | | W.E.B. Du Bois | |
| Titles Used with Names | Mr. | Ms. | Jr. | Sr. | Dr. |
| States | Ky. | Fla. | Tenn. | Calif. |
| Addresses | St. | Blvd. | P.O. Box | |
| Organizations and Companies | Co. | Inc. | Corp. | Assn. |
| Times | A.M. | P.M. | B.C. | A.D. |

Place A.D. before the number and B.C. after the number. For centuries expressed in words, place both A.D. and B.C. after the century.

**EXAMPLES** A.D. 540   31 B.C.   sixth century B.C.   third century A.D.

When an abbreviation with a period ends a sentence, another period is not needed. However, a question mark or an exclamation point is used as needed.

**EXAMPLES** This is my friend J. R.
Have you met Nguyen, J. R.?

A two-letter state abbreviation without periods is used only when it is followed by a ZIP Code.

**EXAMPLE**
Austin, **TX** 78741

NOTE Some widely used abbreviations are written without periods.

**EXAMPLES** UN, FBI, PTA, NAACP, PBS, CNN, YMCA, VHF

NOTE Abbreviations for most units of measure are written without periods.

**EXAMPLES** cm, kg, ml, ft, lb, mi, oz, qt

The abbreviation for *inch* (*in.*) is written with a period to prevent confusion with the word *in.* If you're not sure whether to use periods with abbreviations, look in a dictionary.

 **QUICK CHECK 1**

Add end marks where they are needed in the following sentences.

**EXAMPLE**  1. Japanese haiku are very short poems
  1. *Japanese haiku are very short poems.*

1. Have you ever heard of Little Tokyo
2. It's a Japanese neighborhood in Los Angeles, Calif, bordered by First St, Third St, Alameda St, and Los Angeles St
3. Some friends of ours who live in Los Angeles, Mr and Mrs Cook, Sr, and their son, Al, Jr, introduced us to the area
4. They met our 11:30 AM flight from Atlanta, Ga, and took us to lunch at a restaurant in the Japanese Plaza Village
5. What a great afternoon we had with our friends

## COMMAS

### Items in a Series

**13f.** **Use commas to separate items in a series.**

Words, phrases, and clauses in a series are separated by commas to show the reader where one item in the series ends and the next item begins. Commas are always needed with three or more items in a series. Two items often do not need a comma.

**WORDS IN A SERIES**  *Hammock, canoe,* and *moccasin* are Native American words.

**PHRASES IN A SERIES**  Seaweed was in the water, on the beach, and in our shoes.

**CLAUSES IN A SERIES**  Tell us who was there, what happened, and why it happened.

If all items in a series are joined by *and* or *or,* commas are not needed.

**EXAMPLE**  I voted for Corey **and** Mona **and** Ethan.

**13g.** **Use a comma to separate two or more adjectives that come before a noun.**

**EXAMPLE**  An Arabian horse is a fast, beautiful animal.

### Compound Sentences

**13h.** **Use a comma before *and, but, or, nor, for, so,* or *yet* when it joins independent clauses.**

**EXAMPLE**  I enjoyed *The King and I,* **but** *Oklahoma!* is still my favorite musical.

You may omit the comma before *and, but, or,* or *nor* if the clauses are very short and there is no chance of misunderstanding.

## Interrupters

**13i.** Use commas to set off an expression that interrupts a sentence.

Two commas are needed if the expression comes in the middle of the sentence. One comma is needed if the expression comes at the beginning or the end of the sentence.

**EXAMPLES**    Yes, my favorite gospel singers, BeBe and CeCe Winans, were on TV, Ed.

**(1) Use commas to set off a _nonessential_ participial phrase or a _nonessential_ subordinate clause.**

A _nonessential_ (or _nonrestrictive_) phrase or clause adds information to the sentence but can be omitted without changing the main idea of the sentence.

**NONESSENTIAL PHRASE**    Orpheus, **mourning his bride,** entered Hades.

**NONESSENTIAL CLAUSE**    Orpheus, **who was a musician,** met a cruel fate.

> **NOTE** Do not set off an **_essential_** (or **_restrictive_**) phrase or clause. It cannot be omitted without changing the meaning of the sentence.
>
> **ESSENTIAL PHRASE**    All the spirits **toiling in Hades** stopped and listened.
>
> **ESSENTIAL CLAUSE**    The song **that Orpheus sang** charmed the king of Hades.

**(2) Use commas to set off an appositive or an appositive phrase that is nonessential.**

**APPOSITIVE**    The gray ferryman, **Charon,** did not charge him any fare.

**APPOSITIVE PHRASE**    Even Cerberus, **the dog at the gate,** listened.

**(3) Use commas to set off words used in direct address.**

**EXAMPLE**    Do you know, **Elena,** when the next bus is due?

**(4) Use commas to set off a parenthetical expression.**

A _parenthetical expression_ is a side remark that either adds information or relates ideas in a sentence. Some of these expressions are not always used as interrupters. Use commas only when the expressions are parenthetical.

**EXAMPLES**    What, **in your opinion,** is the best solution to this problem? [parenthetical]
I have faith **in your opinion.** [not parenthetical]

## Introductory Words, Phrases, and Clauses

**13j.** Use a comma after certain introductory elements.

**(1) Use a comma after _yes, no,_ or any mild exclamation such as _well_ or _why_ at the beginning of a sentence.**

**EXAMPLE**    Yes, King Midas had been foolish.

**(2) Use a comma after an introductory prepositional phrase if the phrase is long or if two or more phrases appear together.**

**EXAMPLES**   **Long ago in a land called Lydia,** King Midas lived.
**In the garden of his palace,** he met Silenus.

**(3) Use a comma after a participial phrase or an infinitive phrase that introduces a sentence.**

**PARTICIPIAL PHRASE**   **Threatened by Midas,** the satyr struck a bargain.

**INFINITIVE PHRASE**   **To reward Midas,** Dionysus offered a gift.

**(4) Use a comma after an introductory adverb clause.**

**EXAMPLE**   **When his daughter arrived,** he warned her to stay away.

## Conventional Situations

**13k.   Use commas in certain conventional situations.**

**(1) Use commas to separate items in dates and addresses.**

**EXAMPLES**   They met on June 17, 1965, in Erie, Pennsylvania.
My address is 520 Cocoa Lane, Orlando, FL 32804.

**(2) Use a comma after the salutation of a friendly letter and after the closing of any letter.**

**EXAMPLES**   Dear Aunt Margaret,        Sincerely yours,

 *QUICK CHECK 2*

Insert commas where they are needed in the following sentences.

**EXAMPLE**   **1.** This story the tale of King Midas warns us about greed.
       **1.** *This story, the tale of King Midas, warns us about greed.*

**1.** Horrified by the sight of his daughter Midas wept.
**2.** Well Midas left the palace went to Dionysus and begged relief.
**3.** Dionysus sometimes a merciful god told him to go to Pactolus.
**4.** In the deep strong waters of the river Midas washed himself.
**5.** My friend do not make Midas's error or you may not find mercy.

## Semicolons

**13l.   Use a semicolon instead of a comma between independent clauses when they are not joined by** *and, but, or, nor, for, so,* **or** *yet.*

**EXAMPLE**   Our parents settled our dispute; they gave us each half.

 **NOTE**   Use a semicolon rather than a period between independent clauses only when the ideas in the clauses are closely related.

**EXAMPLE**   I called Leon; he will be here in ten minutes.

## Using Semicolons

Semicolons are most effective when they are not overused. Sometimes it is better to separate a compound sentence or a heavily punctuated sentence into two sentences rather than to use a semicolon.

**ACCEPTABLE** In the jungles of South America, it rains every day, sometimes all day; the vegetation there, some of which is found nowhere else in the world, is lush, dense, and fast-growing.

**BETTER** In the jungles of South America, it rains practically every day, sometimes all day. The vegetation there, some of which is found nowhere else in the world, is lush, dense, and fast-growing.

## Colons

**13m.** Use a colon before a list of items, especially after expressions like *as follows* or *the following*.

**EXAMPLE** Minimum equipment for camping includes the following: bedroll, utensils for eating, warm clothing, and rope.

**13n.** Use a colon in certain conventional situations.

**(1) Use a colon between the hour and the minute.**

**EXAMPLES** 11:30 P.M.    4:08 A.M.

**(2) Use a colon after the salutation of a business letter.**

**EXAMPLES** Dear Ms. Gonzalez:    To Whom It May Concern:

### ✓ QUICK CHECK 3

Insert a colon or semicolon wherever one is needed in each sentence.

**EXAMPLE** 1. Daedalus made Minos the following furniture, weapons, and armor.

1. *Daedalus made Minos the following: furniture, weapons, and armor.*

1. Some reptiles like a dry climate others prefer a wet climate.
2. The first lunch period begins at 11 00 A.M.
3. Icarus flew too high his wings melted.
4. In Ruth 1 16, Ruth pledges her loyalty to Naomi.
5. The frogs wanted a king they got one.

---

### Try It Out ✎

Decide whether each of the following sentences is better expressed as a single sentence or as two or more sentences. Then, write the sentence accordingly. Revise the sentence for style and clarity as well.

1. The frogs wanted a king, one who could amuse them with royal customs; they thought a strong ruler would be exciting.
2. Jupiter heard their request; he granted it; he felt they were foolish.
3. Jupiter threw down a large log; the log landed next to the frogs.
4. Was this strange, new king fearsome; was he peaceful?
5. Strangely enough, these spoiled, bored frogs were not grateful; they petitioned Jupiter, who again granted their wish.

---

 **NOTE** Never use a colon directly after a verb or a preposition. Omit the colon, or reword the sentence.

**INCORRECT** My stepsister's favorite sports are: basketball, tennis, swimming, and bowling.

**CORRECT** My stepsister's favorite sports are basketball, tennis, swimming, and bowling.

 **NOTE** Use a colon between chapter and verse in referring to passages from the Bible.

**EXAMPLES** John 3:16 Matthew 6:9–13

**LANGUAGE HANDBOOK**

# 14 PUNCTUATION

## UNDERLINING (ITALICS)

*Italics* are printed letters that lean to the right, such as *the letters in these words.* In handwritten or typewritten work, indicate italics by underlining.

**TYPED** <u>Born Free</u> is the story of a lion that became a pet.

**PUBLISHED** *Born Free* is the story of a lion that became a pet.

> **COMPUTER NOTE** If you use a computer, you may be able to set words in italics yourself. Most word-processing software and many printers are capable of producing italic type.

**14a.** Use underlining (italics) for titles of books, plays, periodicals, works of art, films, television programs, recordings, long musical compositions, trains, ships, aircraft, and spacecraft.

| TYPE OF TITLE | EXAMPLES | |
|---|---|---|
| Books | *Barrio Boy* | *House Made of Dawn* |
| Plays | *Macbeth* | *Visit to a Small Planet* |
| Periodicals | *Hispanic* | *The New York Times* |
| Works of Art | *The Thinker* | *American Gothic* |
| Films | *Stand and Deliver* | *Jurassic Park* |
| Television Programs | *Home Improvement* | *Wall Street Week* |
| Recordings | *Unforgettable* | *Man of Steel* |
| Long Musical Compositions | *Don Giovanni* | *The Four Seasons* |
| Ships | *Calypso* | USS *Nimitz* |
| Trains | *Orient Express* | *City of New Orleans* |
| Aircraft | *Enola Gay* | *Spirit of St. Louis* |
| Spacecraft | *Apollo 12* | USS *Enterprise* |

> **NOTE** The article *the* before the title of a magazine or a newspaper is usually neither italicized nor capitalized when it is written within a sentence. Some periodicals do include *the* in their titles.
>
> **EXAMPLES** My parents subscribe to **the** *San Francisco Chronicle.*
> On Sundays, we all share ***The*** *New York Times.*

> 👉 For examples of titles that are not italicized but enclosed in quotation marks, see page 776.

**14b.** Use underlining (italics) for words, letters, and figures referred to as such.

**EXAMPLES** What is the difference between the words *affect* and *effect*?
Don't forget to drop the final *e* before you add *–ing* to that word.
Is the last number a *5* or an *8*?

Underline the words that should be italicized in each of the following sentences.

**EXAMPLE**   **I.** Who will play the lead in Brian's Song?
   **I.** *Who will play the lead in <u>Brian's Song</u>?*

1. Sometimes I forget the r in the word friend and write fiend.
2. Pablo Picasso's famous painting Guernica is named for a Spanish town that was bombed during the Spanish Civil War.
3. My father reads the Washington Post because he likes Carl Rowan's column.
4. The movie My Left Foot celebrates the accomplishments of a writer and artist who has serious disabilities.
5. Janice finally found her mistake; she had written the 4 in the wrong column.

## QUOTATION MARKS

**14c.** **Use quotation marks to enclose a *direct quotation*—a person's exact words.**

**EXAMPLE**   "Here is Eric's drawing of the runaway," said Ms. Rios.

**14d.** **A direct quotation begins with a capital letter.**

**EXAMPLE**   Brandon shouted, "Let's get busy!"

**14e.** **When the expression identifying the speaker interrupts a quoted sentence, the second part of the quotation begins with a small letter.**

**EXAMPLE**   "Gee," Angelo added, "the boy in 'A Day's Wait' is a lot like my brother."

   When the second part of a divided quotation is a separate sentence, it begins with a capital letter.

**EXAMPLE**   "Travel is exciting," said Mrs. Ash. "Space travel is no exception."

**14f.** **A direct quotation is set off from the rest of the sentence by a comma, a question mark, or an exclamation point, but not by a period.**

*Set off* means "separated." If a quotation appears at the beginning of a sentence, place a comma after it. If a quotation falls at the end of a sentence, place a comma before it. If a quoted sentence is interrupted, place a comma after the first part and before the second part.

---

**NOTE** Do not use quotation marks for an *indirect quotation,* which is a rewording of a direct quotation.

**DIRECT QUOTATION**
Kaya asked, "What is your interpretation of the poem?"

**INDIRECT QUOTATION**
Kaya asked what my interpretation of the poem was.

**EXAMPLES**   "I just read a story by Amy Tan," Alyssa said.

Mark said, "I've read a couple of her stories, too."

"Alyssa," asked Janet, "what story did you read?"

When a quotation ends with a question mark or an exclamation point, no comma is needed.

**EXAMPLE**   "Have you seen my brother?" Alicia asked.

**14g.** A period or a comma is always placed inside the closing quotation marks.

**EXAMPLES**   Ramón said, "My little brother loves Shel Silverstein's poems."

"My sister does too," Paula responded.

**14h.** A question mark or an exclamation point is placed inside the closing quotation marks when the quotation itself is a question or exclamation. Otherwise, it is placed outside.

**EXAMPLES**   "Is the time difference between Los Angeles and Chicago two hours?" asked Ken. [The quotation is a question.]

Linda exclaimed, "I thought everyone knew that!" [The quotation is an exclamation.]

What did Sandra Cisneros mean in her story "Four Skinny Trees" when she wrote "Keep, keep, keep, trees say when I sleep"? [The sentence, not the quotation, is a question.]

I can't believe that Mom said, "I'm not planning to raise your allowance until next year"! [The sentence, not the quotation, is an exclamation.]

When both the sentence and the quotation at the end of the sentence are questions (or exclamations), only one question mark (or exclamation point) is used. It is placed inside the closing quotation marks.

**EXAMPLE**   Who wrote the poem that begins "How do I love thee?"

**14i.** When you write dialogue (conversation), begin a new paragraph each time you change speakers.

**EXAMPLE**   "Frog, how may we help you?"

"Uh, well, uh, you see," says Frog, "I would like to become a part of your group."

"That's wonderful," says the head bird.

"Yes, wonderful," echo the other birds.

"Frog, you may help us carry our worms," says the head bird.

"That's not what I had in mind," says Frog.

—Linda Goss, "The Frog Who Wanted to Be a Singer"

**14j.** When a quotation consists of several sentences, place quotation marks at the beginning and at the end of the whole quotation.

**EXAMPLE**  "Take the garbage out. Clean your room. Have fun!" said Dad.

**14k.** Use single quotation marks to enclose a quotation within a quotation.

**EXAMPLES**  "I said, 'The quiz will be this Friday,'" repeated Mr. Allyn.
"What poem begins with the words 'I'm Nobody'?" Carol asked.

**14l.** Use quotation marks to enclose titles of short works such as short stories, poems, articles, songs, episodes of television programs, and chapters and other parts of books.

| TYPE OF TITLE | EXAMPLES |
|---|---|
| Short Stories | "Papa's Parrot"        "Amigo Brothers" |
| Poems | "Early Song"        "The Runaway" |
| Articles | "Free Speech and Free Air"<br>"How to Sharpen Your Wit" |
| Songs | "La Bamba"        "Amazing Grace" |
| Episodes of Television Programs | "Heart of a Champion"<br>"The Trouble with Tribbles" |
| Chapters and Other Parts of Books | "Learning About Reptiles"<br>"English: Origins and Uses" |

> ☞ For examples of titles that are italicized, see page 773.

 **QUICK CHECK 2**

Revise the following sentences by adding commas, end marks, quotation marks, and paragraph breaks where necessary.

[1] Gordon, do you ever think about pencils Annie asked [2] I'm always wondering where I lost mine Gordon replied [3] Well said Annie let me tell you some of the things I learned about pencils [4] Sure Gordon said I love trivia [5] People have used some form of pencils for a long time Annie began [6] The ancient Greeks and Romans used lead pencils [7] However, pencils as we know them weren't developed until the 1500s, when people began using graphite [8] What's graphite asked Gordon [9] Graphite is a soft form of carbon Annie explained that leaves a mark when it's drawn over most surfaces [10] Thanks for the information, Annie Gordon said Now, do you have a pencil I can borrow?

# 15 PUNCTUATION

## APOSTROPHES

**15a.** The *possessive case* of a noun or a pronoun shows ownership or relationship.

**(1)** To form the possessive case of a singular noun, add an apostrophe and an *s*.

**EXAMPLES**   a dog's collar      Cinderella's slipper

**(2)** To form the possessive case of a plural noun ending in *s*, add only the apostrophe.

**EXAMPLES**   doctors' opinions      hosts' invitations

**(3)** To form the possessive case of a plural noun that does not end in *s*, add an apostrophe and an *s*.

**EXAMPLES**   women's suits      geese's noise

**(4)** To form the possessive case of some indefinite pronouns, add an apostrophe and an *s*.

**EXAMPLES**   someone's opinion      no one's fault

**15b.** To form a contraction, use an apostrophe to show where letters have been left out.

A *contraction* is a shortened form of a word, figure, or group of words.

**EXAMPLES**   I am . . . . . . . . . . . . . .I'm      they had . . . . . . . .they'd
1996 . . . . . . . . . . . . . .'96      where is . . . . . . .where's
let us . . . . . . . . . . . .let's      of the clock . . . .o'clock

The word *not* can be shortened to *–n't* and added to a verb, usually without changing the spelling of the verb.

**EXAMPLES**   is not . . . . . . . . . .isn't      had not . . . . . . . .hadn't
do not . . . . . . . . .don't      should not . . .shouldn't
**EXCEPTIONS**   will not . . . . . . .**won't**      cannot . . . . . . . . .**can't**

Do not confuse contractions with possessive pronouns.

| CONTRACTIONS | POSSESSIVE PRONOUNS |
| --- | --- |
| **It's** snowing. [*It is*] | **Its** front tire is flat. |
| **Who's** Clifton Davis? [*Who is*] | **Whose** idea was it? |
| **There's** only one answer. [*There is*] | This trophy is **theirs**. |
| **They're** not here. [*They are*] | **Their** dog is barking. |

 **NOTE**   A proper name ending in *s* may take only an apostrophe to form the possessive case if the addition of 's would make the name awkward to pronounce.
**EXAMPLES**
Ms. Masters' class
Hercules' feats

 **NOTE**   Do not use an apostrophe with possessive personal pronouns.

**EXAMPLES**   **His** pantomime was good, but **hers** was better.

**15c.** **Use an apostrophe and an _s_ to form the plurals of letters, numerals, and signs, and of words referred to as words.**

**EXAMPLES**   Your _2_'s look like _5_'s.
Don't use _&_'s in place of _and_'s.

## ☑ QUICK CHECK 1

Add an apostrophe wherever one is needed in the following sentences.

**EXAMPLE**   **1.** Who wrote "A Days Wait," class?
   **1.** _Who wrote "A Day's Wait," class?_

**1.** My cousin Dorothy, everybodys favorite, usually gets all As.
**2.** It isnt correct to use &s in your compositions.
**3.** Many of my friends scores were in the 80s and 90s.
**4.** Theyll meet us later, if its not raining where were going.
**5.** Whos signed up to try out for a part in _Antaeus_?

## HYPHENS

**15d.** **Use a hyphen to divide a word at the end of a line.**

**(1) Divide a word only between syllables.**

**INCORRECT**   Didn't Carrie write her science report on the tyrann-
osaurs, the largest meat-eating dinosaurs?

**CORRECT**   Didn't Carrie write her science report on the tyran-
nosaurs, the largest meat-eating dinosaurs?

**(2) Divide an already hyphenated word at a hyphen.**

**INCORRECT**   I went to the state fair with my sister and my brother-in-law.

**CORRECT**   I went to the state fair with my sister and my brother-
in-law.

**(3) Do not divide a word so that one letter stands alone.**

**INCORRECT**   On our last class trip, all of us stayed o-
vernight in a hotel.

**CORRECT**   On our last class trip, all of us stayed
overnight in a hotel.

**15e.** **Use a hyphen with compound numbers from _twenty-one_ to _ninety-nine_ and with fractions used as adjectives.**

**EXAMPLES**   thirty-five    one-half    forty-eighth

Hyphens are used in some compound names. In such cases, the hyphen is part of the name's spelling.

**PEOPLE**   Daniel Day-Lewis
Orlando Hines-Smith

**PLACES**   Wilkes-Barre [city]
Stratford-on-Avon [borough]

If you are not sure whether a name is hyphenated, consult a reference source.

## PARENTHESES

**15f.** Use parentheses to enclose material that is added to a sentence but is not considered of major importance.

**EXAMPLES**   Mohandas K. Gandhi **(1869–1948)** led India's struggle for independence.

Ms. Matsuo served us the sushi **(sōō′shē)**.

Fill in the order form carefully. **(Do not use a pencil.)**

My great-uncle Chester **(he's Grandma's brother)** will stay with us.

## DASHES

**15g.** Use a dash to indicate an abrupt break in thought or speech.

**EXAMPLES**   Ms. Alonzo—she just left—will be one of the judges.

"You'll find it—oh, excuse me, Sir—over here," said the librarian.

 *QUICK CHECK 2*

For each of the following sentences, insert hyphens, parentheses, or dashes where they are needed.

**EXAMPLE**   **1.** My grandfather, who is seventy five, can recite "The High wayman."

**1.** *My grandfather, who is seventy-five, can recite "The High-wayman."*

1. On Fifty third Street, there is a restaurant called The Highwayman.
2. The restaurant founded in 1925 draws half of its cus tomers from tourists.
3. I painted its one hundred thirty one chairs a tedious job, to say the least.
4. Last night, the restaurant was oh, hi, Ed about one quarter full.
5. It's decorated like an inn my restaurant won't be.

### Punctuating Parenthetical Information

Too many parenthetical expressions in a piece of writing can distract readers from the main idea. Keep your meaning clear by limiting the number of parenthetical expressions you use.

 **NOTE**   Many words and phrases are used *parenthetically;* that is, they break into the main thought of a sentence. Most parenthetical elements are set off by commas or parentheses. Sometimes, parenthetical elements demand stronger emphasis. In such instances, a dash is used.

### Try It Out ✎

Revise the following sentences to eliminate the parentheses. If you think the sentence is best written with parentheses, write *C*.

1. *Survive the Savage Sea* (true stories are my favorites) is about people on a raft.
2. Yellowstone National Park (established in 1872) covers territory in Wyoming, Idaho, and Montana.
3. The writer Langston Hughes (1902–1967) is best known for his poetry.
4. Alligators use their feet and tails to dig holes (called "gator holes") in marshy fields.
5. On the Sabbath we eat braided bread called challah (pronounced khä′ lə).

# 16 SPELLING

## USING WORD PARTS

Many English words are made up of various word parts. Learning to spell the most frequently used parts can help you spell many words correctly.

## Roots

**16a.** The *root* of a word is the part that carries the word's core meaning.

| WORD ROOT | MEANING | EXAMPLES |
|---|---|---|
| –dict– | speak | dictation, dictionary |
| –duc–, –duct– | lead | educate, conductor |
| –ject– | throw | eject, reject |
| –ped– | foot | pedal, biped |
| –vid–, –vis– | see | videotape, invisible |

## Prefixes

**16b.** A *prefix* is one or more letters or syllables added to the beginning of a word or a word part to create a new word.

| PREFIX | MEANING | EXAMPLES |
|---|---|---|
| anti– | against, opposing | antiwar, anticlimax |
| co– | with, together | coexist, codependent |
| in– | not | inaccurate, ineffective |
| re– | back, again | reclaim, rebuild |
| trans– | across, beyond | transport, translate |

## Suffixes

**16c.** A *suffix* is one or more letters or syllables added to the end of a word or a word part to create a new word.

| SUFFIX | MEANING | EXAMPLES |
|---|---|---|
| –able | able, likely | readable, perishable |
| –ance, –ancy | act, quality | admittance, constancy |
| –ate | become, cause | captivate, activate |
| –ize | make, cause to be | socialize, motorize |
| –ness | quality, state | peacefulness, sadness |

# SPELLING RULES

## ie and ei

**16d.** Except after *c*, write *ie* when the sound is long e.

**EXAMPLES**  achieve  believe  chief  field  piece
ceiling  conceit  deceit  deceive  receive

**EXCEPTIONS**  either  protein  neither  seize  weird

**16e.** Write *ei* when the sound is not long e, especially when the sound is long a.

**EXAMPLES**  foreign  forfeit  height  heir  their
freight  neighbor  reign  veil  weigh

**EXCEPTIONS**  ancient  conscience  patient  friend  efficient

### ✓ QUICK CHECK 1

Add the letters *ie* or *ei* to spell each of the following words correctly.

**EXAMPLE**  **1.** bel . . . ve
        **1.** *believe*

**1.** gr . . . f      **5.** . . . ght      **9.** r . . . ndeer
**2.** v . . . n      **6.** perc . . . ve   **10.** p . . . rce
**3.** n . . . ce     **7.** pat . . . nce
**4.** sh . . . ld     **8.** th . . . f

## –cede, –ceed, and –sede

**16f.** The only English word ending in *–sede* is *supersede*. The only words ending in *–ceed* are *exceed, proceed,* and *succeed.* Most other words with this sound end in *–cede.*

**EXAMPLES**  concede  intercede  precede  recede  secede

## Adding Prefixes and Suffixes

**16g.** When adding a prefix to a word, do not change the spelling of the word itself.

**EXAMPLES**  mis + spell = **mis**spell    il + logical = **il**logical

**16h.** When adding the suffix *–ly* or *–ness* to a word, do not change the spelling of the word itself.

**EXAMPLES**  slow + ly = slow**ly**    dark + ness = dark**ness**

**EXCEPTIONS**  For words that end in *y* and have more than one syllable, change the *y* to *i* before adding *–ly* or *-ness.*
happy + ly = happ**ily**    lazy + ness = laz**iness**

---

**NOTE** This time-tested verse may help you remember the *ie* rule.

*I* before *e*
Except after *c*
Or when sounded like *a*,
As in *neighbor* and *weigh*.

The rhyme above and rules 16d and 16e apply only when the *i* and the *e* are in the same syllable.

**NOTE** When adding *–ing* to words that end in *ie*, drop the e and change the *i* to y.

**EXAMPLES**
lie + ing = l**ying**
die + ing = d**ying**

**NOTE** In some cases, the final consonant either may or may not be doubled.

**EXAMPLE**
cancel + ed = cance**led**
*or* cance**lled**

**16i.** **Drop the final silent e before a suffix beginning with a vowel.**

**EXAMPLES** line + ing = lin**ing**  desire + able = desir**able**

**EXCEPTIONS** Keep the final silent *e* in a word ending in *ce* or *ge* before a suffix beginning with *a* or *o*.
*notice + able = noticeable*
*courage + ous = courageous*

**16j.** **Keep the final silent e before a suffix beginning with a consonant.**

**EXAMPLES** hope + less = hope**less**  care + ful = care**ful**

**EXCEPTIONS** nine + th = nin**th**  argue + ment = argu**ment**

**16k.** **For words ending in y preceded by a consonant, change the y to *i* before any suffix that does not begin with *i*.**

**EXAMPLES** try + ed = tr**ied**  duty + ful = dut**iful**

**16l.** **For words ending in y preceded by a vowel, keep the y when adding a suffix.**

**EXAMPLES** pray + ing = pray**ing**  pay + ment = pay**ment**

**EXCEPTIONS** day—da**ily**  lay—la**id**  pay—pa**id**  say—sa**id**

**16m.** **Double the final consonant before a suffix beginning with a vowel if the word**

(1) **has only one syllable or has the accent on the last syllable**

*and*

(2) **ends in a single consonant preceded by a single vowel**

**EXAMPLES** sit + ing = si**tting**  begin + er = begi**nner**

**EXCEPTIONS** Do not double the final consonant in words ending in *w* or *x*.
mow + ing = mo**wing**  wax + ed = wax**ed**

Otherwise, the final consonant is usually not doubled before a suffix beginning with a vowel.

**EXAMPLES** sing + er = sing**er**  final + ist = final**ist**

 *QUICK CHECK 2*

Add the given prefix or suffix to each word listed at the top of the next page.

**EXAMPLE** 1. display + ed
  1. *displayed*

1. im + migrate    5. semi + circle    9. carry + ed
2. re + settle     6. trace + able    10. advantage + ous
3. un + certain    7. jog + er
4. lucky + ly      8. dry + ness

## Forming the Plurals of Nouns

**16n.** For most nouns, add *–s.*

**EXAMPLES**   desk**s**   idea**s**   shoe**s**   friend**s**   camera**s**   Wilson**s**

**16o.** For nouns ending in *s, x, z, ch,* or *sh,* add *–es.*

**EXAMPLES**   gas**es**   fox**es**   waltz**es**   inch**es**   dish**es**   Suarez**es**

**16p.** For nouns ending in *y* preceded by a vowel, add *–s.*

**EXAMPLES**   decoy**s**   highway**s**   alley**s**   Riley**s**

**16q.** For nouns ending in *y* preceded by a consonant, change the *y* to *i* and add *–es.*

**EXAMPLES**   arm**ies**   countr**ies**   cit**ies**   pon**ies**   all**ies**   dais**ies**

**EXCEPTIONS**   For proper nouns ending in *y,* just add *-s.*
Brady—Brady**s**      Murphy—Murphy**s**

**16r.** For some nouns ending in *f* or *fe,* add *–s.* For others, change the *f* or *fe* to *v* and add *–es.*

**EXAMPLES**   belief**s**   thie**ves**   sheriff**s**   kni**ves**
giraffe**s**   lea**ves**   roof**s**   cal**ves**

**16s.** For nouns ending in *o* preceded by a vowel, add *–s.*

**EXAMPLES**   radio**s**   patio**s**   stereo**s**   igloo**s**
Matteo**s**

**TIPS FOR SPELLING**

In some names, marks that show pronunciation are just as important as the letters themselves.

**PEOPLE**   Alemán   Böll   Ibáñez
Khayyám   Janáček   Eugène
**PLACES**   Açores   Bogotá   Camagüey
Gîza   Köln   Sainte-Thérèse

If you're not sure about the spelling of a name, ask the person whose name it is, or check in a reference source.

**16t.** For nouns ending in *o* preceded by a consonant, add *–es.*

**EXAMPLES**   tomato**es**   potato**es**   echo**es**   hero**es**

**EXCEPTIONS**   For musical terms and proper nouns, add *-s.*
alto—alto**s**      soprano—soprano**s**
Blanco—Blanco**s**   Nakamoto—Nakamoto**s**

**16u.** The plural of a few nouns is formed in irregular ways.

**EXAMPLES**   ox**en**   g**ee**se   f**ee**t   t**ee**th   w**o**men   m**i**ce

**16v.** For most compound nouns, form the plural of the last word in the compound.

**EXAMPLES**   bookshel**ves**   push-up**s**   sea gull**s**   ten-year-old**s**

When you use numbers in your writing, follow these guidelines:

- Spell out a number that begins a sentence.

**EXAMPLE**   **Fifty** people received free tickets.

- Within a sentence, spell out numbers that can be written in one or two words.

**EXAMPLE**   In all, **fifty-two** people worked on our play.

- If you use several numbers, some short and some long, write them all the same way. Usually, it is better to write them all as numerals.

**EXAMPLE**   We sold **86** tickets today and **121** yesterday.

- Spell out numbers used to indicate order.

**EXAMPLE**   Our team came in **third** [*not* 3rd] in the track meet.

**16w.** **For compound nouns in which one of the words is modified by the other word or words, form the plural of the word modified.**

**EXAMPLES**   brothers-in-law    maids of honor
eighth-graders    boy scouts

**16x.** **For some nouns, the singular and the plural forms are the same.**

**SINGULAR AND PLURAL**   Sioux   trout   sheep
deer   moose   series

**16y.** **For numerals, letters, symbols, and words used as words, add an apostrophe and –s.**

**EXAMPLES**   *4*'s   *s*'s   *$*'s   *and*'s

✓ *QUICK CHECK 3*

Spell the plural form of each of the following items. [Note: An item may have more than one correct plural form. You only need to give one.]

**EXAMPLE 1.** &
**1.** &'s

1. cargo
2. diary
3. Gómez
4. sit-up
5. child
6. video
7. hoof
8. Japanese
9. *M*
10. *10*

# 17 GLOSSARY OF USAGE

This Glossary of Usage is an alphabetical list of words and expressions that are commonly misused in English. Throughout this section some examples are labeled *standard* or *nonstandard*. **Standard English** is the most widely accepted form of English. It is used in *formal* situations, such as in speeches and writing for school, and in *informal* situations, such as in conversation and everyday writing. **Nonstandard English** is language that does not follow the rules and guidelines of standard English.

**all ready, already**   *All ready* means "completely prepared." *Already* means "before a certain point in time."

**EXAMPLES**   Everyone was **all ready** for the show.
That bill has **already** been paid.

**all right**   Used as an adjective, *all right* means "unhurt" or "satisfactory." Used as an adverb, *all right* means "well enough." *All right* should always be written as two words.

**EXAMPLES**   Linda fell off the horse, but she is **all right.** [adjective]
Does this suit look **all right** on me? [adjective]
You did **all right** at the track meet. [adverb]

**a lot**   *A lot* should always be written as two words.

**EXAMPLE**   She knows **a lot** about computer software.

**anywheres, everywheres, nowheres, somewheres**   Use these words without the final *s*.

**EXAMPLE**   I didn't go **anywhere** [*not* anywheres] yesterday.

**at**   Do not use *at* after *where*.

**EXAMPLE**   Where is it? [*not* Where is it at?]

**bad, badly**   *Bad* is an adjective. *Badly* is an adverb.

**EXAMPLES**   The raw celery did not taste **bad.** [*Bad* modifies the noun *celery.*]
One little boy behaved **badly.** [*Badly* modifies the verb *behaved.*]

**between, among**   Use *between* when referring to two things at a time, even though they may be part of a group containing more than two.

**EXAMPLES**   In homeroom, Carlos sits **between** Bob and me.
Some players practice **between** innings. [Although a game has more than two innings, the practice occurs only *between* any two of them.]

Use *among* to refer to a group rather than separate individuals.

**EXAMPLES**   We saved ten dollars **among** the three of us. [As a group, the three saved ten dollars.]
There was disagreement **among** the fans about the coach's decision. [The fans are thought of as a group.]

**bust, busted**   Avoid using these words as verbs. Use a form of either *burst* or *break.*

**EXAMPLES**   The door **burst** [*not* busted] open and rats teemed in.
What would happen if the window **broke** [*not* busted]?

**choose, chose**   *Choose* is the present tense form of the verb *choose.* It rhymes with *whose* and means "select." *Chose* is the past tense form of *choose.* It rhymes with *grows* and means "selected."

**EXAMPLES**   Did you **choose** "Fish Cheeks" for your report?
Sara **chose** "Miss Awful."

**NOTE**   Many writers overuse *a lot.* Whenever you run across *a lot* as you revise your own writing, try to replace it with a more exact word or phrase.

☞   **among**   See **between, among.**
**as**   See **like, as.**
**as if**   See **like, as if, as though.**

☞   **because**   See **reason . . . because.**

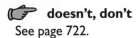

**doesn't, don't**
See page 722.

**could of**   Do not write *of* with the helping verb *could*. Write *could have*. Also avoid *had of*, *ought to of*, *should of*, *would of*, *might of*, and *must of*.

**EXAMPLE**   All of Emily Dickinson's poems **could have** [*not* could of] been lost.

**fewer, less**   *Fewer* is used with plural words. *Less* is used with singular words. *Fewer* tells "how many"; *less* tells "how much."

**EXAMPLES**   We sold **fewer** [*not* less] tickets than they did.
These plants require **less** water than those do.

**good, well**   *Good* is always an adjective. Never use *good* as an adverb. Instead, use *well*.

**EXAMPLE**   Nancy sang **well** [*not* good] at the audition.

*Well* may also be used as an adjective to mean "healthy."

**EXAMPLE**   He didn't look **well** after eating the entire pizza.

**had ought, hadn't ought**   *Had* should not be used with *ought*.

**EXAMPLE**   Eric **ought** [*not* had ought] to help us; he **oughtn't** [*not* hadn't ought] to have missed our meeting yesterday.

**he, she, they**   Avoid using a pronoun along with its antecedent as the subject of a verb. This error is called the **double subject.**

**NONSTANDARD**   Linda Goss she is a famous writer.
**STANDARD**   Linda Goss is a famous writer.

**hisself**   *Hisself* is nonstandard English. Use *himself*.

**EXAMPLE**   Ira bought **himself** [*not* hisself] a polka-dot tie.

**how come**   In informal situations, *how come* is often used instead of *why*. In formal situations, *why* should always be used.

**INFORMAL**   I don't know how come she didn't take the garbage out.
**FORMAL**   I don't know **why** she didn't take the garbage out.

**kind of, sort of**   In informal situations, *kind of* and *sort of* are often used to mean "somewhat" or "rather." In formal English, *somewhat* or *rather* is preferred.

**INFORMAL**   He seemed kind of embarrassed by our applause.
**FORMAL**   He seemed **somewhat** embarrassed by our applause.

**had of**   See **could of.**

**its, it's**   See page 777.

☑ *QUICK CHECK 1*

Revise each of the following sentences to correct any error in usage.

**EXAMPLE**   1. The author she had lived in China.
1. *The author had lived in China.*

1. Alot of stars and planets have names from mythology.
2. Icarus had ought to have listened to his father.
3. If he had listened, he could of survived.
4. I wonder how come he didn't listen.
5. Surely, Daedalus's heart was busted by the death of his son.

**learn, teach**   *Learn* means "gain knowledge." *Teach* means "instruct" or "show how."

**EXAMPLES**   He is **learning** how to play the guitar.
You His grandfather is **teaching** him how to play.

**like, as**   In informal situations, the preposition *like* is often used instead of the conjunction *as* to introduce a clause. In formal situations, *as* is preferred.

**EXAMPLE**   Look in the dictionary, **as** [*not* like] the teacher suggests.

**like, as if, as though**   In informal situations, the preposition *like* is often used for the compound conjunctions *as if* or *as though*. In formal situations, *as if* or *as though* is preferred.

**EXAMPLES**   They acted **as if** [*not* like] they hadn't heard him.
You looked **as though** [*not* like] you knew the answer.

**of**   Do not use *of* with other prepositions such as *inside, off,* and *outside.*

**EXAMPLE**   Did anyone fall **off** [*not* off of] the raft?

**Revising Adverbs in Sentences**

In informal situations, the adjective *real* is often used as an adverb meaning "very" or "extremely." In formal situations, *extremely* or another adverb is preferred.

**INFORMAL**   I'm expecting a real important telephone call.

**FORMAL**   I'm expecting an **extremely** important telephone call.

**reason . . . because**   In informal situations, *reason . . . because* is often used instead of *reason . . . that.* In formal situations, use *reason . . . that,* or revise your sentence.

**INFORMAL**   The reason I did well on the test was because I had studied hard.

**FORMAL**   The **reason** I did well on the test was **that** I had studied hard.

**some, somewhat**   Do not use *some* for *somewhat* as an adverb.

**EXAMPLE**   My writing has improved **somewhat** [*not* some].

   **less**   See **fewer, less.**

**lie, lay**   See pages 732–733.

**might of, must of** See **could of.**

**ought to of** See **could of.**

---

**Try It Out**

Revise the following sentences by substituting another adverb for the word *real.* Use a variety of adverbs.

1. Hercules was real strong.
2. He accomplished many tasks that were real hard.
3. Stories of his labors are real interesting.
4. They have endured a real long time.
5. Even today, real young children know his story from television shows.

---

**should of** See **could of.**

**somewheres** See **anywheres,** etc.

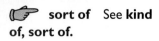 **sort of**   See **kind of, sort of.**

**NOTE**   Here's an easy way to remember the difference between *station-ary* and *stationery*:

You write a lett**er** on station**ery.**

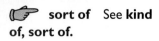 **who's, whose** See page 777.

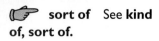 **would of**   See **could of.**

**stationary, stationery**   The adjective *stationary* means "in a fixed position." The noun *stationery* means "writing paper."

**EXAMPLES**   Furnishings in a space capsule must be **stationary.**
I need a new box of **stationery.**

**them**   *Them* should not be used as an adjective. Use *those.*

**EXAMPLE**   The fox couldn't get **those** [*not* them] grapes.

**way, ways**   Use *way,* not *ways,* in referring to a distance.

**EXAMPLE**   They still had a long **way** [*not* ways] to go.

**when, where**   Do not use *when* or *where* incorrectly in a definition.

**NONSTANDARD**   In bowling, a "turkey" is when a person makes three strikes in a row.

**STANDARD**   In bowling, a "turkey" is making three strikes in a row.

**where**   Do not use *where* for *that.*

**EXAMPLE**   I read **that** [*not* where] Pete Sampras won the match.

**who, which, that**   The relative pronoun *who* refers to people only; *which* refers to things only; *that* refers to either people or things.

**EXAMPLES**   Kim is the only one **who** got the right answer. [person]
My bike, **which** has ten speeds, is for sale. [thing]
He is the one person **that** can help you. [person]
This is the ring **that** I want to buy. [thing]

**without, unless**   Do not use the preposition *without* in place of the conjunction *unless.*

**EXAMPLE**   My mother said I can't go **unless** [*not* without] I finish my homework first.

 **QUICK CHECK 2**

Revise the following sentences to correct any error in usage.

**EXAMPLE**   **1.** The team forfeited the game like they had agreed to.
**1.** *The team forfeited the game as they had agreed to.*

1. The reason they forfeited was because Dondré couldn't play there.
2. What was going on inside of their heads?
3. They would not play without their teammate could play, too.
4. That story learned me something about loyalty.
5. True friendship is where people value each other as much as themselves.

# GLOSSARY

The glossary below is an alphabetical list of words found in the selections in this book. Use this glossary just as you use a dictionary—to find out the meanings of unfamiliar words. (Some technical, foreign, and more obscure words in this book are not listed here but instead are defined for you in the footnotes that accompany many of the selections.)

Many words in the English language have more than one meaning. This glossary gives the meanings that apply to the words as they are used in the selections in this book. Words closely related in form and meaning are usually listed together in one entry (for instance, *apprehensive* and *apprehensively*), and the definition is given for the first form.

The following abbreviations are used:

| | |
|---|---|
| *adj.* | adjective |
| *adv.* | adverb |
| *n.* | noun |
| *v.* | verb |

Each word's pronunciation is given in parentheses. A guide to the pronunciation symbols appears at the bottom of each right-hand glossary page.

For more information about the words in this glossary, or for information about words not listed here, consult a dictionary.

**abstracted** (ab·strak′tid) *adj.*: absent-minded.
**accord** (ə·kôrd′) *v.*: give; grant. —*n.*: agreement.
**accordance** (ə·kôrd′′ns) *n.*: agreement; harmony.
**adaptation** (ad′əp·tā′shən) *n.*: change that improves the chance of survival.
**admonish** (ad·män′ish) *v.*: warn or urge.
**ado** (ə·dōō′) *n.*: fuss; trouble.
**advocate** (ad′və·kit) *n.*: person who speaks or writes in support of something.
**afflict** (ə·flikt′) *v.*: cause pain or suffering to.
**agape** (ə·gāp′) *adv.*: with the mouth wide open in surprise or wonder. —*adj.*: wide open.
**agony** (ag′ə·nē) *n.*: intense physical pain.

**alleviate** (ə·lē′vē·āt′) *v.*: relieve; reduce.
**alter** (ôl′tər) *v.*: modify; change. —**altered** *v.* used as *adj.*
**amble** (am′bəl) *v.*: walk easily, without hurrying.
**amiss** (ə·mis′) *adj.*: wrong; improper.
**anachronism** (ə·nak′rə·niz′əm) *n.*: something out of its proper time in history, like a television in the Middle Ages or penicillin in ancient Rome.
**anchorage** (aŋ′kər·ij) *n.*: place that gives or seems to give stability or security.
**anguish** (aŋ′gwish) *n.*: suffering; pain.
**anomalous** (ə·näm′ə·ləs) *adj.*: abnormal; strange.
**appalling** (ə·pôl′iŋ) *adj.*: shocking; horrifying.
**appoint** (ə·point′) *v.*: set; decide upon. —**appointed** *v.* used as *adj.*
**apprehensive** (ap′rē·hen′siv) *adj.*: anxious; uneasy. —**apprehensively** *adv.*
**apt** (apt) *adj.*: quick to learn.
**artful** (ärt′fəl) *adj.*: skillful.
**ascend** (ə·send′) *v.*: move up.
**ashen** (ash′ən) *adj.*: pale.
**assertion** (ə·sʉr′shən) *n.*: statement; declaration.
**assure** (ə·shoor′) *v.*: guarantee; promise confidently.
**astound** (ə·stound′) *v.*: amaze; surprise.
**atrocious** (ə·trō′shəs) *adj.*: very bad.
**attend** (ə·tend′) *v.*: pay attention; wait on.
**awe** (ô) *n.*: mixed feeling of respect, wonder, and fear.

**baleful** (bāl′fəl) *adj.*: wicked or threatening. —**balefully** *adv.*
**ballad** (bal′əd) *n.*: song that tells a story.
**banish** (ban′ish) *v.*: send into exile; get rid of.
**barrage** (bə·räzh′) *n.*: heavy, prolonged attack.
**baton** (bə·tän′) *n.*: slender stick used by a conductor to direct an orchestra or choir.
**beam** (bēm) *v.*: smile warmly. —**beaming** *v.* used as *adj.*
**bear** (ber) *v.*: carry. —**bore** (bôr), **borne** (bôrn)
**belated** (bē·lāt′id) *adj.*: late or delayed.
**berate** (bē·rāt′) *v.*: scold. —**berating** *v.* used as *adj.*
**billow** (bil′ō) *v.*: surge; rise.

at, āte, cär; ten, ēve, is, īce; gō, hôrn, look, tool; oil, out; up, fʉr; ə *for unstressed vowels, as* a *in* ago, u *in* focus; ′ *as in* Latin (lat′′n); chin; she; zh *as in* azure (azh′ər); thin, *the*; ŋ *as in* ring (riŋ)

**blasé** (blä·zā′) *adj.*: bored or unimpressed; not easily excited.

**blissful** (blis′fəl) *adj.*: having great joy or happiness. —**blissfully** *adv.*

**bluff** (bluf) *n.*: steep cliff.

**blunt** (blunt) *adj.*: plain-spoken and abrupt.

**blurt** (blʉrt) *v.*: say suddenly, without stopping to think.

**bore** (bôr) *v.*: See *bear.*

**bout** (bout) *n.*: match; contest.

**brace** (brās) *v.*: make ready for impact.

**bravado** (brə·vä′dō) *n.*: pretended courage.

**breach** (brēch) *n.*: I. break in a wall. 2. breaking of a law or promise.

**brigade** (bri·gād′) *n.*: group of people organized to function as a unit.

**buckle** (buk′əl) *v.*: collapse (usually under pressure).

**calisthenics** (kal′is·then′iks) *n.*: exercises to develop a strong, trim body.

**canister** (kan′is·tər) *n.*: small can.

**capsize** (kap′sīz′) *v.*: overturn (usually said of a boat).

**cascade** (kas·kād′) *v.*: fall like a waterfall.

**cease** (sēs) *v.*: stop.

**cement** (sə·ment′) *v.*: confirm; unite.

**chaotic** (kā·ät′ik) *adj.*: confused; disordered.

**chaperone** (shap′ər·ōn′) *n.*: person who accompanies young people to supervise their behavior.

**charade** (shə·rād′) *n.*: obvious pretense or act.

**chink** (chiŋk) *n.*: narrow opening.

**churn** (chʉrn) *v.*: shake or stir violently, as when milk is made into butter in a churn.

**civic** (siv′ik) *adj.*: of a city or citizenship.

**clamor** (klam′ər) *n.*: loud, confused noise.

**clannish** (klan′ish) *adj.*: very loyal to one's group and hostile to outsiders.

**clarity** (klar′ə·tē) *n.*: clearness.

**clench** (klench) *v.*: close firmly. —**clenched** *v.* used as *adj.*

**coarse** (kôrs) *adj.*: of poor quality; rough or harsh in texture.

**commence** (kə·mens′) *v.*: begin.

**communion** (kə·myoon′yən) *n.*: deep understanding; communication of thoughts without speaking.

**comparable** (käm′pə·rə·bəl) *adj.*: similar.

**compatible** (kəm·pat′ə·bəl) *adj.*: in agreement; in harmony.

**compliance** (kəm·plī′əns) *n.*: giving in to a request or demand.

**condemn** (kən·dem′) *v.*: disapprove strongly of.

**condescending** (kän′di·sen′diŋ) *adj.*: proud; haughty.

**confrontation** (kän′frən·tā′shən) *n.*: face-to-face meeting between opposing sides.

**congregate** (käŋ′grə·gāt′) *v.*: gather into a crowd.

**conjure** (kän′jər) *v.*: call upon, as by a magic spell.

**consensus** (kən·sen′səs) *n.*: opinion of all or most.

**consign** (kən·sīn′) *v.*: send; deliver.

**console** (kən·sōl′) *v.*: make less sad; comfort.

**consolation** (kän′sə·lā′shən) *n.*: comfort.

**consternation** (kän′stər·nā′shən) *n.*: fear or shock that causes helplessness or confusion.

**constriction** (kən·strik′shən) *n.*: limitation.

**consultation** (kän′səl·tā′shən) *n.*: meeting to discuss, decide, or plan something.

**contemplate** (kän′təm·plāt′) *v.*: consider; look at or think about carefully.

**contraption** (kən·trap′shən) *n.*: strange machine or gadget.

**convivial** (kən·viv′ē·əl) *adj.*: sociable or friendly.

**convoluted** (kän′və·loot′id) *adj.*: very complicated.

**copious** (kō′pē·əs) *adj.*: plentiful.

**cosset** (käs′it) *v.*: pamper.

**counter** (kount′ər) *v.*: say in defense.

**cower** (kou′ər) *v.*: crouch and tremble in fear.

**critique** (kri·tēk′) *v.*: evaluate and criticize.

**crow** (krō) *v.*: boast in triumph.

**cultivated** (kul′tə·vāt′id) *adj.*: prepared and used for growing crops.

**curt** (kʉrt) *adj.*: rude and with few words. —**curtly** *adv.*

**dash** (dash) *v.*: knock; strike with violence.

**debris** (də·brē′) *n.*: rough, broken bits of litter.

**defiance** (dē·fī′əns) *n.*: open, bold resistance to authority; opposition.

**deign** (dān) *v.*: consider it appropriate to one's dignity.

**delve** (delv) *v.*: search.

**derange** (dē·rānj′) *v.*: unsettle; make disorderly. —**deranged** *v.* used as *adj.*

**derisive** (di·rī′siv) *adj.*: scornful and ridiculing.

**descend** (dē·send′) *v.*: go down.

**desecrate** (des′i·krāt′) *v.*: show disrespect for something (considered holy).

**desolation** (des′ə·lā′shən) *n.*: lonely grief; misery.

**despondency** (di·spän′dən·sē) *n.*: loss of hope.

**detached** (dē·tacht′) *adj.*: not involved emotionally; indifferent.

**detain** (dē·tān′) *v.*: hold back; delay.

**deteriorate** (dē·tir′ē·ə·rāt′) *v.*: get worse.

**detract** (dē·trakt′) *v.*: take away.

**dignitary** (dig′nə·ter′ē′) *n.:* person holding high, dignified position or office.

**dilate** (dī′lāt′) *v.:* become wider. **—dilating** *v.* used as *adj.*

**diminution** (dim′ə·nōō′shən) *n.:* lessening.

**discontented** (dis′kən·tent′id) *adj.:* not satisfied.

**discrimination** (di·skrim′i·nā′·shən) *n.:* showing of prejudice; actions or policies meant to treat minority groups unfairly.

**dishearten** (dis·härt′′n) *v.:* discourage. **—disheartened** *v.* used as *adj.*

**dislodge** (dis·läj′) *v.:* drive out; force from a position or place.

**dismal** (diz′məl) *adj.:* miserable; gloomy. **—dismally** *adv.*

**dismay** (dis·mā′) *n.:* loss of confidence in the face of trouble or danger.

**disparage** (di·spar′ij) *v.:* show disrespect for; "put down."

**dispel** (di·spel′) *v.:* drive away. **—dispelled**

**disperse** (di·spʉrs′) *v.:* scatter; move in different directions. **—dispersing** *v.* used as *adj.*

**dispute** (di·spyōōt′) *n.:* argument. *—v.:* argue; debate.

**dissipate** (dis′ə·pāt′) *v.:* scatter and disappear.

**distract** (di·strakt′) *v.:* draw attention away; divert. **—distracted** *adj.*

**distress** (di·stres′) *n.:* sorrow; pain.

**domain** (dō·mān′) *n.:* territory.

**dour** (door) *adj.:* gloomy; sullen.

**drone** (drōn) *v.:* talk on and on in a dull way.

**duplicate** (dōō′pli·kāt′) *v.:* make double.

**dutiful** (dōōt′i·fəl) *adj.:* obedient. **—dutifully** *adv.*

**dwindle** (dwin′dəl) *v.:* shrink.

**ease** (ēz) *v.:* move carefully.

**ecstasy** (ek′stə·sē) *n.:* delight; state of absolute joy.

**edible** (ed′ə·bəl) *adj.:* fit to be eaten.

**eerie** (ir′ē) *adj.:* mysterious; weird in a frightening way.

**egotism** (ē′gō·tiz′əm) *n.:* conceit; talking about oneself too much.

**elimination** (ē·lim′ə·nā′shən) *n.:* removal from competition.

**elude** (ē·lōōd′) *v.:* escape by quickness or cleverness.

**ember** (em′bər) *n.:* glowing piece of coal or wood from a fire.

**embolden** (em·bōl′dən) *v.:* give courage; make bold.

**emerge** (ē·mʉrj′) *v.:* come forth into view.

**enervate** (en′ər·vāt′) *v.:* exhaust; weaken. **—enervated** *v.* used as *adj.*

**enigmatic** (en′ig·mat′ik) *adj.:* mysterious; like a riddle.

**ensue** (en·sōō′) *v.:* come after; follow immediately.

**entitle** (en·tīt′l) *v.:* qualify.

**entreaty** (en·trēt′ē) *n.:* earnest request.

**epic** (ep′ik) *adj.:* grand; heroic.

**erode** (ē·rōd′) *v.:* wear away.

**erupt** (ē·rupt′) *v.:* explode or burst forth.

**esoteric** (es′ə·ter′ik) *adj.:* specialized; beyond most people's understanding or knowledge.

**ethnicity** (eth·nis′ə·tē) *n.:* membership in a group with a common cultural background.

**evade** (ē·vād′) *v.:* avoid. **—evading** *v.* used as *adj.*

**evict** (ē·vikt′) *v.:* remove from a rented apartment by legal means. **—evicted** *v.* used as *adj.*

**exaltation** (eg′zôl·tā′shən) *n.:* feeling of great joy.

**exasperate** (eg·zas′pər·āt′) *v.:* irritate. **—exasperated** *v.* used as *adj.*

**exceedingly** (ek·sēd′iŋ·lē) *adv.:* extremely; very.

**excessive** (ek·ses′iv) *adj.:* too great; not moderate. **—excessively** *adv.*

**exertion** (eg·zʉr′shən) *n.:* effort; activity.

**exhalation** (eks′hə·lā′shən) *n.:* breathing out.

**expand** (ek·spand′) *v.:* develop in detail.

**expire** (ek·spīr′) *v.:* die. In Latin, *exspirare* means "to breathe out"; *to breathe out one's last breath* is "to die."

**extensive** (ek·sten′siv) *adj.:* covering a large area; vast. **—extensively** *adv.*

**exuberant** (eg·zōō′bər·ənt) *adj.:* in high spirits. **—exuberantly** *adv.*

**facade** (fə·säd′) *n.:* literally, the front part of a building; a "front" put up to hide real feelings.

**facility** (fə·sil′ə·tē) *n.:* building that makes possible some activity.

**falter** (fôl′tər) *v.:* speak hesitantly; stumble in speech.

**fathom** (fath′əm) *v.:* understand completely.

**fawn** (fôn) *v.:* flatter or lower oneself to make friends. **—fawning** *v.* used as *n.*

**festoon** (fes·tōōn′) *v.:* adorn with flowers, papers, or other decorations.

**fetid** (fet′id) *adj.:* stinking like something rotten.

---

at, āte, cär; ten, ēve, is, īce; gō, hôrn, look, tōōl; oil, out; up, fʉr; ə *for unstressed vowels, as* a *in* ago, u *in* focus; ′ *as in* Latin (lat′′n); chin; she; zh *as in* azure (azh′ər); thin, *the;* ŋ *as in* ring (riŋ)

---

**finesse** (fə·nes′) *n.*: skill; cunning.

**finicky** (fin′ik·ē) *adj.*: fussy and extremely careful.

**flail** (flāl) *v.*: move wildly or excitedly. —**flailing** *v.* used as *adj.*

**flank** (flaŋk) *v.*: surround on either side.

**flare** (fler) *v.*: burst out suddenly in anger.

**flat** (flat) *n.*: low-lying marsh.

**fledgling** (flej′liŋ) *n.*: young bird.

**flimsy** (flim′zē) *adj.*: poorly made; easily broken or damaged.

**fling** (fliŋ) *v.*: throw with force; hurl. —**flung** *v.*

**flourish** (flʉr′ish) *v.*: thrive; grow well.

**fluidity** (flōō·id′·ə·tē) *n.*: grace of movement.

**flung** (fluŋ) *v.*: See *fling.*

**fluster** (flus′tər) *v.*: confuse; upset. —**flustered** *v.* used as *adj.*

**footage** (foot′ij) *n.*: length of film that has been shot.

**forlorn** (fôr·lôrn′) *adj.*: hopeless. *Forlorn* may also mean "deserted" or "abandoned."

**formidable** (fôr′mə·də·bəl) *adj.*: awe-inspiring; impressive.

**frenzied** (fren′zēd) *adj.*: wild.

**frolicsome** (fräl′ik·səm) *adj.*: playful; merry.

**fumble** (fum′bəl) *v.*: search awkwardly.

**furrow** (fʉr′ō) *n.*: narrow groove.

**gait** (gāt) *n.*: way of walking or running.

**gape** (gāp) *v.*: stare with the mouth open, in wonder or surprise.

**garland** (gär′lənd) *n.*: wreath or woven chain.

**garment** (gär′mənt) *n.*: article of clothing.

**ghastly** (gast′lē) *adj.*: horrible; ghostlike.

**gingerly** (jin′jər·lē) *adv.*: carefully; cautiously.

**glint** (glint) *v.*: glitter; shine.

**glower** (glou′ər) *v.*: stare angrily; scowl. —**glowering** *v.* used as *adj.*

**goad** (gōd) *v.*: push or drive. A goad is a stick with a sharp point used to herd oxen.

**grave** (grāv) *adj.*: serious; somber.

**grim** (grim) *adj.*: stern; harsh. —**grimly** *adv.*

**habitual** (hə·bich′ōō·əl) *adj.*: done or fixed by habit; customary.

**haggle** (hag′əl) *v.*: argue about price; bargain.

**harry** (har′ē) *v.*: cause worry; torment. —**harried** *v.* used as *adj.*

**heave** (hēv) *v.*: raise or lift with effort. —**heaved, hove** (hōv) —*n.*: the act of heaving.

**heretical** (hə·ret′i·kəl) *adj.*: against established views.

**horde** (hôrd) *n.*: large, moving crowd.

**hover** (huv′ər) *v.*: **1.** hang in the air. **2.** linger; wait.

**idiocy** (id′ē·ə·sē) *n.*: stupidity; foolishness.

**ignominious** (ig′nə·min′ē·əs) *adj.*: shameful.

**immense** (im·mens′) *adj.*: enormous. —**immensely** *adv.*

**imminent** (im′ə·nənt) *adj.*: about to happen.

**impart** (im·pärt′) *v.*: make known.

**impassive** (im·pas′iv) *adj.*: not showing emotion.

**impel** (im·pel′) *v.*: drive. —**impelled, impelling**

**imperative** (im·per′ə·tiv) *adj.*: absolutely necessary.

**implore** (im·plôr′) *v.*: ask or beg.

**imposing** (im·pō′ziŋ) *adj.*: impressive; grand.

**impostor** (im·päs′tər) *n.*: person who pretends to be someone or something that he or she is not.

**impresario** (im′prə·sä′rē·ō′) *n.*: director or manager of a theater, opera, or ballet.

**inadequate** (in·ad′i·kwət) *adj.*: not sufficient; not equal to what is required.

**incessant** (in·ses′ənt) *adj.*: endless; constant. —**incessantly** *adv.*

**incision** (in·sizh′ən) *n.*: cut (usually in reference to surgery).

**inclined** (in·klīnd′) *adj.*: willing; likely to do.

**inconsolable** (in′kən·sōl′ə·bəl) *adj.*: unable to be comforted; brokenhearted.

**incredulous** (in·krej′oo·ləs) *adj.*: unbelieving. —**incredulously** *adv.*

**indifferent** (in·dif′ər·ənt) *adj.*: uninterested; unconcerned.

**indulgent** (in·dul′jənt) *adj.*: kind or lenient, often to excess.

**industrious** (in·dus′trē·əs) *adj.*: hard-working.

**inert** (in·ʉrt′) *adj.*: inactive.

**infiltrate** (in·fil′trāt) *v.*: gradually enter or sneak into.

**inhabit** (in·hab′it) *v.*: live in; occupy.

**inkling** (iŋk′liŋ′) *n.*: hint; slight indication.

**innumerable** (in·nōō′mer·ə·bəl) *adj.*: too many to be counted.

**insolent** (in′sə·lənt) *adj.*: boldly disrespectful.

**install** (in·stôl′) *v.*: settle; establish in a place.

**instinctive** (in·stiŋk′tiv) *adj.*: natural; inborn.

**integrity** (in·teg′rə·tē) *n.*: literally, completeness. In people, *integrity* usually refers to honor and sincerity.

**intent** (in·tent′) *adj.*: having great concentration. —**intently** *adv.*

**interior** (in·tir′ē·ər) *n.*: inside.

**interweave** (in′tər·wēv′) v.: connect closely; blend.
**—interwove, interwoven**
**interwoven** (in′tər·wō′vən) v.: See *interweave*.
**intricate** (in′tri·kit) adj.: complicated; full of detail.
**invincible** (in·vin′sə·bəl) adj.: unbeatable.
**irreverence** (i·rev′ər·əns) n.: disrespect.
**isolation** (ī′sə·lā′shən) n.: state of being alone; solitude.

**jar** (jär) v.: jolt; shock.
**jostle** (jäs′əl) v.: shove; bump. **—jostling** v. used as *adj.*
**jubilant** (jōō′bə·lənt) adj.: joyful; triumphant.

**keen** (kēn) adj.: sharp and quick in seeing; acute.
**knead** (nēd) v.: form by mixing and working, usually with the hands.

**laborious** (lə·bôr′ē·əs) adj.: involving hard work.
**latitude** (lat′ə·tōōd′) n.: region determined by distance north or south from the equator.
**launch** (lônch) v.: rush; plunge.
**leer** (lir) v.: look at slyly and knowingly. **—leering** v. used as *adj.*
**legislation** (lej′is·lā′shən) n.: laws; the making of laws.
**lithe** (līth) adj.: flexible and graceful.
**lurch** (lʉrch) v.: roll or pitch suddenly forward or to one side.
**lurid** (loor′id) adj.: sensational; shocking.
**lute** (lōōt) n.: old stringed instrument related to the guitar.

**majestic** (mə·jes′tik) adj.: dignified; grand.
**maneuver** (mə·nōō′vər) v.: move skillfully.
**mangle** (maŋ′gəl) v.: tear and crush; ruin. **—mangled** v. used as *adj.*
**maniacal** (mə·nī′ə·kəl) adj.: wildly insane; raging.
**mantle** (man′təl) n.: cloak or cover.
**maritime** (mar′i·tīm′) adj.: having to do with the sea or ships.
**martial** (mär′shəl) adj.: military.
**maw** (mô) n.: mouth (jaw, throat) of a hungry animal. *Maw* suggests a huge, threatening mouth.

**meager** (mē′gər) adj.: literally, very thin; not enough.
**meddlesome** (med′′l·səm) adj.: interfering.
**mercantile** (mʉr′kən·tīl′) adj.: related to trade (the buying and selling of goods).
**mill** (mil) v.: move in a circular or random motion, like cattle or a crowd of people.
**misgiving** (mis′giv′iŋ) n.: doubt; uneasy feeling.
**mobilize** (mō′bə·līz′) v.: make ready for motion.
**molten** (mōl′tən) adj.: melted by heat.
**monotonous** (mə·nät′′n·əs) adj.: having little variety; boring.
**morose** (mə·rōs′) adj.: gloomy.
**mortify** (môrt′ə·fī′) v.: cause to feel ashamed and hurt. **—mortified** v. used as *adj.*
**mottled** (mät′′ld) adj.: blotchy, streaked, and spotted.
**multitude** (mul′tə·tōōd′) n.: mass; large number.
**muster** (mus′tər) v.: call forth.

**namesake** (nām′sāk′) n.: person with the same name as someone else.
**notable** (nōt′ə·bəl) adj.: remarkable; outstanding.
**nurture** (nʉr′chər) v.: nourish; raise.

**objective** (əb·jek′tiv) n.: aim; goal.
**obscure** (əb·skyoor′) adj.: unclear; not easily understood. **—v.:** hide; conceal.
**observatory** (əb·zʉrv′ə·tôr′ē) n.: building equipped for scientific observation.
**officious** (ə·fish′əs) adj.: tending to interfere; bossy, as if in charge. **—officiously** adv.
**ominous** (äm′ə·nəs) adj.: threatening, like a bad sign; warning of something bad.
**ordain** (ôr·dān′) v.: order or decree.
**ordeal** (ôr·dēl′) n.: difficult and painful experience.
**organism** (ôr′gə·niz′əm) n.: individual plant or animal.

**pallid** (pal′id) adj.: pale.
**parched** (pärcht) adj.: very hot and dry.
**particle** (pärt′i·kəl) n.: tiny piece.
**paunch** (pônch) n.: potbelly.
**peer** (pir) v.: look closely.
**peevish** (pēv′ish) adj.: irritable; ill-humored.

---

at, āte, cär; ten, ēve; is, īce; gō, hôrn, look, tōōl; oil, out; up, fʉr; ə *for unstressed vowels, as* a *in* ago, u *in* focus; ′ *as in* Latin (lat′′n); chin; she; zh *as in* azure (azh′ər); thin, *the*; ŋ *as in* ring (riŋ)

---

**pensive** (pen′siv) *adj.*: thoughtful. **—pensively** *adv.*

**perish** (per′ish) *v.*: die.

**permissive** (pər·mis′iv) *adj.*: allowing freedom; tolerant of behavior disapproved of by others.

**persist** (pər·sist′) *v.*: continue firmly or steadily.

**perturb** (pər·turb′) *v.*: disturb; trouble. **—perturbed** *v.* used as *adj.*

**pestilential** (pes′tə·len′shəl) *adj.*: causing disease; deadly.

**phonetic** (fō·net′ik) *adj.*: having to do with speech sounds.

**pious** (pī′əs) *adj.*: deeply religious.

**pivot** (piv′ət) *v.*: rotate; turn around as if on an axis.

**plait** (plāt) *n.*: braid of hair.

**pliant** (plī′ənt) *adj.*: easily bent.

**poise** (poiz) *v.*: balance.

**pomp** (pämp) *n.*: showy display; splendor.

**ponder** (pän′dər) *v.*: think deeply about.

**portent** (pôr′tent′) *n.*: omen; warning.

**predecessor** (pred′ə·ses′ər) *n.*: person who precedes (goes before) someone else.

**predicament** (prē·dik′ə·mənt) *n.*: difficult and unpleasant situation; problem.

**predicate** (pred′i·kāt′) *v.*: affirm or base on something. **—predicated** *v.* used as *adj.*

**predominant** (prē·däm′ə·nənt) *adj.*: main. **—predominantly** *adv.*

**predominate** (prē·däm′ə·nāt′) *v.*: have authority or influence; prevail.

**presumptuous** (prē·zump′choō·əs) *adj.*: too bold; arrogant.

**proceed** (prō·sēd′) *v.*: move along; advance.

**prod** (präd) *v.*: urge or stir into action.

**prodigy** (präd′ə·jē) *n.*: child genius.

**promenade** (präm′ə·nād′) *n.*: public place for a leisurely walk.

**prop** (präp) *v.*: support or hold in place with a support.

**proposition** (präp′ə·zish′ən) *n.*: something put up for consideration.

**prospect** (prä′spekt′) *n.*: something hoped for or expected.

**prostrate** (präs′trāt′) *v.*: throw oneself on the ground to show humbleness.

**provisions** (prō·vizh′ənz) *n.*: stock of food and other supplies stored for future need.

**provoke** (prō·vōk′) *v.*: cause action or feeling, usually anger or annoyance.

**prow** (prou) *n.*: forward part of a ship or boat.

**prowess** (prou′is) *n.*: ability; skill.

**pungent** (pun′jənt) *adj.*: here, sharp smelling; also sharp tasting. Spicy foods are pungent.

**quaver** (kwā′vər) *v.*: tremble.

**query** (kwir′ē) *n.*: question.

**radiant** (rā′dē·ənt) *adj.*: 1. bright; filled with light. 2. showing well-being.

**ramshackle** (ram′shak′əl) *adj.*: likely to fall to pieces.

**rank** (raŋk) *adj.*: 1. in bad taste. 2. coarse and overgrown.

**raspish** (rasp′ish) *adj.*: rough; grating.

**ravage** (rav′ij) *v.*: ruin; violently destroy.

**reassure** (rē′ə·shoor′) *v.*: comfort; give hope or confidence; from the Latin word *securus,* meaning "secure." Compare with *assure.* **—reassuring** *v.* used as *adj.*

**recede** (ri·sēd′) *v.*: 1. withdraw; become more distant. 2. move back. **—receding** *v.* used as *adj.*

**recitation** (res′ə·tā′shən) *n.*: saying aloud in public something memorized.

**reconvene** (rē′kən·vēn′) *v.*: reassemble.

**reluctance** (ri·luk′təns) *n.*: unwillingness.

**remnant** (rem′nənt) *n.*: what is left over; remaining part.

**render** (ren′dər) *v.*: make; give, hand over, or present.

**replenish** (ri·plen′ish) *v.*: make full or complete again.

**reprehensible** (rep′ri·hen′sə·bəl) *adj.*: deserving blame.

**reproachful** (ri·prōch′fəl) *adj.*: expressing blame; accusing. **—reproachfully** *adv.*

**resolute** (rez′ə·loōt′) *adj.*: firm and purposeful; determined.

**resolve** (ri·zälv′) *v.*: decide; make a formal statement.

**resound** (ri·zound′) *v.*: echo loudly; fill with sound.

**respiration** (res′pə·rā′shən) *n.*: breathing.

**resume** (ri·zoōm′) *v.*: go on again after interruption.

**retort** (ri·tôrt′) *v.*: answer in a sharp, quick manner.

**retrieve** (ri·trēv′) *v.*: get back.

**rickety** (rik′it·ē) *adj.*: weak and shaky.

**rigid** (rij′id) *adj.*: hard and firmly fixed.

**rigor** (rig′ər) *n.*: hardship; difficulty.

**robust** (rō·bust′) *adj.*: strong and healthy.

**rollick** (räl′ik) *v.*: play in a lively, carefree way; romp. **—rollicking** *v.* used as *adj.*

**roster** (räs′tər) *n.*: list of names.

**rouse** (rouz) *v.*: stir up, usually to anger or action; wake.

**rueful** (roo'fəl) *adj.*: having sorrow or pity; regretful. **—ruefully** *adv.*

**rumple** (rum'pəl) *v.*: wrinkle; make untidy. **—rumpled** *v.* used as *adj.*

**rut** (rut) *n.*: set, routine process, usually viewed as dull.

**sage** (sāj) *n.*: wise person, especially an elder.

**salvage** (sal'vij) *v.*: save or rescue cargo, goods, property, and so on. *Salvage* is used especially to mean "save things from a shipwreck." **—salvaged** *v.* used as *adj.*

**saunter** (sôn'tər) *v.*: stroll; walk in an unhurried way.

**savor** (sā'vər) *v.*: enjoy with appreciation.

**scald** (skôld) *v.*: burn or injure with hot liquid or steam.

**scanty** (skan'tē) *adj.*: not enough. *Scanty* and *meager* are synonyms; *scanty* and *copious* are antonyms.

**scathing** (skā'thiŋ) *adj.*: harsh.

**scrawl** (skrôl) *v.*: write quickly and sloppily.

**scrutiny** (skroot''n·ē) *n.*: close examination.

**scuttle** (skut''l) *v.*: run or move quickly; scurry.

**sear** (sir) *v.*: burn the surface of. **—searing** *v.* used as *adj.*

**seep** (sēp) *v.*: flow out slowly through small holes; leak.

**seethe** (sēth) *v.*: be violently angry or disturbed. **—seething** *v.* used as *adj.*

**sentry** (sen'trē) *n.*: guard.

**shrewd** (shrood) *adj.*: clever.

**sidle** (sīd''l) *v.*: move sideways in a sly way.

**simultaneously** (sī'məl·tā'nē·əs) *adj.*: at the same time. **—simultaneously** *adv.*

**singe** (sinj) *v.*: slightly burn.

**skewer** (skyoo'ər) *v.*: pierce and hold with a long pin. **—skewered** *v.* used as *adj.*

**skirt** (skurt) *v.*: narrowly avoid.

**skitter** (skit'ər) *v.*: skip along quickly and lightly.

**slack** (slak) *adj.*: loose.

**sloth** (slôth) *n.*: laziness.

**sober** (sō'bər) *adj.*: serious; calm; thoughtful. **—soberly** *adv.*

**solemn** (säl'əm) *adj.*: formal and serious.

**somber** (säm'bər) *adj.*: serious.

**sow** (sō) *v.*: plant seed for growing. **—sowed, sown**

**sown** (sōn) *v.*: See *sow*.

**sparing** (sper'iŋ) *adj.*: careful in spending or using. **—sparingly** *adv.*

**spate** (spāt) *n.*: outpouring. In Britain, a *spate* is a flash flood.

**specify** (spes'ə·fī') *v.*: describe in detail.

**spectacles** (spek'tə·kəlz) *n.*: eyeglasses.

**squander** (skwän'dər) *v.*: waste.

**stalwart** (stôl'wərt) *adj.*: strong and sturdy.

**stamina** (stam'ə·nə) *n.*: endurance; ability to resist fatigue.

**stately** (stāt'lē) *adj.*: dignified; grand.

**staunch** (stônch) *adj.*: firm; loyal.

**sterile** (ster'əl) *adj.*: barren; lacking interest or vitality.

**stir** (stur) *v.*: move or change position, especially only slightly.

**stoic** (stō'ik) *adj.*: not showing or complaining about pain. Stoics were philosophers of ancient Greece who tried not to let pleasure or pain affect them.

**stolid** (stäl'id) *adj.*: unemotional.

**stride** (strīd) *v.*: walk with long steps; walk vigorously. **—strode** (strōd), **stridden** (strid''n)

**strode** (strōd) *v.*: See *stride*.

**stunt** (stunt) *v.*: cause to grow improperly. **—stunted** *v.* used as *adj.*

**subdue** (səb·doo') *v.*: soften; reduce. **—subdued** *v.* used as *adj.*

**submerge** (səb·murj') *v.*: sink; cover with liquid. **—submerged** *v.* used as *adj.*

**substantial** (səb·stan'shəl) *adj.*: considerable; strong.

**subterfuge** (sub'tər·fyooj') *n.*: sneaky strategy; trick used to deceive others.

**subtle** (sut''l) *adj.*: not open or direct; crafty. **—subtly** *adv.*

**suffice** (sə·fīs') *v.*: be enough.

**sufficient** (sə·fish'ənt) *adj.*: enough.

**suffuse** (sə·fyooz') *v.*: fill with a glow. **—suffused** *v.* used as *adj.*

**suppress** (sə·pres') *v.*: keep back; restrain or put down.

**surge** (surj) *v.*: move in a heavy, swelling motion.

**surly** (sur'lē) *adj.*: bad-tempered, rude, and hostile.

**surname** (sur'nām') *n.*: last name.

**survey** (sər·vā') *v.*: examine; consider carefully.

**sustain** (sə·stān') *v.*: support; strengthen. **—sustaining** *v.* used as *adj.*

**swagger** (swag'ər) *n.*: bold, arrogant stride; strut.

---

at, āte, cär; ten, ēve; is, īce; gō, hôrn, look, tool; oil, out; up, fur; ə *for unstressed vowels, as* a *in* ago, u *in* focus; ' *as in* Latin (lat''n); chin; she; zh *as in* azure (azh'ər); thin, *the*; ŋ *as in* ring (riŋ)

---

**tangible** (tan′jə·bəl) *adj.*: capable of being touched or felt.

**taunt** (tônt) *v.*: mock; jeer at.

**taut** (tôt) *adj.*: tense; showing strain.

**teeter** (tēt′ər) *v.*: wobble.

**tempo** (tem′pō) *n.*: pace.

**tenement** (ten′ə·mənt) *n.*: apartment. Tenement buildings are often cheaply built and poorly maintained.

**tenet** (ten′it) *n.*: belief of a group; doctrine.

**testy** (tes′tē) *adj.*: irritable. —**testily** *adv.*

**tether** (teth′ər) *v.*: tie. —**tethered** *v.* used as *adj.*

**theorist** (thē′ə·rist) *n.*: person having knowledge of, rather than practicing, the principles and methods of an art or a science.

**thrive** (thrīv) *v.*: prosper or grow well.

**throng** (thrôŋ) *n.*: crowd.

**tidings** (tīd′iŋz) *n.*: news.

**tier** (tir) *n.*: layer; row.

**torpor** (tôr′pər) *n.*: sluggishness.

**torrent** (tôr′ənt) *n.*: flood or rush.

**trajectory** (trə·jek′tə·rē) *n.*: curved path of something thrown or passing through space.

**tramp** (tramp) *v.*: step on firmly and heavily.

**transform** (trans·fôrm′) *v.*: change the form or outward appearance of.

**treacherous** (trech′ər·əs) *adj.*: dangerous; untrustworthy. —**treacherously** *adv.*

**trespass** (tres′pəs) *v.*: go on another's land or property without permission.

**trifle** (trī′fəl) *n.*: bit; small amount.

**trigger** (trig′ər) *v.*: set off.

**trundle** (trun′dəl) *v.*: roll along.

**tuft** (tuft) *n.*: bunch or clump of things (such as grass or hair) growing close together.

**tyrant** (tī′rənt) *n.*: cruel, oppressive ruler.

**unbidden** (un·bid′′n) *adj.*: not invited; unasked.

**unceasing** (un·sēs′iŋ) *adj.*: endless; not stopping. —**unceasingly** *adv.*

**uncomprehending** (un′käm·prə·hend′iŋ) *adj.*: without understanding. —**uncomprehendingly** *adv.*

**undaunted** (un·dônt′id) *adj.*: not discouraged; not shocked.

**undulation** (un′dyo͞o·lā′shən) *n.*: wavy movement.

**unison** (yo͞on′ə·sən) *n.*: harmony; unity. When people speak in unison, they are saying the same thing at the same time.

**unrequited** (un′ri·kwīt′id) *v.* used as *adj.*: not returned in kind.

**unwieldy** (un·wēl′dē) *adj.*: heavy and awkward; hard to manage.

**upend** (up·end′) *v.*: set on end; topple.

**usher** (ush′ər) *v.*: bring in.

**utter** (ut′ər) *v.*: speak.

**vacate** (vā′kāt′) *v.*: cause to be unoccupied; leave.

**vain** (vān) *adj.*: useless; without result. —**vainly** *adv.*

**valiant** (val′yənt) *adj.*: brave and determined.

**vengeful** (venj′fəl) *adj.*: seeking to cause injury in return for an injury; seeking revenge.

**venomous** (ven′əm·əs) *adj.*: poisonous; malicious.

**vermilion** (vər·mil′yən) *adj.*: bright red; scarlet.

**vicinity** (və·sin′ə·tē) *n.*: neighborhood.

**vigil** (vij′əl) *n.*: watch; guard.

**vigor** (vig′ər) *n.*: active physical force; energy.

**visualize** (vizh′o͞o·əl·īz′) *v.*: picture.

**wallow** (wäl′ō) *v.*: move heavily and clumsily.

**waver** (wā′vər) *v.*: become unsteady; show doubt or indecision.

**weary** (wir′ē) *v.*: make or become tired or worn out. —**wearied** *v.* used as *adj.*

**wedge** (wej) *n.*: piece that is thick at one end and narrows to a thin edge.

**whimsical** (hwim′zi·kəl) *adj.*: full of silly, fanciful ideas.

**whittle** (hwit′əl) *v.*: cut thin pieces from wood with a knife; carve.

**wholehearted** (hōl′härt′id) *adj.*: hearty; sincere. —**wholeheartedly** *adv.*

**wisp** (wisp) *n.*: thin, light piece.

**wither** (with′ər) *v.*: shrivel; dry up. —**withering** *v.* used as *adj.*

**woeful** (wō′fəl) *adj.*: sad; mournful. —**woefully** *adv.*

**writhe** (rīth) *v.*: twist and squirm.

**zest** (zest) *n.*: excitement; keenness.

# ACKNOWLEDGMENTS

For permission to use copyrighted material, grateful acknowledgment is made to the following sources:

**American Library Association:** From Newbery Award Acceptance Speech by Mildred D. Taylor, 1977.

**Carroll Arnett:** "Early Song" by Gogisgi/Carroll Arnett from *South Line.* Copyright © 1979 by Gogisgi/Carroll Arnett. Published by Elizabeth Press.

**Arte Público Press:** "Immigrants" from *Borders* by Pat Mora. Copyright © 1986 by Pat Mora. Published by Arte Público Press–University of Houston, Houston, TX, 1986. "My Father Is a Simple Man" from *The Sadness of Days: Selected and New Poems* by Luis Omar Salinas. Copyright © 1987 by Luis Omar Salinas. Published by Arte Público Press–University of Houston, Houston, TX, 1987.

**The Associated Press:** "Buddies Bare Their Affection for Ill Classmate" by Associated Press from *Austin American-Statesman,* March 19, 1994. Copyright © 1994 by The Associated Press.

**Atheneum Books for Young Readers, an imprint of Simon & Schuster Children's Publishing Division:** ". . . And Then the Prince Knelt Down and Tried to Put the Glass Slipper on Cinderella's Foot" from *If I Were in Charge of the World and Other Worries* by Judith Viorst. Text copyright © 1981 by Judith Viorst.

**Karma Bene Bambara:** Quote by Toni Cade Bambara about writing short stories.

**Susan Bergholz Literary Services, New York:** "Names/Nombres" by Julia Alvarez. Copyright © 1985 by Julia Alvarez. First published in *Nuestro,* March 1985. All rights reserved. "Cuatro árboles flaquititos" from *La casa en Mango Street* by Sandra Cisneros, translated by Elena Poniatowska. Copyright © 1984 by Sandra Cisneros; translation copyright © 1994 by Elena Poniatowska. Published by Vintage Español, a division of Random House, Inc. All rights reserved. "Four Skinny Trees" from *The House on Mango Street* by Sandra Cisneros. Copyright © 1984 by Sandra Cisneros. Published by Vintage Books, a division of Random House, Inc., New York, and in hardcover by Alfred A. Knopf, Inc., New York, in 1994. All rights reserved.

**BOA Editions, Ltd., 260 East Ave., Rochester, NY 14604:** From "breaklight" and "the 1st" from *good woman: poems and a memoir 1969–1980* by Lucille Clifton. Copyright © 1987 by Lucille Clifton.

**Joseph Bruchac:** "Sky Woman" by Joseph Bruchac. Copyright © 1997 by Joseph Bruchac.

**Arthur Cavanaugh:** "Miss Awful" by Arthur Cavanaugh from *McCall's,* April 1969. Copyright © 1969 by Arthur Cavanaugh.

**Children's Better Health Institute, Benjamin Franklin Literary & Medical Society, Inc., Indianapolis, Indiana:** From "Kachinas: Sacred Drama of the Hopis" by Lonnie Dyer from *Young World.* Copyright © 1976 by Review Publishing Company.

**Columbia TriStar Television:** Slightly adapted from *Brian's Song* by William Blinn. Copyright © 1971 by Screen Gems, a division of Columbia Pictures.

**Don Congdon Associates, Inc.:** "The Naming of Names" by Ray Bradbury from *Thrilling Wonder Stories.* Copyright © 1949 by Standard Magazines, Inc.; copyright renewed © 1976 by Ray Bradbury.

**CRICKET Magazine:** "Wings" by Bronwen Anne Gilbert from *CRICKET,* vol. 18, no. 11, July 1991. Copyright © 1991 by Carus Publishing Company. "Sir Kensley the Brave" by Megan Washam from *CRICKET,* vol. 19, no. 1, September 1991. Copyright © 1991 by Carus Publishing Company.

**Crown Publishers, Inc.:** "Overture" (retitled "The Power of Music") from *Nadja on My Way* by Nadja Salerno-Sonnenberg. Copyright © 1989 by Nadja Salerno-Sonnenberg.

**Delacorte Press, a division of Random House, Inc.:** "User Friendly" by T. Ernesto Bethancourt from *Connections: Short Stories,* edited by Donald R. Gallo. Copyright © 1989 by T. Ernesto Bethancourt.

**Dial Books for Young Readers, a division of Penguin Putnam Inc.:** "The Flight of Icarus" from *Stories of the Gods and Heroes* by Sally Benson. Copyright 1940 and renewed © 1968 by Sally Benson. *Song of the Trees* by Mildred D. Taylor. Copyright © 1975 by Mildred Taylor.

**Doubleday, a division of Random House, Inc.:** Excerpt (retitled "The Only Girl in the World for Me") from *Love & Marriage* by Bill Cosby. Copyright © 1989 by Bill Cosby. "King Midas and the Golden Touch" from *Tales from Ancient Greece* by Pamela Oldfield. Copyright © 1988 by Grisewood and Dempsey, Ltd.

**Esquire Magazine:** "Three Skeleton Key" by George G. Toudouze from *Esquire,* January 1937. Copyright 1937 by Hearst Communications, Inc. All rights reserved. Esquire is a trademark of Hearst Magazines Property, Inc.

**Dr. Clarissa Pinkola Estés and Ballantine Books, a division of Random House, Inc.:** From "Sealskin, Soulskin" from *Women Who Run with the Wolves* by Clarissa Pinkola Estés, Ph.D. Copyright © 1991, 1992, 1995 by Clarissa Pinkola Estés, Ph.D. All performance, derivative, adaptation, musical, audio and recording, illustrative, theatrical, film, pictorial, electronic, and all other rights reserved.

**Firebrand Books, Ithaca, New York:** From "World View" from *Talking Indian: Reflections on Survival and Writing* by Anna Lee Walters. Copyright © 1992 by Anna Lee Walters.

**Samuel French, Inc.:** From "The Dream of Good Fortune: Arabian Nights" from *More from Story Theatre,* by Paul Sills. Copyright © 1981 by Paul Sills. CAUTION: Professionals and amateurs are hereby warned that *More from Story Theatre,* being fully protected under the copyright laws of the United States of America, the British Commonwealth countries, including Canada, and the other countries of the Copyright Union, is subject to a royalty. All rights, including professional, amateur, motion picture, recitation, public reading, radio, television and cable broadcasting, and the rights of translation into foreign languages, are strictly reserved. Any inquiry regarding the availability of performance rights, or the purchase of individual copies of the authorized acting edition, must be directed to Samuel French, Inc., 45 West 25th Street, NY, NY 10010 with other locations in Hollywood and Toronto, Canada.

**Jean Fritz c/o Refna Wilkin:** From "American Bicentennial Reading," prepared by Jean Fritz for The Children's Book Council, Inc. Copyright © 1975 by Jean Fritz. From "George Washington, My Father, and Walt Disney" by Jean Fritz (given on June 6, 1975, at the Sixth Annual Spring Festival of the New England Round Table of Children's Librarians at Kennebunkport, Maine) from *The Horn Book,* vol. LII, no. 2, April 1976. Copyright © 1976 by Jean Fritz.

**Gale Research Inc.:** Quote by Olivia Coolidge from "Olivia Coolidge" from *Something About the Author,* vol. 1, edited by Anne Commire. Copyright © 1971 by Gale Research Inc. Quotes by Anne McCaffrey from "Anne McCaffrey" from *Something About the Author,* vol. 8, edited by Anne Commire. Copyright © 1976 by Gale Research Inc. Quotes by Patricia Lauber from "Patricia Lauber" from *Something About the Author,* vol. 33, edited by Anne Commire. Copyright © 1983 by Gale Research Inc.

**Brooke Garner:** Letter to Holt, Rinehart and Winston from Brooke Garner, November 12, 1991. Copyright © 1997 by Brooke Garner.

**Glamour:** From "Forum: 'To Help the Handicapped, Talk to Them'" by Itzhak Perlman from *Glamour,* vol. 85, no. 3, March 1987. Copyright © 1987 by Condé Nast Publications, Inc.

**Linda Goss:** From "The Frog Who Wanted to Be a Singer" by Linda Goss from *Talk That Talk: An Anthology of African-American Storytelling* by Linda Goss and Marian E. Barnes. Copyright © 1983 by Linda Goss.

**Harcourt Brace & Company:** From "A Note from the Author" from *In the Beginning* by Virginia Hamilton. Copyright © 1988 by Virginia Hamilton. Illustration by Thomas Locker for "Gold" by Pat Mora from *Home: A Journey Through America,* edited by Thomas Locker and Candace Christiansen. Copyright © 1998 by Thomas Locker. "The Algonquin Cinderella," retold by M. R. Cox, from *World Tales: The Extraordinary Coincidence of Stories Told in All Times, in All*

*Places* by Idries Shah. Copyright © 1979 by Technographia, S. A. and Harcourt Brace & Company. "The No-Guitar Blues" from *Baseball in April and Other Stories* by Gary Soto. Copyright © 1990 by Gary Soto. "The Boy and the Wolf" from *The Magic Circle* by Louis Untermeyer. Copyright 1952 by Harcourt Brace & Company; copyright renewed © 1980 by Brian I. Untermeyer.

**HarperCollins Publishers, Inc.:** Poem No. 15 from *Tao-Te Ching by Lao Tzu, A New English Version, with Foreword and Notes* by Stephen Mitchell. Translation copyright © 1988 by Stephen Mitchell. Untitled tall tale from "Painting" from *Whoppers, Tall Tales, and Other Lies Collected from American Folklore* by Alvin Schwartz. Text copyright © 1975 by Alvin Schwartz. "In Search of Cinderella" from *A Light in the Attic* by Shel Silverstein. Copyright © 1981 by Evil Eye Music, Inc. "Sarah Cynthia Sylvia Stout Would Not Take the Garbage Out" from *Where the Sidewalk Ends* by Shel Silverstein. Copyright © 1974 by Evil Eye Music, Inc. "Master Frog" from *The Brocaded Slipper and Other Vietnamese Tales* by Lynette Dyer Vuong. Text copyright © 1982 by Lynette Dyer Vuong.

**Hill and Wang, a division of Farrar, Straus & Giroux, Inc.:** From "Poetry in Practical" from *The Big Sea* by Langston Hughes. Copyright © 1940 by Langston Hughes; copyright renewed © 1968 by Arna Bontemps and George Houston Bass.

**Henry Holt and Company, Inc.:** From "Africa in 1492" by Patricia and Fredrick McKissack from *The World in 1492* by Jean Fritz, Katherine Paterson, Patricia and Fredrick McKissack, Margaret Mahy, and Jamake Highwater. "Africa in 1492" copyright © 1992 by Patricia and Fredrick McKissack. "The Runaway" from *The Poetry of Robert Frost,* edited by Edward Connery Lathem. Copyright 1951 by Robert Frost; copyright 1923, © 1969 by Henry Holt and Company, Inc.

**Holy Cow! Press:** From *Nancy Hanks of Wilderness Road: A Story of Abraham Lincoln's Mother* by Meridel Le Sueur. Copyright 1949 and renewed © 1979 by Meridel Le Sueur.

**The Horn Book, Inc.:** Quote by Cynthia Rylant from "An Interview with Cynthia Rylant" by Anita Silvey from *The Horn Book,* vol. 63, no. 6, November/December 1987. Copyright © 1987 by The Horn Book, Inc.

**Houghton Mifflin Company:** "Ashpet" from *The Grandfather Tales* by Richard Chase. Copyright © 1948 and renewed © 1976 by Richard Chase. All rights reserved. "The Great Musician" (retitled "Orpheus, the Great Musician") and "The Origin of the Seasons" from *Greek Myths* by Olivia Coolidge. Copyright © 1949 and renewed © 1977 by Olivia E. Coolidge. All rights reserved. "Bargain" from *The Big It and Other Stories* by A. B. Guthrie. Copyright © 1960 by A. B. Guthrie. All rights reserved. From "Havana" from *Papa: A Personal Memoir* by Gregory H. Hemingway. Copyright © 1976 by Gregory H. Hemingway. All rights reserved.

**Evelyn Tooley Hunt:** "Mama Is a Sunrise" by Evelyn Tooley Hunt from *The Lyric,* 1972.

**Hyperion Books for Children:** From *Dinorella: A Prehistoric Fairy Tale* by Pamela Duncan Edwards, illustrated by Henry Cole. Text copyright © 1997 by Pamela Duncan Edwards; illustrations copyright © 1997 by Henry Cole.

**Juniper Academy, Redding, CA:** Photo of Juniper Academy students. Text from "Uniforms" from Juniper Academy Web site. Available January 6, 1999, http://shastalink.k12.ca.us/juniper/j9.htm.

**Alfred A. Knopf, Inc.:** "Madam and the Rent Man" and "Epigram" from *The Collected Poems of Langston Hughes.* Copyright © 1957 by Ballantine Books, Inc.; copyright renewed © 1985 by George Houston Bass; copyright © 1994 by the Estate of Langston Hughes.

**Patricia Lauber:** "What an Earthquake Is" and "When the Earth Shakes" from *Earthquakes: New Scientific Ideas About How and Why the Earth Shakes* by Patricia Lauber. Copyright © 1972 by Patricia Lauber.

**Liveright Publishing Corporation:** From "Introduction" to *New Poems* (from *Collected Poems*) and "maggie and milly and molly and may" from *Complete Poems: 1904–1962* by E. E. Cummings, edited by George J. Firmage. Copyright © 1938, 1956, 1966, 1984, 1991 by the Trustees for the E. E. Cummings Trust. "Those Winter Sundays" from *Angle of Ascent: New and Selected Poems* by Robert Hayden. Copyright © 1966 by Robert Hayden.

**Macmillan General Reference USA, a division of Ahsuog, Inc.:** From *Webster's New World Dictionary,* Third College Edition. Copyright © 1988, 1991, 1994, 1996, 1997 by Simon & Schuster, Inc.

**Ashley Deal Matin:** "Antaeus" by Borden Deal. Copyright © 1961 by Southern Methodist University Press. Comment on "Antaeus" by Borden Deal.

**Anne McCaffrey and agent, Virginia Kidd:** "The Smallest Dragonboy" by Anne McCaffrey. Copyright © 1973 by Anne McCaffrey. First appeared in *Science Fiction Tales.*

**Margaret K. McElderry Books, an imprint of Simon & Schuster Children's Publishing Division:** From "The Search Goes On" from *The Mystery of the Ancient Maya* by Carolyn Meyer and Charles Gallenkamp. Copyright © 1985, 1995 by Carolyn Meyer and Charles Gallenkamp.

**Eucario Mendez:** "The Desert" by Eucario Mendez from *Rising Voices: Writings of Young Native Americans,* selected by Arlene B. Hirschfelder and Beverly R. Singer. Copyright © 1990 by Eucario Mendez.

**Merlyn's Pen: The National Magazines of Student Writing:** "Makx a Diffxrxncx!" by Elena Chen from "Letters to the Pen" from *Merlyn's Pen,* December/January 1993. Copyright © 1993 by Elena Chen. First appeared in *Merlyn's Pen: The National Magazines of Student Writing.* All rights reserved. "The Lion, the Witch, and the Wardrobe by C. S. Lewis" by John Belletti from "Reviews and Retrospects" and "As I Gaze Upon My Father" by Maren Stuart from *Merlyn's Pen,* vol. VIII, no. 4, April/May 1993. Copyright © 1993 by Merlyn's Pen. First appeared in *Merlyn's Pen: The National Magazines of Student Writing.* All rights reserved. From "In the Kitchen" by Elly Henry from *Merlyn's Pen,* Middle School Edition, October/November 1994. Copyright © 1994 by Merlyn's Pen. First appeared in *Merlyn's Pen: The National Magazines of Student Writing.* All rights reserved.

**Vinnie Merrill:** "The Clutch Moment" by Vinnie Merrill from *Paw Prints: Simonsen Junior High Literary Magazine,* May 1992. Copyright © 1992 by Vinnie Merrill. Published by the Pen 'n Ink Club of Simonsen Junior High, Jefferson City, MO.

**William Morris Agency, Inc., on behalf of the authors:** Excerpts (retitled "Pic") from *I Am Third* by Gale Sayers and Al Silverman. Copyright © 1970 by Gale Sayers and Al Silverman.

**Morrow Junior Books, a division of William Morrow & Company, Inc.:** From *Earthquakes* by Seymour Simon. Copyright © 1991 by Seymour Simon.

**National Geographic World, the official magazine for Junior Members of the National Geographic Society:** "It's Only Natural" from *National Geographic World,* no. 236, April 1995. Copyright © 1995 by National Geographic Society.

**National Public Radio®:** "Segment #6: Eighth Grade Teacher Finds Grammar Errors on Food Label," a news report by NPR's Scott Simon with Donna Dowling. Copyright © 1995 by National Public Radio®. Originally broadcast on National Public Radio's "Weekend Edition/Saturday" on April 29, 1995. Any unauthorized duplication is strictly prohibited.

**NEA Today:** From "Amy Tan: Joy, Luck, and Literature," an interview by Anita Merina from *NEA Today,* October 1991. Copyright © 1991 by the National Education Association of the United States.

**Newsweek, Inc.:** From "Hollywood Family Values" by Laura Shapiro and Corie Brown from *Newsweek,* August 3, 1998. Copyright © 1998 by Newsweek, Inc. All rights reserved.

**The New York Times Company:** From "Storytelling Art Mixes Fantasy and Wit," an interview with Linda Goss by Esther Iverem from *The New York Times,* October 30, 1986. Copyright © 1986 by The New York Times Company. From "In a Mix of Cultures, an Olio of Plantings" by Anne Raver from *The New York Times,* August 15, 1991. Copyright © 1991 by The New York Times Company.

**Naomi Shihab Nye:** Quote about writing poetry by Naomi Shihab Nye. Copyright © by Naomi Shihab Nye.

**Oxford University Press:** "Oni and the Great Bird" from *Fourteen Hundred Cowries: Traditional Stories of the Yoruba,* collected by Abayomi Fuja. Copyright © 1962 by Oxford University Press.

**Penguin Books Canada Limited:** From *Little by Little: A Writer's Education* by Jean Little. Copyright © 1987 by Jean Little.

## PICTURE CREDITS

# INDEX OF SKILLS

## LITERARY TERMS

The boldface page numbers indicate an extensive treatment of the topic.

Rhyme 338, 339, 398, 460, 463, **688**
  approximate (near, slant) **460,** 463,
    688
  end 338, 688
  exact 460, 463
  eye (visual) 688
  internal 338, 688
Rhyme scheme 338, 339, 685, 687,
    688
Rhythm 338, 339, 340, 348, 349, 398,
    **688–689**
  refrain **420,** 425, **688**
  repetition **350,** 354, 398, 403
  scanning 338, 339, 689
Scanning 338, 339, 689
Screenplay 271, 276, 322
Script 271
Sensory details 134, 166, 355, 460, 488
Setting 78, 96, 98, **152,** 165, 166, 227, 242,
    270, 273, 340, 348, 354, 396, 490, 605,
    636, **689**
Short story 22–23, **689**
  character 42, **80,** 85, 98, 340, **356,** 365,
    635, 646, **682**
  climax 22, 61, 349, 687
  complications 22, 687
  conflict **2,** 19, 22, 42, 61, 96, 118, 199,
    244, 254, 349, **682,** 687
  exposition 687
  plot 22, 96, 98, **687**
  resolution 23, 349
  setting 96, 98, **152,** 165, 340, 348, **689**
  theme 23, **28, 690**
Simile **168,** 171, 397, 520, 577, 684, **689**
Situational irony 685
Slang 255, 442
Slant rhyme **460,** 463, 688
Sound effects (sound devices) 338–339
  alliteration 338–339, 349, **681**
  onomatopoeia 339, **686**
  repetition **350,** 354, 398, 403
  rhyme 338, 339, 398, 460, 463, **688**
  rhythm 338, 339, 340, 348, 349, **688–**
    **689**
Speaker **689**
Stage 270
Stanza **690**
Static character 682
Stereotype 367
Storytelling, oral 661
Style 85, 511, 564, 648
Subjective writing 122, 686
Supporting details 149, 241
Suspense **64,** 77, 271, 440, 604, **690**
Symbol **24,** 27, **690**
Tall tale 551, **690**
Teleplay 271, 272, 276
Theme 23, **28,** 98, **690.** *See also* Main idea.
Third-person limited point of view 203,
    216, 687
Title 26, 85, 119, 141, 149, 165, 223, 272,
    322, 323, 396, 398, 659, 660
Tone **226,** 229, **690**
Topic 443
Topic sentence 685
Verbal irony 684

## READING AND CRITICAL THINKING

Active reading 2
  assignments (Dialogue with the Text) 2,
    4–5, 19, 45, 105, 194, 340, 341, 350,
    420, 421, 424, 500, 501, 594
  student models 4–5, 105, 194, 341, 421,
    501, 594
Analogies, word 143, 706
Analysis questions (Shaping Interpretations)
    19, 26–27, 42, 61, 77, 85, 118, 131, 141,
    149, 165, 171, 199, 213, 223, 229, 241,
    254, 300, 322, 348, 354, 365, 383, 391,
    396, 402–403, 424–425, 430, 440, 457,
    463, 467, 479, 509, 518, 527, 537, 551,
    562, 575, 604, 622, 635, 646, 659
Anticipation/response survey 522
Arguments, analyzing 492
Author's point of view, analyzing 266, 696
Author's purpose, identifying 468, 480
Brainstorming 95, 104, 132, 181, 224, 262,
    267, 323, 329, 386, 431, 434, 444, 558,
    605, 673
Building on prior knowledge 558, 562
Causal chain 356, 365
Cause and effect 323, 433, 440, 509, 562
  analyzing 434, 440
  recognizing 356, 365
Causes, recognizing 356, 365
Charts 61, 62, 77, 79, 85, 87, 95, 96, 100,
    133, 142, 143, 166, 167, 168, 204, 213,
    230, 241, 261, 300, 322, 323, 324, 327,
    329, 348, 385, 398, 403, 411, 416, 425,
    433, 434, 440, 444, 457, 464, 488, 493,
    510, 511, 518, 521, 551, 558, 562, 576,
    583, 607, 622, 627, 628, 636, 646, 660,
    670, 704
  how to read 704
Chronological order 184, 205, 329, 332,
    334, 412, 426, 430, 489, 588, 671, 674,
    704
Chronology, recalling with 426, 430
Cluster map 119, 255, 262, 480
Comparing texts 398, 403, 607, 622
Comparison and contrast 123, 124, 132,
    166, 213, 223, 230, 244, 402, 403, 457,
    518, 622, 628, 647
Comparisons, making 27, 61, 99, 168, 391,
    432, 457, 479, 584, 607, 646, 648
Comprehension, monitoring 45, 46, 152,
    188
Comprehension questions (Reading Check)
    19, 42, 61, 77, 85, 118, 131, 141, 149,
    165, 199, 213, 223, 241, 254, 300, 322,
    348, 365, 383, 391, 424, 430, 440, 457,
    479, 509, 518, 527, 537, 551, 562, 575,
    604, 622, 635, 646, 659
Comprehension strategies 45, 204, 272,
    433, 521, 529
Conclusions, drawing 78, 189, 230, 241,
    492, 509
Conflict resolution 417
Connotation 44, 120, 682
Context clues 62, 192, 201, 255, 334, 521,
    522, 529
  analyzing 192, 201

Cultural sayings 216, 223
Decision making 272
Deduction, understanding 492
Denotation 44, 120, **682**
Dialogue with the Text 2, 4–5, 19, 45, 105,
    194, 340, 341, 350, 420, 421, 424, 500,
    501, 594
Dictionary, using a 167, 255, 385, 511,
    **701–702**
Drama, analyzing 270–271
Editorial 266
Effects, recognizing 356, 365
Evaluation 510, 519, 528, 538, 552, 563,
    576, 582–586
Evaluation questions (Challenging the Text)
    19, 61, 85, 141, 149, 165, 213, 223, 241,
    254, 301, 365, 440, 527, 575, 604, 635,
    646, 659
Evaluation strategies for reading 492
Evidence 77, 230, 262, 264, 443, 527, 530
Fables, analyzing 565
Fact 104, 118
Fact and opinion, analyzing 104, 118, 367,
    368
Fiction, analyzing 22–23, 123, 202–203
Flexibility in reading 512, 518
Flowchart 356, 365, 692–693, 704
Folk tales, analyzing 625–626
Format of text 272
Generalizations, making 28, 530, 538
Geography book, reading a 416
Glossary, using a 167
Graphic organizers 28, 42, 61, 62, 77, 79,
    85, 86, 87, 95, 96, 100, 119, 123, 132,
    133, 142, 143, 166, 167, 168, 183, 204,
    213, 215, 230, 241, 244, 255, 261, 262,
    263, 272, 300, 322, 323, 324, 327, 329,
    330, 348, 356, 365, 367, 385, 398, 403,
    411, 416, 425, 433, 434, 440, 444, 457,
    458, 464, 480, 488, 493, 510, 511, 518,
    521, 522, 551, 554–557, 558, 562, 576,
    583, 588, 607, 622, 627, 628, 636, 646,
    659, 660, 670, 673, 692–693, 700, 704
Graphs 272, 440, 493
  how to read 704
  types of 704
Headings in texts 100
Identifying author's purpose 468, 480
Independent reading 188
Index, searching an 416, 539, 694
Induction, understanding 492
Inferences 521, 685, 690
  making 80, 85, 118, 213, 430, 509
Judgment 510, 519, 528, 552, 563, 576,
    582–586
Key passage 443
Knowledge questions (Reading Check) 19,
    42, 61, 77, 85, 118, 131, 141, 149, 165,
    199, 213, 223, 241, 254, 300, 322, 348,
    365, 383, 391, 424, 430, 440, 457, 479,
    509, 518, 527, 537, 551, 562, 575, 604,
    622, 635, 646, 659
KWL chart 434, 440
Language structure, applying knowledge of
    192, 201
Letter-sound correspondences, applying
    knowledge of 243

## LANGUAGE (GRAMMAR, USAGE, AND MECHANICS)

## SPEAKING, LISTENING, AND VIEWING

# INDEX OF ART

## FINE ART

# INDEX OF AUTHORS AND TITLES

## STUDENT WRITERS